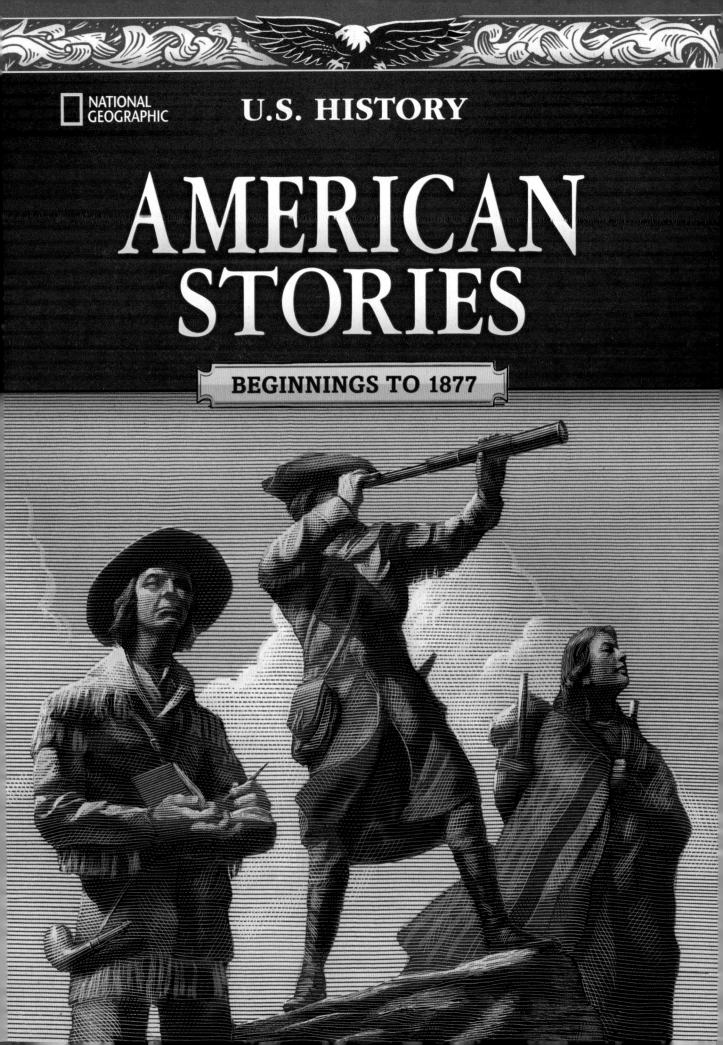

NATIONAL GEOGRAPHIC

U.S. HISTORY

AMERICAN STORIES

BEGINNINGS TO 1877

Lewis, Clark, and Sacagawea

In 1803, Thomas Jefferson sent explorers Meriwether Lewis and William Clark on an expedition into the uncharted territory of the American West. Jefferson wanted them to gather information about the geography, plants, and animals of this region, and befriend Native American tribes. After encountering both friendly and unfriendly tribes during their journey, Lewis and Clark realized they needed the help of someone who knew the local terrain and people. They hired Sacagawea, a young Shoshone woman, to be their interpreter and guide. Her knowledge of languages and the land was invaluable, and Sacagawea became an important member of Lewis and Clark's expedition.

For more information on Lewis and Clark (above) and Sacagawea (right), read the American Story in Chapter 9.

"National Geographic", "National Geographic Society" and the Yellow Border Design are registered trademarks of the National Geographic Society ® Marcas Registradas

For product information and technology assistance, contact us at Customer & Sales Support, 888-915-3276

For permission to use material from this text or product, submit all requests online at **www.cengage.com/permissions**

Further permissions questions can be emailed to **permissionrequest@cengage.com**

Acknowledgments

Grateful acknowledgment is given to the authors, artists, photographers, museums, publishers, and agents for permission to reprint copyrighted material. Every effort has been made to secure the appropriate permission. If any omissions have been made or if corrections are required, please contact the Publisher.

Credits

Wrap Cover: Mark Summers/National Geographic Learning

Acknowledgments and credits continue on page R77.

National Geographic Learning | Cengage
1 N. State Street, Suite 900
Chicago, IL 60602

Cengage is a leading provider of customized learning solutions with office locations around the globe, including Singapore, the United Kingdom, Australia, Mexico, Brazil, and Japan. Locate your local office at **www.cengage.com/global.**

Visit National Geographic Learning online at **NGL.Cengage.com/school**

Visit our corporate website at **www.cengage.com**

ISBN: 978-133-711-136-2

Printed in the United States of America.

Print Number: 03
Print Year: 2018

Senior Consultants

Fredrik Hiebert

Fred Hiebert is National Geographic's Archaeologist-in-Residence. He has led archaeological expeditions at ancient Silk Roads sites across Asia. Hiebert was curator of National Geographic's exhibition "Afghanistan: Hidden Treasures from the National Museum, Kabul," and its most recent exhibition, "The Greeks: Agamemnon to Alexander the Great."

Peggy Altoff

Peggy Altoff's career includes teaching middle school and high school students, supervising teachers, and serving as adjunct university faculty. Altoff served as a state social studies specialist in Maryland and as a K–12 coordinator in Colorado Springs. She is a past president of the National Council for the Social Studies (NCSS) and served on the task force for the 2012 NCSS National Curriculum Standards.

Fritz Fischer

Fritz Fischer is a professor and Director of History Education at the University of Northern Colorado, where he teaches U.S. History and Social Studies Education courses. Fischer is also Chair Emeritus of the Board of Trustees of the National Council for History Education (NCHE), the largest national membership organization focusing on history education at the K–12 level.

Program Consultants

Terence Clark
Director, Shíshálh Archaeological
Research Project
University of Saskatchewan

William Parkinson
Associate Curator of Anthropology,
Field Museum of Natural History
National Geographic Explorer

Ken Garrett
National Geographic
Photographer

Robert Reid
Travel Writer
National Geographic
Digital Nomad

Kathryn Keane
Vice President, National
Geographic Exhibitions

Andrés Ruzo
Geothermal Scientist
National Geographic Explorer

National Geographic Teacher Reviewers

National Geographic works with teachers at all grade levels from across the country.
The following teachers reviewed chapters in *U.S. History: American Stories*.

Wesley Brown
Ravenscroft School
Raleigh, North Carolina

Crystal Culp
McCracken
Regional School
Paducah, Kentucky

Karen Davis
St. Joseph School
Conway, Arkansas

Jessica Lura
Bullis Charter School
Los Altos, California

Tama Nunnelley
Guntersville
Middle School
Guntersville, Alabama

Ann Viegut
John Muir Middle School
Wausau, Wisconsin

Natalie Wojinski
West Contra Costa USD
Richmond, California

National Geographic Society

The National Geographic Society contributed significantly to *National Geographic U.S. History: American Stories*. Our collaboration with each of the following has been a pleasure and a privilege: National Geographic Maps, National Geographic Education and Children's Media, and National Geographic Missions programs. We thank the Society for its guidance and support.

National Geographic Exploration

National Geographic supports the work of a host of anthropologists, archaeologists, adventurers, biologists, educators, writers, and photographers across the world. The individuals below each contributed substantially to *U.S. History: American Stories*

Ken Garrett

National Geographic Photographer

John Kelly

Archaeologist

National Geographic Explorer

William Kelso

Archaeologist

National Geographic Explorer

Robert Reid

Travel Writer

National Geographic Digital Nomad

Pardis Sabeti

Computational Geneticist

National Geographic Explorer

Donald Slater

Educator

National Geographic Explorer

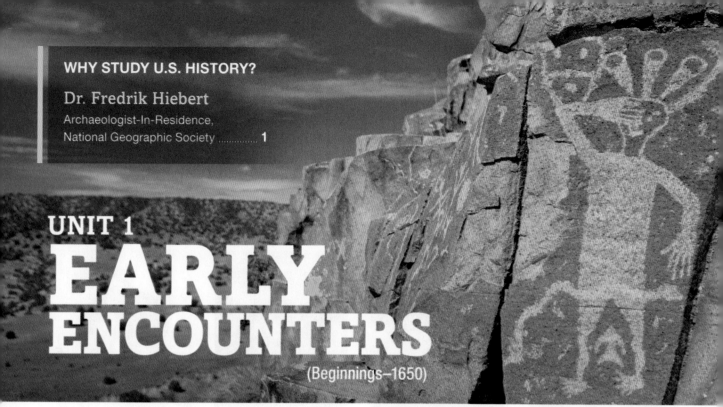

UNIT 1
EARLY ENCOUNTERS
(Beginnings–1650)

UNIT 2
ENGLISH SETTLEMENT (1585–1763)

UNIT 3
A NEW NATION (1763–1791)

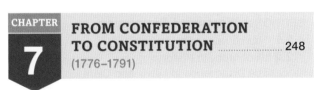 **Colonial Vernacular Architecture**

CHAPTER **7** **FROM CONFEDERATION TO CONSTITUTION** 248
(1776–1791)

 Philadelphia, Summer of 1787

AMERICAN **GALLERY** ONLINE **Historic Philadelphia**

UNIT 4
THE EARLY REPUBLIC
(1789–1844)

UNIT 5
PUSHING NATIONAL BOUNDARIES
(1821–1860)

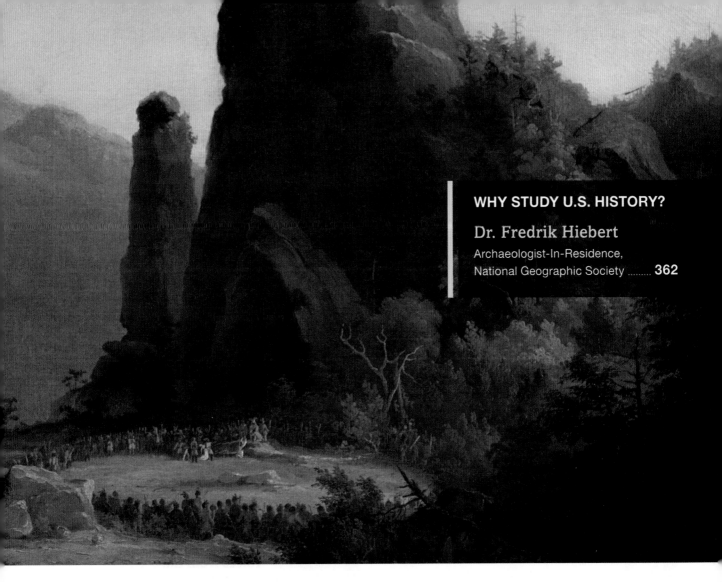

UNIT 6
CIVIL WAR AND RECONSTRUCTION
(1846–1877)

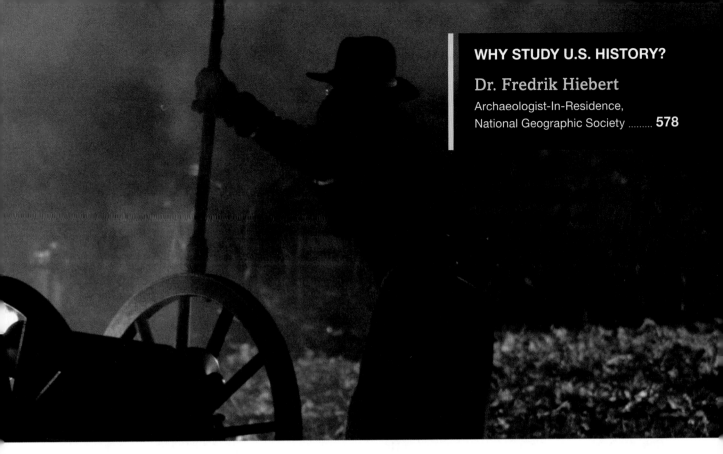

WHY STUDY U.S. HISTORY?

Dr. Fredrik Hiebert
Archaeologist-In-Residence,
National Geographic Society **578**

National Geographic Features

Maps

Mask carved by New Vancouver Tribe

National Geographic Explorer Pardis Sabeti

National Geographic Explorers

Document-Based Questions

Valley Forge National Historical Park, Pennsylvania

American Stories

American Stories Online

Student Handbooks

Geography in History

American Voices Biographies

American Places

Special Features

Thomas Jefferson

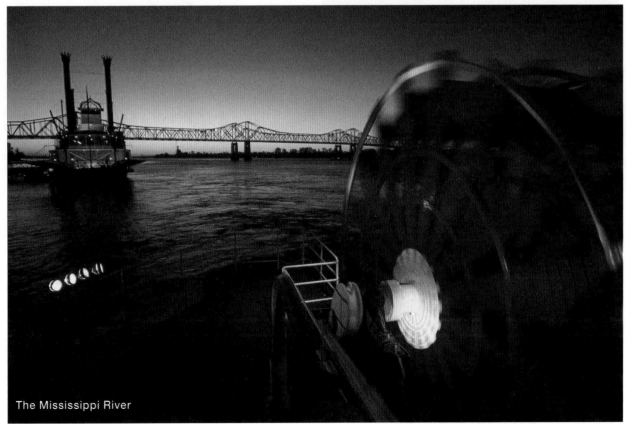

The Mississippi River

Why Study U.S. History?

I'm Fred Hiebert, National Geographic's Archaeologist-in-Residence. Like you, I live in the United States. But my work takes me all over the world, and that gives me a chance to view the United States from a global perspective. I think a lot about what it means to be an American.

The history of the United States is a chronicle of different regions that today are pulled together on a cultural basis. In the early years, our identity as a nation was defined on a military or political basis—and we're still struggling with those differences.

As we look back on U.S. history, we'll consider the role of justice and American values in giving people an opportunity to make a life for themselves and to move between these regions. One of our freedoms is the ability to move across the country and experience different ideas about what it means to be American.

HISTORY NOTEBOOK

Find "Why Study U.S. History?" in your History Notebook. The questions and activities will help you begin to find meaning in what you're reading. Use the notebook to record your ideas and questions as you read.

What makes the history of the United States special?

PERSONAL FREEDOM

THE PROMISE OF JUSTICE FOR ALL

AN OPEN SOCIETY

U.S. history is a microcosm of world history; think of it as a mini–world history. It includes the history of our natural resources and how they've been conserved—or not. It involves the defense of our nation and the United States' role in the world. U.S. history examines our collective identity as American citizens or people who call this country home. And on a personal level, U.S. history explores how our identity has been shaped by critical events from the past and the key women and men who brought them about.

Has anyone ever said to you, "Who *are* you?" What did that person mean by asking that? How did you respond? And how does that question relate to U.S. history?

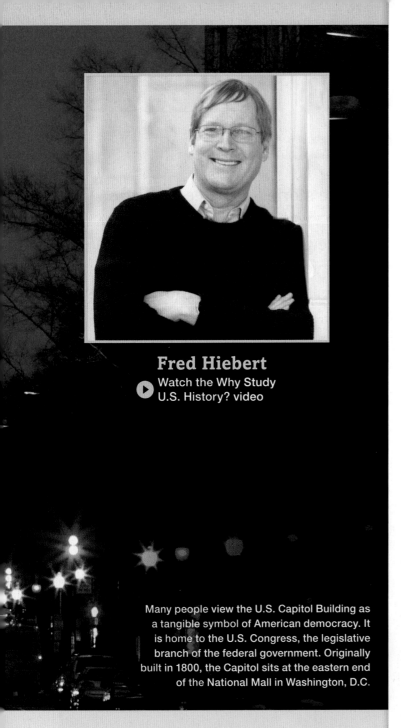

Fred Hiebert

▶ Watch the Why Study
U.S. History? video

Many people view the U.S. Capitol Building as a tangible symbol of American democracy. It is home to the U.S. Congress, the legislative branch of the federal government. Originally built in 1800, the Capitol sits at the eastern end of the National Mall in Washington, D.C.

The fact is your life today is the result of events and ideas that make up the history of the United States. We study history to learn how we became who we are at this place and at this time, which helps us actually answer that question for ourselves.

History really can tell you something about yourself and your identity.

Think about ways in which you are unique: What factors affect your personal identity, your home, your family, your community, your country? How can you shape who you are and who you want to be?

National Geographic Framework for U.S. History

The **Framework for U.S. History** can help you use your text to explore these questions—and to start a dialogue with your classmates about the history and culture of the United States. Your *American Stories* textbook divides history into these general categories:

UNITS 1 AND 2
Core Populations

The United States is made up of indigenous peoples as well as people from other lands, other traditions, and other cultures, including north Asian, Scandinavian, Spanish, English, French, and African.

UNITS 3, 4, AND 5
Primary Development of the American Republic

The early American republic unifies as a new nation and begins to develop a national identity. Americans act on a spirit of boundless possibility as they push westward and stretch national borders.

UNIT 6
Second Stage of National Development

The United States endures deep political divisions that result in the Civil War. Postwar changes lead to new freedoms for formerly enslaved people but leave unanswered questions about the future direction of the country. An urge to capture the state of American society as a new century approaches leads to the World's Columbian Exposition, hosted in Chicago to celebrate the 400th anniversary of Columbus's landing in the New World.

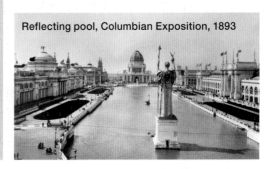
Reflecting pool, Columbian Exposition, 1893

To explore what it means to be an American

U.S. history is full of stories. Some of those stories may seem a little slow-moving, but others couldn't be more exciting. You live in the United States, and whether you are a citizen or not, those stories belong to you and to all of us—and you have your own story to tell. Use Fred Hiebert's personal story below as a model for capturing your own story about life in this country.

FRED'S AMERICAN STORY

My great-great-grandparents were invited to homestead in the Great Plains region of Kansas and raise a new strain of wheat that is planted in the fall and harvested in the spring. This type of wheat revolutionized farming in this country.

Both my mom's and dad's families came from the same Kansas community. Their way of life was disrupted by the Great Depression of 1929, a financial low point in American history during which many farmers found themselves greatly in debt.

Fred's grandmother, Helen Hiebert, is shown here on her father's farm about 1912, bringing lunch to harvesters.

This postage stamp—shown here on its first day of issue in 1974—celebrates the centennial of the introduction of winter wheat to the Great Plains, where it became an important commercial crop. Winter wheat usually produces higher crop yields than other types of wheat. This intersection between the lives of individual Americans like Fred Hiebert's grandparents and the development of the United States into a major economic force still happens today in large and small ways across the country.

My parents' families lived in the Dust Bowl, the area within the Great Plains of the Midwest where extended drought and soil erosion sometimes made farming impossible. That forced my dad's family to move to Nebraska and later to California.

My mom's family stayed in Kansas, and my parents met at a local college before World War II. During the war, my dad got interested in health care and, like his brothers and sisters, went to college. Eventually they settled in cities from Bakersfield, California, to Chicago, Illinois. I was born in Washington, D.C., while my dad was interning in a hospital, and I grew up in Michigan.

For the last 18 years, my hometown has been in Haverford Township, Pennsylvania, close to Philadelphia. I'm connected by train service to New York City and Washington, D.C., where my office at the National Geographic Society is located. Today, from my suburban hometown I am linked to the world through Internet, telephone, and a close airport, making me a "global citizen."

As You Read

We all have our own stories about life in the United States. The important thing is to share our experiences and be good listeners, showing respect and tolerance for the storytellers.

In your History Notebook, write a paragraph on what the term *identity* means to you. Think about how the events you read about might connect to your own life and how these events helped shape the community and country you live in today. And finally, think about how you might answer this question:

What does it mean to be an American?

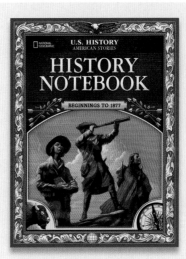

THE STORY
OF A
CONTINENT

BY DR. WILLIAM PARKINSON

National Geographic Explorer
Associate Curator of Anthropology
Field Museum of Natural History

CRITICAL VIEWING This artist's rendering shows the Laurentide Ice Sheet, which, at times, covered large parts of North America during the Pleistocene epoch. Present-day glaciers, particularly in Canada, are remnants of this ice sheet. What does the image reveal about this glacial period?

EARTH'S TIME LINE —— 100 Million Years

Earth Forms	First Life Appears on Earth
4.5 Billion Years Ago	3.8 Billion Years Ago

Close your eyes for a minute. Try to imagine the United States without any of the familiar trappings of 21st-century life—no smartphones, hoverboards, or tablets. No iTunes, YouTube, or video games.

Imagine moving from place to place without paved roads to follow—in fact, with no roads at all, and no wheeled vehicles or even horses to carry you. Instead of strip malls, fast-food chains, and electric streetlights, there are lush, dark forests, pristine rivers and streams, and abundant plant and animal life as far as your eye can see.

Take a deep breath—you're in for an adventure. Travel back to the earliest history of North America, from the beginnings of civilization and even further back to a time when mammoths and mastodons, saber-toothed cats, and giant ground sloths roamed the lands of North America. It was a time when your own species, *Homo sapiens*, evolved and spread throughout the world.

This is the moment in a play just before the main curtain rises on North America—a continent with a story much longer than you may think.

GEOLOGY AND LANDSCAPE

North America is geologically dramatic. It features towering mountains, vast deserts, sandy beaches, and rolling hills. But the landscape that Europeans like Christopher Columbus encountered when they arrived in the "New World" just a few hundred years ago was profoundly different from the world that the earliest humans experienced when they first came to North America.

Let's go way back in time. The first modern humans arrived in North America at the end of a period geologists refer to as the **Pleistocene epoch** (PLEIS-toh-seen EH-puhk). The Pleistocene lasted over 2 million years. During this period, the climate and ecology of North America was completely different from the climate and ecology of today. It included supersized animals and plants that no longer exist. During the Pleistocene epoch, modern humans across the world honed their skills in hunting, created early artwork, developed fire, and began to use language.

Many people think the climate during the Pleistocene was always cold. In fact, there were dramatic fluctuations in temperature over relatively short periods of time. At some points, the climate during the Pleistocene was about the same as it is today. During **glacial periods**, or **ice ages**, when glaciers expanded across Earth's surface, the global average annual temperature was significantly colder.

There were more than 20 cycles of glacial periods during the Pleistocene epoch. The movement of ice and water during these cycles changed the landscape and shorelines of the continents drastically, especially around the edges of the Arctic Circle and in present-day Europe, Asia, and North America.

◄ 2.6 MILLION YEARS AGO

TODAY ►

PLEISTOCENE EPOCH ┗━━━┛ 100 Thousand Years
2.6 Million to 11,700 Years Ago

People Arrive in North America 18–12,000 Years Ago
Modern Humans Evolve 75,000 Years Ago

HOLOCENE EPOCH
11,700 Years Ago to Today

North America Splits from Pangea
200 Million Years Ago

TODAY ►

BRIDGING THE CONTINENTS

In Europe, Asia, and Africa, modern humans evolved between 75,000 and 35,000 years ago—long before they arrived in North America. By the end of the Pleistocene, about 12,000 years ago, the only surviving hominid species was modern humans.

Scientists love debates, and one of the biggest debates in archaeology centers around the arrival of the earliest modern humans in North America. We know that when the Pleistocene ended, there were modern human societies living throughout the continent. The debate revolves around pinpointing when during the Pleistocene the first people migrated to the Americas and whether they came by boat or walked. Could people have *walked* from Europe and Asia to the Americas? Yes! But the continents are separated by oceans!

Remember during the Pleistocene, there were glacial periods when ice sheets covered the continents. The oceans contained less water, and the coastlines of the continents were much larger. After the last major glacial period, about 20,000 years ago, the two ice sheets that covered northern North America began to melt. North America was temporarily connected to Asia by a large stretch of land between modern-day Alaska and Siberia that scientists call the **Bering Land Bridge**. About 11,000 to 12,000 years ago, the land bridge disappeared as the ice melted, the oceans filled with the water, and the coastlines receded.

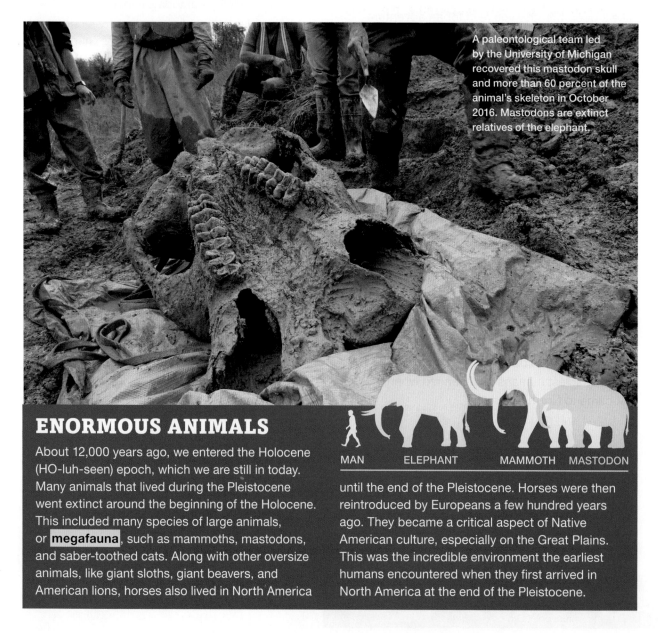

A paleontological team led by the University of Michigan recovered this mastodon skull and more than 60 percent of the animal's skeleton in October 2016. Mastodons are extinct relatives of the elephant.

MAN   ELEPHANT   MAMMOTH   MASTODON

ENORMOUS ANIMALS

About 12,000 years ago, we entered the Holocene (HO-luh-seen) epoch, which we are still in today. Many animals that lived during the Pleistocene went extinct around the beginning of the Holocene. This included many species of large animals, or **megafauna**, such as mammoths, mastodons, and saber-toothed cats. Along with other oversize animals, like giant sloths, giant beavers, and American lions, horses also lived in North America until the end of the Pleistocene. Horses were then reintroduced by Europeans a few hundred years ago. They became a critical aspect of Native American culture, especially on the Great Plains. This was the incredible environment the earliest humans encountered when they first arrived in North America at the end of the Pleistocene.

THE GREAT DEBATE

Until recently, scientists believed that the earliest people—**hunter-gatherers**—arrived in the Americas just before the land bridge disappeared. They specialized in hunting large herd animals that migrated back and forth across the continent. Archaeologists call them the Clovis Culture, based on a kind of stone tool—a Clovis point—that people made at that time.

But there is growing evidence that other groups may have reached the Americas before the Clovis Culture. Sites in Chile and Pennsylvania suggest that there was a pre-Clovis occupation of North America, and some scientists even speculate that people may have arrived by boats earlier in the Pleistocene, perhaps from Europe rather than Asia.

By the end of the Pleistocene, the climate began to stabilize, and modern humans spread throughout the Americas. They were specialized, mobile hunters and gatherers like their contemporaries elsewhere in the world, and they used the same technology—Clovis points—to hunt. These points have been found throughout North America, and similar ones have appeared as far south as Venezuela. People began to settle in different regions of the North American continent. These regions can be distinguished according to the specialized stone tools that were made and used in the Holocene.

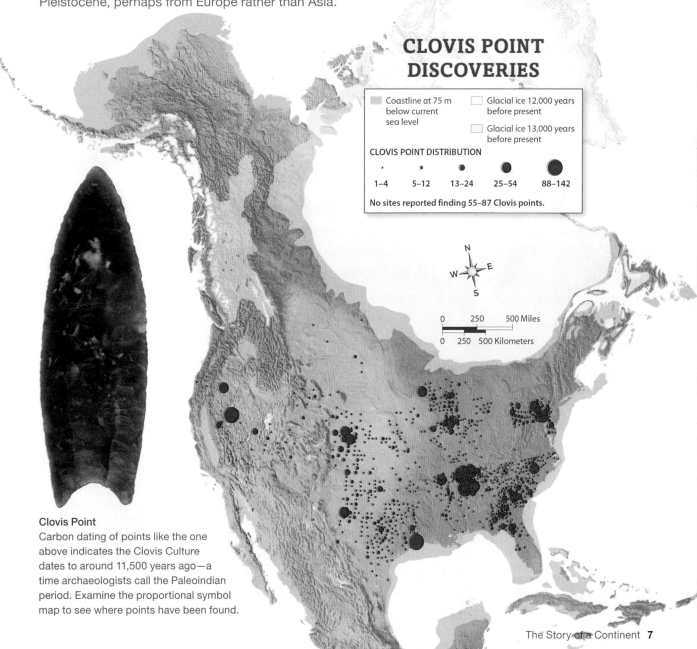

CLOVIS POINT DISCOVERIES

- Coastline at 75 m below current sea level
- Glacial ice 12,000 years before present
- Glacial ice 13,000 years before present

CLOVIS POINT DISTRIBUTION

| 1–4 | 5–12 | 13–24 | 25–54 | 88–142 |

No sites reported finding 55–87 Clovis points.

Clovis Point
Carbon dating of points like the one above indicates the Clovis Culture dates to around 11,500 years ago—a time archaeologists call the Paleoindian period. Examine the proportional symbol map to see where points have been found.

CORN EVOLVES

Corn's wild ancestor is a grass called *teosinte*, which doesn't look much like corn but has a very similar genetic makeup. After corn was introduced to North America 6,000 to 10,000 years ago, it spread from Mexico into the American Southwest and across the continent. Early farmers learned to grow types of corn with qualities they valued, such as resistance to pests and the ability to grow in different types of soil. That led to a great diversity of species.

teosinte

modern corn

Greater Southwest c. 1000 B.C.

Corn cobs and kernels found in Bat Cave in New Mexico were carbon-dated to around 1000 B.C. and had characteristics similar to older corn remnants found in Mexico.

East Coast c. 100 B.C.

Corn was probably first grown in the area that is now the eastern United States around 100 B.C., but people in this region had been domesticating other crops, like beans, gourds, and sunflowers, for thousands of years. Once introduced, maize quickly spread across agricultural communities.

Mexico c. 5000 B.C.

Samples from archaeological sites in Oaxaca and Tehuacán, Mexico, are believed to represent the earliest examples of farmed corn on the North American continent, including teosinte and later, more domesticated varieties.

THE SPREAD OF CORN

Analyze the map above. What do you observe about the movement of corn across the North American continent?

THE AGRICULTURAL REVOLUTION

For several thousand years during the Holocene, people continued to live in small groups and move frequently throughout the year. Everything changed when some groups of mobile hunters and gatherers started to experiment with planting their own crops. This transition from relying on gathering wild plants and hunting animals to planting crops and raising animals is called the **Agricultural Revolution**.

The practice of bringing plants and animals under human control is called **domestication**. Almost all the foods we eat today are domesticated instead of wild. This means that they have been modified from their wild forms and are to some extent reliant upon humans for their existence. Corn, for example, is the domesticated form of a plant called *teosinte* (TAY-oh-SIN-tay), and cows are the domestic form of a wild herd animal called an *aurochs* (OR-auks). Domestication had a dramatic impact on society. Once people settled down and became reliant upon domestic plants and animals, human life transformed.

Out of all the plants domesticated in North America thousands of years ago, the real game changer was corn. The hunters and gatherers who began experimenting with the domestication of corn had no idea of the impact their little experiment would have on the world in the years to come. Corn is now grown almost everywhere in the world and tied to almost everything Americans eat. It's even used to make toothpaste and gasoline. But the biggest impact corn had in North America was its unparalleled ability to feed large populations.

This c. 1250 cedar mask was discovered in Fulton, Illinois, and provides evidence of Mississippian cultures outside of Cahokia.

SETTLING DOWN

It took a while for corn to be adopted and widely used in North America. In eastern North America, for example, it wasn't a major part of the human diet until about 1,000 years ago. Growing crops like corn and remaining in one location allowed social groups to grow larger and develop more complex political systems. In some places, these groups built massive cities and had extensive trade networks that moved goods across the continent.

One of these cities was located in present-day Illinois along the Mississippi River near the modern town of St. Louis, Missouri. Founded around A.D. 800, Cahokia would come to be the capital of a large community called a **chiefdom**. By A.D. 1250, Cahokia was a thriving community. This large city controlled a massive geographic area at the confluence of three rivers (the Missouri, Illinois, and Mississippi), and at its height may have had a population of about 15,000 people. It is considered the most sophisticated prehistoric native civilization north of Mexico.

The fertile soil of Cahokia was easy to farm and well suited to growing corn. As a result, people farmed more and hunted less. And archaeological evidence unearthed from the site indicates the people of Cahokia ate well.

Although Cahokia and other similar sites in the southeastern United States were heavily dependent upon domestic crops like corn, communities in other parts of North America were not. They continued to hunt and gather wild resources as a major part of their diet.

A CULTURAL MOSAIC

Before the 1500s, the Americas, Europe, and Africa had been isolated from one another. But as Europeans began looking beyond their shores for riches and resources, Africa's mighty empires wanted to show their strength. Both continents were on a collision course with the Americas, but the Europeans got there first.

When the Europeans arrived in the "New World," they experienced a mosaic of diverse cultures and landscapes. From the hierarchical chiefdoms of Florida to the more mobile, less hierarchical groups of the Great Basin, the cultures of North America made up a patchwork quilt of societies with distinct languages, economic practices, political systems, and traditions as varied as the landscape.

This bird-shaped tobacco pipe was found in Canada in the Pacific Northwest region of North America.

Groups such as the Chumash, who settled along the California coastline, fished from canoe-like boats made of rushes.

Chumash fishing hook, carved from a shell

As you read in Why Study U.S. History, everyone has a personal American story to tell, and those stories often reflect the diversity of our cultural mosaic. That diversity is one of the best things about life in the United States. It's not always easy to build consensus or get everyone "on the same page," but that's what's exciting. With so many opinions and perspectives and our dogged American drive, we have the potential to develop amazingly creative solutions to 21st-century issues.

Believed to be 1,000 years old, the Pilling Figurines from the Fremont group in Utah were named for the rancher who discovered them in 1950.

So raise the curtain on this incredibly rich and varied landscape, well equipped to sustain and nurture the promise of a unique new country and a vibrant people. The action and the drama are just about to begin.

NORTHWEST

PLATEAU

BASIN

CALIFORNIA

SOUTHWEST

THINK ABOUT IT

What does the fact that these diverse cultures all expressed themselves through art suggest about early humans?

Like other groups in the Southwest, the Hohokam of southern Arizona frequently painted birds on items, such as the pot from which this shard came.

ARCTIC

SUBARCTIC

PLAINS

NORTHEAST

SOUTHEAST

In the Woodlands culture, a bird stone like this one found in Jefferson County, New York, was used to properly weight a throwing stick, or atlatl.

This hand made by a Hopewell artist from the Ohio River Valley was cut from a type of soft rock called mica.

These ear spools, which were carved from shells and worn in large holes in the earlobes, were unearthed from an Oklahoma mound.

Carved from wood and bone, this Mississippian mask fuses a human face with deer antlers and dates to between 800 and 1500.

The ruins of more than 600 cliff dwellings where the ancient Pueblo lived between 500 and c. 1300 can be seen at Mesa Verde National Park in Colorado.

EARLY
ENCOUNTERS

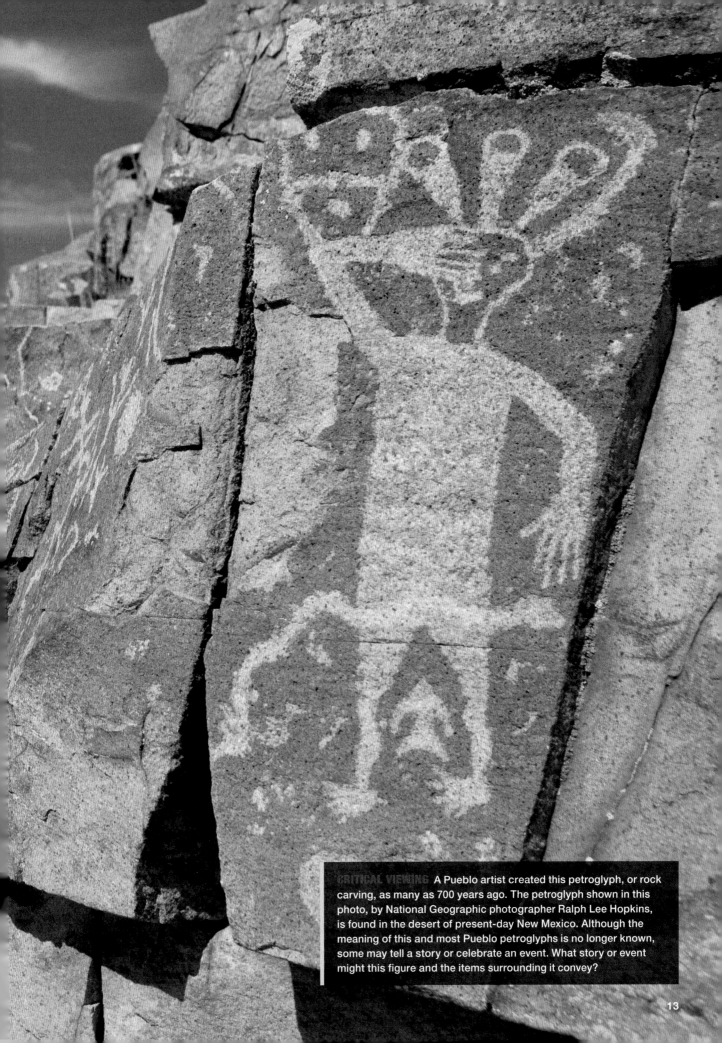

CRITICAL VIEWING A Pueblo artist created this petroglyph, or rock carving, as many as 700 years ago. The petroglyph shown in this photo, by National Geographic photographer Ralph Lee Hopkins, is found in the desert of present-day New Mexico. Although the meaning of this and most Pueblo petroglyphs is no longer known, some may tell a story or celebrate an event. What story or event might this figure and the items surrounding it convey?

THE
AMERICAS

1325
The Aztec found Tenochtitlán
and build a great civilization.
*(Aztec mosaic of a serpent,
possibly used in religious
ceremonies)*

A.D. 250
The Maya Classic Period begins.
(Maya temple in Tikal, Guatemala)

1200
More than 20,000
people live in the
Mississippian city
of Cahokia.

1200

c. 1000 B.C.
The ancient Pueblo begin
to farm in the southwestern
region of North America.

A.D. 1

1000 B.C.

THE
WORLD

c. 500 AFRICA
Ghana becomes the
first great trading
state in West Africa.

1200 AFRICA
The empire of Mali,
built on trade and gold,
arises in West Africa.
*(terra cotta horse and
rider created in Mali
around the early 1300s)*

A.D. 476 EUROPE
The Western Roman Empire
falls, and the period known as
the Middle Ages soon begins
in Western Europe.

HISTORICAL THINKING: DETERMINE CHRONOLOGY

What activities were undertaken throughout much of the world beginning in the 1400s?

1450
The Inca build Machu Picchu in the Andes Mountains. *(golden Inca artifact)*

1519
Hernán Cortés leads the invasion of Mexico and conquers the Aztec.

1492
Columbus makes the first of several voyages to the Americas.

t' Fort nieuw Amsterdam op de Manhatans

1626
The Dutch buy Manhattan Island from Native Americans and found New Amsterdam (present-day New York City) on the site. *(fine art image of the New Amsterdam settlement)*

1400

1800

1405 ASIA
Zheng He begins the first of seven voyages from China, exploring Asia and Africa.

1650 AFRICA
More than 40 trading posts on Africa's west coast send slaves to the New World.

1300 EUROPE
The Renaissance begins in Europe. *(Renaissance artist Leonardo da Vinci's painting, the Mona Lisa)*

CHAPTER 1

THREE WORLDS
BEFORE 1500

ESSENTIAL QUESTION
How were early civilizations in the Americas, Africa, and Europe both similar and different?

AMERICAN **STORIES**   Land of Plenty

SECTION 1 Societies of the Americas
KEY VOCABULARY

civilization	irrigation	physical geography
domesticate	kayak	potlatch
geographic perspective	matrilineal	slash-and-burn agriculture
human geography	migrate	tepee
Iroquois League		tundra

SECTION 2 Societies of Europe
KEY VOCABULARY

caravel	manor system	Protestant
feudalism	navigation	serf
hierarchy	printing press	vassal
humanism	profit	

SECTION 3 Societies of West Africa
KEY VOCABULARY

caravan	oasis	steppe
convert	pilgrimage	trans-Saharan

AMERICAN **GALLERY**
ONLINE   Cahokia: A Native American City

READING STRATEGY

COMPARE AND CONTRAST
To compare and contrast, note similarities and differences between two or more people, places, events, or things. As you read, use a graphic organizer like this one to compare and contrast the societies discussed.

Americas	Europe	Africa
empires		

"All things are bound together. All things connect."

—Seattle, Duwamish leader

CRITICAL VIEWING Rivers, brooks, and waterfalls flow through the rugged landscape of Vermont's Green Mountain National Forest. The 400,000-acre forest also holds archaeological evidence of the Native American "Original Vermonters" dating back 10,000 years. What natural resources can you identify in the photo that Native American populations might have used to survive?

LAND OF
PLENTY

BY DR. TERENCE CLARK

Director, Shíshálh Archaeological Research Project,
University of Saskatchewan

What does *plenty* mean to you? For the first people who lived in North America, the concept of plenty revolved around food. Hunting, gathering, and growing food took up a lot of their time. Lucky for them, they lived in a Land of Plenty.

As you have just read, North America is one of the most geographically varied places in the world. It has towering mountain ranges, wide, grassy plains, rocky coasts, and gentle valleys. Networks of powerful rivers support rich soil. Countless species thrive in every part of the continent. For thousands of years, North America's varied environments have provided people, both ancient and modern, with lush natural resources. Whether bison on the Great Plains, berries from a rain forest, elk in the Rocky Mountains, or fish along the coasts, the first residents had plenty to eat.

In addition, Native Americans across the continent developed ways to produce even more food. In the southwestern deserts, they raised crops like corn, beans, and squash. In the eastern woodlands, they devised a slash-and-burn method to create land on which to farm. Native Americans knew a great deal about the world around them, and they understood the delicate balance of taking from nature in moderation and with respect.

How might the concept of plenty have defined people who lived in North America in the past?

CRITICAL VIEWING Deer run through Tuolumne Meadows in California's Yosemite National Park. What details in this photo represent North America as a "land of plenty"?

CULTURES OF THE NORTHWEST COAST

Let's take a look at one region in particular—the Pacific Northwest—that demonstrates the powerful relationship between Native Americans and the natural world. The Pacific Northwest is a geographic and cultural area that stretches from what is now northern California to present-day Alaska. It includes coastal areas, inland forests, and several mountain ranges. It is also where the massive Columbia River flows through the Cascade Mountains and into the Pacific Ocean.

One unique feature of the Pacific Northwest is its temperate rain forests, which are characterized by heavy rainfall—as much as 14 feet per year—and by moderate temperatures. These rain forests are also home to some of the biggest trees in the world, including Sitka spruce, giant sequoia, and Douglas fir. These trees can grow to more than 250 feet tall and live for hundreds of years.

The first people who lived in the Pacific Northwest developed distinctive cultures, including the Kwakiutl (kwah-kee-YOO-tuhl), the Tlingit (KLING-kit), the Haida (HIGH-dah), the Chinook (SHIH-nuhk), and many others.

Because they lived among giant trees, these cultures mastered skills in woodworking. They built huge cedar plank houses, some large enough for hundreds of people. They also carved sturdy and seaworthy boats out of enormous tree trunks.

Northwest Coast people used woodworking in other ways, too. Intricately carved and painted totem poles towered over villages. Totems demonstrated village or family identities and indicated families' positions in the tribal social structure. They incorporated colorful representations of Pacific Northwest wildlife, including bears, ravens, whales, and eagles, as well as human figures and supernatural spirits. Totems functioned as collective histories, and the stories they told have been passed down among the generations.

Woodcarving also played a role in Northwest Coast ceremonies. Several ceremonies marked important times of the year or life events, and others reinforced social ties. Shamans, or people who were believed to be able to help others communicate with the spirit world, guided the carving of masks used during some ceremonies.

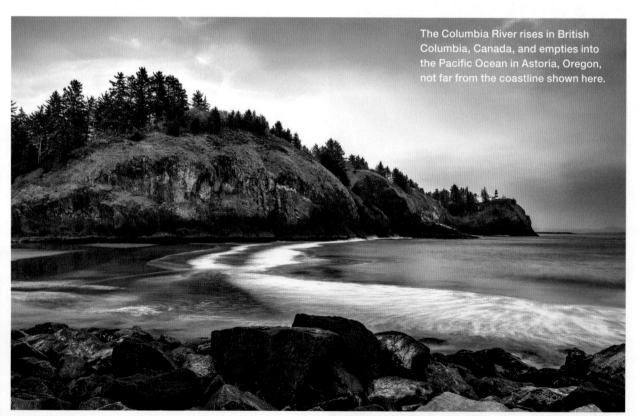

The Columbia River rises in British Columbia, Canada, and empties into the Pacific Ocean in Astoria, Oregon, not far from the coastline shown here.

OCEANS, FORESTS, AND RIVERS

Unlike groups in many other areas of North America, the coastal people of the Pacific Northwest did not farm to obtain food. Instead, they relied on the plentiful natural resources available to them. The many rivers that flow into the Pacific Ocean nourished the land and provided a welcome habitat for hundreds of species of plants and animals.

Perhaps the most important of these was the salmon. Since the earliest days of North America, five species of salmon born in rivers and lakes have traveled downstream to live their adult lives in the ocean. They only return to fresh water to spawn, or reproduce, and die. These spawning events, when millions of fish return to the streams and lakes where they were born, are some of the greatest migrations on Earth.

For early Northwest Coast people, abundant and predictable salmon migrations, or runs, provided the backbone of their traditional economies. The spring salmon runs in April and May were, and continue to be, incredibly important in providing food for Northwest Coast people. After a long winter of subsisting on dried foods—including smoked and dried salmon—spring was a time of plenty as fresh foods returned to the menu. Historically, the coming of the salmon often saved tribes from starvation as their winter supplies dwindled.

In addition to salmon, Northwest Coast people harvested a variety of shellfish, including clams, cockles, mussels, and oysters. They also hunted many land animals and birds, gathered a wide variety of plants and berries, and even hunted whales in some areas.

Northwest Coast totem poles are truly distinctive, with bright colors, detailed carving, and graphic patterns. What animals can you see on this totem?

A UNIQUE WORLDVIEW

Northwest Coast people saw themselves as an important part of their environment. Respect for the natural world was at the core of their worldview. They believed the plants and animals around them were as important as their human neighbors. How does this compare with the view people today have about the relationship between humans and nature?

Northwest Coast cultures also believed that many animals possessed human-like abilities. Some could even change into human form and take on traits such as anger if they were not treated with respect. If someone didn't hunt or fish in a respectful way, the animal might tell its kin to refuse to be caught in the future. All this added up to one clear point: survival required living in balance with animals and plants and respecting the natural world. Living a balanced life would ensure that food would be available year after year. Not doing so would bring dire consequences to the tribe.

Northwest Coast people adapted to and were shaped by their environments. In what ways does your environment shape who you are?

KING OF THE SALMON

Northwest Coast cultures performed special ceremonies to honor nature and to show respect for the plants and animals that kept them alive. One of the most important of these was the First Salmon ceremony. After a grueling winter of cold rain, with little access to fresh foods, spring brought new hope and abundance. People anxiously awaited the arrival of the salmon to usher in a season of plenty.

The first salmon to return to the river was called the King of the Salmon. People believed that as the leader, the King of the Salmon had the power to encourage other salmon to come and be caught or to scare away the other fish. If he was not treated with respect, the entire salmon run could be affected. To welcome the King of the Salmon, shamans conducted the First Salmon ceremony. Whole communities gathered to pay respect.

Although the First Salmon ceremony varied among different groups, three steps (described at right) characterize this ritual, which is still performed today. Once the ceremony is complete, the salmon fishing season is declared officially open and everyone can begin catching fish for food.

Students at the Lummi Nation School in Bellingham, Washington, prepare to bring in the First Salmon at their annual celebration of this traditional ceremony.

1. **Catching and welcoming the salmon**
   The chief selects a fisherman to catch the King of the Salmon. Once caught, tribal members carry it to the chief on a bed made of cedar.

2. **Cleaning, cooking, and eating the fish**
   Cooks delicately remove the meat from the fish. The head, entrails, and bones are set aside. Then community members eat the fish.

3. **Returning the remains to the water**
   Tribal members place the remains, which are considered sacred, in a cedar basket with its head facing upstream, pointing the way home. Then the salmon is released back into the water, where it is believed it will become whole again to continue its journey.

A master of ceremony named La-mos lifts the King of the Salmon to the sky as part of the Lummi Nation's First Salmon ceremony in May 2010.

CULTURAL REVIVAL

When European settlers arrived in the region in the early 1800s, two different worldviews came into contact with one another. In many cases, this contact led to changes among native traditions and practices.

Missionaries introduced Christianity and pressured native people to change their traditions. Europeans frowned on native beliefs that elevated the natural world to the level of humans, so they halted some ceremonies and declared others illegal. Along with ceremonies and religious beliefs, Europeans also replaced native foods with Western ones. Over time, Northwest Coast people began to shift away from traditional practices and focused on trade with the newcomers. By the late 1800s, the First Salmon ceremony began to die out.

During the 20th century, large commercial fisheries depleted salmon stocks all along the Pacific Coast. Development, overfishing, and pollution endangered the rivers and streams where the salmon migrated to spawn. According to the Native American worldview, this lack of respect for nature led to negative consequences, which included much smaller salmon runs than had been historically known.

In the 1970s, the Lummi people of Puget Sound, near Seattle, Washington, decided to bring back the First Salmon ceremony. They had never lost their belief in the importance of the plants and animals around them. And they felt the ceremony could help the salmon and the Lummi people.

In addition to reviving the First Salmon ceremony, the Lummi have also reclaimed salmon spawning habitats. They have restored streams to their natural state, ensuring the vital environment that salmon need to reproduce. The Lummi's efforts are paying off. Growing numbers of salmon are returning to their territory, and the Lummi are able to teach their children about the importance of respecting nature.

THINK ABOUT IT

The Lummi revived a ceremony to reinforce their connection to the natural world. What kinds of ceremonies or celebrations do you participate in that reinforce beliefs in your family and community?

A CEREMONIAL BLESSING

After the King of the Salmon is caught, cleaned, and cooked, it is ready to be eaten—after a blessing.

Among the Kwakiutl, this blessing is recited to honor the First Salmon. It has likely been handed down from generation to generation of Kwakiutl and is delivered before the salmon can be enjoyed. From this primary source, what can you conclude about how the Kwakiutl viewed their relationship with the King of the Salmon?

PRIMARY SOURCE

We have come to meet alive, Swimmer.
Do not feel wrong about what I have done to you,
friend Swimmer, for that is the reason why you come
that I may spear you, that I may eat you,
Supernatural One, you, Long-Life-Giver,
you, Swimmer.
Now protect us, (me) and my wife, that we may keep
well, that nothing may be difficult for us.

Source: from *The Religion of the Kwakiutl Indians*, by Frank Boas, New York: Columbia University Press, 1930, p. 207

1.1 Early American Civilizations

The Americas were never a blank slate, waiting for someone to "discover" them. People began arriving in the region about 20,000 years ago. Over time, they developed cultures that would influence all of the Americas and the world.

MAIN IDEA Civilizations emerged and thrived in Mesoamerica and South America for thousands of years.

MESOAMERICA

Long before 1492, great **civilizations**, or complex societies, arose in the Americas. The earliest of these civilizations began in **Mesoamerica**, which stretches from southern Mexico into part of Central America. Mesoamerica's landscape consists of two main areas: highlands and lowlands. The highlands lie between the mountains of the Sierra Madre (see-AIR-uh MAH-dray), a mountain system in Mexico. The lowlands are found along the coast of the Gulf of Mexico and in the jungles of the Yucatán (yoo-kuh-TAN) Peninsula. Both areas provided fertile land for agriculture.

The fertile land allowed several civilizations to develop in Mesoamerica. The **Olmec**, **Maya**, and **Aztec** thrived at different times from around 1200 B.C. to about A.D. 1520. The oldest civilization, the Olmec society, settled along present-day Mexico's Gulf Coast. The Maya, who were influenced by Olmec culture, mainly lived in parts of the countries we now call Mexico, Guatemala, and Belize. The Aztec were the last of the major Mesoamerican civilizations, establishing their empire in central and southern Mexico.

SOUTH AMERICA

To the south of Mesoamerica lies South America, a continent twice the size of the United States. South America contains coastal plains, dry forests and deserts, and vast river basins covered by dense rain forests and grasslands. The Andes Mountains rise along the continent over a distance of about 5,500 miles, extending from the northwestern coast all the way down to the southern tip. The mountains divide the Pacific coast from the continent's interior and separated the early civilizations in lands that are now the countries of Peru, Bolivia, Argentina, and Chile.

The **Moche** (MOH-chay) and the **Inca** were two of the most important early civilizations. The Moche lived on the arid northern coast of present-day Peru between about A.D. 100 and 800. They developed a complex **irrigation** system that channeled water to their crops. The rise of the Inca started in the 12th century. They established a capital city in Cusco (KOOS-koh), Peru, and later built the complex and mysterious city of Machu Picchu (MAH-choo PEE-choo) high in the Andes Mountains.

Moche Metalworking
The Moche were known for their vibrant murals, fine pottery, and advanced metalwork. Gold monkey-head beads, like this one, were often buried with members of the Moche nobility.

HISTORICAL THINKING

1. **READING CHECK** Which three civilizations developed in Mesoamerica?

2. **COMPARE AND CONTRAST** How were the highlands and lowlands of Mesoamerica similar?

3. **INTERPRET MAPS** How do you think the Andes Mountains benefited both the Moche and the Inca?

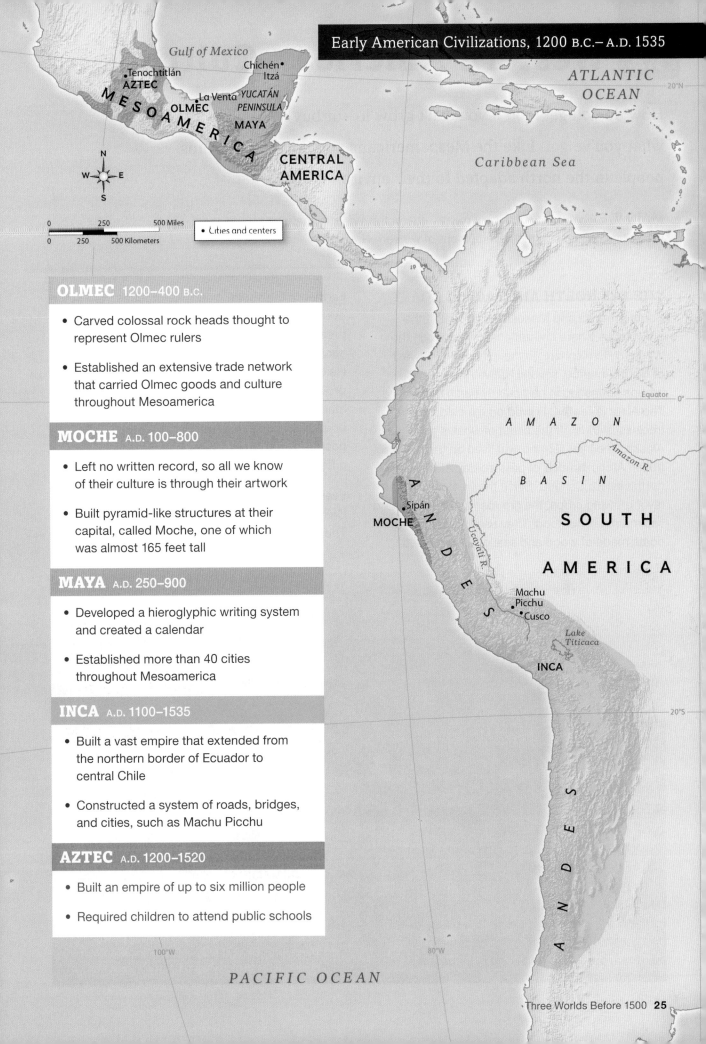

Gulf of Mexico

ATLANTIC OCEAN

20°N

Chichén Itzá

Tenochtitlán
AZTEC

La Venta YUCATÁN PENINSULA
OLMEC

MESOAMERICA

MAYA

CENTRAL AMERICA

Caribbean Sea

N
W E
S

500 Miles
0 250

0 250 500 Kilometers

• Cities and centers

OLMEC 1200–400 B.C.

- Carved colossal rock heads thought to represent Olmec rulers

- Established an extensive trade network that carried Olmec goods and culture throughout Mesoamerica

MOCHE A.D. 100–800

- Left no written record, so all we know of their culture is through their artwork

- Built pyramid-like structures at their capital, called Moche, one of which was almost 165 feet tall

MAYA A.D. 250–900

- Developed a hieroglyphic writing system and created a calendar

- Established more than 40 cities throughout Mesoamerica

INCA A.D. 1100–1535

- Built a vast empire that extended from the northern border of Ecuador to central Chile

- Constructed a system of roads, bridges, and cities, such as Machu Picchu

AZTEC A.D. 1200–1520

- Built an empire of up to six million people

- Required children to attend public schools

Equator 0°

AMAZON

Amazon R.

BASIN

SOUTH

AMERICA

ANDES

Sipán
MOCHE

Ucayali R.

Machu Picchu
Cusco

Lake Titicaca

INCA

20°S

ANDES

100°W

80°W

PACIFIC OCEAN

1.2 Western American Cultures

How do you get food if you can't grow it—or buy it? You work with what you've got. Like the Mesoamericans and South Americans, people in the north adapted to their environments.

> **MAIN IDEA** A variety of environments, characterized by climate and landforms, influenced the development of western North American cultures.

THE FAR NORTH AND PACIFIC COAST

South America and Mesoamerica weren't the only places where civilizations developed in the Western Hemisphere. In the extreme northwest of North America, several Native American groups flourished in particularly harsh climates. The Aleut (a-lee-OOT) lived on the cold, nearly treeless islands off the coast of what is now Alaska. The Inuit (IH-noo-wit) lived on the flat, frozen Arctic **tundra** of present-day Alaska and northwestern Canada. Since the weather did not favor growing crops, the groups fished and hunted sea mammals for food. They used **kayaks**, light boats made of wood and seal or walrus hides.

Farther to the south, a number of tribes lived in the evergreen forests that swept down the coast from present-day British Columbia to Oregon. Groups such as the Kwakiutl (kwah-kee-YOO-tuhl) and Haida (HI-duh) hunted and fished, and the ocean provided plenty of food. The abundance of trees made wood the preferred material for houses, boats, and household goods. The Kwakiutl also hosted **potlatches**, feasts where families gave gifts to guests to show social rank and wealth.

Even farther down the coast, in what is now California, the Pomo lived as hunter-gatherers. The Pomo didn't need to farm because the

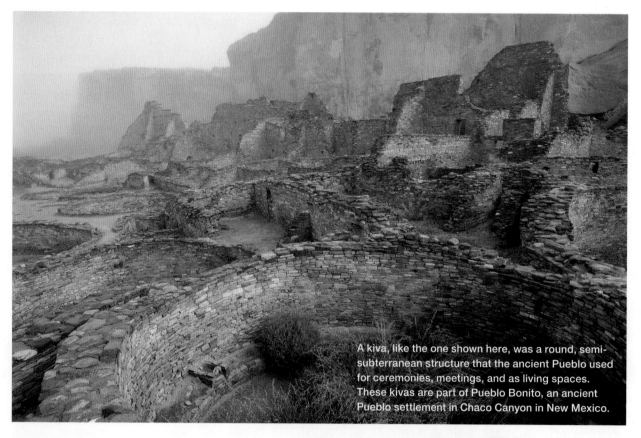

A kiva, like the one shown here, was a round, semi-subterranean structure that the ancient Pueblo used for ceremonies, meetings, and as living spaces. These kivas are part of Pueblo Bonito, an ancient Pueblo settlement in Chaco Canyon in New Mexico.

streams were full of fish, and plenty of edible wild plants, nuts, and berries grew on the land. The Pomo had a unique religion. Worshippers dressed as animal spirits and other beings to sing, dance, and distribute gifts.

THE DESERTS AND PLAINS

Like the people of the North and the West, Native Americans living in the Southwest and Great Plains had to adapt to special climates and conditions. In the arid American Southwest, the **ancient Pueblo** (PWAY-bloh) and the **Hohokam** (ho-ho-KOM) thrived during the time of the Maya. In fact, Mesoamerican culture heavily influenced these groups. Not only did the Hohokam trade with Mesoamericans, they also **domesticated**, or grew, similar crops for food. They irrigated their crops in the dry climate. The Hohokam grew cotton, squash, beans, and maize, or corn, by digging canals from their fields to nearby rivers. Having extra food allowed the population to grow.

Early North American Civilizations, c. 1400

Around A.D. 1000, both the Hohokam and the ancient Pueblo built large adobe (uh-DOH-bee) homes made of sun-dried clay and straw bricks. These dwellings were similar to apartment buildings with multiple floors. For example, Pueblo Bonito, pictured to the left, once had as many as five floors and at least 600 rooms.

The ancient Pueblo were once referred to as the Anasazi, a name given them by the Navajo. In the 1990s, descendants of the ancient Pueblo protested the use of the term, pointing out that it means "enemy ancestor." Today many historians use the term "ancient Pueblo."

Northeast of the Hohokam, the Great Plains tribes experienced a very different way of life. Vast grasslands stretched from the Mississippi River to the Rocky Mountains. Native Americans who lived in the eastern part of the Great Plains, such as the Mandan and Pawnee, lived the settled lives of farmers, building villages of earthen lodges. In the western grasslands, the Blackfoot and other

tribes like them **migrated**, or moved from place to place, hunting herds of bison (also commonly called buffalo) and other game for food and clothing. **Tepees**, or tents made of bison hides, served as their portable homes.

At this time, tribes herded bison on foot. They steered the animals over cliffs or into corrals where men could kill them with arrows. Nonetheless, Plains Indian tribes considered the bison sacred. They used every part of the animal: meat for food, skin and fur for clothes and tepees, and bones for tools and crafts.

HISTORICAL THINKING

1. **READING CHECK** How did the tribes of northern and western North America adapt to their environments?

2. **COMPARE AND CONTRAST** How did lifestyles differ among Great Plains tribes?

3. **DRAW CONCLUSIONS** What can you conclude about similarities between the Maya culture and those of the ancient Pueblo and the Hohokam?

1.3 Eastern American Cultures

You climb to the top of the tower at Serpent Mound in southern Ohio and look down at the amazing sight below. It really does appear to be a gigantic, grass-covered snake slithering across the landscape with an egg or a jewel in its mouth. How did it get here? Who made it, and when?

MAIN IDEA Native Americans in eastern North America established stable agricultural societies and specialized burial and religious practices.

Ancient Mounds
Serpent Mound in Adams County, Ohio, resembles a writhing snake. The mound stretches more than 1,300 feet. It is estimated to be between 1,000 and 2,000 years old.

THE MOUND BUILDERS

Serpent Mound and other mounds like it began dotting the North American landscape around 1000 B.C. The people who created these structures are known as the **Mound Builders**. They lived in the river valleys of the Midwest and eastern United States. These earthen mounds came in different shapes and sizes and served a variety of purposes. Some housed the dead, and others served as temples.

The Adena and Hopewell were two cultures that built mounds. Both groups lived chiefly in the southern part of present-day Ohio, where Serpent Mound is located. They also settled in the region we now call Indiana, Kentucky, West Virginia, Michigan, Wisconsin, and Pennsylvania. Both groups were primarily hunter-gatherers, though the Hopewell farmed as well. Studies of the Hopewell Mound Group have determined that their mounds served as ancient burial sites.

A couple of hundred years after the Hopewell culture died out, the Mississippians emerged. Beginning in about A.D. 700, this group spread across North America from present-day Georgia to Minnesota. The Mississippians topped their mounds with grand temples or chiefs' residences. Cahokia (kuh-HO-kee-yuh), a grouping of mounds located in Illinois, served as the culture's capital. At the Cahokia Mounds site, Monks Mound stands nearly 100 feet high. Its base is larger than that of the Great Pyramid of Giza in Egypt.

Unlike the hunter-gatherer cultures of the Adena and Hopewell, the Mississippians were largely agricultural. For food, they planted crops such as corn, beans, and squash. Having a large and dependable harvest helped them feed a large population. Cahokia alone may have housed as many as 15,000 people.

PEOPLE OF THE WOODLANDS

Just as the Mississippians depended on farming for their livelihoods, so too did the tribes who lived after them in the woodlands of eastern and southeastern North America.

The mild climate of the Southeast made it an ideal place to grow crops. The Chickasaw and Choctaw of present-day Mississippi and Alabama grew corn, beans, and pumpkins. Women planted and harvested the crops. They also cooked, cared for the children, and made baskets, clothes, and other goods. Men cleared the land, constructed buildings, hunted, served as warriors, and engaged in trade. Both the Chickasaw and Choctaw societies were **matrilineal**, meaning they traced their family lines through their mothers.

Agriculture was so important to these groups that one of their religious ceremonies was a Green Corn festival. The festival was held each summer as the corn began to ripen. Over a series of days, people fasted, feasted, danced, played games, and prayed.

The region in which the Eastern Woodlands people lived was heavily wooded, which explains its name. The tribes of the Eastern Woodlands practiced a technique known as **slash-and-burn agriculture**. This method involved cutting down and burning trees to clear land, and it supported the groups' pattern of moving frequently. Their farms were not permanent.

Two groups, named for the languages they spoke, lived in the Eastern Woodlands: the Algonquian (al-GAHN-kwee-uhn) and the Iroquois (IHR-uh-kwoy). The Algonquian lived along the Atlantic coast. The Iroquois primarily lived in the central part of present-day New York State. In Algonquian groups, men were the heads of households, but Iroquois society was matrilineal, and women shared political power with men. Five Iroquois-speaking nations banded together to form the **Iroquois League**: the Mohawk, Oneida, Onondaga, Cayuga (kah-YOO-guh), and Seneca. This brought long-lasting peace among them. The Iroquois nations still exist to this day.

HISTORICAL THINKING

1. **READING CHECK** How did farming help maintain a large population in Cahokia?

2. **IDENTIFY PROBLEMS AND SOLUTIONS** How did the Eastern Woodlands people solve the problem of growing food in forests?

3. **MAKE INFERENCES** Why would the mild climate of the Southeast have made it an ideal place to grow crops?

The Birdman Tablet depicts a man with wings and was found on the east side of Monks Mound.

Mounds
on the Mississippi

"Cahokia has changed our ideas about ancient Native American culture." —John Kelly

Once one of the greatest cities in North America, Cahokia went largely unstudied for hundreds of years. Then in the 1950s, President Dwight Eisenhower initiated the interstate highway program with a provision for archaeological excavations along the new roads. What the archaeologists found at the East St. Louis, Illinois, mound center astounded them: over a thousand houses that had been built in an amazingly short span of time. What had drawn so many people to the site? Who were they? Archaeologist **John Kelly** has been working on the answers to these and other questions for about 40 years.

^
Highways run on either side of Cahokia's Monks Mound, the largest pyramid north of Mesoamerica. A temple may have once stood on the platform atop the mound. After climbing to the top, a priest would have had a magnificent view of Cahokia's vast floodplain, known as the American Bottom.

MAIN IDEA Archaeologist John Kelly's excavations of the Cahokia Mounds have provided insight into the city's culture and its rise and fall.

CITY OF MYSTERY

National Geographic Explorer John Kelly has his work cut out for him. We know very little about Cahokia. The people who lived there didn't have a written language. We don't even know what they called themselves or the city they lived in. Cahokia was the name of people who lived briefly on the site in the 1700s, long after the city had disappeared. Archaeologists have pieced together what evidence they've found to expand our understanding of Cahokia. But as Kelly admits, "People still aren't really sure what it was."

According to Kelly, one thing we do know is that people had been living in Cahokia for years. The area was easy to reach along the Missouri, Illinois, and Mississippi rivers, and the land was good for growing a variety of crops, including corn. But why did the population swell from about 7,000 to 15,000 people between 1000 and 1100? One surprising theory states that people arrived after an extremely bright star called a supernova appeared around this time.

For whatever reason, people arrived in Cahokia in large numbers to build a ritual city with houses, farmland, and great plazas for religious celebrations. Above all—literally—they built the mounds. Monks Mound was the tallest. Named for the French monks who once lived in its shadow, the mound rose 100 feet in the center of the city. Laborers toiled on it for about 25 years using only baskets and stone hoes.

RISE AND FALL

Over time, the Cahokians built at least 110 other mounds. Some of these were used as burial sites. Archaeologists working at one called Mound 72 unearthed the remains of a man surrounded by ornaments and weapons. They also discovered the bodies of men and young women buried with and near him. Some were likely human sacrifices.

Kelly has spent much of his time investigating a mound that wasn't used for burials: Mound 34. Actually, his research takes him underneath the mound. The Cahokians constructed a building on

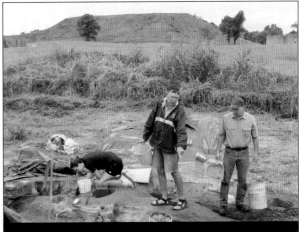
Kelly (center) works with students at the site of Cahokia's Mound 34. They are actually standing underneath the mound, which was removed. Artifacts suggest that a special society of hunters or warriors may have used the building that stood on top of the mound. Monks Mound rises in the background.

top of the mound's platform, but other buildings and a copper workshop stood beneath the mound. According to Kelly, the buildings may have been placed there and covered with earth to represent the view of the world as existing in three layers: the beneath world with Earth Mother, this world, and the upper world. As Kelly says, "We focus on the mounds, but the history's really about the building that was there before the mound!"

Around the end of the 1100s, a different kind of construction began in Cahokia. Walls were erected around the city, possibly as protection against attack. But by then, the population had already begun to dwindle and the city to decline. Some say climate change or disease may have led to the fall of Cahokia. Kelly says that a massive flood may have covered the city and caused the people to leave for a brief time. Over a century later, a long drought may have led to the eventual abandonment. What we do know is that, for some reason, by the late 1300s, the residents had left the city. Cahokia remains mysterious to the end.

HISTORICAL THINKING

1. **READING CHECK** What did the Cahokians build in their city?

2. **ANALYZE CAUSE AND EFFECT** Why did Cahokia decline?

1.5 National Museum of the American Indian Washington, D.C.

The National Museum of the American Indian (NMAI) is located in Washington, D.C., on the National Mall. The museum and its grounds were designed with the help of tribes and communities from across the hemisphere to share the sense and spirit of Native Americans with its many visitors. NMAI has a tremendous collection of Native American arts and artifacts—over 800,000 items representing more than 1,200 cultures throughout the Americas and over 12,000 years of history. Visitors experience everything from ancient tools and weapons to modern Native American art, cultural and religious artifacts, and everyday items. Which of the items below were used for everyday activities and which ones served a different purpose?

Tlingit Canoe Paddles

These Tlingit paddles date to the early 1900s. The Tlingit are indigenous people of the Pacific Northwest in North America, where fish are abundant. For the Tlingit, canoes and paddles are tools necessary for survival.

Odawa Moccasins

This pair of beaded Odawa (Ottawa) moccasins was purchased by a trader at Crown Point, Indiana, a fur trade depot. The moccasins feature folded-down silk cuffs decorated with small beads arranged in dashed lines, a pattern often found on this type of Odawa moccasins. Silk teardrops and diamond shapes also decorate the moccasins and are outlined with even smaller white glass beads.

What do you observe about the craftsmanship of these Odawa moccasins?

Chief of the Undersea Mask

This colorful carved wood mask is made of western red cedar. It represents the chief of the undersea kingdom. He is believed to live in a copper home under the ocean, guarded by sea monsters. Ceremonial masks like this one usually depict characters from family histories or from the supernatural. This mask was carved by a master carver from the New Vancouver Tribe in western Canada in the late 1800s or early 1900s.

The U-shaped designs that surround the face represent the scales of a fish or a sea creature. They may have been added to the mask later by a second artist.

"We seek to bring the Native voice into **every school, every library, every university,** indeed, every home."
—Kevin Gover (Pawnee)
Director, National Museum of the American Indian

The paddles are made of yellow cedar and ornately painted with a wolf design.

1.6 Native American Environments

MAIN IDEA Before European settlement, 500 Native American tribes inhabited North America. Geography helped to shape their diverse cultures.

PHYSICAL AND HUMAN GEOGRAPHY

When you examine how geography affected people and culture, you are taking a **geographic perspective**. That is, you are looking at culture through the lens of geography. You can examine two aspects of geography: physical geography and human geography.

Physical geography refers to the physical characteristics of a region. It includes the surface of the earth, soil, bodies of water, climate, and glaciers and ice sheets. It also includes plant and animal life.

Human geography examines how people and their cultures are affected by physical geography, and how human activities affect the environment. For example, geography has a great impact on how people make a living. People who live near the sea often make a living by fishing, and in regions with fertile soils, farming is usually an important economic activity.

Use physical geography and human geography to study these Native American tribes before the arrival of Christopher Columbus in the Americas. For each group, you will find an explanation of their physical geography and human geography.

Carved polar bear knife handle, Alaska

Native American Nations, 1491

0   250   500 Miles
0   250 500 Kilometers

ARCTIC AND SUBARCTIC

NORTHWEST COAST

GREAT BASIN AND PLATEAU

GREAT PLAINS

NORTHEAST

Great Lakes

SOUTHEAST

SOUTHWEST

PACIFIC OCEAN

Earthenware bowl, New Mexico

Stone point, Eastern Woodlands

PHYSICAL GEOGRAPHY	HUMAN GEOGRAPHY

ARCTIC AND SUBARCTIC

The Inuit, Aleut, and other tribes of this region lived in one of the harshest environments on Earth—the land that we now call Alaska. It is a land of snow and ice, with little vegetation in the winter.

The people living in the far north creatively adapted to their harsh environment. They hunted for seals and whales and built igloos out of ice to protect themselves from the extreme cold.

NORTHWEST COAST

The tribes of the Northwest Coast lived in the region that is now the states of Washington and Oregon and the Canadian province of British Columbia. It is a rich environment with lush forests and rivers filled with fish.

The tribes of the Northwest included the Chinook and the Tlingit. They fished and hunted for bears and other large game. The abundance of the region allowed families to accumulate wealth. Families gained honor by giving away part of their wealth in a ceremony called the potlatch.

GREAT BASIN AND PLATEAU

This region, west of the Great Plains, features soaring mountains and plateaus with long stretches of grassland. The land supported large mammals, including antelope, moose, elk, mountain goat, and bison.

The Utes, Shoshone, and other tribes hunted for game and fished in the rivers for salmon and trout. Some Native Americans even created dances to mimic the movement of the grass in the wind.

SOUTHWEST

The Southwest, which includes today's Arizona and New Mexico, is a region of deserts with very little rainfall. The climate is harsh, with temperatures soaring to 110 degrees Fahrenheit or more in the summer. But the region also has rivers.

The rivers are critical to this region because of the lack of rainfall. The Pueblo tribes, who lived near the Rio Grande in what is now New Mexico, planted maize (corn) and other crops near the river.

GREAT PLAINS

The Great Plains stretch from present-day Iowa to Wyoming. The region is flat, with plains and tallgrass prairies. The most important resource was once the bison, or buffalo, which numbered at least 30 million in the 1400s.

The Great Plains had many tribes, including the Lakota, the Blackfoot, and the Mandan. These tribes had one thing in common—they used the bison for food, shelter, and clothing.

NORTHEAST

The Northeast region spans the present-day states from Virginia to Maine. This land has ample rainfall, many rivers and streams, and a wealth of natural resources, including wild game, fish, and fertile soil.

The Algonquian- and Iroquois-speaking people who lived in this region used the many rivers and streams as highways. They built canoes out of wood and birchbark to use for long-distance trading.

SOUTHEAST

The Southeast reaches from today's North Carolina to Florida and offers many natural gifts: a mild climate, plentiful rainfall, and fertile soil.

The Cherokee, the Choctaw, and other groups grew maize, beans, squash, and other crops in the fertile soil. Because of the mild climate, the land supported a large population and tribes thrived.

THINK LIKE A GEOGRAPHER

1. **IDENTIFY MAIN IDEAS AND DETAILS** How did different Native American groups adapt to the amount of rainfall they received?

2. **MAKE INFERENCES** What does the potlatch reveal about the attitudes toward wealth among Native Americans of the Northwest?

2.1 The Middle Ages

For hundreds of years, the Roman Empire united much of Europe. So when the western part of the empire fell in A.D. 476, its laws and social structures collapsed, too. With the empire no longer in control, "Now what?" could well have been the question on almost everyone's mind.

MAIN IDEA During the Middle Ages, Western Europe underwent many political, economic, and social changes.

A FEUDAL SOCIETY

Political, economic, and social problems led to the decline of the Western Roman Empire. As the empire weakened, Germanic tribes from Northern Europe invaded Western Europe and overthrew the emperor.

The end of the Western Roman Empire signaled the beginning of a period known as the **Middle Ages**, which lasted from about A.D. 500 to 1450. With no central government after the fall of Rome, Western Europe largely consisted of small kingdoms ruled by Germanic tribes, such as the Franks, Visigoths, and Vikings. Over time, the kingdoms grew and became very powerful.

To help the leaders of these kingdoms hold onto their land and protect their subjects, a political and social system called **feudalism** developed. Feudalism helped ensure the defense and security of kingdoms, which were constantly at war with one another. It achieved this security by maintaining a strict social **hierarchy**, or order.

Kings sat atop this structure. They gave pieces of their land to noblemen, known as lords. A lord, in turn, granted parts of this land to lesser noblemen called **vassals**. Vassals paid taxes on the land and pledged their military service to the lord.

Structure of Feudal Society

A *king* inherited his position, but none could rule without the support of the noblemen.

Church officials and noblemen often exercised more power than the king.

Knights guarded their lord's castle and fought for him according to a strict code of conduct.

Serfs worked the land. In exchange for protection, a serf provided loyalty, labor, and crops.

The Plague Doctors

When the bubonic plague swept through medieval Europe in the 1300s, medical science was still 500 years away from understanding its cause. At that time, some doctors believed the plague was spread by bad air or odors. In the 1600s, a French physician created the costume, shown here, to protect against such odors and supposedly against the plague. But the problem was not odors. The problem was infected rats and their fleas. Rats spread throughout medieval cities, which lacked sanitation. Fleas living on the rats spread the disease by biting people. The victim then often suffered swelling, vomiting, back pain, delirium, and, finally, death.

Many vassals themselves were soldiers in the army and served as knights, who were warriors on horseback. Peasants called **serfs** were at the bottom of the heap.

The **manor system** emerged as a result of feudalism. The system consisted of peasants bound to a lord's land, or manor. Landowners maintained a tight grip on both their land and their workers, while the peasant workers received a level of military protection they could not provide for themselves. Feudalism and the manor system remained in place throughout the Middle Ages, providing some stability to Western Europe.

WARS, TRADE, AND TOWNS

Still, feudalism was not the only source of stability. The Roman Catholic Church served as the strongest unifying force in medieval Europe. Late in the 11th century, the Church waged the **Crusades**, wars against the spread of **Islam**. That religion's followers, called **Muslims**, had seized control of the Holy Land—the city of Jerusalem and the surrounding area. They'd also begun to attack the Christian Byzantine Empire, once the eastern half of the Roman Empire.

The Crusades continued for two centuries, allowing Crusaders to acquire land in areas previously conquered by Muslims. The land acquisition led to the establishment of trade centers. Though the Crusaders were ultimately unsuccessful—they eventually lost any land they captured—their actions increased trade between Europe and the eastern Mediterranean region.

As trade increased in Europe, businesses and the economy grew. Towns grew, too, as people left their positions on the manors for better jobs.

Outbreaks of a devastating disease called the bubonic plague also created jobs. In the 14th century, the plague killed as many as one-third of all Europeans. Those laborers lucky enough to survive the illness found better work prospects as a result of the decline in population. Less competition led to greater opportunities for those who survived.

The plague, along with the movement to cities and towns, helped bring about the decline of feudalism and the end of the Middle Ages. Europe began to experience cultural changes that would mark the beginning of a new age of creativity.

HISTORICAL THINKING

1. **READING CHECK** How are the manor system and feudalism similar to each other?

2. **EVALUATE** In what way were the Crusaders both successful and unsuccessful?

3. **COMPARE AND CONTRAST** How did feudalism and the Church affect Europe similarly and differently?

CRITICAL VIEWING During the Renaissance, artists often painted secular, or nonreligious, subjects in everyday settings. What do the details in this painting tell you about this woman's everyday life?

▥ J. Paul Getty Museum, Los Angeles

Francesco Ubertini (1494–1557), known as Bacchiacca, was a Renaissance painter from Florence, Italy. This painting, *Portrait of a Woman with a Book of Music*, reflects the new styles and techniques employed by Renaissance artists. For example, look at the column and vase in this painting.

By painting them proportionally smaller, Bacchiacca has produced the impression that these items are placed well behind the woman. This technique, called perspective, gives the illusion of depth and distance and helped Bacchiacca create a work that looks three-dimensional.

2.2 Renaissance and Reformation

In the 1300s, a revolution began to brew in Europe. But this revolution didn't involve weapons and war. It involved ideas. People focused on the individual and believed every person had unlimited possibilities. These, indeed, were revolutionary ideas.

MAIN IDEA The Renaissance marked a time of curiosity, learning, experimentation, communication, and change.

REBIRTH OF ART AND LEARNING

Historians called the revolutionary movement that began at the end of the Middle Ages the **Renaissance**, which means "rebirth." The Renaissance originated in Italy and spread to other parts of Europe. The movement had its roots in the classical writings of ancient Greece and Rome and the philosophy of **humanism**. Humanists encouraged freedom of thought and the development of new ideas.

The Renaissance also saw the revival of elements of ancient Greek and Roman architecture, such as columns and arches. This revival enabled generations of artists and architects to achieve levels of artistic creation not seen in Europe for a thousand years. Painters such as Raphael and Michelangelo, and architects such as Brunelleschi, created works that still inspire awe in people today. **Leonardo da Vinci** is considered by many to be the ideal Renaissance figure. Leonardo not only painted artistic masterpieces, but he was also an inventor, sculptor, and architect. His studies of anatomy and other sciences proved to be ahead of their time.

The ideas of the Renaissance also had an effect on literature. In the mid-1400s, **Johann Gutenberg's** invention of the **printing press**, which used movable metal type to print pages, allowed for mass distribution of classical and humanist literary works. As the availability of printed materials increased, more people learned to read, and the philosophy of the Renaissance and humanist movement began to spread rapidly across Europe.

DIVISIONS IN THE CHURCH

Around the time of the Renaissance, the Catholic Church began to lose some of its power. Some members charged the Church with corruption and called for reform. This gradual progression toward change within the Church eventually led to the **Reformation**, a split from the Catholic Church that took place in the early 16th century. **Martin Luther**, a German pastor and university professor, led this movement. He believed biblical scripture was more important than the pope's authority. He also believed that Christians achieved God's favor through faith rather than by doing good works. Luther was eventually excommunicated, or expelled, from the Catholic Church for his teachings.

Followers of the Reformation became known as **Protestants**, and the Church split between the Protestants and Catholics. Over time, many different Protestant churches, called denominations, developed, each with its own set of beliefs within the framework of Christianity.

HISTORICAL THINKING

1. **READING CHECK** From which ancient cultures did the Renaissance receive inspiration?

2. **DESCRIBE** Why was the printing press such an important invention during the Renaissance?

3. **DRAW CONCLUSIONS** Why do you think the Catholic Church excommunicated Martin Luther?

2.3 Trade Expands

Just as the Renaissance spurred an expansion in people's thoughts and attitudes, it also inspired a spirit of adventure and curiosity about the world. Sea voyagers set out to explore new lands and, above all, to find new trading opportunities and markets.

MAIN IDEA New sea routes and developments in sailing technology allowed for an expansion of trade between European societies and the East.

EXPANDING TRADE WITH ASIA

In the mid-15th century, the Turks of the Ottoman Empire captured the city of Constantinople. Located on a peninsula between Europe and Asia, Constantinople joined the two continents. Capturing the city gave the Turks complete control of the land trade routes that connected the continents. This control allowed the Turks to charge Europeans high prices for Asian goods. Turkish merchants could then make a **profit**, or earn more money than they spent, on the goods.

To avoid trading with the Turks over land, Europeans explored new sea routes to Asia. At the end of the 15th century, Portuguese navigator **Vasco da Gama** sailed to India via one of these routes. He and his fleet traveled around the Cape of Good Hope at the southern tip of Africa. Portuguese navigator **Bartholomeu Dias** had first discovered this route about a decade earlier. Da Gama was able to return from his trip with Indian spices. This journey helped reestablish direct trade between Europe and the East.

PORTUGAL AND AFRICA

In the early 1400s, **Prince Henry the Navigator** established a school on the Atlantic coast in Sagres, Portugal. The school consisted of mathematicians, mapmakers, astronomers, instrument makers, and other instructors who taught students about sailing. Henry's goal was to train sailors about shipbuilding and **navigation**, or planning and following a route. He wanted to send his students on ocean explorations.

Students learned, among other lessons, how to build a special new ship called a **caravel**. The caravel was a light sailing ship that was both quick and able to sail windward, or into the wind. These characteristics made the ship a particularly good choice for the long voyages Henry had in mind.

Caravels made it possible for explorers to sail farther down the West African coast—and elsewhere. Even Christopher Columbus used two caravels during his historic voyage to the Americas in 1492. In the 1420s, Henry began funding caravel expeditions to Africa. Though Henry himself never joined these expeditions, he instructed his sailors to return with goods from Africa's western coast. During part of the Middle Ages, Portugal was under Islamic rule, and Muslim traders had long told stories about a "land of gold" near the African coast. A series of powerful African empires had inspired these stories. And the stories weren't that far from the truth.

HISTORICAL THINKING

1. **READING CHECK** What was the new sea route that Bartholomeu Dias first discovered and Vasco da Gama later followed to get to India?

2. **ANALYZE CAUSE AND EFFECT** Why did Europeans want to find new sea routes to Asia in the 15th century?

3. **EVALUATE** What might have been some of the advantages and disadvantages of taking a long voyage in a caravel?

3.1 The Kingdom of Ghana

After Arab traders reached West Africa during the 700s, they talked of a land where even the horses were draped in gold cloth. This was the land of Ghana, and for centuries it was the wealthiest kingdom in West Africa.

MAIN IDEA West Africa's location made it a major trade center, leading to the rise of the kingdom of Ghana and the spread of Islam.

Trans-Saharan Trade Routes, c. 1050–1500

Travelers had to carry enough fresh water to last until the next **oasis**, one of those rare areas in the desert that contain freshwater sources.

People who traveled across the Sahara discovered that camels were well suited to the desert climate and could carry humans and goods long distances through the Sahara. Camels can survive traveling up to 100 miles without water, and they can carry heavy loads. Nomadic traders began to lead camel **caravans**, or groups of people traveling together. In their caravans, they carried goods on **trans-Saharan** trade routes between sub-Saharan Africa and northern Africa, which lay within reach of Europe and Southwest Asia. Market towns started to flourish where trading routes met.

GOLD AND SALT IN GHANA

To reach the golden land, the kingdom of Ghana in West Africa, traders had to cross the largest hot desert in the world, the **Sahara**. Covered in dunes, rippling sheets of sand, and rocky formations, the desert extends over an area a little smaller than the United States. South of the desert is a **steppe** region of West Africa called the Sahel. Steppes are flat grasslands with very few trees.

The Sahara could have easily isolated the lands south of it. Extreme heat and a lack of water made travel through the region difficult for humans.

Two kinds of goods dominated trans-Saharan trade: gold and salt. Gold was mined in the forests south of Ghana and was regularly used as a trade item. Salt, however, was not produced naturally in this area. People had to look north to the Sahara, which had an abundance of this valuable and essential nutrient. In fact, buildings in the Saharan trading town of Taghaza were constructed of salt blocks because that was the building material in largest supply.

A POWERFUL KINGDOM

Gold and salt traders met in West Africa, with gold flowing north and salt moving south. Near the midway point, the **kingdom of Ghana** grew and profited from the rising economy as the king collected taxes on the import and export of goods.

By the ninth century, Ghana was rich and powerful and able to conquer nearby lands with its strong army. The kingdom was structured according to a feudal system, with many princes ruling over various parts of the kingdom on behalf of the king.

In addition to goods, traders from North Africa carried their Islamic faith. Islam was the dominant religion of much of southwestern Asia at this time. Rising Muslim empires in North Africa made efforts to **convert**, or change, the people of West Africa to Islam and take over Ghana's trade, which weakened the power of the kingdom's rulers.

These efforts were so successful that in the mid-11th century, a historian named al-Bakri from al-Andalus (now Spain) described Ghana's capital as consisting of two towns. One was home to Muslim traders. The other was the palace of the king. By 1100, Ghana had declined as a result of droughts and unrest, providing an opportunity for a new Muslim empire to take control of the region.

HISTORICAL THINKING

1. **READING CHECK** How did Ghana's location help it become wealthy?

2. **INTERPRET MAPS** Identify two geographic features that the people of West Africa would have to travel through to trade with others.

3. **MAKE INFERENCES** Why did the movement of traders help spread the influence of Islam?

CRITICAL VIEWING The Great Mosque in Djenné (jen-AY), Mali, is an architectural wonder. A mosque is a Muslim place of worship. What distinctive features does the photo show?

3.2 Mali and Songhai

In the 1300s, new legends spread to Europe about an impossibly wealthy king from West Africa who traveled with hundreds of camels and thousands of servants. This man, Mansa Musa, gave away so much gold that it led to a decline in the precious metal's value in parts of Africa.

MAIN IDEA Wealth from the kingdoms of Mali and Songhai spread along trans-Saharan trade routes to northern Africa and Europe.

MALI TAKES OVER GHANA

After Ghana's decline in the 1200s, the kingdom of **Mali** took control of the gold and salt trades in West Africa. Mali's first king was **Sundiata Keita** (sun-JAHT-ah KAY-tah). Sundiata led military forces to defeat the weakened kingdom of Ghana, uniting the conquered lands into a peaceful, prosperous empire stretching along the Niger River and up into the Sahara.

Though Sundiata ruled well, it was **Mansa Musa** who first introduced Mali to the world. Musa became king in the 1300s. As a Muslim, he decided to make a **pilgrimage**, or religious journey, to the holy city of Mecca in 1324. He took thousands of servants and dozens of camels. The caravan gave gold and other luxurious goods to people along the way. Europeans and Asians, upon hearing accounts of the generous king, became more motivated to trade with the wealthy empire.

Mansa Musa returned from Mecca a year later with new knowledge and ideas. He turned the city of Timbuktu into a center for culture and learning. He also encouraged his people to learn Arabic so they could study the holy book of Islam, the Qur'an.

SONGHAI

The **Songhai** people lived to the east of the Mali Empire. Their capital city, Gao, became such a wealthy, thriving city that the Mali Empire conquered it in 1325 and ruled over it for the next 50 years. When the Songhai finally retook their capital city, they began to build their own empire. In the process, Songhai assumed control of trans-Saharan trade. The Songhai ruler Askia Mohammed then continued to expand the kingdom and strengthen ties with other Muslims. He also reformed government, banking, and education. Later rulers fought each other for control, making the Songhai vulnerable to the ambitions of their envious neighbors. Songhai lost Timbuktu and its capital, Gao, when Morocco captured the two cities in 1591. The invasion by Morocco marked the end of the Songhai Empire.

As Ghana, Mali, and Songhai rose and fell, other West African cultures developed. The Hausa (HOW-suh) and Yoruba (YOR-uh-buh) practiced agriculture and crafts. While the Hausa and Yoruba were allied with each other, they never combined forces to engage in war for other territories. The kingdom of Benin (buh-NEEN) rose to power in the late 1400s, conquered many of its neighbors, and successfully engaged in trade with Europeans.

The Europeans, meanwhile, had set their sights on other lands by the late 1400s. Soon they would be exploring territory in the Americas.

HISTORICAL THINKING

1. **READING CHECK** How did the rise of Mali and Songhai affect trans-Saharan trade?

2. **ANALYZE CAUSE AND EFFECT** How did Mansa Musa's pilgrimage lead to changes in Timbuktu?

3. **COMPARE AND CONTRAST** How were the empires of Mali and Songhai similar?

3.3 Impressions of Mali

Travelers have long recorded their observations as they explore new places. Travel journals from the past reveal details about places as they were long ago and also give us insight into how people reacted to different cultures.

This painting is an illustration from an Arabic manuscript from the 1200s and shows a wealthy pilgrim on his hajj, or pilgrimage to Mecca in present-day Saudi Arabia. Moroccan traveler Ibn Battuta (IBH-uhn bah-TOO-tuh) began his travels by going on his hajj in 1325. This was one year after Mansa Musa made his hajj. Stopping in Cairo, Ibn Battuta heard about Mansa Musa. The two never met, but later Ibn Battuta visited Mali. There he met Mansa Musa's brother Mansa Suleyman and began recording his observations.

CRITICAL VIEWING What mood does the painting convey?

DOCUMENT ONE

Primary Source: Atlas
from the *Catalan Atlas, c. 1375*

Drawn by a European mapmaker, this detail from a medieval map shows West Africa and Mansa Musa, the man wearing a gold crown and holding a ball of gold. The map was made after Mansa Musa's pilgrimage to Mecca, which literally put West Africa on the map.

CONSTRUCTED RESPONSE What does this image suggest about the impression Mansa Musa made on people outside of Mali?

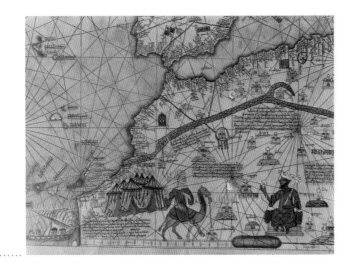

DOCUMENT TWO

Primary Source: Travel Memoir
from *Travels in Asia and Africa 1325–1354*, by Ibn Battuta

Ibn Battuta traveled throughout Africa, Europe, and Asia and wrote about his experiences. His writings help us understand the history and cultures of the places he visited. In this excerpt from his writing, he describes the entrance of the sultan, or ruler, of Mali, Mansa Suleyman.

CONSTRUCTED RESPONSE What impression do you think the sultan made on his audience?

On certain days the sultan holds audiences in the palace yard, where there is a platform under a tree, with three steps. . . . The sultan comes out of a door in a corner of the palace, carrying a bow in his hand and a quiver on his back. . . . His usual dress is a velvety red tunic, made of the European fabrics called "mutanfas." The sultan is preceded by his musicians, who carry gold and silver guimbris [two-stringed guitars], and behind him come three hundred armed slaves. He walks in a leisurely fashion. . . . As he takes his seat the drums, trumpets, and bugles are sounded.

DOCUMENT THREE

Primary Source: Travel Memoir
from *Travels in Asia and Africa 1325–1354*, by Ibn Battuta

As a Muslim, Ibn Battuta was interested to see how people in other regions practiced his religion. In this excerpt, he notes what he witnessed about the observance of Islam in Mali. He admired the commitment of the people there to the religion.

CONSTRUCTED RESPONSE What does this description tell you about the importance of Islam in Mali?

On Fridays, if a man does not go early to the mosque, he cannot find a corner to pray in, on account of the crowd. It is a custom of theirs to send each man his boy [to the mosque] with his prayer-mat; the boy spreads it out for his master in a place befitting him [and remains on it] until he comes to the mosque. . . . Yet another is their zeal for learning the Koran [Qur'an] by heart. They put their children in chains if they show any backwardness in memorizing it, and they are not set free until they have it by heart.

SYNTHESIZE & WRITE

1. **REVIEW** Review what you have learned about travel, trade, and religion in West Africa.

2. **RECALL** Think about your responses to the constructed response questions above. What details in the documents caused you to form these impressions?

3. **CONSTRUCT** Write a topic sentence that answers this question: What impressions did Mali make on those who traveled there?

4. **WRITE** Using evidence from this chapter and the documents, write a paragraph that supports your topic sentence.

REVIEW

VOCABULARY

Use each of the following vocabulary terms in a sentence that shows an understanding of the term's meaning and its connection to the information in this chapter.

1. **civilization**
   Once humans started growing their own food, cities and civilizations could grow.

2. **migrate**

3. **matrilineal**

4. **slash-and-burn agriculture**

5. **feudalism**

6. **navigation**

7. **trans-Saharan**

8. **caravan**

READING STRATEGY
COMPARE AND CONTRAST

If you haven't already, complete your table to list the characteristics of the three societies discussed in the chapter. List at least four characteristics of each. Then answer the question.

Americas	Europe	Africa
empires		

9. What conflicts might arise among these three societies based on what you've learned about them?

MAIN IDEAS

Answer the following questions. Support your answers with evidence from the chapter.

10. How did the land in Mesoamerica contribute to the rise of civilizations there? **LESSON 1.1**

11. What determined whether a group of people in North America took up farming or continued to live as hunter-gatherers? **LESSON 1.2**

12. What was the significance of the Green Corn festival in the lives of the people of southeastern North America? **LESSON 1.3**

13. Why did the Roman Catholic Church begin the Crusades? **LESSON 2.1**

14. How did the Renaissance influence religious thought and pave the way for the Reformation? **LESSON 2.2**

15. Why did Prince Henry the Navigator establish a school to train sailors? **LESSON 2.3**

16. What caused the eventual decline of the kingdom of Ghana? **LESSON 3.1**

17. How did Mansa Musa increase his trade business on his pilgrimage to Mecca? **LESSON 3.2**

18. Why are the writings of Ibn Battuta considered such an important source for understanding West Africa in the 1300s? **LESSON 3.3**

HISTORICAL THINKING

Answer the following questions. Support your answers with evidence from the chapter.

19. **SUMMARIZE** What purposes did mounds serve in the Adena, Hopewell, and Mississippian cultures?

20. **ANALYZE CAUSE AND EFFECT** Why did trading across continents become important to European merchants?

21. **MAKE INFERENCES** What do you think happened to the kingdom of Songhai as other kingdoms and empires arose in the region?

22. **DRAW CONCLUSIONS** In what way did the Crusades help weaken feudalism?

23. **FORM AND SUPPORT OPINIONS** Which South American, Mesoamerican, or North American civilization do you think was most advanced? Explain and support your answer.

INTERPRET MAPS

Look closely at this map of Vasco da Gama's voyage around Africa to reach India and return to Europe. Then answer the questions that follow.

Da Gama's Voyage, 1498–1499

24. As you have read, overland trade routes were used for centuries to link Europe and Asia. Why did Vasco da Gama sail all the way around Africa to reach the same Asian trading centers?

25. Do you think Europeans who followed da Gama traded only with Indian merchants? What information on the map helped you answer the question?

ANALYZE SOURCES

Here is an account of an experience from Vasco da Gama's ship's log. The encounter he describes took place near the southern tip of Africa in 1498. Read the passage and answer the question.

> On the following day (November 10) fourteen or fifteen natives came to where our ships lay. The captain-major landed and showed them a variety of merchandise, with the view of finding out whether such things were to be found in their country. This merchandise included cinnamon, cloves, seed-pearls, gold, and many other things, but it was evident that they had no knowledge whatever of such articles, and they were consequently given round bells and tin rings.

26. Why do you think the captain-major wants to know if "such things were to be found in their country"?

CONNECT TO YOUR LIFE

27. **ARGUMENT** Think about the way trading across societies and continents affected the civilizations you have read about in this chapter. Today, nations still trade with one another. Does modern trade have the same cultural impact as it did 600 years ago or more? Write a paragraph stating your opinion, and offer reasons to support your opinion.

TIPS

- Look back on the chapter and list ways in which trading affected the cultures. Then think about how trade affects cultures today. What are the similarities and differences? Make notes and then review them to help you formulate your opinion.

- Include examples of similarities or differences to support your opinion. Use evidence from the text and two or three key terms from the chapter to make your point.

- Conclude your argument by restating your opinion and summarizing your reasoning.

EUROPEAN EXPLORATION OF
THE AMERICAS
1492–1650

ESSENTIAL QUESTION

What impact did European exploration have on the Americas?

 The Missions of New Mexico

SECTION 1 **Spain Claims an Empire**

KEY VOCABULARY

conquistador   missionary   viceroy

mercantilism   smallpox   viceroyalty

SECTION 2 **Europe Fights Over North America**

KEY VOCABULARY

circumnavigate   Northwest Passage   privateer

galleon   persecute   watershed

heretic

SECTION 3 **Spanish Rule in the Americas**

KEY VOCABULARY

Columbian Exchange   hacienda   mestizo   plantation

encomienda   immunity   mission   quinine

SECTION 4 **Slavery Begins in the Americas**

KEY VOCABULARY

African diaspora   institution   slavery

chattel slavery   Middle Passage   triangular trade

 The Inca Empire

READING STRATEGY

DRAW CONCLUSIONS

Drawing conclusions between ideas and events in informational texts is important to building understanding. As you read this chapter, use a chart like this one to note specific details about how European exploration affected the Western Hemisphere.

"Set sail...
at 8 o'clock, and proceeded
with a strong breeze till sunset."
—Christopher Columbus

A reproduction of one of Columbus's ships sets
sail more than 500 years after that world-changing
voyage in 1492. Today, replicas of the *Niña* and the
Pinta make stops in ports along the East Coast, the
Great Lakes, and the Mississippi River as traveling
museums for visitors to enjoy.

1.1 The Age of Exploration

Imagine setting sail in a direction no one you know has ever gone. Would you be excited or scared? European explorers probably felt both as they set out without smartphones, GPS, or even accurate maps. Now, that's an adventure!

> **MAIN IDEA** The search for a western route to Asia during the late 15th and early 16th centuries opened the Americas to European settlement.

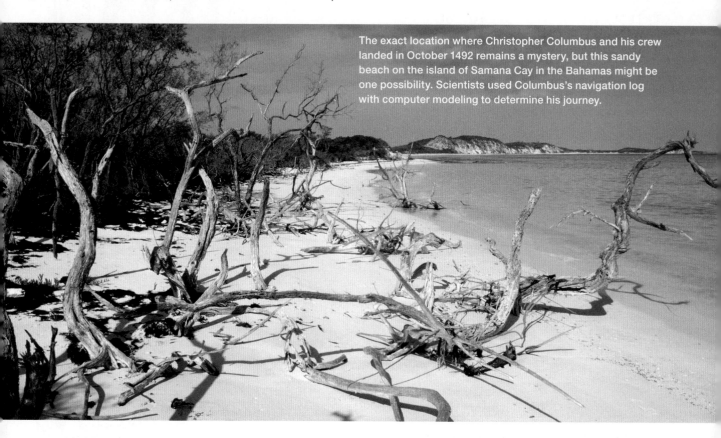

The exact location where Christopher Columbus and his crew landed in October 1492 remains a mystery, but this sandy beach on the island of Samana Cay in the Bahamas might be one possibility. Scientists used Columbus's navigation log with computer modeling to determine his journey.

COLUMBUS SETS SAIL

In the 1440s, Portugal established trade on the West African coast. Seeing the success of the Portuguese, merchants from other countries also tried to participate. However, Pope Nicholas V gave Portugal sole possession of the African and Indian coasts in 1455.

King Ferdinand and **Queen Isabella** of Spain were determined to continue trading despite the pope's decree. They found a strong willed and obsessed navigator to search for a western route to Asia. **Christopher Columbus** gladly accepted the challenge for the Spanish monarchs. In October 1492, Columbus and his fleet of ships arrived in the Bahamas. As he traveled from island to island, he believed—incorrectly, of course—that he was exploring islands south of China. He encountered people called the **Taino** (TIE-noh) and received gold in return for his goods. Leaving a few men behind, Columbus set out for home in January 1493. When he returned a year later, he discovered that the Taino had killed all his crew after his men had abused and badly harmed them. The men's actions were the start of the mistreatment of Native Americans that would last for centuries.

Ferdinand and Isabella petitioned Pope Alexander VI to allow them to colonize the lands Columbus claimed for Spain. Spain's economy was based on **mercantilism**, a system in which countries kept the sole right to trade with their colonies. Under this system, more colonies equaled more wealth—and power.

In 1494, the **Treaty of Tordesillas** established a boundary—called the **Line of Demarcation**—that passed vertically through the Atlantic and present-day Brazil. The boundary gave Portugal a portion of South America to colonize, control of the sea routes around Africa, and control of the Atlantic slave trade. Spain received permission to colonize all of the land west of the line.

Both Portugal and Spain also sent **missionaries**, or people who travel to other places to spread their own religion, to these new lands. The two countries wanted to convert the people who lived there to Christianity.

EXPLORING NEW LANDS

As Europeans continued exploring lands in the Western Hemisphere, they realized that Columbus had not reached Asia. In 1499 and 1501, the Italian captain **Amerigo Vespucci** (uh-MEHR-ih-goh veh-SPOO-chee) made two voyages—one for Spain and one for Portugal. His explorations revealed that South America was a huge landmass, which he later named **Mundus Novus**, meaning "New World" in Latin. Of course, the land was only new to the Europeans; Native Americans had already been living there for centuries. Vespucci's explorations inspired a German cartographer to name the continents *America*, after Vespucci's given name, *Amerigo*.

In 1513, Vasco Núñez Balboa led explorers across the Isthmus of Panama, and they became the first Europeans to see the eastern rim of the Pacific Ocean. Balboa claimed everything he saw for Spain.

Six years later, Ferdinand Magellan departed Spain with five ships to sail around South America and on to Asia. But the Pacific Ocean was much wider than the navigator expected. By the time the ships reached the island of Guam, the sailors were near starvation. After inhabitants killed Magellan, another sailor, Sebastian del Cano, took command of the one remaining ship. He returned to Spain after a three-year voyage, completing the first navigation around the world.

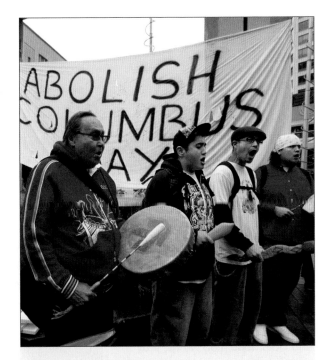

The Controversy Over Columbus Day
Was Christopher Columbus a great explorer or a ruthless invader? The question is at the heart of the controversy over Columbus Day, an annual mid-October holiday that celebrates the explorer's "achievements."

Supporters of the holiday argue that Columbus opened two continents to trade and further settlement, forever changing the world. Opponents say the holiday glorifies a man who nearly destroyed the livelihood of the native peoples of the Americas. They argue instead for celebrating Indigenous Peoples Day to remember the native peoples lost through European colonization. Various city councils have replaced Columbus Day observances with celebrations of Indigenous Peoples Day. The state of South Dakota renamed the holiday Native Americans' Day.

HISTORICAL THINKING

1. **READING CHECK** Why did the Spanish want to find a western route to Asia?

2. **DRAW CONCLUSIONS** In what ways did the Treaty of Tordesillas support Spain's mercantilist economy?

3. **IDENTIFY MAIN IDEAS AND DETAILS** How did further exploration prove that Christopher Columbus had not landed in Asia?

1.2 Christopher Columbus 1451–1506

"By prevailing over all obstacles and distractions, one may unfailingly arrive at his chosen goal or destination." —Christopher Columbus

Of course, since Christopher Columbus's chosen goal was Asia, he didn't actually arrive at his destination. He got distracted by North America, which he confused with India. And Columbus didn't know that a group of Vikings led by Leif Eriksson got to North America more than 500 years before him. Still, in a very real sense, Columbus didn't fail at all. His discoveries and the impact they had were far greater than the route he set out to find.

EXPLORATION OBSESSION

Like many boys born in the coastal city of Genoa, Italy, in the 1400s, young Christopher Columbus sought his fortune on the sea. He first set sail in 1465, when he was just a teenager. About 10 years later, he was on a ship bound for the Mediterranean when the vessel was sunk by pirates. Luckily, Columbus was able to cling to a bit of wreckage from the ship and swim to shore.

Hero or villain? The debate over Columbus's legacy has raged, particularly over the last several decades. Whether he's seen as the discoverer of the New World or the destroyer of native peoples, the fact is that Columbus's voyages opened up the world. Our global society wouldn't exist without him.

With perhaps even greater luck, he ended up in Lisbon, Portugal, where the exploration craze was at its height. There, Columbus studied navigation, cartography (mapmaking), and astronomy, and became obsessed with finding a westward route to Asia. He also read accounts of the riches of the East and decided he would try to bring these precious items back to Europe.

Columbus planned his journey to Asia based on the misinformation that most Europeans of the time accepted as fact—including an underestimation of Earth's circumference. Based on what he thought he knew, Columbus calculated the distance from Portugal to Japan and determined that the seagoing vessels of the day could handle it. Plan in hand, he looked for a sponsor to fund his journey. He finally found his backers in King Ferdinand and Queen Isabella of Spain.

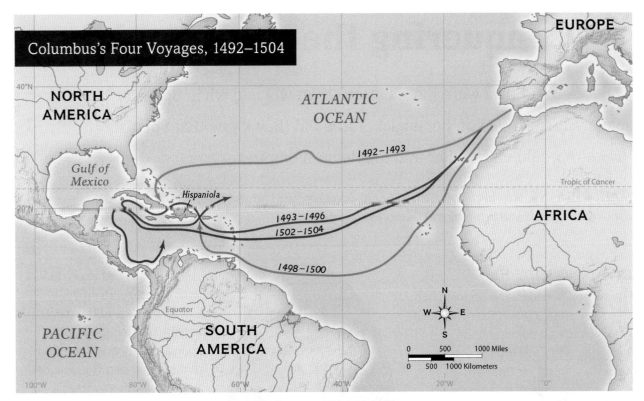

Columbus's Four Voyages, 1492–1504

EUROPE

40°N

NORTH AMERICA

ATLANTIC OCEAN

1492–1493

Gulf of Mexico

Tropic of Cancer

Hispaniola

20°N

1493–1496

1502–1504

AFRICA

1498–1500

Equator

PACIFIC OCEAN

SOUTH AMERICA

N W E S

0   500   1000 Miles
0   500   1000 Kilometers

100°W   80°W   60°W   40°W   20°W   0°

Portraits of Columbus

These three portraits of Columbus are very different because no one really knows what he looked like. But his contemporaries described him as a tall man with blond or red hair and beard and blue eyes.

VOYAGES TO THE "NEW WORLD"

On October 8, 1492, as Columbus neared the island he would call San Salvador, he declared "the air soft as that of Seville [a city in Spain] in April, and so fragrant that it was delicious to breathe it." It must have seemed a promising beginning, but his voyages did not turn out the way he hoped.

On the first voyage, he established a settlement on the island of Hispaniola. On the second voyage, he discovered the settlement had been destroyed. He left his two brothers in charge and then returned on his third voyage to find the colonists in revolt. The situation got so bad that a new governor was sent to the island, and Columbus was brought back to Spain in chains. Ferdinand and Isabella eventually pardoned him and even funded his fourth voyage. But he returned from this final trip empty-handed.

Columbus died a few years later, still believing he had found a route to Asia. No matter, though. While he hadn't discovered the riches he dreamed of, he had blazed a trail from Europe to what came to be known as the West Indies. He had opened up a "new world" to exploration and colonization and changed the course of history.

HISTORICAL THINKING

1. **READING CHECK** How did Columbus plan to sail to Asia?

2. **ANALYZE CAUSE AND EFFECT** What happened as a result of Columbus's voyages?

3. **MAKE INFERENCES** What qualities do you think Columbus must have possessed to plan and carry out his voyages?

1.3 Conquering the Aztec and Inca

The Aztec and Inca were more curious than worried when Spanish soldiers first arrived on horseback. Little did they know that Spanish invaders would enlist allies and topple both empires.

> **MAIN IDEA** A variety of factors helped Spanish soldiers and adventurers conquer the Aztec and Inca empires in the 16th century.

INVADING MEXICO

For several decades, the Spanish had little interference from other Europeans in exploring and colonizing the Americas. **Conquistadors** (kon-KEE-stuh-dohrz), or Spanish soldiers and adventurers, conquered the native tribes of many Caribbean islands, claiming the lands for Spain. They then moved through present-day Mexico and Central America. By 1543, Spanish settlements extended south to Chile, north to present-day Florida, and west to California.

Hernán Cortés was one of the most successful conquistadors. In 1519, he launched an expedition into the vast Aztec Empire in Mexico. As Cortés and his small Spanish force moved toward the Aztec capital of Tenochtitlán (tay-nohch-teet-LAHN), they recruited allies from some Native American tribes that were dissatisfied with

Aztec rule. They seized the Aztec emperor **Moctezuma** (mahk-tuh-ZOO-muh), who believed the light-skinned, bearded Spaniards signaled the return of the Aztec god Quetzalcoatl (kwet-sul-kuh-WAH-tuhl). Some historians think this is one reason Cortés was able to capture Moctezuma.

Controlling Tenochtitlán proved more difficult. When the Spanish outlawed human sacrifice—an important part of Aztec religion—and demanded more gold, the Aztec rebelled. They forced the Spanish and their allies to retreat, killing many in the process. After Cortés regrouped, he returned in May 1521 with more Spanish troops and allies and laid siege to Tenochtitlán.

The Aztec fought bravely, even though they were already weakened by a deadly outbreak of a disease the Spanish carried, called **smallpox**. In the end, though, the Spanish destroyed the city of Tenochtitlán. Over time, the Spanish colonizers spread their culture throughout Mexico. In fact, the Spanish built Mexico City on the ruins of Tenochtitlán.

🏛 The Museum of Fine Arts, Houston

The Inca were spectacular artisans. This figure, fashioned from silver, copper, shell, and polished stone, dates from between 1200 and 1532. The Spanish melted most such figures to reuse the precious metals.

CONQVISTA DE MEXICO POR CORTES. A 7

PIZARRO'S QUEST FOR GOLD

When the Spanish arrived in the Americas, the Inca already controlled a powerful empire stretching along the Andes Mountains in South America. Stories of Inca gold and silver interested the Spanish conquistador **Francisco Pizarro**. So in the 1530s, with around 180 men and a small number of horses, Pizarro set out from Panama to conquer the Inca.

In 1532, the Inca emperor **Atahualpa** invited Pizarro and his men to a meeting in the northern part of present-day Peru. At the meeting, Atahualpa and Pizarro exchanged gifts to show goodwill toward each other. Atahualpa was confident that the presence of his 6,000 warriors would discourage Pizarro from attacking. But the emperor was wrong.

Pizarro's men opened fire on the mostly unarmed Inca and took Atahualpa prisoner. Atahualpa offered Pizarro gold and silver, which Pizarro took. Then he had Atahualpa killed. By 1537, the Spanish had crushed Inca opposition.

Several factors helped the Spanish conquer the Aztec and the Inca. Smallpox and other European diseases killed or weakened many Aztec, Inca, and Native Americans. The Spanish were masterful at forming alliances with Native American groups, especially with tribes opposing the Aztec. Aztec and Inca weapons were no match for the guns and swift horses of the Spanish. Finally, the Spanish used violence and forced labor to control Native American populations and put down revolts.

HISTORICAL THINKING

1. **READING CHECK** What was the goal of the Spanish conquistadors?

2. **ANALYZE CAUSE AND EFFECT** What factors helped the Spanish defeat the Aztec and Inca?

3. **DRAW CONCLUSIONS** What might have led Aztec and Inca leaders to underestimate the Spanish invaders?

1.4 Conquistadors in the North

When conquistadors eager for riches, power, and fame heard news of Cortés's and Pizarro's triumphs, they may have thought to themselves, "How hard could it be?" As it turned out, it was pretty hard.

MAIN IDEA Conquistadors exploring North America in the 1540s were less successful than Cortés and Pizarro.

EXPLORERS REACH FLORIDA

In their search for wealth and new lands, the Spanish did not limit their American explorations to Mesoamerica and South America. Soon they set their sights northward. **Álvar Núñez (NOO-nyez) Cabeza de Vaca** was part of an expedition that sailed from Spain in 1527 aiming to claim North America for the king. After he and his fellow voyagers landed on the west coast of present-day Florida, they marched north through insect- and snake-infested swamps. They kidnapped a Native American chief, which triggered an attack from his people. They fled on hastily built rafts, quickly became lost in the Gulf of Mexico, and were captured by Native Americans after a hurricane washed them up on an island near the western shore of the Gulf.

After befriending and living with their captors for several years, de Vaca and three others escaped. They traveled west, passing through southwestern deserts all the way to the Gulf of California. Finally, they encountered other Spaniards near the Pacific coast of Mexico in 1536. De Vaca later commented that on that day the men were "dumbfounded at the sight of me, strangely dressed and in the company of Indians." In his tales, de Vaca mentioned the possibility of riches to the north, which inspired more explorers to try their luck. He returned to Spain the next year and became a governor and judge, standing up for better treatment of Native Americans.

In 1539, **Hernando de Soto**, the governor of Cuba, launched a three-year expedition through the southeast part of North America. His expedition also landed on the west coast of Florida and then trekked northward on foot. The group traveled through the Southeast to the Tennessee River Valley and then turned south toward the Gulf of Mexico, destroying Native American communities, stealing from them, and enslaving or killing people who resisted them. De Soto caught a fever and died in 1542, and the survivors of the expedition returned to Spain.

THE SEARCH FOR GOLDEN CITIES

As the Spanish explored and conquered new lands in the Americas, they set up a system to rule these faraway places. **Viceroys** were colonial leaders who were appointed by the king. Viceroys governed **viceroyalties**, or territories in the Americas "owned" by Spain.

In 1540, the viceroy of one of these territories, **New Spain,** ordered **Francisco Vásquez de Coronado** to lead an expedition of 336 Spaniards and nearly 1,000 Native Americans through the American Southwest. The expedition was to search for the golden cities described in Native American legends.

Conquistador Spur
This sparkling spur is similar to those worn by Spanish explorers on their boots to control their horses. It is an early version of the types of spurs some American cowboys wear today.

Conquistador Routes, 1527–1542

Key:
- Álvar Núñez Cabeza de Vaca
- Hernando de Soto
- Francisco Vásquez de Coronado
- Juan Rodríguez Cabrillo

Map labels: Snake R., ROCKY MOUNTAINS, GREAT PLAINS, Missouri R., Grand Canyon, Ohio R., Arkansas R., Mississippi R., De Soto, 1539–1542, ATLANTIC OCEAN, Coronado, 1540, Cabrillo, 1542, Rio Grande, Cabeza de Vaca, 1528–1536, Gulf of California, NEW SPAIN, Gulf of Mexico, CUBA, PACIFIC OCEAN, Caribbean Sea, Hispaniola, Mexico City, 120°W, 100°W, 80°W, 20°N

Traveling through the Southwest and the Great Plains, Coronado and his men saw and experienced many things not known to the Spanish before. They encountered the Hopi, Native Americans who lived in the Southwest. They also saw giant herds of buffalo, and some of the party stood on the rim of the Grand Canyon. But they found no gold. They returned to Mexico empty-handed.

Two years later, **Juan Rodríguez Cabrillo** (kuh-BREE-yoh) led a voyage of exploration north from Mexico along the California coast in search of a northern water route from the Pacific to the Atlantic Ocean. His expedition may have traveled as far as the Pacific Northwest before turning back south, but he never returned home. He died from injuries received in a battle with Native Americans, and his crew brought his ships back to Mexico.

None of these conquistadors found cities of gold or riches. Despite these failures, Europeans' interest in claiming land in the Americas continued. As you will learn, these interests would lead to international tensions and even war.

Cities of Gold

De Soto, de Vaca, Coronado, and Cabrillo explored a great deal of southern North America. De Soto hunted the southeastern forests of North America for Cofitachiqui (koh-FEE-tah-CHEE-kee), a rich Native American city. De Vaca and his shipmates searched the Southwest looking for a kingdom called Cíbola (SEE-bow-lah). Coronado also searched for Cíbola in lands farther north on the southern Great Plains. Cabrillo hoped to find wealthy civilizations as he sailed along the California coast. In the end, none of these explorers found what they were looking for because the rumored cities of gold had never existed.

HISTORICAL THINKING

1. **READING CHECK** Why weren't Spanish explorations successful in North America?

2. **ANALYZE CAUSE AND EFFECT** What social impact did conquistadors have on native populations of the American Southwest and Southeast?

3. **INTERPRET MAPS** Look at the routes of the conquistadors on the map. What is one common feature of each of these expeditions?

2.1 Competing Claims

You're probably used to friendly competitions in your classroom or among friends. For European countries in the 1500s, however, intense competition for land and resources in North America led to some not-so-friendly conflicts.

MAIN IDEA Struggles arose in Europe when other countries challenged the claims Spain and Portugal had made in the Americas.

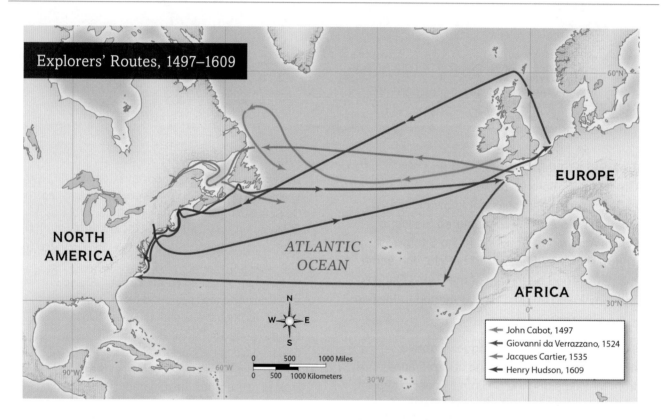

Explorers' Routes, 1497–1609

→ John Cabot, 1497
→ Giovanni da Verrazzano, 1524
→ Jacques Cartier, 1535
→ Henry Hudson, 1609

THE NORTHWEST PASSAGE

European kings and queens hoped to find a water route to Asia through the Western Hemisphere. Several monarchs sent explorers to find such a route, or a **Northwest Passage**. In 1497, King Henry VII of England commissioned the Italian navigator **John Cabot**. Cabot left the harbor at Bristol, England, and sailed to Newfoundland, in present-day Canada, where he claimed land for the king. France sent another Italian, **Giovanni da Verrazzano**, to the Americas in January 1524. His ship *La Dauphine* landed near Cape Fear, North Carolina, and continued north along the coast to Newfoundland.

Ten years later, French seafarer **Jacques Cartier** explored the coast of Canada and the St. Lawrence River three different times. His interactions with the Native Americans there led to the name *Canada*. The name is derived from the Huron-Iroquois word *kanata*, meaning "village or settlement."

After voyaging to the Americas twice for England, an explorer named **Henry Hudson** made his final trip in 1609—this time for the Dutch in the Netherlands. Hudson sailed along the Atlantic coast after failing to navigate the Arctic Ocean. Today, a river, a strait, and a bay carry his name.

Just as the conquistadors who searched for golden cities failed, none of these explorers found what they were looking for: a western route to Asia. However, the knowledge gained from these explorations did prove useful. It aided the countries when they later laid claim to land in North America.

TENSIONS GROW

While explorers searched for a Northwest Passage, religious and political unrest grew in Europe. The Spanish were already angry with the French and English for claiming lands in the New World. Tensions increased when France and England challenged Catholicism, the dominant faith in Spain.

As you have read, the Reformation began in 1517 when a German monk named Martin Luther accused the Catholic Church of corruption. At the time, Catholic priests were selling indulgences, which forgave sins in exchange for money. In response, Luther put together a document called the 95 Theses, which pointed out the Church's hypocritical and greedy practices. Luther's teachings divided European Christians, as some common people and rulers alike adopted his Protestant beliefs. Some of Luther's followers formed the branch of Protestantism that now bears his name: Lutheranism. The Catholic Church officially excluded him from Church rituals and membership. In addition, the Catholic Church **persecuted**, or punished, all followers of Protestantism.

One Protestant group, the French Huguenots, looked to the Americas for refuge. They tried settling in Brazil and South Carolina before founding a colony near St. Augustine, Florida, around 1564. This enraged Spain's **King Philip II**, but not only because he was Catholic. The Huguenots had chosen South Carolina with the intention of attacking Spanish ships carrying silver. It was not enough that they were **heretics**, or people who held beliefs different from teachings of the Catholic Church. Philip perceived them as a menace. The king sent General Pedro Menéndez de Avilés to remove the Huguenot colony. After a brief encounter at sea, Menéndez captured the French settlement at Fort Caroline. Most of the men who refused to return to Catholicism were killed.

King Philip II of Spain

HISTORICAL THINKING

1. **READING CHECK** What was Spain's response to the claims of other European countries in North America?

2. **INTERPRET MAPS** Based on the sea routes shown on the map, which countries were likely competing over land claims in the Western Hemisphere?

3. **DRAW CONCLUSIONS** How did the Protestant Reformation influence European relations in the Americas?

2.2 Defeat of the Spanish Armada

Fans of any sport love a major upset. In much the same way, when England's small but mighty fleet of ships defeated Spain in 1588, the world took notice.

MAIN IDEA Because of England's strong naval fleet, an English victory at sea challenged Spanish dominance in Europe and the Americas.

MONARCHS AND SEA DOGS

Spain had a head start on settling North America, but England started to catch up, largely because of **Queen Elizabeth I**. The Protestant queen ascended to the English throne in 1558. She saw Spain as a threat to England's independence. Her brother-in-law, Philip II of Spain, like many Catholics, wished to see Elizabeth unseated from the throne. He supported Mary, Queen of Scots, Elizabeth's Catholic cousin and the heir to the English throne. But after being implicated in a plot to take Elizabeth's life, Mary was arrested, tried, and beheaded for conspiracy.

Both Philip and Elizabeth had powerful navies. Spain's fleet was made up of large, full-rigged sailing ships called **galleons**, mainly used to transport goods from the Americas. They were heavily armed, but their cannons weren't secured to the deck, which made these large weapons difficult to reload and discharge.

By contrast, English ships were nimble. They carried fewer goods and soldiers, but their mounted artillery was more quickly discharged. English ships were also fast, and their sailors, the **Sea Dogs**, appreciated this quality.

Perhaps the most famous of these sailors was Francis Drake. Drake and other Sea Dogs were **privateers**, or seafarers licensed by a monarch to attack enemy ships. Drake sailed the world stealing treasure from Spanish ports and ships. He and his crew were the first Englishmen to **circumnavigate**, or sail around, the globe.

ENGLISH VICTORY

Under the leadership of Elizabeth I, England challenged Spain's claims to the Western Hemisphere. England supported the Dutch revolt against Philip II. When part of the Netherlands declared its independence from Spain and became the United Provinces in 1585, Elizabeth sent aid there. In doing so, she was essentially declaring war on Spain.

King Philip sent his "invincible" navy to conquer England in May 1588. The **Spanish Armada** was a fleet of about 130 warships. Knowing their vessels

Queen Elizabeth I
In a society where women rarely held any political authority, Elizabeth ruled as a popular, strong, and capable monarch. During the 45 years of her reign, England prospered and became one of the most powerful nations in history. In this portrait, painted around 1588, the English fleet appears behind Elizabeth, likely an acknowledgment of England's increasing naval power.

were slower and had fewer and smaller cannons than the English, the Spanish captains hoped to take advantage of their own greater numbers. Their plan was to have their men board the enemy ships and defeat the English in hand-to-hand combat.

Stormy weather delayed the armada. This gave English admiral Charles Howard, commander of England's fleet, a chance to join up with Francis Drake's advance force. England's fleet had smaller ships and fewer soldiers, but its superior speed and artillery demolished the Spanish. Many thousands of Spanish men were killed, while England lost several hundred. With only 60 ships remaining, the Spanish returned home in shame.

The defeat of the Spanish Armada was a blow to Spain's position as the dominant world power in both Europe and the New World. Through its victory, England ensured its own continued independence from foreign domination while preserving the Netherlands' United Provinces.

Spain's power weakened further as Sea Dogs continued to harass Spanish vessels and ports. At the same time, Protestant sects in Europe and later in the New World would continue to challenge the supremacy of Spain and the pope on colonization and commerce. Spain found itself on the defensive.

HISTORICAL THINKING

1. **READING CHECK** What political changes did England's defeat of the Spanish Armada bring to Europe?

2. **COMPARE AND CONTRAST** What were the different advantages and disadvantages of the Spanish and English ships?

3. **DRAW CONCLUSIONS** How did the Spanish captains' strategy to combat the English fleet lead to their own defeat?

CRITICAL VIEWING French artist Philippe-Jacques de Loutherbourg painted *Defeat of the Spanish Armada, 8 August 1588* in 1796. How does the artist use color to show the drama of the battle?

2.3 French and Dutch Colonies

If you visit a coffee shop in Burlington, Vermont, you might see a menu that has both French and English descriptions. Walk around New York City and you'll see Dutch names for streets. Different languages and names are the remnants of European exploration in the 17th century.

MAIN IDEA The French and Dutch claimed North American lands as rich sources of trade and wealth, but they had trouble establishing colonies.

OUTPOSTS IN NEW FRANCE

In 1608, explorer and cartographer **Samuel de Champlain** established a fur-trading base at a point along the St. Lawrence River that became the first permanent French settlement in North America. For two decades, Champlain explored the **watershed** lands, or the area drained by rivers, surrounding his post. As he explored, he strengthened trading ties with the Huron, the Algonquian, and the Montagnai. Champlain also allied with these Native Americans against the Iroquois. Champlain's new trading partners brought him valuable furs, which he then shipped to Europe to be sold. Hearing of Champlain's success, other French traders joined him. This system resulted in an international fur trade so robust the country claimed the region, naming it **New France**.

Population growth in New France was slow. Twenty years after Champlain began his business, the post, which was later named Quebec (kuh-BEK), was home to only about 100 people. By comparison, Jamestown, Virginia, grew from 105 people at its founding in 1607 to 1,240 people in 1622.

In an effort to encourage French people to settle in New France, Champlain's company expanded its charter to include lands from Florida to the Arctic. The company sent Jesuit priests to Native American villages in the hope of learning their languages and converting them to Christianity in accordance with France's Catholic beliefs. However, the French government's refusal to allow Protestants, the most likely immigrants, to settle in the Americas kept the outposts' populations small.

Another factor limiting population growth in New France was its social structure. France was still a feudal society, and settlers brought this system to the Western Hemisphere. Large manors belonged to wealthy settlers. All others worked as tenant farmers. Peasants living in France saw little chance to improve their status in the Americas, where they still could not own and work their own land.

CONFLICT IN NEW NETHERLAND

As you have read, Henry Hudson was searching for a passage to Asia through North America when he discovered the river that would bear his name in what is today New York State. On behalf of the Dutch, Hudson sailed up the river, trading European knives and beads for furs from the Native Americans. The pelts brought a good price in Holland, the Dutch homeland, which is also known as the Netherlands. Traders responded by setting up a post near Albany, New York. In 1614, the Dutch built **Fort Nassau** in that same area. Like the French, the Dutch cooperated with local tribes to establish a thriving fur trade, and the colony of **New Netherland** was established.

The Dutch purchased the island of Manhattan from Native Americans in 1626. They developed the community of New Amsterdam, named for the capital of the Netherlands, but there was a misunderstanding. The Native Americans believed they had sold rights to share the land and could continue using it themselves. The Dutch believed they had purchased exclusive rights to the land. By 1640, the Dutch and the Native Americans were at war over the misunderstanding.

AMERICAN PLACES
Manhattan, New York

Long before skyscrapers towered above its shores, members of the Lenape tribe lived on this island at the mouth of the Hudson River. They called it Mannahatta, "the island of many hills." Compare and contrast the two views of Manhattan shown below. The photo on top is a computer model that suggests what the island might have looked like when Henry Hudson arrived in 1609. The photo at the bottom shows Manhattan 400 years later, in 2009. Manhattan is a borough of New York City, which is the largest city by population in the United States.

The conflict over Manhattan represented a larger issue. Native American tribes, such as the Abenaki and Powhatan, had been living in eastern North America for centuries before Europeans arrived. English settlements in New England and near Chesapeake Bay were agricultural societies, while the French, Dutch, and Swedes focused on trade. Conflicts over land arose between Europeans and Native Americans in these areas. Different European groups sometimes involved Native American trading partners in their arguments over trading opportunities. Some disputes ended in violence. Additionally, many Native Americans succumbed to European diseases, resulting in a decrease in their populations.

HISTORICAL THINKING

1. **READING CHECK** How did explorers influence international trade during the 17th century?

2. **FORM AND SUPPORT OPINIONS** In your opinion, what could the French have done differently to attract settlers and grow the population of New France? Support your opinion with evidence from the text.

3. **INTERPRET VISUALS** What physical features might have made Mannahatta an attractive place for the Dutch to build a community?

3.1 Spanish Colonial Rule

Imagine invaders from far away taking over your town. They would know little about your culture and would likely try to change it. When the Spanish claimed territory in the Americas, they forced a number of social and economic changes, many of which were far from positive.

MAIN IDEA Spanish colonial social and agricultural practices in the Americas had a dramatic effect on Native American cultures.

A SOCIAL PYRAMID

As you have read, to control such a huge and distant territory in the Americas, the king of Spain divided it into two viceroyalties. Viceroys governed New Spain and Peru from their capitals, Mexico City and Lima, respectively.

Society in Spanish colonies was hierarchical, or organized like a pyramid. Spanish-born people and their American-born children, called Creoles, were the smallest but most powerful group. **Mestizos** (mes-TEE-zohs), people of mixed Spanish and Native American ancestry, occupied the middle part of society. Native Americans and enslaved Africans were the least powerful but most numerous group.

The Spanish government gave the wealthiest Spanish colonists **haciendas** (hah-see-YN-dahz), or tracts of land to farm. On Caribbean islands, most haciendas were sugarcane **plantations**, or large farms. Sugarcane was an important crop from which colonists made sugar and molasses, which they traded with Europe.

With the hacienda came an **encomienda** (en-coe-mee-AYN-dah), a grant to owners of a certain number of Native American laborers. In return for their labor, the Native Americans received protection from enemies, but never any payment. Native Americans had little power within this social and labor system. Additionally, so many Native Americans died from working in hot and dangerous conditions that the Spanish began to import enslaved Africans to replace them.

IMPACT OF THE CHURCH

The Catholic Church played a major role in Spanish colonization by establishing hundreds of **missions**, or religious settlements, in the Americas. Priests and missionaries wanted to convert Native Americans to Christianity and they also taught skills such as masonry and carpentry.

Some priests brutally punished those who would not adopt Spanish culture. **Bartolomé de Las Casas**, a Spanish priest himself, wrote about the abuses of Native Americans that he'd witnessed. He convinced the Spanish king to pass laws to protect Native Americans from mistreatment, but landowners forced the reversal of those laws.

In 1680, a Pueblo leader named **Popé** led a revolt in present-day New Mexico and drove the Spanish from the area. Popé freed the region of Spanish influence, but Spain restored its control after his death in 1692. By 1700, Spain controlled much of the Americas and remained a powerful presence and a major social influence into the 1800s.

HISTORICAL THINKING

1. **READING CHECK** Who were the mestizos and where did they fit in Spanish colonial society?

2. **COMPARE AND CONTRAST** How did the encomienda and mission systems compare?

3. **ANALYZE CAUSE AND EFFECT** How did the Spanish mission system affect Native American societies?

Carmel Mission, California

Founded in 1771, Carmel Mission served as the center of the Catholic mission system in California until 1834. Its founder, Father Junipero Serra, dedicated his life to building seven more missions in California. Today, visitors to the mission can tour an exhibit of his living quarters.

Genetics, Disease, and Native Americans

"The impact that science has on the world around us is something I'm enthralled with." —Pardis Sabeti

Meet National Geographic Explorer **Pardis Sabeti**. She is a research scientist, a musician, a teacher, and a volleyball player. She also doesn't sleep much. When Sabeti is not teaching a class at Harvard University, you might find her analyzing data in her lab, playing bass with her band, collecting virus samples in West Africa, or using mathematics to understand the latest epidemic.

^
Pardis Sabeti, shown here in her Harvard University lab, loves to engage with her students and collaborate with colleagues all over the world to prevent major outbreaks of deadly diseases.

MAIN IDEA Modern scientific research can help explain how diseases from Europe impacted Native Americans in North America.

Doctors dread seeing the smallpox virus, shown here, in patients. Smallpox is highly contagious and could cause a major human catastrophe if uncontrolled.

REFUGEE TO RESEARCH SCIENTIST

When Pardis Sabeti was two years old, she and her family escaped Iran just before its 1979 revolution and settled in Florida. In school, Sabeti learned that she loved math. That's right: math. She followed her interests into medical school, where she fell in love with research and data analysis. That's right: research and data analysis.

While in graduate school, Sabeti developed a pathbreaking algorithm, or a procedure for solving a problem or analyzing data using a computer. She used this algorithm to analyze a specific gene, or the part of a cell that controls growth, appearance, and traits. She knew she'd made a great discovery. She recalls, "I realized I'd found a trait that had to be the result of natural selection—a trait that likely helped the population I was looking at cope with malaria better than others. It was an amazing feeling because at that moment I knew something about how people evolved that nobody else knew."

Today, Sabeti specializes in the study of infectious diseases, or diseases that spread from person to person. She uses mathematical and computer science tools to analyze the different ways diseases change over time and how they influence changes in human biology. Sabeti works in her lab at Harvard University and in countries impacted by diseases such as malaria and Lassa fever.

UNDERSTANDING DISEASE

Sabeti's research has an urgency, and it's risky. Recently, she led a research team during an outbreak of Ebola in Sierra Leone, a country in West Africa. She and her colleagues determined that the Ebola virus actually spread through human-to-human contact, not from contact with bats or other animals. This knowledge helped health professionals stop, or at least slow down, the epidemic and save many lives.

Her research also reveals how infectious diseases have been some of the most important factors in human history. According to Sabeti, more soldiers have died of infections or from exposure to new climates—and therefore new diseases—than from battle itself. Disease also played an enormous role when Europeans and Native Americans came into contact with each other. Europeans brought diseases to North America, including tuberculosis and smallpox. Europeans likely had inherited immunity, or a genetic protection, against these diseases. But Native Americans had not yet been exposed to them. Smallpox, especially, ravaged Native American populations. This disease also became a weapon of war when European colonizers realized the effect that blankets infected with smallpox could have on native populations.

If you ask Sabeti what she most enjoys about her work, she'd likely respond with more than one answer. She's inspired by colleagues in Africa researching the treatment and prevention of Lassa fever. She thrives on working with her students in classes and in the lab. And she's thrilled to be utilizing her skills in math, research, and data analysis to help develop new treatments for devastating diseases like malaria, a disease that kills more than 1 million people every year.

HISTORICAL THINKING

1. **READING CHECK** What kind of research does Pardis Sabeti do?

2. **SUMMARIZE** In what ways have infectious diseases shaped human history?

3. **MAKE INFERENCES** In what ways might understanding how diseases change over time help doctors prevent future epidemics?

3.3 The Columbian Exchange

One of the best parts about traveling to different places is encountering new and unusual foods, plants, and animals. Beginning in the 1500s, European explorers and colonists encountered and introduced hundreds of new and amazing things.

MAIN IDEA The Columbian Exchange was a significant biological event that changed societies and environments around the world.

TWO WORLDS CONNECT

Millions of years ago, the landmasses of North and South America were connected to Eurasia and Africa. Over time, they drifted far apart and an ocean filled the gap between them. The two hemispheres developed in isolation from each other, resulting in distinct plants and animals evolving in each half of the world. Farmers in the two hemispheres developed and planted different crops and raised different livestock.

The European encounter with the Americas coincided with improved methods of sea travel and the desire to explore and conquer new lands. The combined impact was enormous. Places and people that were once isolated from one another became part of a global exchange network. The contact and trade between these far-flung lands helped some people—and harmed others.

When Europeans crossed the Atlantic in 1492, they carried more than just their ideas—they also brought plants and animals. As they prepared to sail home, they packed new plants and animals they found in the Americas to introduce to the people of Europe. This period of biological mixing between the New World of the Americas and the Old World of Europe, Africa, and Asia is known as the **Columbian Exchange** —named after Christopher Columbus. This momentous swap of biological matter had major economic and social effects in the Americas, both good and bad.

Some of the species the Europeans introduced to the Americas caused significant environmental changes. For example, the Spanish transported livestock, including cattle, horses, sheep, and goats, to the Americas. These animals' roaming and grazing habits altered native landscapes. Europeans also slashed and burned forests to clear lands for farming.

Additionally, Europeans introduced deadly new diseases to the Western Hemisphere. Because they had already encountered diseases such as smallpox, Europeans had developed an **immunity**, or a natural protection, to those diseases. They could even carry the diseases without showing symptoms or appearing sick.

Native Americans had not been exposed to European diseases, so they did not have immunity to them. Epidemics of smallpox, influenza, measles, and other diseases spread quickly after Europeans arrived in the Americas. Between 1519 and 1565, the native population of Central America fell from about 25 million to 2.5 million due to disease alone. Within three centuries of Columbus's landing, about 90 percent of the Native American population had died of disease.

CHANGES FOR THE BETTER

Not all of the consequences of the Columbian Exchange were so negative, however. The great transatlantic swap introduced positive things to both sides. Europeans imported pigs, chickens, and other domesticated animals and brought horses with them, which Native Americans incorporated into their cultures. Europeans also introduced new crops to the Americas. Wheat, barley, rye, rice, and cotton were some of the plants introduced to the Western Hemisphere.

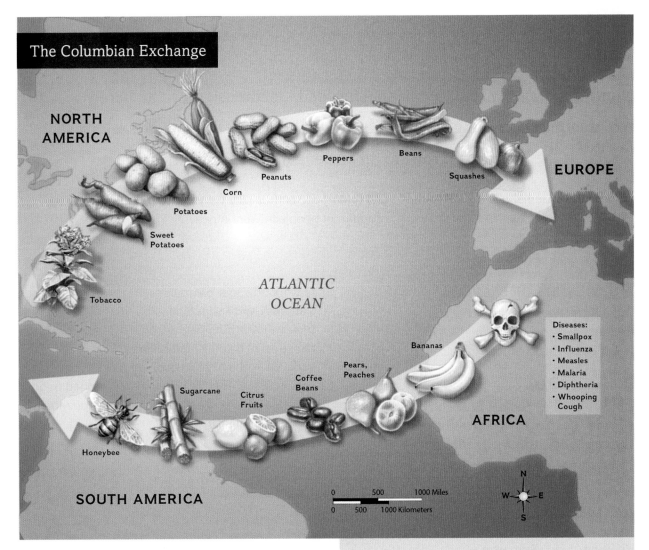

The Columbian Exchange

NORTH AMERICA

EUROPE

Peppers

Beans

Peanuts

Squashes

Corn

Potatoes

Sweet Potatoes

Tobacco

ATLANTIC OCEAN

Bananas

Diseases:
• Smallpox
• Influenza
• Measles
• Malaria
• Diphtheria
• Whooping Cough

Pears, Peaches

Coffee Beans

Sugarcane

Citrus Fruits

AFRICA

Honeybee

SOUTH AMERICA

0   500   1000 Miles
0   500   1000 Kilometers

N W E S

Other crops included bananas, coffee beans, and sugarcane, all of which grew especially well in Central and South America.

The Western Hemisphere also contributed an important medicine called **quinine** to Europe, Africa, and Asia. Europeans learned about quinine, which comes from the bark of a tree in South America, in the 1600s. For about 300 years, it served as the only effective remedy for malaria, which is carried by mosquitoes. Quinine's use as a treatment for malaria benefited millions of people, but it allowed Europeans to later colonize malaria-ridden areas of the world.

The Columbian Exchange affected the lives of people throughout the world. Some changes were positive, such as improved nutrition because of a greater variety of foods. However, the effect of the Columbian Exchange on native populations in the Americas was disastrous.

More Options, New Troubles

The exchange of crops and animals increased agricultural options and enriched diets on the continents of Europe, North America, Africa, and South America. Some elements of the exchange, such as tobacco and a host of European diseases, were not as positive.

HISTORICAL THINKING

1. **READING CHECK** Why was the Columbian Exchange such an important phenomenon in world history?

2. **INTERPRET MAPS** Based on what you notice on the map, what foods do you enjoy today that originated in the Americas?

3. **DRAW CONCLUSIONS** Which hemisphere benefited most from the Columbian Exchange and why?

4.1 A New Kind of Slavery

Hundreds of newly enslaved people chained together so they can barely move sounds horrifying, because it was. In the 1600s, Europeans seeking wealth in the Americas turned to an ancient and brutal practice: slavery.

MAIN IDEA Demand for labor in Europe and the Americas drove the development of a new kind of slavery, beginning with the capture of people in West Africa.

A NEW FORM OF SLAVERY

Slavery is a social system in which human beings take complete control of others. It has existed throughout human history. In ancient societies around the world, prisoners of war were a main source of slaves. People also bonded themselves into slavery to pay off debts. Such slaves rarely stayed in bondage all their lives. They could usually buy or work for their freedom, and many of them had certain legal rights. Their children almost never became slaves themselves.

However, during European colonization of the Americas, a new kind of slavery developed. Under **chattel slavery**, people were classified as goods with virtually no human rights. Their bondage—and that of their children—was permanent.

Chattel slavery originated in the mid-1400s when the Portuguese started to trade with West African kingdoms for slaves to work on sugar plantations. Kingdoms such as Dahomey and Ashanti became powerful centers of slave trade commerce, partly by capturing people in raids on inland villages. Raiders marched captives in chains to the coast and locked them in holding pens. The slave traders exchanged goods for the newly enslaved people and shipped them across the Atlantic.

Slave Ship Diagram
The slave trade involved a lot of money and investment on the part of slave traders, merchants, and ship captains. This slave ship diagram shows the precise planning that went into transporting humans across the Atlantic Ocean.

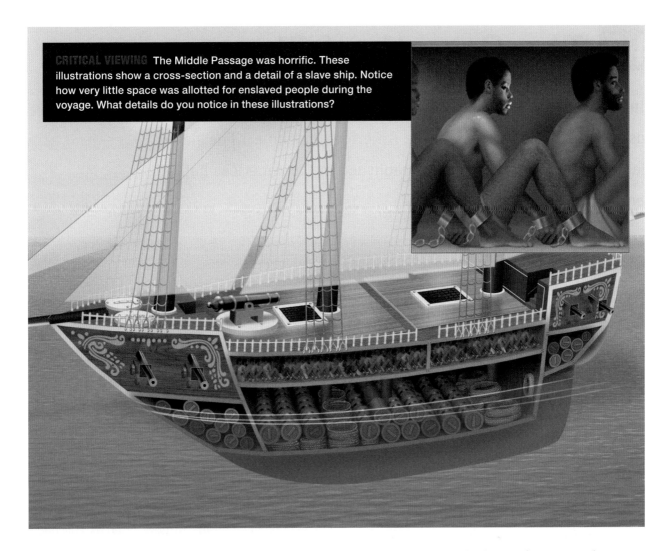

The Middle Passage was horrific. These illustrations show a cross-section and a detail of a slave ship. Notice how very little space was allotted for enslaved people during the voyage. What details do you notice in these illustrations?

THE TRIANGULAR TRADE

As you read earlier in this chapter, the Columbian Exchange transformed the Americas and Europe through a massive transfer of plants, animals, and diseases. Another exchange also transformed the Americas, only this one included humans as goods. This exchange formed part of the **triangular trade**, a three-part system of trade that connected Europe, Africa, and the Americas during the 17th and 18th centuries.

In the first leg of the triangular trade route, traders from Europe brought goods to West Africa to exchange for captured and enslaved Africans. The second and most infamous leg was the **Middle Passage**. Slave traders forced enslaved Africans onto ships where they were confined in sickening, often fatal conditions. The 5,000-mile voyage took from three weeks to three months. Approximately 10 to 15 percent of the people held captive on slave ships died of disease or despair before reaching the Americas.

Once the ships reached port, the captured Africans were sold again or traded for goods. On the third leg of the voyage, ships loaded with products from the Americas returned to Europe, and the pattern repeated.

The triangular trade lasted until the slave trade was abolished in the early 1800s. Meanwhile, the people who were captured, transported, and sold were unlikely ever to taste freedom again.

HISTORICAL THINKING

1. **READING CHECK** How was chattel slavery different from most forms of slavery practiced in ancient societies?

2. **SUMMARIZE** What was the triangular trade?

3. **INTEGRATE VISUALS** How would you describe the Middle Passage? Use details from the illustrations and the text in your description.

4.2 The Growth of Slavery

In 2015, author Ta-Nehisi Coates described enslaved Africans as "people turned to fuel for the American machine." The slave labor system that Europeans established in the Americas had an enormous human cost.

MAIN IDEA European access to African slave labor paved the way for the growth of slave labor in the Americas and the expansion of the slave trade.

SLAVERY IN THE AMERICAS

The encomienda and hacienda systems established in Spain's American colonies encouraged the growth of sugar plantations in the West Indies and set the stage for the growth of slavery in North America. These plantations supplied the European market with sugar, and they required a considerable workforce in order to grow and process enough sugarcane to make a profit.

At first, the Spanish forced the islands' Native American populations to work in the sugarcane fields, but ultimately this plan failed. Many Native Americans died of European diseases, while others escaped their bondage.

The inability to force Native Americans into slavery led Spain to turn to Africa as a source of captive labor. At first, the Spanish bought Africans who had been enslaved on the Portuguese plantations. Soon, however, they began buying enslaved Africans directly from West Africa. By the end of the 1500s, 75,000 enslaved Africans were working on Spanish plantations in the Caribbean. The North American slave trade expanded from there.

FAR FROM HOME

Europeans began to buy and ship so many people to the Americas that West African slave hunters had to travel farther into the continent in order to capture and enslave more people to meet the demand. The forced march to the coast was even longer and more brutal, and many people died before they even boarded a ship. Because the slave raiders captured the youngest and most productive members of inland societies, the transatlantic slave trade devastated entire cultures and economies in Africa.

Altogether, the slave trade between Africa and the Americas lasted for about 400 years. From the 16th to the 19th century, traders shipped between 7 and 10 million people to the Western Hemisphere. The removal of so many Africans from their homeland to the Americas is known as the **African diaspora**.

Slavery became an **institution**, or an established and accepted practice, in North America, particularly in the Southern Colonies and then in the new nation, the United States. The international slave trade ended in 1807, and the United States abolished slavery completely in 1865. There is no doubt that slavery as an institution shaped the social, economic, and cultural development of the United States and that it still casts its shadow today.

HISTORICAL THINKING

1. **READING CHECK** How did the slave trade change as demand for African slaves grew?

2. **MAKE INFERENCES** In what ways did the African diaspora change the population of the African continent?

3. **DRAW CONCLUSIONS** How did Portuguese slave trading off the western coast of Africa help contribute to the development of slavery in the Americas?

The Jamaica Train

When sugar refining first began, enslaved workers used four vats of decreasing size called the Jamaica Train. One of the most dangerous jobs on a sugar plantation was boiling the sugarcane water in vats like the ones shown here. When enough liquid had evaporated from one vat, the water was ladled into the next, smaller, vat. The process occurred two more times with more batches following. Enslaved workers had to move quickly so that all the vats were always full.

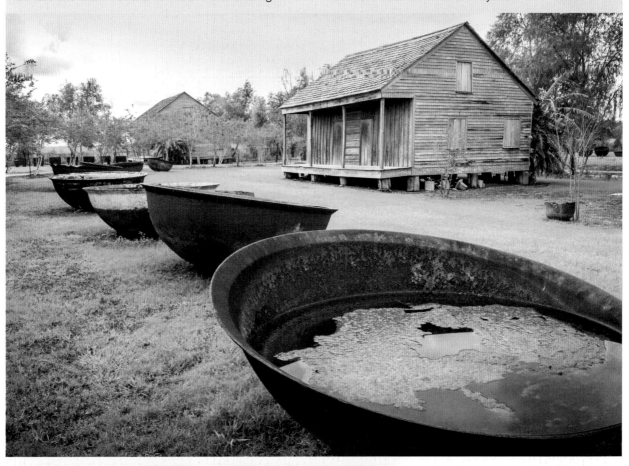

Indoor Sugar Refining

This painting by William Clark captures work in a large sugar plantation after technology improved the sugar refining process. Moving this process indoors better regulated the heat. Using brick ovens reduced the number of fires needed to boil the sugarcane, but these advances did not make the work much easier for enslaved workers. They still faced scalding, heat exhaustion, and grueling physical labor.

In 1843, Norbert Rillieux invented an evaporating machine. Additional inventions, such as steam power and a process that lowered the boiling point of liquid, continued to improve the sugar refining process.

REVIEW

VOCABULARY

Use vocabulary words to complete the sentences.

1. In the 1500s, Spain's economy was based on _____.

2. King Philip II considered Protestants to be _____ because they held beliefs different from those of the Catholic Church.

3. Francis Drake and his crew were the first Englishmen to _____ the globe.

4. Francisco Pizarro was a _____ who conquered the Inca in the 1530s.

5. Spain divided the lands it claimed in the Americas into two _____.

6. The Catholic Church _____ followers of Protestantism in the 16th century.

7. _____ were large tracts of land granted to wealthy Spanish colonists.

8. Native Americans did not have _____ against diseases carried by Europeans.

READING STRATEGY
DRAW CONCLUSIONS

If you haven't already, complete your chart to analyze how European exploration affected the Western Hemisphere. List three details, and then answer the question.

9. What were the ways in which Europeans transformed the Western Hemisphere?

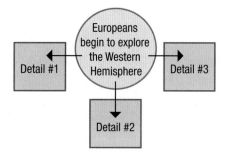

MAIN IDEAS

Answer the following questions. Support your answers with evidence from the chapter.

10. Why were European countries seeking a western route to Asia? **LESSON 1.1**

11. What strategies did the Spanish use to topple the Aztec and the Inca? **LESSON 1.3**

12. What challenges did the conquistadors encounter in North America? **LESSON 1.4**

13. Why did the French Huguenots feel they needed to escape Europe? **LESSON 2.1**

14. Why did King Philip II want Mary, Queen of Scots, to rule England instead of Queen Elizabeth I? **LESSON 2.2**

15. How did the feudal system hinder the growth of New France? **LESSON 2.3**

16. What effect did Spanish rule have on Native American cultures? **LESSON 3.1**

17. What were some of the effects of the Columbian Exchange? **LESSON 3.3**

18. In what ways did the slave trade change cultures and economies in Africa? **LESSON 4.1**

19. Why did the Spanish and Portuguese choose to use slave labor in their New World colonies? **LESSON 4.2**

Answer the following questions. Support your answers with evidence from the chapter.

20. **DRAW CONCLUSIONS** How did competition for land and resources in the Americas lead to conflicts in Europe?

21. **MAKE GENERALIZATIONS** How did the use of slave labor by Europeans in the Americas differ from its use in ancient societies?

22. **MAKE INFERENCES** Why did Bartolomé de Las Casas set himself apart from other Spaniards?

23. **COMPARE AND CONTRAST** What was similar about the colonization of New France and New Netherland? What was different?

24. **FORM AND SUPPORT OPINIONS** What do you think was the most important social or economic effect of the Columbian Exchange? Support your opinion with evidence.

This bar graph shows numbers of enslaved Africans who got on (embarked) and got off (disembarked) slave ships from West Africa between 1500 and 1807. Study the graph and answer the questions below.

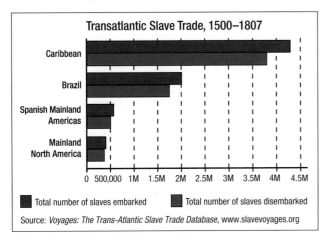

Transatlantic Slave Trade, 1500–1807

Caribbean

Brazil

Spanish Mainland Americas

Mainland North America

0 500,000 1M 1.5M 2M 2.5M 3M 3.5M 4M 4.5M

■ Total number of slaves embarked   ■ Total number of slaves disembarked

Source: *Voyages: The Trans-Atlantic Slave Trade Database*, www.slavevoyages.org

25. Which region in the Americas imported the most enslaved Africans between 1500 and 1807?

26. What do the two bars for each region show, and what evidence about the Middle Passage do they provide?

In 1524, Giovanni da Verrazzano wrote a letter to King Francis I of France. He described an encounter with Native Americans that he'd witnessed. Read the passage and answer the question.

We sent one of our young sailors swimming ashore to take the people some trinkets, such as little bells, mirrors, and other trifles, and when he came within four fathoms of them, he threw them the goods and tried to turn back, but he was so tossed about by the waves that he was carried up onto the beach half dead. Seeing this, the native people immediately ran up; they took him by the head, the legs, and arms and carried him some distance away. Whereupon the youth, realizing he was being carried away like this, was seized with terror, and began to utter loud cries.

27. Based on the excerpt, do you think the young sailor misread the intentions of the Native Americans? Explain your answer.

28. **EXPLANATORY** In his letter, Verrazzano describes a crew member's first interaction with a new culture. Connect your knowledge about cultural encounters in the 1500s to a time in your life when you experienced something new for the first time. Write a paragraph connecting the two events.

TIPS

• After you decide on a story of your own to share, use a Venn diagram to organize similarities and differences between your story and Verrazzano's story.

• Use text evidence to compare or contrast the crew member's behavior with actions in your own story.

• After you have finished writing, reread your paragraph to make sure the essay does not slip into informal language, especially when telling your own story.

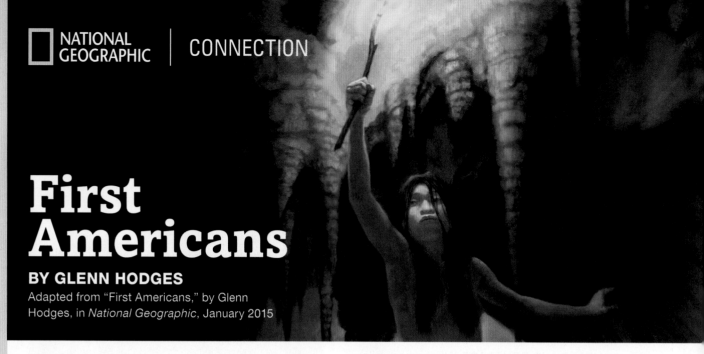

NATIONAL GEOGRAPHIC | CONNECTION

First Americans

BY GLENN HODGES

Adapted from "First Americans," by Glenn Hodges, in *National Geographic*, January 2015

The story begins with an unlucky teenage girl who fell to her death in a cave in Mexico's Yucatán about 12,000 to 13,000 years ago. But her prehistoric bad luck is modern science's good fortune. The skeleton, called Naia (NY-ah), turned out to be one of the oldest ever found in the Americas, and it provides evidence of North America's first inhabitants.

In 2007, a team of Mexican divers led by Alberto Nava made a startling find: an immense submerged cavern they named Hoyo Negro, the "black hole." At the bottom of the abyss, their lights revealed a bed of prehistoric bones, including a nearly complete human skeleton. It was intact enough to provide a foundation for a facial reconstruction. Geneticists were even able to extract a sample of DNA.

Together, these clues may help explain a mystery about the peopling of the Americas. If Native Americans are descendants of Asian trailblazers who migrated into the Americas toward the end of the last Ice Age, why don't they look like their ancient ancestors?

By all appearances, the earliest Americans were a rough bunch. If you look at the skeletal remains of Paleo-Americans, more than half the men have injuries caused by violence. Their wounds do not appear to have been the result of hunting accidents or warfare. Instead, it appears that these men fought violently among themselves. Female skeletons do not reveal the same kinds of injuries. Additionally, female skeletons are much smaller than male skeletons, and they show signs of malnourishment.

Jim Chatters, archaeologist and co-leader of the Hoyo Negro research team that found Naia, theorizes that the earliest Americans were bold pioneers whose behaviors and physical traits changed as they became more settled. This change over time, he explains, is why the earliest Americans' facial features look so different from those of later Native Americans.

According to this hypothesis, men fought for dominance in the group. They also ate better, grew larger, and lived longer than the women did. The men who were able to establish their dominance in the group were the ones who were able to pass on their genes. As a result, their strong traits and features were selected over the softer and more domestic features evident in later, more settled populations.

Chatters's hypothesis is speculative, but his team's findings are not. Naia has the facial features typical of the earliest Americans as well as the genetic signatures common to modern Native Americans. This means that the two groups do not look different because later groups from Asia replaced the earliest populations. Instead, they look different because the first Americans changed after they got here.

For most of the 20th century, anthropologists pointed to spearpoints found near Clovis, New Mexico, and dated to 13,000 years ago as the oldest evidence of ancient hunters. They concluded that the first Americans had followed mammoths and other prey out of Asia, across Beringia, and then south into North America. But in 1997, archaeologists confirmed new evidence of human occupation in Monte Verde, Chile, and the story of the peopling of the Americas was thrown wide open. How did they get there? Given that the Monte Verde people made it all the way to southern Chile more than 14,000 years ago, it would be surprising if they hadn't journeyed by boat.

The story of how and when humans began to inhabit the Americas continues to develop. What is clear is that the Americas hosted diverse communities of people long before the Clovis culture began to spread across North America. We may never know the whole story, but each new discovery gets us closer to a more complete one.

For more from National Geographic, check out "Scurvy Struck Columbus's Crew" online.

UNIT INQUIRY: Establish an Empire

In this unit, you learned about three worlds before 1500 and about the European exploration of the Americas. Based on your reading, what happened when people from Europe, Africa, and the Americas encountered each other on African and American soils? Which societies fared better than others, particularly when Europeans began to establish empires in North, Central, and South America? Why did Europeans establish empires? Which empires were more successful and why?

ASSIGNMENT

Design an empire you think would be successful today. Consider factors such as geography, government, the economy, social structure, and culture. Be prepared to present your plan for an empire to the class.

Gather Evidence As you design your empire, gather evidence from this unit about the factors that made European empires successful and what factors eventually led to their fall. Make a list of both sets of factors. Then develop a plan about how you would use similar or different strategies in your empire. Use a graphic organizer like this one to help organize your thoughts.

Produce Use your notes to produce detailed descriptions of each component of your empire. Write a short paragraph describing your empire's geography, government, economy, social structure, and culture. To support your ideas, make sure to use evidence from the chapters in this unit.

Present Choose a creative way to present your empire to the class. Consider one of these options:

- Write an introduction to a travel guide that describes your empire. Use a narrative style that gives your audience a "tour" of your empire.

- Draw a map of your empire to accompany the descriptions you provide. Include a legend, geographic features, and other details that help give a visual summary of your empire.

- Create a multimedia presentation using photos, drawings, text, and maps to illustrate your empire and its various components.

NATIONAL GEOGRAPHIC | LEARNING FRAMEWORK ACTIVITIES

Create a Map

SKILLS Observation, Collaboration
KNOWLEDGE Our Living Planet

Team up with a partner to create a map of the continents discussed in this unit. Include as many civilizations, landforms, bodies of water, and labels on your map as possible. Draw arrows to represent migration routes, or how groups of people began to move from place to place. You might also consider using arrows to show these civilizations' trade routes and drawing icons to represent products that were traded along those routes. When you have finished your map, compare it to other teams' maps. Offer your own observations, and ask your classmates to make observations about your map.

Think Like an Archaeologist

ATTITUDE Curiosity
KNOWLEDGE Our Human Story

Civilizations leave behind clues about what they were like and how people lived. Archaeologists all over the world follow very strict procedures when they excavate a site to ensure that no information is lost. They also have to make sure that in digging, they don't destroy or ruin artifacts, structures, or art. In groups of four, imagine that you are in charge of a dig site in the location of one of the civilizations covered in this unit. Make a list of items you might find on your site and describe what challenges you think your crew might face on the dig. Then share your imagined dig experience with the class.

ENGLISH SETTLEMENT

CRITICAL VIEWING In this 1941 painting by Newell Wyeth, the Pilgrims watch the *Mayflower* depart on its return voyage to England in April, 1621. What mood does the artist convey by showing the Pilgrims as they watch their ship return to England?

ENGLISH SETTLEMENT

COLONIAL AMERICA

1607
English settlers found Jamestown in Virginia. *(sealing wax stamp owned by Jamestown resident)*

1620
Pilgrims sign the Mayflower Compact, establishing a self-governing colony at Plymouth, Massachusetts.

1676
Nathaniel Bacon leads a rebellion against the governor of Virginia and demands war against the Native Americans.

1585
Roanoke, the first English colony, is established. *(engraving showing the English arriving in Virginia in 1585)*

1600

1500

c. 1620 AFRICA
The West African kingdom of Dahomey, which would become rich in part through the Atlantic slave trade, is founded.

1644 ASIA
The Manchus overthrow the Ming and found the Qing dynasty in China. *(lion statue before palace of Ming and Qing emperors)*

THE WORLD

1735
John Peter Zenger is tried for printing articles criticizing the English governor of New York. *(block of movable type used in 1700s America)*

HISTORICAL THINKING: DETERMINE CHRONOLOGY

What two events, nearly 70 years apart, indicate the American and British concern with the power of government?

1763
After the French and Indian War ends, the Proclamation of 1763 is issued.

1692
The Salem witch trials are held in Massachusetts.

1754
The French and Indian War between Great Britain and France is fought on American soil. *(pipe tomahawk, a blend of Native American and European cultures)*

1800

1700

1688 EUROPE
Britain's Glorious Revolution begins and results in greatly increased power for Parliament.

c. 1750 EUROPE
The Industrial Revolution begins in Great Britain. *(spinning jenny, which helped industrialize Britain's textile production)*

1722 ASIA
Chinese emperor Kangxi dies after reigning for 61 years.

CHAPTER

3

THE THIRTEEN
COLONIES
1585–1732

ESSENTIAL QUESTION
How did early settlers cope with challenges as they established the first 13 colonies?

 The Lost Colony of Roanoke

SECTION 1 Early Colonies Have Mixed Success

KEY VOCABULARY

charter	joint-stock company
indentured servant	traitor

SECTION 2 New England Colonies

KEY VOCABULARY

banish	King Philip's War	Mayflower Compact
dissenter	levy	self-governance
Fundamental Orders of Connecticut		separatist

SECTION 3 Middle and Southern Colonies

KEY VOCABULARY

alliance	natural resource	raw material
confederacy	neutrality	royal colony
doctrine	proprietor	tributary
economic activity		

AMERICAN GALLERY
ONLINE

A Portrait of the Pilgrims

READING STRATEGY

MAKE INFERENCES
When you make inferences, you use what you already know to figure out the meaning of the text. Use a chart like this one to make inferences about the challenges settlers faced as they established the first 13 colonies.

I READ	I KNOW	AND SO
The settlers lived under difficult conditions.	Many settlers died of diseases.	

"As a **city upon a hill,** the eyes of all people are upon us."
—John Winthrop

Founded in 1947, Plimoth Plantation, a living museum in Plymouth, Massachusetts, provides an experience of what life was like for the Pilgrims and the Native Americans after the Pilgrims' arrival in 1620. From details in the photo, what materials can you identify that Pilgrims used to build houses and objects that were once part of daily life?

Dasamonquepeuc

Roanoac

CRITICAL VIEWING Which groups are represented in this historical map of Roanoke Island, and how did you identify them?

torasck

THE LOST COLONY OF
ROANOKE

Have you ever read about an unsolved mystery
that really haunts you? Something unexplainable has
happened, and you just can't get it out of your mind. The
"Lost Colony" of Roanoke is an unsolved mystery that has
haunted Americans since the late 1500s, when a group of
118 English colonists disappeared from the shore of North
Carolina sometime between 1587 and 1590.

TRYING TO COLONIZE

In 1584, nearly 100 years
after Christopher Columbus
had landed in North America,
Queen Elizabeth of England
grew tired of watching the
Spanish grow rich off the "New
World." Eager for the wealth and
fame that the colonies might
bring, and for the opportunity
to expand English control, she
granted nobleman Walter Raleigh
permission to set up a colony in North
America. Raleigh sent more than 100 colonists
to Roanoke Island, part of the island chain now
known as the Outer Banks of North Carolina.

Watercolor by John White
of the Roanoke Colony

The colony lasted less than
a year. The colonists had
no farming or fishing skills
and had to rely on trade
with Native Americans
named the Roanoac to feed
themselves. Foolishly, they
soured relations with the
tribe by treating them with
suspicion and ordering the
killing of a Roanoac chief. When
the explorer Sir Francis Drake
arrived with his fleet in June 1586, the
colonists were sorely in need of food and supplies
and desperate to leave. They gladly accepted
Drake's offer to bring them back to England.

SOMETIMES, EVIDENCE GROWS ON TREES

Scientists who study tree rings have offered an intriguing clue about the fate of the lost colony. Trees grow a new outer layer of wood each year during the growing season— that's why you can tell the age of a tree by counting its rings. In years with good growing conditions, a wider ring forms. Narrow rings indicate poor years for growth. Long-lived trees, such as the bald cypress trees in some North Carolina rivers, can help researchers determine what growing conditions were like centuries ago.

By studying local trees, scientists have determined that Roanoke Island experienced one of its worst droughts in centuries during the years 1587–1589. Which explanation for the colony's disappearance do you think this evidence supports?

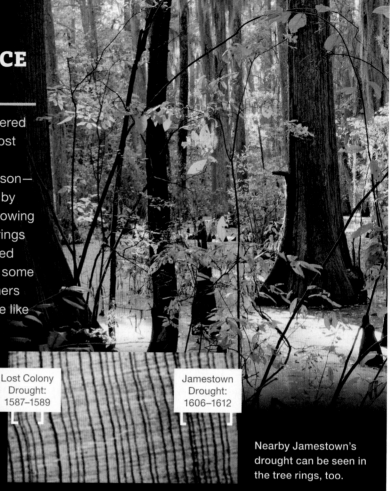

Lost Colony Drought: 1587–1589

Jamestown Drought: 1606–1612

Nearby Jamestown's drought can be seen in the tree rings, too.

FOUND AND LOST

Soon, Raleigh decided to try again, this time with a different type of colony. Unlike the all-male group that made the first attempt, these colonists would be a mixed group of men, women, and some children—families aspiring to be planters in the new colony. The governor would be John White, who had been a member of the earlier, failed expedition and had some knowledge of the local geography and tribes. Among the settlers were White's pregnant daughter Eleanor and her husband Ananias Dare.

The colonists reached Roanoke Island in July 1587. Because of the first colony's experiences, they were wary of the Roanoac, but they began a friendly relationship with a different local tribe, the Croatoan. On August 18, 1587, Virginia Dare was born, the first English baby born in North America.

The settlers soon realized they would need more supplies to get through the coming winter. In

August, John White returned to England with the ships that had brought the colonists, intending to ask Raleigh for the much-needed goods. But because of England's war with Spain, White was unable to return to Roanoke for three years.

When John White came ashore on an eerily silent Roanoke Island in August 1590, not a single human—colonist or Native American—was present. White found the word *CROATOAN* carved into a post in the former settlement's gate, and a nearby tree bore the letters *CRO.* According to his journal, White concluded that the settlers were "safe . . . at Croatoan, where . . . the Savages of the Island [are] our friends." But he would never learn whether his assumption was correct.

The next day, a strong storm blew up, forcing White's ships away from the Outer Banks. Under an onslaught of continuing bad weather, the small fleet had no choice but to retreat to England. White never succeeded in mounting another expedition to Roanoke or finding the missing colonists.

This woodcut shows John White examining the carved word *Croatoan*. What can you infer from the men's expressions and body language?

LOST COLONY FOUND?

Like John White in 1590, researchers today wonder about what happened to the missing colonists. Were the colonists indeed with the Croatoan, just a few miles away from White as he searched the ruined settlement? Did baby Virginia Dare grow up in America? Many plausible explanations exist. The colonists may have moved in with the Croatoan and eventually become part of the tribe. It is also possible they were killed by a hostile native group or by soldiers from a passing Spanish ship.

In recent years, two teams of researchers have found new evidence about the colony's possible fate. In 2012, one group took a closer look at a map of the region drawn by John White. Underneath a paper patch on the map, they found a star-shaped symbol indicating a spot about 50 miles inland from Roanoke. Archaeologists digging at the spot, which they named Site X, uncovered pottery in a style that was also used by the Roanoke colonists.

Meanwhile, researchers digging at Cape Creek on Hatteras Island, where the Croatoan lived, have also discovered a number of objects that may have come from the Roanoke colony.

Many believe the finds at Cape Creek and Site X indicate that the Roanoke colonists left the island to live with different native tribes. Definite proof of the colonists' fate, however, remains tantalizingly out of reach. Charles Ewen, an archaeologist at East Carolina University, sums up the situation. "We still don't know what happened," he reflects, "and we are waiting to be persuaded."

THINK ABOUT IT

How does the story of Roanoke remind you of fictional mystery stories you have read or watched?

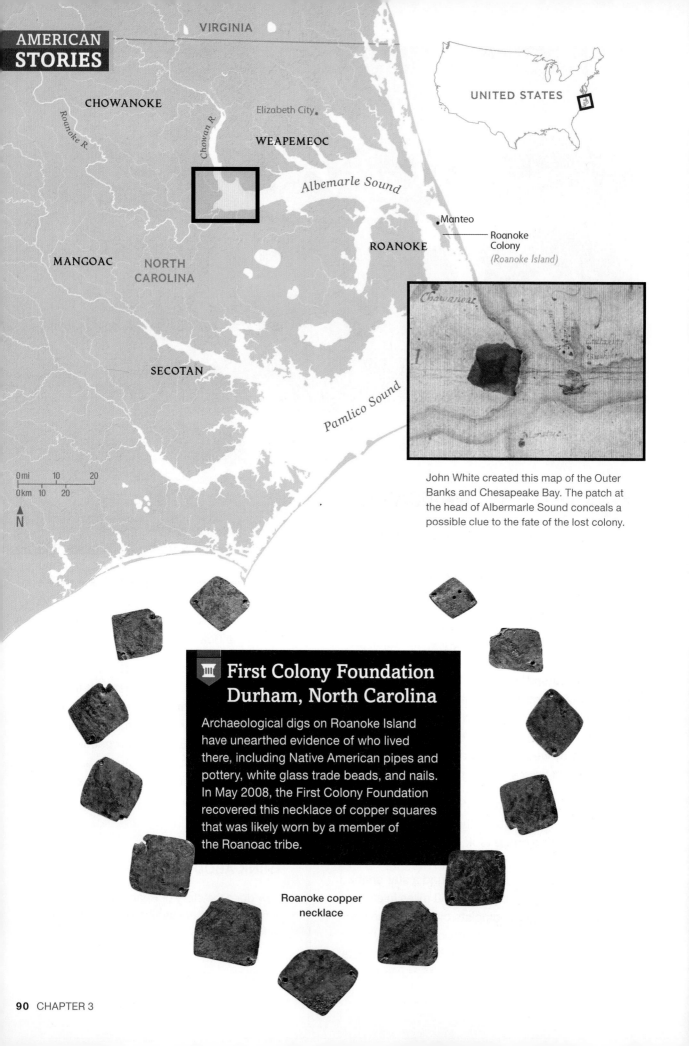

VIRGINIA

UNITED STATES

CHOWANOKE

Roanoke R.

Chowan R.

Elizabeth City.

WEAPEMEOC

Albemarle Sound

.Manteo

Roanoke
Colony
(Roanoke Island)

ROANOKE

MANGOAC

NORTH
CAROLINA

SECOTAN

Pamlico Sound

0mi   10   20
0km 10 20

N

John White created this map of the Outer
Banks and Chesapeake Bay. The patch at
the head of Albermarle Sound conceals a
possible clue to the fate of the lost colony.

First Colony Foundation
Durham, North Carolina

Archaeological digs on Roanoke Island
have unearthed evidence of who lived
there, including Native American pipes and
pottery, white glass trade beads, and nails.
In May 2008, the First Colony Foundation
recovered this necklace of copper squares
that was likely worn by a member of
the Roanoac tribe.

Roanoke copper
necklace

THE ARTWORK OF JOHN WHITE

John White was an accomplished artist and cartographer. In 1585, he voyaged from England to the Outer Banks. During his year-long stay at Roanoke, he created more than 70 watercolor drawings of indigenous people, plants, and animals to give the English a sense of the environment in the "New World."

John White's watercolor of the Native American town of Pomeiooc

MANTEO AND WANCHESE

Manteo and Wanchese were two of the first Native Americans to have extensive contact with the English. Manteo was a Croatoan chief, and Wanchese was from the Roanoac tribe. Both men encountered a scouting party that Walter Raleigh sent before the first Roanoke colony, and both returned with the group to England.

Wanchese came to dislike the English and felt like a prisoner in England. Manteo, on the other hand, became friendly with the English and remained loyal to them for years. Both Manteo and Wanchese came to Roanoke with the first colony. Wanchese rejoined his people, but Manteo stayed with the English as an interpreter and guide. When the first colony failed, Manteo returned to England with the former settlers. Later, he accompanied White's group of colonists, once again serving as an interpreter and helping to smooth relations with the Croatoans. In August 1587, before White left for England, Manteo was baptized and officially converted to Christianity.

John White's watercolor of a Native American chief

1.1 Colonizing Virginia

Imagine settling in an entirely new place, far across an ocean from your home. How would you prepare for this adventure? The founders of Jamestown, Virginia, found out the hard way just what it was like.

MAIN IDEA Virginia's first colonists struggled with starvation, wars, and disease before finally finding success in their new home.

FOUNDING JAMESTOWN

In the early 1600s, England began establishing colonies in America. As with Spain and its colonies, England pursued the economic policy of mercantilism, giving it a trade monopoly with its colonies. The colonies provided raw materials to England, where workers made them into goods. Finished goods were then shipped back to the colonies and sold or traded, helping England increase its wealth.

At the same time, merchants and investors developed a new type of business, called a **joint-stock company**. Wealthy individuals invested in a venture, or business project. Their funds paid for the endeavor, and the individuals shared ownership in the venture. This business raised money for

AMERICAN PLACES
The Chesapeake Bay

The Chesapeake Bay is a large inlet that extends through the present-day states of Virginia and Maryland. It is a rich ecosystem, with more than 150 rivers and streams flowing into it. The area around the bay provided rich farmland to colonists who established farms and plantations there.

exploring trade routes and establishing markets in new locations. In late 1606, a joint-stock company called the **Virginia Company** funded the first English settlement at **Jamestown** in the colony of Virginia. King James I had provided a **charter**, or written grant detailing rights and privileges, to the company to settle the colonies. After a difficult winter voyage across the Atlantic Ocean, more than 100 settlers arrived in the **Chesapeake Bay** and established a fort along the James River.

The settlers were ill-equipped to establish a colony. They had little experience with farming, hunting, or fishing and were more interested in searching for gold. Soon they were starving. To make matters worse, Jamestown was located in a low-lying area—perfect for mosquitoes that carried malaria, a disease that killed many settlers.

Colonial officer John Smith established a mutually beneficial trade relationship with the Powhatan, a Native American tribe. The Powhatan grew corn that the settlers could use, and the English had goods that the Powhatan wanted, such as weapons. In 1608, Smith became president of the colony and put the settlers to work planting crops, fishing, and building houses. The state of the colony improved.

Then in September 1609, Smith was injured and returned to England. That same year, the Virginia Company angered Chief Powhatan, who then cut off trade with the settlers. Winter came, and the settlers began to starve again. Any colonist who left the fort risked being attacked. Only 60 colonists survived the winter. In 1614, Chief Powhatan's daughter, Pocahontas, married colonist John Rolfe. The marriage helped usher in peace between the two groups.

SUCCESS AT LAST

In about 1612, Rolfe started to grow a new variety of tobacco in Virginia. He used seeds he had acquired in the West Indies. Rolfe's new tobacco was less bitter than the variety that had been grown in the colony, and by the following year, he began shipping it to England, where it became very popular. Tobacco farmers tried to produce enough to meet rising demand, and tobacco became a driving economic force in the colonies.

In 1619, the Virginia Company tried to persuade English citizens to move to Virginia to build this labor force. Some citizens were freeholders who

Pocahontas
Artists have portrayed Pocahontas in various ways, almost always based on information rather than actually seeing her. The top left painting as Lady Rebecca Rolfe in England (1616) is the only known portrait of her from life. Other artists have imagined her as the Powhatan princess who captivated John Rolfe (top right, painting dated 1945), and shortly after her marriage to Rolfe in 1614 (painting dated c. 1852).

paid their own transportation and received land in exchange. Others were **indentured servants**, who gave up several years of freedom to have their travel fees paid by the company or another person. Indentured servants were bound for a certain length of time to work to pay off their traveling expenses.

Also in 1619, the Virginia Company established an assembly of elected delegates in Virginia, called the **House of Burgesses**. It became the first representative assembly in the American colonies, and it gave the colonists more local control.

HISTORICAL THINKING

1. **READING CHECK** What was the purpose for establishing an English settlement in Virginia?

2. **FORM AND SUPPORT OPINIONS** How important do you think John Smith was to the settlers? Use evidence from the reading to support your opinion.

3. **MAKE INFERENCES** Why did John Rolfe's marriage to Pocahontas bring about peace between the Powhatan and the colonists?

1.2 Voorhees Archaearium Jamestown, Virginia

Located near the site of the original Jamestown Settlement, America's first permanent English colony, the Voorhees Archaearium captures the story of Virginia in the 1600s. Artifacts from the arrival of English colonists to Jamestown in 1607 and the earliest cultural encounters and events are housed in this archaeology museum. Visitors can explore the cultures of the Native Americans, Europeans, and Africans who intersected in 17th-century Virginia, and trace Jamestown's beginnings in England. They can even climb aboard replicas of the three ships, moored nearby, that crossed the Atlantic, bringing the earliest colonists from England to Virginia. What can you infer about the lives of the colonists based on the artifacts below?

Lead Toy Horse

A collection of tiny toy horses like this one was found in a trash heap along with food remains, broken pottery, and shattered glassware from the James Fort. Long ago, this horse may have carried a toy rider in its saddle and had wheels so a child could push or pull it around.

Gaming Dice

Excavations have revealed more than 60 gaming dice at the James Fort. Many of the dice are made of animal bone, but some are made of ivory or lead. It's possible that the lead dice may have been made by a soldier who also made lead shot (fired by weapons) at the fort. Like modern dice, the opposing sides of the Jamestown dice add up to seven. Soldiers passed the long hours at the remote fort playing dice games.

Brass Thimble

This 16th-century thimble was made in Nuremberg, Germany, and is one of 11 brass thimbles found at the James Fort. Several tailors joined the Jamestown colonists in 1607 and 1608, and their ability to sew and repair cloth was important to the frontier settlement. Other tailoring tools have also been found, including needles, irons, and pins.

Ear Picker

Believe it or not, a Jamestown colonist once used this silver sea creature to scrape teeth, clean dirt from fingernails, and scoop out earwax. Gold and silver grooming tools were often worn like jewelry in Europe during the late 1500s and early 1600s. The first settlers at Jamestown included a surgeon and a barber who could perform basic medical care like removing infected teeth—and excessive earwax.

Tailors sometimes used earwax to make their thread stronger if they had no beeswax!

Why might the English have felt it was safer to drink wine than water in the early 1600s?

Monogrammed Wine Bottles

Discovered by Jamestown archaeologists, these wide glass bottles were made in England between 1680 and 1700 and found upright on the dirt floor of a rectangular cellar. One of the intact bottles is marked with the initials *FN,* which reveals it once belonged to someone of wealth and status. During the 17th century, high-ranking gentlemen liked to order wine bottles from England stamped with their personal seal.

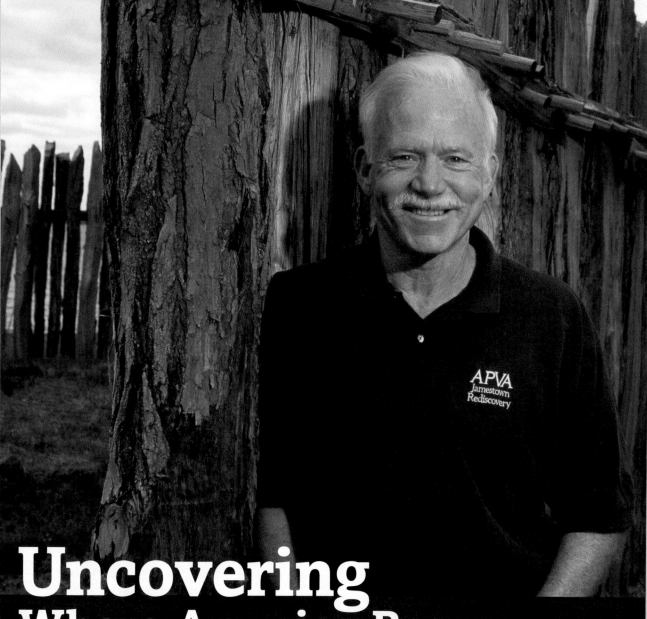

Uncovering
Where America Began

"The American dream was born on the banks of the James River." —William Kelso

The experts said the Jamestown fort had washed away without a trace, but **William Kelso** didn't believe them. He saw something in a glassed-in cross-section of dirt exhibited at the Jamestown ranger station that suggested something might still lie below the surface. So, in 1994, Kelso set out alone with his shovel and hit pay dirt almost immediately: earth stained dark by logs that had decayed long ago. Thus began his quest for Jamestown's buried truths.

^
Kelso stands next to a portion of the Jamestown fort that he and his team reconstructed. The archaeologist has worked for more than 20 years in Jamestown in part because, as he says, "This is America's site. It belongs to the people."

MAIN IDEA Archaeologist William Kelso has uncovered evidence at Jamestown that is changing how people view the settlement.

This map shows the triangular Jamestown fort and the houses that stood within it. Chief Powhatan sits at the top right of the map, while ships full of settlers arrive on the island along the James River.

EARLY DISCOVERIES

National Geographic Explorer William Kelso's search began in 1994. In anticipation of the 400th anniversary of Jamestown's founding, the Association for the Preservation of Virginia Antiquities had announced plans to investigate the island. Kelso volunteered for the job.

About all he had to go on were some historical accounts and documents, including a roughly drawn Spanish map from 1608 showing the triangular Jamestown fort. But he also knew that the only aboveground ruins that had survived in Jamestown were parts of a church tower. Kelso reasoned that the settlers would have built the fort near the church, so he began there. Fragments of early 1600s ceramics and the dark-stained dirt told him that he was on the right track.

THE TRUTH ABOUT JAMESTOWN

In time, Kelso identified evidence of all but one corner of the fort's structure as well as thousands of artifacts. He and his team—at this point, Kelso wasn't working alone anymore—began reconstructing the fort, using the materials and tools available to the Jamestown settlers. During this process, he discovered just how tough the settlers had been. Kelso says, "They were cutting down trees, digging holes, building forts, building buildings, digging ditches." The skeletons that Kelso has excavated also reveal how hard the settlers' lives were. Many died during the starving time of the early years and in the wars with Native Americans. Others couldn't adapt to the new environment. Lifespans were short.

One misconception about Jamestown is that it was a failure, but the settlers got many things right. Historians have often faulted them for establishing their colony in what was basically a marsh. But they needed to find a place where they could defend themselves against the Spanish. Locating their settlement on an island worked—the Spanish never attacked. Above all, they developed a new form of government. Around 1619, the settlers organized a representative assembly that met at the church. According to Kelso, "That's when liberty got out of the bag, and nobody could stuff it back in."

These findings have told us a lot about the site, and Kelso hopes to uncover more. But now the sea level around Jamestown Island is rising. Soon, important evidence may disappear. And Kelso believes the site is worth preserving. For, as he says, "This is where America began. This is where the English settlers first became American."

HISTORICAL THINKING

1. **READING CHECK** What did Kelso learn about the Jamestown settlers from his excavations?

2. **ANALYZE CAUSE AND EFFECT** Why did the settlers choose Jamestown as the site for their colony?

3. **DRAW CONCLUSIONS** What action on the settlers' part was key to the development of American constitutional democracy?

1.4 Conflicts with Native Americans

When something that belongs to you is taken away, it can be difficult to keep the peace. Native Americans in the 1600s faced this challenge when colonists began to take over their ancestral lands.

MAIN IDEA Wars between Native Americans and Virginian colonists raged on and off for decades as each group laid claim to the land.

WARS WITH THE POWHATAN

For about eight years after John Rolfe and Pocahontas were married, the Jamestown colonists and the Powhatan lived in peace. During that time, the Powhatan helped the colonists plant corn, catch fish, and capture wild fowl. But as thousands of new colonists arrived to work for the Virginia Company, the Powhatan saw their land and culture taken away. In 1622, one Powhatan leader staged a rebellion against the English and their European and Christian customs. Colonists killed him, and the Powhatan responded by launching an attack on the colony, killing hundreds of settlers.

This attack set off a 10-year war. When peace finally came, it lasted for more than a decade. But even during the peaceful years, the colonists' desire for land continued to provoke the Powhatan. As the demand for tobacco as a cash crop increased, colonists, claiming the English king owned the colony and its land, simply grabbed land they deemed to be unoccupied. Although no one lived on the land, the Powhatan hunted, fished, and farmed on it. Two years later, the Powhatan attacked the colony again, triggering yet another war. In 1646, the Powhatan surrendered. Their leader was captured and later killed.

The two groups signed a treaty that required the Powhatan to live on lands north of the York River. They also had to make a yearly payment to the colonists of 20 beaver skins. The Powhatan had lost their power in Jamestown.

BACON'S REBELLION

As years passed, conflicts between Native Americans and colonists increased. In the 1660s, the governor of Virginia, William Berkeley, urged colonists to interact peacefully and maintain trading to avoid a costly war. However, by 1670, tensions surfaced among colonists who owned land and those who did not. Landless freemen resented their lack of property and wanted a stronger voice in Virginia's government.

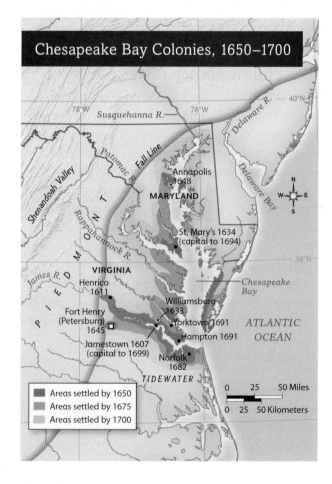

Chesapeake Bay Colonies, 1650–1700

Many of them had the right to purchase land, but low tobacco prices and high land prices made it difficult for them to find land they could afford to buy. They also claimed that the Powhatan controlled too much land, even though this land had been granted to the Native Americans by the 1646 treaty.

A young councilman and wealthy planter named Nathaniel Bacon, who was actually Berkeley's cousin by marriage, challenged Berkeley's leadership. He argued that the governor held too much power and that the colonists should be more involved with the government. He also wanted to claim more land from the Powhatan. Bacon and a group of landless followers attacked Native Americans in 1676 in an attempted revolution later called **Bacon's Rebellion**.

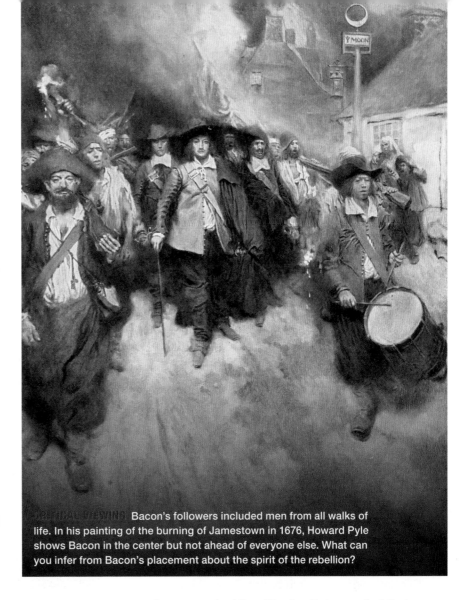

CRITICAL VIEWING Bacon's followers included men from all walks of life. In his painting of the burning of Jamestown in 1676, Howard Pyle shows Bacon in the center but not ahead of everyone else. What can you infer from Bacon's placement about the spirit of the rebellion?

Berkeley accused Bacon of being a traitor, or someone disloyal to his or her own people or cause, because he believed Bacon had challenged the power of the governor and his fellow wealthy planters. Bacon had growing public support, however. Bowing to this pressure, Berkeley agreed to be lenient with Bacon if he turned himself in and went to England to be tried before King Charles II. But the House of Burgesses did not approve of Berkeley's leniency. They forced Bacon to apologize to Berkeley. The power struggle between Bacon and Berkeley continued for several months. Bacon and his army even burned Jamestown to the ground in September 1676.

The rebellion ended a month later when Bacon died unexpectedly. Berkeley ordered Bacon's fellow leaders to be executed. Angered by these events, King Charles II demanded that Berkeley return to England. Some historians have interpreted Bacon's Rebellion as a fight against the authority of the local government, while others have described it as a power struggle between a powerful governor and a wealthy colonist. However, the Native Americans who were driven from their lands were ultimately the ones who lost the most.

HISTORICAL THINKING

1. **READING CHECK** How did the treaty of 1646 lead to Bacon's Rebellion?

2. **INTERPRET MAPS** How does the map reflect Native American concerns about land?

3. **MAKE INFERENCES** Why did Nathaniel Bacon have public support for his rebellion?

2.1 Pilgrims and Puritans

"Are we there yet?" You've probably asked this question during a long car ride. Imagine sailing across an ocean in a cramped wooden ship. Colonists who braved the long voyage from England to North America may have thought they'd never arrive.

MAIN IDEA The New England colonies became a new home for groups who wished to create societies centered on their religious principles.

THE PILGRIMS FIND A HOME

During the early 1600s, European settlers continued to arrive in the American colonies, despite ongoing conflicts between Native Americans and colonists. At this time in England, religious **dissenters**, or people who disagreed with the beliefs of the Church of England, could be imprisoned or fined. Dissenters yearned for religious freedom so intensely that they left their homes, sailed across the ocean, and settled in the colonies. They became **separatists**, or people who created their own congregations outside of the Church of England.

The **Pilgrims** were one such group. They did not believe in the reforms instituted by the Church of England and saw complete separation as their only spiritual option. In September 1620, a group of Pilgrims boarded the *Mayflower* in England, bound for the northern part of Virginia. The ship strayed off course and landed on Cape Cod. Once they realized they would not land in Virginia, the Pilgrims established and signed the **Mayflower Compact**. This agreement laid out a plan for governing a new colony.

From Cape Cod, the Pilgrims moved to the area around what is now Plymouth, Massachusetts. During their first winter, half of the Pilgrims died from illness or exposure to the cold. The following spring, Native Americans who lived nearby, including Squanto, a member of the Pawtuxet, helped the Pilgrims grow their own food. They identified which crops grew best and when to plant them. They also showed the Pilgrims how to use herring, a local fish, to fertilize the crops. As experienced local planters, Native Americans also shared their knowledge of how to plant corn, beans, and squash together for the best results. The two groups celebrated the Pilgrims' first harvest in a three-day celebration considered the first Thanksgiving.

Eyeglasses with wooden case

🏛 Pilgrim Hall Museum Plymouth, Massachusetts

Even Pilgrims wore spectacles. These eyeglasses, on display at Pilgrim Hall Museum in Plymouth, Massachusetts, were probably made in England sometime in the 17th century. They are made of glass, horn, wood, and leather. The case is carved from pinewood.

A CITY UPON A HILL

Like the Pilgrims, the **Puritans** believed that the Church of England needed additional reform. Unlike the Pilgrims, however, the Puritans wanted to reform the church from within.

Beginning in 1630, the Puritans began their migration from England to Massachusetts Bay. They arrived as part of the Massachusetts Bay Company, believing God wanted them to create a moral community. As Puritan leader John Winthrop said, the colony would be "as a City upon a Hill, the Eyes of all people are upon us."

The Puritans' system of self-governance was called the New England Way. The church was the center of the community, and all citizens were required to attend. Puritans believed that a congregation, bound by a sacred oath, held all authority and could punish members who disagreed with church doctrine. People who tried to leave a congregation could lose their property. The Puritans were dissenters who did not allow dissent within their own communities.

Not all Puritans agreed with the New England Way. In 1636, clergyman Thomas Hooker and a group of Puritans left Massachusetts to found a new colony in Connecticut. Three years later, in a sermon, Hooker provided inspiration for the **Fundamental Orders of Connecticut**. This document established a General Assembly of representatives from many towns. Unlike in Massachusetts, church membership was not a condition for voting.

In 1631, religious dissenter and Pilgrim minister **Roger Williams** arrived in Massachusetts Bay Colony. He attacked laws requiring church attendance and tax support of Puritan churches and was **banished**, or sent away from the colony. In 1636, he bought land from the Narragansett and founded the colony of Rhode Island. He based this new colony on the idea that church and state affairs should be kept separate.

In 1637, Massachusetts Bay Colony leaders banished another dissenter. **Anne Hutchinson** had angered orthodox Puritans by teaching that people had to respond directly to God, not the church, for their actions. Hutchinson also believed that ministers were unnecessary. She founded a settlement in the colony of Rhode Island.

Built in England in 1956, the *Mayflower II* is a full-scale replica of the vessel that brought the Pilgrims from England to North America in 1620. Upon completion, it sailed from England to New England following the Pilgrims' route. It remains a working sailing ship, moored at Plymouth, Massachusetts.

HISTORICAL THINKING

1. **READING CHECK** What was the Mayflower Compact and why was it important?

2. **MAKE INFERENCES** Why did the Puritans link citizenship to church membership?

3. **MAKE GENERALIZATIONS** Why did some groups leave the Massachusetts Bay Colony to establish new colonies?

2.2 Squanto
c. 1580–1622

"[Squanto] was a special instrument sent of God for [the Pilgrims'] good beyond their expectation."

—from the journal of William Bradford, governor of Plymouth Colony

The Pilgrims certainly couldn't have expected that a fluent English-speaking Native American would happen on the scene and choose to act as their interpreter and guide. So Squanto, also known as Tisquantum, must have seemed like a gift indeed. He taught the Pilgrims how to grow maize and where to catch fish, and generally showed them the ropes so they could survive in Plymouth. Squanto even died in the Pilgrims' service. What we don't know for sure is exactly what came before.

EARLY LIFE

Part folk hero, part myth, much of what we know—or think we know—about Squanto comes from often conflicting eyewitness accounts. According to some sources, he was kidnapped from his Massachusetts home in 1605 by Englishman George Weymouth and taken to England. While there, he was apparently treated well and taught English—the idea being that he would serve as an interpreter for those settling the colonies. John Smith, one of the founders of Jamestown Colony, is said to have returned him to America for that purpose around 1615.

Remarkably, Squanto was kidnapped a second time, an event on which most authorities agree. One of Smith's men,

Wooden sculpture of Squanto

🏛 Pilgrim Hall Museum
Plymouth, Massachusetts

The nation's oldest continuously operating public museum, Pilgrim Hall, tells the founding story of America: the Pilgrims' arrival, struggles, and first Thanksgiving in Plymouth. This 19th-century sculpture of Squanto forms part of the museum's collection. It shows what one artist thinks the Native American guide might have looked like.

Squanto was known for his role as the Pilgrims' guide. But stories have also circulated about trouble he caused. For example, fearful of losing his position of power, Squanto tried to pit the Pilgrims against the Native Americans. He spread rumors that Massasoit was joining forces with other tribes in a plan to attack the Pilgrims.

When Squanto's plot was uncovered, Massasoit demanded that Squanto be turned over for punishment. Certain that the Wampanoag chief would execute Squanto, William Bradford refused. With more colonial ships arriving in the area, Bradford knew that he and the new settlers would need Squanto more than ever.

Before long, Squanto became an indispensable member of the colony. He taught the settlers how to plant local crops and served as their ambassador on trading expeditions. He even helped negotiate a peace treaty between the Pilgrims and the Wampanoag chief, Massasoit. In the fall of 1621, the Wampanoag, the Pilgrims, and Squanto celebrated the peace and Plymouth's successful harvest with the first Thanksgiving.

Squanto's time in Plymouth turned out to be brief. While guiding William Bradford on an expedition around Cape Cod, the Native American contracted a fever and died. According to some sources, Squanto said to Bradford on his deathbed, "Pray for me, Governor, that I might go to the Englishmen's God in heaven." Apparently, the Pilgrims had had a powerful influence on Squanto. He could have no idea that his own influence and aid had helped secure the survival of the colonists.

Thomas Hunt, took Squanto and several other Native Americans to Spain where the Englishman hoped to sell them into slavery. Fortunately, Squanto managed to get away. Some say Spanish priests rescued him. Most accounts, though, have him escaping to England and befriending merchants in London. This period, then, may have been when Squanto learned English. In 1619, he sailed with the merchants to New England to help them establish trade with the Native Americans.

LIFE AMONG THE PILGRIMS

Squanto returned to his homeland only to find that most of his people—the Pawtuxet—had been wiped out by disease. For a time, he lived with the Wampanoag (WAHMP-uh-noh-ag). Then, in early 1621, a Native American named Samoset brought Squanto to Plymouth Colony. Samoset had been the first Native American to greet the Pilgrims. But, with his limited understanding of English, he couldn't really speak to them. Squanto, he knew, had a far better command of the language.

HISTORICAL THINKING

1. **READING CHECK** How did Squanto help the Pilgrims in Plymouth?

2. **FORM AND SUPPORT OPINIONS** Do you think the treaty with the Wampanoag could have been created without Squanto? Why or why not?

3. **DRAW CONCLUSIONS** Based on his dying words, what did Squanto learn from the Pilgrims?

2.3 Foundations of Democracy

Democracy is founded on a number of principles, one of which is equality. Throughout history, legal documents have outlined rights and created rules for governing communities fairly. Some of these writings inspired the authors of the Declaration of Independence and the Constitution.

In colonial New England, the Puritans established a style of governing that revolved around town hall meetings. These meetings were some of the first experiments in American democracy. Certain requirements limited who could vote in the meetings, however. In most cases, only male, property-owning church members had a vote. Today, all citizens can participate fully in town hall meetings, regardless of gender, race, or wealth.

CRITICAL VIEWING Old Town Hall, located in Canterbury, New Hampshire, was built in 1736. It continues to function as a meeting and polling place. Below, a Canterbury citizen leaves Old Town Hall after voting in a primary during the 2012 election. What details from the photo indicate that the citizens of Canterbury value their town hall?

DOCUMENT ONE

Primary Source: Legal Document
from the Magna Carta, 1215

The Magna Carta, or "Great Charter," served as a peace treaty between King John of England and his barons, who rebelled against the heavy taxes the king **levied** on them, or required that they pay. The original document contained 63 clauses detailing laws that everyone was expected to follow. Principles in the Magna Carta were later embodied in the 1689 English Bill of Rights, such as the right to a trial by jury and protection from excessive fines and cruel punishment.

CONSTRUCTED RESPONSE Why is it significant that the Magna Carta includes the phrase "lawful judgment of his equals"?

No free man shall be seized or imprisoned, or stripped of his rights or possessions, or outlawed or exiled, or deprived of his standing in any other way, nor will we proceed with force against him, or send others to do so, except by the lawful judgment of his equals or by the law of the land.

DOCUMENT TWO

Primary Source: Legal Document
from the Mayflower Compact, 1620

Just prior to settling Plymouth, Massachusetts, the settlers-to-be signed the Mayflower Compact on board their ship. The agreement established **self-governance**, or control of the colony based on the democratic principle of common consent.

CONSTRUCTED RESPONSE What reasons do the Mayflower Compact signers give for working together as a "civil body politic"?

Having undertaken . . . a voyage to plant the first colony in the northern parts of Virginia, do . . . solemnly and mutually in the presence of God and one another, covenant [promise], and combine ourselves together into a civil body politic, for our better ordering and preservation, and furtherance of the ends aforesaid; and . . . to enact, constitute, and frame such just and equal laws . . . as shall be thought most meet and convenient for the general good of the colony.

DOCUMENT THREE

Primary Source: Legal Document
from the Fundamental Orders of Connecticut, 1639

The founders of Connecticut drafted a plan of government called the Fundamental Orders of Connecticut. The document created an assembly of elected representatives from each town in the colony. The ideas captured in this document were later reflected in the U.S. Constitution.

CONSTRUCTED RESPONSE Why do you think it was important to the colony founders that the representatives lived in the towns they represented?

It is Ordered . . . and decreed, that there shall be yearly two General Assemblies or Courts. The first shall be called the Court of Election, wherein shall be yearly chosen from time to time, so many Magistrates and other public Officers as shall be found requisite [necessary] . . . which choice shall be made by all that are admitted freemen and have taken the Oath of Fidelity [loyalty], and do cohabit within this Jurisdiction . . . of the Town wherein they live.

SYNTHESIZE & WRITE

1. **REVIEW** Review what you have learned about the Magna Carta, the Mayflower Compact, and the Fundamental Orders of Connecticut.

2. **RECALL** On your own paper, write the main ideas about government expressed in the Magna Carta, the Mayflower Compact, and the Fundamental Orders of Connecticut.

3. **CONSTRUCT** Construct a topic sentence that answers this question: How is the Magna Carta, written in 1215, similar to the Mayflower Compact and the Fundamental Orders of Connecticut?

4. **WRITE** Using evidence from this chapter and the documents, write a paragraph that supports your topic sentence in Step 3.

2.4 War and Witch Trials

The continued takeover of Native American lands by colonists caused conflicts in the 1670s. Conflicts also arose among colonists, and in one New England town, accusations of witchcraft and wickedness flew.

MAIN IDEA In the late 1600s, wars with Native Americans raged in the New England colonies and witch trials nearly tore the town of Salem apart.

KING PHILIP'S WAR

In 1671, because of increasing tensions with Native Americans, the Plymouth government forced the Wampanoag to surrender their guns. Four years later, a chain of events led to a bloody war.

A Native American named John Sassamon was a convert to Christianity and an interpreter for English colonists. Soon after he warned of an impending attack by a Wampanoag leader named **Metacom**, he was found dead. With little or no evidence, authorities tried and hanged three Wampanoag for his murder.

In response, Metacom and his troops attacked 52 towns throughout New England, destroying 12 of them completely. By the next summer, Metacom's troops were suffering from disease, hunger, and a shortage of weapons, so the campaign came to an end.

English settlers had given Metacom the nickname "King Philip"—no one remembers why—and these attacks became known as **King Philip's War**. Around 600 colonists and thousands of Native Americans died in the war, including Metacom.

ACCUSATIONS IN SALEM

In February 1692, authorities in the village of Salem, Massachusetts, accused three women of witchcraft. Presumably, the charges stemmed from the strange behavior of some village girls. But it didn't take long for people to believe that witches existed and were living in Salem.

Authorities began to arrest people accused by fellow villagers. Nearly 200 women and men were accused and brought to trial for witchcraft.

"Evidence" consisted largely of accusations and little more. Twenty of the accused were put to death, most by hanging.

Historians think the issue underlying the trials may have been women's ownership of property. In Puritan society, women were rarely allowed to own property. When a man died, his son or sons usually inherited his property. If he had no male children, his wife or daughter could inherit.

Many Salem residents accused of witchcraft were women who had inherited property. Their status as property owners went against the societal norm and threatened to challenge traditional gender roles. The threat posed by women as property owners may have driven many witchcraft accusations.

Governor William Phips and Increase Mather, an influential minister, initially supported the trials but then realized things had gone too far. By May 1693, Phips had pardoned all of those still imprisoned. Additionally, courts dismissed charges and returned not-guilty verdicts in the remaining cases. The strange episode of the Salem witch trials was over.

HISTORICAL THINKING

1. **READING CHECK** Why did Metacom attack New England towns?

2. **ANALYZE CAUSE AND EFFECT** What effect did King Philip's War have on Native Americans in the region?

3. **MAKE INFERENCES** Why were landowning women targets of witchcraft accusations?

The Wonders of the Invisible World.

OBSERVATIONS

As well *Historical* as *Theological*, upon the NATURE, the NUMBER, and the OPERATIONS of the

DEVILS.

Accompany'd with,

I. Some Accounts of the Grievous Molestations, by DÆ-MONS and WITCHCRAFTS, which have lately annoy'd the Countrey; and the Trials of some eminent *Malefactors* Executed upon occasion thereof: with several Remarkable Curiosities therein occurring.

II. Some Counsils, Directing a due Improvement of the terrible things, lately done, by the Unusual & Amazing Range of EVIL SPIRITS, in Our Neighbourhood: & the methods to prevent the *Wrongs* which those *Evil Angels* may intend against all sorts of people among us; especially in Accusations of the Innocent.

III. Some Conjectures upon the great EVENTS, likely to befall, the WORLD in General, and NEW-EN-GLAND in Particular; as also upon the Advances of the TIME, when we shall see BETTER DAYES.

IV. A short Narrative of a late Outrage committed by a knot of WITCHES in *Swedeland*, very much Resembling, and so far Explaining, *That* under which our parts of *America* have laboured!

V. THE DEVIL DISCOVERED: In a Brief Discourse upon those TEMPTATIONS, which are the more Ordinary *Devices* of the Wicked One.

By **Cotton Mather**.

Boston Printed by *Benj. Harris* for *Sam. Phillips.* 1693.

The fiery New England preacher named Cotton Mather wrote a book on the Salem witch trials. At left is a page from his book. In the 1890s, 200 years after the Salem witch trials, illustrator Joseph E. Baker reimagined the events reported to have taken place in Salem. What are the different ways witches are portrayed in Mather's writing and these drawings?

3.1 The Middle Colonies

Have you ever traveled to a new place and discovered a culture different from that of your hometown? A colonist traveling south from New England to the Middle Colonies would meet people from European countries who were forging a unique colonial identity.

MAIN IDEA The Middle Colonies included a diverse mix of cultures and religions as people from different countries began to settle in the region.

NEW NETHERLAND TO NEW YORK

Situated in the mid-Atlantic region of North America, the **Middle Colonies** included New York, New Jersey, Pennsylvania, and Delaware. Settlers from countries such as England, France, the Netherlands, Germany, Sweden, and Portugal came to the colonies for different reasons. Some were fleeing religious wars in their home countries. Others were conducting trade.

The first Dutch settlers arrived about 1614 and began trading with Native Americans. In 1624, Cornelius Jacobsen May, working on behalf of the Dutch West India Company, founded New Netherland to provide a base for trade in the Hudson River region. The first settlers of New Netherland worked for the company.

For about 15 years, colonists maintained good relations with Native Americans. However, disputes over land ownership grew. In particular, Native Americans objected to the Dutch settling on lands without a clear agreement that they could do so. Eventually, wars broke out.

In 1664, King Charles II of England gave his brother James, the duke of York, permission to force the Dutch out. The overwhelming English presence in the area made doing so easy and ensured the English complete control of eastern North America. James took over the colony and renamed it New York, and the English made peace with Native Americans living there.

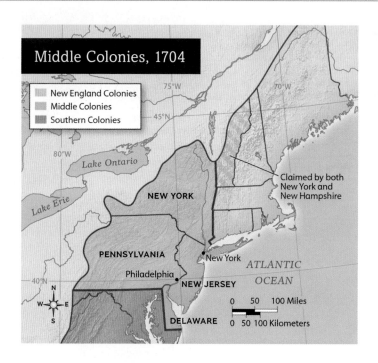

Middle Colonies, 1704

- New England Colonies
- Middle Colonies
- Southern Colonies

Lake Ontario
Lake Erie
NEW YORK
Claimed by both New York and New Hampshire
PENNSYLVANIA
New York
Philadelphia
NEW JERSEY
ATLANTIC OCEAN
DELAWARE
0   50   100 Miles
0 50 100 Kilometers

PENN'S WOODS

After assuming control of New York, James granted land between the Delaware and lower Hudson rivers to Lord John Berkeley and Sir George Carteret, who named the area New Jersey. New Jersey eventually split into West Jersey and East Jersey.

In 1681, Charles II granted a charter for a colony to an Englishman named **William Penn**. Penn wanted to establish a safe home for his fellow **Quakers**—members of the Religious Society of Friends, a Christian movement devoted to peaceful principles. Quakers emphasized education and equality and rejected formal worship and ministry. Because they were perceived by others as

CRITICAL VIEWING In 1682, William Penn met with leaders of the Lenni Lenape under an elm tree at a spot on the Delaware River in present-day Philadelphia. There they signed a treaty together promising cooperation. In this relief from the U.S. Capitol Rotunda, Penn is in the center, gesturing toward the activity around the chest. What details in this relief reveal the reactions of the participants in this treaty signing?

anti-authority and even dangerous, thousands of Quakers were persecuted in England and even in the American colonies. Penn named his colony Sylvania, which means "woods." Charles II renamed it Pennsylvania, after Penn's father.

Penn set out to create a colony based on the Quaker **doctrine**—a principle or policy accepted by a group—that all are equal in the eyes of God. By applying this doctrine, he made Pennsylvania into an extremely diverse society, partly by encouraging religious minorities to settle there. Quaker doctrine also emphasized tolerance for others. In Pennsylvania, all colonists, no matter their religion, could worship in their own way.

Penn encouraged diversity in other ways, too. He kept peace with Native Americans, such as the Lenni Lenape. He purchased land from them, which he then sold to a variety of buyers—people from other colonies, different countries in Europe, and the West Indies. The Swedes, Finns, and Dutch who already inhabited the area became English subjects under Penn.

European settlers who lived in the "Lower Counties" in the southern part of the colony did not like living under Penn's government and at times clashed with Pennsylvania's authority. Penn tried unsuccessfully to unite the English and the Europeans, but in 1704, after two decades of difficulties, he allowed Delaware to form its own assembly. Elsewhere, and following Penn's death, conflicts between Native Americans and colonists continued.

HISTORICAL THINKING

1. **READING CHECK** What factors contributed to the diversity of the Middle Colonies?

2. **ANALYZE CAUSE AND EFFECT** What caused William Penn to allow Delaware to form its own assembly?

3. **INTERPRET MAPS** Locate Delaware on the map. Why does it make sense that Penn might have difficulty uniting people who settled there with the settlers who lived in the rest of Pennsylvania?

3.2 Forming Alliances

Have you ever heard the phrase "strength in numbers"? In the 1600s, as Native Americans and Europeans battled with each other in the Middle Colonies, they discovered that it's sometimes better to be part of a larger group than to stand alone.

MAIN IDEA The Iroquois Confederacy consisted of five tribes that worked together to defeat other Native American tribes and the French.

CLASHES AMONG CULTURES

As white colonists continued moving into New England and the Middle Colonies, two groups of Native Americans began to feel increasingly threatened by their presence.

One group that banded together was the Algonquian (al-GAHN-kwee-uhn). It consisted of the tribes who lived along the Atlantic coast and spoke similar languages. The Pequot tribe resided in New England. The Lenape inhabited the region that became the Middle Colonies. The Algonquian were hunters and gatherers. While they also fished and planted crops, they moved each season to follow the supply of food and lived in temporary camps while away from their villages.

Historically, the Algonquian were the enemies of another united group of tribes, the Iroquois (IHR-uh-kwoy). The Iroquois lived in what is currently central New York State. The French gave these Native Americans the name *Iroquois*, but they called themselves the Haudenosaunee (hah-duh-NAH-suh-nee), or "People of the Longhouse," for the style of home that they built and lived in with their families.

Native American Nations, 1650

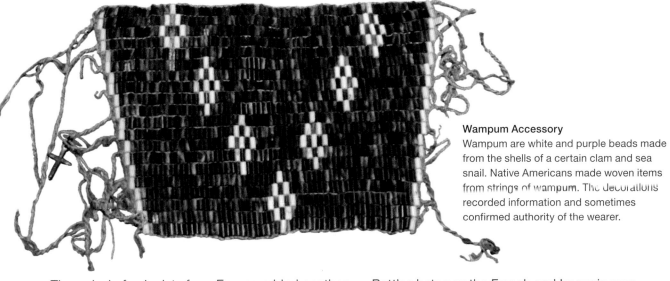

Wampum Accessory
Wampum are white and purple beads made from the shells of a certain clam and sea snail. Native Americans made woven items from strings of wampum. The decorations recorded information and sometimes confirmed authority of the wearer.

The arrival of colonists from Europe added another source of tension to the region. Yet another wave of settlers was now occupying disputed tribal territories, disrupting hunting grounds, communities, and sacred sites.

UNITED WE STAND

Even before Europeans began colonizing and claiming land in North America, conflicts among groups of Native Americans led some of them to form **alliances**, or agreements, with one another. One of the most important alliances was the **Iroquois Confederacy**. A **confederacy** is an agreement among several groups to protect and support one another in battle or other endeavors. In about 1600, the Iroquois Confederacy joined together five tribes: the Mohawk, Onondaga, Oneida, Cayuga, and Seneca, ending the fighting that had once raged among them. The addition of the Tuscarora about 120 years later would change the confederacy's name to the Six Nations.

By banding together, Native Americans hoped to protect their lands and culture and prevent further strife, but they also formed alliances with the French and British. These alliances shifted over time. Sometimes Native Americans even pitted the French, British, and colonists from other countries against one another.

The Iroquois—the Mohawk, in particular—often traded furs with Dutch and British settlers in exchange for firearms. In this way, the trading partners came to rely on each other, and they supported each other in battle. Likewise, the Lenape and the Huron, both enemies of the Iroquois, allied with the French.

Battles between the French and Iroquois over control of the fur trade continued. Due to high demand for their fur, beavers became scarce in the East by the mid-1600s. As a result, the Iroquois Confederacy moved west to gain greater access to beavers in the region, warring with competing tribes along the way. The Iroquois also attacked New France in the North, hoping to end French fur trading in the Ohio Valley and beyond.

In 1689, the Iroquois attacked the settlement of Lachine, near Montreal, in present-day Canada. The attack was in response to a raid two years earlier in which the French had destroyed Iroquois corn. The Iroquois killed about 250 settlers and burned the settlement. More back-and-forth retaliation followed until both sides grew weary of conflict. The weakened Iroquois made peace and, in 1701, signed a treaty of **neutrality**, in which they agreed not to take sides in future wars. But the conflict over land and furs was to grow even more.

HISTORICAL THINKING

1. **READING CHECK** How did forming alliances help the members of the Iroquois Confederacy?

2. **MAKE INFERENCES** In what ways did the demand for beaver fur affect alliances among Native Americans and Europeans?

3. **INTERPRET MAPS** How does the map help you understand why some Native Americans living near the Great Lakes might have been easy targets for the Iroquois Confederacy?

3.3 The Southern Colonies

Have you ever made a plan that didn't work out as you expected? Leaders developed detailed plans for the Southern Colonies. But as more colonists arrived, some of the plans worked better than others.

MAIN IDEA The Southern Colonies provided economic opportunities and social challenges for the colonists who settled in them.

COLONIAL EXPANSION AND COMMERCE

As you have read, in 1607 Jamestown became the first colonial settlement. In 1699, Williamsburg became the new capital of the Virginia colony. Over time, Europeans established settlements in many parts of the South. Maryland, Virginia, North Carolina, South Carolina, and Georgia together formed the **Southern Colonies**.

In 1632, King Charles I of England granted a charter to George Calvert, who held the title Lord Baltimore, to establish a new colony called Maryland, made up of the northern part of Virginia. Most of its settlers were small landowners and renters. Upon Calvert's untimely death, his son became Lord Baltimore and Maryland's **proprietor**—the person responsible for the colony. Maryland's location on the Chesapeake Bay provided easy access to trade, and the region's rich, fertile soil was ideal for growing tobacco. Wealthy plantation owners and merchants built docks on **tributaries**, or small rivers that flow into larger bodies of water, of the Chesapeake Bay. There, they could more easily load ships with tobacco for export and receive ships from around the world loaded with goods.

By 1670, Carolina had become a colony. By 1691, it had split into two colonies: North Carolina, already settled by small planters from Virginia, and South Carolina. Many of South Carolina's settlers came from Barbados in the West Indies. They established large plantations where they grew tobacco, rice, cotton, sugarcane, and other crops. They purchased enslaved Africans to work these plantations. By 1729, both Carolinas had become **royal colonies**, or colonies with a governor and council appointed by the king.

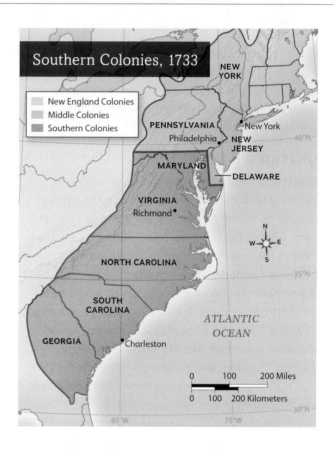

Southern Colonies, 1733

- New England Colonies
- Middle Colonies
- Southern Colonies

GEORGIA: A GRAND EXPERIMENT FAILS

Most of Britain's American colonies were founded for profit or religious freedom. But Georgia, the last mainland British colony in North America, began with a different idea. **James Oglethorpe** and Viscount John Percival envisioned a colony in which debtors and the very poor could make a new start.

King George II wasn't interested in helping the poor, but he understood that Georgia could be a military buffer between Spanish Florida and South Carolina. He granted the charter, placing control of the colony in the hands of trustees who could neither receive financial gain from Georgia nor own

CRITICAL VIEWING Tobacco was one of the major crops in the Southern Colonies. Today, the work of planting, harvesting, and preparing tobacco for market is much the same as it was during the colonial period. In the top photo, a man in Tennessee harvests the whole tobacco plant by chopping it at its base. In the bottom photo, bundles of tobacco hang to cure, or dry and preserve. Based on details you notice in both photos, what kinds of challenges do you think tobacco farmers encounter?

land within it. As governor, Oglethorpe required that all colonists follow three rules based on his own beliefs: no slaves, no liquor, and limited land ownership for each settler. His lofty vision did not last long.

Settlers began arriving in 1733. Many of them found the colony's strict policies unreasonable, so Georgia's population grew slowly. Its role as military buffer between the Spanish and British colonies soon became a source of conflict. The Spanish, suspecting the British of smuggling slaves and goods into Spanish provinces, began searching British ships. Then, in 1740, Oglethorpe attacked Florida, in an attempt to drive the Spanish out. The Spanish, in turn, invaded Georgia in 1742. After a number of other conflicts, both sides gave up, and calm was restored to the buffer zone.

The trustees recognized that Georgia would not thrive under Oglethorpe's strict rules. By 1750, laws allowed liquor and slavery, and there were no limits on land ownership. In 1752, control of Georgia returned to Great Britain. The grand experiment had failed.

HISTORICAL THINKING

1. **READING CHECK** In what ways was Georgia different from the other Southern Colonies?

2. **MAKE INFERENCES** Why might James Oglethorpe have insisted on limiting the amount of land a settler could have?

3. **INTERPRET MAPS** Find the city of Charleston on the map. What advantages do you think this city enjoyed due to its geographic location?

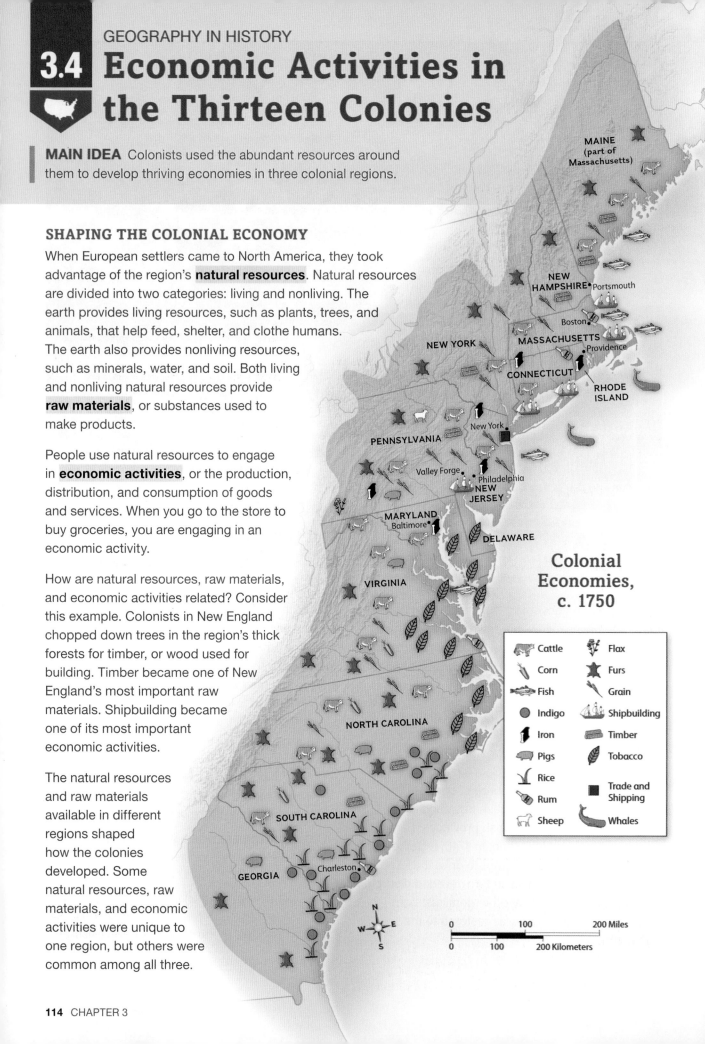

GEOGRAPHY IN HISTORY

3.4 Economic Activities in the Thirteen Colonies

MAIN IDEA Colonists used the abundant resources around them to develop thriving economies in three colonial regions.

SHAPING THE COLONIAL ECONOMY

When European settlers came to North America, they took advantage of the region's **natural resources**. Natural resources are divided into two categories: living and nonliving. The earth provides living resources, such as plants, trees, and animals, that help feed, shelter, and clothe humans. The earth also provides nonliving resources, such as minerals, water, and soil. Both living and nonliving natural resources provide **raw materials**, or substances used to make products.

People use natural resources to engage in **economic activities**, or the production, distribution, and consumption of goods and services. When you go to the store to buy groceries, you are engaging in an economic activity.

How are natural resources, raw materials, and economic activities related? Consider this example. Colonists in New England chopped down trees in the region's thick forests for timber, or wood used for building. Timber became one of New England's most important raw materials. Shipbuilding became one of its most important economic activities.

The natural resources and raw materials available in different regions shaped how the colonies developed. Some natural resources, raw materials, and economic activities were unique to one region, but others were common among all three.

Colonial Economies, c. 1750

Legend:
- Cattle
- Corn
- Fish
- Indigo
- Iron
- Pigs
- Rice
- Rum
- Sheep
- Flax
- Furs
- Grain
- Shipbuilding
- Timber
- Tobacco
- Trade and Shipping
- Whales

COLONIAL TRADE

The American colonies exported raw materials and agricultural products such as timber and tobacco to Europe. In exchange, they imported manufactured goods from Europe.

NORTH AMERICA

EUROPE

→ RAW MATERIALS AND AGRICULTURAL PRODUCTS

← MANUFACTURED GOODS

AMERICAN COLONIES

	CLIMATE	PHYSICAL FEATURES	RAW MATERIALS	ECONOMIC ACTIVITIES
NEW ENGLAND COLONIES				
MASSACHUSETTS	mild, short summers; long, cold winters	mountains, forests, rivers, poor soil	fish, whales, timber, cattle, wheat	farming, fishing, shipbuilding, rum production
CONNECTICUT	mild, short summers; long, cold winters	mountains, rivers, and poor, rocky soil	cattle, iron	shipbuilding, rum production
MIDDLE COLONIES				
NEW YORK	humid summers; cold, snowy winters	mountains, plains, hills, rivers	furs, timber, cattle, wheat	trade and shipping, shipbuilding, farming
PENNSYLVANIA	mild summers; mild winters	mountains, plains, fertile soil, rivers	flax, wheat, sheep, cattle, pigs	farming, shipbuilding
SOUTHERN COLONIES				
VIRGINIA	warm, humid; plentiful rainfall	rich soil, rivers, coastal lowlands	furs, cattle, pigs, wheat, corn, tobacco, fish	farming, fishing, rum production
NORTH CAROLINA	warm, humid; plentiful rainfall	deep forests, rivers, grasslands	indigo, tobacco, furs, timber, pigs, cattle, rice, corn	farming

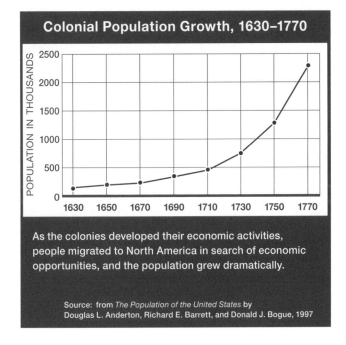

Colonial Population Growth, 1630–1770

As the colonies developed their economic activities, people migrated to North America in search of economic opportunities, and the population grew dramatically.

Source: from *The Population of the United States* by Douglas L. Anderton, Richard E. Barrett, and Donald J. Bogue, 1997

THINK LIKE A GEOGRAPHER

1. **IDENTIFY MAIN IDEAS AND DETAILS** For each colonial region, identify an example of a natural resource that helped the region develop a specific economic activity.

2. **INTERPRET CHARTS** In what ways are the raw materials and economic activities of the New England Colonies and the Southern Colonies alike and different?

3. **ANALYZE ENVIRONMENTAL CONCEPTS** In what ways did the quality and quantity of natural resources impact population growth in the 13 colonies?

3.5 Werowocomoco, the Powhatan Capital

In 1607, Europe had long-established capital cities such as London, Paris, and Madrid. When the Jamestown colonists first met the Native American chief they called Powhatan, they visited him in an equally sophisticated capital.

MAIN IDEA In the 1600s, Werowocomoco was the capital of the Powhatan tribes. Today researchers are exploring its site to learn about the tribes and their interactions with English colonists.

SEAT OF POWER FOR A CHIEFDOM

It was in Werowocomoco (wayr-wuh-KAH-muh-koh) that John Smith first met Powhatan's daughter Pocahontas, who eventually married colonist John Rolfe. Smith would later tell a dramatic tale of being rescued by Pocahontas from certain execution at the hands of Chief Powhatan's warriors. Historians suspect the true story of the meeting was a little less exciting, but it nevertheless was a key moment in the relationship between the colonists and the Powhatan people.

The village of Werowocomoco must have presented a real contrast to the Jamestown Colony in 1607. While Jamestown had been built on swampy ground, Werowocomoco was built on bluffs above the Pamunkey River, which the Europeans later renamed the York River, in present-day Virginia.

The village had many geographical advantages. River bluffs and nearby creeks served as natural defenses against attackers. Nearby waterways were a source of drinking water and fish. The surrounding

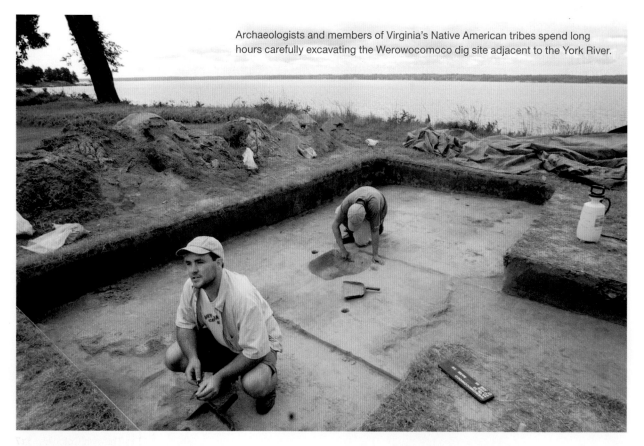

Archaeologists and members of Virginia's Native American tribes spend long hours carefully excavating the Werowocomoco dig site adjacent to the York River.

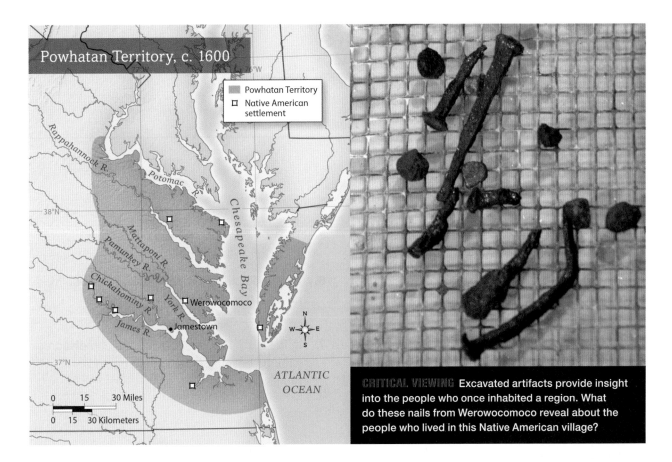

Powhatan Territory, c. 1600

Powhatan Territory
☐ Native American settlement

Rappahannock R.
Potomac R.
Chesapeake Bay
38°N
Mattaponi R.
Pamunkey R.
Chickahominy R.
York R.
Werowocomoco
James R.
Jamestown
37°N
ATLANTIC OCEAN

0   15   30 Miles
0   15   30 Kilometers

CRITICAL VIEWING Excavated artifacts provide insight into the people who once inhabited a region. What do these nails from Werowocomoco reveal about the people who lived in this Native American village?

land was suitable for farming, and nearby forests provided wood for building and fires.

Archaeological evidence suggests that Virginia Indians had lived on the Werowocomoco site since around 8000 B.C. By the early 1600s, the village was the seat of power for Chief Powhatan. He ruled over a group of more than 30 Algonquian-speaking tribes spread out over more than 8,000 square miles around Chesapeake Bay.

EXPLORING WEROWOCOMOCO TODAY

Today, Werowocomoco's wealth lies in the knowledge it reveals about Powhatan society. In 1609, Chief Powhatan abandoned the village, and in time the location of Werowocomoco was forgotten. Then in 2003, researchers announced they had used evidence from historical maps and documents to pinpoint the village's location. Since then, archaeologists have been actively excavating the site.

Finding Werowocomoco has allowed researchers to learn not only about how Powhatan society evolved but also about the meeting of the English and Native American cultures that took place between 1607 and 1609. Archaeologists found a number of English artifacts that closely

resembled lists of trade goods John Smith kept in his Jamestown journals. These included several copper-alloy items such as a pot, fragments of a spoon, and small beads. In order to enhance his importance among local tribes, Chief Powhatan had tried to maintain an exclusive trade in objects such as these with the English.

Within a few years, the English and the Powhatan would be at war. Werowocomoco preserves evidence that for brief but significant moments before the conflict, the two sides engaged in mutual bonds of trade and cultural exchange.

HISTORICAL THINKING

1. **READING CHECK** What types of items did the Powhatan and the Jamestown settlers trade with each other?

2. **MAKE CONNECTIONS** Think about what you learned about Jamestown in this chapter. In what ways did geography affect the relationship between Jamestown and Werowocomoco?

3. **MAKE GENERALIZATIONS** What purposes do exploring and preserving sites like Werowocomoco serve?

3 REVIEW

VOCABULARY

Use vocabulary words to complete the sentences.

1. _____ had to work for a set number of years to pay off their passages to the colonies.

2. Governor Berkeley accused Nathaniel Bacon of being a _____ .

3. The Virginia Company was known as a _____ because its shareholders also owned stock in the company.

4. When Lord Baltimore died, his son became the _____ of the Maryland colony.

5. The company had received a _____ from King James I to establish a colony in Virginia.

6. Governed by the crown through an appointed governor and council, Carolina was a _____ .

7. In the early 1600s, a _____ who disagreed with the beliefs of the Church could be punished.

READING STRATEGY
MAKE INFERENCES

If you haven't already, complete your chart of inferences about the challenges of establishing the first 13 colonies. List at least four inferences. Then answer the question.

8. What kind of physical dangers did settlers face in the colonies?

I READ	I KNOW	AND SO
The settlers lived under difficult conditions.	Many settlers died of diseases.	

MAIN IDEAS

9. How did John Smith help keep the settlers from starving at Jamestown? **LESSON 1.1**

10. What caused the conflict between colonists at Jamestown and the Powhatan? **LESSON 1.4**

11. Why did Nathaniel Bacon stage a rebellion? **LESSON 1.4**

12. How were the Pilgrims' and Puritans' involvement with the Church of England different? **LESSON 2.1**

13. What was the reason for massive arrests in Salem in 1692? **LESSON 2.4**

14. How did England benefit from taking control of New Netherland? **LESSON 3.1**

15. How did William Penn's Quaker beliefs help influence the diverse makeup of Pennsylvania? **LESSON 3.1**

16. Why did the Iroquois attack New France? **LESSON 3.2**

17. How did Maryland's access to the Chesapeake Bay benefit the colony? **LESSON 3.3**

Answer the following questions. Support your answers with evidence from the chapter.

18. **EVALUATE** In what ways was control of land central to struggles between Native Americans and European colonists?

19. **SYNTHESIZE** Why did the American colonies represent a safe haven for religious groups willing to move to a new place in the 17th and 18th centuries?

20. **COMPARE AND CONTRAST** How were the settlers in the New England colonies different from and similar to settlers in the Middle Colonies?

21. **FORM AND SUPPORT OPINIONS** Why do you think some Puritans in Salem might have felt threatened by women owning property? Use information from the chapter to support your opinion.

22. **DISTINGUISH FACT AND OPINION** Was the idea that Georgia could help debtors and the very poor overcome their difficulties a fact or an opinion? Explain why you think so.

INTERPRET MAPS

Look closely at the map of the Pilgrims' intended route and where they actually sailed. Then answer the questions that follow.

23. What was the Pilgrims' planned destination?

24. Between what latitudes did the Pilgrims go off their planned course, and where did they land?

Pilgrims' Route, 1620

ANALYZE SOURCES

Transcriptions of court records from the 1692 Salem witch trials include testimony from the accused. In the following transcription, Reverend Increase Mather relays information about his conversation with prisoner Mary Bridges. Read the passage and answer the question.

> Goodwife Bridges said that she had confessed against herself things which were all utterly false; and that she was brought to her confession by being told that she certainly was a witch, and so made to believe it,—though she had no other grounds so to believe.

25. What does Mather's statement reveal about the likely cause of many people's confessions?

CONNECT TO YOUR LIFE

26. **INFORMATIVE** Think about how and why people left their homelands to settle in the 13 colonies. Then think of a present-day group of people who have moved to a new place. Write a paragraph that connects the two groups.

TIPS

- Before you start writing, organize your ideas in a two-column chart. On the left, list your two groups. On the right, list the reasons why each group decided to move.

- Include textual evidence and one or two vocabulary terms from the chapter.

- Conclude the paragraph with your observations about the reasons why colonists came to America and why the group you selected decided to move to a new place.

CHAPTER 4

COLONIAL DEVELOPMENT
1651–1763

ESSENTIAL QUESTION
How did a developing American identity unite the colonies?

Colliding Cultures: The Fur Trade

Colonial Graveyards

READING STRATEGY

IDENTIFY MAIN IDEAS AND DETAILS
To identify a main idea and details, state the most important idea and find facts that support it. Use a diagram like this one to find a main idea and details about the development of the colonies as you read the chapter.

Colonial Development

Main Idea:
Detail:
Detail:
Detail:

"The ground is very fruitful,
and produceth plentiful crops with great speed."
—Nathaniel Shrigley, author and British Army officer

CRITICAL VIEWING The Piedmont in Virginia and North Carolina, shown here, is a land of rolling hills and rich farmland. How does the photo illustrate the description in the quotation above?

Sperm whales, like the one shown here, have huge heads and a full set of teeth along the inside of their long jaws. Colonial whalers frequently hunted this type of whale, venturing far out to sea to search for them. The oil of these whales burned more brightly than other whale oils and made finer candles, which became important export items.

1.1 Harvesting Land and Sea

In 17th-century New England, you basically had two choices: toil day and night as a farmer, or toil day and night as a sailor. Neither option left much time for anything else.

MAIN IDEA New England's colonial economy was based on agriculture, commerce, and small-scale manufacturing.

FARMING HILLY, ROCKY LAND

Most New England colonists were farmers. Their farms were small and were frequently located on hilly and forested land with rocky soil. The long, cold winters made for a short growing season.

Farmers relied on their large families to clear the fields, plant and harvest the crops, and care for the farm animals. This all added up to something called **subsistence farming**. This means the farmers produced about enough food to provide for their family with only a little, if any, left over to sell or trade. In other words, they were barely scraping by. Without much in savings or extra food, a poor year of farming could ruin a family.

Because farming was so tough, the size and quality of a family's farmland mattered. Colonists were at the mercy of their town's powerful Puritan founders, who led the church and the town. The founders decided the location and amount of land a family received. One man might be given 50 acres with grazing fields attached, another only 3 acres with grazing fields a mile away. It wasn't fair, and these differences in land ownership created distinct social classes within the town.

Harpoon
Whalers used harpoons to stun and capture their prey. Sailors launched whaleboats from the ship, surrounded the whale, and threw their weapons. Once the whale was fully pierced by harpoons, which were attached to ropes, the sailors towed the huge animal back to the ship.

FISHING, WHALING, AND TRADE

The Atlantic Ocean provided greater economic opportunities than agriculture. Colonial fishers could engage in international trade, selling their catch to London merchants in exchange for goods such as shoes, textiles, and metal products. Whaling provided the colonists with many commercial products, including whale oils and waxes, meat, fat, bones, and leather. Colonists sold and exported the whale meat and blubber, or fat. People used the blubber to light oil lamps, make candles, and soften leather.

Fishing and whaling led to the growth of a shipbuilding industry. New England's plentiful forests supplied the shipyards with timber—and employment. Building a single ship could employ 200 workers. Shipbuilders also kept sawmills, rope makers, and iron foundries busy. By the end of the 1700s, New England built one-third of all British ships and almost all of its own merchants' and fishers' ships. This economic activity made New England a natural center of colonial trade.

HISTORICAL THINKING

1. **READING CHECK** What four economic activities were important in New England?

2. **DRAW CONCLUSIONS** What conclusion can you draw about the relationship between a family's farm and its social class?

3. **ANALYZE CAUSE AND EFFECT** In what ways were the goods provided by the Atlantic Ocean essential to the livelihood, economy, and culture of the New England colonists?

1.2 Colonial Trade

It was good to be a trader in New England. The region's shipyards turned out many ships that carried goods along the North American coast and across the Atlantic. If colonial trade were a race, the merchants of New England were winning.

MAIN IDEA New England merchants expanded the colonial economy through Atlantic trade.

TRADE IN THE ATLANTIC

As its fishing and whaling industries continued to thrive, New England found itself at the center of America's trade. New England merchants traded with other colonies. They also engaged in direct trade with Europe. Soon the New England merchants became the chief traders along the coast from Newfoundland to Georgia.

The merchants also conducted business through the triangular trade. As you have learned, the triangular trade routes crossed the Atlantic and connected North America, Europe, and Africa. New England merchants sent goods such as rum and cotton to Europe. The merchants received imported goods including wine, fruit, and salt from islands off the coast of North Africa. Molasses, rum, sugar, and dyes came from the Caribbean. Food and drink weren't the only goods New England merchants traded. As you know, the merchants also acquired enslaved people from Africa in exchange for rum and other goods.

The growth of trade across the Atlantic created great demand for sailors and other workers. Shipbuilders and sailmakers crafted vessels.

Triangular Trade, c. 1700

Sugar, tobacco, rum, cotton (to Europe)

Manufactured goods (to Africa)

Slaves (to the Americas)

NORTH AMERICA

SOUTH AMERICA

ATLANTIC OCEAN

EUROPE

AFRICA

Colonial Trade Routes and Goods

The colonial economy depended on ships trading goods between North America, Europe, and Africa. So did the economies of most European countries. France, England, the Netherlands, Portugal, and Spain were willing to fight for a share of the wealth the trade routes generated. Many ships on the triangular trade routes sailed only between North America and Africa or Europe and Africa. Some ships bound for New England also stopped in Brazil or the Caribbean, where some of the enslaved Africans onboard were sold.

Suppliers stocked ships with **provisions**, which consisted of the food, water, and other supplies needed for the voyages. Dockworkers loaded and unloaded goods that laborers transported in carts. As a result of the thriving trade, port cities sprang up in New York, Philadelphia, and Charleston after 1750. Colonial trade was no longer dominated entirely by the merchants of Boston and other port cities in Massachusetts and Rhode Island.

Blackbeard the Pirate

Smuggling was not the only illegal activity on the high seas. Pirates prowled the Atlantic looking for ships and cargo to steal. One such pirate was called Blackbeard.

According to some, the English pirate's real name was Edward Teach. He tried to make his appearance frightening by putting pieces of burning rope under his hat, as shown in the illustration. For two years, he and his pirates terrorized merchant ships in the Atlantic and the Caribbean. In 1718, Blackbeard met his end at the hands of Lieutenant Robert Maynard of the Royal Navy. Maynard chopped off the pirate's head and threw his body overboard.

ENGLAND'S CUT OF THE PROFITS

When New England began to earn huge profits from trade, the English decided to begin taking their cut. To ensure their share of the profits, the English passed a series of laws called the **Navigation Acts** in 1651. The acts required that goods brought to England or its colonies in Asia, Africa, or America be carried on English ships or ships made in the colonies. Furthermore, the acts identified a list of colonial products that could only be sold to England or its colonies. These products included tobacco, sugar, cotton, and dyes.

The acts also made sure that England controlled—and taxed—all trade to and from the colonies. So, for instance, all European goods bound for the colonies had to go to England first. There, English dockworkers would unload, inspect, and reload the goods back onto English or colonial-made ships. These ships then carried the goods to colonial ports where the English charged additional taxes on the imports. Worst of all for the colonists, the English taxed all colonial goods that were not going to be shipped to England.

Not surprisingly, the colonists resented the additional charges to products going in both directions. Some colonists turned to trading goods illegally, or **smuggling**. The colonists proved hard to control as they resisted attempts to enforce the acts.

While New England colonists protested their treatment at the hands of the English government, many in their own society had far more cause for complaint. But enslaved African Americans and some Protestant groups were powerless to change their situation.

HISTORICAL THINKING

1. **READING CHECK** What different types of trade did New England merchants carry out?

2. **ANALYZE CAUSE AND EFFECT** Why did Parliament pass the Navigation Acts?

3. **INTERPRET MAPS** How do the items sent from North America differ from those exported from Europe?

1.3 Society and Religion

In New England, some African Americans performed tasks that were not available in other colonies—small consolation for their far-from-equal treatment.

> **MAIN IDEA** New England was different from other colonial regions in terms of its use of enslaved labor and its religious views.

ENSLAVED LABOR IN NEW ENGLAND

Enslaved African Americans accounted for only 2 to 3 percent of New England's population. But this wasn't really due to colonial opposition to enslavement. Some of the wealthiest New England merchants made their money in the slave trade. The low percentage was due to geography and economics. New England farms were generally small. Most colonial farmers had no need for large numbers of enslaved workers, and they couldn't afford them, anyway.

The enslaved African Americans who came to New England worked as household servants, farmhands, artisans, and laborers. In the Southern Colonies, slaveholders generally wanted to purchase enslaved people who could work in the fields immediately, but slaveholders in New England were often more willing to purchase young people who could be trained for specific household or business duties.

Enslaved people generally lived in their masters' houses and worked by their sides. They practiced carpentry, printing, baking, and making cloth, shoes, and clothing, among other trades. In seaport towns, enslaved African Americans sometimes worked alongside free African Americans in the shipyards and on the docks as fishers, whalers, and shipbuilders.

Some African Americans were born free, but most free African Americans spent part of their lives in enslavement. Some achieved freedom by fulfilling the terms of a work contract. Some escaped. Others were freed by their master for faithful service or as part of their master's will. Although both enslaved and free African Americans in New England enjoyed some legal rights, they were not treated equally. For example, a 1703 Massachusetts law stated that African Americans could not be outdoors after 9:00 P.M. unless they were on business for their masters.

THE DECLINE OF PURITANISM

Some religious groups were treated unfairly, although not to the extent suffered by African Americans. The Puritans saw other Protestant groups, such as the Quakers and Baptists, as a threat to the harmony of their society. Therefore, Puritan leaders allowed only the male members of the Puritan church to vote and hold most public offices. Puritans clashed with other Protestant sects that disagreed with their teachings. They punished citizens who did not share their beliefs and even hanged several Quaker missionaries. They also objected to a newly emerging merchant class and its focus on commercial values and worried that the younger generation was only concerned with making money.

Beginning in 1650, membership in the Puritan church had begun to decline, especially among men. Quakers who had been deported from Massachusetts kept coming back. King Charles II of England sent a letter forbidding the execution of Quakers. Quaker communities and Baptist congregations began to flourish throughout New England.

The crown gave the Puritans two options: they could either obey the terms of the colonial charter of Massachusetts Bay or they could have the charter revoked. And the charter guaranteed **religious freedom**, or the right to practice the religion of one's choosing, for all.

But the Puritan leaders believed themselves to be the highest authority in Massachusetts and did not feel that they answered to the king. Charles II disagreed. In 1684, the king canceled the colonial charter of Massachusetts Bay. Charles died in 1685, but that didn't do the Puritans any good. Charles's successor, James II, tried to strengthen English control even more. He combined Massachusetts with other northern colonies to form the **Dominion of New England**.

Eventually, the Dominion included Massachusetts Bay, Plymouth, New Hampshire, Maine, Rhode Island, Connecticut, New York, and New Jersey. Both the decision to create the Dominion and to appoint its new governor were extremely unpopular with the colonists. They felt stripped of the rights and freedoms they had enjoyed under their own colonial charters.

In 1691, Massachusetts received a new charter to replace the one King Charles had canceled. It guaranteed religious freedom for all Protestants, further undermining Puritan influence. It also opened up the right to vote to any man owning property, regardless of his religion. The number of property owners was much greater than the number of churchgoers. As a result, the charter led to a large increase in the number of voters in New England.

As Puritanism declined, education in New England was on the rise. Acquiring knowledge was becoming a new priority in the colony.

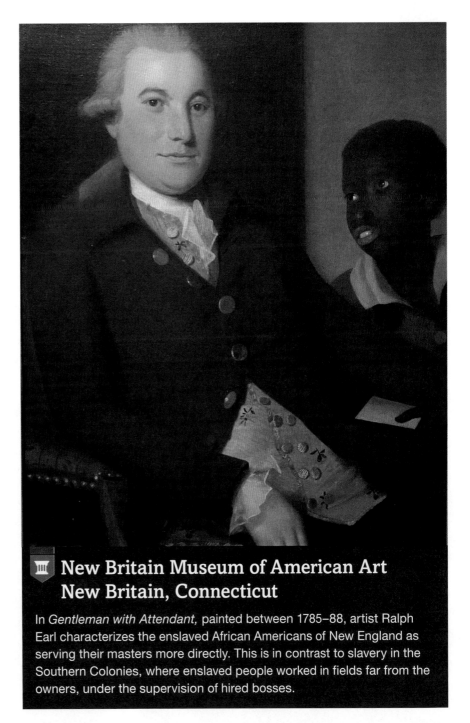

🏛 **New Britain Museum of American Art New Britain, Connecticut**

In *Gentleman with Attendant,* painted between 1785–88, artist Ralph Earl characterizes the enslaved African Americans of New England as serving their masters more directly. This is in contrast to slavery in the Southern Colonies, where enslaved people worked in fields far from the owners, under the supervision of hired bosses.

HISTORICAL THINKING

1. **READING CHECK** Why was the percentage of enslaved African Americans low in New England?

2. **IDENTIFY MAIN IDEAS AND DETAILS** What types of tasks did most enslaved and free African Americans in New England perform?

3. **ANALYZE CAUSE AND EFFECT** What impact did the 1691 Massachusetts charter have on Puritanism?

1.4 Education and Literacy

Why do you read? Probably for fun or to learn new things. Colonial children mostly learned to read so they could understand the Bible.

MAIN IDEA Education and literacy were important to New England colonists and had a major impact on the region's economic and social development.

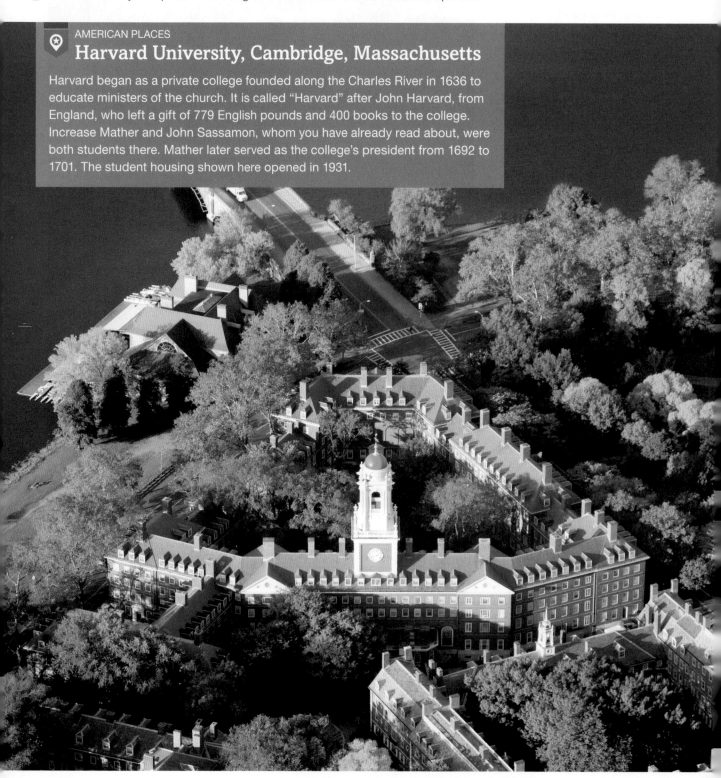

⊙ AMERICAN PLACES
Harvard University, Cambridge, Massachusetts

Harvard began as a private college founded along the Charles River in 1636 to educate ministers of the church. It is called "Harvard" after John Harvard, from England, who left a gift of 779 English pounds and 400 books to the college. Increase Mather and John Sassamon, whom you have already read about, were both students there. Mather later served as the college's president from 1692 to 1701. The student housing shown here opened in 1931.

A NEW ENGLAND EDUCATION

New Englanders believed people needed to be able to read so they could learn about God. They set up schools that focused on the Bible, religious study, and texts that taught moral behavior. In the 1640s, the Massachusetts legislature established **common schools**, the colonial name for elementary schools, and secondary schools called Latin grammar schools. Connecticut and other colonies followed with similar legislation. Eventually, more people in New England were able to read than in any other colony.

Early education also involved teaching children skills that would help them thrive in their community. For many colonial boys, this meant becoming an **apprentice**. An apprentice lived with a master craftsman for a set number of years in order to learn a trade, such as butchering, baking, or carpentry. Girls, on the other hand, often stayed with their mothers to learn cooking, sewing, and other skills necessary to manage a household.

Communities established colleges for older students. The Puritans founded Harvard College in Massachusetts in 1636 and Yale College in Connecticut in 1701. Harvard and Yale joined William and Mary College in Virginia to make up the only three colleges in the colonies. All three have grown into modern universities that offer a wide range of subjects and the chance to earn many different degrees. Most of the graduates of colonial colleges became members of the clergy. None, however, were women. Colonial colleges only admitted men.

NEWSPAPERS AND BOOKS

The rising rate of literacy throughout the colonies created a big demand for newspapers and books. Starting in 1704, newspapers popped up in Boston, Philadelphia, New York, and Charleston. These early newspapers focused on European events and politics. They helped colonists feel less separated from faraway Europe and more connected to England.

The general reading tastes of colonial people ranged across many subjects, but readers especially enjoyed topics unique to the American experience. In New England, books about being captured by Native Americans attracted interest. One of the most popular of these was by **Mary Rowlandson**. In her account, she describes being taken prisoner with her three children during King Philip's War. The Native Americans who had captured her then released her for 20 pounds' ransom. After her husband, a Puritan minister, died, Rowlandson moved to Boston and wrote the story for which she is famous.

Another favorite genre, the almanac, stuffed many types of useful information together in one volume. *Poor Richard's Almanack*, published by **Benjamin Franklin**, proved a best seller. It mixed calendars, information about the weather and planting, medical advice, and witty proverbs, such as "Fish and visitors stink after three days." Also around this time, writers began to compose the first histories of their lives in the colonies. Meanwhile, to the south, life was very different—particularly for African slaves.

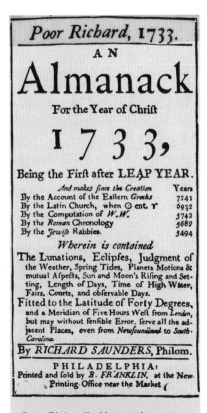

Poor Richard's Almanack
Ben Franklin created the almanac under the name Richard Saunders, but he credited himself as the volume's printer.

HISTORICAL THINKING

1. **READING CHECK** What types of schools did colonial New Englanders establish?

2. **DRAW CONCLUSIONS** What role did religion play in the importance of education in New England?

3. **MAKE GENERALIZATIONS** Why would a newspaper's emphasis on European events and politics be helpful to colonial merchants?

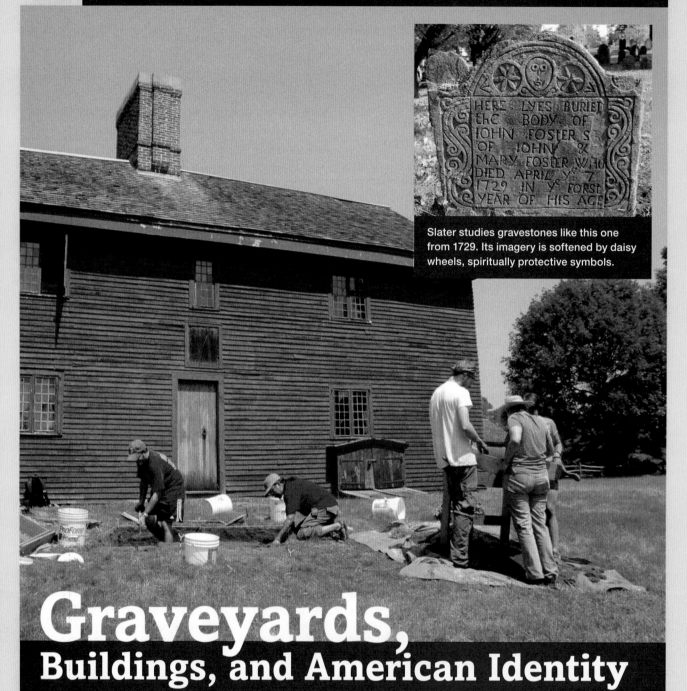

Slater studies gravestones like this one from 1729. Its imagery is softened by daisy wheels, spiritually protective symbols.

HERE LYES BURIED the BODY OF JOHN FOSTER S OF JOHN & MARY FOSTER WHO DIED APRIL Yᵉ 7 1729 IN Yᵉ FORST YEAR OF HIS AGE

Graveyards,
Buildings, and American Identity

"Archaeology is an adventure. Even graveyards and buildings have exciting tales to tell." —Donald Slater

When **Donald Slater** was growing up in Massachusetts, his parents drove him to a swim club during the summer. On the way, they passed an old graveyard that always caught his eye. It stood abandoned and disordered, with gravestones tilted every which way—some nearly falling over. "I knew there was a story there," Slater remembers thinking. Years later, he became an archaeologist and decided to uncover the stories at such sites himself.

^
Donald Slater enjoys providing students with hands-on archaeological experience. Here, Slater (far left), his colleagues, and students work at a dig at the Rebecca Nurse Homestead to learn about Nurse, who was believed to be a witch and hanged in 1692.

MAIN IDEA Archaeologist Donald Slater
investigates colonial New England graveyards
and architecture to learn about American culture.

THE GRAVE WHISPERER

National Geographic Explorer Donald Slater
studies graveyards from the 1600s and 1700s.
Luckily for him, he lives in New England where
there are lots of graveyards from those periods.
One of his favorites is the Old Burying Ground,
established in 1634 in Ipswich, Massachusetts.
It contains the region's oldest documented
gravestones, including those of the wife and child
of John Winthrop, Jr., the town's chief founder.

As Slater examines a graveyard, he pays particular
attention to the iconography of the gravestones—
the stone's carved design. Although the details
are hotly debated among scholars, Slater believes
that changes in the designs point to evolving
religious ideas in the New England Colonies.
A death's head, showing a stylized skull with
wings or crossed bones, appeared on most early
gravestones. As the 18th century progressed,
however, death's heads were replaced by winged
cherub, or angel, heads.

Slater believes a religious movement that began
in the 1720s caused the graveyard iconography
to soften. The movement—called the Great
Awakening—which you'll learn more about later
in this chapter, emphasized the idea that people
could ascend to heaven by demonstrating their
faith in God. Earlier Puritan beliefs held that
people's place after death—heaven or hell—was
predestined, or determined, by God at birth.

Around the same time, the epitaphs, or
inscriptions, carved on the gravestones also
became more hopeful. Instead of focusing on
mortality, later epitaphs celebrate the deceased's
reward in heaven for a life well lived. Some provide
a brief narrative of the person's life. According
to Slater, one such epitaph reveals that the man
buried was born a slave but died free.

OUR AMERICAN IDENTITY

Like gravestones, colonial architectural styles also
evolved over time. Some of these changes reflect
cultural change—and the increasing American
identity of the colonies. In the early 1600s, builders

Slater reads a gravestone at the South Parish Burial
Ground in Andover, Massachusetts. Established in 1709,
the cemetery is Andover's oldest museum.

in New England based their structures on English
architecture. But instead of brick, the colonists
most often used wood and other rustic building
materials, which resulted in a uniquely American
style. Builders adapted structures to conditions in
the colony. For example, they constructed summer
kitchens at the rear of a house to avoid heating up
the entire home, applying construction techniques
they used in England.

Much of New England is a treasure trove of
colonial sites and artifacts. But what if you don't
live there? Slater suggests you visit your local
historical society to learn about early American
sites in your community, including those of Native
Americans, or ask your neighborhood librarian
for information. All these sources can help you
discover your American identity. And Slater
believes this is important. For, as he says, "There
is no better way to preserve our cultural heritage
than to educate today's youth on the subject,
because it is they who will be making tomorrow's
decisions that will determine whether sites are
protected or destroyed."

HISTORICAL THINKING

1. **READING CHECK** What does Slater study
   when he investigates colonial graveyards?

2. **ANALYZE CAUSE AND EFFECT** According to
   Slater, why might a cherub head have replaced
   the death's head on later graves?

3. **MAKE INFERENCES** What do you think the
   architectural developments by the early 1700s
   suggest about New England colonists?

2.1 Slavery Expands

A person journeying from New England to the Southern Colonies would be amazed by its large plantations—quite a contrast to New England's small farms. And the warm climate would probably make the traveler shed his or her jacket. What a difference geography makes!

MAIN IDEA The Southern Colonies developed a system of plantation agriculture that relied on increasing numbers of enslaved Africans.

PLANTATION CROPS

The geography of New England was very different from that of the Southern Colonies. The fertile land and milder climate of the Southern Colonies—Maryland, Virginia, the Carolinas, and Georgia—made it possible to grow **cash crops**, crops grown for sale rather than for use by the farmers themselves. The main cash crops were tobacco, rice, and **indigo**, a plant whose leaves provide a source of blue dye for cloth. Tobacco thrived in the hot and humid growing season of Virginia and coastal Maryland. Rice was well suited to the swampy lowlands and tidal areas of coastal rivers in the Carolinas. However, the colonists had no experience in rice cultivation. They depended on enslaved Africans, who had been taken from rice-growing regions in West Africa, to farm the rice and ensure successful yields.

Plantations sprang up along the rivers so planters could use the water for their rice fields. Ships sailed up tributaries from the Chesapeake Bay and docked at the plantations. Because of the ease of transporting goods directly from their farms, southern colonists had little need for port cities.

One exception was the busy seaport of **Charles Town** (now called Charleston). As Carolina planters developed cash crops, Charles Town grew as a port. Many plantation owners lived there part of the year to escape the isolation of their plantations. Although Charles Town became the fourth-largest colonial city, after Boston, Philadelphia, and New York, it never grew larger because English and New England shippers controlled its trade. Without a strong merchant community, the city failed to attract large numbers of new workers.

NEW SLAVE TRADING

Planters in the Southern Colonies originally hired white indentured servants to work for several years in exchange for a plot of land. But in 1698, England gave all English merchants permission to participate in slave trading. As a result, planters who lived in the **Chesapeake**, the settled land around the Chesapeake Bay, turned to enslaved Africans to farm their land. In 1660, only 900 Africans resided in the Chesapeake, some of whom had arrived as servants and lived free. By 1720, one-fifth of the population of that area were Africans. By 1770, that number ranged from one-third to one-half. African populations in Virginia and the Carolinas also increased dramatically during this period. By 1750, African Americans accounted for over 40 percent of Virginia's total population and more than half of South Carolina's. More than 90 percent of the total African-American population was enslaved.

HISTORICAL THINKING

1. **READING CHECK** Why were tobacco and rice good cash crops for Virginia, Maryland, and the Carolinas?

2. **ANALYZE VISUALS** After which step in the rice process are the grains of rice collected?

3. **IDENTIFY MAIN IDEAS AND DETAILS** What factors led to the expansion of slave labor in the Southern Colonies?

RICE PRODUCTION

Rice production required many steps and many people to grow enough grain to make a profit. Below are some of the steps of this labor-intensive process.

1 Flooding

Farmworkers built flood gates and dug ditches. They planted, then opened the floodgates to fill the rice fields with water. After the seeds sprouted, the fields were drained so the women could weed. Then the fields were reflooded.

2 Harvesting

Workers harvested, or reaped, the ripened rice plants with a cutting tool called a scythe (SIGHTH).

3 Threshing

On colonial plantations, threshing meant beating the plants with a stick called a flail until the grains fell from the plants.

4 Winnowing

Winnowing was the process of tossing the rice grains in a basket to separate them from their tissue-like outer coating, or chaff.

5 Pounding

The winnowed rice was poured into a hollowed-out log and pounded with a staff called a mortar. This removed the tough outer husk from the grain.

In 1915, when these photographs were taken, slavery had been abolished, but workers still used tools similar to ones that had been used more than 200 years ago.

2.2 From Plantations to the Backcountry

There's a saying that "the rich get richer," and it seemed to be true on the large plantations. More land and slaves meant more cash crops—and more money.

MAIN IDEA Life in the coastal areas of the Southern Colonies differed greatly from life further inland, and revolved extensively around slavery.

WEALTH AND CLASS

Over time, wealthy planters in Maryland, Virginia, and the Carolinas bought more and more land and slaves. The expanding plantations produced increasing amounts of tobacco, rice, and indigo. The owners reaped the profits.

Not all farmers became wealthy, but the owners of the largest plantations became so wealthy and powerful that distinct classes formed among southern farmers. With their luxurious homes and leisurely lifestyle, rich landowners lived like nobles in Europe.

An army of slaves made this way of life possible. The work the slaves performed depended on where they lived. In South Carolina, each enslaved person received certain jobs to complete each day—a field to hoe, a fence to build. In the Chesapeake, most enslaved people worked on the plantation for a specific number of hours or until the **overseer**, or supervisor, told them to stop. As a result, many slaves worked long into the night.

While some plantation owners treated enslaved people fairly well, others did not. But the terrible workload took its toll on all the laborers. As work increased and the hours grew even longer, death rates among enslaved people surged dramatically.

THE BACKCOUNTRY

A different kind of culture arose as some settlers in the Southern Colonies sought their fortune in the backcountry. The **backcountry** stretched along the Appalachian Mountains from Pennsylvania south through the Shenandoah Valley to the Carolinas. This region included the rich soil, rolling hills, and deep forests of the **Piedmont**, a relatively flat area between the mountains and the coastal plain.

In the early 1700s, European settlers such as the Scots-Irish, immigrants from the northern part of Ireland, came to the colonies. They began settling in the backcountry and establishing farms outside the first English settlements, carving their farmland out of the forests.

Backcountry farmers learned to be self-sufficient. They used one of the most plentiful natural resources of this region—timber—to build simple log cabins. They hunted and raised enough crops and livestock to feed their families. Women in the backcountry worked in the home, the fields, and the wild. Many of them carried guns. Also, unlike many people in the Southern Colonies, most of the immigrants living in the backcountry didn't rely on slaves.

HISTORICAL THINKING

1. **READING CHECK** What was the social structure like in the Chesapeake in the 1700s?

2. **COMPARE AND CONTRAST** How did work patterns differ for slaves in South Carolina and the Chesapeake?

3. **ANALYZE CAUSE AND EFFECT** How did the environment of the backcountry affect how the people settling there made a living?

Shenandoah Valley

In the 1700s, Scots-Irish settlers who had come to Pennsylvania began moving into the Shenandoah Valley in present-day West Virginia and Virginia. The rich soil of the valley made it a dream for farming, and at the time, the Scots-Irish had little competition from other Europeans. They did, however, compete for the land with Native Americans who had long called the region home.

2.3 Life Under Slavery

After days of hard work, enslaved Africans gathered together—sometimes secretly—on Sundays. They cooked African foods and played music based on African rhythms. As much as they could, they hung on to pieces of their past.

MAIN IDEA Plantation slaves kept their African culture and traditions alive, even though their living and working conditions were often very difficult.

LIVING CONDITIONS

As you've read, most plantation slaves—both men and women—spent long hours planting, weeding, and harvesting tobacco, rice, and indigo. Overseers sometimes used whips and other harsh instruments and measures to force workers to work harder or more productively. Some owners also recruited slaves, called drivers, to push their fellow workers to pick up the pace.

Work in the slaveowner's household was sometimes less brutal. Both men and women cooked and did gardening chores. Women often took care of the children as well. Some

men became **artisans**, or skilled workers who crafted things by hand. Some women served as nurses and weavers.

Marriage between slaves was illegal in the colonies. An enslaved couple had to obtain their master's permission to live together as husband and wife. Slave marriages were torn apart when

Slave Housing

Only nine of the 27 slave houses that once stood at Boone Hall Plantation near Charleston, South Carolina, still remain. The houses together make up what is called a "slave street." The nine houses, five of which appear in this photograph, were home to the servants at the plantation house. Each house was divided into two rooms and had either a dirt or a wooden floor. Dirt floors were common in the houses provided for slaves.

one of the pair was sold to a different slaveowner. In those cases, slaves often walked long distances at night to visit and hold the family together.

Slaves often built their own houses, which were typically one-room cabins. Many planters provided only basic foods for their enslaved workers, such as corn and a little pork. Enslaved people often planted gardens with vegetables like yams and squash to enhance their diet. They also raised hogs and chickens and hunted and fished for extra food.

People from different parts of West Africa often found themselves thrown together on large plantations. To speak to each other, they blended African languages with English. By this means, such African words as *yam* and *tote* were introduced into the English language.

Africans influenced colonial culture, as well as that of early national America, in many other ways. Their music, with its rhythmic beat, had a huge impact on jazz and blues. They made clay pottery, baskets, and musical instruments with African designs. They also popularized new foods, including okra, melons, and bananas. In Boston, a slave taught his owner the practice of vaccination, which he had learned in Africa. As a result of the slave's help, the city's people were protected from a smallpox outbreak.

ACTS OF REBELLION

Enslaved people did what they could to cope with their situation, but many actively rebelled against their treatment. They resisted the slave owner's power by staging slowdowns, faking illness, and secretly destroying crops and tools. Others ran away. Some enslaved people became violent, killing the slave owners or setting fire to fields and homes.

In 1739, a group of more than 50 enslaved people revolted near the Stono River in South Carolina. Their leader was a literate slave named Jemmy (also known as Cato) whose master had taught him to read and write. When armed planters defeated the rebels in battle, some of the slaves headed to St. Augustine, Florida, where the Spanish government had promised them freedom. But the South Carolina militia pursued them, putting to death everyone suspected of being involved. Although similar rebellions had already taken place in the Middle Colonies, the **Stono Rebellion** sent fear throughout the American colonies.

The South Carolina legislature enacted a harsh slave code in 1740 in an effort to prevent future revolts. The new code made all enslaved people and their children permanent slaves. In addition, the code prohibited enslaved people from learning to read and write. In spite of these new laws, some slaves did learn to read and write. And they used this knowledge to tell their stories and let the world know what was happening to them.

Banjo
Africans on plantations played instruments made of a gourd cut in half with a goatskin stretched over it, a stick, and three strings. The banjo shown here was made in Baltimore, Maryland, in 1845. In this banjo, the gourd has been replaced with a circular wooden frame and the stick with a flat piece of wood. In other modern versions, the frame is sometimes made of metal.

HISTORICAL THINKING

1. **READING CHECK** What measures did owners use to force slaves to work harder?

2. **IDENTIFY MAIN IDEAS AND DETAILS** What are some of the ways in which enslaved people asserted their humanity and kept their traditions alive?

3. **ANALYZE CAUSE AND EFFECT** What were the long-term negative consequences of the Stono Rebellion on enslaved people?

2.4 Slave Narratives

After gaining their freedom, some former slaves wrote about their experiences and the cruelty they'd endured. They wanted to open up people's eyes to the true nature of slavery.

Olaudah Equiano (oh-LOW-duh ehk-wee-AHN-oh) was born in Benin, an empire in Africa that you have learned about previously. Equiano was sold into slavery at the age of 11. About 10 years later, he bought his freedom from his last owner, a Quaker from Philadelphia. He made his way to England, where he lectured on the evils of slavery.

In 1789, in London, Equiano published his autobiography, an excerpt from which appears on the next page. He had the image shown here created for the book. Copies sold quickly, and the popularity of *The Interesting Narrative of the Life of Olaudah Equiano* contributed to a law being passed in England in 1807 that made slavery illegal in England and its colonies. By then, as you will learn, America was no longer a British colony.

CRITICAL VIEWING Why do you think Equiano wanted to have his portrait show him holding a book?

Engraving of Olaudah Equiano from his book, *The Interesting Narrative of the Life of Olaudah Equiano*

DOCUMENT ONE

Primary Source: Autobiography
from *The Interesting Narrative of the Life of Olaudah Equiano*, 1789

In this excerpt from his autobiography, Equiano describes the brutal conditions aboard the slave ship during the passage from Africa to the Americas—the notorious Middle Passage.

CONSTRUCTED RESPONSE What details help you understand the horror the slaves endured in the Middle Passage?

I was soon put down under the decks, and there I received such a salutation [greeting] in my nostrils as I had never experienced in my life: so that, with the loathsomeness of the stench [smell], and crying together, I became so sick and low that I was not able to eat, nor had I the least desire to taste any thing.

. . . Many a time we were near suffocation from the want [lack] of fresh air, which we were often without for whole days together. This, and the stench of the necessary tubs, carried off [killed] many.

DOCUMENT TWO

Primary Source: Autobiography
from *A Narrative of the Most Remarkable Particulars in the Life of James Albert Ukawsaw Gronniosaw, An African Prince, as Related by Himself*, 1772

James Albert Ukawsaw Gronniosaw was sold into slavery at age 15. Upset with his family, Gronniosaw had believed the promise of a slave merchant and voluntarily left his home in Africa. He realized his mistake too late.

CONSTRUCTED RESPONSE How does the merchant make the idea of going with him sound like a fascinating adventure rather than the entry into a nightmare?

About this time there came a merchant from the Gold Coast. . . . He told me that if I would go with him I should see houses with wings to them walk upon the water, and should also see the white folks; and that he had many sons of my age, which should be my companions; and he added to all this that he would bring me safe back again soon. I was highly pleased with the account of this strange place, and was very desirous of going.

DOCUMENT THREE

Primary Source: Autobiography
from *A Narrative of the Life and Adventures of Venture, a Native of Africa: But Resident Above Sixty Years in the United States of America*, 1798

Venture Smith was born in West Africa, captured as a young child by an enemy army, and then sold as a slave in Rhode Island. He published his autobiography in 1798. The excerpt details how he obtained freedom for his family.

CONSTRUCTED RESPONSE What can you infer about the personal qualities that enabled Venture Smith to accomplish all that he describes?

Being thirty-six years old, I left Col. Smith once for all . . . [having] paid an enormous sum for my freedom. . . . When I had [raised enough money to purchase] my two sons, I had then left more than one hundred pounds. . . . The rest of my money I laid out in land, in addition to a farm which I owned before, and a dwelling house thereon . . . [In] my forty-fourth year, I purchased my wife Meg . . . Being about forty-six years old, I bought my oldest child Hannah . . . I had already redeemed from slavery, myself, my wife and three children.

SYNTHESIZE & WRITE

1. **REVIEW** Review what you have learned about the slave trade and slavery in colonial America.

2. **RECALL** On your own paper, write the main ideas expressed in each document.

3. **CONSTRUCT** Construct a topic sentence that answers this question: How did formerly enslaved persons endure and overcome slavery?

4. **WRITE** Using evidence from this chapter and the documents, write an informative paragraph that supports your topic sentence in Step 3.

3.1 Agricultural Production

The basics of farming haven't changed. Farmers today need fertile soil and a good climate to grow abundant crops, just like their counterparts in the colonies. Good climates in the Middle Colonies attracted immigrant farmers from Britain and other parts of Europe.

MAIN IDEA The fertile land of the Middle Colonies allowed farmers to raise cash crops and livestock for sale and export, resulting in a booming economy.

FARMLAND AND FREEDOM

Just like the settlers of New England and the Southern Colonies, immigrants who came to the Middle Colonies of New York, New Jersey, Pennsylvania, and Delaware found ways to support themselves in their new environment. There were navigable rivers and harbors, and rich farmland rolled across the region. The area's weather was warmer than New England's but avoided the sticky heat farther south. Settlers soon discovered that grains such as wheat, corn, rye, and barley thrived in the climate. As a result, the region earned the nickname "breadbasket of the colonies."

Immigrants from all over Europe heard about the **arable**, or fertile, land and decided to move to the Middle Colonies. Attracted by cheap land, limited government control, and religious tolerance, more than 100,000 Germans immigrated to the area between 1683 and 1783.

The majority of Germans headed for the backcountry of Pennsylvania. They brought with them new farming techniques, such as providing shelter for their animals in the winter. Some farmers used indentured servants and enslaved people to tend their fields. As the settlers grew wealthier, they sold more of their harvest as cash crops and raised livestock for sale and export.

The residents of the breadbasket enjoyed more prosperous lives than farmers in New England. Unfortunately, there was a cost—though not directly to the settlers. Their growing farms continued to edge out the Native Americans who lived on the land.

GRIST FOR THE MILL

Many Middle Colony farmers grew grains, and wheat was the most popular grain in colonial America. The plant made a finer flour than corn, which in turn produced softer bread. Colonists enjoyed wheat bread with their meals, but making the flour required grinding. Grinding the grain by hand took a long time and resulted in flour that was rough in texture. Farmers found they could save time and energy by taking their wheat to a **gristmill**, a building that housed machinery for grinding grain.

Since human and animal labor was in short supply in the Middle Colonies, many colonists built their gristmills near a river and harnessed the power of water to operate the gristmill. At that time, water mills were the latest technology. The water spun a wheel outside that turned grinding stones within the gristmill.

Workers called millers ran the gristmills and generally took a portion of the flour they ground as payment. They also took other goods in exchange. Some millers opened stores to sell the surplus flour, grain, or other goods. These stores became the centers of communities. Neighbors would gather there to exchange goods and catch up on news. As demand grew, some millers bought larger mills or moved their mill to a spot on the river with a faster current.

But not all of the immigrants who came to the Middle Colonies became farmers or millers. Some settled in the cities hoping to find greater opportunities in the fast-growing coastal towns.

How a Gristmill Works

With the exception of a few metal parts and the stone grinding blocks, most colonial gristmills were made of wood. Some had foundations of stone. A channel called a millrace was dug from a stream or river to direct fast-running water to the waterwheel. Water falling from the millrace turned the wheel. The moving waterwheel then turned gears inside the building, which rotated the top grinding block. This block could be raised and lowered to vary its closeness to the bottom block, depending upon the size of the grain being ground between the stones. As the top block turned, it pressed and rolled the grains, cracking away the hard outer layers and grinding all the parts into soft flour.

grain

sluicegate

hopper

millrace

top stone (rotates)

bedstone (stays still)

waterwheel

flour

HISTORICAL THINKING

1. **READING CHECK** Why were farmers in the Middle Colonies able to raise cash crops and livestock for sale and export?

2. **IDENTIFY MAIN IDEAS AND DETAILS** Why were the Middle Colonies called the "breadbasket of the colonies"?

3. **ANALYZE VISUALS** Use the diagram to explain how the flour got into the sacks.

3.2 A Diverse Society

What would you look for if you were searching for a new homeland? You might look for a place that was prosperous and productive and tolerant of differences. For many immigrants, the Middle Colonies seemed like such a place.

MAIN IDEA In addition to being economically successful, the Middle Colonies were culturally diverse.

GROWTH OF CITIES

A stream of settlers, hungry for new opportunities, moved to cities along the Atlantic coast, especially the ports of New York City and Philadelphia. As the colonies produced more and more goods, trade from these ports also grew, and people could find a variety of work in the cities.

Founded in 1681, Philadelphia was the fastest-growing city in the colonies. It started out as a village on the Delaware River and grew to more than 2,000 people in 1700. By 1760, the population had rocketed to roughly 23,000 people, outstripping New York and Boston. The city thrived on crops and trade. Philadelphia's merchants forged relationships with farmers who needed to sell their wheat, livestock, and lumber and with dealers who wanted to market these **commodities**, or goods, in the West Indies and elsewhere.

Philadelphia was an attractive city. Pennsylvania's founder, William Penn, drew up plans for Philadelphia while establishing his own colony. He conceived the city as a large "green country town," with wide streets in a grid pattern, public parks, ample lots, and brick houses.

One of Philadelphia's most famous brick buildings is Independence Hall, which was called the Pennsylvania State House when it was first established in 1753.

Meanwhile, New York City was also expanding. The English acquired the city in 1664 as part of their takeover of the Dutch colony New Netherland. The brick houses with low-sloping tile roofs that lined the city's cobblestoned streets looked exactly like those in Dutch towns. As the city expanded, the English made their mark by building houses of brick and wood in their own style.

After the English took over the city, New York merchants maintained ties with the Netherlands and its colony, the Dutch West Indies. They continued to ship grain, flour, dried fish, timber, and other goods to Amsterdam. Because of these ties, New York City's population more than doubled between 1720 and 1760.

American Products
Cities in the colonies wouldn't have grown without the work of artisans like Cornelius Kierstede of New York. He made this silver teapot around 1720. He shaped the spout into the form of a bird and engraved the purchaser's initials into the side.

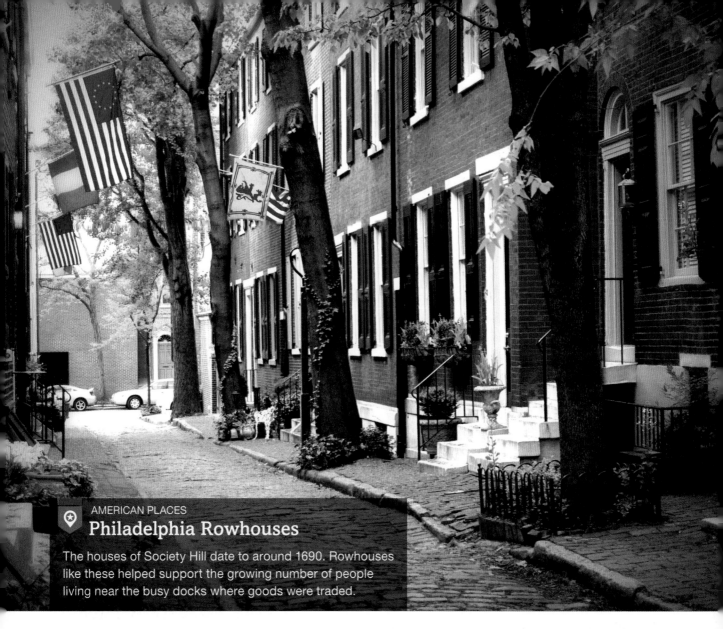

Philadelphia Rowhouses

The houses of Society Hill date to around 1690. Rowhouses like these helped support the growing number of people living near the busy docks where goods were traded.

VARIETY OF IMMIGRANTS

When the English took possession of New Netherland, it was already home to the Dutch, Swedes, Finns, Norwegians, French Protestants, Jews, and other settlers. This **diversity**, or wide variety of people, was partly due to the Dutch, who had opened immigration to many different groups. It made the population of the Middle Colonies unique among the regions of America.

After the English takeover, most new immigrants came from England and Germany. German artisans created the Pennsylvania long rifle for hunting. They also designed the **Conestoga wagon**, which was capable of carrying up to four tons of cargo. Other German artisans were ironworkers and makers of glass, furniture, and kitchenware.

The farmland and cities drew immigrants to the Middle Colonies. But immigrants also came to enjoy something that was much less concrete but, perhaps, even more important: religious freedom.

HISTORICAL THINKING

1. **READING CHECK** What ideas or events caused the populations of Philadelphia and New York City to change over time?

2. **COMPARE AND CONTRAST** What caused the population of the Middle Colonies to differ from that of New England and the Southern Colonies?

3. **IDENTIFY MAIN IDEAS AND DETAILS** How did German immigrants contribute to the success of the Middle Colonies?

3.3 Cultures of the Middle Colonies

You probably know this from your own experience with your classmates: Things just go better if you try to get along. For the most part, that's what people in the Middle Colonies discovered, too.

MAIN IDEA While the Middle Colonies made an honest attempt to tolerate different religions, tensions still existed between different races.

RELIGIOUS TOLERANCE

With people from all walks of life pouring into the Middle Colonies, neighbors needed to show religious **tolerance**, or acceptance of others, in order to establish community. This open-mindedness was part of the legacy of the Dutch. In the Netherlands, Jews practiced their religion freely and became citizens. The Dutch also welcomed many Protestant groups not recognized by the church, including Puritans, Quakers, and Lutherans. In fact, the Pilgrims who settled at Plymouth, Massachusetts, had originally gone to live in the city of Leiden in the Netherlands because of the religious tolerance they found there. The Dutch carried their practice of tolerance across the sea to New Netherland, where it continued after the English took over.

Less than 100 miles away, William Penn founded Pennsylvania as a free colony—not just for Quakers, but for other religions as well. He promised equal rights and opportunities. As a result, the colony attracted many different Protestant faiths, including the Amish. This group emphasized personal faith and a simple life. They also valued humility and submission.

Quakers believed all people were equal in the eyes of God. They saw religion as a personal matter, and they did not demand **conformity**, or obedience, to a strict set of beliefs. Quakers were also the first group in America to ban slaveholding.

TENSIONS BETWEEN RACES

But most people in the Middle Colonies didn't share the Quakers' view. When the English acquired New Netherland in 1664, an estimated 20 percent of the population was African. The Dutch West India Company provided "half freedom" to older enslaved Africans. This meant that the company released the older slaves, but not their children, from slavery. Other slaves worked for wages to buy their freedom. As a result, by 1664, one-fifth of all Africans were free. But tolerance for diversity did not extend to these Africans and African Americans, whether they were free or slaves.

Most African Americans in the Middle Colonies lived in New York City. By 1711, about 40 percent of white households there had at least one slave. Many enslaved people were skilled workers and lived and worked next to free and indentured whites.

Enslaved African Americans whose owners had run out of tasks for them often sought work on their own, looking for paid work throughout New York. However, the sight of so many African Americans on the streets of New York made white people fearful. A law was put into effect requiring that all hiring of slaves be done at one place, the slave market. This put still more restrictions on the lives of the African Americans, and in turn, white people began to worry about a slave rebellion.

These fears became reality on the night of April 6, 1712, when about 20 enslaved people set fire to a building, attacking the white men who came to put it out. Nine white people were killed, and terror spread up and down the Atlantic coast.

As in the case of later slave revolts and conspiracies, the revenge taken on the African-American community far outweighed any

🏛 Museum of Fine Arts, Boston

Like many Protestant groups, Quakers did not have a paid clergy. Instead, they believed every individual should decide how to worship. People sat silently at Quaker meetings, thinking and praying, until they felt that God moved them to speak. They wore plain clothes and spoke plainly, even to nobility. This painting by an unknown artist from the late 1700s or early 1800s captures the feeling of a Quaker meeting.

violence the rebels had committed. In the wake of the New York revolt, 13 enslaved African Americans were hanged, 3 were burned at the stake, 1 was tortured, and another starved to death in chains.

Some white colonists, however, questioned the morality of slavery. Wasn't it a violation of the Bible's golden rule, which says to act toward others as you want others to act toward you? A person who enslaves another certainly would not like to be enslaved in return. Other whites opposed slavery simply because they feared slave rebellions. Despite these considerations, slavery became a part of early American culture and would remain so for more than 150 years.

HISTORICAL THINKING

1. **READING CHECK** How did the Dutch colonists show tolerance for religious diversity in New Netherland?

2. **MAKE INFERENCES** Why do you think Quakers accepted other religions and races?

3. **EVALUATE** The text claims that "the revenge taken on the African-American community far outweighed any violence the rebels had committed." What evidence supports this?

4.1 Colonial Men and Women

As a girl, can you imagine rights reserved only for boys? As a boy, can you imagine being denied rights because of your family's lack of wealth? That's the way it was in the colonies.

MAIN IDEA Rights and wealth were not evenly distributed across religions, social classes, races, and genders in colonial American society.

RIGHTS AND WEALTH

Between 1720 and 1763, the diverse American population experienced changes in many aspects of their lives. In science, doctors made strides in understanding how diseases spread. People reexamined traditions and laws. The changes spread throughout the colonies.

However, other ideas were resistant to change. Voting was restricted to white men—and to a select group. Only landowning men could vote. But there were exceptions. Men who were Catholic or Jewish were denied the vote based on religion. Servants, slaves, and men without property were also barred. Men with a small amount of land or personal property had to pay to vote.

Although land was plentiful and industry booming, wealth in the colonies was not evenly distributed. This was especially visible in the cities. Fabulously wealthy merchants built mansions and bought coaches with income from trade with other nations or colonies. Less fortunate city dwellers worked for low wages or lacked employment altogether. For instance, seamen and artisans who relied on trade could be out of a job if the demand for goods decreased. In addition, the **burgeoning**, or quickly growing, towns lacked sanitation, putting many people at risk from the spread of disease.

ROLE OF WOMEN

Life was tough for both colonial men and women, but the women had even fewer choices. In rural areas, white wives cooked, cleaned, sewed, reared children, and helped with farm tasks. Many also made candles, soap, and other items to sell or exchange for goods. Most African-American women were enslaved. They worked in the fields, cooked, cleaned, and tended to the slaveholder's family. Only the wives of plantation owners led an easy life. They supervised the household slaves and servants and oversaw meal preparation.

In cities, women cared for their children and the household. Wealthier wives employed servants, and some depended on slaves. Some worked alongside their husbands in shops and businesses. Other women served as **midwives**, helping deliver babies. Poor women often made money by mending, washing, and ironing clothes or providing domestic services. Few women worked outside the home.

Women had few legal rights throughout most of the colonial period. They could not vote. They lost the right to manage their property and earn a living once they married. Many women relied on the church for their social life. Soon, all colonists would be asked to pay more attention to their spiritual lives as well.

HISTORICAL THINKING

1. **READING CHECK** What requirements did a person have to meet to be eligible to vote in colonial America?

2. **IDENTIFY MAIN IDEAS AND DETAILS** What details support the idea that wealth was not evenly distributed in colonial American cities?

3. **ANALYZE VISUALS** Which household task may have posed the biggest problem for colonial women? Use the information in the visual to explain your answer.

hatch lever

handle

hatch door

hatch

slug

box

soleplate

BOX IRON

Easy-care fabrics did not exist in colonial times, so ironing was an essential part of laundry, which was hard work at every stage. The box iron had a hatch in the back where the woman inserted a hot metal piece called a slug. One slug sat on the fire until the one in the iron cooled. Then the woman switched them.

The first electric iron was introduced in 1882.

slug heated in the fire

slug placed in box

ALL IN A DAY'S WORK

In the days before electricity and grocery stores, colonial women—and, later, the women of early national America—labored to maintain their homes and families. There was cream to churn into butter, and there were fires to stoke and clothes to iron, along with all the other aspects of making sure the family was fed and warm.

BUTTER CHURN

For a colonial woman, making butter began with milking a cow. The milk sat in a container until the cream rose to the top. Then the woman skimmed off the cream and put it into a butter churn. She moved the dasher up and down and in circles, churning the cream. After what could be minutes or hours, butter formed, along with buttermilk. The final step was to strain the butter to separate the two.

The first U.S. butter factory opened in 1856.

dasher

splasher top

cream

plunger disc

BED WARMER

Heat from the fireplace of a colonial home did not spread from room to room. If the house couldn't be heated, however, the beds could. A colonial woman filled the pan of a bed warmer with glowing coals and took it from room to room. She moved the pan around under the covers to distribute the heat evenly. Then she went along to the next bed.

The first electric blanket was introduced in 1912.

holes to vent

hot coals, rocks, or brick

4.2 Great Awakening and Enlightenment

Have you ever listened to someone who made you think about a familiar topic in a new way? Something like that happened to colonists in the early 1700s and reawakened their dedication to religion.

MAIN IDEA The Enlightenment, emphasizing reason, and the Great Awakening, a religious renewal, helped shape colonial thought.

THE GREAT AWAKENING

You probably remember that many of the first colonists came to America to seek religious freedom. But once they'd achieved it, they began to focus on the material concerns of everyday life. People concentrated on their work and their homes. As a result, by the early 1700s, people's passion for religion had begun to die down. Some even stopped going to church regularly.

Many Protestant ministers feared that colonists were losing sight of the importance of God. In an effort to inspire people to recommit to their spiritual beliefs, these ministers gave stirring—and sometimes frightening—sermons during a series of religious revivals known as the **Great Awakening**.

One of the most effective of these ministers was **Jonathan Edwards** of Massachusetts. In 1734, he began preaching sermons on **salvation**, or the deliverance from sin. In his most famous sermon, "Sinners in the Hands of an Angry God," Edwards compared his listeners to spiders. God, he said, held them by a string over the fires of hell. If they failed to seek salvation, he warned, God would simply let go of the string.

Another minister, **George Whitefield**, came from Britain to preach salvation to the colonists. With his theatrical gestures and thundering words, he appealed to people's emotions and brought them to tears. Some even fainted.

The revivals of the Great Awakening changed how people viewed religion and morality. People began to believe they did not need church officials to

A Ray of Hope

Jonathan Edwards delivered "Sinners in the Hands of an Angry God" in 1741 to a congregation in Connecticut. Unlike George Whitefield, Edwards spoke in a quiet voice and used few gestures, but his message caused near-hysteria in his listeners. In this excerpt from the sermon, after threatening his audience with damnation, Edwards offers them a chance to be saved. How do you think Edwards's listeners responded to his words of hope?

PRIMARY SOURCE

And now you have an extraordinary opportunity, a day wherein Christ has thrown the door of mercy wide open, and stands in the door calling and crying with a loud voice to poor sinners. How awful is it to be left behind at such a day! To see so many rejoicing and singing for joy of heart, while you have cause to mourn for sorrow of heart. How can you rest one moment in such a condition? Therefore let every one that is out of Christ [that has not accepted Christ], now awake and fly from the wrath [fury] to come.

–from "Sinners in the Hands of an Angry God," by Jonathan Edwards, 1741

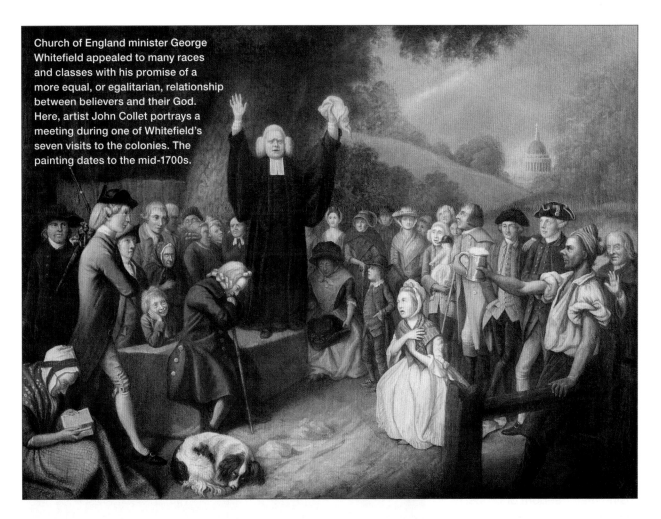

Church of England minister George Whitefield appealed to many races and classes with his promise of a more equal, or egalitarian, relationship between believers and their God. Here, artist John Collet portrays a meeting during one of Whitefield's seven visits to the colonies. The painting dates to the mid-1700s.

connect with God. Even more dangerously, they began to challenge authority and think themselves equal to those in power.

THE ENLIGHTENMENT

The Great Awakening was not the only movement that helped pave the way for revolutionary fervor. The intellectual movement known as the **Enlightenment** spread from Great Britain to the colonies in the 1700s. Enlightenment thinkers believed that the "light" of human reason would shatter the "darkness" of ignorance, superstition, and unfair authority. In part, they were influenced by the **Scientific Revolution**, which began in Europe around the mid-1550s and used logical thinking to answer scientific questions. The Enlightenment encouraged people to use logic and ask questions instead of just accepting what religious and political figures told them.

The ideas of **John Locke**, a 17th-century English philosopher, greatly influenced Enlightenment thought. Locke asserted that humans were born free and equal with **natural rights** , or rights such as life or liberty that a person is born with. He

also claimed that a leader could rule only with the consent of the people. If a ruler failed to protect the people's rights, Locke believed they had the right to overthrow him.

These ideas would prove hugely influential in the colonies. American Enlightenment leaders included Benjamin Franklin, who devoted his life to public service and science. In time, Franklin and many other American founders would start to demand their own rights and freedoms.

HISTORICAL THINKING

1. **READING CHECK** What was the Great Awakening?

2. **IDENTIFY MAIN IDEAS AND DETAILS** What were some of John Locke's beliefs?

3. **DRAW CONCLUSIONS** What did the Enlightenment and the Great Awakening contribute to colonial views about equality and government?

4.3 Rights in England and the Colonies

The colonists considered themselves English and felt they were entitled to the same rights that the citizens of England enjoyed. And for a while, the English government let them think that.

MAIN IDEA Political changes in England that balanced the power between Parliament and the king helped set the American colonies on the path to democracy.

ENGLISH PARLIAMENT

Of course, the English themselves hadn't always enjoyed many rights. As you have learned, the Magna Carta, or Great Charter, began to change all that. The Magna Carta put protections in place to keep the English people from losing their freedom or property unless the law of the land ruled against them.

This important document helped give rise to **Parliament**, the legislative body of England, and later, Great Britain. Parliament consisted of two houses: the House of Lords, made up of nobles and high church officials, and the House of Commons, whose members were elected by male landowners.

Parliament's power grew in the late 1600s after clashing with King James II, who was a Catholic. Fearing James would make England a Catholic country under authoritarian rule, parliamentary leaders exiled him to France. They then invited his Protestant daughter, Mary, and her husband, William, to take the throne.

The Magna Carta and the Colonies

This stained glass in the Mansion House in London, England, home to the city's Lord Mayor, depicts the signing of the Magna Carta. The document established that the king was not above the law. Henry III, John's successor, reissued slightly revised Magna Cartas in 1216, 1217, and 1225. The 1225 version became English law in 1297. Hundreds of years later, the English colonists believed that they, too, possessed the rights guaranteed in the Magna Carta. During the American Revolution, colonists drew on principles in the Magna Carta for their Declaration of Independence and rebellion against the tyranny of King George III.

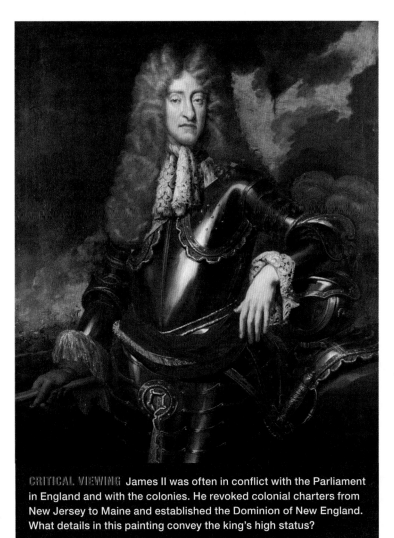

CRITICAL VIEWING James II was often in conflict with the Parliament in England and with the colonies. He revoked colonial charters from New Jersey to Maine and established the Dominion of New England. What details in this painting convey the king's high status?

COLONIAL ASSEMBLIES

The American colonies modeled their governments after Parliament by forming elected assemblies similar to the House of Commons. The colonial assemblies consisted of representatives elected by property owners. The assemblies could collect money through taxes and decide how to spend it.

Unlike the English legislature, however, elected officials in the assemblies lived in the area they represented. The colonists believed that representatives who lived among the people who elected them would better understand local interests and needs.

As colonists came to enjoy making decisions and managing some of their own affairs, they began to resent English authority. The colonists had no representatives in Parliament and sometimes felt they were treated unfairly—especially when Parliament passed laws the colonists didn't like.

For the most part, though, the English government was busy fighting foreign wars and dealing with disagreements within the country itself. So the government adopted a policy of **salutary neglect** toward the colonies. Under this policy, the English government did not strictly enforce its colonial policies. As a result, the colonies grew happily accustomed to living in relative isolation from British authority and largely governing themselves. They were generally content with British rule. But that state of affairs was about to change.

At the same time, Parliament permanently limited the English monarch's power. It established Parliament's control of taxation, and its right to pass laws, and it also secured the independence of the courts. Parliament's consent was necessary for raising an army in peacetime and in the case of any foreign invasions. The bloodless overthrow of James II and the transferring of power to Parliament was called the Glorious Revolution. Parliament created the **English Bill of Rights of 1689** (more formally known as "An Act Declaring the Rights and Liberties of the Subject and Settling the Succession of the Crown") to officially protect the rights of English citizens and Parliament.

Many believed the balancing of powers would prevent a single individual or social group from becoming too dominant. Power shared by the king, the nobles, and the common people was thought to be the way to avoid more destructive forms of government that could threaten the liberty of some portion of the population.

HISTORICAL THINKING

1. **READING CHECK** How did Parliament influence the growth of representative government in the colonies?

2. **SUMMARIZE** How did the Magna Carta pave the way for the English Bill of Rights?

3. **IDENTIFY MAIN IDEAS AND DETAILS** What rights did Parliament establish in the English Bill of Rights?

4.4 John Peter Zenger and Free Speech

Today, we expect talk show hosts to joke about politicians and criticize our government. We take for granted that people in the media are free to say what they want. That was not always the case in the colonies.

MAIN IDEA The trial of John Peter Zenger helped pave the way for freedom of the press.

LIBEL OR FREE SPEECH?

Under Great Britain's policy of salutary neglect, the colonists became used to determining what they could and couldn't do. In 1733 by British law, it was illegal to criticize the government in print. But **John Peter Zenger**, the publisher of the *New-York Weekly Journal,* did it anyway. In his newspaper, he printed a series of articles about the British colonial governor of New York, William Cosby. A few years before, Cosby had removed a judge who had ruled against him and then tried to rig, or tamper with the outcome of, an election.

Another person, a lawyer named James Alexander, wrote the articles, but his name didn't appear in the paper. Unable to determine the author, Cosby went after Zenger. Police arrested Zenger for **libel**, the publishing of lies, in November 1734. He remained in jail until his trial in August 1735.

Governor Cosby expected the trial to be an open and shut case. Any criticism of the government, true or not, was considered libel. The paper had definitely criticized the governor—there was no question about that—so as far as Cosby was concerned, the jury had to find Zenger guilty.

Andrew Hamilton, John Peter Zenger's lawyer, reasoned convincingly on Zenger's behalf. In this illustration from 1877, Hamilton makes his case before the judge.

High Court Upholds Students' Peaceful Protest

Continued From Page 1, Col. 4

demonstrate and would embroil the Supreme Court in public school affairs.

Justice Abe Fortas emphasized in the Court's opinion that school children's free speech rights are limited to conduct that does not disrupt discipline or interfere with the rights of others.

He also said that their rights included only political expression, and that the Federal courts would not become involved in disputes over the permissible length of students' hair

and more acid in recent years, spoke extemporaneously for about 20 minutes this morning. At one point he used mocking tones to quote from an old opinion with which he disagreed, and he finished by stating that "I want it thoroughly known that I disclaim any sentence, any word, any part of what the Court does today."

Justice Black will observe his 83d birthday next Thursday.

The events leading to today's decision go back to December, 1965, when antiwar groups in Des Moines began to plan the armband protest. The Board of Education voted to prohibit the

The suit, sponsored by the American Civil Liberties Union, was brought in the names of three of the suspended students: John F. Tinker, then 15; his sister Mary Beth, then 13, and Christopher Eckhardt, 16.

The father of the Tinker children is a Methodist minister employed by the American Friends Service Committee. Young Eckhardt's mother is an officer in the Women's International League for Peace and Freedom.

The United States District Court in Des Moines refused to enjoin the school officials from forbidding the armband

ZENGER CLEARED

Although he was confident of the outcome, Cosby didn't want to take any chances. He packed the jury with his own supporters. However, Zenger's wife Anna found out and revealed Cosby's misdeed in the *New-York Weekly Journal*, which she had continued to publish while her husband was in jail. The judge replaced Cosby's jury with a jury of colonists, but Zenger's problems continued. The judge dismissed Zenger's lawyers when they challenged the judge's authority. Meanwhile, Zenger's friends brought Andrew Hamilton, a famous Philadelphia lawyer, to take over the case.

Hamilton took a novel approach. He admitted that Zenger had printed articles criticizing Cosby. Hamilton argued, however, that the jury should consider the fact that the criticisms were true. Should Zenger be jailed for doing his job correctly as a newspaper publisher by printing the truth? Hamilton went on to argue that freedom of the press was especially important in the colonies because it acted as a check against the abuses of colonial governors. In his closing, Hamilton urged

the jury to grant "that, to which Nature and the Laws of our Country have given us a Right, . . . both of exposing and opposing arbitrary Power . . . by speaking and writing Truth."

After a short time, the jury returned to the court with a verdict of not guilty, and Zenger was released. The victory paved the way to gaining freedom of the press. It also unified the colonists in their pursuit of their rights. But the colonists still considered themselves British citizens. Soon, they'd unite and join forces with Britain in war.

HISTORICAL THINKING

1. **READING CHECK** Why was John Peter Zenger charged with libel?

2. **IDENTIFY MAIN IDEAS AND DETAILS** Why did William Cosby assume that John Peter Zenger would be found guilty?

3. **SYNTHESIZE** How was the outcome of *Tinker* v. *Des Moines* similar to the outcome of Zenger's trial?

Battles in New France, 1754–1760

Louisbourg,
1758

Fort Beauséjour, ✴
ACADIA   1755

NOVA SCOTIA

• Halifax

MAINE
(part of Massachusetts)

N E W   F R A N C E

St. Lawrence River

Québec,
1759

Montréal
(Surrendered,
1760)

St. Lawrence R.

Lake
Champlain

Fort Ticonderoga,
1758, 1759
NEW
HAMPSHIRE

Fort Frontenac,
1758

Fort William Henry,
1757

Boston •

MASS.

Fort Oswego, 1756
NEW YORK

Lake Ontario

CONN.

RHODE ISLAND

Fort Niagara,
1759

Lake Huron

Hudson R.

ATLANTIC
OCEAN

Lake Erie

Allegheny R.

PENNSYLVANIA

NEW
JERSEY

New York •

Susquehanna R.

Philadelphia •

Monongahela,
1755

Fort Duquesne

Fort
Necessity,
1754

DELAWARE

MARYLAND

OHIO VALLEY

VIRGINIA

Ohio R.

James R.

Roanoke R.

NORTH CAROLINA

SOUTH
CAROLINA

N
W   E
S

British territory
French territory
Disputed territory
✴ British victory
✴ French victory

0   100   200 Miles

0   100   200 Kilometers

154

5.1 War Begins

Finders keepers. That's what the French might have said when they claimed prime real estate in the Ohio Valley for themselves. But the British and the American colonists begged to differ.

MAIN IDEA Competition for land and furs involved France and Great Britain in many years of war in North America, starting with the French and Indian War.

SEEDS OF CONFLICT

When French fur traders first came to North America in the 1600s, they set up a few forts and **trading posts** in the St. Lawrence Valley. As you may recall, the French traded with the Huron and Algonquian there for almost 100 years. But after French trappers killed many of the animals in the area and fur supplies dwindled, they resettled in the Ohio Valley. This land was also claimed by Great Britain. So in the 1740s, the British joined forces with the Iroquois and pushed the French traders out of the valley.

The fertile land of the Ohio Valley appealed to colonial settlers. In 1749, they were eager to buy land shares from the Ohio Company of Virginia, which promoted the westward settlement of colonists from Virginia. But the French hadn't given up their claim to the land. They built a number of forts there, including Fort LeBoeuf (luh-BUHF) in northwest Pennsylvania. Then in 1752, the French destroyed Pickawillany, a colonial trading post. In an effort to settle the dispute over the Ohio Valley peacefully, the British governor of Virginia sent a young colonial army leader named **George Washington** to Fort LeBoeuf to ask the French to leave. Not surprisingly, they refused.

COLONIAL INVOLVEMENT

In 1754, the British decided to take more forceful measures and sent the newly promoted Colonel Washington and a small number of troops to capture Fort Duquesne (doo-KAYN) in present-day Pittsburgh. When he arrived, Washington quickly realized he was outnumbered. Scrambling to defend his troops, he built a wooden barrier, or stockade, which he fittingly named Fort Necessity. But the situation was hopeless. French and Native American troops surrounded the fort and attacked, causing heavy losses for Washington's troops. Defeated, Washington surrendered and abandoned the fort.

Many consider this battle the beginning of the **French and Indian War**. For Britain and France, this war would become part of a larger one, called the Seven Years' War, that officially began in 1756. It pitted these two great powers in a struggle over land in Europe.

The colonists, meanwhile, were concerned with land in North America. Seven colonies sent delegates to a congress in Albany, New York, to discuss uniting the colonies to fight the French for that land. The delegates adopted Benjamin Franklin's **Albany Plan of Union**, which proposed granting a central government the power to tax, pass laws, and oversee military defense for the colonies. When the delegates returned home with the proposal, none of the colonies approved it. But the colonists were united in their determination to fight for land they considered theirs. And they soon persuaded the British to help them.

HISTORICAL THINKING

1. **READING CHECK** How did the fur trade cause conflict between the French and the British?

2. **INTERPRET MAPS** Around what bodies of water were many of the battles fought?

3. **IDENTIFY MAIN IDEAS AND DETAILS** What was the purpose of the Albany Plan of Union?

5.2 Quebec and the British Victory

The stakes were high in the French and Indian War. Ultimately, the outcome of the war would determine which countries controlled North America.

MAIN IDEA The British and French fought for control of North America in the French and Indian War, with extensive losses on both sides.

EARLY BRITISH LOSSES

In response to the colonists' request for help, the British jumped into the fight. In 1755, they sent British general Edward Braddock and two regiments to North America to destroy French forts. George Washington accompanied Braddock as he marched with his more than 2,000 soldiers through the Virginia backcountry on a mission to capture Fort Duquesne. Braddock was confident that his highly trained soldiers would quickly defeat the enemy.

He was wrong. The British soldiers were totally unprepared for fighting on the frontier. Their wagons were too big for the paths, and they offended many of the Native American scouts they'd recruited to lead the way, causing most of them to abandon the soldiers. The army's slow progress gave the French plenty of notice of their clumsy arrival.

As a result, the French and Native American troops were lying in wait for them. In the **Battle of the Monongahela**, fought just east of present-day Pittsburgh, they hid behind trees and ambushed Braddock's army as it marched by. Used to fighting on battlegrounds where both sides formed neat rows, the British soldiers were caught completely off guard. Washington suggested they break ranks and fight from behind trees like the French, but Braddock refused. Within a few hours, nearly two-thirds of the British forces lay dead or wounded. Braddock himself soon died of his wounds. Washington, his uniform ripped by bullets, helped lead the retreat.

Losses continued to plague the British in the early years of the war. In New York, the French seized Fort William Henry, Fort Oswego, and 2,000 British soldiers at Lake George. The British defeats emboldened Native American tribes allied with the French to attack British settlements in the backcountry, where they killed and captured hundreds of settlers. Things looked bleak for the British and colonial forces.

Native American club
Braddock and his men likely faced Native Americans holding weapons like this one, made of wood and brass. The maker of the weapon carved the ball on the end from wood. Two-and-a-half feet, or nearly one yard, long, these clubs could be devastating weapons.

FRENCH DEFEATS

The tide turned after British statesman **Sir William Pitt** poured money and men into the war. In July 1758, the British captured Louisbourg in Nova Scotia (NOH-vuh SKOH-shuh). Alarmed, the French pulled their troops from the Ohio Valley so they could protect Quebec and Montreal. The retreat allowed the British to take control of the west. Cut off from French supplies and weakened by smallpox, Native Americans ended their war in the backcountry.

Even with extra troops, the French could not save Quebec. The British captured the city in 1759 during the **Battle of Quebec.** Encouraged by these victories, the Iroquois joined forces with Britain. In 1760, the British captured Montreal, ending French control of Canada.

The defeat of the French in Canada marked the end of the war with France in North America. A treaty would be signed, but the war had a lasting impact on everyone who had taken part in it. For one thing, thousands of colonists had joined the British army. They found that, at best, the British soldiers and officers looked down on them, and at worst, the British dealt out severe punishments to soldiers for small offenses. Colonial soldiers didn't feel they'd been treated like allies. The war would also cause great suffering to Native Americans. Soon settlers would invade even more of their homeland.

HISTORICAL THINKING

1. **READING CHECK** How did Braddock's defeat at Fort Duquesne show that the British were not ready to fight a frontier war?

2. **IDENTIFY MAIN IDEAS AND DETAILS** What turned the tide of the French and Indian War?

3. **DETERMINE CHRONOLOGY** What happened after Braddock and Washington marched to capture Fort Duquesne?

5.3 Impact of the War

The colonists celebrated Britain's victory in the French and Indian War. New York City even raised a statue of King George III. Would the colonists' love of the king endure? We'll see.

MAIN IDEA Victory in the French and Indian War expanded British territory but led to conflict with Native Americans in the Ohio Valley.

THE TREATY OF PARIS

In 1763, diplomats from Britain and France met in Paris to negotiate a **treaty**, or peace agreement. The resulting **Treaty of Paris** officially ended the French and Indian War.

According to its terms, France lost all of its territory—and thus all of its power—in North America. As Britain's ally, Spain acquired New Orleans and the Louisiana Territory west of the Mississippi. The British gained Canada from France and Florida from Spain in exchange for Cuba and the Philippines. Britain now controlled all of the land in North America east of the Mississippi River.

The colonists also reaped some rewards from the treaty. They received the right to fish in the North Atlantic off the coast of Canada. The colonists also assumed they were now free to settle the Ohio Valley.

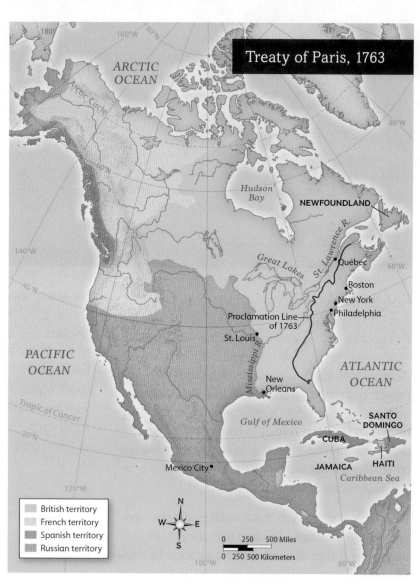

PONTIAC'S REBELLION

Not everyone in North America was happy when the French and Indian War ended. The war had been a disaster for Native Americans. While the French had presented them with gifts each year, the British ended this custom and then raised prices on trade goods. Worse yet, the British government limited what—and how much—Native Americans could trade. Additionally, white settlers streamed into the Ohio Valley after the war, in clear violation of existing treaties.

The British trade policies and land-grabbing drove large numbers of Delaware, Shawnee, Iroquois, and other Native Americans to take up arms.

When I go to see the English commander and say to him that some of our comrades are dead, instead of bewailing their death, as our French brothers do, he laughs at me and at you. If I ask for anything for our sick, he refuses with the reply that he has no use for us. From all this you can well see that they are seeking our ruin. Therefore, my brothers, we must all swear their destruction and wait no longer.

—Chief Pontiac in a speech to a council of Native Americans near Detroit, May 1763

Ottawa leader **Pontiac** urged Native Americans in the region to band together and rise up against the British. Many listened.

Pontiac had fought alongside the French in the French and Indian War. In 1763, he led Native Americans in launching what came to be called **Pontiac's Rebellion**. His forces defeated 13 British outposts. However, the British successfully defended their most important forts, including Fort Pitt, sometimes by ruthless means.

When Pontiac launched his rebellion, he needed help to replenish ammunition supplies and strengthen the Native Americans' ranks throughout the Great Lakes region and western Pennsylvania. He counted on the French to come to his aid. But they never did. Then, when British commanders met with Native American leaders at Fort Pitt, they are said to have given them smallpox-infested blankets and handkerchiefs as gifts, hoping to spread disease among many of the tribes.

Fighting continued for two more years. Sick of war, the king issued a proclamation that colonists could not settle west of a line drawn along the crest of the Appalachian Mountains from Maine to Georgia. This angered colonists, who wondered what they had been fighting for. They also resented the continued presence of British troops in their homeland. The soldiers and their somewhat coarse behavior served as a daily reminder of the mother colony. In time, colonists began to regard British authority more critically.

HISTORICAL THINKING

1. **READING CHECK** How did the Treaty of Paris affect power in North America?

2. **INTERPRET MAPS** Which countries gained the most territory after 1763?

3. **SYNTHESIZE** How did the outcome of the war impact Native Americans?

CHAPTER COLONIAL DEVELOPMENT
4 REVIEW

VOCABULARY

Use each of the following vocabulary words in a sentence that shows an understanding of the term's meaning.

1. subsistence farming
   If a family practices subsistence farming, they usually harvest just enough food to survive and sometimes will have a little left over to sell.

2. provisions

3. religious freedom

4. apprentice

5. cash crop

6. backcountry

7. gristmill

8. diversity

9. libel

10. trading post

READING STRATEGY
IDENTIFY MAIN IDEAS AND DETAILS

If you haven't done so already, complete your chart to identify details about the development of the colonies. Then answer the question.

Colonial Development

Main Idea:
Detail:
Detail:
Detail:

11. Why did the use of enslaved African labor grow over time in the Southern Colonies?

MAIN IDEAS

Answer the following questions. Support your answers with evidence from the chapter.

12. Why was fishing important to the economy of New England? **LESSON 1.1**

13. How did triangular trade contribute to the expansion of slavery? **LESSON 1.2**

14. Why did Charles Town remain smaller than the largest northern cities? **LESSON 2.1**

15. What was the Stono Rebellion? **LESSON 2.3**

16. How did gristmills affect the economy of the Middle Colonies? **LESSON 3.1**

17. What were indicators of racial tension in New York City in the early 1700s? **LESSON 3.3**

18. In what ways did women add to the colonial economy? **LESSON 4.1**

19. How did ministers like Jonathan Edwards and George Whitefield contribute to the Great Awakening? **LESSON 4.2**

20. What led to the creation of the Albany Plan of Union? **LESSON 5.1**

21. Why did Pontiac rebel? **LESSON 5.3**

HISTORICAL THINKING

Answer the following questions. Support your answers with evidence from the chapter.

22. **MAKE INFERENCES** How did the Navigation Acts lead to an increase in smuggling?

23. **ANALYZE CAUSE AND EFFECT** How did the beliefs of the Puritans lead to the growth of education in the colonies?

24. **COMPARE AND CONTRAST** How was society in the backcountry different from society in the Chesapeake and South Carolina?

25. SYNTHESIZE How did the Great Awakening and the Enlightenment contribute to revolutionary thought?

26. FORM AND SUPPORT OPINIONS Were the Native Americans better off dealing with French fur traders or the British settlers? Support your opinion with evidence from the chapter.

27. DRAW CONCLUSIONS How did the British victory in the French and Indian War change the distribution of power in North America?

INTERPRET MAPS

Look closely at the map of the African-American population in the British colonies around 1760. Then answer the questions that follow.

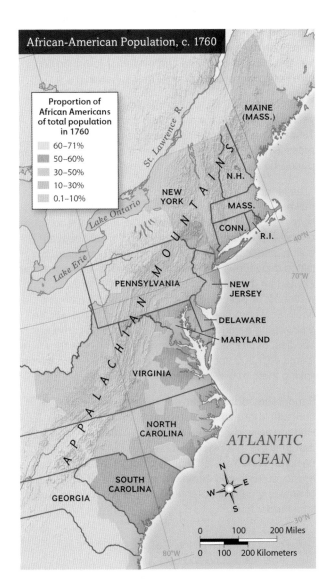

African-American Population, c. 1760

Proportion of African Americans of total population in 1760
- 60–71%
- 50–60%
- 30–50%
- 10–30%
- 0.1–10%

28. Which two areas had the highest proportion of African Americans in their population?

29. How did the African-American population in South Carolina differ from that in Virginia?

ANALYZE SOURCES

In 1704, French and Native American forces attacked Deerfield, Massachusetts, killing 50 people and taking 112 captives. Stephen Williams, an 11-year-old captive, kept a journal while a prisoner. Here he describes the attack. Read the excerpt and answer the question.

> The French and Indians came and surprised our fort and took it. And after they had broken into our house and took us prisoners, they barbarously murdered a brother and sister of mine as they did several of our neighbors. They rifled our house and then marched away with us that were captives, and set our house and barn afire as they did the greatest part of the town.

30. How does this source help to develop an understanding of the attack?

CONNECT TO YOUR LIFE

31. NARRATIVE Think about the tasks and adjustments of someone who moves and starts at a new school. What work is involved in physically moving? What does a person do to get to know new neighbors, teachers, and friends? Write a paragraph in which you make connections between this experience and that of the colonists.

TIPS

- List the challenges that the colonists faced coming to British America. Then make a list of the challenges involved in moving.

- Use two or three vocabulary terms from the chapter in your narrative.

- Conclude the narrative with a comment that ties the colonists' experiences to that of a modern student's move.

Before New York

BY PETER MILLER

Adapted from "Before New York," by Peter Miller, in *National Geographic*, September 2009

Of all the visitors to New York City in recent years, one of the most surprising was a beaver named José. No one knows exactly where he came from. He just showed up one wintry morning in 2007 on a riverbank in the Bronx Zoo, where he built a lodge.

During the early 17th century, when the city was the Dutch village of New Amsterdam, beavers were widely hunted for their pelts, which were fashionable in Europe. The fur trade grew into such a profitable business that a pair of beavers earned a place on the city's official seal, where they remain today.

Because of the high demand for their pelts, the real animals vanished. According to Eric Sanderson, an ecologist at the Wildlife Conservation Society (WCS) headquartered at the Bronx Zoo, "There hasn't been a beaver in New York City in more than 200 years." That's why he was skeptical when a colleague told him he'd seen evidence of a beaver during a walk along the river. But it was true. Sanderson and his colleague found José's lodge, and a couple of weeks later, they ran into José himself.

The beaver's return to the Big Apple was hailed as a victory by those who have spent more than three decades restoring the health of the Bronx River, once a dumping ground for abandoned cars and trash. José was named in honor of José E. Serrano, the congressman from the Bronx who'd secured more than $15 million in federal funds to support the river cleanup.

For almost a decade, Sanderson has led a project at WCS to imagine and digitally recreate what the island of Manhattan might have looked like before the city took root. The Mannahatta Project, as it's called (after the Lenape name for "island of many hills"), is an effort to turn back the clock to 1609, just before Henry Hudson and his crew sailed into New York Harbor and spotted the island.

Long before its hills were bulldozed and its wetlands paved over, Manhattan was a wilderness of chestnut, oak, and hickory trees. It was full of salt marshes and grasslands with turkey, elk, and black bear—and "as pleasant a land as one can tread upon," Hudson reported. Sandy beaches ran along stretches of both coasts on the narrow, 13-mile-long island where the Lenape feasted on clams and oysters. More than 66 miles of streams flowed through Manhattan.

"You might find it difficult to imagine today, but 400 years ago there was a red maple swamp right here in Times Square," Sanderson mentioned while waiting to cross Seventh Avenue. "Just over there was a beaver pond," he said, as a bus rumbled by.

"The landscape in Manhattan is so transformed, it makes you wonder what was here before," Sanderson remarked. As a landscape ecologist, his goal is to figure out how wild places work. So he and his colleagues built a landscape from the bottom up. They began by listing the various ecosystems they could safely assume existed on the island, such as old-growth forests, wetlands, or plains. In all, they identified 55 different ecological communities. Then they filled in the wildlife, discovering a dense network of relationships among species, habitats, and ecosystems. In the end, they identified 1,300 species and at least 8,000 relationships linking them to one another and their habitats.

Sanderson hopes his project will stimulate a new curiosity about what existed on Manhattan before Hudson arrived. "I'd like every New Yorker to know that they live in a place that had this fabulous ecology," he said. "New York isn't just a place of fabulous art, music, culture, and communications. It's also a place of amazing natural potential—even if you have to look a little harder here."

For more from National Geographic, check out "America, Found and Lost" online.

UNIT INQUIRY: Envision an Ideal Community

In this unit, you learned about the visions different groups had about what newly founded communities should be. Some groups built communities based on shared religious beliefs. Other groups focused on profiting from the rich natural resources the new continent offered. Based on your understanding of the text, what factors are involved in envisioning a new community? How might some groups' visions conflict with others?

ASSIGNMENT

Envision an ideal community. All new colonies began with people who imagined a new way of living or a new world. Consider factors such as what the "goal" of your community is, what sort of rules would govern your community, and how the community would thrive. Be prepared to present your community to the class.

Gather Evidence As you envision your community, gather evidence from this unit about the various factors that founders of new communities had to consider. Make a list of categories and subcategories that you consider the most important. Review the unit to gather evidence that supports your vision. Use a graphic organizer like this one to help organize your thoughts.

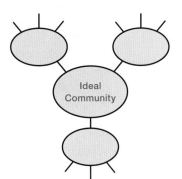

Produce Use your notes to produce a detailed vision of your new community. Write a short paragraph on each component, using evidence from this unit to support your ideas.

Present Choose a creative way to present your ideal community to the class. Consider one of these options:

- Create a commercial to persuade people to move to your new community. Include details that describe where it is, who would prosper there, what the "goal" of the community would be, and what people who move there might expect.

- Organize teams and hold a classroom discussion on establishing a new community. Explore questions such as who would hold power, who might be included (or excluded), and how the community would support its residents.

- Design a flag or symbol for your new community. Describe how the elements you include on your flag represent your community and why these factors would be important to people who might choose to settle there.

NATIONAL GEOGRAPHIC | LEARNING FRAMEWORK ACTIVITIES

Prepare a Leadership Memo

ATTITUDE Responsibility

SKILLS Observation, Problem-Solving

Effective leaders possess solid diplomatic, communication, and problem-solving skills. Choose a leader that you read about in this unit and, using evidence from the reading, prepare a memo from that leader's point of view. In your memo, outline what you as that leader accomplished—or wish you had—by approaching problems in your community or colony with diplomacy. Offer examples of specific events or problems that your leader participated in or encountered. Then present your leadership memo to the class.

Create a Trade Network

SKILL Collaboration

KNOWLEDGE Our Human Story

Work with a team of classmates to create a trade network. Decide what products or resources you would trade with other groups and what products or resources you would like to acquire. Collaborate with your classmates on setting prices and quantities for products and resources to be traded. Then determine how your network will exchange goods. Illustrate your trade network on a classroom whiteboard. When all groups have added their networks to the board, discuss the ways in which the networks are similar to and different from each other.

A NEW NATION

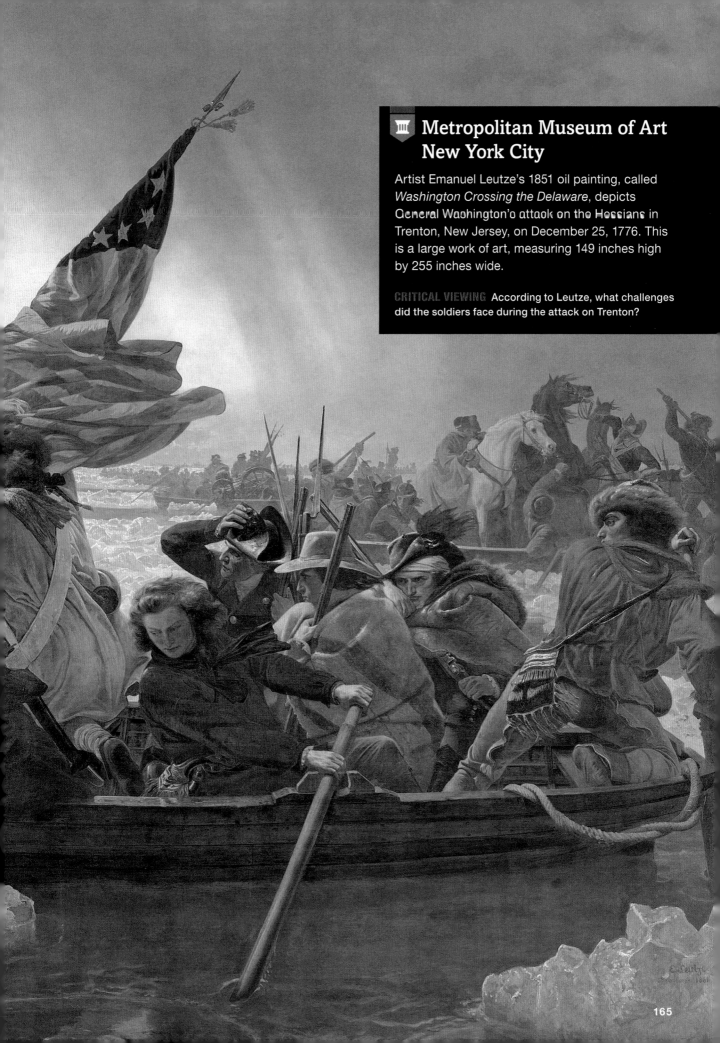

Artist Emanuel Leutze's 1851 oil painting, called *Washington Crossing the Delaware*, depicts General Washington's attack on the Hessians in Trenton, New Jersey, on December 25, 1776. This is a large work of art, measuring 149 inches high by 255 inches wide.

CRITICAL VIEWING According to Leutze, what challenges did the soldiers face during the attack on Trenton?

THE UNITED STATES

1776

The Declaration of Independence, which announces the formation of the United States of America and its independence from Britain, is adopted on July 4. *(the original Declaration of Independence)*

1775
After a shot is fired in Lexington, Massachusetts, the American Revolution begins.

1773
Colonists board three ships in Boston Harbor and throw 342 boxes of tea overboard to protest the Tea Act. The protest comes to be known as the Boston Tea Party.

1765
The Stamp Act is imposed, requiring American colonists to pay a tax on nearly every piece of paper they use. *(colonial teapot protesting the Stamp Act)*

1770

1760

1765 ASIA
China invades Burma and begins a war with that country.

THE WORLD

1770 OCEANIA
British captain James Cook explores the east coast of Australia and claims the region for Great Britain. *(replica of James Cook's ship, the* Endeavour*)*

1763 AMERICAS
France is defeated in the French and Indian War and surrenders most of its North American colonies to Britain and Spain.

HISTORICAL THINKING: DETERMINE CHRONOLOGY

What world events occurred at the same time as events leading to the formation of the United States?

1789
George Washington becomes the first president of the United States. *(Statue on the steps of New York's Federal Hall celebrates the site of Washington's inauguration.)*

1787–1788
Delegates at the Constitutional Convention draft, sign, and ratify the U.S. Constitution, which becomes the supreme law of the land.

1791
The Bill of Rights, guaranteeing individual rights, is added to the U.S. Constitution.

1783
The United States defeats Britain, and the American Revolution ends when representatives from both sides sign the Treaty of Paris.

1790

1791 AMERICAS
In the French colony of Saint-Domingue on the Caribbean island of Hispaniola, slaves rebel against French authority.

1800

1780

1779 AFRICA
Luanda, a city on Africa's Atlantic coast, becomes the leading port in the African slave trade.

1789 EUROPE
Inspired by Enlightenment thinkers, the French people attack the Bastille, a prison in Paris, and start a revolution. (Storming of the Bastille *by Jean-Pierre Houël*)

A New Nation **167**

CHAPTER 5

THE ROAD TO
REVOLUTION
1763–1776

ESSENTIAL QUESTION
Why did the colonists decide to break from Britain?

AMERICAN STORIES Our American Identity

SECTION 1 British Control
KEY VOCABULARY

boycott	militia	repeal	Stamp Act
Currency Act	Proclamation of 1763	revenue	Sugar Act
duty	Quartering Act	Sons of Liberty	tyranny
grievance			

SECTION 2 Rebellion in the Colonies
KEY VOCABULARY

Boston Massacre	committee of correspondence	Townshend Acts
Boston Tea Party	Tea Act	writ of assistance

SECTION 3 Lexington and Concord
KEY VOCABULARY

First Continental Congress	Loyalist	Patriot
Intolerable Acts	minutemen	

SECTION 4 Declaring Independence
KEY VOCABULARY

artillery	earthwork	Second Continental Congress
Continental Army	geology	terrain
Declaration of Independence	Hessian	unalienable right
drumlin		

AMERICAN GALLERY ONLINE Colonial Boston

READING STRATEGY

ANALYZE CAUSE AND EFFECT
When you analyze cause and effect, you note the consequences of an event, an action, or a condition. As you read the chapter, use a graphic organizer like this one to identify the causes of the colonies' separation from Britain.

Causes   Effect

The colonies declare independence from Britain.

In this photo by National Geographic photographer Kenneth Garrett, reenactors stage a battle in Leesburg, Virginia. What details in the photo convey what fighting on the front lines of this battle might have been like?

"These are the times that try men's souls."
—Thomas Paine

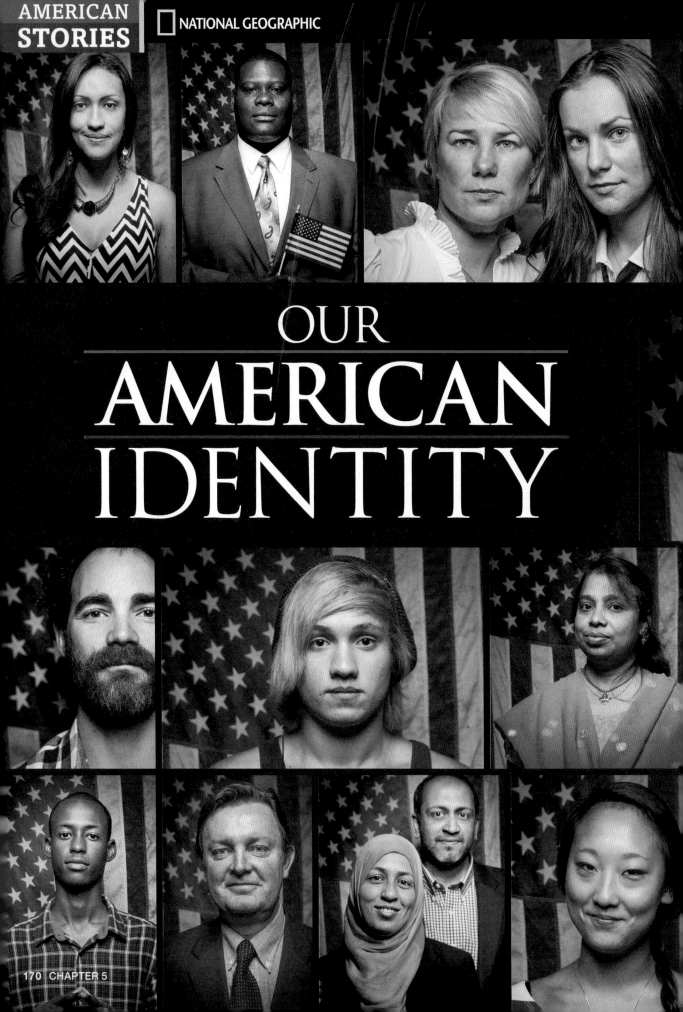

NATIONAL GEOGRAPHIC

OUR
AMERICAN
IDENTITY

The American flag is one of the most recognizable national symbols. For many of us, seeing it at just the right moment or in just the right setting sends shivers down our spines, raises goosebumps on our arms, or brings tears to our eyes.

Why does a simple piece of cloth have the power to provoke such a physical reaction in so many people? The answer may be simple: identity. For many, being an American is part of our identity, and the flag may be a symbol of that part of us. It reminds us that being part of a country influences who we are as individuals.

The Stars and Stripes solemnly drapes the caskets of fallen heroes returning from battle, sheltering them with the gratitude of their country as they are laid to rest. The flag waves proudly at sporting events, representative of the strength and perseverance the United States was built upon and the country's passion for sports and competition. Clothing that bears the flag is often worn to make a statement—to identify the wearer. It says: I'm a firefighter. I'm a soldier. I'm a Girl Scout. I'm an astronaut. I'm a veteran. I'm an athlete. I'm a relief worker. I live in the United States. I represent the United States. I support the United States.

Where did this important icon come from, and what does its story tell us about the establishment of national identity?

Their faces may be different, but these individuals all identified as Americans and first-time voters in the 2012 presidential election. Here they are shown posing in front of the American flag after casting their ballots in Bridgeport, Connecticut.

On July 4, 1776, representatives of the 13 American colonies approved the Declaration of Independence, formally announcing their break with Britain. Soon after the Declaration was drafted, the Continental Congress passed an act establishing an official flag for the new nation: "Resolved, that the flag of the United States be thirteen stripes, alternate red and white; that the union be thirteen stars, white in a blue field, representing a new constellation." This description doesn't fit the look of the flag as we know it today, but it describes the first of many versions of the flag—the earliest official national symbol and the emblem of independence from Great Britain.

Fast forward to September 13, 1814. The War of 1812 rages on, with British and American troops battling fiercely at Fort McHenry in Baltimore, Maryland. At this point in history, the American flag featured 15 stars and 15 stripes. Fort McHenry served both as the military stronghold that stood between the harbor and the city and as the United States' last hope to prevent a major British military victory. As British rockets and bombs flew from ships, letting loose a deadly deluge of shrapnel and fire over the fort, American gunners responded with their own fire, pushing the British back. The fighting continued all night as a young Washington lawyer named Francis Scott Key watched from a boat in the harbor. While the fiery battle carried on, Key wondered which country would emerge victorious and whose flag he would see flying above the fort in the morning.

It was the American Stars and Stripes—a huge flag measuring 30 feet by 42 feet, made out of red, white, and blue wool by a Baltimore seamstress. The sight of the flag flying proudly over Fort McHenry that morning was so moving it inspired Key to draft the original version of the poem that would become our national anthem: "The Star-Spangled Banner."

CRITICAL VIEWING Think about a time you attended an event or game that began with "The Star-Spangled Banner," and consider this photograph of the stadium. What might a person from another country infer about American identity from these traditions?

THE STAR-SPANGLED BANNER

O say can you see, by the dawn's early light,
What so proudly we hail'd at the twilight's last gleaming,
Whose broad stripes and bright stars through the perilous fight
O'er the ramparts we watch'd were so gallantly streaming?
And the rocket's red glare, the bombs bursting in air,
Gave proof through the night that our flag was still there,
O say does that star-spangled banner yet wave
O'er the land of the free and the home of the brave?

Inspired by the sight of the American flag after a U.S. victory over the British during the War of 1812, Francis Scott Key wrote the 1814 lyrics that were set, ironically, to the tune of a popular British song and became "The Star-Spangled Banner." This song is still the go-to musical expression of patriotism in the United States.

After the United States entered World War I, patriotic music was often played at professional baseball games. In game one of the 1918 World Series, the Cubs and Red Sox players faced the American flag while the band played "The Star-Spangled Banner" with the crowd singing along. This sparked the tradition of playing the song at U.S. sporting events, even though it wouldn't be declared the national anthem by Congress until 1931.

This three-cent stamp honoring Francis Scott Key was issued August 9, 1948. It features Key's portrait and home, the American flags of 1814 and 1948, and Fort McHenry.

For the next 100 years, American military families cared for and proudly displayed the famous Fort McHenry flag. During the Civil War, they hid the flag to keep it safe. Until 1880, small pieces of the flag were even cut and given to war veterans and others—something considered disrespectful and unpatriotic by today's standards. The flag finally landed safely in the Smithsonian National Museum in 1912, 98 years after it flew over Fort McHenry. It remains part of the Smithsonian collection today.

The look of the American flag has evolved along with the nation. Stars and stripes have been added and relocated as the country has expanded, endured the horrors of civil and global wars, and acquired new territories. But the impact and symbolic value of the flag has remained steadfast to many Americans. Many of us view the American flag as a symbol of our identity as U.S. citizens, but it's not the only symbol of national identity, nor does a person have to attach to *any* symbol in order to establish his or her identity. Maybe your identity as an American is revealed in a different way. Or maybe a different symbol of national identity has more meaning to you. A person. A logo. A slogan. A poem. When it comes to what defines your unique identity, you have many rich and wonderful choices.

THINK ABOUT IT

What type of symbol represents your identity as an American? Why?

THE PLEDGE OF ALLEGIANCE

I pledge allegiance to the flag of the United States of America, and to the republic for which it stands, one nation under God, indivisible, with liberty and justice for all.

If you go to school in the United States, you've probably recited the Pledge of Allegiance many times. Written in 1892 by Francis Bellamy, a Baptist minister from New York, the pledge was intended as a salute to the American flag, to be read in unison by schoolchildren. Over time, its words have been changed and debated—especially the phrase "under God," which some people feel violates the constitutional separation of church and state. What do you think?

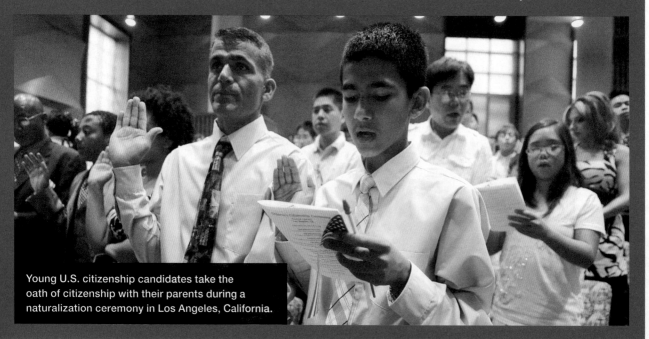

Young U.S. citizenship candidates take the oath of citizenship with their parents during a naturalization ceremony in Los Angeles, California.

A SYMBOL OF A NATION

You'd expect to see the American flag on American soil, but the Stars and Stripes can be seen in many interesting and meaningful places across the world—and out of this world!

Why might people visiting faraway destinations want others to know about their nation's flag? Maybe it's the item they feel identifies them most clearly as Americans. Think about what symbol of national identity you might use when visiting another country.

1 Marchers carry American and Cuban flags at a 2015 rally focused on human rights abuses by the Castro regime. The United States restored diplomatic ties with Cuba in late 2014 after 53 years of distrust.

2 The famous sculpture at the Marine Corps Memorial in Arlington, Virginia, depicts U.S. Marines raising the flag on the island of Iwo Jima, Japan, after a major victory during World War II. The sculpture is based on a photo of the actual flag-raising captured by photographer Joe Rosenthal in February 1945.

3 This customized version of the flag was used at a peaceful protest at the Washington Monument in 1969.

4 Astronaut Buzz Aldrin posed for this 1969 photograph beside the American flag he and Neil Armstrong planted on the moon.

PRESERVING THE STAR-SPANGLED BANNER

The enormous flag raised over Baltimore's Fort McHenry to announce the American victory over the British during the War of 1812 has seen better days. Time, use, and questionable storage have rendered it dirty and fragile, and the flag itself—this important relic of American history—is now at risk of falling apart.

Beginning in 1998, great efforts have been made to preserve this 1814 flag, the inspiration for Francis Scott Key's composition of "The Star-Spangled Banner." The flag has been safely housed in the National Museum of American History since the early 1900s. It is now stored with attention to preservation, at a 10-degree angle in a low-oxygen, low-light chamber. Experts routinely examine the flag's delicate fibers with microscopes, looking for signs of decay or damage.

As you read about the events leading up to the American Revolution in this chapter, consider why having a flag to represent an emerging American identity would have been important to the colonists.

CRITICAL VIEWING What details from these photographs reveal how this museum balances preserving the flag with displaying it for public view?

1 For more than 30 years, the Star-Spangled Banner hung in the central Flag Hall at the museum. But in 1998, the flag entered a 10-year-long restoration process.

2 To repair the flag, the conservation team had to first remove its soiled linen backing. This meant clipping about 1.7 million stitches that had held the backing in place since 1914 and using tweezers to lift each one away.

3 The team used dry sponges to gently remove dirt from the side of the flag that had been covered by the linen. The dirt itself was analyzed to learn more about the flag's history.

4 Much of the restoration of the flag was done in a special lab that allowed museum visitors to watch the process through a glass wall. A movable bridge called a gantry allowed conservation team members to hang above the flag as they restored it.

1.1 Limits on Freedom

As far as the British were concerned, 1763 was a great year. They had won the French and Indian War—a major victory. Business in the colonies was booming, which put money into the British economy. What could possibly go wrong?

MAIN IDEA After the French and Indian War, the British government enacted laws that restricted some of the colonies' freedoms.

PROBLEMS ARISE

At the end of the French and Indian War, the British colonists in North America had plenty of reasons to be optimistic about their future as British subjects. The colonies' **militias**, or groups of local men who organized to protect their town or colony, had proven themselves to be able fighters alongside British soldiers. After decades of economic growth, the colonies were prosperous. Still, some of the colonists felt a growing dissatisfaction.

The British colonies were the only European settlements in North America where ordinary people could vote for their local legislatures. This freedom to govern, however, was limited by **King George III** and the British Parliament. King George believed the role of a colony was to support the mother country. He was determined to maintain control of Britain's North American colonies.

Concerned about the high cost of the French and Indian War, the king was eager to limit contact between the Native Americans and the colonists in order to keep the peace. As you have read, the king issued a law requiring colonists to stay east of a line drawn on a map along the crest of the Appalachian Mountains. This law was called the **Proclamation of 1763**.

Settlers in the western areas objected to the proclamation. They felt the king was restricting their freedom to expand colonial territories westward. In fact, people continued to settle west of the line decreed by the proclamation. The British government, weighed down by debt from the French and Indian War, could not afford to send soldiers to enforce the law.

SOLDIERS IN THE COLONIES

Soon, colonists along the eastern coast also found themselves frustrated by laws they found oppressive. After the war, many British soldiers were moved into port cities such as New York and Boston to help enforce laws. In 1765, the British Parliament passed the **Quartering Act**. The Quartering Act required colonists to provide

CRITICAL VIEWING This hand-colored engraving (right) shows British soldiers housed in an American home during the 1770s. What do the details in this image help you infer about the colonists' reactions to the Quartering Act?

The Proclamation of 1763

This historical map shows the land assigned to the colonists and Native Americans by the Proclamation of 1763. The colonists resented the proclamation, and many continued to push west of the Appalachians into land long inhabited by Native Americans. This migration weakened an agreement called the Covenant Chain. A covenant is an agreement or promise between two parties.

The Covenant Chain was a complicated system of alliances established between the nations of the Iroquois League and the northernmost colonies. The chain originated around 1677 and lasted for a century. It helped European settlers and some Native American groups maintain mostly peaceful relationships, but that friendship was tested as new settlers began to claim Native American lands.

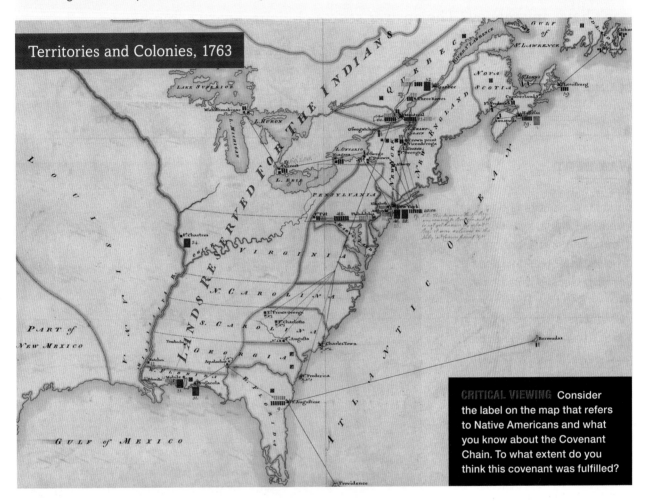

Territories and Colonies, 1763

CRITICAL VIEWING Consider the label on the map that refers to Native Americans and what you know about the Covenant Chain. To what extent do you think this covenant was fulfilled?

housing for British soldiers. If a city did not have barracks to house the soldiers, the men were housed in local inns, homes, and stables, or vacant houses or barns.

While the Quartering Act did not allow the British troops to kick people out of their homes, local governments and residents still resented being forced to house the soldiers. The New York colonial assembly refused to enforce the Quartering Act. In all the colonies, the presence of British troops provoked tension and hostility between soldiers and the civilians who had begun to identify less with the British and more as Americans.

HISTORICAL THINKING

1. **READING CHECK** What were the goals of the Proclamation of 1763 and the Quartering Act?

2. **COMPARE AND CONTRAST** In what ways were the complaints of eastern and western colonists similar and different?

3. **DETERMINE WORD MEANING** What does *prosperous* mean in the sentence, "After decades of economic growth, the colonists were prosperous"?

1.2 Taxation Without Representation

If you borrow money from a friend to buy an amazing pair of sneakers, eventually you'll have to pay off your debt. But how can you do that if you don't have any money? The answer seems obvious—earn some money. But it wasn't that simple for King George and Parliament.

> **MAIN IDEA** British attempts to impose taxes and exert greater control over the colonies caused growing anger and resentment among colonists.

WAR DEBT

The French and Indian War had been an expensive undertaking for the British government. Maintaining and supplying an army in distant colonies had left King George with a hefty debt. In addition, Britain was still keeping 10,000 soldiers in North America to protect the colonies. The British government needed **revenue**, or income, to pay off its debts and expenses.

King George appointed a new prime minister, George Grenville, who agreed that the colonies should be strictly controlled by Britain. Grenville concluded that the colonies should pay for the war debt and the continuing maintenance of the troops in North America. After all, he reasoned, the colonies had benefited the most from the French and Indian War. To raise the money, Grenville sought ways to tax the colonies directly, rather than allowing colonial assemblies to pass taxes. What followed was a series of acts that would have big consequences.

King George III

King George III (1738–1820) ruled Britain for 59 years. "Born and educated in this country," he said, "I glory in the name of Britain." But the war with America was hard on George. He became seriously ill around 1788 and continued to decline until 1811, when his son, George IV, became the acting king and eventually took the throne. A 2005 study of a hair sample from George III suggested that the king may have become ill and died from arsenic poisoning.

Colonial Currency
Colonial currency came in different shapes, and its designs were very detailed, as the five-pound note (left) issued in New York in 1759 shows. The Pennsylvania 15-shilling note below was produced by Benjamin Franklin and issued on January 1, 1756. It featured multiple anti-counterfeiting processes invented by Franklin, including the blue thread that ran through the note.

ACTS OF PARLIAMENT

The **Sugar Act** of 1764 was among the first of the new taxes. This law was designed to raise revenue as well as to reinforce British control over the colonies. The Sugar Act actually lowered the **duty**, or tax, on the imported molasses used to produce rum in the colonies. The goal of the Sugar Act was to encourage merchants to pay the lower duty instead of smuggling molasses into the colonies to avoid paying the tax, as they had been doing before. This would then increase revenue to the British government.

The **Currency Act**, also passed in 1764, aimed to more tightly control the colonial economy. Previously, different colonies had issued their own paper money. The Currency Act declared that only British currency could be used in the colonies. As colonists discarded the now-useless colonial paper money, the resulting shortage of British currency in the colonies created a number of economic difficulties.

Not surprisingly, the colonists voiced several **grievances**, or objections, to Britain's attempts to tax and control them. They had come to resent the policy of mercantilism—trade designed to bring wealth primarily to the mother country—which was now strengthened by the Sugar Act and Currency Act. The colonists were further frustrated when a new prime minister tightened the Navigation Acts, which controlled colonial trade and shipping, to benefit Britain.

Some accused the British of **tyranny**, or unjust rule by an absolute ruler. They used the slogan "no taxation without representation." Colonists argued that Parliament did not have the right to impose direct taxes on them because they did not have representatives in Parliament who could vote on taxes.

HISTORICAL THINKING

1. **READING CHECK** In what ways did the British government try to raise revenue and control the colonies at the same time?

2. **MAKE INFERENCES** How did the Sugar Act and Currency Act reinforce Britain's policy of mercantilism?

3. **ANALYZE CAUSE AND EFFECT** What impact did these acts likely have on the ways colonists did business?

1.3 The Stamp Act

In 1765, the easiest way to become unpopular with your neighbors was to be appointed by the king to collect his latest tax.

MAIN IDEA An attempt to impose a new type of tax sparked open protests and violent action, which forced the British government to repeal the tax.

A NEW KIND OF TAX

Passed by Parliament in 1765, the **Stamp Act** provoked an even greater storm of protest. Unlike previous laws, the Stamp Act did nothing to further Britain's mercantilist aims. Instead, it was designed purely to raise revenue to pay for the soldiers stationed in the colonies.

The Stamp Act required that all printed materials have a special government stamp. Items subject to the law included newspapers, playing cards, court documents, and sales receipts for land. So, for example, a person selling or buying a piece of land would also pay a British official to stamp the sales document. Colonists could only pay officials for the stamp with gold or silver coins—both of which were rare in the colonies. British courts enforced the Stamp Act by taking away any land or property involved in sales conducted without the stamps.

To the colonists, the Stamp Act was a shocking example of taxation without representation. Philadelphia merchant John Reynell said, "The point in dispute is a very important one, if the Americans are to be taxed by a Parliament where they are not nor can be Represented, they are no longer Englishmen but Slaves."

PROTESTING BRITISH GOODS

Colonial reactions to the Stamp Act were increasingly angry. **Patrick Henry** was a young politician and newly elected to Virginia's House of Burgesses. He persuaded the assembly to pass a series of resolutions that defended the colonists' right to tax themselves rather than to be taxed by Parliament. The resolutions declared that "the General Assembly of this colony . . . have the sole right . . . to lay taxes and impositions upon its inhabitants." When newspapers spread word of

Stamp Act Resistance
The hated Stamp Act was scheduled to take effect on November 1, 1765. Philadelphia newspaper printer William Bradford designed the October 31 "tombstone edition" of the *Pennsylvania Journal* with this skull and crossbones "stamp" to represent the death of the newspaper due to the Stamp Act. Bradford then ignored the act and continued publishing his paper.

Virginia's action, other colonies responded. Rhode Island instructed officials to ignore the stamp tax. Several other colonies passed resolutions similar to Virginia's resolution.

Colonists in cities such as Boston and Philadelphia soon realized they had more in common with each other than with Britain, and they began to organize. In Boston, a group rioted against the Stamp Act.

Museum of Fine Arts, Boston

Paul Revere was a father, husband, silversmith, and member of the Sons of Liberty. He left his mark on America by crafting many treasures relating to the American Revolution. Some of Revere's finest work is housed in Boston's Museum of Fine Arts.

The Sons of Liberty Bowl featured the engraved names of 92 members of the Massachusetts House of Representatives. In 1767, they refused to retract a letter sent throughout the colonies protesting the Townshend Acts, which taxed paper, tea, glass, and other goods imported from Britain. This act of peaceful protest by the "Glorious Ninety-Two" was a major step leading to the American Revolution.

In the same year that Paul Revere crafted the Sons of Liberty Bowl, artist John Singleton Copley (KOP-lee) honored the silversmith by painting his portrait. Copley's decision to represent Revere as an artisan at work embodies the concept of Americans as builders and crafters throughout history.

Sons of Liberty Bowl Commissioned by the Sons of Liberty and made by Paul Revere, this silver bowl joins the Declaration of Independence and the Constitution as the nation's three most precious historical treasures.

Paul Revere In 1768, Copley painted Paul Revere engraving a teapot. It is his only finished portrait of an artisan at work.

They damaged the home of Andrew Oliver, the official in charge of stamping documents, and destroyed the governor's house. Oliver promptly resigned. Protestors in other colonies also acted to prevent the distribution of stamps. By the end of 1765, the stamp distributors in all the colonies except Georgia had resigned.

Some of the men who led the angry crowds called themselves the **Sons of Liberty**. They were mostly merchants, shopkeepers, and craftsmen. The Sons of Liberty also organized a **boycott**, a form of protest that involves refusing to purchase goods or services. Merchants in New York City, Boston, and Philadelphia agreed to stop importing goods from Britain.

In 1766, the protestors succeeded. Parliament **repealed**, or canceled, the Stamp Act. The colonists had taken their first major step toward independence from Britain and creating a new American identity.

HISTORICAL THINKING

1. **READING CHECK** How did the Stamp Act raise revenue for the British government?

2. **MAKE INFERENCES** Why did the Stamp Act provoke such a strong response?

3. **ANALYZE CAUSE AND EFFECT** What events led up to the repeal of the Stamp Act?

1.4 Benjamin Franklin 1706–1790

"To succeed, jump as quickly at opportunities as you do at conclusions."—Benjamin Franklin

Benjamin Franklin seized just about every opportunity that came his way. When he was 17, he ran away from his home in Boston to seek a fresh start in a new city. He eventually ended up in Philadelphia. There, the multitalented Franklin worked as a printer, an inventor, and a scientist. His experiments on the nature of electricity, conducted with his famous kite, brought him international fame. But it is as a statesman that he is best known—and honored.

A REPRESENTATIVE IN ENGLAND

When the Stamp Act was passed in 1765, Franklin was in England, serving as a colonial representative. He'd been in the country off and on since 1757 and, by all accounts, enjoyed his stay there. Franklin liked to dine in fine restaurants and go to the theater—comforts that the more rustic colonies lacked. He opposed the Stamp Act but didn't think it could be stopped. Franklin had even ordered British stamps to be used in his Philadelphia printing firm.

The colonists' response to the passage of the act took him completely by surprise. Franklin learned that mobs of Americans were joining together to prevent the act's enforcement. He also discovered that his acceptance of the despised Stamp Act

🏛 The National Portrait Gallery Washington, D.C.

French artist Joseph Siffred Duplessis painted two very similar portraits of Benjamin Franklin, but only this one hangs in the National Portrait Gallery. For the most part, only the color and style of Franklin's coat differ in the two paintings. In both, as one person noted, the subject's "large forehead suggests strength of mind" and his expression conveys "the smile of an unshakeable serenity."

Our American Identity

You may have seen the "Join, or Die" cartoon before, but did you know that Franklin was the artist? The pieces of the snake are meant to roughly represent the 13 colonies. "N.E." stands for the New England colonies of New Hampshire, Massachusetts, Rhode Island, and Connecticut.

Franklin's cartoon found its most popular meaning later, when the colonists' futures were at risk. For many, the choice to support the colonies in North America involved abandoning their identity as Europeans and, instead, identifying themselves as Americans at a time when no one knew what that might mean. The stakes were high, but the eloquent words of people like Franklin carried the day.

JOIN, or DIE

had begun to tarnish his reputation. Stirred to action, Franklin spoke eloquently to Parliament, condemning the act and explaining the colonists' position. His speech was instrumental in the act's repeal. The experience made Franklin feel what he called his "Americanness" as never before. He also began to question his loyalty to Britain and its treatment of the colonies.

A SUPPORTER OF INDEPENDENCE

Over the next few years, Franklin tried to smooth over the differences between Britain and the colonies and help each side understand the other. To achieve that goal, he worked closely with Thomas Hutchinson, the governor of Massachusetts. Hutchinson was supposed to defend the rights of the colonists, but he really acted on behalf of King George. Secretly, he was working to limit the colonists' rights. When Franklin uncovered letters that detailed Hutchinson's intentions, he sent them to America. The letters fueled the colonists' anger with British rule.

The letters' release also led the British government to condemn Franklin, who shortly thereafter returned to America. His experiences in England had convinced him that the colonies should break away from Britain. At the outset of the French and

Indian War in 1754, Franklin had created a political cartoon called "Join, or Die" to urge the colonies to unite and fight with Great Britain against the French. Now the cartoon came to symbolize colonial unity against the British.

As colonial protests mounted against Britain and the king, Franklin became a strong voice for independence and democracy. He would help draft the Declaration of Independence and was among the first to sign it, saying as he did so, "We must indeed all hang together, or most assuredly we shall all hang separately."

HISTORICAL THINKING

1. **READING CHECK** What official role did Franklin have while he lived in England?

2. **ANALYZE CAUSE AND EFFECT** What realization led to Franklin's dissatisfaction with British rule?

3. **MAKE INFERENCES** Franklin said he was feeling his "Americanness" as never before. How might Franklin have described the American identity at that time in history?

2.1 Colonial Protests Grow

You're a young Boston colonist in 1768. "Sorry, son. There's no tea today," your mother says at breakfast. "We're boycotting British imports again." How would you feel about doing without your favorite food or drink to make a point?

MAIN IDEA Britain's attempt to raise revenue and control the colonies through the Townshend Acts led to protests and violence.

THE TOWNSHEND ACTS

Colonists celebrated the Stamp Act's repeal. However, the British government insisted that it had not lost any authority over the colonies. But with the Stamp Act repealed, Britain had to figure out other ways of gaining revenue.

In 1767, Parliament passed the **Townshend Acts**, named after Charles Townshend, a British royal treasurer. The acts placed duties on tea, glass, paper, lead, and paint—all goods that the colonies were required to purchase only from Britain. The revenue from the Townshend Acts would be used by the British to pay the salaries of colonial governors and judges. Previously, these officials had been paid by the colonial assemblies. By paying officials directly, the British government would establish greater control over the day-to-day running of the colonies.

The Townshend Acts also required colonial courts to provide **writs of assistance**, or search warrants, so officials could search houses and businesses for smuggled goods. Writs of assistance had existed for several years, and colonists had protested them. To the colonists, the writs allowed the British to search without cause and to justify random searches, and the Townshend Acts only expanded their use.

THE COLONISTS REACT

Colonists once again protested and accused the British government of tyranny. The protestors were strongly influenced by the 17th century British philosopher **John Locke**, who wrote that a leader could rule only with the consent of the people.

Daughters of Liberty

In the 1770s, colonial women contributed significantly to the anti-British movement. They even spun yarn to reduce colonial dependence on British textiles, prompting Samuel Adams to declare, "With the ladies on our side, we can make every Tory tremble."

This image of a colonial woman holding a flintlock musket appeared on a broadside, a single-sided newspaper, around 1779. A symbol of strength and patriotism, she wears a man's hat, holds her weapon and powder horn, and is pictured in front of a British fort.

He stated that government exists to uphold natural rights, or rights such as life or liberty that a person is born with. Any government that failed in this task should be overthrown. The colonists strongly identified with Locke's way of thinking.

Samuel Adams was a follower of Locke's philosophy, a member of the Massachusetts Assembly, and a leader of the Sons of Liberty. In 1768, Adams cowrote a letter with lawyer James Otis to the other colonial assemblies. The letter objected to the new duties and proposed a boycott of British goods. The British governor of Massachusetts threatened to dismiss the assembly if it did not take back the letter. Defiantly, the assembly refused, and it was disbanded.

Samuel Adams and the Sons of Liberty vigorously continued to support actions against the Townshend Acts. Colonists in Boston signed an agreement to boycott British imports, and merchants in New York soon followed. Women also used their purchasing power to protest the Townshend Acts. A group called **Daughters of Liberty** boycotted imported tea and clothing. To replace imported cloth, they wove their own fabric, known as homespun, from American yarn and wool.

The Great Awakening of the 1730s and 1740s also helped push the colonists toward rebellion and independence. During that revival movement, believers challenged the authority of their church leaders. They learned to use their own judgment in matters of religion. The habit of thinking independently spread throughout the colonies. By the 1770s, the ideas of the Great Awakening had helped create a revolutionary fervor among the colonists, which led them to challenge Britain's authority.

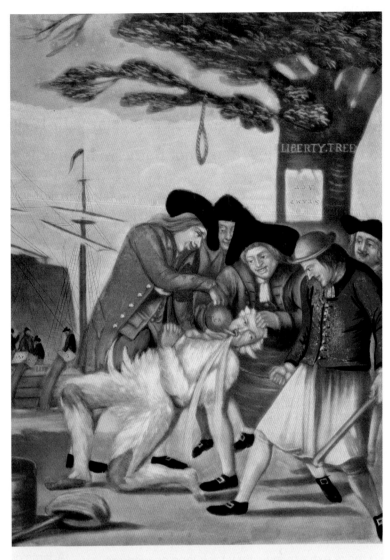

Tar and Feathers

Sometimes angry protestors used tar and feathers to punish people who supported British taxes. Victims would be dragged to a public place. Then they would be coated with hot, sticky tar and covered in feathers, as shown in this 1774 political cartoon. Tarring and feathering was often portrayed in a humorous way, but it was in fact horribly painful.

HISTORICAL THINKING

1. **READING CHECK** How were the Townshend Acts intended to accomplish Britain's goals in the colonies?

2. **ANALYZE CAUSE AND EFFECT** In what ways did Locke's philosophy influence the colonists in their protest against British actions?

3. **MAKE PREDICTIONS** What might result from the boycotts against the Townshend Acts?

2.2 The Boston Massacre

If you place a flame too close to a powder keg full of explosive gunpowder, it will blow up spectacularly. In 1770, Boston was like a powder keg, and a hot flame was quickly approaching.

MAIN IDEA Tensions between the British troops and the colonists in Boston reached a breaking point when some soldiers fired on an angry crowd of citizens.

TENSIONS RISE

In response to growing protests and increasing unrest among colonists, British authorities brought additional troops to Boston. Some of the soldiers camped out on Boston Common, an open area that was intended for all Bostonians to use.

This arrangement made for a tense situation. Frequent fights broke out between soldiers and civilians. To annoy the British soldiers, children followed them in the streets, taunting them and calling them names such as "redcoats" and "lobsterbacks" because of the bright red uniforms they wore.

In addition, the British soldiers were poorly paid. To make extra money, they took jobs as workers during their off-duty hours. This took jobs away from some Bostonians, who were angry at losing work to soldiers they already despised.

On March 5, 1770, a boy began yelling insults at a British soldier standing guard at a government building. The soldier hit the boy with his gun. A rowdy crowd gathered around the commotion, and Captain Thomas Preston led a group of seven additional soldiers out to diffuse the situation. The crowd grew larger, throwing snowballs, ice, and sticks at the soldiers. Then someone hit a soldier with a club, knocking his gun out of his hands.

TENSIONS EXPLODE

Suddenly Preston's men were firing at the crowd. Five townspeople were killed and six were injured. This event soon became known as the **Boston Massacre**. To the colonists, the killings would come to symbolize all that they hated about British rule.

The first man shot and killed was **Crispus Attucks**, an African American and former slave who worked as a sailor and rope maker in Boston. Attucks is considered to be the first person to die in the quest for American independence.

After the shooting, the soldiers were arrested and put on trial for murder. At the trial, they were represented by lawyer **John Adams**, a cousin of Samuel Adams. This surprised some people because John Adams was a well-known Patriot, or supporter of colonial self-rule, in addition to being a respected lawyer. But he was also a firm believer in the right to a fair trial for everyone, no matter how unpopular they were.

Adams claimed that the soldiers had fired in self-defense. He made his case so eloquently that Captain Preston and all but two of the soldiers were found not guilty. Many people, including John Adams, thought this trial would be the end of his legal career. Yet in the end, Bostonians came to respect Adams for making the unpopular but ethical choice. He went on to have a distinguished career in politics, including serving as the first vice president and second president of the United States.

HISTORICAL THINKING

1. **READING CHECK** What events led up to the Boston Massacre?

2. **MAKE INFERENCES** What was the general feeling in Boston in 1770?

3. **ANALYZE VISUALS** What similarities and differences can you identify in the two depictions of the Boston Massacre at right?

The Bloody Massacre

American Patriot Paul Revere wasn't the first person to use a tragic incident to sway people's opinions, but he did it particularly effectively in the engraved print on the left. Titled *The Bloody Massacre in King Street*, the print shows a line of British soldiers firing into an unarmed crowd when, in fact, violence erupted on both sides. If you look closely at the white building on the right—the Customs House—you can also see that Revere changed its name to "Butcher's Hall." You may also notice that Crispus Attucks isn't represented in the print.

In fact, Attucks wouldn't be portrayed as a person of color until artist William L. Champney depicted him at the event in his 1855 drawing *Boston Massacre*. The antislavery movement was at its height, so the artist placed Attucks squarely in the center of the action. He also shows the colonists taking a more active role in the fight—probably a more accurate depiction of the incident.

A GLOBAL PERSPECTIVE We may be an ocean apart, but the people of the United States and France are similar in many ways. When a protest march was cancelled in Paris's Place de la Republique in 2015 due to concerns about terrorism, protestors placed thousands of pairs of shoes in the square as a silent yet effective expression of their protest and presence. How does this public protest compare to the Boston Tea Party?

The Boston Tea Party

Sit-ins, marches, posters, and chants are the tools of peaceful protest. They help people express displeasure or opposition without violence. The colonists were angry with the British, but sometimes they found ways to make their feelings known without lifting a weapon.

> **MAIN IDEA** When Parliament imposed new laws to regulate tea, colonists responded by throwing a cargo of British tea into Boston Harbor.

NEW LAW, OLD TAX

At about the same time as the Boston Massacre, the British government decided to repeal most of the Townshend Acts. The taxes on all the items listed in the act were lifted, except for the tax on tea. There were fewer protests, and for two years, the relationship between Britain and the colonies was generally calm.

But in 1772, Patriots in Rhode Island burned a British ship that had been searching local boats for smugglers. When news of the attack reached England, Parliament once again began passing laws to gain greater control over the colonies. In Massachusetts, Samuel Adams responded by forming a **committee of correspondence**. This group made a list of British offenses against the colonies' rights and published it in Massachusetts. Other colonies joined in the movement by forming their own committees.

The committees soon had a new complaint. In 1773, Parliament passed the **Tea Act**, allowing the British East India Company to sell tea directly in the colonies. This lowered the price of tea, but it also took money away from colonial tea merchants. The prime minister also refused to repeal the Townshend Acts' tax on tea.

Despite the fact that cheaper tea would now be available, the new law fanned the flames of colonial resentment toward Britain. Colonial tea merchants were close to going out of business, and Parliament was still taxing the colonists without representation.

TEA OVERBOARD!

At first, the colonists protested by making it difficult for the British East India Company to deliver shipments of tea. Workers in major cities refused to unload shipments of tea from ships in port. In New York and Philadelphia, the ships' captains were told to return to England.

On the night of December 16, 1773, members of the Sons of Liberty disguised themselves as Native Americans and boarded three ships loaded with tea in Boston Harbor. Without harming the ships' other cargo, they dumped the tea into the icy water while thousands of people on shore watched the events of the **Boston Tea Party** unfold.

The Boston Tea Party was not the only act of colonial defiance that involved tea. On October 14, 1774, in Annapolis, Maryland, a ship with a cargo of tea was set on fire. King George was furious. Soon Parliament would enact new laws to punish the colonists for their actions, and the stage would be set for further conflicts.

HISTORICAL THINKING

1. **READING CHECK** In what ways did the colonists protest the Tea Act?

2. **FORM AND SUPPORT OPINIONS** Was the Boston Tea Party an effective form of protest? Support your opinion with evidence from the text.

3. **MAKE GENERALIZATIONS** How did the Tea Act reflect the attitude of the British government toward the colonies?

2.4 Museum of the American Revolution, Philadelphia

The Museum of the American Revolution is located in the heart of historic Philadelphia. Visitors find themselves across the street from Carpenter's Hall, the first meeting place of the Continental Congress, and a short walk to the home of founding father Benjamin Franklin. The museum's rich collection of artifacts includes many personal belongings of George Washington, early American weapons, artwork, documents, and thousands of other items that date to the American Revolution. These items help tell the earliest stories of American independence from Britain. How would each of the artifacts shown have been used during the war?

American War Drum

This drum dates to 1740, well before the American Revolution had begun. It is believed to be the second-oldest dated American drum that exists. The drum is inscribed with the name of its maker, Robert Crosman, from Taunton, Massachusetts.

Considered a piece of standard equipment for New Englanders, drums and small, shrill flutes called fifes served as signal instruments for the infantry. They provided musical "commands" to soldiers in the battlefield and around camp. Fife and drum music also distracted soldiers from the drudgery of long marches.

What role did fife and drum music play in the American Revolution?

The stamp or brand on this musket is unique. It reads "U. States," which was a label required by the Congress to show that this gun was American-made, not European.

Engraved Powder Horn

Virginia rifleman William Waller used this ornate powder horn as he fought British and Hessian soldiers during a battle at Fort Washington on November 16, 1776. Waller was captured.

Made of cow, ox, or buffalo horn, this elaborate version bears popular slogans from the American Revolution, including "Liberty or Death," and "Kill or be Kill(e)d." Powder horns were vital pieces of equipment for soldiers during the American Revolution. Riflemen used them to carry and protect the gunpowder they needed to fire their rifles.

Riflemen often engraved their horns with names, dates, and artwork to personalize them.

"The need for wider, **deeper understanding of the Revolution,** and respect for those who championed the cause at the time, has never been greater than now."

—David McCullough
Pulitzer Prize-winning author

The design on the musket's flintlock was modeled after the Continental three-dollar bill.

American Military Musket

Made around 1775, this musket is pretty rare. By 1777, weapons imported from France and other countries had replaced American-made firearms from the early days of the American Revolution. This particular musket features a flintlock mechanism. The flintlock creates a spark that lights the gunpowder stored in the barrel of the gun. What challenges might the use of this weapon have posed to soldiers?

3.1 Preparing to Fight

King George had reached his limit. He believed the colonies were out of control and had to be reined in. Maybe the king didn't understand that the colonists had reached their limits, too. Could there be a war on the horizon?

MAIN IDEA Britain enacted a series of laws to punish Boston and force the colonies into obedience, but the colonies united to resist the laws.

INTOLERABLE LAWS

Parliament decided to punish the Bostonians. It passed a series of laws called the Coercive Acts. In the colonies, these laws quickly became known as the **Intolerable Acts**.

The Intolerable Acts prevented Massachusetts from governing itself. The Massachusetts Assembly would no longer be made up of representatives elected by the people of the colony. Instead, it was to be replaced by a ruling council of officials appointed by the king. The Quartering Act was strengthened. Now, if no barracks were available, troops could take over private homes. In addition, the port of Boston would be closed until the residents could pay for the tea they had destroyed.

The British government expected the new laws to isolate Boston and convince the other colonies to be obedient. Instead, towns near Boston sent much-needed supplies to the city and took in Bostonians looking for work. Other colonies called for a meeting to decide on a united response to the Intolerable Acts. According to the Virginia House of Burgesses, "an attack made on one of our sister colonies . . . is an attack made on all British America."

Patrick Henry
Patrick Henry was known for crafting speeches on the spot with no notes. In one of his most famous speeches, given on March 23, 1775, Henry ended with the now-famous phrase, "Give me liberty or give me death!"

AMERICAN PLACES

Carpenters' Hall Philadelphia

Books were hard to find in the 1700s, so in 1731, Benjamin Franklin established the Library Company of Philadelphia, America's first lending library. For the first time, the public had access to a collection of books that could be borrowed and shared. In September 1773, the library moved to Carpenters' Hall (left).

Members of both Continental Congresses used the library, making it the first unofficial Library of Congress. Officers of the British Army were also permitted to borrow books, provided that they returned them in good condition.

SEEDS OF WAR

The meeting of the colonies—called the **First Continental Congress**—took place in Philadelphia on September 5, 1774. Every colony except Georgia sent delegates. The 56 representatives included Patrick Henry, Samuel and John Adams, and George Washington. The main purpose of the First Continental Congress was to discuss ways to have the Intolerable Acts repealed.

The delegates wanted to assert the rights of the 13 British colonies in North America. One of the resolutions they passed stated that the Intolerable Acts were "gross infractions of those rights to which we are justly entitled by the laws of nature, the British constitution, and the charter of this province." However, the First Continental Congress was not ready to declare independence. In the end, the delegates simply voted to end all trade with Britain and Ireland—still a significant step.

Several delegates believed it was also time to start training for a possible fight with Britain. One of the other resolutions stated that everyone qualified to fight should learn "the art of war as soon as possible." Some delegates may have believed that if there was any fighting, it would be over quickly. But others, like Patrick Henry, expected all-out war.

HISTORICAL THINKING

1. **READING CHECK** How did the colonies react to the Intolerable Acts?

2. **MAKE INFERENCES** What might learning "the art of war" have meant to colonists?

3. **ANALYZE CAUSE AND EFFECT** What were the Intolerable Acts, and how did they backfire on the British government?

3.2 The Midnight Ride of Paul Revere

If you wanted to spread important news, you'd probably text it or put it out on social media for everyone to see. In 1775, spreading information wasn't that simple. "Social media" meant a man on a horse racing from town to town.

MAIN IDEA The British wanted to take control of military supplies in the colonies, but Paul Revere and others warned colonists of the coming attack.

STORED ARMS

After the First Continental Congress, militia units across the colonies began to step up their training and stockpile supplies. Remember, militias were not professional soldiers; they were groups of local men who organized to protect their town or colony. Companies of handpicked, specially trained militia members called **minutemen** were also assembled. The minutemen were known for their ability to be ready to fight with practically no warning—in a "minute."

Revere's Lantern
This iron and glass piece of American history was identified as one of the two lanterns used to signal that the British were coming by sea. It's an important artifact. Without it, the minutemen might not have been prepared for the arrival of the British troops, and Paul Revere's late-night ride might have been in vain.

General Thomas Gage, the British governor of Massachusetts, was ordered by the British government to take forceful action against the militias. In April 1775, he learned that the Massachusetts militia was storing military supplies in the town of Concord. He decided to take the supplies and also to arrest Samuel Adams and **John Hancock**. Both men were staying in Lexington, on the road from Boston to Concord. Like Adams, Hancock was a leading figure in the protests against British laws and a member of the First Continental Congress.

ONE IF BY LAND, TWO IF BY SEA

Gage's plans were leaked, however. Paul Revere, a silversmith who had taken part in the Boston Tea Party, formed a plan to warn the Massachusetts militias. He arranged to signal the Sons of Liberty in Charlestown when the British soldiers left for Concord. He would use lanterns in the Old North Church steeple, which was visible from Charlestown. If the British troops left Boston by land, there would be one lantern in the steeple. If they left by water, there would be two lanterns.

On the night of April 18, 1775, Revere learned that British soldiers were preparing to cross the bay. He had a friend hang two lanterns in the steeple, and he rowed to Charlestown in a small boat. There, the Sons of Liberty had a horse waiting for him, and he set off on his famous ride, stopping at houses and villages to warn the local militias that the British troops were coming.

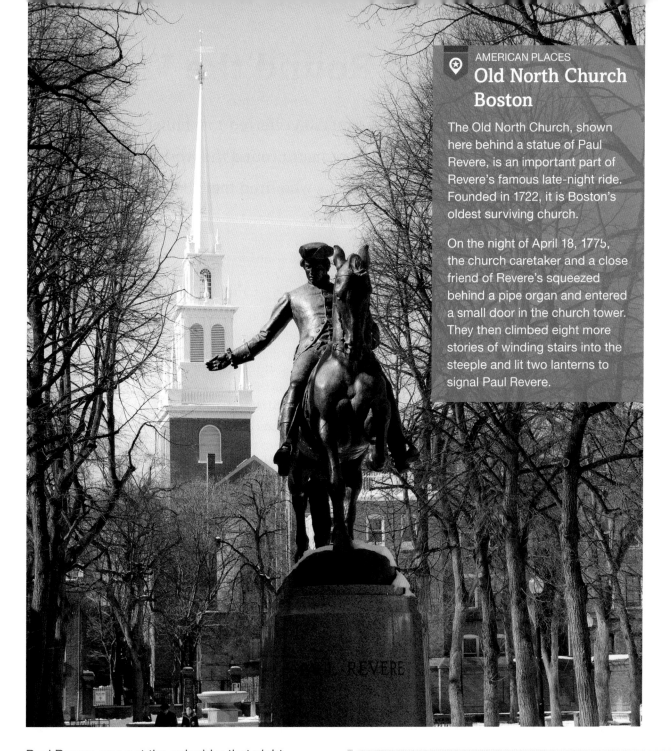

Old North Church Boston

The Old North Church, shown here behind a statue of Paul Revere, is an important part of Revere's famous late-night ride. Founded in 1722, it is Boston's oldest surviving church.

On the night of April 18, 1775, the church caretaker and a close friend of Revere's squeezed behind a pipe organ and entered a small door in the church tower. They then climbed eight more stories of winding stairs into the steeple and lit two lanterns to signal Paul Revere.

Paul Revere was not the only rider that night. When he stopped in Lexington to tell Adams and Hancock that the troops were on their way, he was joined by William Dawes. A third rider, Dr. Samuel Prescott, caught up with Revere and Dawes farther down the road.

Soon, a patrol of British soldiers stopped the riders. Dawes and Prescott escaped, but Revere was held and questioned by the soldiers. Prescott was able to complete the ride and alert the militia in Concord. When the British troops arrived, the minutemen were ready.

HISTORICAL THINKING

1. **READING CHECK** How did Paul Revere and others alert the Massachusetts militia about the approaching British soldiers?

2. **INTERPRET VISUALS** How do the photo and caption above help you understand the events described in the text?

3. **FORM AND SUPPORT OPINIONS** Is Paul Revere an important figure in American history? Why or why not?

3.3 Shot Heard Round the World

In 1837, American poet Ralph Waldo Emerson referred to a bullet fired in Lexington, Massachusetts, as "the shot heard round the world" in his poem "Concord Hymn." Nobody knows who fired that shot, but it started a revolution that changed the world.

MAIN IDEA The American Revolution began when Massachusetts militia fought the British forces in the towns of Lexington and Concord.

THE REVOLUTION BEGINS

As the British Army marched toward Concord, they heard church bells and saw lights in windows. The colonists were awake and aware. Soon after sunrise on April 19, the troops reached Lexington. There, they met about 70 armed militiamen, nearly half of the town's adult males. But the Lexington militia was inexperienced and faced a much larger British force.

The scene was chaos as both the British commander and the militia leader called orders to their troops. The British officer, Major John Pitcairn, wanted to disarm the Americans, not engage in battle. But as the British advanced, a shot rang out. Then there were several more. Pitcairn tried to stop his troops, but the shooting continued for 20 minutes, leaving eight Lexington men dead and 10 wounded. Only one British soldier was wounded and none were killed.

The British reached Concord at about eight o'clock in the morning. Using previously hidden military supplies, the Americans inflicted more casualties than the British did this time. The British soldiers attempted an orderly retreat back to Boston. But hundreds of militiamen fired at them from behind trees, walls, rocks, and buildings and forced many British soldiers to panic. The British countered by sending advance parties to set fire to homes and kill residents along the way back to Boston.

The fighting at **Lexington and Concord** is considered the first battle of the American Revolution. By the end of the day, British losses totaled 73 dead and 200 wounded or missing. The Americans counted 49 killed and at least 39 wounded or missing.

CHOOSING SIDES

As tensions between Britain and the colonies turned into open violence, colonists took sides in the conflict. Those who called themselves **Patriots** supported the right of the colonies to rule themselves. At first, not all Patriots wanted to separate from Britain. Over time, however, those on the Patriot side became convinced that independence was necessary.

The **Loyalists**, colonists who supported Britain, increasingly found themselves an uncomfortable minority. As time went on, it became dangerous to sympathize with the British cause. Some Loyalists were beaten or saw their homes burned by fellow colonists. In 1775, a Loyalist who spoke openly about his opinions was ordered to leave Maryland by the Maryland Provincial Convention.

HISTORICAL THINKING

1. **READING CHECK** What were the results of the fighting at Lexington and Concord?

2. **ANALYZE CAUSE AND EFFECT** Why did the battles of Lexington and Concord increase tensions between Patriots and Loyalists?

3. **IDENTIFY MAIN IDEAS AND DETAILS** What details support the idea that the Patriots won the battles?

LOYALISTS CALLED THE **PATRIOTS**

Whig! Rebel! Yankee!

COLONIAL ARMY **SOLDIER**

PATRIOTS CALLED THE **LOYALISTS**

King's Man! Royalist! Tory!

BRITISH ARMY **SOLDIER**

FAMOUS **PATRIOTS**

George Washington

Thomas Jefferson

James Madison

Patrick Henry

John Adams

Alexander Hamilton

Benjamin Franklin

FAMOUS **LOYALISTS**

John Howe

Mary Dowd

Myles Cooper

William Franklin

Thomas Hutchinson

DAILY COLONIAL ARMY RATIONS

1 1/2 lb. Bread or Flour

4 oz. Whiskey

1 lb. Beef or 3/4 lb. Pork

DAILY BRITISH ARMY RATIONS

1 1/2 lb. Bread or Flour

8 oz. Rum

1/4 pint Canned Peas and 1 oz. Rice

1 oz. Butter

1 lb. Beef or 1/2 lb. Pork

COLONISTS VS BRITISH

ALLIES

France   Spain

United Netherlands

ALLIES

Many Native American Tribes

Hessian Troops

2.5 Million American Colonists

20% Supported Britain

BATTLES WERE FOUGHT ACROSS THE **GLOBE**

Europe

North America

Caribbean

11 Million People in Great Britain

2.5 Million Colonists in America

SOURCE: Civil War Trust Online

3.4 North Bridge
Concord, Massachusetts

North Bridge is more than just a quaint path over the Concord River in Massachusetts. Located in **Minute Man National Historical Park**, it's a solemn place—American hallowed ground. It is also the site where some of the first shots of the American Revolution were fired on April 19, 1775. The original "battle bridge" that existed when the war broke out has long since been replaced, but the symbolism of this historical landscape remains. Based on what you see here, how might the geography of this place have impacted colonial and British soldiers?

CRITICAL VIEWING The 1875 bronze Minute Man statue (right background) was made from melted Civil War cannons for the 100th anniversary of the battle in this location. It symbolizes the colonial farmers who replaced their plows with muskets to defend their land and liberty. What does this tell you about how the colonial soldiers differed from British soldiers?

The Road to Revolution 201

4.1 Colonial Army Forms

You nervously count and recount your bullets as you and your fellow militiamen stand at the top of the hill. Below, a line of red-coated British soldiers marches toward you, pausing only to fire in unison. This is it. This is war.

MAIN IDEA Colonial leaders remained reluctant to fully declare independence, but battles between the British and colonial militias continued to break out.

CRITICAL VIEWING Originally built by the French in 1755, Fort Ticonderoga was constructed to guard a strategic strip of land that connected New France and the American colonies. What do you observe about the fort's location that may have been significant during the American Revolution?

VICTORY AT FORT TICONDEROGA

The next battle in the growing conflict took place on May 10, 1775. At dawn that morning, **Ethan Allen**, a Patriot and colonial leader from Vermont, and **Benedict Arnold**, from Connecticut, led a troop of militia in an attack on Fort Ticonderoga in northeastern New York. In a classic example of "timing is everything," the militia known as the Green Mountain Boys surprised the sleeping British soldiers and captured the fort without firing a shot.

The victory at Fort Ticonderoga gave the colonial forces an important advantage. The Green Mountain Boys captured the fort's **artillery**, or large guns that could fire a long distance. In all, they claimed 59 cannons and 19 other pieces of heavy artillery for the colonies. It was an epic gain.

On the same day that Ethan Allen took Fort Ticonderoga, the **Second Continental Congress** met in Philadelphia. Many of the delegates had also been part of the First Continental Congress. New delegates included Thomas Jefferson of Virginia and Benjamin Franklin of Pennsylvania.

The Congress recognized the need to prepare for war and wanted to make sure the army would be under its control. So it appointed **George Washington** as the commander in chief of the colonial forces, which would now be called the **Continental Army**. Despite this warlike decision, however, many of the delegates were still opposed to declaring independence.

BATTLE OF BUNKER HILL

Before Washington could even take command of the troops, another battle broke out. The militia around Boston learned that the British were planning to seize the hills overlooking the city. On June 16, a troop of militiamen occupied Bunker Hill and Breed's Hill to prevent the British from taking the high ground.

The next morning, the British troops attacked. The militia fighters were greatly outnumbered. They were also short of ammunition, so they had to make every shot count. Colonel William Prescott, their commander, is said to have told his men, "Don't fire until you can see the whites of their eyes."

An American Traitor

Benedict Arnold was an early hero in the American Revolution who went on to become one of the most infamous traitors in American history. After helping capture Fort Ticonderoga in 1775, Arnold continued his support of the American war efforts but felt his work went unrecognized. In 1779, he secretly negotiated with the British to turn over an American post in exchange for a commanding position in the British army and a cash reward. Arnold's plot was discovered by the Americans, but he escaped to British territory.

The militia did have one key advantage: the British troops had to charge uphill to reach them. The redcoats tried storming Breed's Hill three times. The first two attempts failed, resulting in a huge loss of lives. On the third try, the Patriots were overrun by the redcoats. Britain won the battle, but at an enormous cost. Today, the encounter is known as the Battle of Bunker Hill, even though most of the fighting took place on Breed's Hill.

HISTORICAL THINKING

1. **READING CHECK** What happened at the battles of Fort Ticonderoga and Bunker Hill?

2. **ANALYZE CAUSE AND EFFECT** Why did the Second Continental Congress decide to prepare for war?

3. **FORM AND SUPPORT OPINIONS** Do you think peace between Britain and the colonies could have been possible in 1775? Why or why not?

4.2 How Geology Shapes the Battlefield

MAIN IDEA Geologic forces shape the landscape, impacting the outcome of many battles.

By Andrés Ruzo, **National Geographic Explorer**

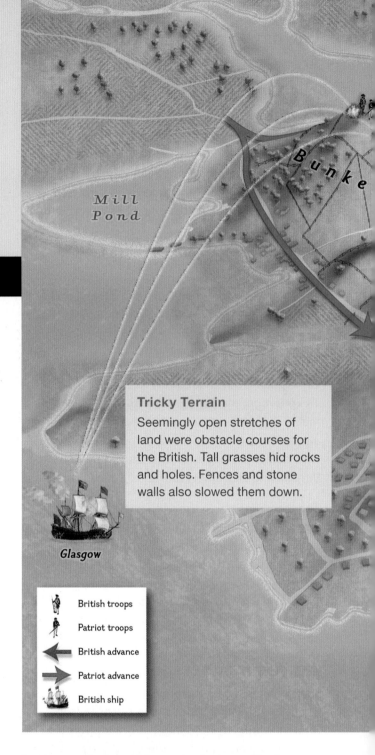

Mill Pond

Bunke

Glasgow

Tricky Terrain
Seemingly open stretches of land were obstacle courses for the British. Tall grasses hid rocks and holes. Fences and stone walls also slowed them down.

British troops

Patriot troops

British advance

Patriot advance

British ship

TAKE THE HIGH GROUND

Taking advantage of a battlefield can mean the difference between victory and defeat, and there is a geologic story behind every great battle. An area's **geology**—the local geologic features such as rocks, landforms, and the processes that created and shaped them—can define a battlefield. Over millions, even billions of years, colliding tectonic plates and volcanic activity give rise to great landforms like mountain ranges. Erosion from weathering, moving glaciers, and other destructive forces break down these landforms. The eroded material is transported and re-deposited, customizing each region with its distinctive **terrain**, the physical features of the land.

Throughout history, successful commanders were the ones who understood how to use the local terrain to their advantage. The names of American Revolution battle sites like Brooklyn Heights (New York), Bunker Hill (Massachusetts), and Kings Mountain (South Carolina) are clues to the importance of battlefield geology. Hills, cliffs, bluffs, and other elevated landforms played a key role in the war. Elevation gave soldiers a strategic military advantage. Think about running uphill with a heavy rifle straight into enemy gunfire. Now consider the benefits of firing down on your enemies from a well-fortified position as they advance up difficult terrain. It's no wonder military commanders try to "take the high ground."

BUNKER HILL

Study the map of Bunker Hill. This landscape tells a geologic story. Over 20,000 years ago, a massive melting glacier slowly began to reveal the landscape that would one day become Boston. Geologically, Bunker Hill and Breed's Hill are called **drumlins**, smooth-sloped hills made of glacial sediments. In 1775, the Americans took the high ground and fortified these drumlins by building 6-foot **earthworks**, human-made land modifications, out of the silty glacial soils. This put the Americans in an ideal defensive position overlooking the battlefields.

But taking the high ground doesn't always ensure victory. At Bunker Hill, the Americans held their ground until they ran out of ammunition. As you

Breed's or Bunker?
On June 16, 1775, more than 1,000 colonists set out to fortify Bunker Hill, but they passed it in the dark and fortified Breed's Hill instead.

Mystic River

Hill

Warren's Redoubt

Breed's Hill

CHARLESTOWN

Falcon

Lively

BOSTON ↘

Taking the High Ground
The colonists didn't have many cannons, and they weren't very good at firing the ones they did have. But they did have a strong position on high ground, just across the water from Boston. This forced the British to attack before they were fully ready to do so.

have read, the British won the battle, but at a terrible cost. Over 1,000 British soldiers were killed or wounded, compared to over 400 Americans. This showed that the Patriots could hold their own against a better-trained, better-equipped, and far larger British force. Clearly local terrain played a role in how the battle unfolded.

War commanders probably don't think much about the geologic story that shaped their battlefields, but that doesn't mean the geology isn't significant.

THINK LIKE A GEOLOGIST

1. **IDENTIFY MAIN IDEAS AND DETAILS** If you were a commander defending your city, where would you set up troops? Why?

2. **DESCRIBE** What advantages or disadvantages would your local terrain present in battle?

3. **INTERPRET MAPS** Aside from hills, which geologic features do you think affected the battle?

4.3 Breaking with Britain

Congress has always had a difficult job, making decisions that will impact a large number of people. In 1775, the Second Continental Congress faced a hard choice: pursue peace or prepare for war.

MAIN IDEA The Second Continental Congress made one last attempt to make peace with Britain, but fighting continued and public opinion moved toward declaring independence.

PEACE REJECTED

During the summer of 1775, the Continental Congress made moves toward both peace and war. In an attempt to restore peace with Britain, delegates sent the king a petition. They asked him to resolve the conflict between the colonies and Parliament. Instead, he proclaimed that the colonies were in "an open and avowed rebellion."

At the same time, Congress sent an army north to invade Canada and take on the British forces there. This proved to be a poor decision. The Canada campaign was long, bloody, and unsuccessful. British troops successfully pushed the colonial army back into New York.

In December 1775, Parliament decided to punish the colonies by cutting off all trade. Then in January 1776, King George signed a treaty with Germany that allowed him to hire more than 20,000 German soldiers and send them to the colonies. These soldiers for hire were known as **Hessians**, and they had a reputation as fierce fighters. For many Americans, these actions proved that the British government intended to crush the colonies both militarily and economically, at any cost.

TIME TO PART

Meanwhile, the colonial army was meeting with greater success in Boston. George Washington had arrived there during the summer of 1775, determined to drive the British from the city. The following winter, he sent troops to drag the heavy guns from Fort Ticonderoga and install them on high ground overlooking Boston. In the spring of 1776, under the threat of the looming artillery, the British withdrew from the city. They sailed north to Canada in preparation for an eventual invasion of New York City. More than a thousand Loyalists left with the British because they feared they would not be safe from angry Patriots if they stayed in Boston.

Alarmed by the colonists' show of force in Boston, the British government sent a massive force to put down the revolt. Nearly 400 ships set sail from England carrying 32,000 troops, including at least 12,000 Hessians. The soldiers would join the British troops already gathering in Canada for an attack on New York City. The warships would attack seaports and disrupt colonial shipping.

Hessian miter cap

 National Museum of American History Washington, D.C.

This hat, called a miter cap, was worn by a Hessian infantry soldier from the Fusilier Regiment, which served under the British Army during the American Revolution. The cap has a cloth body covered with a brass cap plate and is stamped with a Hessian lion.

Printing *Common Sense*

Colonial printers working on printing presses similar to the one shown here created publications one page at a time. They carefully folded paper onto set and inked letters and then used a lever to press the images and words onto the page.

Thousands of copies of *Common Sense* were printed, sold, and read aloud in meeting rooms and inns throughout the colonies. Because it was originally anonymous, many initially attributed *Common Sense* to Ben Franklin. As you have read, before he was a scientist and revolutionary, Ben Franklin was a printer and publisher in Philadelphia. He even owned his own printing press, so it is not a surprise that some would think he published *Common Sense.*

Printing Press

Ink Ball
The printer uses the ink ball to apply an oil-based ink onto the type.

Press
The printer rolls the type box under the press and uses the handle to imprint letters onto the paper.

Paper Holder
The printer inserts paper in the holder and folds it onto the inked type.

Type Box
The printer arranges the letters in the type box.

In January 1776, **Thomas Paine** published a pamphlet called *Common Sense* to argue the case for independence. In the pamphlet, Paine made several practical arguments for independence. He claimed that France and Spain would only aid the colonies if they broke with Britain. He also pointed out that European countries would continue to purchase American exports if the colonies declared independence. "'Tis time to part," he urged his readers. As the eventful year unfolded, more and more Americans agreed with him.

HISTORICAL THINKING

1. **READING CHECK** Which events in 1775 and 1776 led the colonies toward independence?

2. **ANALYZE CAUSE AND EFFECT** Why did the British government respond with overwhelming force to events in North America, and what was the colonial response?

3. **IDENTIFY MAIN IDEAS AND DETAILS** What was Thomas Paine's principal argument in favor of independence?

4.4 Drafting the Declaration

Every Fourth of July, the air fills with the sound of marching bands and the night sky with fireworks—all to celebrate a piece of paper? It's not just any piece of paper. It's the document that launched a new country and gave a name and an identity to the United States of America.

MAIN IDEA In 1776, the Continental Congress formally declared the independence of the United States of America from Great Britain.

MOVING TOWARD INDEPENDENCE

By the spring of 1776, the Continental Congress was making decisions for the colonies as a whole, serving in effect as the colonial government. In this role, the Congress declared that American ports would accept ships from any country—except, however, for Great Britain. The Congress also encouraged the colonies to establish their own independent governments.

Then, on June 7, Richard Henry Lee of Virginia placed a shocking resolution before the delegates. It stated that "these United Colonies are, and of right ought to be, free and independent States."

Not all the delegates were in favor of Lee's resolution to separate completely from Britain. Still, the Congress appointed a committee to draft an official statement to declare independence. **Thomas Jefferson** of Virginia, a brilliant scholar and persuasive writer, would be the principal author.

John Adams and Benjamin Franklin were also on the committee to create the document. Franklin had lived in England for several years, serving as a representative from several colonies to the British government. Adams suggested that Jefferson should write the first draft. Franklin gave Jefferson advice and helped revise the document.

On July 2, 1776, the Continental Congress voted to approve independence from Britain. Two days later, the Congress adopted Jefferson's document, the **Declaration of Independence**.

Thomas Jefferson
In addition to drafting the Declaration of Independence, Jefferson served his country for more than 50 years as a historian, public official, president, and founder of the University of Virginia. His famous words captured the voice and identity of a new America like no one else's could.

SELF-EVIDENT TRUTHS

Many of the ideas expressed in the Declaration of Independence can be traced to John Locke. The first part states, "We hold these truths to be self-evident, that all men are created equal, that they are endowed by their Creator with certain unalienable Rights, that among these are Life, Liberty, and the Pursuit of Happiness." An **unalienable right** is one that cannot be taken away.

Yet the unalienable rights of two large groups were not discussed in the Declaration. In his first draft, Jefferson had listed slavery as one of the king's offenses. After an intense debate, this section was removed. The Declaration was silent on the rights of women, too, even though John Adams's wife, Abigail, had pleaded with him in a letter to "remember the ladies and be more generous and favorable to them than your ancestors."

The second part of the Declaration listed the offenses of the king against the colonies. These included refusing to approve laws passed by the colonial assemblies, placing a standing army in the colonies, and imposing taxes without colonial consent. For these reasons and more, the Continental Congress declared the 13 colonies "free and independent states," the United States of America.

HISTORICAL THINKING

1. **READING CHECK** What are the principal parts of the Declaration of Independence?

2. **ANALYZE LANGUAGE USE** What is an "unalienable right," and how did the inclusion of these words in the Declaration point to a new philosophy of governing?

3. **MAKE CONNECTIONS** What laws did Jefferson refer to when he listed the complaints against the British king?

4.5 Declarations of Freedom

Beginning in the late-1600s, political thinkers put forth new ideas about natural rights and human equality in books, articles, essays, and pamphlets. These writings set the stage for a revolution that created a nation and transformed the world.

This painting by John Trumbull, titled *Declaration of Independence,* depicts the moment on June 28, 1776, when the first draft of the document was presented to the Second Continental Congress in the Pennsylvania State House. In the painting, Thomas Jefferson, thought to be the main author of the document, places the document in front of John Hancock, who was the president of the Congress, surrounded by members of the committee who helped create the draft.

CRITICAL VIEWING What do you notice about the people who are gathered for the presentation of the first draft of the Declaration of Independence?

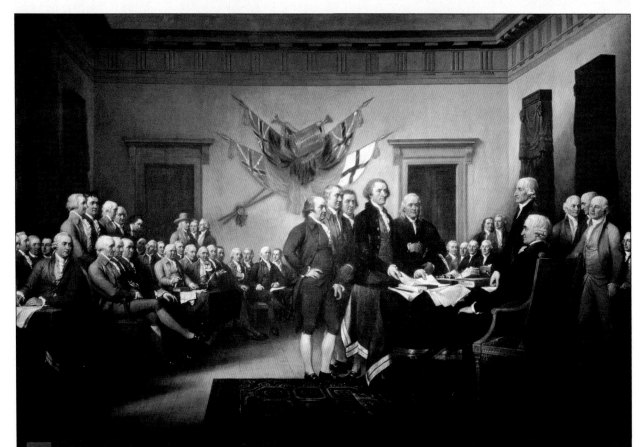

🏛 **U.S. Capitol Rotunda, Washington, D.C.**

Declaration of Independence, John Trumbull, 1817

This is the first of four Revolutionary-era scenes that the U.S. Congress commissioned from John Trumbull. The artist had created a smaller version of this painting to document the events of the American Revolution, and he enlarged the painting for the Rotunda between August 1817 and September 1818. It was installed in the Rotunda in 1826, along with three other Trumbull paintings.

DOCUMENT ONE

Primary Source: Legal Document
from the Declaration of Independence, 1776

The Declaration of Independence begins with a clear statement of its writers' beliefs. The goal of the Declaration was to unify the colonies as one new nation in opposition to Great Britain.

CONSTRUCTED RESPONSE In what ways is this vision of governing different from how the British monarchy governed?

We hold these truths to be self-evident, that all men are created equal, that they are endowed by their Creator with certain unalienable Rights, that among these are Life, Liberty and the pursuit of Happiness. That to secure these rights, Governments are instituted among Men, deriving their just powers from the consent of the governed, That whenever any Form of Government becomes destructive of these ends, it is the Right of the People to alter or to abolish it, and to institute new Government.

DOCUMENT TWO

Primary Source: Legal Document
from the Declaration of Independence, 1776

The second part of the Declaration contains a long list of offenses by the king against the colonies. In total, Jefferson included 27 grievances that referred to the Quartering Act, the Intolerable Acts, and several other British attempts to impose their will on the colonies.

CONSTRUCTED RESPONSE Why do you think the writers included such a complete list of grievances against the king?

To prove this, let Facts be submitted to a candid world.

He has refused his Assent to Laws, the most wholesome and necessary for the public good.

He has dissolved Representative Houses repeatedly, for opposing with manly firmness his invasions on the rights of the people.

He has kept among us, in times of peace, Standing Armies without the Consent of our legislatures.

DOCUMENT THREE

Primary Source: Essay
from *Two Treatises on Government,* by John Locke, 1689

Nearly a century before the American Revolution, John Locke outlined his theories of government in two treatises, or essays. In the second treatise, he explained his thoughts on liberty and the consent of people to be governed. Thomas Jefferson drew heavily on Locke's political theories when creating the Declaration.

CONSTRUCTED RESPONSE In what ways did Locke's ideas directly influence the actions of the colonies and the writing of the Declaration of Independence?

Men being . . . by nature, all free, equal, and independent, no one can be put out of this estate, and subjected to the political power of another, without his own consent. The only way . . . any one divests himself of his natural liberty, and puts on the bonds of civil society, is by agreeing with other men to join and unite into a community, for their comfortable, safe and peaceable living one amongst another.

Read the full Declaration of Independence in the Citizenship Handbook.

SYNTHESIZE & WRITE

1. **REVIEW** Review what you have learned about the events leading up to the Declaration of Independence.

2. **RECALL** On your own paper, write the main ideas about government expressed in the Declaration of Independence and Locke's *Second Treatise on Government.*

3. **CONSTRUCT** Construct a topic sentence that answers this question: How did beliefs about the nature of government and human freedom lead to the colonies' break with Britain?

4. **WRITE** Using evidence from this chapter and the documents, write an informative paragraph that supports your topic sentence in Step 3.

5 REVIEW

VOCABULARY

Use each of the following vocabulary words in a sentence that shows an understanding of the term's meaning.

1. **revenue**
   Because the British government needed money after the French and Indian War, it imposed taxes to raise revenue.

2. unalienable right

3. militia

4. tyranny

5. boycott

6. committee of correspondence

7. repeal

8. artillery

READING STRATEGY
ANALYZE CAUSE AND EFFECT

If you haven't already, complete your chart to analyze the causes that led up to the colonies' break with Britain. List at least four key causes. Then answer the question.

Causes → Effect

The colonies declare independence from Britain.

9. What changes in the way Britain treated the American colonies caused the colonies to revolt?

MAIN IDEAS

Answer the following questions. Support your answers with evidence from the chapter.

10. What changes did the British government make in the colonies after the French and Indian War? **LESSON 1.1**

11. Why did the colonists protest the Sugar Act and Currency Act as forms of "taxation without representation"? **LESSON 1.2**

12. How did the colonists bring about the repeal of the Stamp Act? **LESSON 1.3**

13. Why did the colonists consider the Townshend Acts to be oppressive? **LESSON 2.1**

14. Why did the Tea Act result in such violent opposition? **LESSON 2.3**

15. In what ways did the Intolerable Acts build on earlier British laws? **LESSON 3.1**

16. What was the result of the battles at Lexington and Concord for the British and the colonists? **LESSON 3.3**

17. How did the Second Continental Congress pursue both peace and war? **LESSON 4.1**

18. What were the main goals of the two parts of the Declaration of Independence? **LESSON 4.4**

HISTORICAL THINKING

Answer the following questions. Support your answers with evidence from the chapter.

19. **SYNTHESIZE** How did the events of the French and Indian War help lead to the American Revolution?

20. **MAKE INFERENCES** Why did the Patriots find the ideas of John Locke appealing?

21. **ANALYZE CAUSE AND EFFECT** How did the passage of the Townshend Acts lead to the Boston Tea Party?

22. **EVALUATE** Were boycotts an effective form of protest against British taxes and laws? Explain.

23. **FORM AND SUPPORT OPINIONS** Which of the British laws and taxes placed the greatest burden on the colonies? Support your opinion with evidence from the chapter.

INTERPRET MAPS

Look closely at the map of eastern North America in 1763. Then answer the questions that follow.

Territories and Colonies, 1763

Legend:
— Proclamation Line of 1763
Thirteen colonies
FOX Native American settlements
Other British territory
Spanish territory

24. What groups were impacted the most by the Proclamation of 1763?

25. How did the geography of the Proclamation Line make it hard for the British to enforce it?

26. Compare this historical map to a present-day map of the eastern part of the United States. What similarities do you observe? What differences? How might those similarities and differences be explained?

ANALYZE SOURCES

In *Common Sense*, published in January 1776, Thomas Paine included a variety of arguments in favor of independence. In addition to the reasons you have already read, he stated the one below. Read the passage and answer the question.

> As to government matters, It is not in the power of Britain to do this continent justice: The business of it will soon be too weighty, and intricate, to be managed with any tolerable degree of convenience, by a power, so distant from us, and so very ignorant of us; for if they cannot conquer us, they cannot govern us.

27. What argument does Paine make about the British government in this passage?

CONNECT TO YOUR LIFE

28. **NARRATIVE** Think about the events that led up to the Declaration of Independence and why the colonists felt they had to separate from Great Britain. Make a connection between that time in history and a recent protest that you have read about, heard about, or seen. Write a paragraph connecting the two events.

TIPS

- Make a time line of the principal events leading up to the colonists' action or decision. Then make a time line showing what led up to the present-day protest you have chosen.

- Use textual evidence and two or three vocabulary terms from the chapter in your narrative.

- Conclude the narrative with a comment that ties the colonists' actions to those of people today.

CHAPTER

6

THE AMERICAN
REVOLUTION
1775–1783

ESSENTIAL QUESTION
What factors helped America win the war?

AMERICAN STORIES **Bitter Winter at Valley Forge**

AMERICAN GALLERY
ONLINE **Colonial Vernacular Architecture**

READING STRATEGY

FORM AND SUPPORT OPINIONS
You often form opinions while reading. As you read the chapter, decide what factor was most important in achieving an American victory in the Revolution. Use a graphic like this one to write your opinion and record your reasons for supporting it.

Opinion:

Supporting statement:

Supporting statement:

Supporting statement:

Supporting statement:

"It is a common observation here that **our cause is the cause of all mankind.**"

—Benjamin Franklin

BITTER WINTER AT
VALLEY FORGE

Valley Forge is now a National Historical Park in Pennsylvania. These re-created soldier cabins in the park give visitors a sense of what the living conditions were like for the Continental Army in the winter of 1777–78.

COLD, HUNGRY, AND SICK

Think of the images you have seen of U.S. Army units marching on parade. The soldiers are strong, healthy, and clothed in matching uniforms. They move with assurance and discipline, each soldier knowing his or her place in the formation. It's a sight that inspires confidence in the armed forces.

In the winter of 1777, the sight of George Washington's troops straggling into Valley Forge would have inspired anything but confidence. Instead, some viewers felt pity and shock. The army had been defeated twice by the British, and now the soldiers were going into winter quarters to rest and regroup. The city of Philadelphia, 20 miles away, was in British hands.

The soldiers were in desperate need of relief. They were exhausted, underfed, diseased, and freezing. Albigence Waldo, an army doctor, described their plight in his journal: "There comes a Soldier, his bare feet are seen thro' his worn out Shoes." Joseph Plumb Martin, an army private, later recalled his fellow soldiers walking barefoot "till they might be tracked by their blood upon the rough frozen ground." At one point during the long winter, 7,000 soldiers were too sick to be on duty.

NO RELIEF IN SIGHT

George Washington was well aware of his men's suffering. In a letter to Congress, he wrote, "I am now convinced, beyond a doubt that unless some great and capital change suddenly takes place . . . this Army must inevitably be reduced to one or other of these three things. Starve, dissolve, or disperse in order to obtain subsistence [food] in the best manner they can."

Congress, however, did not send Washington the relief he needed in the form of either supplies or money. Instead, some members pressured him to send his starving army against the British troops in Philadelphia. Some, including John Adams, had lost confidence in General Washington and wanted to replace him. Another Patriot, Alexander Hamilton, demonstrated his faith in Washington by joining the general's staff in 1777, a position he would hold until 1781.

Of even greater concern was the trust of Washington's officers and men. In all, 1,000 soldiers deserted during that harsh winter, and several hundred officers resigned. Most, however, remained loyal to their general and their cause. Joseph Plumb Martin wrote, "We had engaged in the defense of our injured country and were . . . determined to persevere."

Boots weren't exactly weatherproof in the 1700s. Valley Forge soldiers lucky enough to have footwear wore boots like these. Others simply wrapped their feet in rags, which provided little protection from the hard ground and cold snow.

Valley Forge

After British forces took control of Philadelphia, George Washington and his troops fled 20 miles northwest to take refuge at Valley Forge. This location was close enough to put pressure on the British but far enough away to make an enemy attack unlikely.

Schuylkill River

Star Redoubt

Varnum's Brigade

Huntington's Brigade

McIntosh's Brigade

Huntington's Quarters

General Varnum's Quarters

Washington's Headquarters

Ft. Huntington

Adjutant General's Quarters

Conway Huts

Redan

GRAND PARADE

Ft. Greene

Redan

SITE OF 2004 EXPERIMENT

Conway's Brigade

Muhlenberg's Brigade
Weedon's Brigade
Patterson's Brigade
Learned's Brigade
Glover's Brigade

Redan

Ft. Muhlenberg

Maxwell's Brigade

Gulph Road

OUTER LINE OF DEFENSE

Knox's Artillery Brigade

Mount Misery

Valley Creek

Mount Joy

INNER LINE OF DEFENSE

Ft. Washington

Scott's Brigade

1st Pa. Brigade

2nd Pa. Brigade

Poor's Brigade

Covered bridge

Woodford's Brigade

OUTER LINE OF DEFENSE

Lord Stirling's Quarters

Maxwell's Quarters

Knox's Quarters

Lafayette's Quarters

> Army engineers laid out the camp wisely in a triangle shape. Each side of the triangle measured seven miles. On two sides, the ridgeline and two high hills provided the camp's main defenses. The Schuylkill River, a natural barrier to enemies, made up the third side of the triangle.

Legend:
- ▦ Brigade
- ☐ Fort/Redoubt
- ■ Hut/Cabin

N

| 0 mi | 0.25 | 0.5 |
| 0 m | 250 500 | |

TOLERABLY COMFORTABLE

In 2004, a team of park rangers and volunteers used "experimental archaeology" to discover how well cabins like those the soldiers built and lived in at Valley Forge sheltered the soldiers during the winter of 1777. First, the team reviewed historical documents and soldiers' personal accounts for details about their living experiences. Then the team spent six days and five nights living in a re-created cabin at Valley Forge, capturing temperature, humidity, and weather data. While conditions weren't cozy, the study led the team to conclude the soldiers' cabins were well-built and relatively comfortable.

CABIN FLOOR PLAN

> Soldiers built the cabins using logs harvested from the surrounding woods and a mix of mud and straw as mortar.

log walls

14 Feet

door

dirt floor

hearth

lower bunk
middle bunk
upper bunk

16 Feet

> The cabin door was usually located on the south end of the cabin to let in sunlight for added warmth.

> Bunks closest to the hearth were the warmest. Higher-ranking officers, sick soldiers, and those who did hard manual labor may have earned warmer bunks.

> 8–12 soldiers shared about 200 square feet of living space.

> The hearth kept the soldiers warm and dried the dirt floor and log walls.

> The team measured temperatures inside the re-created cabin up to 50° F warmer than outdoor conditions during the day, and up to 35° F warmer at night. They concluded that the well-designed structures likely made the soldiers feel like it was **"April inside while it was January outside."**

SOURCE: National Park Service

GATHERING STRENGTH AND TRAINING

The painful irony was that the Continental Army was starving in a land of plenty. The area around Valley Forge was fertile farmland. However, the Americans were competing with the British for the region's resources, and the British were very effective at buying—or taking—what they wanted.

Once the soldiers were fed, they would also need training to fight the well-equipped, professional British Army. The soldiers came from state militias that were each organized differently. They did not know how to work together as an effective force.

Fortunately, Washington had two men at Valley Forge who could address these problems. He put General Nathanael Greene in charge of supplies. Greene organized groups of soldiers to go foraging, or seeking food, in the countryside. Greene found ways to help the army get food and horses, and he set up a system of supply sites and roads for moving the goods. By springtime, the troops were properly fed and supplied.

At Ben Franklin's suggestion, Friedrich von Steuben (FREE-drihk von STOO-buhn), formerly an officer in the Prussian Army, came to Valley Forge to train Washington's troops. Von Steuben was an expert in the military tactics used by modern armies. A colorful figure, he barked out commands in German, drilling the soldiers for hours each day. Private Martin recalled, "I was kept constantly, when off other duty, engaged in learning the Baron de Steuben's new Prussian exercise." The Americans emerged from von Steuben's special brand of boot camp ready to fight like professionals.

The Continental Army marched out of Valley Forge on June 19, 1778. The tattered, starving, desperate group had been transformed into a confident, disciplined army. A week later, Washington's soldiers fought the British Army at the Battle of Monmouth. There was no turning back on the path to independence.

THINK ABOUT IT

How would you feel if you were a soldier in the Continental Army and you felt you lacked the support of Congress?

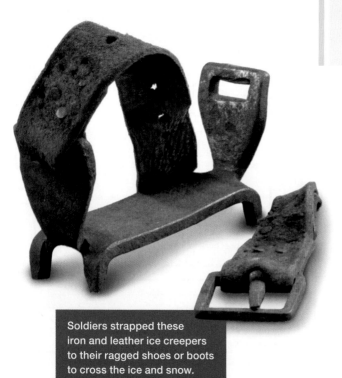

Soldiers strapped these iron and leather ice creepers to their ragged shoes or boots to cross the ice and snow.

LIFE GOES ON

While the soldiers starved, struggled, and battled illness at Valley Forge, life went on as usual in Philadelphia. This is evident in these two wildly different personal accounts of the same time period. Read and compare these primary sources.

PRIMARY SOURCE

You can have no idea of the life of continued amusement I live in. I can scarce have a moment to myself. I have stole this while everybody is retired to dress for dinner . . . and most elegantly am I dressed for a ball this evening at Smith's where we have one every Thursday.

—from a letter by Rebecca Franks, 1778

PRIMARY SOURCE

I lay two nights and one day, and had not a morsel of any thing to eat all the time, save half of a small pumpkin, which I cooked by placing it upon a rock, the skin side uppermost, and making a fire upon it; by the time it was heat through I devoured it with as keen an appetite as I should a pie made of it at some other time.

—from *Memoir of a Revolutionary Soldier*, by Joseph Plumb Martin, 1830

Despite the grim living conditions—or perhaps because of them—the men at Valley Forge found ways to have fun when they were not drilling or scouting for food. Sometimes, soldiers would play "base," a very early form of baseball. George Washington himself once joined a group of men playing cricket, a British sport that also involves a type of bat and ball. Some officers put on plays in a stone building on the Valley Forge site. The men were not allowed to play cards or gamble, but many ignored this rule to pass the time with a friendly card game or two. After all, the winter nights at Valley Forge were long, dull, and uncomfortable.

Soldiers also played games of dice by shaking ivory dice in this leather cup and rolling them out.

These French paper playing cards somehow made their way into the hands of bored Continental soldiers trying to pass the time at Valley Forge.

1.1 War in the Middle States

Have you ever been surprised when a team that seems to have no chance at all actually wins the big game? The Continental Army was that kind of team.

> **MAIN IDEA** Despite its disadvantages, the Continental Army managed to win important battles early on in the American Revolution.

CREATING AN ARMY

In 1775, Great Britain had one of the most powerful armies in the world. Its soldiers were well-trained, experienced professionals, and about 42,000 of them came to fight in the colonies. Great Britain was prepared to meet the troops' needs for arms and other supplies. As you have read, the British also hired Hessian soldiers to join them in the colonies—about 30,000 men. These **mercenaries**, or soldiers who are paid to fight for a country other than their own, further swelled the number of British forces.

On September 9, 1776, the Continental Congress voted to rename the colonies the "United States of America," but the new nation did not have a strong central government. Congress did not have the power to provide funding for arms, other supplies, or soldiers' pay.

This situation didn't change until the next year, when the Continental Congress drafted and adopted the **Articles of Confederation** in 1777. Under the Articles of Confederation, the 13 states mostly governed themselves as small **republics**. A republic is a form of government in which the people elect representatives to speak for them and enact laws based on the people's needs. James Madison helped organize the state government of Virginia. The Articles granted Congress the authority to call on states to help fund the war.

Compared with the British Army, the young Continental Army was ill prepared and disorganized. The Patriots had other problems as well. George Washington faced a huge challenge in turning a collection of local militias into a disciplined, united fighting force. He also had trouble recruiting more troops. Few eligible men had formal military training, and many were unwilling to leave their farms or jobs. Also, not everyone was eager for independence. Families and communities found themselves split between Loyalists and Patriots.

Both free and enslaved African Americans were in a unique situation when it came to deciding where their loyalties lay. The British promised freedom to many enslaved people if they promised to fight on the British side. Other African Americans, both free and unfree, were motivated to try to secure freedom for all and served in the war with the Patriots.

In 1776, only around 20,000 men had joined the Continental Army, but despite this and its numerous other problems, the Continental Army did have some advantages over the British. Most importantly, its soldiers were fighting a **defensive war**, or a war to protect one's own land, on familiar ground, while the British Army was far from home. And Americans were fighting for their homes and way of life.

EARLY VICTORIES AND DEFEATS

Even though the Revolution started in New England, it quickly spread to the Middle States of New York, New Jersey, Pennsylvania, and Delaware. In July 1776, British troops landed on New York's Staten Island and pushed American troops back to Manhattan Island and then New Jersey. The Continental Army soon had to escape across the Delaware River into Pennsylvania.

But the Continental Army had a change of luck by the end of the year. When they crossed the icy Delaware River on Christmas Day, Washington and his troops surprised and defeated the Hessian defenders in Trenton, New Jersey. The Hessian commander had received orders to build defenses

GREAT NEWS FROM NEW-YORK.

Each December, the Old Barracks Museum in Trenton, New Jersey, hosts a reenactment of the battle that showed the determination of American troops as they marched in blinding snow. The leaflet shown here provides an account of the battle—which lasted only 35 minutes—and the American victory. It took the news 11 days to reach Salem, Massachusetts, and appear in print on January 6.

around Trenton, but he had ignored them. On the night before the battle, he got a message informing him that the Continental Army was on its way. He ignored this as well, and the result was a major defeat for the British. After this American victory, called the **Battle of Trenton**, British general **William Howe** withdrew most of his army back to New York. In the words of one British officer, the Americans had "become a formidable [fearsome] enemy." This victory resulted in a wave of support and enthusiasm for the American cause, which encouraged recruitment—and greater victories.

HISTORICAL THINKING

1. **READING CHECK** What advantages and disadvantages did the Continental Army have at the start of the American Revolution?

2. **FORM AND SUPPORT OPINIONS** How do you think questions over national identity might have affected military recruitment? Explain why.

3. **ANALYZE CAUSE AND EFFECT** How did the Articles of Confederation impact the American Revolution?

1.2 The Struggle for New York

One of the worst things you can do is underestimate an opponent. The Americans looked like a ragtag bunch, but they had advantages the more disciplined British failed to see, and this oversight cost them.

MAIN IDEA Due to poor planning, the British expectation that they would dominate the Hudson River Valley proved to be incorrect.

HUDSON RIVER VALLEY

Even though Washington's troops were victorious in New Jersey, the British still controlled New York City. From there, they planned to capture the Hudson River Valley. They hoped to divide New England from the rest of the states and bring a swift conclusion to the colonial rebellion.

General Howe, a lieutenant general of British forces in North America, planned to seize the Hudson River Valley using three armies. In 1777, he sent a regiment under the command of British general **John Burgoyne** from Boston to Canada. Burgoyne's troops were to move by boat down Lake Champlain. Howe's own troops would move north to meet them. Another force, led by British lieutenant colonel Barry St. Leger, would move east from western New York along the Mohawk River to link up with the other two armies in Albany, New York.

On their way south from Lake Champlain, Burgoyne's troops took Fort Ticonderoga, but they quickly ran into problems. Burgoyne had overloaded his troops with baggage, including cartloads of his own clothing. American forces chopped down trees and rolled boulders into the path of the British troops, making a march of 23 miles take 24 days. Then, near Saratoga, New York, the Americans surrounded Burgoyne's troops. When Burgoyne called

Revolutionary Battles in New York, 1777

for **reinforcements**, or more soldiers and supplies, from New York, he found that Howe had changed his plans. Instead of joining Burgoyne's troops, Howe had decided to head for Philadelphia. His route there was roundabout. He sailed around Delaware and up Chesapeake Bay to Pennsylvania. Washington tried and failed to block Howe's advance through Pennsylvania. The British

A Mohawk Loyalist

Joseph Brant was born by the Ohio River and educated at an Indian charity school in Connecticut. His sister married a British Army officer, whom Brant followed into battle during the French and Indian War. His loyalties remained with the British throughout the American Revolution, and he skillfully led Iroquois Loyalist troops in battle throughout the Mohawk Valley. After the war, he worked for peace on the frontier. For his service, the British awarded him land in Canada, where he and his followers eventually settled.

Thayeadanegea, Joseph Brant, the Mohawk Chief

A gorget was worn by officers to protect their throats during battle. King George gave this gorget to Brant as a gift.

occupied and successfully defended Philadelphia and nearby Germantown against another attack by Washington's troops in October 1777.

ALONG THE MOHAWK RIVER

Meanwhile, St. Leger continued to push toward Albany. After crossing Lake Ontario, he led his army along the Mohawk River. And he was not alone. Iroquois warriors from the region supported St. Leger's troops.

The Six Nations of the Iroquois had formed their alliance around 1720. They signed a treaty with Britain in 1768 to establish a boundary between Native American and European lands. Then, in 1775, as the American Revolution approached, the Six Nations agreed to remain neutral. However, after war broke out, both the Americans and the British pressured the nations in the alliance to choose sides. Eventually the Six Nations decided to split their loyalties. The Mohawk sided with the British.

Mohawk chief **Joseph Brant** commanded his troops as they fought alongside St. Leger in the Mohawk River Valley. But they encountered American resistance at Fort Stanwix in 1777. When they heard that officer Benedict Arnold was approaching from the east with more American troops—and Native American allies—St. Leger and his Iroquois allies retreated. Their flight and Howe's change of plans meant that no one would be coming to help Burgoyne once he got to Albany.

HISTORICAL THINKING

1. **READING CHECK** What errors did Burgoyne make as he headed to the Hudson River Valley?

2. **INTERPRET MAPS** Along what river did most of the American victories occur in 1777?

3. **FORM AND SUPPORT OPINIONS** Do you think Burgoyne and Howe were ready for battle in America? Why or why not?

1.3 Battles of Saratoga

Sometimes things just don't go as planned. Unexpected events can derail even the best strategy—events like being hopelessly outnumbered, for example.

MAIN IDEA American planning and coordination, along with British miscalculation, led to Patriot victories at Saratoga and a turning point in the American Revolution.

AMERICAN PLACES
Saratoga Battlefield, New York

In order to hold off British forces, American troops under General Horatio Gates built two fortified walls along Bemis Heights, overlooking the Hudson River and the road beside it. They lined up 22 cannons along the walls, which helped them successfully defend their line. Today, the battlefield where these important American victories were won is open to all as part of the Saratoga National Historical Park.

A TURNING POINT

As you have read, General Burgoyne found himself in a tricky situation as he moved south—without backup—toward Albany after his victory at Fort Ticonderoga. He expected to be joined by British troops moving north from New York, but that support never came.

Here's what happened: In September 1777, 12,000 members of the Continental Army under General Horatio Gates surrounded Burgoyne and his 5,800 men at Saratoga, New York. The Americans were well prepared for this clash. Gates and Polish military engineer Tadeusz Kościuszko (tah-DAY-oosh kos-CHOOS-ko) had overseen a plan to build up American **fortifications**, or structures built to protect a place from attack.

They had brought in reinforcements from other states as well, including the Light Horse Volunteers commanded by Colonel John Langdon. One of Langdon's men was Wentworth Cheswell, an African-American government official from Massachusetts. Though the British Army had been more welcoming of African-American volunteers, soldiers such as Cheswell had started to support the Patriot cause in larger numbers.

On September 19, 1777, the British and Continental armies clashed at what would later be known as the First Battle of Saratoga, also called the Battle of Freeman's Farm. Burgoyne failed to cross Gates's lines. The British struck at the Americans again on October 7, but General Benedict Arnold staged a strong American **counterattack**, or attack in response, in what would be known as the Second Battle of Saratoga. At this point, 20,000 American troops surrounded Burgoyne's men. Burgoyne had requested that General Howe send reinforcements, but, as you may recall, Howe and his troops were on their way to Philadelphia. Greatly outnumbered, Burgoyne surrendered at Saratoga on October 17.

An African-American Hero of the Revolution

Wentworth Cheswell is most often remembered today as one of the early African-American heroes of the American Revolution. As the town messenger of Newmarket, New Hampshire, Cheswell once had to ride all night to warn his community of an impending British invasion. He also served in the Continental Army with John Langdon's Light Horse Volunteers.

But this was just one facet of a man whose career in politics lasted nearly 50 years. His ancestry was part European, part African American. Formally educated in Byfield, Massachusetts, the ??-year-old Cheswell was elected in 1768 to his first political office—town constable of Newmarket. Over the course of his impressive career, he held other prominent posts, including justice of the peace for Rockingham County, New Hampshire.

A NEW ALLY

The **Battles of Saratoga** proved to be an important turning point in the American Revolution. As with the Battle of Trenton, the victories boosted Americans' morale and gave them hope that they could defeat a larger, well-established army.

Success at Saratoga also earned the Americans a valuable asset: an alliance with France. France was already supporting the United States with economic and military assistance, and these victories convinced the French government that the Americans could win the war. No longer feeling outmatched, the Americans now had military help from a wealthy nation, and they had experienced significant victories themselves.

HISTORICAL THINKING

1. **READING CHECK** Why were the battles of Saratoga important for the Continental Army?

2. **ANALYZE CAUSE AND EFFECT** How did an error in strategy affect the outcome of the Battles of Saratoga?

3. **IDENTIFY PROBLEMS AND SOLUTIONS** What problems did the Continental Army face at Saratoga, and what steps did it take to solve them?

Seeking Help from Europe

It's hard to face a tough challenge alone. This is especially true in times of war. During the Revolution, America looked for help from other countries.

MAIN IDEA Assistance from European powers and from heroes of various backgrounds helped Americans overcome some of their disadvantages in the American Revolution.

POWERFUL FRIENDS

The alliance between France and the United States did not happen immediately. Taking advantage of the Continental Army's momentum, the Continental Congress sent Benjamin Franklin and John Adams to Europe. Congress hoped to persuade France to become an official ally of the United States. The French considered Britain to be their main enemy and wanted to avenge their loss in the French and Indian War. These considerations helped Franklin and Adams convince France to sign the Treaty of Alliance in February 1778 and provide the United States with financial assistance.

France and Spain were allies, and they both had lost significant lands in North America at the end of the French and Indian War. In addition to money and supplies, France provided the Americans with troops. Both nations helped the Americans by drawing Britain's military and naval attention in different directions. The French navy engaged the British in the West Indies, pulling resources away from the North American mainland. Spanish military leader Bernardo de Gálvez forced the British to send troops to the Mississippi Valley to defend forts formerly held by the Spanish. Then Gálvez helped defeat the British in Florida and claimed that territory for Spain.

HEROES FROM HOME AND ABROAD

France and Spain also played pivotal roles in affecting the course of the war. You've learned that Tadeusz Kościuszko from Poland helped win the Battles of Saratoga. You've also read about the contributions of Prussia's **Baron Friedrich von Steuben** at Valley Forge. From von Steuben, the inexperienced American soldiers rapidly

learned skills such as marching, making quick decisions in combat, and using weapons, including the **bayonet** (BAY-uh-net), a sharp blade attached to a musket.

The **Marquis de Lafayette** (mar-KEE duh lah-fy-EHT), a French nobleman, had already offered his assistance to the American war effort and had become a general in the Continental Army. He took a break from the fighting and returned to France to help Franklin and Adams get funding and support from the king. With that goal accomplished, Lafayette came back to America and took part in many battles, including the one that would end the war.

Although the Continental Army did not actively welcome African Americans, those who sympathized with the Patriot cause found ways to help. An enslaved man named **James Armistead** was allowed by his owner to spy for Lafayette. Gaining the trust of British officers, Armistead gathered information that helped the Americans win key battles.

Even with France and Spain helping to pay for some of the costs of the war, the United States faced major economic challenges during the conflict. Before the war, Britain and the West Indies had been markets for American goods and sources of goods for the American markets. Now British ships **blockaded** American ports by refusing to let vessels enter or leave these harbors. Towns and farms were destroyed as battles raged near or around them. And war is expensive. American troops had to be fed, and they needed uniforms, dependable weapons, and a steady supply of ammunition. Battle wounds and

In this 1853 painting by Andre Jolly, Benjamin Franklin is shown as the center of attention among French royalty at the home of Princess Elizabeth. Diane de Polignac, placing a laurel wreath on Franklin's head, ran the household. Elizabeth stands behind her brother, King Louis XVI, who is seated at the right. To his right is his wife, Marie-Antoinette, the queen.

outbreaks of disease led to an increasing need for medical supplies. And, of course, the soldiers expected to be paid.

Unfortunately, Congress did not have the power to collect taxes to help fund the war. Instead, Congress decided to make up for the shortfall by printing more money, even though it had no real wealth to back it up. In 1782, John Adams obtained a loan from Dutch bankers but also looked to American citizens for additional help.

Many Americans contributed what they could to the cause. For example, American Jewish **financier** Haym Salomon lent funds to help pay the costs of the revolution. A financier raises and provides funds for a business or undertaking. Salomon's generous gesture was never repaid, however, and he died in 1785 without a penny to his name. Financial problems were not the only challenges Americans faced, however. The war was still far from over.

HISTORICAL THINKING

1. **READING CHECK** How did France and Spain help the Americans?

2. **MAKE INFERENCES** Why did other nations offer to help the Americans?

3. **DRAW CONCLUSIONS** How did Britain wage war against the Americans off the battlefield?

2.2 Hardship and Challenges

Even the most satisfying success can be short-lived, especially in wartime. You're up one day and down the next. Challenging as it may be, you just have to hang in there.

MAIN IDEA The Continental Army faced hardship and challenges at Valley Forge and on the frontier.

VALLEY FORGE

As you have read, the victory at Saratoga boosted American morale, but there was much more work to be done. The focus of the war shifted to Pennsylvania, where General Howe now occupied Philadelphia. You probably remember that the Continental Army set up camp at **Valley Forge**, northwest of the city, in the dead of the winter of 1777. George Washington set up camp alongside his men high atop a series of hills. Washington vowed to "share in the hardship" and "partake of [take part in] every inconvenience" his soldiers

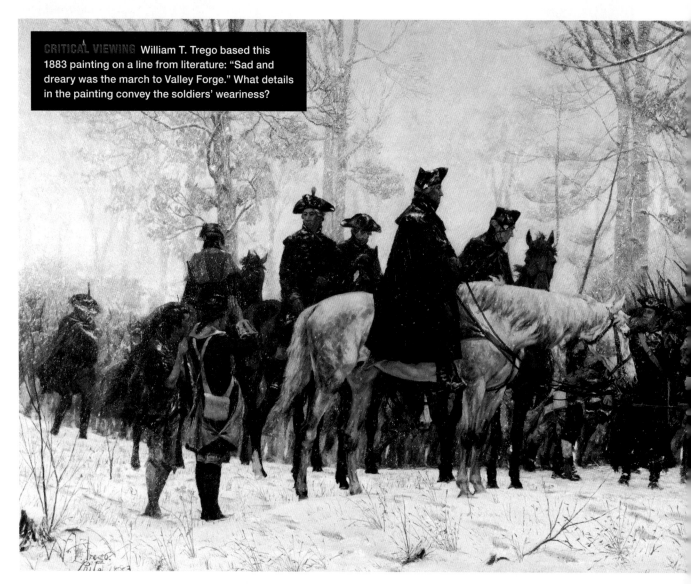

CRITICAL VIEWING William T. Trego based this 1883 painting on a line from literature: "Sad and dreary was the march to Valley Forge." What details in the painting convey the soldiers' weariness?

experienced. While Washington certainly suffered, he lived with his aides in a stone house at Valley Forge. His men lived in the small wooden huts they'd built themselves and used straw they gathered for bedding.

Meanwhile, General **Henry Clinton** had become the new commander of British forces in North America. In contrast to the Americans, Clinton and his men settled into quarters in Philadelphia, where they lived in relative comfort. Loyalist families gave them places to stay, and Clinton and his officers enjoyed parties and good food.

As you've read, the soldiers in the Continental Army suffered greatly from the cold and a lack of food, and some chose to **desert**, or run away from the army. But despite the horrible conditions, most soldiers chose to stay. Loyal to General Washington and determined to keep up the fight, they spent the winter training under von Steuben.

As winter wore on, others arrived to help the American cause. Lafayette came to command a division at Valley Forge. In addition to sharing his men's hardships, the Frenchman provided uniforms and muskets to those who needed them.

Spring's arrival brought not only better weather but also great news. Word of the alliance between America and France reached the camp. To celebrate, Washington had his men line up and shoot their guns in the air. They were poised and ready to do battle at Monmouth.

WAR ON THE FRONTIER

Pennsylvania wasn't the only place where war raged. From New York to Georgia, **skirmishes**, or small, short battles, took place along the rural western boundary of the frontier. Small divisions of the British Army guarded forts in this region, supported by Native American volunteers. Remember that at the outset of the American Revolution, many Native Americans supported the British. They feared that if the Americans won, they would take over more Native American land.

British general Henry Hamilton and his Native American allies planned to invade the frontier. But American frontiersman George Rogers Clark heard of these plans and led a small force in a surprise attack on one of the British bases, Fort Vincennes (vihn-SEHNZ). Hamilton surrendered, and the joint British–Native American offensive was halted.

Despite Clark's victory at Vincennes, American settlers found themselves constantly battling Iroquois forces. The fighting caused homelessness and food shortages in many communities.

HISTORICAL THINKING

1. **READING CHECK** What did George Washington's men have to do when they first arrived at Valley Forge?

2. **COMPARE AND CONTRAST** How did the experiences of the British and Continental armies in the winter of 1777–78 differ?

3. **IDENTIFY MAIN IDEAS AND DETAILS** How and why did Native Americans participate in the American Revolution?

2.3 Women's Roles in the Revolution

If colonial women could time travel to the present day, many would probably be surprised to see American women working alongside men in most settings. But some would feel right at home.

MAIN IDEA Even though they could not officially serve in the army, women played many key roles in the American Revolution.

BEFORE THE REVOLUTION

Colonial women had long stood with men against the British. For instance, do you remember that before the American Revolution, the Daughters of Liberty helped organize a boycott of British goods? **Mercy Otis Warren** was an outspoken supporter of these boycotts. She became active in colonial politics through one of the committees of correspondence and went on to become a notable historian of the Revolutionary era.

John Adams's wife, **Abigail Adams**, also played a vital role from the earliest days of the Revolution. Along with Mercy Otis Warren and the governor's wife, Hannah Winthrop, Adams was appointed by the Massachusetts Colony General Court to question and report on local women suspected of being Loyalists. Both Adams and Warren were sharp thinkers and skilled writers who freely voiced their ideas about liberty, independence, women's rights, and a new government.

DURING THE REVOLUTION

As often happens in wartime, women took over many duties at home traditionally performed by men. Women ran farms, shops, and businesses. They also supported soldiers who passed through their communities, giving them housing and food. Some women took more direct action. They traveled with the troops, working as nurses, cooking men's meals, and washing their clothes.

You may be surprised to learn that some women excelled at **espionage**, or spying. This was due in great part to the fact that men tended to underestimate them. Many of these spies worked as maids or cooks for British officers and so had access to valuable information. Some women even took part in combat, disguising themselves as men or at times simply stepping into battle. They risked not only the dangers of combat but also jail if it were discovered that they were women.

In 1777, **Sybil Ludington** rode more than 40 miles in a single night to warn forces commanded by her father of a British attack in Connecticut. The British planned to destroy American supplies there. She also warned the people along the way.

When women did not have a defined role in the war, they were resourceful in finding ways to help—some of which could be very risky. Abigail Adams's appeal to her husband still did not bring equal rights to American women. But colonial women had shown their ability to participate in the building of a new nation.

HISTORICAL THINKING

1. **READING CHECK** How did women contribute to the success of the American Revolution?

2. **FORM AND SUPPORT OPINIONS** Which woman named in this lesson do you think contributed most to the American Revolution? Use evidence from the text to explain and support your opinion.

3. **DRAW CONCLUSIONS** In what way do Abigail Adams's comments to her husband reflect ideas in the Declaration of Independence?

Remember the Ladies

The four women featured on this page—Abigail Adams, Anna Smith Strong, Mary Ludwig Hays McCauly, and Phillis Wheatley—provide examples of women who were every bit as involved and took the same or greater risks in the American Revolution as the men.

Abigail Adams wrote the following to her husband, John Adams, affirming that women were as much a force behind the war as men and deserved to be heard.

"In the new Code of Laws which I suppose it will be necessary for you to make I desire you would **Remember the Ladies** . . . we are determined to foment a Rebellion, and will not hold ourselves bound by any Laws in which we have no voice, or Representation."

—Abigail Adams in a letter to John Adams, March 31, 1776

Portrait of Abigail Adams by Benjamin Blyth, c. 1766

Molly Pitcher at the Cannon's Mouth postcard, 1909

Mary Ludwig Hays McCauly carried water to cool off the soldiers and the hot cannon her husband was firing during battles. This earned her the nickname Molly Pitcher. She also worked with her husband to fire the cannon. Other women served in combat during the war. One of them was Margaret Corbin, who is buried and honored with a monument at the United States Military Academy at West Point, New York. The woman in the postcard above represents not just Molly Pitcher but all the brave women who faced combat during the Revolution.

Phillis Wheatley proved the pen could also be a mighty weapon. She was born in Africa, enslaved as a young girl, and sold to a family of Boston Quakers who provided her with a good education. She became a poet who called for freedom for all, praised George Washington, and supported the American Revolution. She was the first African-American poet to have her work published.

Anna Smith Strong was a member of a spy ring on the coast of New York. She used a code based on how she hung out her laundry to let other members of the ring know when a messenger with information was arriving. A black petticoat on her clothesline meant the messenger was coming. The number of handkerchiefs scattered on the line indicated the cove in which he would land.

2.4 War at Sea

When you're used to walking on land, it can be hard to adjust to the tossing and swaying of a boat. Some people refer to this as "getting your sea legs." Sailors in the Continental Navy were about to get theirs.

MAIN IDEA The Continental Navy needed teamwork, determination, and strategy as it faced almost impossible odds against Britain's Royal Navy.

ATTACKS ON MERCHANT SHIPS

On land, Americans had the advantage of fighting on familiar terrain, or landforms and other physical features. And even though the British sent great numbers of troops to fight in North America, they were spread out across vast distances, so the Continental Army often faced smaller numbers of British troops at a time. In this way, it was able to hold its own.

The war at sea was a different story. Through the efforts of John Adams, the Continental Congress had established the Continental Navy in 1775, but the navy never had many ships. In contrast, Britain's Royal Navy was the largest and most powerful in the world, capable of causing great damage to the Americans' forces and economy. Even as the American Revolution began, British naval vessels had blockaded American harbors. Now they were attacking both American naval and merchant ships. The tiny Continental Navy could not hope to match its enemy's strength and resources.

Quickly building up and supporting a naval fleet was much more difficult than recruiting troops for land conflict. However, Benjamin Franklin's visit to France paid off. The French and Spanish navies helped swell the ranks of the Continental Navy.

Americans also turned to privateers—privately owned ships authorized to participate in warfare—to help protect their own shipping industry and damage Britain's. The Continental Congress granted privateers official permission to attack any British naval and merchant ships they encountered. During the war, as many as 2,000 vessels were put into use for privateering.

Privateer crews included a number of African-American sailors, both enslaved and free. Slave catchers rarely tried to capture runaway slaves who had stowed away on a ship. And the pay onboard was good, even though all privateer sailors worked in dangerous conditions. In fact, they were often captured and taken as prisoners of war.

Teenage African-American crewmember **James Forten** was taken aboard a British ship when it captured his vessel, the *Royal Louis*. The British captain assigned Forten to care for his young son, and the two became fast friends. As a result, the

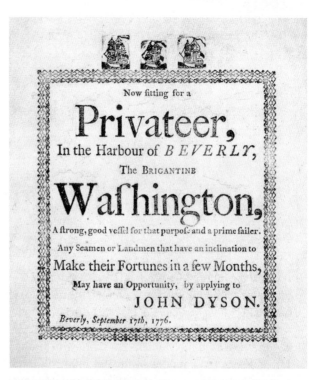

Calling All Able Sailors
This handbill advertised for experienced sailors to sail with the *Washington*, a vessel that went on to capture several enemy ships.

The Ordeal of John Paul Jones

Illustrator Anton Otto Fischer captures the drama on the *Bonhomme Richard* as
John Paul Jones (background, right) and his crew fight to keep sailors on the British ship
Serapis from boarding their ship. About 150 people were killed on each side in this battle.

captain's son asked his father to grant Forten his
freedom instead of turning him over to a prison
ship. The captain offered Forten a chance to
return to Britain with them, but Forten refused.
He believed in the principles of the American
Revolution, especially the natural rights of freedom
and the opportunity for democracy.

JOHN PAUL JONES

What the Continental Navy lacked in ships it
made up for in determination, strategy, and sheer
heroism. One American captain, **John Paul Jones**,
had all three of these strengths. In September
1779, Jones was in command of a ship called the
Bonhomme Richard when he encountered the
British ship *Serapis*. The *Serapis* was escorting
British merchant ships carrying military supplies.
Jones attacked the *Serapis*, and the battle was on.

Disaster struck for the American ship when
its main gun battery exploded. Soon after, the
Bonhomme Richard caught fire and was damaged

beyond repair. Legend has it that with both ships
fighting side by side, the British called on Jones
to surrender. But he yelled back, "I have not yet
begun to fight!" The battle raged on, and soon
it fell to the British to surrender. Jones boarded
and took control of the *Serapis*. In a war with few
victories for the Continental Navy, Jones's success
boosted American morale as the conflict moved
into its final stage.

HISTORICAL THINKING

1. **READING CHECK** How was the Continental
   Navy able to hold its own against Britain's
   Royal Navy?

2. **ANALYZE CAUSE AND EFFECT** How were
   France and Spain affected by the war at sea?

3. **MAKE INFERENCES** What do you think
   James Forten hoped to gain by fighting to
   uphold the American principles of freedom?

3.1 War in the Southern Colonies

When you're losing a game, sometimes it helps to change your strategy. That's what the British decided to do. But would moving the war south help or hurt them?

MAIN IDEA At first, southern battles went badly for the Continental Army, but the Patriots soon found ways to torment the British.

EARLY LOSSES

The British deployed a new strategy in the Southern Colonies in 1778. They counted on Loyalist and African-American support in Georgia, the Carolinas, and Virginia. They used the islands of the British West Indies to gather and transport supplies and recruits for the British and their allies.

But French-held territory in the Caribbean provided aid to the Continental Army's southern campaign. The French Colonial Army recruited many soldiers for the American cause from its islands, such as Saint-Domingue (san dom-ANG), or present-day Haiti. Their numbers included enslaved men willing to fight against the British.

Enslaved African Americans in the Southern Colonies were also recruited to fight for the British. General Henry Clinton offered freedom to enslaved men who joined the British Army. As a result, African-American support for the British grew in the Southern Colonies.

CRITICAL VIEWING In 1780, Francis Marion lured a British force 26 miles into the heart of a South Carolina swamp. Will Anderson illustrated this episode in a mural he painted in 2001. Why do you think the British (on horseback) might have had a difficult time fighting on the Swamp Fox's terms?

In 1778, Clinton sent thousands of troops to Georgia. There they captured Savannah and Augusta, followed by Charleston, South Carolina. In an effort to combat the British onslaught, in July 1780, American general Horatio Gates arrived to build a new southern army. But Gates failed to prepare these troops properly for battle. **Lord Cornwallis**, the British commander, had learned of Gates's movements and attacked the Americans at Camden, South Carolina. The British scored an overwhelming victory that spelled disaster for the Continental Army and disgrace for Gates.

THE SWAMP FOX

While the Continental Army suffered major losses in the South, nontraditional military units strengthened the American cause. **Guerrilla** units, or independent military groups that used methods such as sneak attacks, thrived in the rural wetlands of the American Southeast. South Carolina officer **Francis Marion** and his small group of guerrillas harassed British troops through the swamps of Georgia and the Carolinas. Because he was so clever and good at dodging the British, Marion soon earned the nickname "the Swamp Fox."

Marion had once been a regular soldier fighting for the Patriots. But General Gates dismissed him before the disastrous Battle of Camden to focus on defending other territories. Marion soon discovered his genius for guerrilla warfare—conducting surprise attacks on the British, gathering intelligence about the enemy, and winning the loyalty of local people. Despite the many early American defeats in the Southern Colonies, guerilla leaders such as Marion caused enough trouble for the British to keep the United States competitive—and, eventually, on the path to victory.

HISTORICAL THINKING

1. **READING CHECK** What early wins did the British score in the Southern Colonies?

2. **IDENTIFY MAIN IDEAS AND DETAILS** What role did France play in the war in the Southern Colonies?

3. **DRAW CONCLUSIONS** What characteristics of a fox did Francis Marion demonstrate as a guerrilla leader?

Major Battles of the American Revolution, 1775–1781

Québec, 1775

Montréal

BRITISH NORTH AMERICA
(CANADA)

MAINE
(part of
Massachusetts)

45°N

St. Lawrence

Lake Champlain

Fort Ticonderoga, 1777

NEW
HAMPSHIRE

Lexington, 1775

Bunker Hill, 1775

Saratoga, 1777

Concord, 1775

Boston

Lake Superior

Lake Michigan

Lake Huron

Lake Ontario

Lake Erie

NEW YORK

MASSACHUSETTS

CONNECTICUT

Hudson R.

70°W

RHODE
ISLAND

New York

40°N

Princeton, 1776

Monmouth Court House, 1778

PENNSYLVANIA

Valley Forge

Trenton, 1776

Brandywine Creek, 1777

Philadelphia

NEW
JERSEY

MARYLAND

DELAWARE

Wabash R.

VIRGINIA

Chesapeake
Bay

Cahokia, 1778

Vincennes, 1779

Ohio R.

Richmond

James R.

Yorktown, 1781

Kaskaskia, 1778

NEW SPAIN

Cumberland R.

Roanoke R.

35°N

Guilford Court House, 1781

Mississippi R.

NORTH CAROLINA

Kings Mountain, 1780

Tennessee R.

Cowpens, 1781

Camden, 1780

ATLANTIC
OCEAN

SOUTH CAROLINA

Alabama R.

GEORGIA

Charleston, 1780

Chattahoochee R.

Savannah, 1778

▢	British colonies
✴	American victory
✴	British victory
✴	No clear victor
—	Proclamation Line of 1763

WEST FLORIDA

EAST
FLORIDA

N
W E
S

Gulf of Mexico

30°N

0   100   200 Miles

0   100   200 Kilometers

90°W   85°W   80°W   75°W

3.2 The Tide Turns

Sometimes a new leader brings new energy and ideas to a situation and makes all the difference. That's just what happened when a new commander was brought in to lead the southern troops.

MAIN IDEA A change in leadership and a victory in the Carolinas helped change the course of the war in the Southern Colonies.

A NEW GENERAL

The tide of the war in the Southern Colonies began to turn in 1780. That's when General **Nathanael Greene** replaced Horatio Gates as commander of the Continental Army's southern troops. As a Quaker, Greene should have been a **pacifist**, or a person who stood against war and violence. So when Greene expressed his desire to organize troops against the British, the Quakers expelled him. After serving with Washington and leading troops in New York, New Jersey, and Pennsylvania, Greene was sent to the Southern Colonies to try to change the direction of the war for the Americans.

Greene's strategy involved increasing the Continental Army's mobility and agility. Spread out over the Southern Colonies, the large British Army had trouble moving quickly and changing plans. Greene used smaller forces to draw British troops away from strategic locations. He also benefited from a growing southern dislike of the British, whose troops and supporters had destroyed local houses and farms, executed prisoners of war, and made false promises of protection. Greene impressed southern colonists, including Loyalists, by protecting their property and enforcing order. Growing numbers in the Southern Colonies joined Greene's army or guerrilla forces.

PATRIOTS AND LOYALISTS CLASH

While the Americans changed their strategy, the British did not. British strategy in the Southern Colonies depended heavily on Loyalist support. The British relied on pitting American Loyalists and Patriots against each other, with little British troop involvement. That strategy failed at the **Battle of Kings Mountain**.

In the fall of 1780, Lord Cornwallis headed north from South Carolina, believing the time had come for British forces to conquer all the Southern Colonies. His troops met with heavy resistance. At Kings Mountain, near the border between the Carolinas, 2,000 Patriots, fighting independently from the Continental Army, clashed with an enemy force made up almost entirely of other Americans. These frontier Patriots dealt a resounding defeat to 1,100 Loyalist soldiers fighting under Major Patrick Ferguson, the only British Army member at the battle. Patriot fighters put to death some Loyalists who surrendered, perhaps as revenge for recent British executions of American prisoners.

The Battle of Kings Mountain was the first of many victories for the Patriots in the Southern Colonies. Loyalists sustained big losses at Cowpens in South Carolina, and Cornwallis and his troops suffered casualties at Guildford Court House in North Carolina. As a result, Cornwallis headed back toward Virginia. Because of the importance of the Battle of Kings Mountain, Thomas Jefferson called it "the turn of the tide of success."

HISTORICAL THINKING

1. **READING CHECK** How did Nathanael Greene's leadership affect the war in the Southern Colonies?

2. **INTERPRET MAPS** Why might frontiersmen have fought the Battle of Kings Mountain?

3. **SUMMARIZE** Why did Cornwallis's plan to control the Southern Colonies by enlisting the aid of Loyalists fail?

3.3 The War Ends

How often does winning against impossible odds happen in real life?

When that first shot was fired in Lexington, no one could have predicted

that 13 small colonies would defeat one of the world's greatest armies.

MAIN IDEA The British defeat at the Battle of Yorktown
brought an end to the American Revolution.

A PIVOTAL YEAR

As you've read, British hopes for victory in the South began to fade after their defeat at Kings Mountain. In 1781, American general Nathanael Greene moved south to regain South Carolina and Georgia, where the British still had 8,000 men spread thinly throughout the large region. Greene's 1,500 Continental soldiers and the guerilla units helping them were able to defeat small groups one by one. Americans were able to take back most of the area. Meanwhile, in Virginia, Lord Cornwallis replaced

Benedict Arnold as commander of the British forces in the area. In Yorktown, with an army of almost 8,000 men, Cornwallis camped on a peninsula facing the York River. His aim was to protect the harbor for the use of the British fleet. Cornwallis requested more troops from New York, but the British were slow in sending them.

🏛 U.S. Capitol Rotunda, Washington, D.C.

John Trumbull's painting *Surrender of Lord Cornwallis* depicts the British surrender in Yorktown. In the painting, American troops (on the right) and French troops (on the left) are all on horseback. Cornwallis's soldiers appear in the center of the painting. Why do you think the British soldiers are all on foot?

Setting up camp on the peninsula would prove to be a fatal mistake for Lord Cornwallis and his soldiers.

THE WORLD TURNED UPSIDE DOWN

American and French troops surrounded Cornwallis's camp by land and by sea. French naval officer admiral Comte de Grasse (duh-GRAHS) commanded a French fleet on the York River. He approached the British camp from the water. Meanwhile, a combined army of French soldiers, commanded by Comte de Rochambeau (ROH-sham-BOH), and Americans, led by General George Washington, marched south from New York, approaching the camp by land. In a show of military **expertise**, or skill, these three commanders led their 17,000 troops against Cornwallis, trapping him on the peninsula. Cornwallis had no choice but to surrender.

Charles O'Hara, second in command to Cornwallis, tried to surrender his general's sword to Rochambeau, but the French leader steered him to Washington instead. The British military band played a song called "The World Turned Upside Down," a fitting comment on the victory. The **Battle of Yorktown** was the last major battle of the war. In 1782, more than six years after the first shots were fired, the British Parliament officially voted to end the war.

The impact of this victory was staggering. Once only the dream of a group of visionaries seeking freedom from unreasonable laws and taxes, the young country had come through the fire of war to take its place as a full-fledged nation. In the decades and centuries that followed, the United States of America—established with the promise of equality for all—would rise to become one of the most powerful and influential nations on Earth. In time, people in many countries around the world would draw inspiration from America's example and fight for their own freedom and independence.

Remembering the Victors

This stamp commemorates the 150th anniversary of the victory at Yorktown. We all know George Washington, who is shown in the middle, but what about the other two leaders who helped the Americans win at Yorktown?

Comte de Rochambeau (on the left), was born in Vendôme, France. Commissioned into the French army at age 17, he was a veteran of 14 military sieges in Europe. King Louis XVI sent him to lead the French force in America in 1780.

Comte de Grasse (on the right), was born in Le Bar, France, and started working on ships when he was only about 12 years old. At 18, he joined the French navy. DeGrasse was fighting the British in the West Indies when General Washington asked for his help in Virginia against Cornwallis. The rest is history.

HISTORICAL THINKING

1. **READING CHECK** What factors led to the American victory at Yorktown?

2. **DRAW CONCLUSIONS** What statement was Rochambeau making when he made O'Hara surrender the British general's sword to Washington?

3. **ANALYZE CAUSE AND EFFECT** What happened as a result of the American victory in both the long- and short-term?

3.4 An Ally in the American Victory

MAIN IDEA The physical and human characteristics, as well as the "site" and "situation," of locations have helped shape events in history.

In 1776, no one in the world believed the American colonists could defeat the mighty British Army. Yet throughout history, geography has affected how events have unfolded, and this was certainly the case during the American Revolution. The Continental Army had several types of geographic advantages: terrain, population distribution, distance, and climate. For example, the Continental Army spent the winter of 1777–78 at Valley Forge in Pennsylvania. The climate there was cold—and the cold shaped events. As you know, the soldiers suffered greatly from a lack of sufficient clothing and shelter. Yet the bad weather prevented the British from attacking them.

The Catskill Mountains in New York State are covered with thick forests that provided cover for the Continental Army and challenges for the British as they approached.

Study these examples of the geographic advantages that favored the Continental Army. Consider the information provided about each site—the physical characteristics of the example given. Then consider the situation or the location of each site in relation to other places.

European Claims in North America, 1776

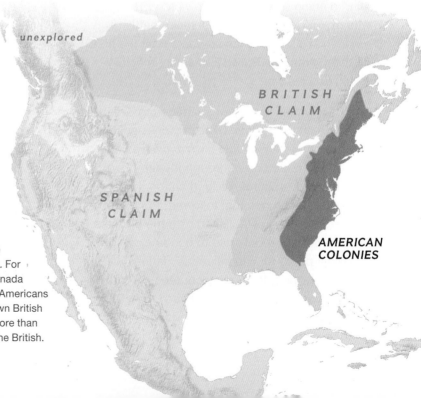

unexplored

BRITISH CLAIM

SPANISH CLAIM

AMERICAN COLONIES

TERRAIN

SITE The terrain of upstate New York is mountainous and heavily forested, with many rivers and streams.

SITUATION The Americans were familiar with the terrain, which gave them an enormous advantage. For example, in 1777, British troops marched from Canada toward New York to attack the Continental Army. Americans cut down trees and wrecked bridges, slowing down British troops. This gave the Americans time to gather more than 11,000 troops at Saratoga, where they defeated the British.

40,000 people
population of Philadelphia in 1776

POPULATION DISTRIBUTION

SITE The area of the colonies was large, but the population was relatively small—about 2.5 million people. Cities were also small, as most people lived on farms, so the population was widely scattered.

SITUATION The population was so widely distributed that the British couldn't simply attack one or two cities to defeat the Americans. In addition, the Continental Army could hide from British troops in unpopulated territory.

97 miles
from New York City to Philadelphia

370 miles
from New York City to Fort Pitt

COLONIAL POPULATION, 1776

Philadelphia, PA	40,000
New York, NY	25,000
Boston, MA	15,000
Charleston, SC	12,000
Newport, RI	11,000

Source: *The Economist*

1,580 miles
from northern border of Maine to southern border of Georgia

DISTANCE

SITE The colonies stretched more than 1,500 miles from north to south and more than 350 miles from east to west.

SITUATION The 13 colonies were located more than 3,000 miles from Great Britain. The distance created enormous problems for the British. They had to transport soldiers, supplies, and munitions by sailing ships. When the troops reached North America, they took weeks to march from one field of combat to another.

3,460 miles
from London, England, to New York City

CLIMATE

SITE The British were not used to the cold winters of the northern states. The heat and humidity of the southern states were unfamiliar to the British, too.

SITUATION The Americans used their knowledge of the climate during the war. In the winter of 1775, Washington wanted artillery transported from New York to Boston. Colonel Henry Knox used 42 sleds pulled by oxen to transport the artillery over snow and ice. The Americans used the weapons to drive the British out of Boston.

763 miles
from New York City to Charleston

THINK LIKE A GEOGRAPHER

1. **IDENTIFY MAIN IDEAS AND DETAILS** Why did distance pose problems for British troops during the American Revolution?

2. **ANALYZE CAUSE AND EFFECT** How did the Americans use geography to gain an advantage over the British?

3. **FORM AND SUPPORT OPINIONS** Of the four geographic factors, which one do you think had the greatest impact on the war? Explain your reasons.

3.5 Legacy of the War

With the war finally over, the young country assessed its costs and looked toward the future. The citizens of the United States had some hard decisions to make. What direction would the new country take?

MAIN IDEA Once a formal treaty was negotiated and signed, the United States began to forge its new identity as an independent nation.

NEGOTIATING THE PEACE

The American Revolution was over. It would soon inspire other nations, including France and the French colony of Haiti, to revolt and demand democracy. But war always comes at a high price. Thousands of soldiers—both American and British—lost their lives in combat, and even more died of disease. Now it was time to heal and begin building the nation. First, though, the United States and Great Britain had to make peace. The two countries did so in the **Treaty of Paris of 1783**.

Benjamin Franklin, John Jay, and John Adams negotiated skillfully for the United States. The treaty they produced included two extremely important **provisions**, or legal conditions, that aided the country. The British agreed both to recognize the independence of the United States of America and to approve the new American boundaries. The new country was bounded on the west by the Mississippi River, on the north by Canada, and on the south by Florida. The United States would have plenty of growing room.

Florida, from which Britain had created **East Florida** and **West Florida**, went back to Spain in a separate agreement. The British also made a separate agreement with France over parts of the West Indies and Canada.

A NEW IDENTITY

Not all Americans were happy with the outcome of the war. Many Loyalists and Native Americans, furious that their British allies had signed away their lands, moved to Canada. Some former slaves freed by the British also made their way to Canada, but others were returned to slavery. The majority of Americans, though, stayed right where they were and began rebuilding. Britain's economic control and taxation had spurred the Revolution. Freedom of trade took firm hold, laying the groundwork for growing commerce and industry.

Liberty and equality were central to the new national identity as well. In 1781, an enslaved woman named Mum Betts sued and won her freedom in court. Taking the name **Elizabeth Freeman**, she inspired Massachusetts to become the first state to abolish slavery. In Delaware, **Richard Allen** bought his freedom and later founded one of the first independent black churches in Philadelphia.

The most difficult task facing the United States was establishing a plan for government. Citizens favored **republicanism**, a system with no king or queen, where the people choose representatives to make their laws. They also stressed civic republicanism, or responsibility for the common good. Americans hoped to blend civic republicanism and ideals of classical liberal principles, including private property and individual and religious freedoms, to create their new government.

HISTORICAL THINKING

1. **READING CHECK** How did the Treaty of Paris of 1783 secure the future of the United States?

2. **DESCRIBE** How did the U.S. government plan reflect the ideals of civic republicanism, classical liberal principles, and English parliamentary traditions?

3. **FORM AND SUPPORT OPINIONS** Do you think African Americans were better off after the revolution? Explain why or why not.

The solemn Ratifications of the present Treaty expedited in good and due Form shall be exchanged between the contracting Parties in the Space of six Months or sooner, if possible, to be computed from the Day of the Signature of the present Treaty. In Witness whereof We the undersigned their ministers Plenipotentiary have in their Name and in Virtue of our full Powers, signed with our Hands the present Definitive Treaty, and caused the Seals of our Arms to be affixed thereto.

Done at Paris, this third Day of September In the Year of our Lord, one thousand, seven hundred and Eighty three. —

D Hartley

John Adams.

B Franklin

John Jay

CHAPTER 6

THE AMERICAN REVOLUTION

REVIEW

VOCABULARY

Match the following vocabulary terms with their definitions.

1. mercenary
2. blockade
3. skirmish
4. desert
5. pacifist
6. provision
7. republicanism
8. espionage

a. legal condition or requirement
b. the act of spying to gather information
c. to leave military service illegally
d. a soldier who is paid to fight for a country other than his or her own
e. a small, short battle
f. a form of government in which the people elect representatives
g. to use ships or other means to keep ships and commerce from entering a port
h. a person who stands against war and violence

READING STRATEGY
FORM AND SUPPORT OPINIONS

If you haven't already, complete your chart listing your opinion and supporting statements regarding the factor that most helped secure an American victory in the Revolution. Then answer the following question.

9. What factor was key to the U.S. victory in the American Revolution? Include your supporting statements in your answer.

Opinion:
Supporting statement:
Supporting statement:
Supporting statement:
Supporting statement:

MAIN IDEAS

Answer the following questions. Support your answers with evidence from the chapter.

10. What disadvantages did the Americans face at the beginning of the war? **LESSON 1.1**

11. How did the alliances and treaties made by Native Americans affect their relationships with both the Patriots and the British? **LESSON 1.2**

12. How did other nations come to the aid of the Americans? **LESSON 2.1**

13. Compare the experiences of the American and British armies in the winter of 1777–78. **LESSON 2.2**

14. Why did Abigail Adams ask her husband to "Remember the Ladies"? **LESSON 2.3**

15. What strategy did the Americans use to face the powerful British Navy? **LESSON 2.4**

16. How did Nathanael Greene and Francis Marion help change the course of the war in the Southern Colonies? **LESSON 3.2**

17. How did the Americans earn a victory at Yorktown? **LESSON 3.3**

18. How did American calls for independence inspire other nations, such as France and the French colony of Haiti? **LESSON 3.5**

Answer the following questions. Support your answers with evidence from the chapter.

19. **ANALYZE CAUSE AND EFFECT** Besides the death toll, what was a negative effect of the war?

20. **SYNTHESIZE** How did American women and men work together in the war?

21. **DRAW CONCLUSIONS** What groups of people did not benefit from the Revolution?

22. **FORM AND SUPPORT OPINIONS** What British mistake led most directly to their defeat?

INTERPRET MAPS

Look closely at the map of the Battle of Yorktown. Then answer the questions that follow.

Battle of Yorktown, 1781

23. According to the map, what happened in the Battle of the Capes?

24. How does the map illustrate cooperation between the Americans and the French?

ANALYZE SOURCES

Timothy Pickering, Jr., was an officer in the Continental Army. In 1778, when he read that his father, a Loyalist, was dying, Pickering wrote him a letter. Read the excerpt from the letter and answer the question.

> When I look back on past time, I regret our difference of sentiment in great as well as (sometimes) in little politics; as it was a deduction [subtraction] from the happiness otherwise to have been enjoyed. Yet you had always too much regard to freedom in thinking & the rights of conscience, to lay upon me any injunctions [commands] which could interfere with my own opinion of what was [my] duty. Often have I thanked my Maker for the greatest blessing of my life—your example & instructions in all the duties I owe to God, and my neighbor. They have not been lost upon me.
>
> —Letter from Timothy Pickering, Jr., to Timothy Pickering, Sr., February 23, 1778

25. What emotions does Pickering express toward his father?

CONNECT TO YOUR LIFE

26. **EXPOSITORY** Think about the different people you read about in the chapter. How did individuals, both Americans and others, show heroism in the American Revolution? Write a paragraph about two individuals mentioned in the chapter, explaining why they should be considered heroes.

TIPS

- Review the chapter and choose two individuals whom you consider heroes. Write a topic sentence about their heroism during the American Revolution.

- Support your choices with evidence from the chapter.

- Conclude your paragraph with a summary of the individuals' heroism.

FROM CONFEDERATION TO
CONSTITUTION
1776–1791

ESSENTIAL QUESTION
How did ideas about the role of state and national government evolve?

AMERICAN STORIES ONLINE Philadelphia, Summer of 1787

SECTION 1 **The Confederation Era**

KEY VOCABULARY

constitution	ordinance
constitutionalism	Ordinance of 1785
credit	ratify
federal	Shays's Rebellion
Northwest Ordinance of 1787	sovereign

SECTION 2 **Drafting the Constitution**

KEY VOCABULARY

checks and balances	executive branch	legislative branch
commerce clause	federalism	separation of powers
common market	Framers	slave importation clause
delegate	fugitive slave clause	Supreme Court
dual sovereignty	judicial branch	Three-Fifths Compromise
electoral college		

SECTION 3 **Ratification and the Bill of Rights**

KEY VOCABULARY

amendment	Bill of Rights	statute
antifederalist	federalist	

AMERICAN GALLERY ONLINE Historic Philadelphia

READING STRATEGY

DETERMINE CHRONOLOGY
When you analyze chronology, you determine how ideas and events unfold over time. As you read the chapter, use an organizer like this one to record how ideas about state and national government developed in the United States.

"The people are the only legitimate fountain of power."

—James Madison

249

1.1 State and National Governments

The last thing revolutionaries who have broken free from oppressive rulers want is the same way of governing. American revolutionaries wanted a new style of government—and one with limited power.

MAIN IDEA The Articles of Confederation limited the power of the new national government, while state governments retained much of their independence.

CREATING ORDER

Part of the legacy of the American struggle for independence included the establishment of a government based on republicanism, or the idea that government's power comes from its citizens and their representatives. Even as the war raged, each state moved forward and set up its own government.

Elected representatives from each state met and drafted a **constitution**, or a plan for government. Many state constitutions included lists of rights to which every citizen was entitled, such as the freedom to practice any religion. Once the constitutions were drafted and revised, the state representatives **ratified**, or approved, them.

Many states decided to organize their governments with governors and two-house legislatures elected by the people. Organizing legislatures into two parts, instead of one, ensured that lawmakers would have to share power and limited the power of governors. Some states, such as Pennsylvania, opted for no governor at all.

State constitutions were a new concept at the time. Most western European countries did not grant such power to elected legislatures. The

ARTICLES
OF
CONFEDERATION
AND
PERPETUAL UNION
BETWEEN THE
STATES
OF
NEW-HAMPSHIRE, MASSACHUSETTS-BAY, RHODE-ISLAND AND PROVIDENCE PLANTATIONS, CONNECTICUT, NEW-YORK, NEW-JERSEY, PENNSYLVANIA, DELAWARE, MARY-LAND, VIRGINIA, NORTH-CAROLINA, SOUTH-CAROLINA AND GEORGIA.

The Articles of Confederation went through six drafts between 1775 and 1777 before Congress finally approved it and then submitted it to the 13 states for ratification.

process of writing and ratifying state constitutions served as a model for the new national government to introduce future political institutions and ideas. One of the new ideas that emerged was a constitution that would govern all American states.

A NATIONAL PLAN

After the states ratified their constitutions, they decided to band together to defeat the British. Representatives from many of the states started meeting regularly to draft a plan for unification called the Articles of Confederation.

The Articles of Confederation gave Congress the ability to make decisions about the military. They also outlined a national plan of **sovereign**, or self-governing, states. The **federal**, or national, government would have little power of its own, nor would it include a president or a federal court system. It would simply serve as an administrator to help unify the states. This limited federal government reflected the ideals first put forth in the Declaration of Independence, which stated that a government should derive its powers "from the consent of the governed."

The Articles of Confederation assigned foreign affairs and relations with Native Americans, the ability to declare war and peace, and the postal

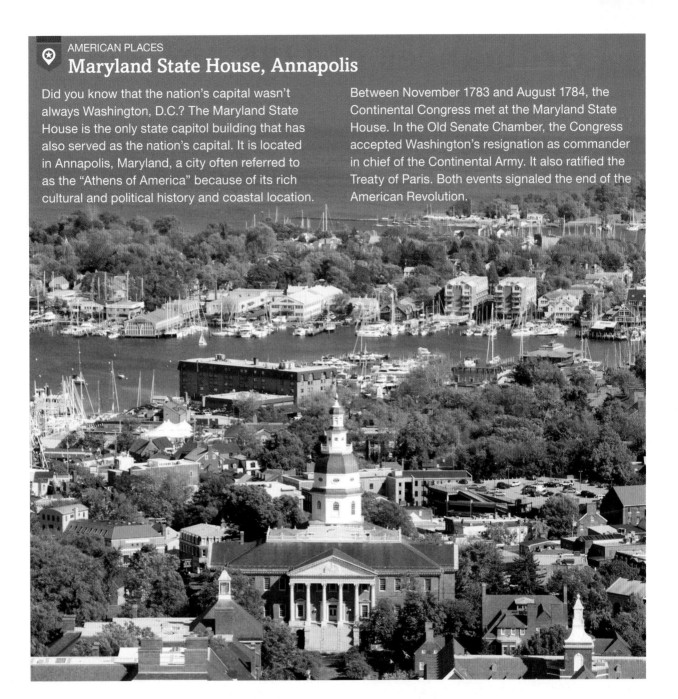

AMERICAN PLACES
Maryland State House, Annapolis

Did you know that the nation's capital wasn't always Washington, D.C.? The Maryland State House is the only state capitol building that has also served as the nation's capital. It is located in Annapolis, Maryland, a city often referred to as the "Athens of America" because of its rich cultural and political history and coastal location.

Between November 1783 and August 1784, the Continental Congress met at the Maryland State House. In the Old Senate Chamber, the Congress accepted Washington's resignation as commander in chief of the Continental Army. It also ratified the Treaty of Paris. Both events signaled the end of the American Revolution.

service to Congress. The national government could produce money but not levy taxes. If it needed money, it had to ask the states for funds. Congress needed to approve any legislation that would affect the country.

Americans liked these ideas because they addressed liberties denied to them under British rule. They also laid the foundation for **constitutionalism**, an approach to government that strictly defines and limits its powers. In March 1781, all 13 states finally ratified the Articles of Confederation, which would serve as the first constitution of the United States for eight years.

HISTORICAL THINKING

1. **READING CHECK** What responsibilities did the national government have under the Articles of Confederation?

2. **ANALYZE CAUSE AND EFFECT** How did the development of state constitutions influence the national plan for government?

3. **IDENTIFY MAIN IDEAS AND DETAILS** How were the ideals put forth in the Declaration of Independence reflected in the new American government?

1.2 Ordinances of 1785 and 1787

When large groups of people get together but have few rules to follow, things can get wild fast. As settlers moved into territory northwest of the Ohio River, the new United States struggled to maintain law and order beyond its official boundaries.

MAIN IDEA The ordinances of 1785 and 1787 allowed the federal government to better regulate westward expansion and distribute land to new settlers.

GO WEST!

You have read that the Treaty of Paris of 1783 granted the United States most of the territory from the Atlantic Ocean to the Mississippi River. This land extended north to the St. Lawrence River and the Great Lakes and south to the Spanish colony of Florida. Under the Articles of Confederation, the national government controlled all this territory.

Fertile soil attracted white settlers to the land beyond the Appalachian (a-puh-LATCH-uhn) Mountains. Settlers had begun arriving there in 1775, when frontier adventurers such as

Daniel Boone and some companions created a route through the Appalachian Mountains from Virginia to Kentucky. The new route, called the **Wilderness Road**, enabled large numbers of people to move west. The "western lands," as they were called, included present-day Ohio, Indiana, Illinois, Michigan, Wisconsin, and part of Minnesota.

THE NORTHWEST TERRITORY

Territorial expansion and its consequences created a new set of problems for the federal government. Congress recognized the need to provide safety and order within the new settlements, and it also wanted to establish a strong governmental presence in the western lands. Operating under the Articles of Confederation, Congress passed a series of **ordinances**, or laws, for settling the western lands. These ordinances established an orderly system for transferring federally owned land into private holdings, townships, and states. The first ordinance, passed in 1784, divided the territory into a small number of self-governing districts that could later become states.

The second ordinance was the **Ordinance of 1785**. It called for surveying and organizing districts into townships. The townships would be further divided into lots that the government would sell at a minimum of $1 per acre. Each township also had to set aside land for a school.

Finally, the **Northwest Ordinance of 1787** renamed the land the **Northwest Territory**. The ordinance provided for ownership of land by individuals and for the creation of new states out of this territory. Because it applied a portion of funds

Northwest Territory, 1787

Boundaries indefinite

Northwest Territory
Present-day state boundary

L. Superior

BRITISH NORTH AMERICA (CANADA)

Mississippi R.

L. Michigan

L. Huron

L. Erie

SPANISH LOUISIANA

PENN.

Ohio R.

VIRGINIA

KENTUCKY
Cumberland Gap

NORTH CAROLINA

TENNESSEE

0   100   200 Miles
0 100 200 Kilometers

50°N
40°N
90°W
80°W

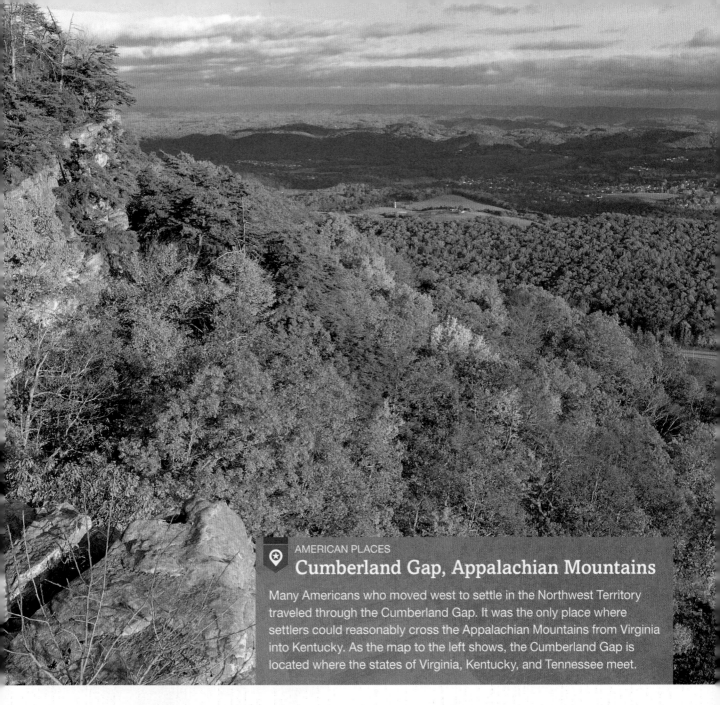

Cumberland Gap, Appalachian Mountains

Many Americans who moved west to settle in the Northwest Territory traveled through the Cumberland Gap. It was the only place where settlers could reasonably cross the Appalachian Mountains from Virginia into Kentucky. As the map to the left shows, the Cumberland Gap is located where the states of Virginia, Kentucky, and Tennessee meet.

from the sale of lands toward building schools, it established the first system of public education and reinforced the Founders' belief that the success of a republican government relies on an educated people. The ordinance prohibited slavery in the Northwest Territory. It guaranteed the rights of the people who settled there and stated that "the utmost good faith shall always be observed" toward Native Americans. The ordinances of 1785 and 1787 created a plan for westward expansion. They also caused some unforeseen problems for the new nation. One of these problems would be growing conflict with Native Americans in the Northwest Territory.

HISTORICAL THINKING

1. **READING CHECK** What problems did territorial expansion create for the new nation?

2. **DETERMINE CHRONOLOGY** How did the Articles of Confederation and each of the land ordinances build on one another to pave the way for settlement?

3. **INTERPRET MAPS** Based on what you see on the map, what major waterways were newly available to settlers in the Northwest Territory?

1.3 Controversies About the Articles

Have you ever thought of a brilliant solution to a problem that only led to more problems? In the 1780s, the Articles of Confederation were exactly that: a solution that led to more problems.

MAIN IDEA The Articles of Confederation limited the federal government's effectiveness and led to economic problems and challenges to its authority.

THE PRICE OF WAR

The Articles of Confederation provided a governing structure during the Revolution but quickly proved inadequate for the needs of the new nation. The Articles created 13 sovereign states instead of one unified nation. So when the national government faced growing economic problems, it did not have an effective system in place to solve them.

One economic problem was the amount of debt that remained after the Revolution. By 1790, the U.S. government owed around $50 million to American merchants and farmers and also to the French government. The shortfall in funds also meant soldiers could not be paid, which led to angry protests.

Because of the limitations of the Articles, Congress could not impose taxes or regulate trade. Individual states refused to contribute enough money to help the national government pay these debts. Rewriting the Articles so that Congress could levy taxes was nearly impossible because the representatives of all 13 states had to approve such a measure. Few, if any, states were likely to offer their support, so the debts went unpaid.

Before the war, many Americans relied on receiving **credit**, or the privilege of purchasing something and paying the cost back over time. British companies wanted to encourage the colonists to buy their goods, and giving credit made that possible. As British subjects, farmers could repay their debts with goods, such as livestock and crops. After the war, British manufacturers demanded that all debts be repaid with money instead of goods. At the same time, state governments started to impose heavy taxes upon their citizens. Few farmers had cash on

Tricorn hat

🏛 Memorial Hall Museum Deerfield, Massachusetts

Tricorn hats like this one, dated 1775, were popular in Europe and America in the 1700s. Notice how the tricorn hat appears in the illustration on the opposite page, flying off the head of the man attacking the official. Other men in the scene are wearing tricorn hats as well.

hand, and many Americans, especially farmers, faced financial ruin. When farmers failed to repay their debts, they often faced prosecution and the loss of their farms.

In some states, those who owed money demanded new laws that would allow them to settle their debts and pay taxes with goods. Citizens also wanted fewer requirements for voting so that they would have better representation in state governments. When governments did not respond, citizens challenged their authority and legitimacy by rebelling.

SHAYS'S REBELLION

In the fall of 1786, Daniel Shays, a veteran of the American Revolution, led rifle-carrying farmers into various Massachusetts courthouses and demanded the end of debt hearings. The Massachusetts government frantically asked Congress for help to put down the armed rebellion. In turn, Congress requested that the states help by sending money and soldiers, but the states refused. Its inability to respond to the domestic crisis of citizen rebellion revealed how ineffective Congress was under the Articles of Confederation.

Citizens became angrier when the state of Massachusetts passed the Riot Act, which prohibited armed groups from gathering in public. To prove its point, the state government sent armed troops, who defeated Shays's men easily. Shays and his supporters risked losing their voting rights and even imprisonment. However, **Shays's Rebellion** inspired other people to stand up to the government. One effect of the uprising was that in the following year's election, voter participation increased dramatically. Citizens wanted input into how problems such as debt repayment could be resolved.

CRITICAL VIEWING A protestor attacks an official during Shays's Rebellion in an attempt to disrupt court proceedings in Springfield, Massachusetts. Protests over the repayment of debts occurred in many states but reached a higher level of intensity in Massachusetts. Confrontations between farmers and government officials also occurred in the Massachusetts towns of Northampton, Concord, and Worcester. What details in the illustration convey the drama of Shays's Rebellion?

HISTORICAL THINKING

1. **READING CHECK** How did the Articles of Confederation limit the effectiveness of the federal government?

2. **DETERMINE CHRONOLOGY** In what ways did the economics of the American Revolution lead to Shays's Rebellion?

3. **ANALYZE CAUSE AND EFFECT** What effect did Shays's Rebellion have on the election of 1787?

2.1 The Constitutional Convention

Would you like to travel for weeks by horse-drawn wagon along bumpy dirt roads in bad weather to help decide your country's fate? That's what 55 government representatives did to attend a meeting in the spring of 1787.

MAIN IDEA American leaders met at the Constitutional Convention to debate and decide how to reform the national government.

Legend
1 James Madison   3 George Washington   5 Gouverneur Morris
2 George Mason   4 Benjamin Franklin   6 Alexander Hamilton

CRITICAL VIEWING This mural is one of two large-scale scenes painted by Barry Faulkner in 1936. It hangs in the Rotunda for the Charters of Freedom in the National Archives. What do you think the artist meant to convey by the setting he created for James Madison's presentation of the U.S. Constitution to George Washington?

DELEGATES GATHER

By 1787, it was clear the Articles of Confederation were not very effective. The United States was growing geographically and economically, and the Articles were not able to address complications from that growth. Robert Morris of Pennsylvania and **Alexander Hamilton** of New York pointed to Shays's Rebellion and other crises as evidence in support of their message. Morris and Hamilton believed the country needed a stronger government in order to deal with its problems.

Leaders called for a meeting to discuss reform. The meeting, held in Philadelphia on May 25, 1787, was called the **Constitutional Convention**.

Every state sent **delegates**, or representatives, except Rhode Island. The tiny state did not trust the concept of a powerful federal government, which it feared would be the outcome of the Constitutional Convention. Rhode Island's decision not to send delegates irritated many, including the normally even-tempered George Washington.

Independence Hall Philadelphia

When Washington presided over the Constitutional Convention, he occupied this chair, called the Rising Sun chair. Note the intricate, carved detail of the sun that would appear behind the head of its occupant. John Folwell designed and carved the Rising Sun chair in 1779. Today, it is housed in the Assembly Room at Independence Hall.

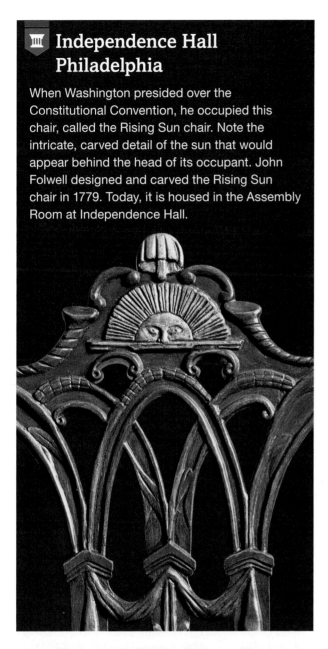

Those who gathered at the Convention to create the Constitution became known as the **Framers**. The Framers were wealthy, influential, and well educated. Many of the Framers had also been leaders during the Revolution, including Pennsylvania delegate Benjamin Franklin. The Framers elected George Washington from Virginia to lead the Convention.

Of the Framers at the Convention, James Madison, from Virginia, was the best prepared to craft a constitution for the new nation. His research and knowledge proved the most influential in shaping the ideas the delegates debated and ultimately included in the final document. Because of his active role, Madison is often called the "Father of the Constitution."

Some notable American leaders did not attend. Thomas Jefferson and John Adams were serving as ministers to France and Great Britain. Patrick Henry refused to attend because he fiercely opposed a strong central government.

GOALS AND CHALLENGES

The delegates debated for four months. Because of their experience, the Framers aimed to create a government that was neither too strong, like the British monarchy, nor too weak, as under the Articles of Confederation. The delegates wanted national, state, and local governments to share governing power, an idea called **federalism**. They also felt **dual sovereignty**, or giving state governments certain powers that the national government could not overrule, was important.

Delegates at the Convention agreed upon other main principles. One was republicanism. In a republican government, citizens elect officials to represent them, and these officials must act and govern according to the law. Another principle that guided the delegates was that elections and legislative votes would be decided by majority rule. Majority rule requires that the candidates or legislation receive at least one more than one-half of all votes, even when there are more than two choices. Majority rule means that support for a successful candidate or law must be strong.

Convention delegates supported the idea of federalism but debated how to divide state-federal power. They disagreed about how much power state and national governments should have and about how much authority they should grant the three branches of the federal government.

HISTORICAL THINKING

1. **READING CHECK** In what ways did James Madison contribute to the Constitutional Convention?

2. **DESCRIBE** What were the main issues of debate among delegates at the Constitutional Convention?

3. **FORM AND SUPPORT OPINIONS** Which principle under debate at the Convention do you think was most important to the new nation? Support your opinion with evidence from the text.

2.2 The Big Question: How to Divide Power

Imagine listening in on the debates at the Constitutional Convention. Delegates from more populous states want more representatives than smaller states. Other delegates want the same number of representatives for all states. How do they resolve this issue? They compromise.

MAIN IDEA Delegates at the Constitutional Convention decided how to divide power in the government and how to elect the president.

THE GREAT COMPROMISE

As you have read, the Constitutional Convention embraced the idea that the federal government should rely on three branches of government based on the principles of **separation of powers** and **checks and balances**. Each branch would have unique powers. None would have more power than any other, and each branch would be a check on the other two. The **legislative branch** would create and pass legislation, or make laws. The **executive branch** would lead the nation and enforce laws, and the **judicial branch** would interpret laws.

Most delegates agreed on a judicial branch headed by a **Supreme Court** and that one leader, a president, should head the executive branch. But they could not agree on how the legislative branch should work. Delegates Edmund Randolph and William Paterson proposed two different plans, the **Virginia Plan** and the **New Jersey Plan**, shown at right. Smaller states, such as Delaware, Maryland, and New Jersey, were uncomfortable with the Virginia Plan. Larger states didn't like the New Jersey Plan. Delegates voted for the Virginia Plan as the draft framework for the Constitution, but many remained dissatisfied.

Roger Sherman of Connecticut combined the best ideas from both plans to craft the **Great Compromise**. He proposed a legislative branch with two houses. Delegates voted in favor of Sherman's plan and established the legislative branch that exists today.

PRESIDENTIAL ELECTIONS

The delegates agreed on the executive role of the president of the United States, but not on how to select this leader. Some argued for a direct election—the candidate with the majority of votes would win. Others wanted Congress or the state legislatures to choose, fearing that the people might elect someone unqualified for the job.

The Convention delegates landed on another compromise: the **electoral college**. States would be granted a specific number of electors equal to their numbers of senators and representatives in Congress. States would then choose their electors, who would cast their votes for president based on their voters' preferences. Though voting rights would eventually expand over time, after the Revolution, voting was limited to white males.

HISTORICAL THINKING

1. **READING CHECK** What compromises did the Convention delegates reach when planning for the legislative and executive branches?

2. **DETERMINE CHRONOLOGY** What two proposals preceded the Great Compromise?

3. **FORM AND SUPPORT OPINIONS** Of the Virginia Plan and the New Jersey Plan, which do you think best reflected the spirit of the new nation? Support your opinion with evidence from the text.

TOTAL POPULATION OF THE UNITED STATES, 1790: 3,929,214

Population of Virginia
19%, 747,610

Population of New Jersey
4.7%, 184,139

= one representative from New Jersey

(Pie chart labels: SC, PA, NC, NY, MA, MD, CT, DE, RI, KY, GA, VT, ME, NH)

= one representative from Virginia

Edmund Randolph's
Virginia Plan
TWO HOUSES

UPPER HOUSE

LOWER HOUSE

The number of representatives from each state is **proportionate to the state's population.**

This plan made delegates from small states nervous.

William Paterson's
New Jersey Plan
ONE HOUSE

Each state has an equal number of representatives, **regardless of population.**

Delegates from larger states didn't like this plan.

ROGER SHERMAN'S

GREAT COMPROMISE

HOUSE OF REPRESENTATIVES

The number of representatives from each state is **proportionate to the state's population.**

SENATE

Each state has an equal number of representatives, **regardless of population.**

SEPARATION OF POWERS

THREE BRANCHES OF GOVERNMENT

LEGISLATIVE BRANCH	EXECUTIVE BRANCH	JUDICIAL BRANCH
MAKES LAWS	ENFORCES LAWS	INTERPRETS LAWS

2.3 Slavery and Trade

When people in power make decisions, the consequences are often immediate and long-lasting. That was the case during the Constitutional Convention when the Framers made decisions about slavery and trade.

MAIN IDEA Before the delegates approved the final draft of the Constitution, they had to compromise about slavery and settle issues about commerce.

SLAVERY AND REPRESENTATION

Even though the word *slavery* does not appear in the original body of the Constitution, slavery was a major topic at the Constitutional Convention. In fact, the delegates negotiated several compromises that firmly preserved the institution of slavery.

All delegates, whether from the North or the South, were especially concerned with how the practice of slavery affected state representation in Congress. Southern states depended more on enslaved labor than northern states. As a result, southern delegates wanted enslaved people to be counted as members of a state's population. Doing so would increase the number of delegates representing southern states in the House of Representatives. It would also increase the region's electoral votes. Northerners argued that enslaved people should not be counted because they were legally defined as property.

As part of the Great Compromise, the Convention delegates decided that five enslaved Americans would count as three free persons and approved inserting what is called the **Three-Fifths Compromise** into Article 1 of the Constitution. The Three-Fifths Compromise increased the power of white voters in the South at the expense of enslaved African Americans, who were each counted as less than a full person.

Article 1 also included a **slave importation clause** stating that Congress could not ban the importation of slaves for 20 years and that the tax on importing an enslaved person could not exceed $10 per person. Southern delegates also supported

Enslaved Population, 1790

Region	Total Population	Enslaved Population	Percentage of Population
New England	1,009,522	3,886	0.38%
Middle Atlantic	1,017,726	45,371	4.46%
South	1,866,387	645,023	34.56%
TOTAL	3,893,635	694,280	17.83%

Source: United States Census Bureau

the addition of the **fugitive slave clause** into Article 4 of the Constitution. This clause barred people who had escaped slavery in the South from living as free people in northern states.

Some delegates, especially those from northern states, wondered if the nation's ideals of freedom, liberty, and democracy could coexist alongside slavery. Benjamin Franklin wanted to abolish slavery from Pennsylvania altogether, but other representatives from northern free states approved the provisions. Most did not oppose slavery.

FREE AND OPEN TRADE

The southern representatives' other concern was the government's taxation of exports. The South's strong agricultural economy depended on the export of goods to other countries. Southerners believed that requiring foreign buyers to pay taxes on exported goods would hurt this trade. A weakened agricultural trade, in turn, would hurt the southern economy. The delegates agreed.

The Constitution placed few limits on the nation's commerce. One exception was the **commerce clause**, which gave Congress the power "to

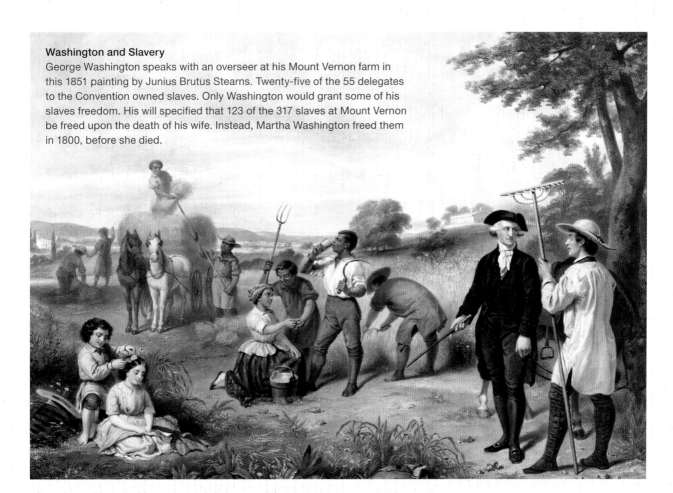

Washington and Slavery
George Washington speaks with an overseer at his Mount Vernon farm in this 1851 painting by Junius Brutus Stearns. Twenty-five of the 55 delegates to the Convention owned slaves. Only Washington would grant some of his slaves freedom. His will specified that 123 of the 317 slaves at Mount Vernon be freed upon the death of his wife. Instead, Martha Washington freed them in 1800, before she died.

regulate commerce with foreign nations, and among the several states, and with the Indian tribes." Under the commerce clause, Native American tribes were considered sovereign governments and were not subject to the same regulations as states. The coinage clause required all states to use common coinage, or the same kind of money. Finally, according to the full-faith and credit clause, all states were required to respect the public acts, records, and judicial proceedings of all other states. Together, these three clauses gave Congress the authority to oversee interstate commerce and keep trade free and open among states. Delegates decided the country's economy would work under a **common market**, which meant that no tax could be charged on trade between states.

At last, the delegates had settled the most important issues for the new nation. Gouverneur Morris, a delegate from New York, perfected the wording of the proposed Constitution and organized it into seven articles, or main sections. On September 15, 1787, the delegates approved the final draft. They signed it two days later. As he observed the signing of the Constitution, Benjamin

Franklin commented that the sun on George Washington's chair at the Convention must be a rising sun. The United States was at the beginning, and not the end, of its time.

Thirty-nine of the 55 Convention delegates, or more than two-thirds, signed the document. Some delegates who approved of the final draft did not sign it because they were not in attendance. After it was signed, the Constitution was sent to the states for ratification and became the subject of yet more debate.

HISTORICAL THINKING

1. **READING CHECK** How did the Constitution reflect specific concerns of southern states?

2. **ANALYZE DATA** Why did southern delegates want to insert clauses about slavery into the Constitution? Use evidence from the population chart and the text to support your answer.

3. **MAKE GENERALIZATIONS** What advantages did the states experience under the common market?

3.1 Federalists and Antifederalists

Sometimes a fight between two people can spread until everyone takes a side. After the Constitutional Convention, citizens in the new nation faced this situation as two separate groups argued that their ideal vision was the right one.

> **MAIN IDEA** Americans with opposite views about a strong central government engaged in intense debates over the ratification of the Constitution.

DIFFERENT POINTS OF VIEW

September 17, 1787, was a big day for the new United States. It was the day its Framers signed the Constitution. However, after it was signed, much more work was yet to come. Every state legislature had to ratify this new document. Given the spirited debates at the Constitutional Convention itself, it is not surprising that legislators and citizens quickly split into two factions. Those who supported the Constitution as it was written were known as **federalists**. Those who opposed all or parts of the Constitution were called **antifederalists**.

As you have read, federalism is a principle of governing in which a strong national government shares powers with the states. Federalists tended to live in big coastal cities and work in commerce. They hoped for more international trade and wanted to establish a strong and stable federal government. Some federalists were also frontier settlers, and they believed a strong central government could help defend them against attacks by Native Americans.

Antifederalists believed the Constitution did not provide strong enough barriers against the potential abuse of power by the federal government. They favored giving more power to state governments and believed only a government closest to the people could properly protect their liberties. Antifederalists tended to be from more rural areas, and they perceived the federal government as distant and separate from their interests. Antifederalists Patrick Henry and **George Mason**, a delegate from Virginia, gave impassioned speeches criticizing the Constitution.

Many newspapers supported the federalist cause. In New York, James Madison, Alexander Hamilton, and **John Jay**, who had been working behind the scenes in helping to craft the new government, published a series of essays in newspapers that argued in favor of the Constitution. In the spring of 1788, they published a book of the 85 essays called *The Federalist*. Despite these convincing essays, some key states, such as North Carolina, Virginia, and New York, resisted ratification at first.

RATIFYING THE CONSTITUTION

Each state held a convention to debate and vote on the Constitution. Delaware was the first to ratify, followed by Pennsylvania, New Jersey, Georgia, Connecticut, and Massachusetts. Except for Pennsylvania, all these states had small populations. Delegates to conventions in these states understood the advantages of joining a union in which their representation was equal to that of larger states. In Pennsylvania, federalists led by James Wilson moved quickly to secure ratification before antifederalists in the rural west could organize.

Many state constitutions already included a bill of rights, and the federalists argued that for this reason, another bill of rights was unnecessary. But in Virginia, antifederalists George Mason and Patrick Henry argued that adding a bill of rights to the Constitution was necessary to protect individuals and states and to prevent abuse of power by the federal government. Political writer Mercy Otis Warren also advocated for a bill of rights. In 1788, horrified by the violence she witnessed during Shays's Rebellion, she argued that the revolutionaries did not fight against Britain only to meet with more tyranny.

CRITICAL VIEWING In 1939, Congress commissioned artist Howard Chandler Christy to paint *Signing of the Constitution* in honor of the 150-year anniversary of the Constitution. It is an enormous work, 20 by 30 feet in size, and it hangs in the House wing of the U.S. Capitol. In this painting, Christy depicts the events of September 17, 1787.

George Washington stands in front of his Rising Sun chair during the signing, which was held at Independence Hall. The 81-year-old Ben Franklin listens to something Alexander Hamilton is telling him, and Richard Spaight signs the document. How does this painting convey the importance of the event it depicts?

By July 1788, all but two states— North Carolina and Rhode Island— had voted for ratification. Rhode Island, again a holdout, refused to ratify the Constitution until a list of changes was included. The vote for ratification was so close that James Madison finally proposed to Congress that a set of 12 official **amendments**, or changes, be added to the Constitution to provide greater constitutional protection for individual liberties. The states ratified 10 of these amendments, and Congress added them to the Constitution. These amendments, which place specific restrictions on governmental power, became known as the **Bill of Rights**. Together, the Constitution and the Bill of Rights have provided the foundation for the U.S. government for more than 200 years.

HISTORICAL THINKING

1. **READING CHECK** What were the main arguments between the federalists and the antifederalists?

2. **COMPARE AND CONTRAST** What are some general characteristics of the people who identified as federalists and those who identified as antifederalists?

3. **DESCRIBE** Why did Congress add the Bill of Rights to the Constitution?

3.2 Constitutional Debates

Legislators and ordinary citizens had a lot to say both for and against ratifying the proposed Constitution. As people on both sides of the debate published their arguments, it became clear that some kind of compromise was necessary for this plan of government to survive.

Federalists and antifederalists circulated their opinions to appeal to and persuade their audiences. As you have read, Alexander Hamilton, John Jay, and James Madison published *The Federalist* in support of ratification of the Constitution as written. Writer George Mason argued against the Constitution without certain guarantees. Writing under the pen name of "A Columbian Patriot," Mercy Otis Warren presented a strong antifederalist argument, which antifederalist newspapers used to challenge federalist ideas.

CRITICAL VIEWING John Singleton Copley painted this 1763 portrait of Mercy Otis Warren. Warren grew up in a wealthy and politically active family. Though she did not receive a formal education, she became a poet, a playwright, and a historian. Her social position allowed her a unique view of the events of the American Revolution. What details in her portrait convey her social status?

DOCUMENT ONE

Primary Source: Essay
from "Federalist No. 1," by Alexander Hamilton, 1788

Originally appearing as an anonymous series of 85 newspaper essays in favor of the Constitution, the authors' work was bound into the book *The Federalist* in 1788. These essays are considered among the most important examples of political philosophy in American history. This excerpt, from the first essay, was written by Hamilton.

CONSTRUCTED RESPONSE What was the author's opinion about a strong government versus the opinions of those who advocated for more rights for the people?

History will teach us that [dangerous ambition] has been found a much more certain road to the introduction of despotism [government with an absolute ruler] than the [firmness and efficiency of government], and that of those men who have overturned the liberties of republics, the greatest number have begun their career by paying . . . court to the people; commencing demagogues [absolute rulers], and ending tyrants.

DOCUMENT TWO

Primary Source: Essay
from "Objections to the Constitution of Government Formed by the Convention," by George Mason, 1787

During the Constitutional Convention in 1787, George Mason wrote an essay about why he refused to sign the Constitution. In his essay, which was published in the *Virginia Journal,* Mason predicted what would become of the union if individual rights weren't made clear. His ideas reflected principles in the Declaration of Independence.

CONSTRUCTED RESPONSE How does Mason's essay about government differ from ideas expressed in *The Federalist?*

This government will set out a moderate aristocracy [a class system based on birth or wealth]: it is at present impossible to foresee whether it will, in its operation, produce a monarchy, or a corrupt, tyrannical aristocracy; it will most probably vibrate some years between the two, and then terminate in the one or the other.

DOCUMENT THREE

Primary Source: Essay
from "Observations on the New Constitution," by Mercy Otis Warren, 1788

As a woman in the new United States, Mercy Otis Warren could not vote or take part in any conventions or lawmaking. That did not stop her from voicing a strong antifederalist viewpoint in the hopes of swaying those who had the power to ratify or reject the Constitution.

CONSTRUCTED RESPONSE What concerns about the Constitution did Warren express?

[The] Constitution, which, by the undefined meaning of some parts, and the ambiguities of expression in others, is dangerously adapted to the purposes of . . . tyranny. There is no security in the proffered [presented] system, either for the rights of conscience, or liberty of the press. There are no well-defined limits of the Judiciary Powers. The Executive and Legislative are so dangerously blended as to give just cause of alarm.

SYNTHESIZE & WRITE

1. **REVIEW** Review what you have learned about the arguments for and against the ratification of the Constitution.

2. **RECALL** On your own paper, write details about the arguments in favor of and opposed to the ratification of the Constitution, as revealed by the three excerpts.

3. **CONSTRUCT** Construct a topic sentence that answers this question: What were the main philosophies that supported the arguments for and against the ratification of the Constitution?

4. **WRITE** Using evidence from this chapter and the documents, write an informative paragraph that supports your topic sentence in Step 3.

3.3 The Bill of Rights

Americans enjoy many rights every day, from freely expressing opinions in public and in the press to protesting government actions. These and other fundamental rights are part of our identity as a nation, and we have the Framers of the Constitution to thank for them.

MAIN IDEA The Framers included a Bill of Rights in the Constitution to protect the fundamental rights and individual liberties of all citizens.

AMENDING THE CONSTITUTION

In 1787, the United States Constitution represented a bold new way of governing based on the consent of the governed. It also established a government that has survived for more than 200 years. Its survival has resulted from the control of power and interests through a system of checks and balances. Through Article 5, the Constitution provided a process by which it could adapt to the needs of a changing society. This process made possible a series of amendments protecting individual liberties from governmental abuses.

In order to amend, or change, the Constitution, Congress or two-thirds of the state legislatures must propose an amendment. Then three-fourths of the state legislatures must approve it. If they do, the amendment is ratified. This vigorous process helps protect citizens from unreasonable amendments.

Congress added the first 10 amendments, known as the Bill of Rights, to the Constitution in 1791. The amendments were intended to protect the freedoms of life, liberty, and the pursuit of happiness—all ideals that were put forth in the Declaration of Independence.

INDIVIDUAL FREEDOMS

The First Amendment protects fundamental individual freedoms: freedom of religion, freedom of speech and the press, and freedom of peaceful assembly and petitioning. In 1786,

THE BILL OF RIGHTS

FIRST AMENDMENT	Freedoms of speech, religion, the press, and the right to peacefully assemble and to petition the government
SECOND AMENDMENT	The right to form a well-regulated militia and to keep and bear arms
THIRD AMENDMENT	Protection from being forced to quarter soldiers
FOURTH AMENDMENT	Protection against searches and seizures without a warrant based on reasonable grounds
FIFTH AMENDMENT	The right of an arrested individual to know what he or she is accused of; protection against being tried for the same crime twice; protection against unjustified deprivation of life, liberty, or property; the right to refuse to testify against oneself
SIXTH AMENDMENT	The right to a fair and speedy trial by jury; the right to a lawyer
SEVENTH AMENDMENT	The right to a jury trial in certain civil cases
EIGHTH AMENDMENT	Protection against excessive bail and cruel or unusual punishment
NINTH AMENDMENT	Protection against others taking away rights not mentioned in the Bill of Rights
TENTH AMENDMENT	The right of states and citizens to retain powers not given to the federal government

See the Citizenship Handbook for the full text of the United States Constitution.

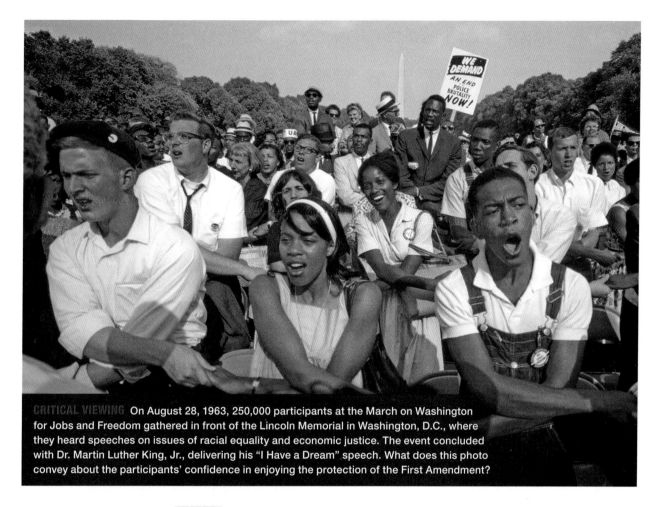

CRITICAL VIEWING On August 28, 1963, 250,000 participants at the March on Washington for Jobs and Freedom gathered in front of the Lincoln Memorial in Washington, D.C., where they heard speeches on issues of racial equality and economic justice. The event concluded with Dr. Martin Luther King, Jr., delivering his "I Have a Dream" speech. What does this photo convey about the participants' confidence in enjoying the protection of the First Amendment?

Thomas Jefferson wrote a **statute**, or a law written by a legislative body, for the state of Virginia that served as a forerunner to the First Amendment. In the Statute for Religious Freedom, Jefferson strongly advocated for religious liberty and the separation of church and state. Some delegates objected to including this idea in the Constitution, believing that the Constitution should reflect the nation's Christian foundation. Other delegates, such as James Madison, contended that safeguarding people's "natural right" to worship freely, or not worship at all, was more important. Because of the First Amendment, Americans have the right to practice any religion or no religion without fear of discrimination or persecution.

Freedom of the press, another First Amendment right, was a new concept in the 1780s, when governments routinely blocked the publication of stories they disliked. Governments also forced newspapers to print articles that suited their own purposes. The First Amendment made both acts illegal, and today the American press can report and publish freely. The First through Eighth

Amendments focus on individual rights. The Ninth Amendment protects any personal freedoms not specified in the Bill of Rights. The Tenth Amendment allows citizens and states to keep any powers not mentioned in the Constitution.

Throughout our nation's history, we, the people, have added additional amendments to the Constitution to expand and clarify our rights. These amendments have been vital to the development of an American identity. They have established many of the essential freedoms Americans enjoy today.

HISTORICAL THINKING

1. **READING CHECK** Why was protecting the rights and freedoms listed in the Bill of Rights important to citizens of the new nation?

2. **MAKE GENERALIZATIONS** In what ways are natural rights protected in the Bill of Rights?

3. **EXPLAIN** What requirements are involved for proposed and ratified amendments, and why is this process in place?

VOCABULARY

Write a sentence for each group of words that explains the relationship between them.

1. federalist / antifederalist
2. commerce clause / common market
3. legislative branch / executive branch / judicial branch
4. Bill of Rights / amendment
5. separation of powers / checks and balances
6. constitution / constitutionalism
7. statute / ordinance
8. sovereign / dual sovereignty
9. delegates / Framers

READING STRATEGY
DETERMINE CHRONOLOGY

If you haven't done so already, complete your sequence chain to show how the roles of state and federal governments evolved in the early United States. Then answer the question.

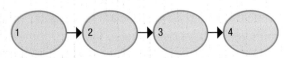

10. From 1776 to 1791, how did the role of the federal government develop in the United States?

MAIN IDEAS

Answer the following questions. Support your answers with evidence from the chapter.

11. In what ways did the Articles of Confederation limit the effectiveness of the national government? **LESSON 1.1**

12. What did the ordinances of 1785 and 1787 regulate? **LESSON 1.2**

13. What were Daniel Shays and his followers protesting? **LESSON 1.3**

14. What was the purpose of the Constitutional Convention of 1787? **LESSON 2.1**

15. What three principles did delegates at the Constitutional Convention want to include? **LESSON 2.1**

16. Why did the Framers insist on separation of powers in the Constitution? **LESSON 2.2**

17. How did the Great Compromise help both large and small states? **LESSON 2.2**

18. What was the Three-Fifths Compromise and who did it benefit? **LESSON 2.3**

19. How did James Madison, Alexander Hamilton, and John Jay present the arguments of the federalists? **LESSON 3.1**

20. Why was the Bill of Rights added to the Constitution? **LESSON 3.3**

HISTORICAL THINKING

Answer the following questions. Support your answers with evidence from the chapter.

21. **ANALYZE CAUSE AND EFFECT** What factors prompted leaders to work to replace the Articles of Confederation with a new constitution?

22. **IDENTIFY PROBLEMS AND SOLUTIONS** What problem did the establishment of the electoral college solve?

23. **SYNTHESIZE** How does the Bill of Rights represent the ideals that Americans fought for in the American Revolution?

24. **FORM AND SUPPORT OPINIONS** Do you think the Constitution reflects a fair balance between federalist and antifederalist arguments? Support your opinion with evidence from the chapter.

25. EVALUATE How did the Framers reconcile the ideals of freedom, liberty, and democracy with slavery?

26. EXPLAIN Why did James Wilson want a quick ratification of the Constitution?

ANALYZE VISUALS

This statue, called *Guardianship,* stands in front of the National Archives building in Washington, D.C., where the foundational documents of the United States are housed. The inscription at the base of the statue reads, "Eternal vigilance is the price of liberty." Study the statue and its inscription. Then answer the questions below.

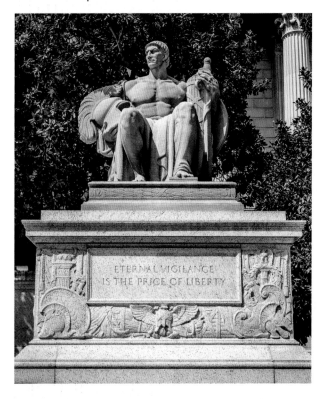

27. Why might the inscription on this statue refer to "eternal vigilance," or keeping a careful watch over something, as the "price of liberty"?

28. *Guardianship* means taking care of something. In what ways were the Framers guardians of the new nation?

ANALYZE SOURCES

In 1788, as part of "Federalist No. 38," James Madison wrote the following opinion about the process of forming a government through history. Read the passage and answer the question.

> It is a matter both of wonder and regret, that those who raise so many objections against the new Constitution should never call to mind the defects of that which is to be exchanged for it. It is not necessary that the former should be perfect; it is sufficient that the latter is more imperfect.

29. What is Madison saying to those who disagree with the new Constitution?

30. To what is Madison referring when he mentions "the defects of that which is to be exchanged for it"?

CONNECT TO YOUR LIFE

31. NARRATIVE Review the rights granted by the First Amendment. Think about a time when one of the rights played a role in your own life or that of someone you know. Write a paragraph connecting that right to your life as an American today.

TIPS

- Read through the text of the First Amendment. List the specific freedoms mentioned. Then choose a freedom that has had an impact on your life.

- Use textual evidence from the amendment in your paragraph. Cite the specific language used to describe the freedom, and then explain the impact that freedom has had on your life.

- Conclude the paragraph with a comment about what you think is most important about the First Amendment.

NATIONAL GEOGRAPHIC | CONNECTION

Patriots in Petticoats

BY LONNELLE AIKMAN

Adapted from "Patriots in Petticoats," by Lonnelle Aikman, in *National Geographic*, October 1975

Schooled in an untamed land of hardships, the women of colonial America were conditioned to independence. They grew their own food, sewed their own clothing, and made their own medicines. All this, while rearing children and running their families.

Given their willingness to endure, women in colonial America were more than ready to give up imported luxuries rather than submit to British taxation. Better, they said, to wear plain homespun dresses than to wear European imports. As for British tea, there were plenty of native substitutes—such as sage and currant—which they brewed and served as Liberty Tea. As the war began and spread, women of all classes, from frontier wives to managers of great plantations, participated fully in the conflict. Throughout the colonies, women replaced soldier-husbands in fields and shops and often spied on the enemy.

Abigail Adams, one of the first American women patriots, promoted activities from sewing uniforms to making bullets. She fed and sheltered soldiers and welcomed temporary refugees from neighboring towns. She also provided military and political intelligence to her husband by reporting on enemy troops and ships, as well as on Tories, inflation, and other American problems. John Adams appreciated Abigail's specific and accurate information, saying that she supplied him "with dearer and fuller Intelligence, than I can get from a whole Committee of Gentlemen."

Martha Washington traveled with General Washington throughout the war, which may astonish those who think of her as a sheltered elite. She was with him in New York City, Morristown, Valley Forge, and Middlebrook, and she helped him through two mutinies by his starving troops. Even after the guns were silent, Martha was with George while both waited impatiently for news of the final peace treaty in 1783.

If following the army was hard on the general's wife, it was more challenging for the ordinary women who trudged with the troops. Armies reluctantly allowed women to work alongside their husbands and other men of the corps, to carry water, to swab cannons, and to ease the wounded on the battlefield.

Some women fought side-by-side with men, including Margaret Cochran Corbin. When her husband John joined an artillery corps, Margaret went along. "Molly," as her comrades called her, helped the gunner's team swab out the bore and ram down the ammunition. When John was shot and killed, Margaret jumped into his battle station. Then she, too, went down, her shoulder torn by grapeshot. She never regained the use of her arm. Recognizing her courage under fire, Congress made her the first woman to receive a pension from the United States.

An equally brave woman posed as a man in order to fight. When Deborah Sampson was a child, poverty forced her widowed mother to give her up for indentured service. She emerged a strong woman, quite able to take on men's work. When the Revolution began, she made herself a man's suit, walked to a recruiting post in another town, and enlisted as Robert Shurtleff. She was wounded twice but managed to keep her secret until she went to Philadelphia as a general's orderly. There she came down with a "malignant fever" and was sent to a hospital, where a startled doctor discovered that she was a woman.

Martha Washington, Deborah Sampson, and Abigail Adams were women of strength who continue to capture the spotlight of history. Behind them stand all those others, the nameless Founding Mothers, without whom independence would have been impossible.

For more from National Geographic, check out "Two Revolutions" online.

UNIT INQUIRY: Prepare an Argument

In this unit, you learned about the factors that led to the American Revolution, the war itself, and the creation of the Constitution. Use what you learned from the text and do further research if necessary to determine why all colonists didn't support separating from Great Britain.

ASSIGNMENT

Prepare an argument for or against independence from Great Britain from the perspective of a Patriot and a Loyalist, respectively. Your arguments should offer examples of the benefits and drawbacks or risks involved in becoming independent from Great Britain. Be prepared to present both sides to your class.

Gather Evidence As you consider both sides of the argument, use what you learned in this unit to think of the reasons an American colonist would have either supported or opposed the separation from Great Britain. Make a list of these reasons, and try to incorporate them into your argument. Use a table like this one to help organize your evidence.

Patriot Reasons	Loyalist Reasons

Produce Use your notes to craft a solid argument for both sides of the issue—thinking like a Loyalist and like a Patriot. You may wish to write the arguments in paragraph form or bullet points on index cards and label them either "Patriot" or "Loyalist."

Present Choose a creative way to present both sides of this debate to the class. Consider one of these options:

- Use two different props, such as different hats, to transform yourself into a Patriot and a Loyalist. Wearing the Patriot hat, give a short speech expressing why it makes sense for the colonies to separate from Great Britain. Then put on the Loyalist hat and give a short speech expressing the other side of the debate. Alternate between Patriot and Loyalist hats to change your persona and add to each side of the argument.

- Organize your classmates into teams (Patriots and Loyalists). Familiarize each team with one side of the argument, and have a classroom debate about the benefits or dangers of separating from Great Britain.

NATIONAL GEOGRAPHIC | LEARNING FRAMEWORK ACTIVITIES

Research a Colonial American

ATTITUDE Curiosity

KNOWLEDGE Our Human Story

Choose one of the historical figures from this unit that you are still curious about, and do online research to learn more about him or her. Develop a biography for this individual in a traditional written format, or do something more visual, such as a poster or digital presentation. You could even give a costumed speech to your class as that individual. Be sure your biography—in whatever form it takes—includes common information such as birth and death dates, where the person lived, and the work he or she did. Also consider including information about how this person influenced colonial America, how the American Revolution or the Constitution might have been different without him or her, and the legacy this person left behind.

Build a Time Line

SKILLS Collaboration, Communication

KNOWLEDGE Our Human Story

Work with a partner or small group to capture the "story" of the formation of the United States in the form of a time line. First discuss how your time line will work. For example, decide if it will flow left to right or top to bottom, how it will be divided into intervals, and when the time line will start and end. Then refer to the chapters in this unit to determine which significant events will be included on your time line. Once you have gathered the information you need, work together to craft the physical time line. Consider the following questions: Will you use a symbol or color to represent types of events, such as battles? Will you use each side of the time line to represent different events or eras? What will make your time line clear and easy to read?

National Geographic photographer Dan Westergren
captured this photograph of 12-year-old Alex Lamont,
a Native American of the Lakota Sioux. Alex performs
traditional dances at gatherings called powwows.

Native American
Confederacies & Nations

BY DR. TERENCE CLARK

Director, Shíshálh Archaeological Research Project, University of Saskatchewan, Canada

You've read about how the Founding Fathers worked tirelessly to unite the colonies and create a form of government different from the hierarchies in Europe. But long before the United States was formed, many Native American tribes had determined they were stronger if they banded together. They already had democratic and inclusive governments in place. Some had even established voting rights for all, as well as basic law-making and amendment processes.

We don't know exactly how much the framers of the U.S. Constitution borrowed ideas from early Native American nations and confederacies. We do know that Thomas Jefferson, James Madison, James Monroe, and Benjamin Franklin were familiar with the governmental structure of Native American nations such as the League of the Iroquois. The framers even visited this group to learn from its strength and organization and observe its practices. Franklin in particular was so impressed by the organization of Native American governments, he felt it should be studied—and possibly imitated—by the colonies. And it was.

The Native American confederacy has persevered throughout history, through conflict, land loss, and relocation. Today, there are more than 550 of these federally recognized nations in the United States, including over 200 in Alaska alone. The nations are self-governing, which ensures they can retain and preserve their distinct cultural identities. As you read about two of the largest and most influential North American confederacies, the confederacies of the West and the Iroquois Confederacy, consider how these great nations formed and their impact on Americans and the U.S. government.

LIFE BEFORE CONFEDERACIES

As you have read, the Great Plains are the geographic heart of North America, stretching from the eastern slopes of the Rocky Mountains to the shores of the Mississippi River, from Texas well into Canada. Although they vary geographically, the Great Plains are primarily made up of open grasslands, wooded river valleys, and upland areas. This "sea of grass" has served as a habitat for huge numbers of bison, deer, pronghorn antelope, and other animals—resources relied upon by many Native American groups.

The Native American groups of the northern and western Great Plains, including the Blackfoot, Cheyenne, and Comanche, relied upon hunting large game, fishing, and gathering plants. Groups of the eastern Great Plains, such as the Hidatsa, Mandan, and Arikara, settled in villages and grew maize, beans, and squash, much like their Eastern Woodland neighbors.

Until the 1800s, the Native Americans of the Great Plains lived in small groups and made several short migrations each year. Camps were small but well connected. Trade and social gatherings brought people together into bigger groups to renew social ties and find marriage partners.

CONFEDERACIES OF THE WEST

As American settlers began moving into the Great Plains in the early and mid-1800s, independent Native American groups felt the need to create alliances to protect themselves from the settlers and from potentially hostile Native American neighbors. As you know, westward expansion drew miners, trappers, and traders to the region in search of their own fortunes, and the expansion of the railroad changed the trickle of newcomers to a torrent. As a result, Native American alliances grew and the great confederacies of the West were born.

Two of the most powerful western confederacies were the Sioux (SOO) Confederacy and the Blackfoot Confederacy. These were political and military powerhouses whose territories included large areas of the region. With neighboring communities competing for land and resources and threatening the culture and way of life of local peoples, confederacies gave Native Americans of the Great Plains strength and unity.

Bison and wildflowers fill the sweeping landscape of Wind Cave National Park in present-day South Dakota, traditional lands of the Sioux and Blackfoot Confederacies.

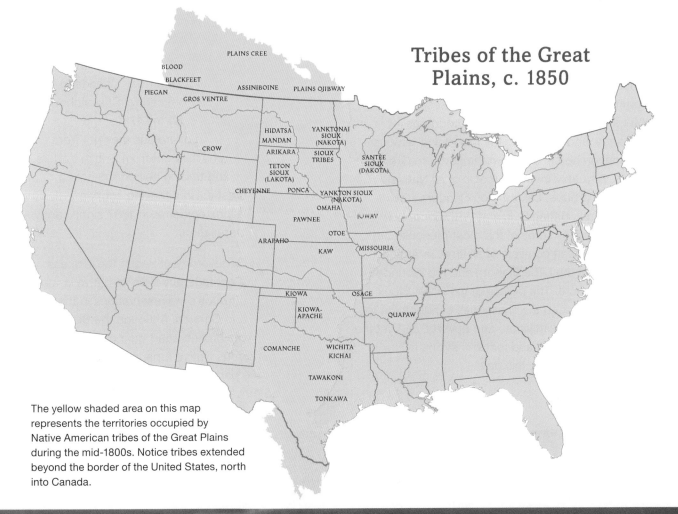

Tribes of the Great Plains, c. 1850

PLAINS CREE

BLOOD

BLACKFEET

ASSINIBOINE   PLAINS OJIBWAY

PIEGAN

GROS VENTRE

HIDATSA   YANKTONAI SIOUX (NAKOTA)

MANDAN

CROW   ARIKARA   SIOUX TRIBES

SANTEE SIOUX (DAKOTA)

TETON SIOUX (LAKOTA)

CHEYENNE   PONCA   YANKTON SIOUX (NAKOTA)

OMAHA

PAWNEE   IOWAY

OTOE

ARAPAHO   MISSOURIA

KAW

KIOWA   OSAGE

KIOWA-APACHE   QUAPAW

COMANCHE   WICHITA   KICHAI

TAWAKONI

TONKAWA

The yellow shaded area on this map represents the territories occupied by Native American tribes of the Great Plains during the mid-1800s. Notice tribes extended beyond the border of the United States, north into Canada.

THE SIOUX AND THE BLACKFOOT

The Great Sioux Nation is a confederacy of groups that speak different dialects, or forms, of the Siouan language: Dakota, Nakota, and Lakota. You have probably seen the Sioux—especially the Lakota Sioux—in famous photographs, paintings, and movies as the proud and famous warriors on horseback from the northern Great Plains. Arguably the most iconic of all Native American groups, Lakota Sioux leaders include Crazy Horse, Sitting Bull, and Red Cloud. Lakota history contains some of the most recognizable Native American conflicts of all time, including the Battle of the Little Bighorn and the Wounded Knee Massacre. The people of the Great Sioux Nation have faced the challenges of relocation to reservations, assimilation, and poverty, and yet the nation has endured and remains strong in North and South Dakota to this day.

The Blackfoot Confederacy was once one of the largest Native American groups in the northern Great Plains. Its territory ran from the North Saskatchewan River in present-day Canada to the Yellowstone River, and from central Saskatchewan to the Rocky Mountains. By the 1750s, the Blackfoot were hunting on horses they got from other tribes with guns they got from British traders. Hunting, raiding, and trading helped the nation gain power and establish a thriving economy. However, a smallpox epidemic in 1837 significantly weakened the population.

In 1855, the U.S. government began the process of removing the confederacy from its native lands and dispersing groups onto reservations in the United States and Canada. Although the Blackfoot Confederacy was broken apart during the removal process, numerous Native American groups that were once part of the nation survived, and continue to thrive in the Great Plains and Canada.

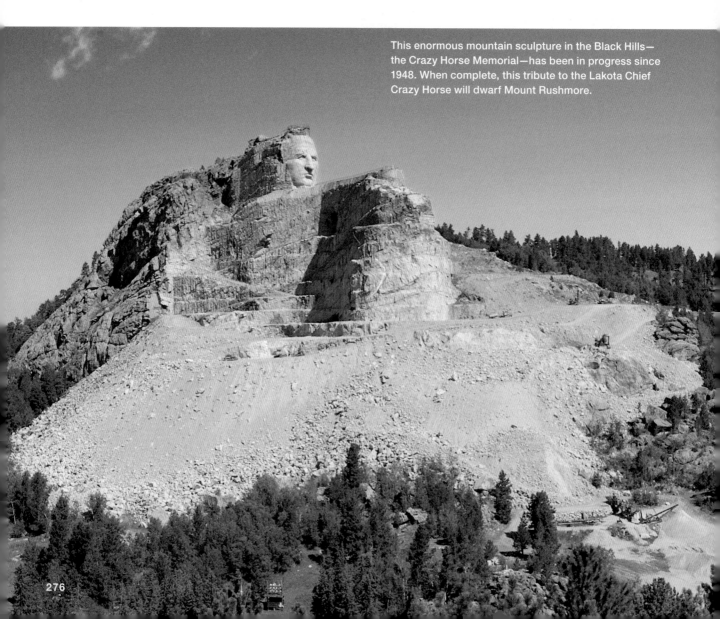

This enormous mountain sculpture in the Black Hills— the Crazy Horse Memorial—has been in progress since 1948. When complete, this tribute to the Lakota Chief Crazy Horse will dwarf Mount Rushmore.

"INDIANS" IN HOLLYWOOD

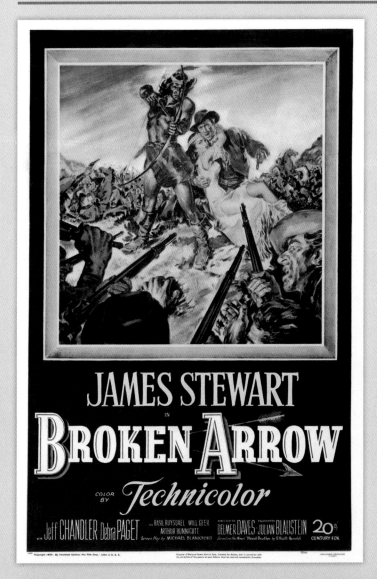

In the 1950s and 1960s, Westerns—fictional television series about the American West in the late 1800s—were on nearly every channel. Movie screens were filled with the same stories of scheming outlaws pursued by handsome lawmen, and noble cowboys protecting cattle from thieves and "civilized" white people from "uncivilized" Indians.

Some Native Americans played a legitimate role in Westerns that required skilled horse riders, but most Westerns represented Native American people as less than human. They were given few spoken lines, and were often shown being shot down or killed. Similarly, women in Westerns were often shown in need of rescue. Yet in reality, many women of the West were fiercely independent, taking on non-traditional roles and responsibilities. And contrary to their portrayal in movies, Native American women had great influence over their tribes and were sometimes warriors.

The 1950 Technicolor Western *Broken Arrow* featured several non-Native American actors playing the roles of Native American chiefs and being paid far more than Native-American actors.

DAVID BALD EAGLE

David Bald Eagle lived an extraordinary life. By the time of his 2016 death at the age of 97, he had been a Lakota tribal chief, a war hero, a champion dancer, a rodeo cowboy, a touring musician, an actor, a professional baseball player, and a race car driver. There was nothing he hadn't tried.

But most importantly, Bald Eagle was an advocate for Native people, a tribal leader, and an elder of the United Native Nations. His grandfathers entertained him with war stories to give him something to remember them by, making him a key connection between the past and present, the traditional and modern cultures.

Traditional Iroquois longhouses, like the one above in northern New York State, were made of tree bark.

The interior of this reconstructed 17th-century Seneca longhouse (left) represents how the people of the Iroquois Confederacy would have sheltered and lived.

THE IROQUOIS CONFEDERACY

Another example of a strong Native American nation is the Iroquois Confederacy, which you may remember reading about earlier in this book. This nation formed between 1570 and 1600. At first, this union of five tribes lived in present-day upstate New York and included the Mohawk, Oneida, Onondaga, Seneca, and Cayuga. The tribes were at one time enemies, but a Mohawk chief and an Onondaga speechmaker persuaded them they would be stronger if they united into a single confederacy, or nation. The tribes found security in this bond, forming what is known as the Great Law of Peace, which continues through today and is arguably the longest-lasting treaty in North America. In 1722, a sixth tribe, the Tuscarora, joined the League, and its territory expanded.

You might recall that together, the tribes in the Iroquois Confederacy became known as Haudenosaunee (hoe-dee-no-SHOW-nee)—People of the Longhouse—because of the types of dwellings they lived in. Their government revolved around a Council of Fifty, made up of representatives from the five tribes. This Council gathered to address issues and solve problems involving multiple tribes. All laws had to be passed unanimously, meaning a single person on the Council could block the law. That meant every man or woman—and there were women on the Council—had the same amount of power, regardless of how many members of his or her tribe sat on the Council. How does the structure of the Council of Fifty compare to the structure of today's U.S. government?

COMMON GROUND

The Iroquois Confederacy lasted through the 1780s, and at its height, reached from present-day Maine to North Carolina and from the Atlantic Ocean to the Mississippi River. It is possible many of our current U.S. government practices were influenced by those of the League. They include the use of discussion and debate before passing laws, removing leaders who were deemed ineffective, and making leaders accountable to the people. The Iroquois League also distinguished between its military and its civilians, as the United States does today.

It's not difficult to form connections between the tribes that united to form Native American confederacies and the colonies that came together to form the United States. Even the states that came together to form the Union and the Confederacy can be compared in a significant way to the formation of Native American nations: they saw strength in unity. Clearly the influence of Native American nations is evident in the government and social structure of the present-day United States.

Indian Nations have always been considered as distinct, independent political communities, retaining their original natural rights, as the undisputed possessors of the soil. The very term "nation" so generally applied to them, means "a people distinct from others."

—Chief Justice John Marshall, 1832

National Geographic photographer William Albert Allard captured this quiet moment as dancers check their makeup at a powwow on the Rocky Boy Indian Reservation in Montana.

THE EARLY REPUBLIC

The Rotunda, University of Virginia Charlottesville, Virginia

Thomas Jefferson designed the Rotunda, his greatest architectural work, when he was 70 years old. With its domed top and graceful columns, the Rotunda is modeled after a temple in ancient Rome. The Rotunda's interior contains a library, said to be one of the most beautiful rooms in America, as well as classrooms and lecture halls. Jefferson founded the University of Virginia and had that achievement—but not his term as president of the United States—commemorated on his gravestone.

CRITICAL VIEWING What words would you use to describe the Rotunda?

THE EARLY
REPUBLIC

THE UNITED STATES

1797
John Adams, a Federalist, becomes president, while Thomas Jefferson, a Democratic-Republican, becomes vice president.

1803
Thomas Jefferson sends Meriwether Lewis and William Clark on an expedition to explore the western territory included in the Louisiana Purchase. *(coin featuring Sacagawea, Lewis and Clark's Native American interpeter)*

1789
George Washington takes office as president and sets up his government.

1780

1800

1789 EUROPE
France explodes into revolution against the royal ruling class.

1799 EUROPE
Napoleon Bonaparte seizes control of the French government. *(statue of Napoleon on horseback)*

THE WORLD

1812
The War of 1812 erupts between Britain and the United States over British violations of American rights at sea. *(American infantry drum used during the War of 1812)*

HISTORICAL THINKING: DETERMINE CHRONOLOGY

Which strong leaders came to power within ten years of each other?

1813
As the textile industry expands during the Industrial Revolution, the first Lowell mill is built in Massachusetts.

1831
Nat Turner leads an armed rebellion in an effort to free the slaves.

1844
Samuel Morse's invention of the telegraph allows messages to be sent between Washington, D.C., and Baltimore, Maryland. *(early telegraph developed by Samuel Morse)*

1820

1833 EUROPE
Britain abolishes slavery in the British Empire.

1821 AMERICAS
Venezuela gains independence from Spain.

1836 AFRICA
The Boers, farmers of Dutch, French, and German descent, undertake their "Great Trek" through southern Africa.

1840

1839–1842 ASIA
The first Opium War is fought between China and Britain after the Chinese government tries to stop the trade of opium in its country. *(Chinese junk boat similar to those used by China during the Opium War)*

CHAPTER 8

GROWING PAINS
IN THE NEW REPUBLIC
1789–1800

ESSENTIAL QUESTION
What challenges did Americans in the new republic confront?

 George Washington's Mount Vernon

SECTION 1 **Washington's Presidency**

KEY VOCABULARY

attorney general	national debt
Cabinet	precedent
Chief Justice	tariff
inauguration	

SECTION 2 **Politics in the 1790s**

KEY VOCABULARY

Alien and Sedition Acts	radical
cede	sedition
envoy	states' rights
French Revolution	strict interpretation
loose interpretation	Treaty of Greenville
power base	Whiskey Rebellion
	XYZ Affair

AMERICAN GALLERY ONLINE **Federal Washington**

READING STRATEGY

IDENTIFY PROBLEMS AND SOLUTIONS
By identifying problems and solutions, you can better understand why decision-makers took the courses of action they did. As you read the chapter, use a graphic organizer like this one to identify and analyze each problem the new nation faced and how it was solved.

Issue: After the Revolution, the nation and individual states had huge debts.

↓

Problem 1: Foreign governments were waiting to be paid.

Problem 2:

Problem 3:

↓

Solution:

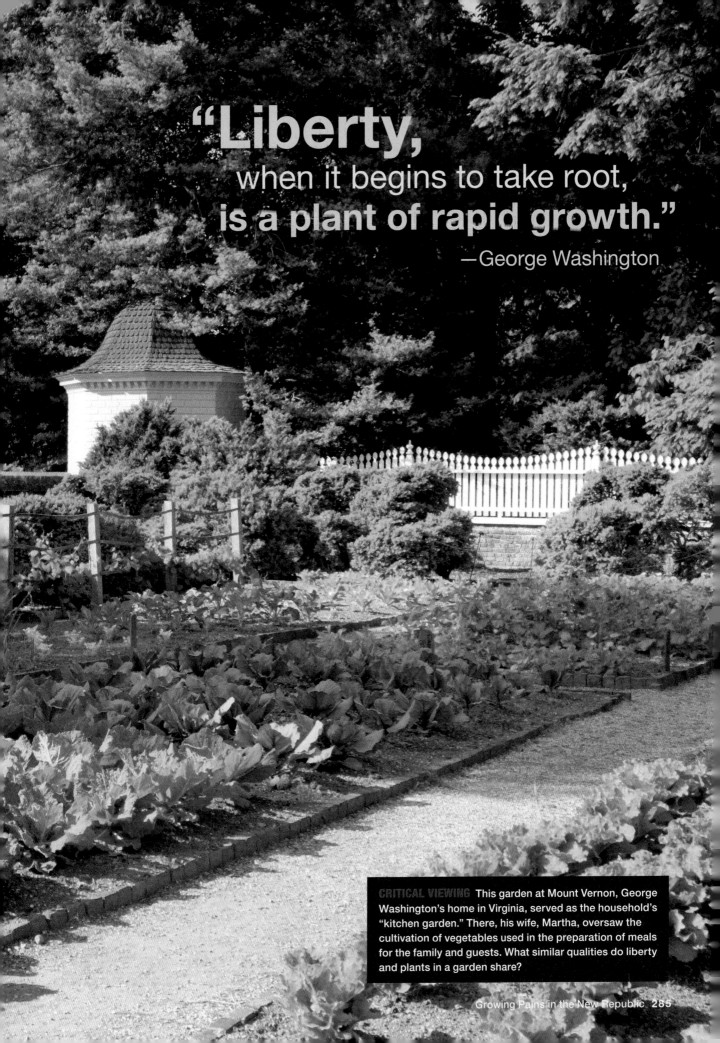

"Liberty,
when it begins to take root,
is a plant of rapid growth."

—George Washington

1.1 Setting Up the Government

Would you want to be president of the United States? You might be surprised to hear that George Washington did *not* want the job. He knew that being the first president of the new country wouldn't be easy. But his countrymen wanted Washington.

MAIN IDEA The Constitution established some guidelines, but for the first president, starting up the new government was a complex and difficult undertaking.

THE FIRST PRESIDENT

George Washington was the obvious choice to be the nation's first president—he was a dignified man of strong character. Better yet, he was a natural leader, which he had proved during the American Revolution. Success in the new republic was not at all assured, but Washington accepted the challenge. Even though he didn't want the job, Washington guided the new government through its early years.

As the newly written Constitution directed, the electoral college determined who would be president in this first election—not the people. Every one of the 69 electors voted for Washington. The reluctant candidate won hands down. John Adams, who was runner-up, became the vice president.

On April 23, 1789, thousands of cheering citizens in New York City, the country's temporary capital, welcomed Washington. He took the oath of office a week later and began his difficult task. Washington had to invent the role of president as he went along. "My station is new; and . . . [I] walk on untrodden ground," he wrote in a letter. Everything he did would set a **precedent**, or establish an example, for all future presidents.

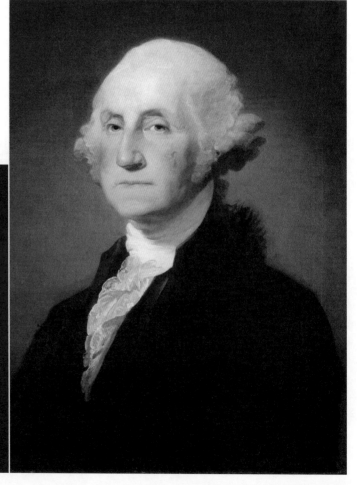

🏛 The Clark Art Institute Williamstown, Massachusetts

Gilbert Stuart painted 104 portraits of George Washington, including the one shown here, which was painted some time between 1796 and 1803. John Jay, whom you may remember as an author of *The Federalist* papers, introduced Washington to the painter. Stuart began creating his likenesses of the president in 1795. Washington became extremely impatient sitting for his portrait, however. Even though Stuart was known as an entertaining conversationalist, Washington remained mostly silent during their sessions.

Washington particularly wanted to make it clear that he was *president* of the United States, not its *king*. He dressed plainly for his **inauguration**, the ceremony that marked the beginning of his presidency, in an American-made brown suit. And he refused to be called "His Excellency" or "Your Highness," as John Adams had suggested. After much debate, Washington decided that "Mr. President" would do just fine.

AN OCEAN OF DIFFICULTIES

Once in office, Washington got to work—and there was a lot to do. As he himself described it, the nation faced "an ocean of difficulties." The new government had to deal with problems within the country as well as conflicts in the Northwest Territory and wars across the Atlantic.

To tackle all these situations, both the president and Congress had certain responsibilities and powers, as spelled out in the Constitution. Essentially, Congress would make the laws, and the president would ensure they were carried out.

But not everything was covered in the Constitution. Here, too, Washington set precedents. For example, he took control of treaty negotiations, bypassing Congress, and established a policy of neutrality in foreign conflicts—insisting it was within the president's power to do so.

Fortunately, the framers of the Constitution did foresee the need for departments to assist the president. Congress had the power to create the departments, and the president decided who would head them. Together, the heads of the departments are called a **Cabinet**.

Washington picked men from a variety of geographical areas and with a mix of political views for his Cabinet. He strongly advocated political moderation and tried to keep himself, as president, above the bickering that went on between political factions. That way, he believed, he could do what was best for the country. Washington appointed a group of highly talented men to his Cabinet—and hoped they'd put aside their political differences, too.

The First Inaugural Address

Washington wasn't required to give a speech at his inauguration, but he decided to do so. Every president since has done the same. To mark the occasion, people attending the ceremony could purchase copper buttons, like the ones below, as souvenirs.

As he gave this First Inaugural Address, Washington was nervous. His hands and voice trembled, but his words were powerful: "The preservation of the sacred fire of liberty, and the destiny of the Republican model of government, are justly considered as deeply . . . staked on the experiment entrusted to the hands of the American people." In other words, the future of the country depended on the success of this new government.

Washington inaugural souvenirs

HISTORICAL THINKING

1. **READING CHECK** Why did George Washington write that he was walking "on untrodden ground"?

2. **IDENTIFY PROBLEMS AND SOLUTIONS** How did Washington deal with treaty negotiations, since no process was spelled out in the Constitution?

3. **MAKE CONNECTIONS** How did Washington's presidency help establish an American identity?

U.S. Treasury Building
Washington, D.C.

In the early years of the nation, the Department of the Treasury was housed in Philadelphia. When the capital moved to Washington, D.C., so did the Treasury. After two Treasury Buildings burned down, construction on a final structure began in 1836—and this time, its architects made it fireproof. A statue of Alexander Hamilton stands before the south entrance of the building, shown here.

1.2 Cabinet and Courts

Imagine trying to play a game of soccer or basketball without any teammates. It wouldn't work. George Washington didn't guide the new country alone, either. He gathered an A-list of team members to help him.

MAIN IDEA The first order of business for George Washington and Congress was to assemble a presidential Cabinet and create a court system.

ASSEMBLING A TEAM

In the summer of 1789, Congress created the Departments of State, Treasury, and War as part of the executive branch. Washington appointed the department heads, called secretaries, and they formed his Cabinet.

To oversee relations with other countries, Washington chose Thomas Jefferson as Secretary of State. As Secretary of War, former general Henry Knox would see to the country's defense. And to manage the government's money, Washington selected Alexander Hamilton as Secretary of the Treasury. Congress also created the office of the **attorney general**, whose primary role was to represent the United States before the Supreme Court. He would be a member of Washington's Cabinet, but unlike the others, he would not head an executive department. Edmund Randolph served as the first attorney general.

The president called his Cabinet secretaries together for regular meetings. However, you might be surprised to learn that Vice President John Adams was *not* invited to these meetings. The vice president soon realized the limitations of his position. "My country," he wrote, "has in its wisdom contrived [designed] for me the most insignificant office that ever the invention of man contrived or his imagination conceived."

THE HIGHEST COURT IN THE LAND

In addition to building the Cabinet, Washington and Congress created a court system. The Constitution established a Supreme Court as the nation's highest court. But it left the question of how many justices would sit on the Court to Congress and didn't specify what its powers would be. So, in 1789, Congress passed the Federal Judiciary Act. It called for the Supreme Court to have six justices—one **Chief Justice** and five associate justices. Today, eight associate justices sit on the court. The Chief Justice presides over the judicial branch of the U.S. government as well as over the Supreme Court itself. John Jay became the country's first Chief Justice.

The act created the world's first dual-court system, with responsibilities split between state and federal courts. Federal courts handled interstate and international cases, disputes regarding the U.S. Constitution, and civil and criminal cases relating to federal laws. State courts dealt with cases involving state laws and civil disputes within states. The act also created lower, or less powerful, federal courts.

The federal government established executive departments and a working system of courts, but more challenges lay in store. For one thing, there was the small matter of a very large war debt to be paid.

HISTORICAL THINKING

1. **READING CHECK** What departments made up Washington's Cabinet?

2. **DRAW CONCLUSIONS** What do the Cabinet departments suggest about what was important to the new government?

3. **MAKE INFERENCES** Why do you think the Federal Judiciary Act created both state and federal courts?

1.3 Hamilton's Economic Plan

Can you spare a cool $54 million? The American Revolution was a success, but that's how much the Patriots had to borrow to pull it off. Now it was time to pay back the debt. The question was how?

MAIN IDEA The United States had to develop an economic strategy for the new nation, but conflicting political points of view made planning difficult.

THE PRICE OF WAR

In addition to America's whopping **national debt**, individual states collectively owed another $25 million. Foreign governments and Americans who had helped finance the war were waiting to be repaid. Secretary of the Treasury Alexander Hamilton wanted the U.S. government to demonstrate it could be trusted to take care of its financial responsibilities. Doing so would improve America's credit and encourage new business.

An ardent federalist, Hamilton suggested that the federal government assume, or take over, the war debts of each state. This strategy would give the government more power to run the country's financial affairs. Under Hamilton's plan, sales of federal lands in the West would finance the repayment of European loans. More money would come from increased **tariffs**, or taxes on imports and exports. Tariffs would also encourage Americans to buy American goods, which would help protect industries from foreign competition.

Hamilton suggested the government pay off the rest of its debts by levying, or charging, certain taxes and by issuing new bonds, or investments promising interest on money

loaned. Investors would buy these bonds because the interest would produce big profits over the long run. Finally, to stabilize the nation's finances, Hamilton proposed a common currency and a National Bank. This bank would collect taxes, hold government funds, and promote business and industry by issuing loans. Hamilton envisioned the United States as a strong industrial nation.

The engraving of Alexander Hamilton, shown here, appears on the ten-dollar bill. Very narrow lines are used to create the engravings on U.S. money, making them so detailed that it is virtually impossible to copy exactly, or counterfeit, paper money.

Silver Dollar

During the American Revolution, individual states and the Continental Congress printed their own paper money. Those notes lost value very quickly and were worth almost nothing by the end of the war. Later, when the Constitution gave Congress the sole power to issue national currency, Alexander Hamilton recommended the nation adopt a silver dollar coin. He also suggested using fractional coins to represent smaller parts of a dollar. The Coinage Act of 1792 established the United States Mint—a facility for manufacturing coins—and regulated the coinage of the United States.

The act established the dollar, half-dollar, quarter-dollar, "disme," "half-disme," cent, and half-cent as the denominations of coins. The word *disme* became what we know as "dime." A "half-disme" is now a nickel.

The first dollar coin, called the "Flowing Hair Dollar," from 1794, showed Liberty as a woman on one side (top) and an eagle surrounded by a wreath on the other (bottom). In 1790, you could have used this coin to buy a bag or two of groceries. Ten of the coins could buy you a cow.

CRITICS WEIGH IN

Thomas Jefferson, on the other hand, envisioned an agricultural nation. He and other antifederalists opposed the strong central government and National Bank that Hamilton envisioned. A National Bank, they feared, would favor the interests of business over agriculture—specifically, the interests of the industrial North over those of the agricultural South. And southern states had even more reasons to oppose Hamilton's plan. Most had already paid their war debts. Hamilton ultimately won the South's favor by promising to relocate the nation's capital to Virginia, in an area that would eventually become Washington, D.C., the current capital of the United States.

Jefferson also opposed a National Bank because he believed it would give the federal government unlimited powers and go against the Constitution. But since the Constitution didn't expressly forbid the creation of a National Bank, Hamilton claimed the federal government had every right to establish one. Congress agreed. In 1791, it passed a bill creating a National Bank for a term of 20 years, and President Washington, who also supported Hamilton's views, signed it into law. In December of 1791, the Bank of the United States opened its doors in Philadelphia. Branches soon were established in major cities such as Boston, New York, Charleston, and Baltimore.

Both Jefferson and Hamilton were dedicated to the success of the new administration and the country. However, each man often advised Washington to ignore the counsel of the other. This made them personal adversaries, or opponents. In a letter to Washington written in 1792, Jefferson claimed that Hamilton's allies in Congress were a "corrupt squadron [military unit]," whose "ultimate object . . . is to prepare the way for a change, from the present republican form of government, to that of a monarchy, of which the English constitution is the model." The very nasty and public feud that developed between Jefferson and Hamilton greatly distressed Washington.

HISTORICAL THINKING

1. **READING CHECK** Why did Hamilton think it was crucial for the United States to repay its debts to European nations right away?

2. **COMPARE AND CONTRAST** Describe Jefferson's and Hamilton's different visions for the new nation.

3. **IDENTIFY PROBLEMS AND SOLUTIONS** How did Hamilton propose to pay off the national debt?

1.4 Broadway, New York City

New York's theater district revolves around a street you've probably heard of—Broadway. Some 40 theaters make up this famous district, including the Majestic, the Gershwin, and the Richard Rodgers Theatre, where *Hamilton: An American Musical* (shown below) made its Broadway debut in 2015. Since the early 1900s, small theaters have nestled between large ones under the glow of colorful signs advertising the latest productions. Countless actors have launched their careers in Broadway shows like *Cats*, *The Phantom of the Opera*, *Mamma Mia!*, and *The Lion King*, because if you've made it to Broadway, you've made it big. How is theater a part of American culture?

"My name is Alexander Hamilton
And there's a million things I haven't done
But just you wait
Just you wait."

—lyrics from the song "Alexander Hamilton"
by Lin-Manuel Miranda

CRITICAL VIEWING Tony Award-winning *Hamilton* is likely the most unique Broadway production in decades. The hip-hop musical tells the story of Founding Father Alexander Hamilton, who authored several of the Federalist Papers. Actor Lin-Manuel Miranda (center) played Hamilton on Broadway to sold-out crowds and critical acclaim. Based on the photo, how do you think *Hamilton* connects a modern audience to American history?

2.1 Political Parties Form

You've probably seen the ads. "Vote for me! Don't vote for" — whomever. The candidates are usually from different political parties. You can thank (or blame) Hamilton and Jefferson for laying the groundwork for such parties.

> **MAIN IDEA** Leaders formed political parties to promote their ideas, forming the basis of the modern American political system.

TAKING SIDES

During the 1790s, many congressional representatives sided with either Hamilton, who fought for a strong central government, or Jefferson, who feared the power such a government could wield. Eventually, the two sides formed two political parties—the **Federalist Party** and the **Democratic-Republican Party**. The Federalists backed Hamilton. The Democratic-Republicans sided more with Jefferson.

The Constitution made no provision for political parties, but it did not prohibit them. Still, the idea of divided political parties shocked the older leaders of the Revolutionary era. Washington warned against their "baneful [harmful] effects." If they were to play any role at all, he said, they needed to be kept in check. But the process was now in motion. Political parties had established themselves as a powerful force, and sides had been taken.

FACING OFF

On one side stood the Federalist Party, whose **power base**, or area of biggest influence, was in New England and the Middle Atlantic states. John Adams, Washington's vice president, joined the Federalists. They favored commercial development, a National Bank, the development of infrastructure to build canals, roads, and schools through land grants, and high tariffs to spur manufacturing. They also believed in a **loose interpretation** of the Constitution—one that gave broad powers to Congress and the president. Federalists were more likely than their opponents to be critical of slavery and so gained the allegiance of free African Americans in both the North and the South. Because their power base

lay in the Northeast, many Federalists didn't back the idea of western expansion and sometimes supported the rights of Native Americans.

On the other side was the Democratic-Republican Party, whose power base was in the South and the West. The party included many former antifederalists. Like Jefferson, the Democratic-Republicans believed in a **strict interpretation** of the Constitution—one that strictly followed the document and honored the rights of states over federal power. They opposed too much federal support for manufacturing and commerce. With its southern backing, the party rejected efforts to abolish slavery. Because it favored westward expansion and had little sympathy for the rights of Native Americans, the party also had the support of westerners on the frontier. The fundamental tension created by the development of a two-party system continues to influence American politics today.

In addition to these internal divisions within the government, the United States had to confront more fundamental challenges to its authority and legitimacy. Trouble was brewing in the Northwest Territory and abroad.

HISTORICAL THINKING

1. **READING CHECK** What regions of the United States supported each party, and why?

2. **IDENTIFY PROBLEMS AND SOLUTIONS** What problems might either a loose or strict interpretation of the Constitution create or solve?

3. **EVALUATE** What are the advantages and disadvantages of political parties?

Two-Party System

Although the parties have changed and shifted over the years, the United States still has two major political parties: the Democrats and the Republicans. A two-party system is relatively unique in the world. Some countries have only one party, while others have many. The symbols of each U.S. party are shown below: a donkey for the Democrats and an elephant for the Republicans. Neither modern party aligns closely with the political ideas of the Federalists or the Democratic-Republicans. However, like the parties in the 1790s, the parties today have regional characteristics. The Republicans tend to be stronger in the South and the West, and the Democrats stronger on the coasts, the Northeast, and the upper Midwest.

The campaign buttons shown are from the second half of the 20th century. Remember, though, that supporters purchased buttons honoring George Washington at his inauguration. In the 1840 election, people wore campaign buttons sewn on clothing. Pins were added around 1860, along with the first photograph to appear on a campaign button—a picture of Abraham Lincoln.

2.2 Competition for Territory and the French Revolution

George Washington had dealt with many challenging situations, but as president, he probably got more than he bargained for. As political conflict grew among U.S. citizens, conflicts over western lands heated to the boiling point.

MAIN IDEA As the young republic pushed west, conflicts both at home and abroad caused a host of challenges for the United States.

CONFLICTS IN THE WEST

The problem area was the Northwest Territory, located north of the Ohio River, between the western boundary of Pennsylvania and the Mississippi River. As you may remember, the Treaty of Paris of 1783 had established new boundaries for the United States and tried to settle claims on this land. But in the 1790s, the land seemed to be up for grabs once again. Spain, Britain, the United States, and Native American groups all claimed parts of the vast expanse for their own.

The United States mostly fought with Native Americans over rights to this land. Americans wanted to settle the land, not only for its rich soil but also for its minerals, such as copper, iron, and silver. Native Americans had lived in this region for thousands of years and attacked settlers who moved onto the land. In response, Washington sent in two military expeditions, but the Miami of Ohio, led by

Chief Little Turtle, defeated them both. Then, in 1794, federal troops defeated the Miami at the Battle of Fallen Timbers. The British, who had usually helped the Miami, refused to protect them this time. They were tired of war. Without British support, the Miami and other Native Americans in the region signed the **Treaty of Greenville**, which **ceded**, or gave up, their lands in present-day Ohio and Indiana to the United States.

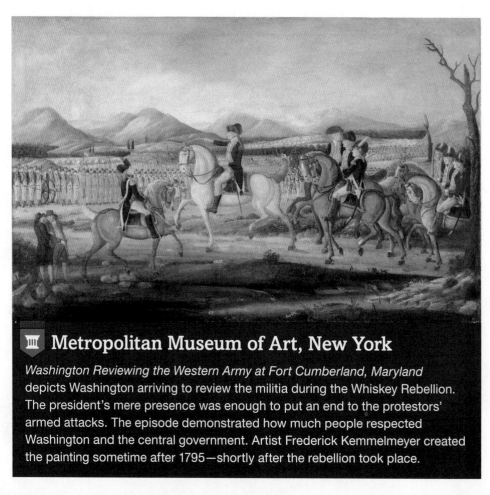

🏛 Metropolitan Museum of Art, New York

Washington Reviewing the Western Army at Fort Cumberland, Maryland depicts Washington arriving to review the militia during the Whiskey Rebellion. The president's mere presence was enough to put an end to the protestors' armed attacks. The episode demonstrated how much people respected Washington and the central government. Artist Frederick Kemmelmeyer created the painting sometime after 1795—shortly after the rebellion took place.

Meanwhile, another conflict brewed in western Pennsylvania. Farmers had been protesting a whiskey tax, claiming it was unfair. The farmers tarred and feathered tax collectors and threatened armed attacks in what is known as the **Whiskey Rebellion**. President Washington sent nearly 13,000 soldiers into the region to demonstrate the power of the federal government. The rebels soon stood down.

THE FRENCH REVOLUTION

Across the Atlantic, the people in France were involved in a rebellion of their own. They sought to put an end to upper-class privilege and demanded equality for the lower classes. Many in the United States, and particularly the Democratic-Republicans, supported the **French Revolution**. But then in 1793, **radicals**, or people who support complete social or political change, executed the French king, Louis XVI. France then declared war on Spain, Britain, and other neighboring nations. In this international conflict, the Federalists sided with Britain, thereby increasing the division between the two American parties. So even though France had supported the American Revolution, Washington declared in 1793 that the United States would remain neutral, not taking sides with anyone.

But Britain made neutrality difficult. Its Royal Navy captured American citizens and forced them to work on British ships. They also blocked trade in the British West Indies and seized American ships. To make peace, Washington sent Chief Justice John Jay to England to work out a deal. Jay's Treaty required the British to pay for the American ships they had damaged, but it failed to reopen trade in the West Indies.

Meanwhile, **Thomas Pinckney**, an American statesman, traveled to Spain and negotiated Pinckney's Treaty in 1796 to maintain friendly relations between the United States and Spain. The treaty opened the Mississippi River to free navigation, allowed Americans to use the Spanish port of New Orleans, and settled a conflict regarding the Spanish colony of West Florida.

Guillotine
One of the most striking images of the French Revolution is the guillotine (GEE-yuh-teen), the machine used to execute thousands, including Louis XVI. The guillotine had a blade that plunged down grooves in two upright posts to slice through the victim's neck, beheading him or her in one stroke.

HISTORICAL THINKING

1. **READING CHECK** Why did farmers in western Pennsylvania stage the Whiskey Rebellion?

2. **IDENTIFY PROBLEMS AND SOLUTIONS** Describe the conflicts between American settlers and Native Americans in the Northwest Territory and how they were resolved.

3. **MAKE INFERENCES** Why do you think the United States wanted to remain neutral during the French Revolution?

2.3 Washington's Farewell Address

At the end of his first presidential term, George Washington wrote a goodbye letter to the American people. Then he ended up running for a second term. The letter—Washington's Farewell Address—was finally published in 1796, and it is an important American document.

When his eighth year as president was drawing to a close, Washington shared the letter with John Jay and Alexander Hamilton. The three men spent four months revising the letter, ensuring that Washington's ideas were crystal clear. Washington handwrote a clean copy of the finished letter—32 pages long—and addressed it to "Friends & Fellow-Citizens." It was published in the Philadelphia newspaper, *American Daily Advertiser,* on September 19, 1796. It was then printed in other newspapers throughout the country. Following his service as president of the United States, Washington moved back to Mount Vernon (shown in the photo), his home and plantation in Virginia. Washington grew up at Mount Vernon and had always dreamed of returning to his home life there. He lived at Mount Vernon until his death in 1799 and is buried there.

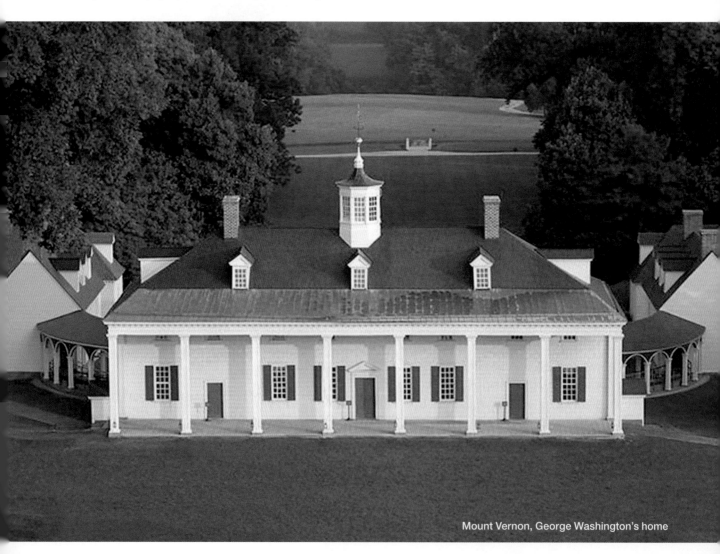

Mount Vernon, George Washington's home

DOCUMENT ONE

**Primary Source: Historical document
from Washington's Farewell Address, 1796**

In this excerpt from his address, Washington tells Americans that they form one united nation. United, he tells them, they are stronger and more secure than they could ever be as separate individuals.

CONSTRUCTED RESPONSE Why does Washington urge people to be proud to be called Americans?

The unity of government . . . is a main pillar in the edifice [structure] of your real independence, . . . of your tranquility at home, your peace abroad; of your safety; of your prosperity; of that very liberty which you so highly prize. The name of American, which belongs to you in your national capacity, must always exalt the just pride of patriotism.

DOCUMENT TWO

**Primary Source: Historical document
from Washington's Farewell Address, 1796**

Washington felt that political parties could pit one group of people against another, posing a threat to national unity. Here, he discusses the dangers of rival political parties.

CONSTRUCTED RESPONSE According to Washington, how might rival political parties affect a community?

In contemplating the causes which may disturb our Union, it occurs as matter of serious concern that any ground should have been furnished for characterizing parties by geographical discriminations [differences], . . . whence [by which] designing men may endeavor to excite a belief that there is a real difference of local interests and views.

DOCUMENT THREE

**Primary Source: Historical document
from Washington's Farewell Address, 1796**

In 1796, France was at war with many other European countries, including Britain. As you've read, some Americans supported the French cause, while others supported Britain. In this excerpt, Washington warns against forming permanent alliances and argues for neutrality in all overseas affairs. He believes such alliances would open the country to foreign influence and unnecessary wars.

CONSTRUCTED RESPONSE What did Washington's speech suggest about the policy the United States should follow with other nations?

Nothing is more essential than that permanent, inveterate antipathies [harsh opposition] against particular nations, and passionate attachments for others, should be excluded and that, in place of them, just and amicable [friendly] feelings towards all should be cultivated. Excessive partiality for one foreign nation and excessive dislike of another cause those whom they actuate [fire up] to see danger only on one side, and serve to veil [cover up] . . . the influence on the other. The great rule of conduct for us in regard to foreign nations is in extending our commercial relations, to have with them as little political connection as possible.

SYNTHESIZE & WRITE

1. **REVIEW** Review what you have learned about Washington's Farewell Address.

2. **RECALL** On your own paper, write the main idea that Washington expressed in each excerpt from his farewell address.

3. **CONSTRUCT** Construct a topic sentence that answers this question: What factors did Washington fear could disrupt the unity and peace of the United States?

4. **WRITE** Using evidence from this chapter and the documents, write an informative paragraph that supports your topic sentence in Step 3.

2.4 The Parties in Conflict

Politicians making negative remarks about each other. Citizens deeply divided over the candidates. A modern-day election? Nope. This happened in 1796, when political parties first competed in an election.

> **MAIN IDEA** Political clashes tested U.S. relationships abroad and the constitutionality of laws passed at home.

ADAMS VS. JEFFERSON

The Federalists and Democratic-Republicans waged a bitter campaign in 1796. John Adams ran on the Federalist side, and Thomas Jefferson represented the Democratic-Republicans. After attacks on both sides, Adams won with 71 electoral votes. He was the first president to govern from Washington, D.C. Jefferson came in second with 68 electoral votes and became vice president. It was not a happy arrangement.

Problems abroad claimed their attention. France began seizing American ships in an effort to prevent U.S. trade with Britain. In response, Adams sent three **envoys**, or ambassadors, to France to settle the problem. The envoys met with French agents known to the American public simply as X, Y, and Z. When the French agents made unreasonable demands and even insisted on being paid a bribe to begin negotiations, the shocked envoys turned them down and returned home.

The **XYZ Affair**, as the negotiations came to be called, further soured American relations with France. It also hurt the reputation of the Democratic-Republicans, who had supported the French Revolution. When Adams made reports of the affair public, most Americans felt their honor had been attacked, and war fever swept the country. Congress expanded the army, established the navy, and authorized naval vessels to attack French ships that threatened American merchant ships. Congress stopped all trade with France and ended the U.S. alliance with the country.

THE ALIEN AND SEDITION ACTS

Americans cheered Adams's response to the French threat. Riding on a wave of popularity, the Federalists passed the **Alien and Sedition Acts**. The Alien Act allowed the president to expel, for any reason, new immigrants, or aliens, living in the United States—most of whom were Democratic-Republicans. The Sedition Act targeted U.S. citizens, including journalists, who criticized the government. **Sedition** is the act of provoking rebellion.

Democratic-Republicans were quick to respond. For example, in the Kentucky Resolutions, Jefferson condemned the excess of the Alien and Sedition Acts, claiming they violated citizens' freedom of speech and freedom of the press. Adams's opponents fought the acts using a theory called **states' rights**, which declares that individual states have rights the federal government cannot violate. By 1802, the acts had expired, but they had undermined Adams's popularity. In the presidential election of 1800, Jefferson defeated him. The election marked the first peaceful transfer of power from one party to another.

HISTORICAL THINKING

1. **READING CHECK** How did Jefferson become Adams's vice president in 1796?

2. **ANALYZE CAUSE AND EFFECT** Why did the XYZ Affair increase Adams's popularity?

3. **SYNTHESIZE** How did the Sedition Acts contradict the rights guaranteed under the First Amendment?

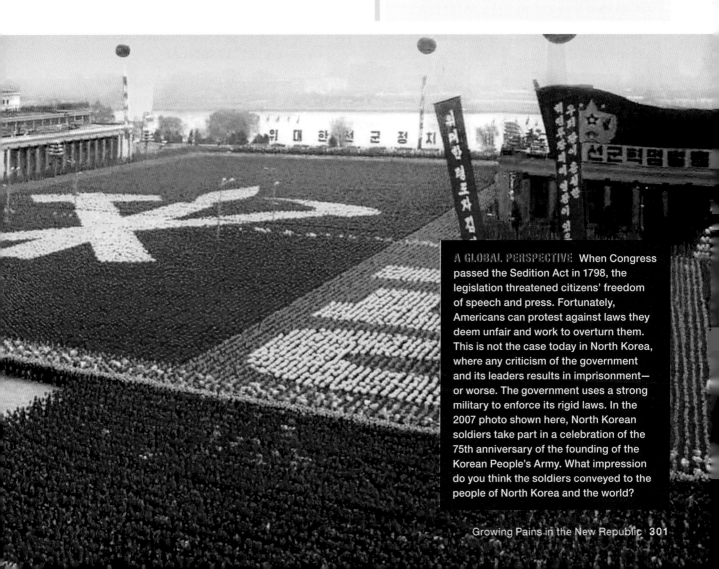

A GLOBAL PERSPECTIVE When Congress passed the Sedition Act in 1798, the legislation threatened citizens' freedom of speech and press. Fortunately, Americans can protest against laws they deem unfair and work to overturn them. This is not the case today in North Korea, where any criticism of the government and its leaders results in imprisonment—or worse. The government uses a strong military to enforce its rigid laws. In the 2007 photo shown here, North Korean soldiers take part in a celebration of the 75th anniversary of the founding of the Korean People's Army. What impression do you think the soldiers conveyed to the people of North Korea and the world?

VOCABULARY

Complete each of the sentences below with one of the vocabulary words or terms from this chapter.

1. The department heads in Washington's _____ did not always agree.

2. Placing a _____ on imported goods helped make American goods more competitive.

3. U.S. journalists who criticized the government could be accused of _____ .

4. Federalists preferred a _____ of the Constitution rather than a rigid one.

5. Antifederalists tended to favor _____ rather than a strong central government.

6. The first presidential _____ took place in New York City.

READING STRATEGY
IDENTIFY PROBLEMS AND SOLUTIONS

Complete your chart to identify the problems the new nation faced. List at least three key problems. Then answer the question below.

Issue: After the Revolution, the nation and individual states had huge debts.

↓

Problem 1: Foreign governments were waiting to be paid.

Problem 2:

Problem 3:

↓

Solution:

7. How did Alexander Hamilton solve the problem of the nation's debt?

MAIN IDEAS

Answer the following questions. Support your answers with evidence from the chapter.

8. Why was George Washington the obvious choice to be the first president? **LESSON 1.1**

9. What three departments did Congress first create to be part of the executive branch? **LESSON 1.2**

10. What did the Federal Judiciary Act call for? **LESSON 1.2**

11. How did Hamilton's economic plan reflect his federalist philosophy? **LESSON 1.3**

12. Why did the South tend to support the Democratic-Republican Party? **LESSON 2.1**

13. Why did Washington warn against divided political parties? **LESSON 2.1**

14. Why did Native Americans in the Northwest Territory sign the Treaty of Greenville? **LESSON 2.2**

15. Why did Congress stop all U.S. trade with France? **LESSON 2.4**

16. What freedoms did the Sedition Act target? **LESSON 2.4**

HISTORICAL THINKING

Answer the following questions. Support your answers with evidence from the chapter.

17. **SYNTHESIZE** How did the choice of George Washington as the country's first president help to shape American identity?

18. **EVALUATE** Why would Washington want to avoid any suggestion that the office of president of the United States was similar to that of a king?

19. MAKE CONNECTIONS Identify a controversial issue mentioned in this chapter that is still causing disagreement today.

20. DRAW CONCLUSIONS Why did George Washington think it was important to leave some parting words to the American people in his farewell address?

21. MAKE INFERENCES Why might Adams have wanted to pass the Alien Act?

22. IDENTIFY PROBLEMS AND SOLUTIONS What new problem did the XYZ Affair cause, and what measures did Congress put in place to solve it?

INTERPRET MAPS

Study this map, which shows the results of the 1796 presidential election between John Adams and Thomas Jefferson. Note that the numbers represent the number of electoral college votes for each state. Remember that the electoral college consists of electors representing each state who vote to elect a president and vice president. The boxed numbers represent the number of electors in that state who voted differently from the others in the state. Then answer the questions that follow.

Electoral College, 1796

- John Adams (Federalist)
- Thomas Jefferson (Democratic-Republican)
- Split electoral vote
- Territories

23. Which state had the most electoral votes?

24. What generalization can you make regarding the geographic distribution of results?

ANALYZE SOURCES

In this excerpt from a letter written on February 28, 1796, by Thomas Jefferson to John Adams, Jefferson explains why he thinks Americans are especially suited to a democratic form of government. Read the passage and answer the question.

> Never was a finer canvas presented to work on than our countrymen. All of them engaged in agriculture or the pursuits of honest industry, independent in their circumstances, enlightened as to their rights, and firm in their habits of order and obedience to the laws. This I hope will be the age of experiments in government, and that their basis will be founded on principles of honesty, not of mere force.

25. How does Jefferson characterize the American people?

CONNECT TO YOUR LIFE

26. EXPLANATORY Think about the election of 1796, the first to involve political parties. Make a connection between that presidential election and a recent one. Write a paragraph explaining how the two elections are similar and different.

TIPS

- Take notes on the two elections. You may wish to use a Venn diagram or other graphic organizer to help organize your ideas.

- State your main idea clearly and support it with relevant facts, details, and examples.

- Use at least two vocabulary terms from the chapter.

- Provide a concluding statement about how the elections are similar and different.

CHAPTER

9

THE JEFFERSON YEARS
1800–1816

ESSENTIAL QUESTION

In what ways did Thomas Jefferson's policies change the country?

AMERICAN STORIES Early Explorers Lewis and Clark

SECTION 1 **Jeffersonian Democracy**

KEY VOCABULARY

incumbent   unconstitutional

judicial review   writ

Judiciary Act of 1801

SECTION 2 **Westward Expansion**

KEY VOCABULARY

Louisiana Purchase   yellow fever

SECTION 3 **The War of 1812 Approaches**

KEY VOCABULARY

customs   prophet

embargo   War Hawks

Embargo Act of 1807   War of 1812

impressment

AMERICAN GALLERY
ONLINE
New Orleans: A French, Spanish, and American City

READING STRATEGY

ANALYZE CAUSE AND EFFECT

When you analyze cause and effect, you note the consequences of an event, an action, or a condition. As you read this chapter, use a graphic organizer like this one to identify the causes that led to a second war with Britain in 1812.

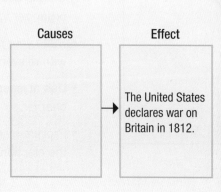

Causes   Effect

The United States declares war on Britain in 1812.

"I hold it that **a little rebellion now and then** is a good thing."

—Thomas Jefferson

CRITICAL VIEWING The Jefferson Memorial, which faces the White House in Washington, D.C., was completed in 1943. Its columns and dome were inspired by ancient Greek and Roman buildings. What other details of the memorial help convey a sense of awe and grandeur?

EARLY EXPLORERS

LEWIS AND CLARK

Captain
Meriwether Lewis

Second Lieutenant
William Clark

In 1803, Thomas Jefferson

sent Meriwether Lewis and William Clark to find a water route to the Pacific and explore the uncharted West. Jefferson believed woolly mammoths, erupting volcanoes, and a mountain of pure salt awaited them. What they found was no less mind-boggling: some 300 species unknown to science, nearly 50 Indian tribes, and the Rocky Mountains.

Lewis was Jefferson's private secretary, an army officer, and an enthusiastic amateur scientist. Clark was a friend of Lewis and also an army officer. On May 14, 1804, the two men set off from a camp near St. Louis, Missouri, accompanied by a group of about 40 men that they dubbed the Corps (KOR) of Discovery. Most of the explorers were soldiers, and one was Clark's African-American slave—a man named York. Packed into three boats along with their supplies, the men headed upstream on the Missouri River toward the regions that now have familiar names such as Kansas, North Dakota, and Idaho. In 1804, this area was called the Louisiana Territory. As far as Jefferson was concerned, it was the great unknown.

National Geographic photographer Sam Abell captured this image of the merging of the Yellowstone River (left) with the Missouri River (right) at one of the locations visited by Lewis and Clark during their expedition.

TO FORT MANDAN AND BEYOND

One of Jefferson's goals for the expedition was to establish friendly relationships with the Indian tribes living in the West. Lewis and Clark had mixed success with this effort. Some tribes welcomed the explorers' gifts and offers of alliance, while others were either uninterested or hostile. The Mandan, living in present-day North Dakota, were among the more welcoming groups. The Corps arrived at the villages of the Mandan and Hidatsa in October 1804. After being warmly received, Lewis and Clark decided to build their winter quarters nearby.

While building their camp, the explorers met Sacagawea (SAK-uh-juh-WE-uh), who would become an important member of the Corps of Discovery. She was a young woman of the Shoshone tribe, which lived just east of the Rocky Mountains. She had been kidnapped from her people as a small child and was now married to a French-Canadian trader named Toussaint Charbonneau. Knowing they would meet the Shoshone later in their travels, Lewis and Clark hired Sacagawea and Charbonneau as interpreters.

In April 1805, the Corps of Discovery broke camp and resumed its journey west. At the same time, they sent a boat back to Thomas Jefferson in Washington, D.C., loaded with 108 botanical specimens, 68 mineral specimens, and a map of the United States drawn by William Clark.

QUITE A SHOPPING LIST

Knowing they would be gone for a long time, Lewis and Clark stocked up on gear for the trip. Below are just a few items from the Corps of Discovery's supply list. Lewis spent $2,324 on supplies for the years-long expedition. That's the equivalent of around $40,000 in 2016 dollars.

Camping Equipment:

- 150 yards of cloth for making tents and sheets
- 25 hatchets
- 10.5 pounds of fishing hooks
- 12 pounds of soap
- 193 pounds of "portable soup"

Medicine:

- 50 dozen of "Rush's Thunderclapper" pills
- syringes
- tourniquets
- 3,500 doses of sweat inducer

Gifts for Native American Tribes:

- 12 dozen pocket mirrors
- 4,600 sewing needles
- 8 brass kettles
- 20 pounds of beads
- 288 brass thimbles

Meriwether Lewis also brought his spyglass on the expedition.

TIME LINE OF EVENTS

1804

May 14, 1804 The Corps of Discovery leaves its camp near St. Louis and begins the journey west.

Early September 1804 The Corps enters the Great Plains. Lewis and Clark begin sighting unfamiliar animal species.

October 24, 1804 The Corps arrives at the villages of the Mandan and Hidatsa tribes near present-day Bismarck, North Dakota.

November 11, 1804 Lewis and Clark hire Sacagawea and Toussaint Charbonneau as interpreters for the rest of the journey.

CRITICAL VIEWING National Geographic photographer Sam Abell captures the White Cliffs of the Missouri River. The Corps of Discovery compared these unique sandstone formations to the ruins of an ancient city. "As we passed on," Lewis wrote in his journal, "it seemed as if those scenes of visionary enchantment would never have an end." Why might the Corps have likened this geologic formation to ancient ruins?

FROM THE ROCKIES TO THE PACIFIC

Throughout the summer, the Corps made progress toward the Rocky Mountains, nervously watching as the imposing, snow-capped peaks grew taller and taller as they approached. When they reached the region we now call northern Montana, Lewis scouted ahead of the expedition, and came across "the grandest sight I ever beheld"—the Great Falls of the Missouri, along with four additional waterfalls immediately upriver. The expedition had no choice but to portage, or carry their canoes over land, for 18.5 miles in order to get around the falls. Extreme summer heat, dangerous storms, prickly pear cacti, and brush made the portage more challenging and time-consuming than anticipated, and the journey took nearly a month.

In August, the Corps reached a Shoshone village just east of the mountains. Here, they hoped to buy horses to help them cross the mountains. The next thing that happened could be described as one of history's most stunning coincidences. The Shoshone villagers recognized Sacagawea. To everyone's shock and delight, she learned that the chief of this group was her long-lost brother.

December 24, 1804 The Corps finishes building Fort Mandan near the Indian villages.

April 7, 1805 The Corps leaves Fort Mandan to resume its westward travel.

May 16, 1805 One of the expedition's boats almost flips over. Sacagawea saves many journals and important papers from going overboard.

August 17, 1805 The Corps reaches the Shoshone camp on the eastern edge of the Rockies. There, Sacagawea realizes the chief is her long-lost brother.

1805

THE CORPS OF DISCOVERY BY THE NUMBERS

PREVIOUSLY UNKNOWN PLANTS DESCRIBED

178

PREVIOUSLY UNKNOWN ANIMALS DESCRIBED

122

INDIAN TRIBES ENCOUNTERED

48

CORPS MEMBER CASUALTIES

ONE

BY NATURAL CAUSES, PROBABLY APPENDICITIS

THE JOURNEY SPANNED OVER **8,000 MILES** AND WENT ON FOR . . .

. . . **863 DAYS.**

JOYFUL ARRIVAL

At the end of August, the expedition set out to cross the Rockies with the 29 horses they had purchased. The crossing was brutal. At one point, the men lost the trail in the midst of a blinding snowstorm. By the time they stumbled out of the mountains, the men and Sacagawea were exhausted, almost frozen, and near starvation. Happily for the Corps, the Nez Perce Indians, who lived on the west side of the Rockies, were welcoming and willing to share their food.

Soon, the explorers were on the last leg of their westward journey, making their way down the swift-flowing Columbia River toward the Pacific Ocean. On November 7, Clark wrote in his journal, "Ocian in view! O! The joy!" In fact, the Corps

had just reached the place where the Columbia widened before meeting the Pacific. The men were still 20 miles from the coast. Three weeks later, after battling fierce storms, the expedition finally reached the shore of the Pacific.

With winter approaching, the Corps built a settlement they named Fort Clatsop, after the Indians living nearby. Lewis and Clark hoped to avoid recrossing the Rockies on the return trip east. American and British trading ships often stopped near the mouth of the Columbia, and the plan was to take passage on one of these ships. However, the expedition never spotted a single ship during a long, dreary winter that had only 12 days without rain.

TIME LINE OF EVENTS CONTINUED

September 11, 1805 The Corps begins climbing up into the Bitterroots, a range of the Rocky Mountains.

September 23, 1805 The expedition completes the mountain crossing and meets the Nez Perce Indians.

October 16, 1805 They reach the Columbia River.

November 24, 1805 The Corps reaches the Pacific Ocean and decides to build Fort Clatsop on the south side of the Columbia.

1806

HOMEWARD BOUND

When spring finally arrived, the expedition was more than ready to leave Fort Clatsop. The trip back to St. Louis was difficult and filled with dangers. The Corps failed in its first attempt to cross the Rockies and had to try a second time. Before leaving the mountains, the expedition split into two to explore more territory, and both groups had hostile encounters with Native American groups. Lewis experienced a dramatic event when he was shot in the leg. The shot, however, was likely by accident from someone in his group. Luckily, it did not result in an injury that was life-threatening. Soon afterward the two halves of the expedition were reunited.

On September 23, the Corps of Discovery came ashore in St. Louis, nearly two and a half years after their departure. The entire city turned out to celebrate the return of the heroes who had been given up for dead. Unlike many earlier explorers, Lewis and Clark did not set off in search of gold or other monetary rewards. Instead, they were returning with a far richer treasure—knowledge about the people, places, plants, and animals in the lands far west of the Mississippi.

THINK ABOUT IT

Use the time line to help you describe the most significant challenges and successes of the Lewis and Clark expedition.

Lewis's silver pocket compass

SACAGAWEA

Kidnapped at the age of 12 by the Hidatsa, Sacagawea, a Shoshone, was taken from the Rocky Mountains to the Hidatsa-Mandan villages in North Dakota. That's where she met the Corps of Discovery in November 1804. Sacagawea's knowledge of languages and the land proved to be very valuable to the Corps as it moved west, passing through the territories of many Native American tribes, some of which had never seen white men before. When tribes saw Sacagawea and her baby traveling with the Corps, they knew the Corps was a friendly group disinterested in war. This statue of Sacagawea stands in a park in Portland, Oregon.

March 23, 1806 The expedition leaves Fort Clatsop to head home.

June 30, 1806 They pause at Traveler's Rest in the Bitterroot Mountains. Lewis and Clark decide to split up and divide the Corps into two groups to cover more ground.

August 12, 1806 The Corps reunites. From here, the swift-flowing Missouri River allows for rapid travel eastward.

September 23, 1806 The Corps of Discovery arrives at St. Louis and receives a hero's welcome.

1807

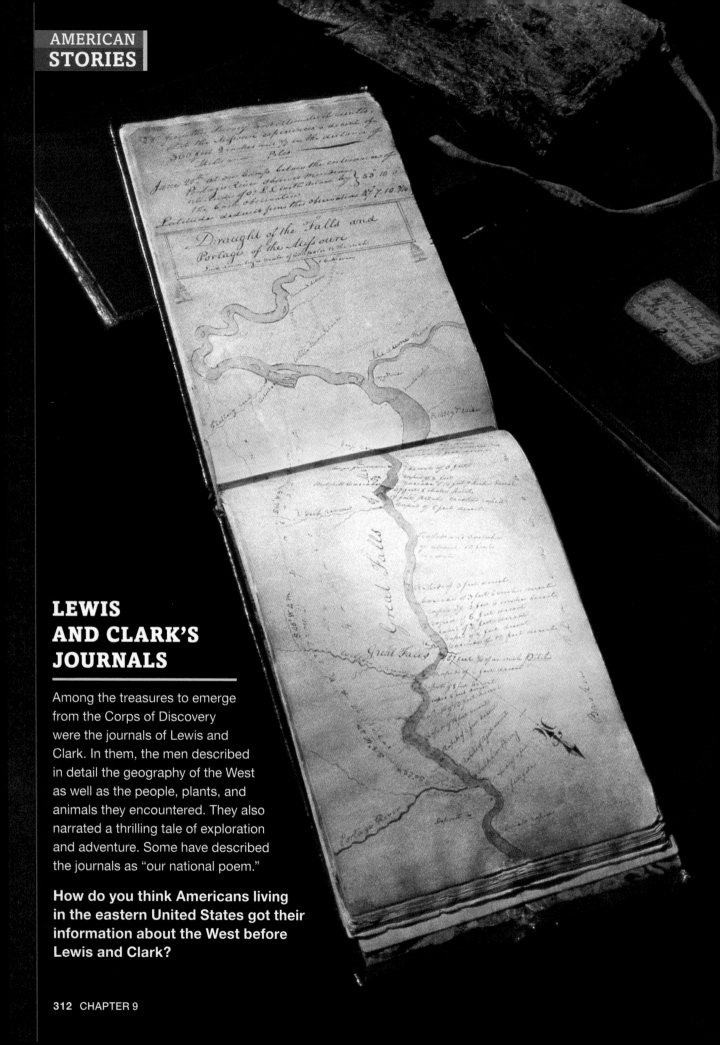

LEWIS AND CLARK'S JOURNALS

Among the treasures to emerge from the Corps of Discovery were the journals of Lewis and Clark. In them, the men described in detail the geography of the West as well as the people, plants, and animals they encountered. They also narrated a thrilling tale of exploration and adventure. Some have described the journals as "our national poem."

How do you think Americans living in the eastern United States got their information about the West before Lewis and Clark?

While it's uncertain exactly how Lewis and Clark assembled their field journals, it's likely that the men first made quick notes in portable notebooks they carried with them, including simple maps and sketches. When they returned to camp, they probably combined their notes and rewrote them into the more clear and detailed pages you see here.

1.1 Jefferson's Vision for America

John Adams and Thomas Jefferson didn't actually come to blows during the election of 1800, but they probably came close. They certainly exchanged insults. But when the dust settled, Jefferson was the winner.

MAIN IDEA After the election of Thomas Jefferson, the nation steered a course to a more limited and less expensive government.

BREAKING THE TIE

The election of 1800 was filled with tension and political divisions, and the fact that the frontrunners were the **incumbent**, or current, president and vice president added to it. President Adams, the Federalist, had spent the past four years building a strong government. Vice President Thomas Jefferson, the Democratic-Republican, believed Adams had favored businessmen from the North. To persuade the nation to elect him, Jefferson promised a limited government and lower taxes.

Jefferson favored Aaron Burr as his candidate for vice president. But remember that, at that time, potential running mates ran on their own. So for Burr to become Jefferson's vice president, Jefferson needed to receive the most votes, and Burr needed to come in second.

As it turned out, Jefferson and Burr received an equal number of votes for president. The tie had to be broken by the Federalist-dominated House of Representatives.

Replicas of Burr-Hamilton dueling pistols

New York Historical Society, New York

In the early 1800s, men engaged in pistol fights called duels to defend their honor. Although dueling was illegal in most states, it was an accepted practice.

On the morning of July 11, 1804, Vice President Aaron Burr and Alexander Hamilton dueled in a field in Weehawken, New Jersey. Burr had challenged Hamilton to the duel; Hamilton had provided the pistols. The men's rivalry had been building for a decade. In 1791, Burr defeated Hamilton's father-in-law in an election. In 1800, Burr publicly shamed Hamilton by publishing a private essay Hamilton had written criticizing his fellow Federalist, President John Adams. The final straw for Burr was when he read a newspaper article that quoted some of Hamilton's negative opinions of him.

Before that fateful morning, Hamilton had written in letters that he had no intention of killing Burr. The aim of Hamilton's first shot is disputed. Some say he pointed his pistol up in the air; others say he fired at Burr and missed. But Burr didn't miss. He shot Hamilton in the stomach, and Hamilton died the next day. Not only did the showdown end Hamilton's life, it also ended the vice president's political career. Burr was charged with Hamilton's death but received no punishment for the crime.

The World's Best Hope

Jefferson tried to unite Americans in his 1801 Inaugural Address and soothe their fears about what had happened in France during the French Revolution. In that country, radical elements in a republican government had seized control and terrorized the French people. In this excerpt from his address, Jefferson explains why he doesn't believe such a thing could happen in the United States. Why does Jefferson believe the United States has the strongest government on earth?

I know, indeed, that some honest men fear that a republican government can not be strong, that this Government is not strong enough, but would the honest patriot . . . abandon a government which has so far kept us free and firm on the theoretic and visionary [imaginary] fear that this Government, the world's best hope, may . . . want [lack] energy to preserve itself? I trust not. I believe this, on the contrary, the strongest Government on earth. I believe it the only one where every man . . . would meet invasions of the public order [would defend the country] as his own personal concern.

—from Thomas Jefferson's First Inaugural Address, March 4, 1801

The House spent six days casting votes 36 separate times. At first, most Federalists supported Burr, but Burr's bitter enemy Alexander Hamilton rallied support for Jefferson. On February 17, 1801, the House cast the final votes. Jefferson became the nation's third president, and Burr became his vice president.

SOOTHING FEARS

Jefferson's inauguration took place the following month, the first to be held in the new capital city of Washington, D.C. The new president was aware of the division in the country following the election. Many Federalists feared what they considered Jefferson's radical views. They saw what had happened during the French Revolution, when extreme revolutionaries took control and executed thousands of people. In his inaugural address, Jefferson tried to soothe their fears by saying, "We are all Republicans; we are all Federalists."

Jefferson's call for unity set the tone for his years in office. He clearly laid out his plan for governing to the people—and followed it. He lowered taxes and reduced the size of the federal judiciary. In addition, Jefferson continued to support the power of the states and championed low government spending. But he did not dismantle all Federalist institutions. He left the military and Hamilton's National Bank mostly intact.

A popular president, Jefferson easily won re-election in 1804. In his second term, Jefferson continued to combine Democratic-Republican beliefs with wise politics, shrinking the federal government, military, and national debt. Further, Jefferson's personal humility, or humbleness, went hand-in-hand with his philosophy of small government. Instead of hosting showy and expensive events, he insisted on meeting personally with members of Congress and foreign leaders for dinner and conversation. A seat at that table would have been a sought-after invitation for most. These dinners showcased not only Jefferson's taste for fine food but also his many talents.

HISTORICAL THINKING

1. **READING CHECK** What was Thomas Jefferson's political philosophy, and how was it reflected in his policies as president?

2. **MAKE INFERENCES** Based on what you have learned about the ideological differences between Jefferson and Hamilton, what can you infer about Hamilton's support of Jefferson in the 1800 election?

3. **DISTINGUISH FACT AND OPINION** What facts and opinions does Jefferson use to reduce the country's fears and unite Americans?

1.2 Thomas Jefferson 1743–1826

"I like the dreams of the future better than the history of the past." —Thomas Jefferson

A gifted writer, architect, scientist—you name it—Thomas Jefferson had the chops to carry out his dreams. He proposed a plan that laid the basis of our school system, restocked the Library of Congress with his own books, and penned America's creed. At a dinner at the White House in 1962, President John F. Kennedy remarked to a group of dignitaries that they represented the greatest talent ever assembled there, "with the possible exception of when Thomas Jefferson dined alone."

MONTICELLO

Because Jefferson was born into one of Virginia's foremost families, he received an education that allowed his natural abilities to flourish. As a young man, he studied law and, in time, developed a successful practice. While trying and winning most of the cases that came his way, the young lawyer met Martha Wayles Skelton, who would become his wife. A few years before they married, Jefferson began to design and build Monticello, which would be their home—aside from his years in the White House—for the rest of their lives.

Jefferson built Monticello on land in Charlottesville, Virginia, that he inherited from his father. The home became his architectural masterpiece, which he

New York Historical Society New York City

American artist Rembrandt Peale painted this portrait in 1805 after Jefferson won reelection in a landslide victory. Jefferson posed for the portrait in the White House, wearing a cape with a fur-lined collar, perhaps to lend an air of informality to the painting.

constantly reimagined and reworked over more than 40 years. The exterior of the house, with its columns and dome, was inspired by ancient Greek and Roman temples. The interior, with its 40-plus

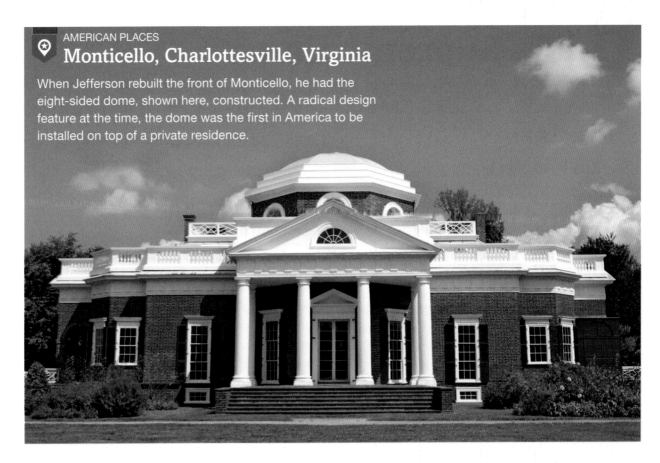

AMERICAN PLACES
Monticello, Charlottesville, Virginia

When Jefferson rebuilt the front of Monticello, he had the eight-sided dome, shown here, constructed. A radical design feature at the time, the dome was the first in America to be installed on top of a private residence.

rooms, held some of Jefferson's own inventions, including a "turning-machine" for holding and rotating the clothes in his closet.

The extensive gardens at Monticello also contained his inventions and improvements, such as a sundial and a plow that could easily lift and turn the soil cut by the machine. Jefferson was a dedicated gardener. He cultivated seeds he'd obtained from Europe and Mexico and even some from Lewis and Clark's westward expedition. Jefferson's gardens were a botanic laboratory where he used the scientific method to determine which seeds and plants grew best in its soil and climate.

MAN OF CONTRADICTIONS

Unfortunately, Jefferson's building projects at Monticello and his lavish lifestyle—he loved to entertain—caused him to fall deeply in debt. This may seem odd for a man who once said, "Never spend your money before you have it," but then, Jefferson was full of contradictions. In the Declaration of Independence, he wrote that "all men are created equal," yet he owned more than 100 slaves. And while George Washington granted freedom to many of his slaves in his will, Jefferson only freed a handful of his. He staunchly supported states' rights, but as president, greatly expanded the power of the national government. In many ways, he embodied the social and political contradictions of America itself.

Jefferson died at Monticello on July 4, 1826—50 years to the day after the signing of the Declaration of Independence. By a strange coincidence, his old friend and rival, John Adams, died on the same day. The pair had often locked horns politically but had always maintained a strong mutual respect. When Adams died, his last words were, "Thomas Jefferson survives." He didn't know that his friend had passed away just a few hours before.

HISTORICAL THINKING

1. **READING CHECK** What were some of Jefferson's talents and accomplishments?

2. **EVALUATE** Why do you think it might have been difficult for Jefferson to live up to his principles?

3. **MAKE INFERENCES** Why do you think Adams might have been thinking of Jefferson in his last moments?

1.3 The Supreme Court

After winning the presidency, Thomas Jefferson might have thought that he and his opponents would be able to put aside their differences and work together. He didn't know John Adams would take one more parting shot.

MAIN IDEA The introduction of judicial review brought greater power to the Supreme Court and greater balance among the three branches of government.

MARSHALL'S COURT

John Adams and the Federalists lost the presidential and congressional elections in 1800, but they made the most of their remaining time in office. Just before the Democratic-Republicans took over, Congress passed the **Judiciary Act of 1801**. The act reduced the number of justices on the Supreme Court from six to five, which would deny Jefferson the chance to appoint a new justice when the next justice died or resigned. This power is important because the position of a Supreme Court justice is a lifetime appointment. The act also allowed Adams to appoint many new, Federalist lower-court judges before he stepped down. Adams worked late into the night of his last day signing commissions for these judges, who became known as "midnight judges."

Adams also chose a new Chief Justice of the United States, **John Marshall**—a Federalist. One of Marshall's earliest and most important cases was *Marbury* v. *Madison*. The case pitted one of Adams's midnight judges, William Marbury, against Jefferson's secretary of state, James Madison.

MARBURY V. MADISON

The case arose because Adams had signed Marbury's commission but left office before it was delivered. Adams believed that his signature alone made the commission valid. Jefferson disagreed and ordered Madison to block the commission. Marbury sued, saying that the Judiciary Act of 1789 required the Supreme Court to force Madison to give him his commission.

It seemed like a straightforward case. The Court had to decide three questions. First, was Marbury entitled to have the commission delivered to him? The Court said yes. Second, was it within the law to have the courts issue a writ, or legal document, commanding Madison to deliver the commission? Again, the Court agreed. Third, was it legal for the Supreme Court to issue this writ? Here, the Court surprised everyone. Marshall answered with a resounding "No!" and decided against Marbury.

Even though the Judiciary Act of 1789 stated that the Supreme Court could issue such writs, Marshall argued that the U.S. Constitution did not give such power to the Court. The Court declared that part of the act to be **unconstitutional**, or against the Constitution. No law had ever been declared unconstitutional before. With his ruling, Marshall established **judicial review**, the power to invalidate any law the Court deems unconstitutional. *Marbury* v. *Madison* established the judiciary's role in the protection of the freedoms and individual rights detailed in the Bill of Rights. The case also strengthened the balance among the three branches of government, promoting the principle of checks and balances. Jefferson, however, would soon test the limits of the power of the branches and the Constitution.

HISTORICAL THINKING

1. **READING CHECK** How was Marbury appointed as a judge?

2. **ANALYZE CAUSE AND EFFECT** What unintended consequence did John Adams's plan to appoint midnight judges bring about?

3. **EVALUATE** What was surprising about Marshall's decision that the Supreme Court did not have the power to issue Marbury's writ?

AMERICAN PLACES

The Supreme Court, Washington, D.C.

Surprisingly, the Supreme Court was not provided with its own building until 1935. Until that time, members of the Court met in several places, including the Capitol Building. Finally, Chief Justice William Howard Taft—who had also served as president—persuaded Congress to construct a permanent home for the Court. When work got underway, the architect built it in the style of an ancient Roman temple, similar to the style of nearby congressional buildings. The result was as Taft wished: "a building of dignity and importance suitable for use as the home of the Supreme Court of the United States."

2.1 The Louisiana Purchase

We all know our nation spans the continent from "sea to shining sea," but in the early 1800s, the western border of the United States was the Mississippi River. Thomas Jefferson took steps to change that.

MAIN IDEA Thomas Jefferson negotiated a deal with France to purchase the Louisiana Territory and doubled the size of the United States.

PORT OF NEW ORLEANS

While the Supreme Court dealt with the midnight judges, Jefferson set his sights on expansion. The population in the region between the Appalachian Mountains and the Mississippi River had grown steadily. Now farmers were settling the area and shipping their crops down the tributaries of the Mississippi to New Orleans. From there, ships carried cargo to ports all over the world. Jefferson wanted to acquire New Orleans. Only France stood in his way.

In 1799, **Napoleon Bonaparte** overthrew the revolutionary government in France and took power. In 1800, he signed a secret treaty requiring Spain to return Louisiana to France. The Spanish government had decided that, with only 50,000 settlers in all of Louisiana, the area was too expensive to maintain and produced too little profit. But Jefferson feared that once France owned Louisiana, it would interfere with American shipping in New Orleans. Fortunately for Jefferson, France now felt as burdened with Louisiana as Spain had and was very willing to sell the territory to another nation. Soon, peaceful negotiations began between Napoleon and the United States.

NAPOLEON'S OFFER

Jefferson began by sending James Monroe to France in 1803 to help negotiate the purchase of territory at the mouth of the Mississippi, including

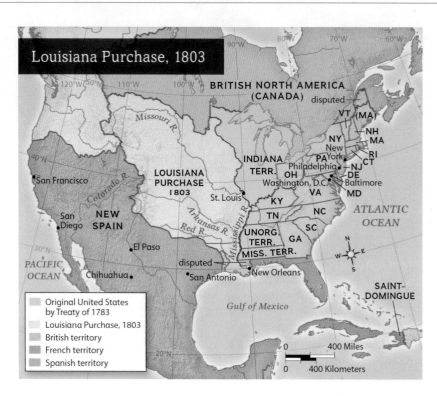

Louisiana Purchase, 1803

Original United States by Treaty of 1783
Louisiana Purchase, 1803
British territory
French territory
Spanish territory

New Orleans. However, negotiations began to stall on the French side. Napoleon was having trouble in another part of the Americas—the Caribbean colony of Saint-Domingue, now known as Haiti, on the island of Hispaniola. In 1791, **Toussaint L'Ouverture** (TOO-sahnt LOH-ver-toor) had led a successful revolution to free slaves in the French colony. L'Ouverture governed the island until 1802, when Napoleon decided he wanted the colony back. But his actions resulted in an all-out war.

Napoleon had had enough of the Americas. His forces had been reduced by **yellow fever**, an often-fatal disease carried by mosquitoes in tropical climates, and he surrendered to Haitian independence. Without Saint-Domingue, Napoleon felt that Louisiana had little value. As a result, the

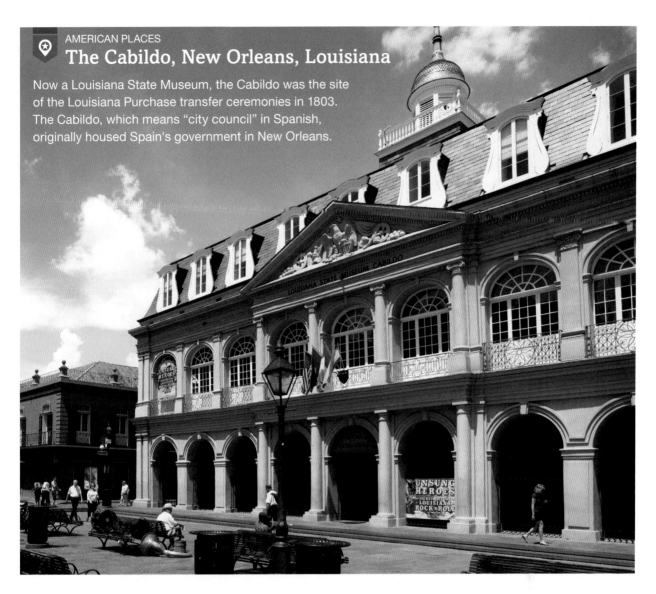

AMERICAN PLACES
The Cabildo, New Orleans, Louisiana

Now a Louisiana State Museum, the Cabildo was the site of the Louisiana Purchase transfer ceremonies in 1803. The Cabildo, which means "city council" in Spanish, originally housed Spain's government in New Orleans.

French leader decided to give up all his territory in continental North America. Instead of selling only New Orleans to the United States, Napoleon suggested selling the entire Louisiana Territory—all 828,000 square miles of it—for $15 million. In October 1803, the U.S. Senate ratified the treaty that established the **Louisiana Purchase**. France officially transferred the land to the United States, doubling the size of the nation.

Jefferson had some misgivings about the deal. He debated the constitutionality of the purchase, saying, "The General Government has no powers but such as the Constitution gives it. . . . It has not given it power of holding foreign territory, and still less of incorporating it into the Union. An amendment of the Constitution seems necessary for this." But Jefferson ended up putting his concerns aside. The land, he believed, would provide space for generations of American farmers and allow people in the region to trade freely on the Mississippi. Soon after the treaty with France was finalized, Jefferson funded an expedition to take a good look at the land and natural resources the country had bought. He could hardly wait to hear what the explorers learned about the plants, animals, and people in the region.

HISTORICAL THINKING

1. **READING CHECK** Why did Jefferson want to purchase Louisiana from France?

2. **ANALYZE CAUSE AND EFFECT** What happened as a result of war in Saint-Domingue?

3. **INTERPRET MAPS** What major river did the United States acquire the rights to in the Louisiana Purchase?

2.2 The Discoveries of Lewis and Clark

MAIN IDEA Lewis and Clark's expedition cleared up some of the geographic unknowns of the new, expansive lands that President Jefferson bought from France.

A SCIENTIFIC EXPEDITION

As you have read, Meriwether Lewis and William Clark's Corps of Discovery traveled almost 8,000 miles from St. Louis, Missouri, to the Pacific Ocean, then back to St. Louis. Few accurate maps of the West existed at that time, and there were many geographic unknowns about the region. Lewis and Clark's recorded observations changed Americans' understanding of the physical landscapes of the West.

Their journey also resulted in the discovery of plants and animals never seen before by European-Americans. Lewis and Clark recorded more than 120 new animal species, including mule deer and coyote. They described 178 new species of plants, like the big leaf maple, the Oregon crabapple, and the ponderosa pine.

Follow the journey of Lewis and Clark on the map below. Then read about three geographic unknowns in the West and the new geographic knowledge the explorers gained through their travels and observations.

Lewis and Clark's Expedition Route, 1804–1806

GEOGRAPHIC UNKNOWN	GEOGRAPHIC KNOWLEDGE

THE MISSOURI RIVER AND THE MARIAS RIVER

In June 1805, Lewis and Clark were sailing up the Missouri River in present-day Montana when they came to another river. One river flowed from the north, and the other flowed from the south. Which one was the main stem of the Missouri River? Which one should they continue to follow?

Most members of Lewis and Clark's expedition wanted to follow the river that flowed from the north. Lewis and Clark were not so sure. They split up, with Clark scouting the river to the south and Lewis scouting the river to the north. They returned from their quick explorations and agreed—the south branch was the Missouri River and the one they should continue to follow upstream. Lewis named the river to the north the Marias River, after his cousin Maria.

THE NORTHWEST PASSAGE

Jefferson had hoped Lewis and Clark would find a Northwest Passage, a water route that would connect the Missouri River to the Pacific Ocean and the riches of Asia. The country that found such a route first would control it. When the explorers arrived at the origin of the Missouri River in August 1805, they expected to have a short portage to the Columbia River, which would carry them to the Pacific.

Lewis reached Lemhi Pass, a two-mile span bridging the gap between the ranges of the Rockies near the border of present-day Montana and Idaho. There, Lewis discovered "immence ranges of high mountains still to the West of us with their tops partially covered with snow." There would not be a short portage to the Columbia River. Instead, the expedition had to cross the rugged Bitterroot Mountains, which took them until October. The hopes for a Northwest Passage had died.

BISON

When Lewis and Clark embarked on their expedition, they knew about bison. However, they had no idea how large the herds were or how vital these animals were to the Native Americans of the Great Plains. They also didn't know where the bison roamed.

As Lewis and Clark traveled west, they found enormous herds of bison and, like the Native Americans, they came to depend on the bison for the animals' nutritious meat. The explorers found no bison west of the Rocky Mountains, but when they took different routes east through the Rockies, the bison reappeared.

THINK LIKE A GEOGRAPHER

1. **IDENTIFY MAIN IDEAS AND DETAILS** How did Lewis and Clark determine that the Northwest Passage did not exist?

2. **ANALYZE ENVIRONMENTAL CONCEPTS** How might settlement in the lands obtained through the Louisiana Purchase affect the biological diversity of the plants and animals Lewis and Clark discovered?

3. **DRAW CONCLUSIONS** How did Lewis and Clark's perceptions of the West change as a result of their expedition?

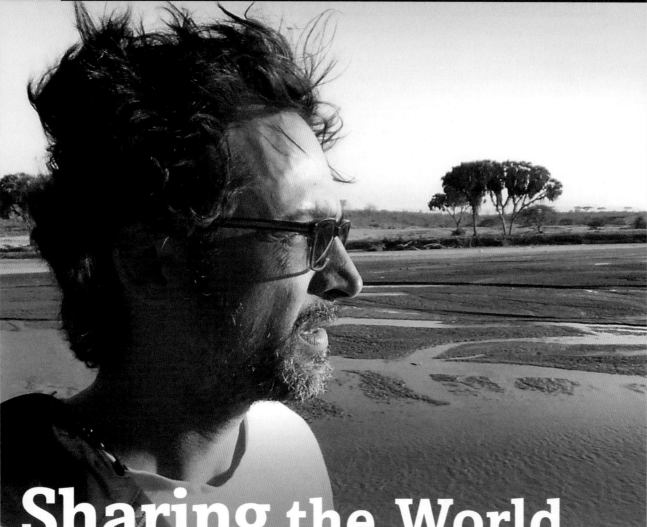

Sharing the World

"Try to say yes when you travel. You'll open yourself up to so many new experiences." —Robert Reid

You might say **Robert Reid** has a pretty great job. As National Geographic's Digital Nomad, he investigates the whys and hows of how we experience the world, sharing his adventures with a global audience via social media, blog posts, and the occasional informal travel video.

Reid has traveled from coast to coast in the United States and extensively abroad, from Vietnam to England to Australia. He's been to Canadian Mountie boot camp, counted mustaches in Siberia, and poked around Atlantic City, New Jersey. He's even parachuted from a World War II-era plane in the middle of Russia. He gets around. Reid uses his own hobbies and interests to build trip itineraries, research articles, and provide a framework for the video storytelling he is famous for. (Look him up!)

^
The East African country of Kenya is only one of the amazing destinations Robert Reid has visited during his career as a travel writer.

MAIN IDEA Digital Nomad Robert Reid explains how travel enriches our lives.

ROAD TRIPPING

In spite of his extensive international travel experience, Reid admits if he could only visit one country for the rest of his life, it would be the United States. "It's so diverse," he explains, highlighting some of his favorite American places. "I love the Great Plains. Mountains are great, but they get in the way of a good view." He's also fond of New York City because of its cultural icons and famous places. Oregon, Reid's home state, is another favorite location. "Oregon is the most underrated state in the country. It has everything. Coastlines. Waterfalls. You name it. It's also where Lewis and Clark ended their great American road trip."

Reid identifies with Lewis and Clark in many ways. "I think the ultimate road trip of all time belongs to those guys," he says. "Their journey was just so American. Americans take road trips to understand their country, and that's what Lewis and Clark were doing." Reid points out the ability of the explorers to travel 8,000 miles—and survive—more than 200 years ago is downright incredible, but explainable. "They didn't overpack. We know that, because they left us lists of exactly what they brought. They knew how important it was to rely on the knowledge of the locals, so they used native guides who knew the language, the terrain, and the culture. And nearly everyone survived the expedition. That's incredible!"

TIPS FROM A TRAVELER

Most importantly to Reid as a travel writer, Lewis and Clark documented their journey. Extensively. So what suggestions does this travel guru have to offer the average tourist today? First, take photographs—lots of them—because they'll help you remember your trip. Secondly, write about who and what you encounter on your journey. Visit a place from different angles and talk to locals who can offer unique perspectives. For example, says Reid, "Go to Wyoming and find a geologist who

When he travels, Robert Reid gets to know the locals—in this case, a Rosie the Riveter reenactor he met in Ronks, Pennsylvania.

is walking every square inch of the state to make maps. That person knows the land better than anyone and knows how to better appreciate things most people miss."

Everywhere he visits, Reid talks to people who live there and tries to see the place from their perspective, not from that of an outsider. "When you travel, do and see the things the locals like to do and see—and make sure you do that with the locals," he advises. Sound advice from someone who knows how to travel.

Check out the Reid on the Road videos online in this history program.

HISTORICAL THINKING

1. **FORM AND SUPPORT OPINIONS** Reid believes it's vital to interact with local residents when you travel. Why does he recommend this? Do you agree? Use evidence in the text to support your answer.

2. **COMPARE AND CONTRAST** What does Robert Reid have in common with Lewis and Clark? How are they different?

This busy port In Seattle demonstrates the strength of
the U.S. economy today, with ships carrying imports and
exports into and out of the harbor. In the early 1800s,
the embargo Jefferson enforced against foreign imports
really only hurt the United States. Once America became
a strong economic power by the 20th century, the
embargoes it placed on other countries, such as Cuba
and Iran, were far more effective.

3.1 Neutrality or War?

When people get into a fight, do you join in or walk away? Thomas Jefferson probably wanted to focus on Lewis and Clark's discoveries in the Louisiana Territory. Unfortunately, the war brewing abroad kept demanding his attention.

MAIN IDEA Jefferson's plan to remain neutral during a war between Britain and France backfired.

JEFFERSON'S FOREIGN POLICY

In his 1801 Inaugural Address, Jefferson had explained his foreign policy. The United States, he said, was "separated by nature and a wide ocean from the exterminating havoc [deadly chaos] of one quarter of the globe." The last part referred to Europe. Among his "essential principles of government" were "peace, commerce, and honest friendship with all nations, entangling alliances with none." In other words, he wished the United States to remain neutral. Easier said than done.

After Napoleon gave up on expansion in North America, he turned to Europe and began a war with Britain in 1803. At first, American merchants profited from U.S. neutrality and sold provisions and weapons to both countries. Yet soon the British and French navies tried to block American ships from supplying their enemy. In addition, Britain authorized its navy to capture American ships and force the sailors to serve the British Navy—an act called **impressment**.

CUTTING OFF TRADE

Although many Americans called for war, the United States remained neutral. But trade with Britain and France became more difficult after Napoleon threatened to seize any ship that engaged in trade with Britain. In response, Jefferson urged Congress to pass the Non-Importation Act, which banned British imports. He also closed U.S. ports and waters to British ships. The British answered by continuing impressment, firing on U.S. coastal towns, and entering the Chesapeake Bay.

In response, Congress passed the **Embargo Act of 1807**. An **embargo** is a law that restricts commerce with one or more nations. The act was supposed to stop all foreign imports from arriving in American harbors, but smugglers still got through. Congress allowed the president to use militia against these illegal traders.

While these steps stopped the smuggling, the embargo had disastrous effects on the U.S. economy. The Treasury's chief source of income— **customs**, or taxes placed on imported and exported goods—dwindled. The embargo particularly affected New England farmers, whose crops were no longer being exported abroad, and New England merchants, who depended on European trade for much of their business. After New Englanders demanded an end to the embargo, Congress passed laws in 1809 that reopened trade with all nations except Britain and France.

Despite the impact of the embargo, Jefferson remained popular. His endorsement of fellow Democratic-Republican James Madison in the 1808 presidential election resulted in a landslide victory against the Federalists. The election proved that Americans still supported the policies of Jefferson's Democratic-Republicans. As it turned out, these policies would soon be tested at home.

HISTORICAL THINKING

1. **READING CHECK** What was Jefferson's foreign policy?

2. **ANALYZE CAUSE AND EFFECT** How did the Embargo Act of 1807 affect Americans?

3. **SUMMARIZE** What foreign actions tested Jefferson's policy of neutrality?

3.2 Native Americans Unite

Thomas Jefferson kept the United States out of war. But in the years shortly after he left office, the threat of war continued to grow. Conflict was in the air, and not only in Europe.

MAIN IDEA Native Americans across North America united to fight against the American government and its increasing expansion into their traditional lands.

TECUMSEH'S IDEA

While the United States was trying to maintain neutrality in the war in Europe, trouble was developing at home. American expansion into the Northwest Territory had increased conflict with Native American nations. Shawnee chief **Tecumseh** (tuh-KUM-suh), in particular, began to speak out against the destruction of native cultures and economies. He also criticized Native American leaders who sold their land to the United States.

A Gift from the British

This ceremonial tomahawk and pipe was a gift to Tecumseh from British colonel Henry Proctor. The two men fought together on the frontier and in Canada, but they fell out over Proctor's reluctance to attack American troops in Ohio. Proctor hoped to win back Tecumseh's respect and friendship by offering him this weapon, which was most likely made in France.

To present a united front against the United States, Tecumseh visited Native American tribes, including the Miami, the Delaware, and the Potawatomi, and spoke to them about forming a confederation, or alliance. In 1809, while Tecumseh traveled the country, the U.S. government negotiated the Treaty of Fort Wayne with several other tribes. According to the terms of the treaty, the Native American leaders who signed the agreement sold 2.9 million acres of their land to the government for a fraction of a penny per acre. This type of "deal" was just what Tecumseh had been trying to prevent. The treaty was the last straw and inspired many more Native American groups to join Tecumseh's cause.

Pipe tomahawk, c. 1810–1812

THE BATTLE OF TIPPECANOE

Meanwhile around 1808, Tecumseh had established **Prophetstown** on the Tippecanoe (tih-pee-kuh-NOO) River in the Indiana Territory. Prophetstown was a community devoted to Native American unity and opposition to U.S. expansion. Tecumseh's brother, Tenskwatawa (tens-qwah-TAH-wah), lived there, and people called him "the Prophet." A **prophet** is someone who is believed to deliver messages that come from God or some other divine source. Tecumseh's brother had become a religious leader in Prophetstown, and many of its inhabitants looked to him to foretell the future. The Prophet promoted a return to traditional ways of life and insisted that Native Americans reject all aspects of European culture.

In 1811, the governor of the Indiana Territory, William Henry Harrison, led about 1,000 men to attack the community and put an end to Tecumseh's confederacy. Tecumseh was away, trying to recruit Native Americans in the South to his cause. Acting against his brother's orders, the Prophet led an attack of his own on Harrison's camp early one morning but was soon forced to retreat. The next day, Harrison's forces found Prophetstown deserted and burned it to the ground. The skirmish came to be known as the **Battle of Tippecanoe**.

The battle infuriated many Americans. Rumors swirled that British forces in Canada had encouraged Tecumseh's confederacy and attacks by Native Americans. Some Americans who favored war, called **War Hawks**, even believed that the British had already formed an alliance with Native Americans against the United States. Many leaders felt, too, that the new nation had to demonstrate its viability, or skill, on the international stage. The War Hawks' anger boiled over in the Capitol, resulting in a call to arms. The shadow of war was falling on the country.

Tecumseh's Eloquence

Tecumseh traveled throughout the United States and Canada, persuading other tribes to join his confederacy. In one speech, he told the Osage that they "belong to one family" and were all "children of the Great Spirit." His goal of confederation, he explained, was "to assist each other to bear our burdens." Tecumseh insisted, "We walk in the same path. . . . We must be united; we must smoke the same pipe; we must fight each others' battles."

HISTORICAL THINKING

1. **READING CHECK** What was Tecumseh's plan, and how did he hope to accomplish it?

2. **ANALYZE CAUSE AND EFFECT** What main factors led Tecumseh to formulate his plan?

3. **EVALUATE** In what ways was Tecumseh's plan a good one, and in what ways was it likely to fail?

3.3 The War of 1812

Americans value their independence. That's what the American Revolution had been about, after all. Turns out, many Americans would be willing to fight for it a second time.

MAIN IDEA The War of 1812 unified the people of the United States and set the stage for expansion and economic prosperity.

A NATION AT ODDS

In June 1812, the War Hawks got their way. Congress declared war against Britain—again. However, despite the widespread belief that the British and Native Americans were working together, Americans had mixed feelings about the **War of 1812**. As you know, the war with Britain was especially unpopular with New England farmers and merchants for economic reasons.

Politicians also wondered how President James Madison planned to pay for the war. The National Bank's charter had expired, leaving only the less stable state banks to provide war loans. Also, you may remember that the United States had ended trade with Britain and France while those two countries were at war. The government had lost a great deal of income from tariffs as a result.

THROUGH THE PERILOUS FIGHT

At first, busy fighting Napoleon, Britain all but ignored the war with the United States. However, Britain had to act when American forces attacked its fort near Detroit, Michigan. The British repelled the attack and even forced the U.S. militia to surrender Detroit. Things were beginning badly for the Americans.

In September 1813, American troops won their first victory when **Oliver Hazard Perry** and his fleet of ships defeated British troops on Lake Erie.

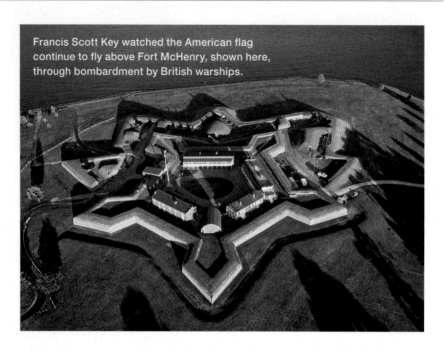

Francis Scott Key watched the American flag continue to fly above Fort McHenry, shown here, through bombardment by British warships.

Soon after, William Henry Harrison's forces retook Detroit and defeated British forces at the Battle of the Thames (tehmz). Shawnee chief Tecumseh died on that battlefield fighting for the British.

By the summer of 1814, Britain's war against Napoleon in Europe was drawing to a close, so the country sent more troops to North America. British forces captured Washington, D.C., and burned down the Capitol and White House. Less than a month later, the British also attacked **Fort McHenry** and Baltimore, Maryland, but failed to take the city. The American flag flying amid the battle's flaming rockets and bombs inspired **Francis Scott Key** to memorialize the scene in his poem "The Star-Spangled Banner." The poem was later set to music and became the national anthem of the United States. (You can read more about Key's famous lyrics and our flag earlier in this text in the American Story, "Our American Identity.")

This painting by Tom Freeman, called *Burning of the White House, 1814*, shows the structure in flames after British soldiers torched it during the War of 1812. Before their arrival, Madison's wife, Dolley, had a full-length portrait of George Washington removed and taken from the building for safekeeping.

CRITICAL VIEWING What emotions is the painting probably meant to inspire?

By the end of 1814, neither Britain nor the United States saw much hope for victory. Delegates from both countries met in Ghent, a city in present-day Belgium, where they signed the Treaty of Ghent and formally ended the war. News of the treaty did not come soon enough to stop one last British naval and ground attack on New Orleans, however. **Andrew Jackson**, a military leader from Tennessee, and his troops countered the attack and killed, captured, or wounded more than 2,000 British soldiers. Jackson lost only 13 soldiers.

The terms of the treaty restored things to the way they were before the war. All territory captured during the war was returned to its original owner, and all prisoners of war were freed.

Although the treaty did not declare a winner, many Americans felt they'd scored a diplomatic victory. The war confirmed U.S. sovereignty and boosted Americans' self-confidence and patriotism. It also encouraged yet more expansion and a new economic prosperity.

HISTORICAL THINKING

1. **READING CHECK** Why were Americans divided over fighting the War of 1812?

2. **ANALYZE CAUSE AND EFFECT** What happened because news of the Treaty of Ghent didn't arrive immediately?

3. **FORM AND SUPPORT OPINIONS** Do you think Americans were justified in their belief that they had won the war? Explain why or why not.

REVIEW

VOCABULARY

Use each of the following vocabulary words in a sentence that shows an understanding of the term's meaning.

1. judicial review
   After judicial review, the Supreme Court decided that the new law was invalid.

2. Louisiana Purchase

3. incumbent

4. unconstitutional

5. impressment

6. customs

7. embargo

READING STRATEGY
ANALYZE CAUSE AND EFFECT

If you haven't already done so, complete your chart to analyze causes that led President Madison to declare war on Britain in 1812. List at least four causes. Then answer the question.

Causes	Effect
	The United States declares war on Britain in 1812.

8. How did Britain's war with France influence the outbreak of the War of 1812?

MAIN IDEAS

Answer the following questions. Support your answers with evidence from the chapter.

9. How was the 1800 election decided? **LESSON 1.1**

10. What were the effects of the Judiciary Act of 1801? **LESSON 1.3**

11. Why did William Marbury think *Marbury* v. *Madison* was a good case? **LESSON 1.3**

12. In what way did the Louisiana Purchase contradict Jefferson's philosophy of government? **LESSON 2.1**

13. What were some difficulties the United States encountered while remaining neutral during the war between Britain and France? **LESSON 3.1**

14. What geographic factor made Tecumseh's plan for union difficult? **LESSON 3.2**

15. What role did the War Hawks play in the War of 1812? **LESSON 3.2**

16. How would you summarize Britain's military situation during the War of 1812? **LESSON 3.3**

17. How was the Treaty of Ghent different from traditional treaties? **LESSON 3.3**

HISTORICAL THINKING

Answer the following questions. Support your answers with evidence from the chapter.

18. **COMPARE AND CONTRAST** How were Jefferson's beliefs similar to and different from those of the Federalists?

19. **ANALYZE CAUSE AND EFFECT** What was the most important lasting effect of the Judiciary Act of 1801?

20. **FORM AND SUPPORT OPINIONS** Do you think the Louisiana Purchase was constitutional? Explain why or why not.

21. **EVALUATE** What were the purpose, challenges, and economic incentives of the Lewis and Clark expedition?

22. **SYNTHESIZE** Why did the War of 1812 increase American patriotism?

23. **IDENTIFY** What experiences contributed to Napolean's loss of interest in the Americas?

INTERPRET MAPS

Look closely at the map below. Then answer the questions that follow.

Western Exploration, 1803–1807

24. Based on the boundaries of the Louisiana Territory, which European nations might have come into conflict with the United States over territorial boundaries?

25. What two explorations does the map show, and which of these went into territory owned by another nation?

ANALYZE SOURCES

In an 1811 letter to Secretary of War William Eustis, William Henry Harrison, governor of the Indiana Territory, described Tecumseh's work in building a confederation to keep U.S. settlers and soldiers off Native American lands. Read the excerpt and answer the questions.

> The implicit [absolute] obedience and respect which the followers of Tecumseh pay to him, is really astonishing, and . . . bespeaks him [suggests that he is] one of those uncommon geniuses which spring up occasionally to produce revolutions. . . . If it were not for the vicinity of the United States, he would, perhaps, be the founder of an empire that would rival in glory that of Mexico or Peru. . . . I hope, however, . . . that that part of the fabric [unity among the tribes] which he considered complete, will be demolished, and even its foundations rooted up.

26. According to Harrison, how do other Native Americans regard Tecumseh?

27. What seems to be Harrison's opinion of Tecumseh?

CONNECT TO YOUR LIFE

28. **NARRATIVE** Choose an important U.S. figure from 1800 to 1816, such as Thomas Jefferson or John Marshall. Make a connection between that historical figure and a well-known person today. Write a paragraph in which you imagine what would happen if the two met.

TIPS

• List the historical figure's qualities and accomplishments. Then make a similar list for the present-day person you have chosen.

• Use textual evidence and vocabulary words from the chapter in your narrative.

• Include dialogue to convey the figures' personalities and philosophies.

• Conclude with a description of the connection that ties the two figures together.

CHAPTER 10

EXPANSION AND GROWTH

1800–1844

ESSENTIAL QUESTION

How did new industries and inventions transform the United States economically, socially, and geographically?

 The Mighty Mississippi

SECTION 1 **America's First Industrial Revolution**

KEY VOCABULARY

factory system	market revolution	strike
Industrial Revolution	reaper	telegraph
interchangeable parts	steamboat	textile

SECTION 2 **Plantations and Slavery Spread**

KEY VOCABULARY

antebellum	interstate slave trade	spirituals
cotton gin	passive resistance	

SECTION 3 **Nationalism and Sectionalism**

KEY VOCABULARY

abolition	monopoly	sectionalism
American System	Monroe Doctrine	subsidy
implied power	nationalism	unorganized territory
Missouri Compromise	republican motherhood	

 The American Railroads

READING STRATEGY

DRAW CONCLUSIONS

When you draw conclusions, you support them with evidence from the text. As you read the chapter, use a graphic organizer like this one to draw conclusions about the expansion and growth of the United States during the 1800s.

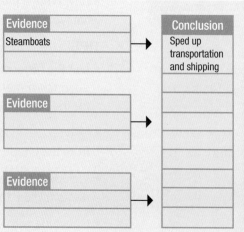

Evidence | Steamboats → Conclusion | Sped up transportation and shipping

Evidence →

Evidence →

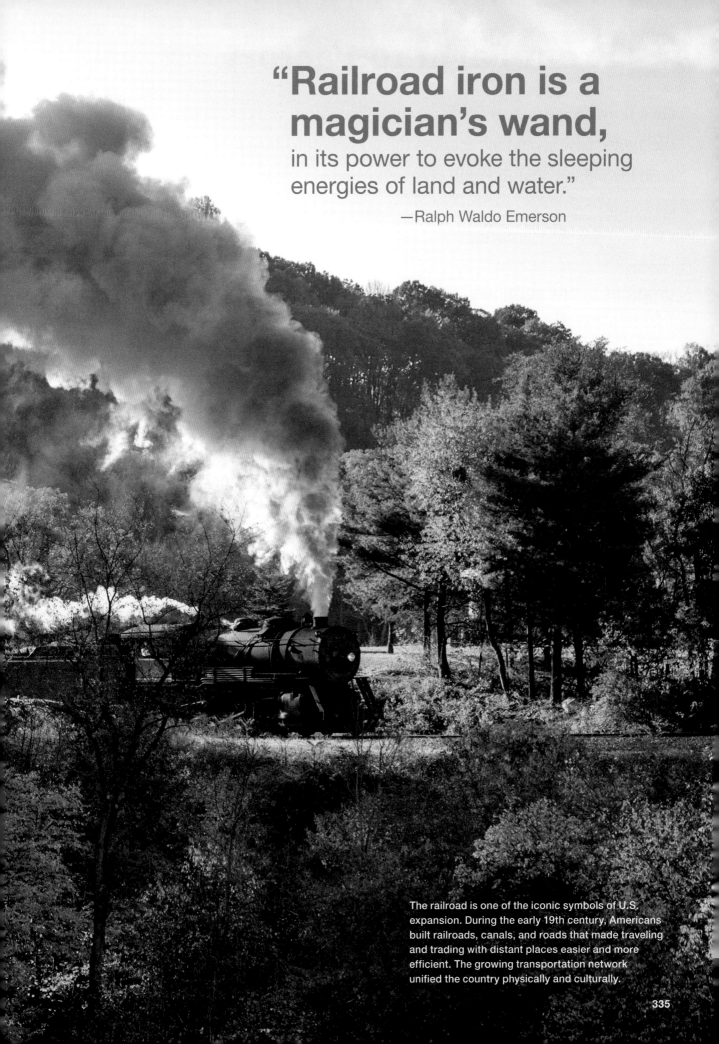

"Railroad iron is a magician's wand, in its power to evoke the sleeping energies of land and water."

—Ralph Waldo Emerson

The railroad is one of the iconic symbols of U.S. expansion. During the early 19th century, Americans built railroads, canals, and roads that made traveling and trading with distant places easier and more efficient. The growing transportation network unified the country physically and culturally.

1.1 From Farm to Factory

On a farm or in a factory—where would you rather work? In the first half of the 1800s, new inventions sparked the growth of factories. Many people left farm life behind, and this shift changed American culture in many ways.

| **MAIN IDEA** Industrialization in the early 19th century transformed the ways in which Americans lived and worked.

CHANGES IN THE ECONOMY

In the early 1800s, different regions of the United States became more interdependent and connected. One factor that made this possible was the **market revolution**, or the transition from a pre-industrial economy to a market-oriented, capitalist economy. In part, this economic transition was prompted by the **Industrial Revolution**, or the widespread production by machinery, that had been underway in Europe since the mid-1700s.

The beginning of the Industrial Revolution in the United States is often dated to 1793, when **Samuel Slater** opened his first cloth factory in Rhode Island. Industrialization in the Northeast transformed social structures and had important consequences for the nation's economy and international position.

Newly introduced machines produced goods more rapidly and efficiently than people could make by hand, one at a time. A **factory system**, or a method of production in which large crews of people perform work in one location, developed. Mechanized production in factories and mills replaced skilled craftspeople. Factory managers recruited men and women from rural areas, many of whom embraced the idea of factory work.

New locations and types of work profoundly affected how people lived and worked. They also transformed the family economy. Furthermore, instead of working together on farms or in shops, men and women began to work in separate spheres. This shift was especially true for the emerging middle class.

THE MILL GIRLS

The United States entered the Industrial Revolution through the **textile** industry, which produced cloth and clothing from cotton and other raw materials. Initially, individual workers wove thread into large pieces of cloth on hand-operated looms. In 1785, an Englishman named Edmund Cartwright introduced the first power loom. Power looms required multiple workers, but by 1813, improvements had eliminated the general need for all but one person. This single-operator model became the basis for a faster, more efficient power loom developed by **Francis Cabot Lowell** at his textile mill in Massachusetts.

A mill town named in Lowell's honor was founded in 1823. Mill owners hired young girls and women because they would work for less pay than men. These female textile workers, some as young as 10 years old, were called the "Lowell girls." The Lowell girls lived in boarding houses and worked in the mills instead of attending school. Their letters home revealed that many enjoyed the independence factory work provided. These young women also published a monthly magazine of poetry and fiction, called the *Lowell Offering*.

Eventually, the Lowell workers' low wages and long hours in dangerous conditions soon became intolerable, so the young women banded together to protest. In the 1830s, the Lowell workers organized several **strikes**, or work stoppages, to protest cuts in wages. Their activism led to the formation of the Lowell Female Labor Reform Association, the first organization of working women in the United States.

A 19th-Century Textile Mill

Textile mills in the 19th century relied on water to power the different machines needed to transform raw materials into textiles. Machines inside the mill performed a variety of tasks, including preparing the cotton and fibers for spinning, spinning fibers into threads, and weaving threads into cloth.

Power Looms
Noisy and fast-moving power looms weave yarn into cloth.

Spinning
Powerful spinning machines combine thread from 10 to 15 different bobbins into strong yarn.

Carding and Drawing
Fine metal teeth in carding machines brush the fibers so they face the same direction. The resulting loosely formed rope is then fed into a drawing frame to combine the fibers into a single strand.

Water Wheel
Moving water turns a geared wheel that drives a series of belts and gears to power the machines inside the mill.

Raw Materials
Bales of cotton arrive at the mill via horse-drawn wagon.

HISTORICAL THINKING

1. **READING CHECK** How did work change in the early 19th century?

2. **INTERPRET VISUALS** Based on the illustration and captions, describe how raw materials were transformed into cloth at textile mills.

3. **DETERMINE CHRONOLOGY** In what ways did the establishment of mill towns in the northeastern United States rely on earlier economic and technological developments?

1.2 Innovations and Inventions

In your lifetime, new ideas and technology have transformed communication in dramatic ways. During the early 1800s, new technologies started speeding up transportation and communication.

> **MAIN IDEA** New inventions made American workers more productive, created new industries, and contributed to the nation's economic growth.

NEW MANUFACTURING METHODS

As industries began to flourish in the United States, innovative thinkers were making manufacturing more efficient and profitable. Eli Whitney, John Deere, Robert Fulton, and Samuel Morse were just a few of the many Americans who introduced new technologies in the early 19th century.

Eli Whitney, one of the most influential of these inventors, was born in 1765 in Massachusetts. From an early age, he showed a natural talent for mechanics and was able to skillfully improve useful items. In 1797, war between the United States and France seemed likely, and the nation's military needed more weapons. Whitney came up with an ambitious plan to supply the federal government

with 10,000 rifles in just two years' time. The challenge was this: Every weapon already in use was unique. Any repair required making a new custom part for that specific gun. So Whitney made his rifles using **interchangeable parts**. Each of his guns had the exact same parts.

Whitney completed the government's order in eight years, but his method of using interchangeable parts set the machine age in motion. The use of interchangeable parts soon spread to the production of nearly all goods. Having all parts ready to use meant that goods could be produced quickly and at a lower cost. This efficiency helped shape the identity of the United States as a nation of problem-solving, ingenuity, and progress.

🏛 John Deere Historic Site, Grand Detour, Illinois

As Americans moved west, they developed new technologies to tackle the challenges they faced. Blacksmith John Deere found the soil of the American prairie to be harder to work with than eastern soil. Farmers typically used cast-iron plows to turn up soil before planting seeds, but their regular plows weren't enough. The dirt just clumped and stuck to the plow.

To solve this problem, Deere developed a plow made of hard, polished steel. The shape and material of his plow kept the soil from clumping, and he began selling his successful invention in 1838. Deere solved an agricultural problem by examining the design and function of a common tool, and paved the way for more improvements in farming technology. Today, Deere & Company manufactures plows and combines, which perform all the tasks associated with crop harvesting in one step.

John Deere's steel plow

CRITICAL VIEWING Today's combine harvesters definitely look different from Deere's original plow. These machines accomplish all the harvesting tasks: they thresh, separate, clean, and collect the grain. What effect do you think these machines have on farm life and food production?

STEAMBOATS AND TELEGRAPHS

New technologies also changed shipping, communication, and agriculture. Robert Fulton's **steamboats**, or boats outfitted with steam boiler engines to power their paddle wheels, revolutionized river travel and made shipping quicker. By 1811, Fulton had designed a steamboat powerful and sturdy enough for the strong currents of the Mississippi River. Soon, an upstream journey on the Mississippi and Ohio rivers from New Orleans to Louisville, Kentucky, was shortened from several months to just 14 days. But even the swiftest ship could not carry a message across miles in a matter of minutes.

Samuel F. B. Morse's **telegraph** sent messages over electrical wires using a series of long and short pulses known as Morse code. An operator in one location tapped out a message on a device called a key. The message moved through wires to a machine that printed it out as dots and dashes punched onto a strip of paper. Another operator then transcribed the code into words. The first telegraph message was transmitted on May 24, 1844. Soon, telegraph wires stretched throughout the nation, and operators could interpret the code in real time. Widespread use of the telegraph for personal, business, and government communication continued for more than 100 years.

Innovations changed life on the farm as well. Cyrus Hall McCormick's horse-drawn mechanical **reaper** quickly cut, or reaped, stalks of wheat from the field and gathered them up for processing. Farmers who used this new machine no longer had to harvest wheat by hand. The reaper helped increase wheat production throughout the Great Plains. It changed not only American farming but also many of the world's farming methods. McCormick's reaper was so successful that he opened a factory in Chicago to produce his machines, advancing both rural farming technology and urban manufacturing techniques.

HISTORICAL THINKING

1. **READING CHECK** What was significant about manufacturing with interchangeable parts?

2. **DRAW CONCLUSIONS** How did McCormick's mechanical reaper contribute to agricultural and urban growth?

3. **MAKE CONNECTIONS** McCormick's reaper connected both rural and urban innovation. How might another invention described in the text connect the country and the city?

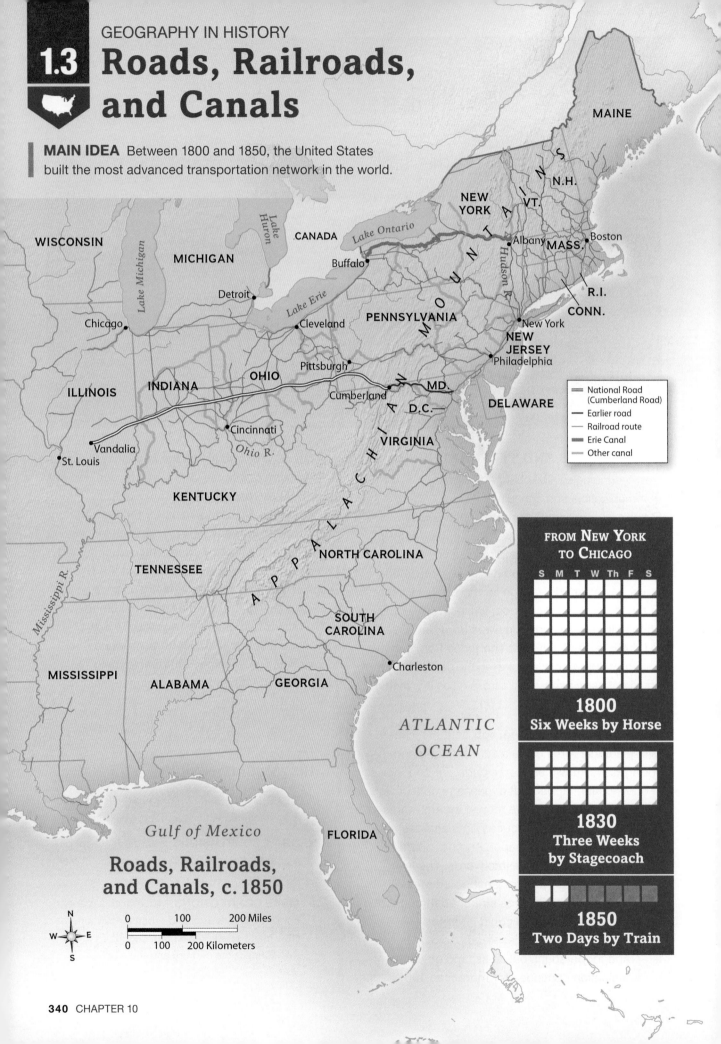

1.3 Roads, Railroads, and Canals

MAIN IDEA Between 1800 and 1850, the United States built the most advanced transportation network in the world.

MAINE

WISCONSIN

Lake Huron

MICHIGAN

CANADA

Lake Ontario

N.H.

NEW YORK

VT.

Albany

MASS.

Boston

Buffalo

Detroit

Lake Erie

Chicago

Cleveland

PENNSYLVANIA

Hudson R.

New York

R.I.

CONN.

NEW JERSEY

Philadelphia

ILLINOIS

INDIANA

OHIO

Pittsburgh

Cumberland

MD.

DELAWARE

D.C.

Cincinnati

Vandalia

Ohio R.

VIRGINIA

St. Louis

KENTUCKY

APPALACHIAN MOUNTAINS

Mississippi R.

TENNESSEE

NORTH CAROLINA

SOUTH CAROLINA

MISSISSIPPI

ALABAMA

GEORGIA

Charleston

ATLANTIC OCEAN

Legend
- National Road (Cumberland Road)
- Earlier road
- Railroad route
- Erie Canal
- Other canal

Gulf of Mexico

FLORIDA

Roads, Railroads, and Canals, c. 1850

N
W E
S

0   100   200 Miles
0   100   200 Kilometers

FROM NEW YORK TO CHICAGO

S M T W Th F S

1800
Six Weeks by Horse

1830
Three Weeks by Stagecoach

1850
Two Days by Train

OVERCOMING OBSTACLES

In the early 1800s, Americans moving west and south soon realized they needed more efficient ways to move people and goods across the country. But they faced several geographic challenges. One of these was distance. Today, you can fly from New York City to Miami, Florida, in a few hours. However, in 1800, that trip took three uncomfortable weeks by horse-drawn stagecoach. Travelers called stagecoaches "shake guts" because they shook so much as they rumbled over roads filled with holes and tree stumps.

The Appalachian Mountains represented another geographic challenge. This mountain range stretches north to south for more than 1,500 miles from Canada to Alabama and is up to 300 miles wide. Often steep and densely wooded, the Appalachians formed a physical barrier between the interior regions of the United States and thriving eastern ports such as New York City, Boston, Charleston, and Philadelphia. Americans innovated new solutions and overcame geographic challenges to build an enormous transportation network that produced major economic benefits.

TRANSPORTATION INNOVATION	ECONOMIC BENEFITS
THE NATIONAL ROAD	
During the early years of the United States, the roads were terrible. But in 1811, the federal government built the National Road, also known as the Cumberland Road. The road stretched west from Cumberland, Maryland, to Vandalia, Illinois. A good stretch of it had pavement, making for a much smoother ride. The states charged travelers tolls for their carriages and wagons—and even for their cattle!	The National Road moved mail, goods, and settlers between the East and the growing states of the Northwest Territory, including Ohio, Indiana, and Illinois. The federal government, states, and private companies soon built more roads connecting the East, the South, and the West. Trade expanded between the nation's interior and its bustling port cities, from Boston south to Charleston.
THE B&O RAILROAD	
During the 1820s, merchants in Baltimore, Maryland, struggled to compete with the merchants of New York City, who had the benefit of the Erie Canal to move goods. In 1826, a group of enterprising businessmen founded the Baltimore & Ohio (B&O) Railroad. They needed a steam-operated railroad to connect Baltimore to the growing cities of the interior, such as Cincinnati, Ohio, and St. Louis, Missouri. A steam locomotive called the Tom Thumb ran on the earliest line and proved that steam-powered cars could handle the steep, winding route.	The B&O proved an enormous success. Trains transported coal from the mines of western Virginia and Pennsylvania to the factories and furnaces of the East. The success of the B&O encouraged companies to build other railroads linking states and territories of the East, South, and West. By the 1850s, railroads were carrying all kinds of products. They transported Chesapeake Bay oysters, Florida oranges, and Georgia peaches to the restaurants of New York City. By 1860, the United States had 30,500 miles of track, about as much as the rest of the world.
THE ERIE CANAL	
Americans built a system of constructed waterways called canals that allowed boats and ships to travel inland to move goods. The largest of them, the Erie Canal, connected the Hudson River to the Great Lakes. It cut through 363 miles of land in upstate New York and linked New York City to growing cities such as Buffalo, Cleveland, Detroit, and Chicago.	Building the Erie Canal took eight years. But after it was completed, farmers in Ohio, Illinois, Indiana, and other states in the Midwest could ship their grain much more cheaply and quickly to the East. Before the canal, farmers had to pay $100 per wagon to ship their grain. By using the canal, their cost was only $10 per shipment. Instead of 20 days, the journey took just eight.

THINK LIKE A GEOGRAPHER

1. **IDENTIFY MAIN IDEAS AND DETAILS**
   What were some geographic challenges the young United States faced?

2. **INTERPRET MAPS** Study the map. How did the road, railroad, and canal systems work together as one transportation network?

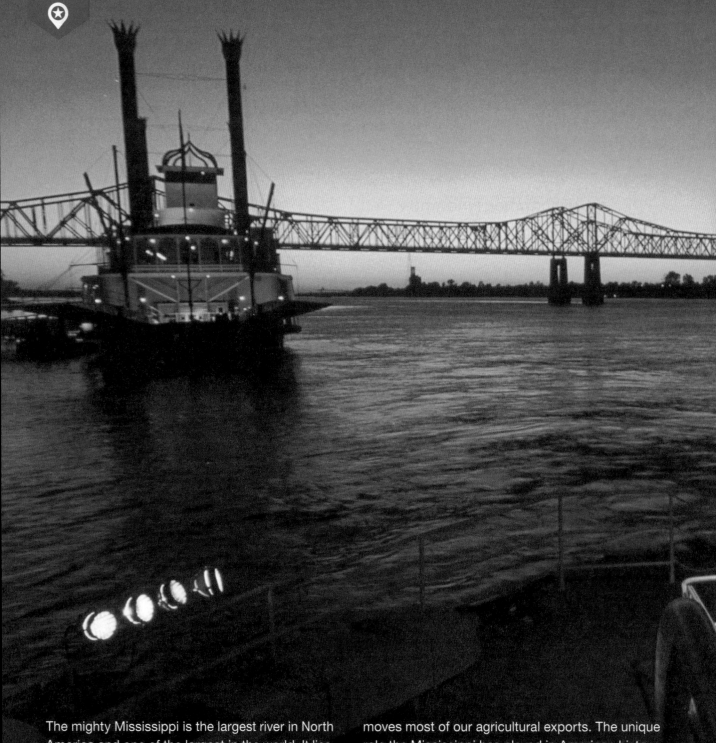

1.4 The Mississippi River

The mighty Mississippi is the largest river in North America and one of the largest in the world. It lies entirely within the United States and flows south from Minnesota, collecting water from the Ohio and Missouri rivers and spilling from Louisiana into the Gulf of Mexico. As one of the world's busiest commercial waterways, the river is the lifeblood of a highly industrialized country. It snakes through some of the nation's most fertile farmland and moves most of our agricultural exports. The unique role the Mississippi has played in American history and literature has woven it deeply into the fabric of the country's folklore. As American author Mark Twain once said, "The Mississippi River will always have its own way; no engineering skill can persuade it to do otherwise." How might a geologic feature like a river serve as a "character" in a book?

2.1 The Henry Ford Museum Dearborn, Michigan

One of the world's wealthiest and most influential innovators, Henry Ford grew up on a farm and never lost his ties to rural life. He became a collector of objects from ordinary people and examples of industrial progress and opened a museum in 1929 to share them with the public. The Henry Ford Museum's mission is to provide unique educational experiences based on authentic objects, stories, and lives that represent America's ingenuity, resourcefulness, and innovation. Its impressive collection of American artifacts includes many items related to the cotton industry. How do the artifacts below reflect the cotton production process?

One bale of cotton can make 1,217 men's T-shirts or 313,600 $100 bills.

Cotton Blossom

Cotton grows on shrubs in 17 states across the southern half of the country. Cotton plants first produce blossoms, which change from white to pink and fall off after a few days. In their place grow small green pods called bolls. Cotton seeds and their attached hairs develop within the bolls, which swell and grow. When the boll is ripe, it bursts into the white, fluffy balls shown here. The seed hair has turned into the fibers used to make cloth and thread.

Once the cotton gin made cotton easier to process, cotton became the primary crop in the American South.

Cotton Gin

Invented by Eli Whitney in 1793, the cotton gin machine revolutionized the process of cleaning seeds out of cotton. Whitney was visiting a friend in the South when he heard about how farmers struggled to efficiently process their cotton crops. He quickly solved their problem with a device that pulled the cotton through a set of wire teeth mounted on a spinning cylinder. The cotton fibers could fit through narrow slots in the machine, but the seeds couldn't.

Spinning Wheel

Spinning fibers into yarn that was then woven into cloth was an important task in many households in the 1600s and 1700s. Young or unmarried women often became experts at this tedious and physically tiring task. This large spinning wheel would have required its spinner to alternate between spinning fibers into yarn and winding the yarn onto the spindle.

Fluffy raw wool or cotton fibers were spun into fine yarn used to make clothing.

"Ford's perspective on history was informed by a strong belief in **the power of learning by doing.**"

—Marc Greuther, Chief Curator, The Henry Ford Museum

Why would advertising thread have been so common during the 1800s?

Cotton Thread Trade Cards

Without cotton, there is no thread, and without thread, there is no clothing! The cotton industry remained strong throughout American history, as demonstrated by these trade cards for "spool cotton" or thread, which date to the late 1800s. Advertisers appealed to customers with colorful ads promoting consumer goods such as thread.

2.2 Growth of the Cotton Industry

Today, economies all over the world are connected to each other in visible and sometimes not-so-visible ways. The same was true for two seemingly very different parts of the United States—the South and the North—in the 19th century.

MAIN IDEA A new invention enabled southern plantation owners to grow more crops and increase profits.

THE COTTON BOOM

The South differed from the North in several ways. For example, the South relied more on an agrarian economy, while the North was rapidly becoming a major industrial center. But one invention brought the two regions closer together.

In 1793, Eli Whitney visited a southern plantation and observed that the system used to remove seeds from picked cotton was slow and labor intensive. To solve this problem, he designed the **cotton gin**, which, as you have read, is a machine fitted with teeth to grab the seeds and separate them from cotton tufts. The cotton gin increased the productivity of enslaved laborers,

and cotton became the main cash crop on many southern farms that had previously grown tobacco. Most southern farmers embraced cotton because years of tobacco cultivation had depleted the soil of the nutrients needed for growing healthy tobacco plants.

Because of more efficient cotton production in the early 19th century, cotton quickly became a central part of the U.S. economy. Both the South and the North relied on this crop. Slave labor produced the cotton and raw materials that enabled northern manufacturers, financiers, and other business interests to thrive. This, in turn, spurred a new consumer culture in individual families connected to the slave-based economy.

CRITICAL VIEWING *Plantation Economy,* by William Aiken Walker, c. 1881, depicts enslaved people working in a southern cotton field. What does the painting convey about the process of cotton production?

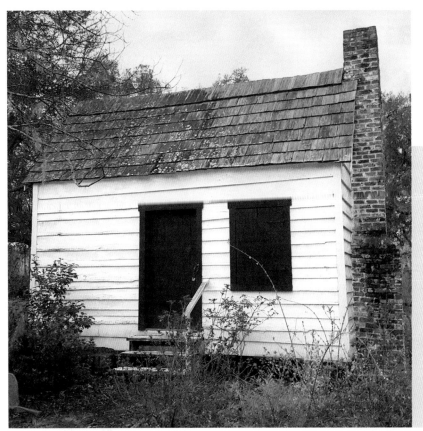

The Slave Dwelling Project

In 2010, Joseph McGill began a series of overnight stays in houses once occupied by slaves. His experiences resulted in the Slave Dwelling Project. Its mission is to preserve the places where enslaved people lived. By 2016, he had visited slave dwellings in 17 states. McGill invites others to visit and sleep in these dwellings. The dwelling featured here is located at Magnolia Plantation in South Carolina.

SLAVERY EXPANDS

Even with the advent of the cotton gin, growing and picking cotton was labor intensive, and the production of cotton relied on the labor system created to support it: slavery. The "peculiar institution" of slavery shaped the South's political, social, economic, and cultural development.

Southern plantation owners who wanted to maximize their profits from cotton production tried to do so by acquiring more land. As you have read, in the early 19th century, the federal government intentionally seized Native American lands. So when some southern landowners and farmers did the same in order to expand their farmlands, they did so with the blessing of the federal government. This land grab forced tribes to leave the Southeast and move to relocation areas in the West. Many Native Americans were permanently displaced from their homes.

Southern plantation owners also tried to maximize profits by increasing their enslaved workforces. In January 1807, Congress passed a new law that would "prohibit the importation of slaves into any port or place within the jurisdiction of the United States...from any foreign kingdom, place, or country." However, the slave importation clause that had been inserted into the Constitution 20 years prior prevented this new law from taking effect until January 1808. Once enacted, the ban caused the **interstate slave trade**, or the slave trade *within* the United States, to increase. Slave owners urged enslaved women to have more children. They then sold some slaves at slave auctions to make a profit and bought others to staff their plantations with specially skilled enslaved workers. Slave auctions separated families. Enslaved communities responded to forced separations by broadening kinship bonds, which meant considering non-blood-related fellow slaves as family members.

HISTORICAL THINKING

1. **READING CHECK** What impact did the cotton gin have on cotton production?

2. **DRAW CONCLUSIONS** How did the interstate slave trade affect enslaved communities?

3. **EVALUATE** In what ways did the institution of slavery shape the economic development of both the South and the North?

2.3 Slavery and Resistance

When one group of people oppresses another, the oppressed group eventually revolts. During the 19th century, enslaved communities and individuals alike rose up.

MAIN IDEA People trapped in the institution of slavery created a culture of survival, resistance, and, ultimately, rebellion.

Shackles

Tax badge

THE SOCIETAL IMPACT OF SLAVERY

The institution of slavery affected all parts of southern society: wealthy or poor, slave or free, white or black. Plantation owners greatly advanced their wealth through slavery. Even though the majority of southern white farmers workers did not own slaves, they supported the practice of slavery. In the **antebellum**, or prewar, South, the poorest whites held higher status than any African Americans.

During the early 19th century, more than 100,000 free African Americans lived in the South, and they most certainly did not support slavery. Though they were free, they could not vote, own property, or receive an education. Legally, their status was constantly in question. Traveling was dangerous because they ran the risk of being accused of being runaway slaves and losing their freedom. In order to prove their free status, free African Americans had to go to court for Certificates of Freedom. Even then, some were kidnapped and sold into slavery.

The greatest impact of slavery, of course, was on enslaved people themselves. Slaves were considered chattel, or property, of their owners and were denied rights, freedom, and sometimes even their lives. Slave owners held a particularly ominous form of power over slaves with the constant possibility of family separation. Just the threat of sale allowed slave owners to exercise enormous control over their slaves. Enslaved parents routinely saw their children sold away from them. Spouses and siblings were separated, and they knew that future contact would be nearly impossible.

🏛 Chicago History Museum, Chicago

The system of slavery relied on preventing escapes. Slave owners placed shackles like these on enslaved people's wrists or ankles. The cuffs were held closed by a screw. In Charleston, South Carolina, enslaved workers who were hired out by their owners had to wear tax badges engraved with tax registration numbers and job categories.

SURVIVAL AND RESISTANCE

Despite the horrific conditions under which they lived, enslaved people resisted the circumstances they faced every day. Many slave owners imposed their own religious beliefs on slaves because they suggested that a belief in Christianity would make slavery an acceptable situation. But enslaved people interpreted scripture for themselves, in ways that encouraged a quest for freedom. They also composed songs called **spirituals** based on scripture and biblical figures such as Moses, who led the Israelites out of slavery in Egypt.

In addition to their own religious practices, enslaved people developed a distinct African-American culture. They retained and adapted traditional customs including music, food, and dancing, as well as varied family structures. They created rich communities bound together by common experiences and shared traditions. In this way, enslaved people asserted their humanity, which could not be taken away by slave owners.

Passive resistance, or the nonviolent refusal to obey authority and laws, was another way enslaved people resisted slavery. Forms of passive resistance included breaking tools, working slowly, pretending to be ill, and learning to read.

Sometimes, though, resistance meant armed rebellion. Inspired by a slave uprising in Haiti, in 1800, a slave named **Gabriel Prosser**, who bore the last name of his cruel owner, Thomas Prosser, planned a revolt in Virginia. In 1822, a freed slave named **Denmark Vesey** used scripture to inspire others to take over arsenals and burn down buildings in Charleston, South Carolina. Most revolts, including these, were put down quickly before whites were killed, and they resulted in the deaths of the enslaved people who had planned the rebellions.

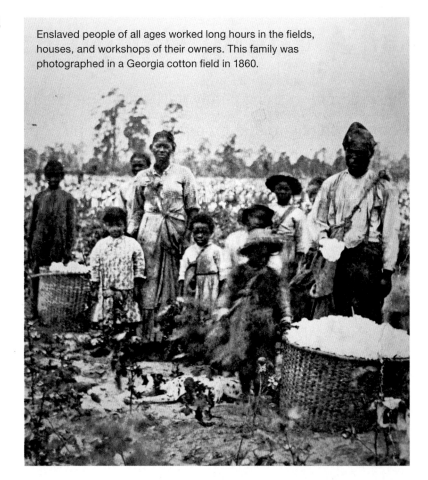

Enslaved people of all ages worked long hours in the fields, houses, and workshops of their owners. This family was photographed in a Georgia cotton field in 1860.

But in 1831, **Nat Turner** led a small group of fellow slaves in a violent rebellion in which more than 50 people were killed in one night. Turner and his men were captured and hanged. Southerners reacted to Turner's rebellion—as they had to others—with violence. Some took matters into their own hands and murdered hundreds of innocent slaves.

Like Gabriel Prosser and Denmark Vesey, Turner was a literate man who led an open, violent revolt against slave-owning whites. Southern authorities reacted to Turner's revolt forcefully and by instituting severe restrictions, including a ban on teaching slaves to read and write.

HISTORICAL THINKING

1. **READING CHECK** In what ways did enslaved people resist slavery?

2. **DRAW CONCLUSIONS** Why did free African Americans need Certificates of Freedom?

3. **MAKE CONNECTIONS** Why was literacy for slaves a threat to slave owners?

3.1 A Young Nation Expands

Being part of a strong family or a successful organization makes members proud to belong to that group. The same kind of pride developed in the early 1800s among Americans witnessing the massive changes in transportation and commerce in the United States.

> **MAIN IDEA** Americans developed a strong national identity during the administrations of presidents James Madison and James Monroe.

TRANSPORTATION AND COMMERCE

The market revolution changed how people worked, traveled, and did business. Eventually, it also encouraged a new philosophy of **nationalism**. Nationalism is the concept of loyalty and devotion to one's nation.

Congressmen **Henry Clay** and **John C. Calhoun** argued for tariffs, or taxes on imported goods, to promote American manufacturing and stimulate commerce. In 1816, Calhoun was instrumental in establishing the Second Bank of the United States. Clay and Calhoun also supported government **subsidies**, or government funds for improvements or support of commerce. Land subsidies, or land granted to private companies by the federal government, became an important part of building roads and railroads. Clay, Calhoun, and others engaged in heated debates with other legislators who favored a more limited federal government role in financing a national infrastructure. Ultimately, tariffs on import goods, the establishment of the National Bank, and government subsidies became known as the **American System**.

Under the American System, improvements in road systems, trains, and waterways united the country geographically and culturally. In 1817, construction began on the **Erie Canal**, which stretched from Buffalo near Lake Erie in western New York to Albany. The Hudson River connected Albany to New York City. When the canal was completed eight years later, farmers could ship their crops within the state and to international destinations through the port at New York City. The canal also encouraged the development of more industrial sites because improved transportation made it easier to move goods to markets.

The **Illinois and Michigan Canal,** completed in 1848, connected Lake Michigan to the Illinois and Mississippi rivers near the city of Chicago. After the construction of these canals, crops and manufactured goods could be shipped all the way from New York City to New Orleans on a water route. The canals also made it easier for people to move their families and belongings west.

NEW BOUNDARIES, NEW DECISIONS

At the same time, the nation was growing in size. General Andrew Jackson became a hero with his successful military campaigns in the War of 1812, including victory in the Battle of New Orleans. His reputation grew when he subdued Native Americans in the Southeast and wrested Florida from Spanish control. Under the terms of the Transcontinental Treaty of 1819, the United States formally received Florida from Spain and gave Spain sovereignty over Texas.

The years that followed the War of 1812 were fairly peaceful and smooth. Territorial conflicts with other nations were temporarily settled, and the economy was growing. The administration of **James Monroe**, who was elected president of the United States in 1816, is remembered as the **Era of Good Feelings**. When Monroe ran for re-election in 1820, the Federalist Party didn't even offer a candidate to oppose him. By 1820, the Federalist Party was no longer a national force.

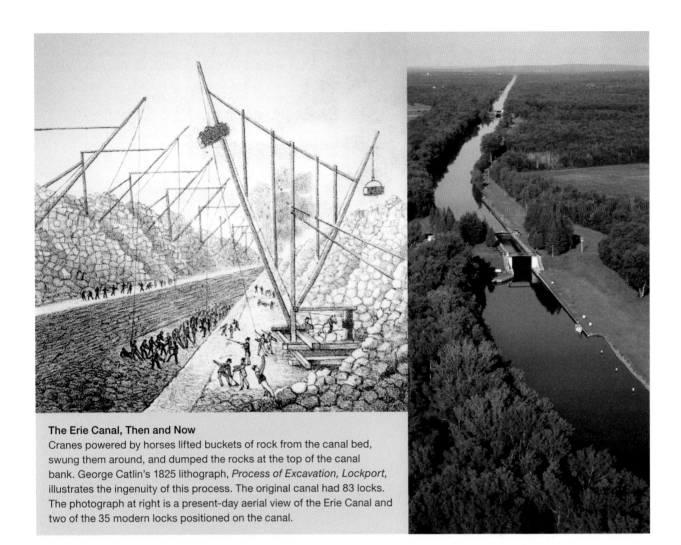

The Erie Canal, Then and Now
Cranes powered by horses lifted buckets of rock from the canal bed, swung them around, and dumped the rocks at the top of the canal bank. George Catlin's 1825 lithograph, *Process of Excavation, Lockport,* illustrates the ingenuity of this process. The original canal had 83 locks. The photograph at right is a present-day aerial view of the Erie Canal and two of the 35 modern locks positioned on the canal.

During this period, important Supreme Court rulings strengthened the federal government's power. In 1819, the Court affirmed the constitutionality of the Second Bank of the United States in the *McCulloch* v. *Maryland* decision. According to the Necessary and Proper Clause in the Constitution, Congress has **implied powers**, or powers not explicitly stated in the Constitution. In short, because a National Bank had previously been established, Congress could establish the Second Bank of the United States. Additionally, the state of Maryland did not have the power to tax that national bank.

In 1824, the case of *Gibbons* v. *Ogden* expanded federal control over interstate commerce, or business affairs between states. Aaron Ogden, who owned steamboats that traveled on the Hudson River, sued Thomas Gibbons for running steamboat operations in the same waters. Gibbons argued that Congress alone had the power to regulate interstate commerce, and that New York had been wrong to grant Ogden the sole right to running his steamboats in the waterway in the first place. The Court ruled in favor of Gibbons to prevent the formation of a **monopoly**, or complete control of an industry by one company. More importantly, the decision solidified the federal government's power to regulate interstate commerce by eliminating the individual states' sole control over it.

HISTORICAL THINKING

1. **READING CHECK** Why did nationalism grow stronger during the administrations of Madison and Monroe?

2. **DRAW CONCLUSIONS** What parts of the American System are still in effect today?

3. **SUMMARIZE** Why is Monroe's presidency remembered as the Era of Good Feelings?

3.2 Increasing Regional Tensions

When people find it impossible to agree, they may need to work out a compromise to resolve the issue. In the early 1800s, Americans wanted to maintain a balance of power between free states and slave states, so they came up with a compromise.

MAIN IDEA As the United States expanded its territory and its power, it negotiated how each new state would deal with the issue of slavery.

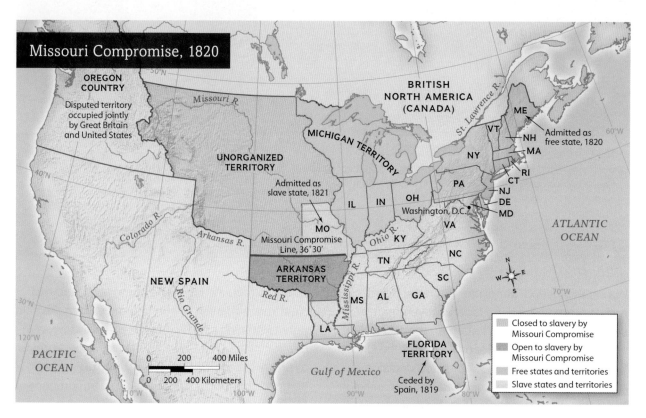

Missouri Compromise, 1820

THE MISSOURI COMPROMISE

Nationalism grew during the years of Madison's and Monroe's presidencies, and so did **sectionalism**. Sectionalism is the identification with and loyalty to a particular part of the country, such as the North or the South. The rise of sectionalism was driven by two main factors: the different economies of these regions and the practice of slavery. For the most part, the North was an industrial region, with mills and wage laborers, while the South was an agricultural region, producing cotton through slave labor.

The federal government wanted to admit the Missouri Territory as the 23rd state. The trick was

how to do so without upsetting the balance of 11 slave states and 11 free states. Americans worried that admitting Missouri would create an imbalance in power between slave and free states. In 1819, the Senate proposed the **Missouri Compromise**. In it, the people of the state of Missouri could own slaves. Missouri would be admitted to the Union at the same time as Maine, a free state, which maintained the balance between the number of slave states and free states. The compromise prohibited slavery in all the lands acquired in the Louisiana Purchase north of the 36° 30' N latitude line. These lands were considered **unorganized territory**, or lands governed by the federal government but not belonging to any state. As a result of the compromise, any states formed from this unorganized territory would be free states. Even so, the compromise stated that enslaved people who escaped to free states could be captured and returned to their owners.

THE MONROE DOCTRINE

In December 1823, President Monroe delivered a speech in which he introduced a new approach to foreign policy. In it he stated, "The American continents, by the free and independent conditions which they have assumed and maintained, are henceforth not to be considered as subjects for future colonization by any European power." Monroe also promised that the United States would not fight in any European wars. In simple terms, the president said, "You stay out of our hemisphere, and we'll stay out of yours." His ideas became known as the **Monroe Doctrine**. Monroe warned European nations against interfering in the Western Hemisphere. Doing so would be considered an act of aggression that would result in military action from the United States. Monroe's declaration was bold because the United States had no actual authority over Central America or South America.

Part of the inspiration for the Monroe Doctrine stemmed from colonies in Central and South America rebelling against European rule. Monroe was concerned about European countries having so much presence and authority in Central and South America. He feared that European countries might try to re-assert their colonial power. He also had concerns over Russia's presence in what is now Alaska. Russia had issued a statement in 1821 that non-Russians could not enter its territory. Monroe did not want Russia to try to expand its North American territory.

Though Russia and Spain denounced the Monroe Doctrine, they tolerated it. Wars among European countries had wearied them, and they had little desire to expand their involvement in the Americas.

The Monroe Doctrine Desk
While serving as a minister to France under President George Washington, James Monroe purchased this mahogany desk in Paris. When he moved into the White House in 1817, he brought this desk with him and likely wrote the Monroe Doctrine while sitting at it. About 100 years after his presidency, Monroe's great-great-grandson discovered letters from Washington, Madison, Franklin, and Jefferson to Monroe, hidden in the desk's secret compartment.

HISTORICAL THINKING

1. **READING CHECK** What was Monroe's concern about Central and South America?

2. **IDENTIFY PROBLEMS AND SOLUTIONS** How did the Missouri Compromise attempt to solve a problem and cause a potential problem at the same time?

3. **INTERPRET MAPS** Based on details you notice on the map, what territories were open to slavery and what territories were closed to slavery?

3.3 The Monroe Doctrine

In the early 19th century, the United States began to position itself as a world power. One part of that new role for the young country, according to President James Monroe, was protecting countries in Central and South America from future interference from European monarchies. The Monroe Doctrine, as his 1823 statement came to be known, would shape U.S. foreign policy for more than a century.

On December 2, 1823, President Monroe delivered his seventh annual message to Congress, or what we know today as a State of the Union address. Monroe touched on many topics, but most significantly, he introduced a new policy toward Europe and the Western Hemisphere.

CRITICAL VIEWING In this 1912 painting by Clyde DeLand, titled *Birth of the Monroe Doctrine*, President Monroe is outlining his new policy to his cabinet in preparation for his address. Notice the map and the globe. What do you think their significance is?

Legend
1 John Quincy Adams
2 William Harris Crawford
3 William Wirt
4 James Monroe
5 John Caldwell Calhoun
6 Daniel D. Tompkins
7 John McLean

DOCUMENT ONE

Primary Source: Speech
from War Message to Congress,
by James Madison, June 1, 1812

The U.S. Navy was young compared to Great Britain's. While navigating Atlantic waters, American sailors had to deal with frequent interference from Great Britain. President Madison delivered this speech as a warning that further activity would initiate an open conflict.

CONSTRUCTED RESPONSE How does Madison's summary of British actions make a case for retaliation?

British cruisers have been in the practice also of violating the rights and the peace of our coasts. They hover over and harass our entering and departing commerce. When called on, nevertheless, by the United States to punish the greater offenses committed by her [Britain's] own vessels, her government has bestowed on their commanders additional marks of honor and confidence.

DOCUMENT TWO

Primary Source: Speech
from Seventh Annual Message to Congress,
by James Monroe, December 2, 1823

In this speech, President Monroe declared that from that point on, European monarchies were not allowed to interfere in Central and South America. At the same time, he promised that the United States would stay out of European affairs.

CONSTRUCTED RESPONSE How does Monroe's speech communicate a strategy for both peacetime and military action, if provoked?

In the wars of the European powers in matters relating to themselves we have never taken any part, nor does it comport with our policy to do so. It is only when our rights are invaded or seriously menaced that we resent injuries or make preparation for our defense. With the movements in this hemisphere we are of necessity more immediately connected, and by causes which must be obvious to all enlightened and impartial [unbiased] observers.

DOCUMENT THREE

Primary Source: Essay
from "The Monroe Doctrine and Spanish America,"
by Juan Bautista Alberdi, c. 1850

Juan Bautista Alberdi, a political thinker from Argentina, expressed concern that Monroe's new policy would threaten the political and economic independence of the countries it promised to protect.

CONSTRUCTED RESPONSE How does Alberdi's opinion of the Monroe Doctrine differ from Monroe's description of his new policy?

The doctrine attributed to Monroe is a contradiction, the daughter of egoism [self-centeredness]. Even though the United States owes everything to Europe, it wants to isolate America from Europe, from any influence that does not emanate [originate] from the United States, which will make the United States the only custom house [official port] for the civilization of transatlantic origin.

SYNTHESIZE & WRITE

1. **REVIEW** Review what you have learned about the position of the United States as a rising world power in the early 1800s.

2. **RECALL** On your own paper, write down the main ideas expressed in the excerpts from Madison's and Monroe's speeches and Alberdi's essay.

3. **CONSTRUCT** Construct a topic sentence that supports or opposes this statement: In the early 1800s, the United States established itself as a world power through a policy of protection and European nonintervention in the Americas.

4. **WRITE** Write a paragraph that presents an argument for or against the statement in Step 3 using evidence from the documents.

3.4 Women in the Early Republic

To people living in the 21st century, the saying "a woman's place is in the home" is not only dated, it's inaccurate. However, in the early years of the republic, home was considered the ideal sphere for a woman's power and influence.

MAIN IDEA Increased access to education and the rise of women's organizations expanded women's roles in the early republic.

REPUBLICAN MOTHERHOOD

In the years after the Revolution, a strong nationalist spirit took hold as the young United States began to grow and prosper. Citizens embraced their new, republican government. As you have read, in the context of the early republic, the word *republican* did not refer to a political party, but to the new form of representative rule. Citizens also embraced the ideal of civic republicanism, or promoting the common good in order to protect liberty. According to the ideal of republicanism, good government and virtuous citizens worked toward the public good instead of private interests.

What did that mean for women in the early republic? Many had fully participated in the American Revolution, just as their husbands and sons had done. But after the war, women returned to their roles as wives and mothers. No matter their race or class, women were not allowed to vote or even, in many cases, to own their own property or hold public office. However, they participated in the republic by teaching republican ideals to their children—especially to their sons, who would grow up to be voters, property owners, and maybe even public officials or statesmen. Historians refer to this set of societal expectations for mothers as **republican motherhood**.

Mother as Teacher
The early 19th-century woman had a lot to live up to. Literature, art, and social expectations defined roles for women in narrow ways. Paintings such as this one cast women in a nearly angelic light and featured them as doting mothers.

Catharine Beecher

In a family portrait taken around 1860, Catharine Beecher is seated second from the left. Beecher championed free public education for all and a rigorous education for women. However, her support of women's education did not extend to other rights for women. She opposed granting women the right to vote. She believed that women should limit their efforts to home and school and that a woman's greatest roles were those of wife and mother. Even so, she never married or had children, and she supported herself throughout her life as an educator, writer, and lecturer.

THE IMPORTANCE OF EDUCATION

In the early 1800s, the ideal woman was pure, religiously devout, and a good housekeeper and mother. She also willingly deferred to all her husband's wishes. Such a role did not require women to be well educated, and few learned more than language arts and basic arithmetic—subjects that aided them in running an efficient home. But without adequate education, how could mothers be expected to teach their children, especially their sons, the basics of civic life and service in a republic?

This question had been brewing since the American Revolution, when Abigail Adams argued that in order to support male education, women should be educated as well: "If we mean to have heroes, statesmen, and philosophers, we should have learned [educated] women."

A few years later, **Judith Sargent Murray,** an American essayist and playwright in the early republic, was known for commenting on public issues, especially women's rights. She wrote that women were not intellectually inferior to men, as some believed. She argued that daughters could not reach their full potential if they were simply trained to be wives, housekeepers, and mothers. In order to teach their children republican values, mothers needed to learn science and higher math, which were traditionally taught only to men.

In 1822, **Catharine Beecher** founded the Hartford Female Seminary, a school for women in Connecticut. Students learned algebra, Latin, logic, and philosophy, among other subjects. The curriculum emphasized physical education and training in home economics. Many women who attended became teachers themselves.

As more girls and women received formal educations, women began to establish organizations that focused on helping others. Many of the organizations had a specific focus, such as helping orphans, people with physical handicaps, or war widows. Members soon began to see the positive effects of their work. Women's organizations grew and expanded, and their leaders became important agents for social change. Some of these women's organizations also laid the groundwork for budding political and social movements, such as securing the vote for women and the **abolition** of, or putting an end to, slavery.

HISTORICAL THINKING

1. **READING CHECK** How does the concept of republican motherhood align with the ideals women were expected to live up to in the early republic?

2. **DRAW CONCLUSIONS** What conclusions can you draw about the work that 19th-century women's organizations did?

3. **MAKE CONNECTIONS** How might a more comprehensive education and the expectation of rearing good citizens lead women to seek broader civic roles for themselves?

VOCABULARY

Use vocabulary words to complete the sentences.

1. Eli Whitney's invention of the _____ made the production of cotton more efficient.

2. *Gibbons* v. *Ogden* declared that a single company could not have a _____ on an industry.

3. _____ made manufacturing more structured and uniform, producing pieces that could fit in any component of its kind.

4. Young girls were recruited to work in mills in the _____ industry.

5. The _____ brought crews of people to one main site where work was done with machinery.

6. Congress used _____ in establishing the Second Bank of the United States.

7. _____ grew as the United States acquired more land, improved its financial system, and encouraged patriotic ideals.

8. The division between the North and the South was an example of _____.

READING STRATEGY
DRAW CONCLUSIONS

If you haven't already, complete your chart with evidence from the text to support conclusions. List at least three key conclusions. Then answer the question.

9. What is one conclusion you can draw about the growth and changes in the United States between 1800 and 1844, and what evidence helped you to draw that conclusion?

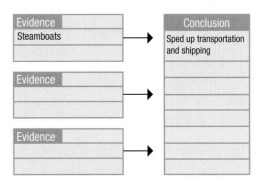

MAIN IDEAS

Answer the following questions. Support your answers with evidence from the chapter.

10. What type of work did the factory system replace? **LESSON 1.1**

11. How did Eli Whitney plan to deliver the most rifles ever produced by one factory? **LESSON 1.2**

12. Why did plantation owners want to use enslaved labor? **LESSON 2.2**

13. How did religion play a role in motivating the leaders of slave rebellions? **LESSON 2.3**

14. How did a strong economy benefit the spread of nationalism during the Era of Good Feelings? **LESSON 3.1**

15. What conditions gave rise to sectionalism in the United States? **LESSON 3.2**

16. What did President Monroe hope to achieve through his message to European powers in the Monroe Doctrine? **LESSON 3.3**

17. How did education help to change women's roles in society? **LESSON 3.4**

Answer the following questions. Support your answers with evidence from the chapter.

18. **MAKE GENERALIZATIONS** How did technological advancements change agriculture in the early 19th century?

19. **SEQUENCE EVENTS** What were the major events of the Industrial Revolution in the United States? Create a time line to illustrate your answer.

20. **DESCRIBE** What were enslaved people's daily lives like in the antebellum South?

21. **EVALUATE** How did the country become more connected in the first half of the 19th century?

22. **FORM AND SUPPORT OPINIONS** Which territorial expansions were of the most value to the United States? Support your opinion with evidence from the chapter.

Cotton spindles are part of cotton spinning machinery. Larger mills had more spindles. Study the map and then answer the questions below.

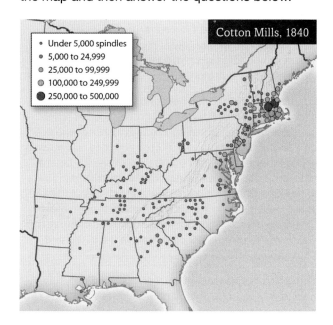

Cotton Mills, 1840

- Under 5,000 spindles
- 5,000 to 24,999
- 25,000 to 99,999
- 100,000 to 249,999
- 250,000 to 500,000

23. Which northern and southern states had the largest mills?

24. According to the map, where might ships carrying raw cotton be headed?

After visiting a plantation in Georgia in 1793, Eli Whitney designed a new machine to remove seeds from cotton. He wrote a letter to his father about his invention. Read the excerpt and then answer the question below.

I tried some experiments. In about ten Days I made a little model, for which I was offered . . . a Hundred Guineas [about $450]. I concluded [decided] to . . . turn my attention to perfecting the Machine. I made one . . . which required the labor of one man to turn it and with which one man will clean ten times as much cotton as he can in any other way before known and also cleanse it much better than in the usual mode. This machine may be turned by water or with a horse, with the greatest ease, and one man and a horse will do more than fifty men with the old machine. It makes the labor fifty times less.

25. What benefits did Whitney point to when describing his new invention?

26. **NARRATIVE** Review the inventions and innovations in this chapter and consider how they changed people's lives. Then think of a new technology that has affected your life. Write a paragraph connecting your experience with the experience of someone in the early to mid-1800s whose life was similarly affected.

TIPS

- Make a list of important engineering or technological advances in the early to mid-1800s.

- Use two or three vocabulary terms from the chapter in your narrative.

- Reflect on new machines, products, or building projects during your lifetime.

- Conclude by stating how you think new technology changes people's lives.

Searching for Sacagawea

BY MARGARET TALBOT

Adapted from "Searching for Sacagawea,"
by Margaret Talbot, in *National Geographic*, February 2003

The glimpses we are allowed of Sacagawea in Lewis and Clark's expedition journals tell us more about her than about almost any other Native American woman of her time. But the very sketchiness of our knowledge has permitted novelists, feminists, and Native American tribes to project what they wish upon Sacagawea. Many see her as a metaphor more than a human being. But who was Sacagawea, really?

From the age of about 13, Sacagawea had lived with the Hidatsa near the confluence of the Missouri and Knife rivers. Lewis and Clark first met Sacagawea when she was about 17 and pregnant with her first child. In November 1804, the Corps of Discovery, as the expedition was known, had arrived among the Mandan and Hidatsa on the upper Missouri River, in what is now North Dakota.

One warm afternoon in 2002, I spent some time there trying to reimagine Sacagawea's world. With me was Amy Mossett, a Mandan-Hidatsa from New Town, North Dakota, and an expert on Sacagawea. On a bluff above the Knife River, Mossett and I look out over shallow, bowl-shaped indentations in the ground where her ancestors' earth lodges once stood. "This is where I feel closest to Sacagawea," says Mossett.

The Corps of Discovery set out from its winter quarters on April 7, 1805. Less than two months after giving birth, Sacagawea gathered up her infant son and embarked with her husband, a French-Canadian fur trader, on a roughly 5,000-mile, 16-month journey. Contrary to her romanticized image, Sacagawea was not the expedition's "girl-guide." Most of the territory they passed through was as unfamiliar to her as it was to Lewis and Clark.

One of Sacagawea's greatest contributions was her mere presence, which seems to have disarmed potentially hostile tribes along the way. The journals record one of those fortunate coincidences.

Sacagawea, who spoke Hidatsa and Shoshone but neither English nor French, was to translate a Shoshone chief's words into Hidatsa for her husband, who was to translate into French for a member of the corps, who would translate into English for the captains. They were just about to begin this unwieldy relay when Sacagawea suddenly recognized the Shoshone chief. He was, of all people, her long-lost brother.

After the 21 months in which Sacagawea's story intersects with that of the expedition, she disappears almost entirely from our view. The best evidence we have suggests that she died in her mid-20s shortly after giving birth to a daughter. For many years, most white Americans wrote about Sacagawea as the archetypal "good Indian"—one who, like Pocahontas, had aided white men. But in recent decades, and especially for Native Americans, Sacagawea has become a different sort of symbol. She is a reminder of the extent to which the Lewis and Clark story is also a Native American story.

Disputes remain about where and when Sacagawea died and even how to spell and pronounce her name. For the 400 or so remaining Lemhi Shoshone who live on a reservation in Idaho, the connection to Sacagawea is one thread on which to hang their hopes for federal tribal recognition and a return of ancestral lands. The Wind River Shoshone in Wyoming insist "Sacajawea" (their spelling) died on their reservation, though most historians dispute this. But the Shoshone's cultural claim on Sacagawea anchors them in the Lewis and Clark story.

Some historians wonder why Sacagawea didn't stay behind with the Shoshone and her brother. Perhaps she had come to feel more like a Hidatsa than a Shoshone. Or perhaps she had been seized with curiosity about what came next and where the journey would take her.

For more from National Geographic,
check out "Lost Missouri" online.

UNIT INQUIRY: Define Good Citizenship

In this unit, you learned about the political, economic, and geographic growth of the United States in the years of the early republic. Based on your understanding of the text, in what ways was good citizenship central to the success of the early republic? What role did citizenship play in how Americans defined themselves and others? Which groups of Americans were excluded from full citizenship, and why?

ASSIGNMENT

Create your own definition for good citizenship. Your definition should include several elements, including a statement of what constitutes good citizenship, why citizenship mattered in the early republic, and why citizenship still matters today. Be prepared to present your definition of citizenship to the class and explain your reasoning.

Gather Evidence As you develop your definition of good citizenship, gather evidence from this unit about the different ways in which concepts of citizenship shaped communities and a young nation. Think about the active roles citizens played in the early republic. Also consider the rights and responsibilities American citizens had—or did not have—and why. Use a graphic organizer like this one to help organize your thoughts.

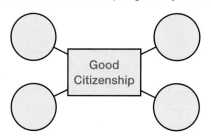

Good Citizenship

Produce Use your notes to produce descriptions of the elements that make up your definition of good citizenship. Write a short paragraph on each element using evidence from this unit to support your ideas.

Present Choose a creative way to present your definition of good citizenship to the class. Consider one of these options:

- Interview citizens in your community about what they think good citizenship entails. Ask them what they do to be good citizens and what rights and responsibilities are the most important to them. Present your interviews to the class.

- Create a good citizenship award. Work with a small team to design the award. Identify a person in your school who you think deserves this honor. Hold an award ceremony and appoint a class member to describe the ways in which your award recipient exemplifies good citizenship.

- Design a collaborative wall mural that illustrates the rights and responsibilities of good citizenship using words and drawings.

NATIONAL GEOGRAPHIC | LEARNING FRAMEWORK ACTIVITIES

Propose a New Invention

`ATTITUDES` Responsibility, Empowerment

`SKILL` Problem-Solving

Part of being a good citizen is taking care of the people and environment around you. The men and women who innovated new technologies in the early republic were all trying to solve some sort of problem or make a process more efficient. Using evidence from the reading, develop a proposal for a new invention. Define the problem that you are solving and how your invention would benefit your community or even the world. Consider including illustrations of your invention. Present your proposal to the class as if you were presenting to a panel of financial backers.

Write a Campaign Speech

`SKILLS` Collaboration, Communication

`KNOWLEDGE` Our Human Story

Political campaigns have been a part of American democracy since it began. Effective campaigns and their candidates have to deliver a clear message to potential voters if they want to win elections. Work with a small team of classmates to write a campaign speech about an important issue during the early republic. Use evidence from the reading to define your issue, craft your message, and select the candidate who would best deliver the speech. Present your team's speech and be prepared to listen to other teams' speeches.

To tell your American story

You've been reading about the founding of the country and the establishment of the American republic. Think about the individuals and families who established their homes in the United States. What does the idea of a "hometown" mean to you? And what can you learn when you investigate your own hometown?

Fred Hiebert
▶ Watch the Why Study U.S. History? video

MAP OF HAVERFORD TOWNSHIP

Proposed Rail Line to Philadelphia

Mrs. W. Taylor's 55 acres

Cobb's Creek

Castle Hill Mills

Nitre Hall Mill

Clinton Mills

This map of Haverford Township, published in 1875, reveals the kind of ground-level details those who lived there would have recognized—homes and farms belonging to prominent citizens, numerous creeks and ponds created for early mills, and the proposed Philadelphia–Chester County rail line.

If you look around my hometown (suburban Philadelphia), it's an area of houses and parks. But there are all sorts of clues to our history—strange names that don't seem to make sense. Like an old building called Nitre Hall on Karakung Drive, or a nearby street on a hillside called Lakeview Avenue (though there is no lake in sight).

So here's what I learned by going to my local library and historical society: This area west of Philadelphia has great agricultural land, watered by streams and creeks, and was acquired from Governor William Penn in 1680 for agricultural development. The largest stream in our part of Delaware County is Cobb's Creek, but the original name given by the Lenape Native Americans was *Karakung* (the place of wild geese). This name is still preserved as a road name.

Electric trolleys similar to this one were introduced in Haverford around the turn of the century. The electric railway transformed settled farmland into a thriving suburb accessible by a growing middle class.

By the early 1800s, the creeks were dammed, and the water flow was used to power mills of all sorts. A gunpowder mill operated from 1810 to 1840, using nitre (saltpeter), charcoal, and sulfur (all brought in), mixed here using the power of the waterwheels. Nitre Hall is actually the original house where the powder master (who mixed the dangerous powder together) lived. At that time, Nitre Hall Powder Mill was the second-largest black powder mill in the United States.

By 1840, the mills were converted to use water power to spin cotton and wool. During the Civil War, cloth for Union soldiers' uniforms was produced here. Following the Civil War and the increased dependence on steam power, the water mills disappeared. The last mill was a sawmill that closed in the mid-20th century.

It was pretty quiet here until—boom!—at the beginning of the 20th century, with the development of electric railways. In 1907, a tramline was built to the region from Philadelphia, and the area opened to provide housing for workers employed in Philadelphia. To increase visitors and make the suburbs more attractive, a large amusement park was built nearby with an artificial lake for boating. Lakeview Avenue was built near Nitre Hall. After three years of bad weather, however, the amusement park was an economic bust and the lake dried up.

Today, Nitre Hall is a local museum located on Karakung Drive, and the name Lakeview Avenue is all that's left of the lake. But together they tell the story of my neighborhood's place in the history of the United States.

What's your American story?

You can begin to recognize the connections between the events of our past and your life today. Look around your neighborhood and find an interesting street name or building name—you can discover your hometown's place in U.S. history, too.

 Use your History Notebook to comment on what you've read. And check out the "Documenting My America" project online to start telling your own American story.

PUSHING NATIONAL BOUNDARIES

CRITICAL VIEWING This painting by Thomas Cole, called *Scene from "The Last of the Mohicans,"* illustrates an event from a novel by American writer James Fenimore Cooper. But Cole, a landscape artist of the Hudson River School, also used the painting to depict the untamed American wilderness, which was soon to be conquered and settled. What challenges might a landscape like the one in this painting have posed to settlers?

PUSHING NATIONAL
BOUNDARIES

1828
Andrew Jackson, a southerner, is elected president. *(Jackson presidential campaign poster)*

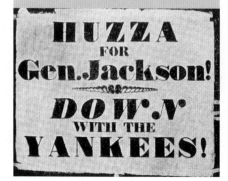

1836
Texans declare independence from Mexico. *(illustration of the Battle of the Alamo, a fort in San Antonio, Texas, where Texans fought Mexican troops)*

1838–1839
The journey of about 17,000 Cherokee forced to leave their homeland becomes known as the Trail of Tears.

1837
A panic over the state of the economy results in a severe depression.

THE UNITED STATES

1840

1830

1820

1821 AMERICAS
Mexico gains its independence from Spain.

1838 AFRICA
Zulus clash with Boers in what is known today as South Africa. *(Zulu shield and weapons)*

1839 AMERICAS
Antonio López de Santa Anna regains control of Mexico and rules as a dictator.

THE WORLD

What was happening in Europe at the same time American women were calling for their rights?

1855
Poet Walt Whitman publishes *Leaves of Grass*, a collection of poems about ordinary Americans. *(brass plate with reversed letters used to print the cover of Whitman's collection)*

VOTES FOR WOMEN

1848
A convention calling for women's rights is held in Seneca Falls, New York. *(sash worn by women's rights activists)*

1849
After gold is found in California's Sacramento Valley, thousands of people rush to the site.

1860
Shoemakers go on strike in Massachusetts, demanding higher wages.

1850

1860

1856 ASIA
The Second Opium War begins in China.

1848 EUROPE
After a revolution in Germany fails, some Germans come to the United States.

1845 EUROPE
The Great Irish Potato Famine kills more than one million people and forces many others to emigrate to the United States.

1847 AFRICA
Freed U.S. slaves and free African Americans establish the republic of Liberia in West Africa. *(The Liberian flag strongly resembles that of the United States.)*

CHAPTER

11

THE AGE OF
JACKSON

1824–1840

ESSENTIAL QUESTION
How did Andrew Jackson's policies impact different groups of people in America?

 The Erie Canal

SECTION 1 **Jacksonian Democracy and States' Rights**
KEY VOCABULARY

agrarian	secession	Tariff of Abominations
doctrine of nullification	slogan	treason
Jacksonian democracy	spoils system	voting rights

SECTION 2 **Jackson's Policy Toward Native Americans**
KEY VOCABULARY

assimilate	Indian Territory	truce
Indian Removal Act	Trail of Tears	

SECTION 3 **Prosperity and Panic**
KEY VOCABULARY

depression	Panic of 1837	Whig Party
inflation	veto	

AMERICAN **GALLERY**
ONLINE **Andrew Jackson**

READING STRATEGY

COMPARE AND CONTRAST
When you compare and contrast two or more things, you note their similarities and differences. Use a Venn diagram like this one to help you compare and contrast the policies of Andrew Jackson and his opponents, such as John Quincy Adams.

"I was born for a storm, and a calm does not suit me."
—Andrew Jackson

CRITICAL VIEWING This statue of Andrew Jackson, created by sculptor Clark Mills, stands in a square across the street from the White House in Washington, D.C. The bronze statue—the first one made in the United States—celebrates Jackson's 1815 victory against the British at the Battle of New Orleans during the War of 1812. Mills obtained the bronze by melting down old weapons provided by the government. The statue was dedicated in 1853, on the 38th anniversary of the battle and 8 years after Jackson's death. What impression of Jackson does the statue convey?

1.1 Expanding Democracy

You back the candidate who's got your back. It's human nature. He or she supports your causes and promises to fix all the things you think are broken. Of course, these promises aren't always kept.

MAIN IDEA Regional differences fueled a battle over the presidency in the 1820s between John Quincy Adams and Andrew Jackson.

THE TIGHT ELECTION OF 1824

The presidential election of 1824 pitted **John Quincy Adams**, the current secretary of state and son of John Adams, against Andrew Jackson, who, as you may remember, fought in the War of 1812. The two candidates embodied the regional differences that divided the country. Adams represented the businessmen of the East. He wanted to build canals and roads to improve the nation's transportation system, and he promoted science and education. Jackson, representing the farmers of the West, supported states' rights. Adams and Jackson were the main candidates in 1824, but other candidates ran as well, including William Crawford, the secretary of the treasury, and Henry Clay, the speaker of the House of Representatives.

Andrew Jackson received the most popular votes in the election by a large margin. He also won the most electoral votes. However, he failed to win more than half of the total electoral votes, which then, as now, is required for victory. As a result, according to the 12th Amendment to the Constitution, the responsibility of choosing a winner among the top three candidates—Jackson, Adams, and Crawford—fell to the House of Representatives. By one vote, the House chose Adams to lead the country.

Adams took office in March 1825 and appointed Henry Clay as the secretary of state shortly thereafter. The appointment outraged Jackson. He believed that Adams and Clay had made a deal in which Clay persuaded other members of the House to vote for Adams in exchange for the prestigious, or highly respected, cabinet position. Jackson called the deal a "corrupt bargain" and claimed the men stole the election from him. As president, Adams didn't gather much backing for his proposed canals and roads, in part because Jackson's supporters in Congress blocked them.

READY FOR A REMATCH

Meanwhile, Jackson had his eyes on the 1828 presidential election. Both Adams and Jackson were Democratic-Republicans, but the party had become deeply split. According to Jackson, on one side stood Adams and the rich easterners whose interests Adams favored. Jackson himself claimed to champion hardworking people whom he called the "common man." Eventually, two new parties arose. Adams and his followers formed the **National Republicans**. Jackson and his camp were known as **Democrats**.

During the 1828 campaign, both parties used speeches, parades, **slogans**, or sayings, and songs to build excitement for their candidate—an approach that changed the way politicians ran for office. Supporters on both sides also took part in mudslinging, or using insults to attack an opponent. In spite of all the name-calling, Jackson easily beat Adams in the election.

Voting rights, or laws that dictate which Americans have the right to vote, had been extended so more people could vote. You may recall that previously, only white men who owned property and paid taxes could vote. By contrast, in 1828, most white men in many states could vote whether they owned property or not. As a result, about 782,000 more "common men" participated in the 1828 election than in the previous one. Most Americans viewed Jackson's win as a victory over the privileged. **Jacksonian democracy** was the

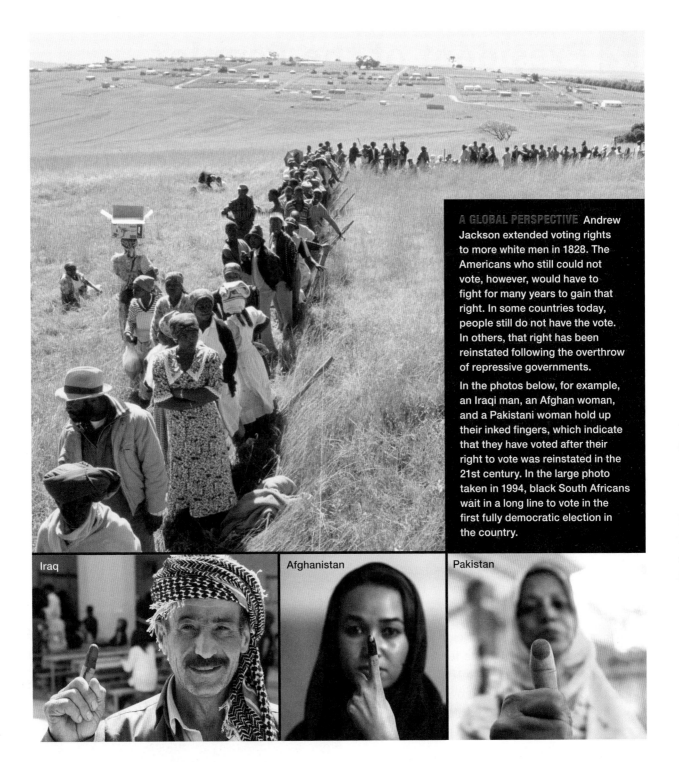

Iraq

Afghanistan

Pakistan

A GLOBAL PERSPECTIVE Andrew Jackson extended voting rights to more white men in 1828. The Americans who still could not vote, however, would have to fight for many years to gain that right. In some countries today, people still do not have the vote. In others, that right has been reinstated following the overthrow of repressive governments.

In the photos below, for example, an Iraqi man, an Afghan woman, and a Pakistani woman hold up their inked fingers, which indicate that they have voted after their right to vote was reinstated in the 21st century. In the large photo taken in 1994, black South Africans wait in a long line to vote in the first fully democratic election in the country.

political movement that celebrated the common man—farmers, craftsmen, laborers, and middle-class businessmen—and defended the will of the people. But women, African Americans, and Native Americans still could not vote or hold office. Nevertheless, Jackson's election in 1828 reflected the steady expansion of white male suffrage, symbolized the shift of political power to the West, and opened a new era of political democracy in the United States. President Jackson was a symbol of his age. People now believed they were represented by one of their own in the White House.

HISTORICAL THINKING

1. **READING CHECK** How was the presidential election of 1824 decided?

2. **COMPARE AND CONTRAST** How was Jacksonian democracy different from what had existed before?

3. **DRAW CONCLUSIONS** Why was Jacksonian democracy such an important development?

1.2 President of the People?

When you're considered an outsider and achieve something big, people expect great things of you. That was the position Andrew Jackson was in when he won the presidency, and now all eyes were on him.

MAIN IDEA Andrew Jackson rose from humble beginnings to become a U.S. president who symbolized a new brand of democracy.

FROM HARDSHIP TO HERO

Andrew Jackson was the first president who didn't come from a wealthy Virginia or Massachusetts family. In fact, he was born into poverty in 1767 and grew up in North Carolina. His father died before his birth, leaving his mother to raise him and his brothers.

During the American Revolution, young Jackson served as a messenger for the Continental Army. British soldiers discovered what he was doing and took him prisoner. While Jackson was being held, a British soldier ordered the boy to clean his boots. Jackson refused, and the soldier slashed him with his sword. Jackson also contracted smallpox and survived, but his mother and brothers weren't as lucky. He was an orphan by the age of 14.

Despite his hard childhood, Jackson achieved great success. He moved to the Tennessee frontier and became a lawyer in 1787. He practiced law in the small but growing town of Nashville and met his future wife, Rachel Donelson Robards, while boarding with her family. Later, he made a successful run for Congress. In 1804, Jackson purchased a

The Cabildo – Louisiana State Museum, New Orleans

In 1815, wearing this uniform coat, Jackson led the American victory at the Battle of New Orleans, which ended the War of 1812. Jackson is also wearing the coat in the 1817 portrait by Ralph E.W. Earl, shown on the opposite page. What details in the coat might indicate that the person wearing it is a general?

425-acre farm, later known as the Hermitage, where he built a plantation and used enslaved people to labor in his fields.

When the War of 1812 broke out between the United States and Great Britain, Jackson served as a general in command of soldiers from Tennessee. After crushing the British at the Battle of New Orleans, Jackson became a national hero.

A CLEAN SWEEP

Jackson's success was crowned by his election as president of the United States in 1828. About 30,000 people witnessed his inauguration in March 1829. But he endured the ceremony with a heavy heart. During the campaign, some of the mudslinging had been directed at his wife's reputation. When she died of a heart attack three months before her husband's inauguration, Jackson believed the personal attacks had caused her death.

Once he took office, however, Jackson assumed the presidency with enthusiasm and began carrying out the government reforms he'd promised to make during his campaign. First, Jackson replaced many of Adams's government officials with his own supporters. These appointees included newspaper editors who had been loyal to Jackson during the presidential campaign.

Critics claimed that what he'd done was corrupt. They believed Jackson was using the appointments to assume greater control of the federal government. But Jackson defended his actions by pointing out that completely removing officials from time to time prevents any one party from maintaining a stranglehold on government. The practice of rewarding political backers with government jobs became known as the **spoils system**, and it continues today. The term comes from the saying, "to the victors belong the spoils [goods or benefits] of the enemy." In this case, the "spoils" were the political positions Jackson had given to his supporters.

Controversy over appointments was just one of the problems Jackson faced early in his presidency. Soon he would find himself in a battle over taxes and states' rights that threatened to tear apart the Union.

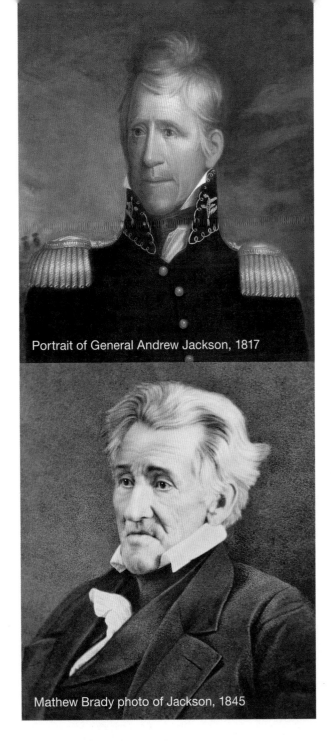

Portrait of General Andrew Jackson, 1817

Mathew Brady photo of Jackson, 1845

HISTORICAL THINKING

1. **READING CHECK** What challenges did Andrew Jackson face growing up?

2. **COMPARE AND CONTRAST** How did Jackson differ from all preceding presidents?

3. **FORM AND SUPPORT OPINIONS** Do you think Jackson was right to initiate the use of the spoils system to appoint government officials? Support your opinion.

1.3 Debating States' Rights

When you get together with friends for a movie, you probably disagree sometimes about which one to see. Will it be sci-fi, a romantic comedy, or a thriller? But the real question is: Do you compromise or split up and see different films?

MAIN IDEA Conflicts over tariffs caused tensions—and triggered threats—in different parts of the country.

TROUBLE OVER TAXES

In the early years of Andrew Jackson's presidency, regions of the country were having trouble compromising. In particular, the Northeast and the South disagreed over tariffs, which are taxes a foreign country charges on its imported goods. The Northeast welcomed tariffs. Many northeasterners worked in manufacturing. Tariffs made foreign goods more expensive than those produced in the Northeast, and so increased sales of local goods. But people in the South didn't like tariffs. The South had an **agrarian**, or agricultural, economy. Southerners were mostly farmers who had to buy manufactured goods from other countries. Tariffs increased the cost of these goods.

So southerners were angry when Congress passed a bill in the last months of John Quincy Adams's presidency that greatly increased tariffs. The bill raised the price of foreign products sold in the United States. It also contained a clause that raised taxes on U.S. raw materials sold abroad. The clause hurt the South because it depended on the overseas sale of such raw materials as cotton and tobacco. Taxes made these items more expensive and, as a result, less attractive to foreign buyers.

The Tariff of 1828, as the bill was called, was a win-win for the federal government and the Northeast. Tariffs were the government's main source of revenue, or income. The fees caused foreign countries to charge more for their goods and helped protect northeastern industries. As you may recall, Adams represented the interests of the Northeast. In fact, the Adams-packed Congress passed the bill to appeal to northeastern voters.

Not surprisingly, southerners were outraged. They called the bill the **Tariff of Abominations**. An abomination is something that stirs feelings of disgust or hatred, which is exactly how southerners felt. But the bill backfired on Adams. The South helped vote him out of office partly in reaction to the tariff hike.

STATE VERSUS FEDERAL POWER

Political leaders in South Carolina hated the bill so much, they began to talk about the state's withdrawal from the Union. To prevent the country from breaking apart, South Carolina senator John C. Calhoun applied the **doctrine of nullification**, also called the states' rights doctrine. According to this doctrine, a state could nullify, or reject, a federal law it considered unconstitutional. By promoting the idea that a state could override a federal law, the doctrine opened up the debate over states' rights versus the authority of the federal government.

The issue placed Jackson in a tough position. He supported states' rights, and he had picked Calhoun to be his vice president. But he disagreed with Calhoun's notion that states should be able to prevent the federal government from acting on behalf of the nation as a whole.

Soon, other politicians joined in. Most famously, two senators took part in the **Webster-Hayne debate** in 1830. **Daniel Webster** from Massachusetts argued against nullification, claiming that it threatened the Union and freedom.

In this painting by George P.A. Healy, *Webster's Reply to Hayne*, Daniel Webster stands and delivers his speech in the Senate. Hayne sits to Webster's right with his hands held in front of him.

In a passionate plea, he called for "Liberty and Union, now and forever, one and inseparable!" Robert Y. Hayne from South Carolina made the case for nullification. He claimed that a state had the right to nullify a federal law, and he criticized those who, as he said, "are constantly stealing power from the States and adding strength to the Federal Government."

To ease the situation, Jackson and Congress agreed to reduce the tariff in 1832, but South Carolina's representatives still thought it was too high. They rejected the tariff in 1828 and 1832. The state's representatives even threatened **secession**, or withdrawal from the country, if the federal government tried to force it to pay the tariffs. Jackson responded by warning the representatives that he would consider secession an act of **treason**, or disloyalty to one's country. And Congress authorized Jackson to use force to collect tariffs.

The crisis finally ended in 1833 when Congress passed yet another bill that gradually reduced tariffs. However, tensions between the North and the South did not go away. On the contrary, tensions would continue to escalate throughout the first half of the 1800s.

But, meanwhile, another crisis was brewing. Americans' demand for more land in the West was driving Native American populations from their homes. Jackson answered with a new set of policies toward Native Americans.

HISTORICAL THINKING

1. **READING CHECK** How did the doctrine of nullification help assert states' rights?

2. **ANALYZE CAUSE AND EFFECT** How did the Tariff of 1828 affect the agrarian economy in the South?

3. **FORM AND SUPPORT OPINIONS** Do you think states should have the right to nullify a federal law? Explain your answer.

2.1 Expanding into Native American Lands

Native Americans had lived in North America for centuries, enduring natural disasters, wars, and disease. Soon they would be forced to try to survive Andrew Jackson's Native American policies.

MAIN IDEA Native Americans lost land to white settlers as Andrew Jackson and the U.S. government forced their westward relocation.

TREATIES AND BATTLES

Andrew Jackson had a long history with Native Americans. After the War of 1812, he battled the Creek in Georgia and negotiated a treaty with them on behalf of the federal government. According to the terms of the treaty, the Creek gave up 22 million acres of land (an area larger than the state of South Carolina) to the government, which then sold pieces of the land to settlers.

More battles and treaties followed with the Creek, Cherokee, Choctaw, and Chickasaw, who held large areas of land throughout the South. Little by little, many of these groups were forced onto lands less suited to farming, as white settlers moved into what had once been Native American territory.

When Jackson became president, he offered Native Americans in the South two choices: either **assimilate**, or adopt, European ways of life and accept the authority of the states in which they lived, or move west of the Mississippi River. More than any other southeastern tribe, the Cherokee assimilated, taking up many aspects of white culture and customs. They dressed in western-style clothing and built plantations and ranches similar to those of white settlers.

One Cherokee named **Sequoya** (sih-KWOY-uh) developed a writing system and began publishing a newspaper. As a result, literacy quickly spread among the Cherokee. They even wrote a constitution, using the U.S. Constitution as a model, and established the **Cherokee Nation**. Despite these efforts, the Cherokee were under constant pressure to leave the region. The pressure came to a head in 1828, when Americans discovered gold on Cherokee lands in Georgia. Now both settlers and miners were eager to grab the land. That's when southern states passed laws allowing them to take over Native American lands.

THE INDIAN REMOVAL ACT

Jackson supported these laws and, in 1830, approved another law that took Native American relocation a step further. The law was the **Indian Removal Act**, which ended the U.S. government's earlier policy of respecting the rights of Native Americans to remain on land they'd lived on for generations. Under this policy, they were forced to move to an area of land that included present-day Oklahoma and parts of Kansas and Nebraska. The area came to be known as **Indian Territory**.

The act required the government to peacefully negotiate treaties with Native Americans and not force them off their land. But the U.S. government and Jackson often ignored this requirement. Jackson considered Native Americans conquered subjects of the United States. As such, he believed the government could decide where they would live.

Not all Americans supported the removal act. Many opposed it because of their dislike of Jackson. Others protested the cruelty of sending Native Americans into an unknown wilderness. Religious groups, such as the Quakers, opposed the act on moral grounds, claiming it wasn't just or right. Many Native Americans gave in and left their homes. But not all would go without a fight.

National Museum of the American Indian, Washington, D.C.

While the Cherokee assimilated European styles, they also held onto their own culture, as the traditional artifacts shown here demonstrate. The man's coat is made from the hide of deer, which the Cherokee hunted. Like all Cherokee baskets, the one shown here was woven by a woman and was used to store all sorts of household goods. The Cherokee would have filled the wooden water drum with a quantity of water to get a deep, echoing sound.

Man's coat, c. 1820

Water drum and drumstick, c. 1890

Basket of woven and dyed rivercane, c. 1900

HISTORICAL THINKING

1. **READING CHECK** What was Jackson's attitude toward Native Americans?

2. **MAKE INFERENCES** What do you think the Cherokee hoped to gain by establishing their own constitution?

3. **COMPARE AND CONTRAST** How were the stated policies toward Native Americans different from what actually occurred?

2.2 Native American Resistance

Sometimes you have to fight for your rights, even when it seems like a losing battle. But the fight is that much harder when the other side doesn't play fair.

MAIN IDEA Some Native Americans took up arms to resist their forced relocation by the U.S. government.

A TRAP IS SET

The **Seminole** were among the Native Americans who refused to leave their homes. They lived near the Everglades, a large wetlands region in southern Florida. After the Seminole rejected a removal treaty, President Jackson and the federal government declared war on them in 1835. But it didn't turn out to be an easy fight.

Seminole villages lay deep within the dangerous swampland of the Everglades, providing plenty of places where the Native Americans could hide and giving them a clear geographic advantage. When American soldiers came on the attack, Seminole leader **Osceola** (ahs-ee-OH-luh) and his warriors took them by surprise. They ambushed the soldiers, killing them with their tomahawks and

Threatened by Oil
Some Native Americans continue to protest their treatment today. In this photo, a Native American member of the Cowboy and Indian Alliance joined other Native Americans and non-native protestors in front of the Capitol in Washington, D.C., in April 2014. The thousands who gathered objected to the building of an oil pipeline through their land in the Great Plains region, saying it threatened water and other natural resources.

Black Hawk

Black Hawk visited Washington, D.C., in 1837 to witness the sale of the last of Sauk land to the United States. During that visit, artist Charles Bird King painted Black Hawk's portrait. Homer Henderson painted this copy in the late 1800s from a print of the original. In the painting, the Native American leader wears a medallion, depicting an unknown man, which he probably received as a treaty gift from U.S. officials.

muskets. The Seminole also burned the homes and crops of American settlers, hoping to drive them from the region.

At the end of 1837, the government arranged to meet with Osceola at a so-called peace conference. The two sides had declared a **truce**, an agreement to stop fighting, while their leaders met to talk. But the meeting was actually a trap. As soon as Osceola arrived, American soldiers took him prisoner. He died three months later in captivity.

Fighting continued off and on for five more years before the Seminole finally surrendered. Some of the Seminole migrated to Indian Territory, but they never entirely left the Everglades. Their descendants continue to live there today.

THE BLACK HAWK WAR

Native Americans in other parts of the country also resisted removal. At first, tribes north of the Ohio River in Illinois, including the Shawnee, Ottawa, Potawatomi, Sauk, and Fox, signed a treaty agreeing to relocate west of the Mississippi River. Once they had moved, however, the Sauk and Fox struggled to grow enough food for their people. They faced starvation. Then, in 1832, they rebelled. A Sauk leader named **Black Hawk** led his people and the Fox back to their lands in Illinois, where they meant to stay.

The U.S. military and Illinois militia had other ideas. To intimidate the Sauk and Fox, troops built large forts in the area. They also recruited members of other Native American tribes to fight Black Hawk and his followers. A young man named **Abraham Lincoln** served as a captain during this campaign. The Black Hawk War dragged on for a few months, but the Sauk and Fox were eventually overpowered. The war was brief but bloody, particularly for the Sauk and Fox. As many as 600 Native Americans died in the fighting, while only about 70 American soldiers perished.

In August 1832, Black Hawk surrendered, and the military imprisoned him for a time in a Virginia fort. He told his captors that he was not sorry for what he'd done. He was defending his land and his people from what he called "cheating men." When the American people read Black Hawk's words, many sympathized with him. Still, the Black Hawk War did not put an end to the government's efforts to drive Native Americans from their lands. Many more would be forced to leave—and at great cost.

HISTORICAL THINKING

1. **READING CHECK** How did Native Americans fight back against attempts to remove them?

2. **COMPARE AND CONTRAST** How were the reactions of Osceola and Black Hawk similar when they were forced to move westward?

3. **MAKE INFERENCES** Who were the "cheating men" Black Hawk referred to, and why did he characterize them in that way?

2.3 The Trail of Tears

When people believe a policy is unfair or unconstitutional, they can take it to the highest court in the land. You would think that everyone would have to abide by a Supreme Court ruling, right?

MAIN IDEA In defiance of a ruling from the Supreme Court, Andrew Jackson forced the Cherokee to relocate to Indian Territory.

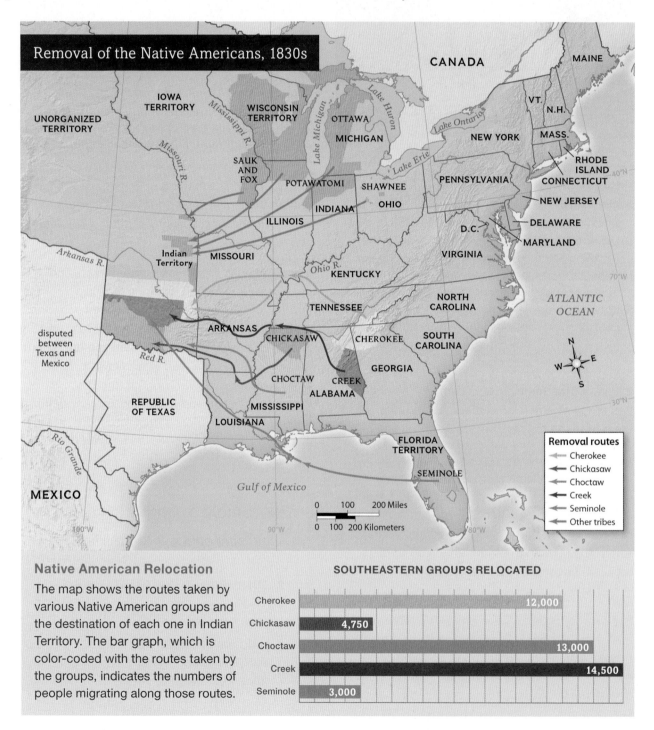

Removal of the Native Americans, 1830s

Removal routes
- ⬅ Cherokee
- ⬅ Chickasaw
- ⬅ Choctaw
- ⬅ Creek
- ⬅ Seminole
- ⬅ Other tribes

Native American Relocation

The map shows the routes taken by various Native American groups and the destination of each one in Indian Territory. The bar graph, which is color-coded with the routes taken by the groups, indicates the numbers of people migrating along those routes.

SOUTHEASTERN GROUPS RELOCATED

Group	Number
Cherokee	12,000
Chickasaw	4,750
Choctaw	13,000
Creek	14,500
Seminole	3,000

ONE LAST STAND

In an 1823 decision, *Johnson* v. *M'Intosh*, the Supreme Court had offered some protection for Native American lands. So, in 1832, the Cherokee turned to the Supreme Court to seek legal means to stay on their land. The Court ruled in their favor, determining that the Indian Removal Act was unconstitutional and that it violated previous treaties with the Cherokee. But the state of Georgia and President Andrew Jackson opposed the Supreme Court's decision. They wanted the Cherokee to go.

A small group of Cherokee signed the treaty, deciding that doing so was their only hope. They soon left for Indian Territory. But most of the Cherokee—about 17,000 people—opposed the treaty and remained on their land. **John Ross**, the principal chief of the Cherokee, led the resistance and tried to negotiate a better treaty. However, Jackson wasn't willing to enter into negotiations. In 1838, he sent General **Winfield Scott** and 7,000 federal troops into Cherokee lands in Georgia and Alabama. The soldiers forced people from their homes and placed them in camps. White settlers then looted and destroyed the Cherokee villages, leaving the Native Americans with only the few possessions they had taken to the camps.

A GRUELING MARCH

After the Cherokee had been confined in the camps for months, American soldiers forced them on a march to Indian Territory. The terrible journey lasted about four months, during the fall and winter of 1838 and 1839. The Cherokee weren't given adequate food, shelter, or clothing as they struggled in the rain and snow. Some soldiers even stole the few supplies that had been provided for the Native Americans.

Trail of Tears Sculpture
This sculpture from the Trail of Tears exhibit at the Cherokee Heritage Center in Tahlequah, Oklahoma, represents a Cherokee couple on the forced march. The exhibit includes a gallery that focuses on how the Cherokee started over after their relocation.

As a result, about 4,000 people died from cold, illness, and starvation on the march. One survivor remembered, "Children cry and many men cry, and all look sad like when friends die, but they say nothing." A witness to the forced migration reported that even old women "were traveling with heavy burdens attached to the back—on the sometimes frozen ground, and sometimes muddy streets, with no covering for the feet." Because of the suffering the Cherokee endured, the journey became known as the **Trail of Tears**.

To add to their burden, the soldiers made the Cherokee pay settlers for passing through their farms and boatmen for transporting them across rivers. By the time the Cherokee reached Indian Territory, they had little money left. They faced other challenges as well. Native Americans already living in the territory resented the newcomers. Not long after the Cherokee resettled, the Osage fought them over land. In addition, many Cherokee sought revenge against those of their tribe who had signed the treaty agreeing to move.

The Cherokee felt they had given up a part of their identity when they left their homeland. They had lost a spiritual connection to their ancestors, and they believed they had been betrayed by the U.S. government. Jackson's policies carried undertones of racial and political superiority and had a devastating impact on Native Americans.

HISTORICAL THINKING

1. **READING CHECK** What happened when some of the Cherokee resisted moving west?

2. **DESCRIBE** What challenges endured by Native Americans on the forced march to Indian Territory caused the journey to be known as the Trail of Tears?

3. **INTERPRET MAPS** Which southeastern Native American tribe traveled the farthest?

3.1 Economic Crises

In the 1830s, people were moving west. New railroads and canals carried people and goods from state to state. These were good times for the country. Most people thought they'd never end.

MAIN IDEA Andrew Jackson helped destroy the Second Bank of the United States, which had a severe impact on the economy.

THE BANK WAR

Andrew Jackson's domestic policies devastated the lives of Native Americans, but for many white Americans, life was good. The U.S. economy prospered during Jackson's presidency. Much of this prosperity was due to the country's powerful National Bank, the Second Bank of the United States, which played a big role in regulating the economy. Founded in 1816 after the first National Bank's charter, or permit to do business, had expired, the Second Bank was a huge federal bank that held power over smaller banks. It controlled the nation's money supply and, by doing so, kept down **inflation**. Inflation is a decrease in the value of money that causes an increase in the price of goods and services. The Second Bank also provided loans to many people who wanted to buy property or launch businesses.

Jackson hated the Second Bank. For one thing, he didn't trust paper currency or any form of money other than gold or silver. For another, Jackson claimed that the bank, led by its president

Bank Notes

The $5,000 bank note (top) is a copy of one that Nicholas Biddle might have issued to customers taking out a loan. As you can see, the Second Bank used the name "Bank of the United States" on its paper currency.

The 6-cent note (below) is actually a political cartoon commenting on the extent to which money had lost its value after 1837. The bank that supposedly issued the note is the "Humbug Glory Bank"—*humbug* means "false or deceiving." And the images at the top of the note may symbolize Andrew Jackson. The donkey represents the Democratic Party to which Jackson belonged, and the hickory leaf may be a reference to his nickname: "Old Hickory."

Land Sales, 1836–1854

The graph shows the impact of the Panic of 1837 on land sales after the government required people to buy land with only gold and silver.

Source: United States Census Bureau

Nicholas Biddle, held a monopoly over all other banks. He thought its policies favored the wealthy over working people. Jackson may also have disliked the bank because it often made loans to members of Congress, possibly giving Biddle influence over the legislators.

The bank became a central issue during the 1832 election. The bank's charter was due to expire in 1836. Jackson's opponent in the 1832 election, National Republican Henry Clay, sponsored a bill to renew the bank's charter early. The bill passed in Congress, but Jackson **vetoed**, or rejected it— and beat Clay in the election.

When Jackson won the presidency in 1832, he believed his victory proved that the people supported his position on the bank. So in the four years that remained of its charter, Jackson waged an all-out war to destroy the bank. He had his treasury secretary withdraw government funds and deposit them in state banks. Jackson's opponents called these state banks his "pet banks." Biddle retaliated by withholding bank loans from customers, but his actions only turned more people against the bank. In time, Jackson got his way, and the Second Bank went out of business.

THE PANIC OF 1837

After the Second Bank closed, people flocked to Jackson's pet banks. These banks made it easier to take out loans. But this easy money led to inflation. During the last years of Jackson's presidency, he required that people use gold or silver to buy land rather than paper money as a way to fight the inflation.

Because the economy still seemed to be in good shape, Jackson's vice president, **Martin Van Buren**, easily won the presidential election in 1836. But within a few weeks of his inauguration, it became clear that the state banks were in trouble. Fear about the condition of the economy spread throughout the country. This widespread fear, or panic, became known as the **Panic of 1837**.

Panicked people ran to the banks to exchange their money for gold and silver, but the banks quickly ran out of the precious metals. When many of the banks closed, businesses collapsed and people lost their jobs and land. Soon, the country sank into a deep economic **depression**, or a period of slow economic activity. States no longer had enough money to finish public projects for developing infrastructure, such as building canals and roads. It wasn't the first depression the nation faced, and it wouldn't be the last. The country's economic problems did not improve during Van Buren's presidency, and he did little to try to resolve them. Van Buren's inaction made him unpopular with the people and set the stage for a change in government and politics.

HISTORICAL THINKING

1. **READING CHECK** Why did Jackson veto the bill to renew the National Bank's charter?

2. **ANALYZE CAUSE AND EFFECT** How did the Panic of 1837 affect the country economically and politically?

3. **INTERPRET GRAPHS** How would you describe land sales between 1836 and 1842?

3.2 A New Party System

When something isn't working, you probably want to change it—out with the old, in with the new. It often works that way in politics, too.

MAIN IDEA A new political party formed to oppose Jackson, and its candidate won the 1840 presidential election.

A CHANGE OF PARTIES

The old way of doing things definitely wasn't working in the United States in the late 1830s. While the economy slumped, the depression dragged on. Most of the factories in the East had let their workers go and closed down. Many of the unemployed in the cities went hungry and lived on the streets.

President Martin Van Buren didn't believe that government should interfere with the economy. But Jackson's old opponent, Senator Henry Clay, disagreed. He and Senator Daniel Webster claimed the government should step in and help fix the economic situation. Clay wanted the government to impose tariffs that would raise the price of imports and encourage Americans to buy domestically produced goods. He believed the federal government should fund infrastructure development by building a network of roads, canals, and railroads. Clay also

called for the establishment of a new national bank. His economic program was called the American System.

In 1834, senators Clay and Webster had formed a new political party, which they called the **Whig Party** after a British political group that had criticized the monarchy. Clay, Webster, and other opponents of Andrew Jackson chose the name because they believed Jackson had exceeded his powers as president. In fact, they often referred to him as "King Andrew." Unlike the Democrats, who supported an agrarian society, the Whigs promoted business and the expansion of industry.

Harrison Campaign Flag

Throughout the 1840 presidential campaign, the Whigs made much of William Henry Harrison's war experience 28 years earlier at the Battle of Tippecanoe, where he won a victory over the Shawnee. The party created this banner, combining a picture of Harrison with the American flag and a label underscoring his heroism at Tippecanoe.

THE ELECTION OF 1840

As the 1840 presidential election approached, the Whigs believed they had a good chance of winning it. Many Americans blamed the country's economic woes on Van Buren and seemed ready for a change. The Whigs nominated William Henry Harrison of Ohio as their candidate for president and **John Tyler** of Virginia as his running mate.

Harrison was a national figure because he had led U.S. Army troops against the Shawnee at the Battle of Tippecanoe in 1811. He'd also been a hero during the War of 1812. Making the most of Harrison's war experience, the Whigs came up with the catchy slogan "Tippecanoe and Tyler too."

Because Harrison lived on a farm, he also gained the reputation as a "common man" of the frontier. As a matter of fact, he came from a wealthy family. But that didn't stop the Whigs from including pictures of a rustic log cabin in banners and Harrison's campaign pamphlets. They also held parades, sang songs, and had their candidate go out on the campaign trail himself. Harrison was the first presidential candidate to do so.

Harrison narrowly defeated Van Buren in the 1840 election, but just 32 days after taking office, he died. He had delivered a long inaugural address—the longest on record—without wearing a hat or overcoat on a cold March day and came down with pneumonia.

Tyler took Harrison's place after his death but received little support from his party. Tyler's views were actually more in line with those of the Democrats. The Whigs had chosen him to attract southern voters. In time, they expelled him from the party and took to calling him "His Accidency." In spite of their differences, Tyler worked well with the mostly Whig Congress. During his single term in office, Tyler focused on strengthening the country by expanding and opening up the West.

DID YOU KNOW?

There is something unique and unusual about each of the presidents you have read about in this lesson.

Martin Van Buren

Eighth president

- First president to be born a U.S. citizen rather than a British subject
- Nicknamed "Old Kinderhook" for his hometown, Kinderhook, New York. The expression "OK" (or *okay*) came into use during his presidency.

William Henry Harrison

Ninth president

- President for only 32 days
- First president to die in office
- Attended medical school to become a doctor, but he could not afford the tuition after his father died. He dropped out and joined the military.

John Tyler

Became tenth president when William Henry Harrison died in office

- Only former U.S. president to side with the Confederacy in the Civil War
- Father of 14 children who lived into adulthood

HISTORICAL THINKING

1. **READING CHECK** Why were the Whigs in a good position to win the 1840 election?

2. **COMPARE AND CONTRAST** How did the agrarians' and the industrialists' views on the economy differ?

3. **MAKE INFERENCES** Why did the Whigs use pictures of a log cabin in Harrison's campaign?

VOCABULARY

Use each of the following vocabulary words in a sentence that shows an understanding of the term's meaning.

1. agrarian

   The economy of the South was mostly agrarian, or based on farming.

2. voting rights

3. depression

4. inflation

5. spoils system

6. doctrine of nullification

7. assimilate

8. truce

READING STRATEGY
COMPARE AND CONTRAST

If you haven't done so already, complete your diagram to compare and contrast the policies of Andrew Jackson and John Quincy Adams. List at least two policies to compare and contrast. Then answer the question.

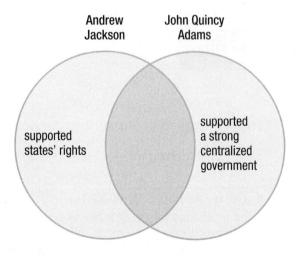

Andrew Jackson — John Quincy Adams

supported states' rights

supported a strong centralized government

9. What were some of the main policy differences between Jackson and Adams?

MAIN IDEAS

Answer the following questions. Support your answers with evidence from the chapter.

10. Why did Andrew Jackson think he had been robbed of the presidential election in 1824? **LESSON 1.1**

11. How does the spoils system work? **LESSON 1.2**

12. Why did Daniel Webster believe nullification would threaten the Union and freedom? **LESSON 1.3**

13. What two options did President Jackson offer Native Americans in the South? **LESSON 2.1**

14. What policy did the Indian Removal Act set in place? **LESSON 2.1**

15. How did the U.S. government trick Osceola? **LESSON 2.2**

16. What did John Ross hope to achieve by resisting the move west? **LESSON 2.3**

17. How did Andrew Jackson bring about the end of the Second Bank of the United States? **LESSON 3.1**

18. How did his opponents react to Andrew Jackson's transfer of funds out of the Second Bank? **LESSON 3.1**

19. What economic factors formed part of Henry Clay's American System? **LESSON 3.2**

HISTORICAL THINKING

Answer the following questions. Support your answers with evidence from the chapter.

20. **SYNTHESIZE** How did Andrew Jackson change the country?

21. **ANALYZE CAUSE AND EFFECT** How did Andrew Jackson's use of the spoils system lead to charges of corruption against him?

22. COMPARE AND CONTRAST In what ways were the rebellions of Black Hawk and the Cherokee similar and different?

23. MAKE CONNECTIONS John C. Calhoun applied the states' rights doctrine to prevent the country from breaking apart. When was states' rights first invoked, and what was it used to fight?

24. DISTINGUISH FACT AND OPINION Both Andrew Jackson and William Henry Harrison were said to represent the "common man." Did this label represent a fact or an opinion?

25. FORM AND SUPPORT OPINIONS Considering the legacy of Jackson's policies, do you think he lived up to his reputation as a hero for common people? Explain your answer.

INTERPRET MAPS

Study the map of the electoral college results for Andrew Jackson and John Quincy Adams in the 1828 presidential election. Then answer the questions that follow.

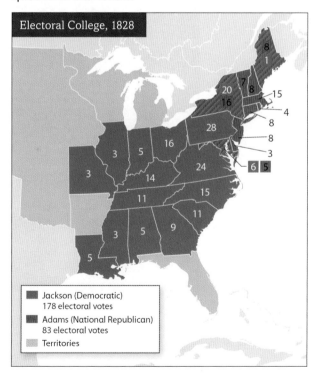

Electoral College, 1828

Jackson (Democratic)
178 electoral votes

Adams (National Republican)
83 electoral votes

Territories

26. Based on the map, what can you conclude about Jackson's victory?

27. Where did Adams gain votes and why?

ANALYZE SOURCES

In 1835, some Cherokee representatives signed, and Congress ratified, the Treaty of New Echota, in which the Cherokee sold all their lands east of the Mississippi River to the United States. The next year, Cherokee leader John Ross wrote a letter to Congress in response.

> Neither myself nor any other member of the regular delegation to Washington, can . . . ever recognize that paper as a Treaty, by assenting to its terms, or the mode of its execution. They are entirely inconsistent with the views of the Cherokee people. Three times have the Cherokee people formally and openly rejected conditions substantially [largely] the same as these. The Cherokee people, in two protests . . . spoke for themselves against the Treaty, even previous to its rejection by those whom they had selected to speak for them.

28. What does this excerpt tell you about Ross's opinion of the Treaty of New Echota?

CONNECT TO YOUR LIFE

29. EXPLANATORY This chapter describes many disputes among different groups of people. Think about disagreements you have had with others in your own life. How were they resolved? Make a connection between what you have learned about problem solving and how this information can be applied to resolve a dispute. Then write a paragraph in which you help two opposing groups overcome their dispute.

TIPS

- Fill in a problem-and-solution chart, listing the problem between the groups at the top, the steps for fixing the problem in the middle, and the plan's conclusion at the bottom.

- Include evidence and one or two vocabulary terms from the chapter.

- Conclude with a comment tying your suggested resolution of the argument to your own life.

CHAPTER 12

MANIFEST DESTINY
1821–1853

ESSENTIAL QUESTION
Why were Americans inspired to move west?

 The Golden City

SECTION 1 **Trails West**

KEY VOCABULARY

annex	individualism	pioneer
Continental Divide	manifest destiny	rendezvous
exodus	mountain men	wagon train

SECTION 2 **The Texas Revolution**

KEY VOCABULARY

margin   presidio   siege

SECTION 3 **The War with Mexico**

KEY VOCABULARY

contiguous	Gadsden Purchase	parallel
diplomat	insurrection	proviso

SECTION 4 **The California Gold Rush**

KEY VOCABULARY

boomtown	forty-niner	rancho
Californio	prospector	

AMERICAN GALLERY ONLINE **The Westward Trails**

READING STRATEGY

IDENTIFY MAIN IDEAS AND DETAILS
When you identify main ideas and details, you determine the most important idea in the text. Finding key details in the text helps you determine the main ideas they support. As you read the chapter, use an organizer like this one to record main ideas and details about the westward movement of Americans.

Main Idea:

Detail:

Detail:

Detail:

"We are the nation of
human progress."

—John L. O'Sullivan

CRITICAL VIEWING A stream winds through a valley in the Rocky Mountains of Colorado, presenting a wide-open vista for people looking for a new home. How does this photo convey the invitation many felt to move west in search of new lives and opportunities?

Three bodies of water surround San Francisco: the Pacific Ocean, the Golden Gate Strait, and the San Francisco Bay. How might the geography of this city influence its population?

THE GOLDEN CITY

San Francisco is a vibrant, modern city known for its unique coastal skyline, diverse neighborhoods, sweeping bridges, and notorious fog. It's the Golden City in the Golden State— a city "built on gold" during the 1848 California gold rush.

This nugget sparked the gold rush after
workers found it near Sutter's Mill in 1848.

It all started on January 24, 1848.
James Marshall set out to inspect the progress
his workers had made on a sawmill they were
building for John Sutter on the American River
near Coloma, California. Overnight, Marshall had
left a trickle of water flowing through the mill to
wash away some loose dirt and gravel. To his
great surprise, some bright flakes of gold were
left behind that morning. Shocked, Marshall
showed the gold to his crew, swearing them to
secrecy. He needed some time to process what
had just happened before he took action. He also
figured he'd better finish building Sutter's Mill.

But an exciting secret like that is impossible
to keep. The word spread quickly, and over
the next few years, hundreds of thousands
of people streamed into California hoping to
get rich. By 1856, around $465 million worth
of gold had been mined in California.

A MINER'S LIFE

The Americans who moved from the East
to California in 1849 in search of gold were
nicknamed the "forty-niners." Most of them came
with the plan to work hard for a short time, find
enough gold to get rich, and return home wealthy.

In reality, mining was then, and still is, brutally
hard work and very dangerous. During the gold
rush, supplies were extremely expensive because
the items were in such high demand. One
miner reported that pork cost $1.25, beans $1,
sugar $.75, and coffee $.50. That sounds pretty
reasonable until you realize that a dollar in 1850
was worth about $30 today. Most miners only
found enough gold to cover their expenses.

The dangerous and difficult nature of the work
caught many new miners by surprise. One of them,
William Swain, described his life in a letter to his
brother back in New York: "George, I tell you this
mining among the mountains is a dog's life."

CHALLENGES FOR IMMIGRANTS

William Swain was joined in his quest for gold
by thousands of immigrants from Mexico, Chile,
Peru, Germany, France, Turkey, China, and other
countries. In China, people dreaming of California
riches sometimes called the United States "the
gold mountain." By 1848, the first Chinese miners
began arriving in San Francisco, leaving behind
China's high taxes and farming challenges. The
arrival of so many different groups to California
shaped the diversity of this exciting new place.

As the number of immigrants grew and as the U.S.
economy weakened, the attitude of Americans
toward the immigrants became increasingly
resentful and discriminatory. In 1850, California's
government placed a $20 tax on each immigrant
miner—a tax American miners did not have to pay.

CRITICAL VIEWING Miners pause for a photo while sluicing, or separating gold from dirt by using water. Early gold rush photographs provide insight into the diversity of many mining operations. What can you observe about this team of sluicers?

The Chinese endured other tough penalties. In 1852, the government imposed another tax on Chinese miners. When California governor John Bigler suggested the wave of Chinese immigrants should be stopped, a Chinese man responded in the *Daily Alta California*: "The effect of your late message has been thus far to prejudice the public mind against my people, to enable those who wait [for] the opportunity to hunt them down, and rob them of the rewards of their toil."

Many of the Chinese men who came to California were literate and eager for new possibilities, but the state's increasingly hostile social climate made mining unwise—and unsafe—for them to continue. Forced out of mining, they found other work, building railroads and operating laundries and stores. Despite ongoing discrimination, thousands of Chinese immigrants stayed in California, seeking refuge in the San Francisco neighborhood known as Chinatown, and contributing greatly to the state's economy and culture.

Gold Rush Mine Locations

· Historic gold mine location

Marysville

Sacramento R.

Lake Tahoe

UTAH TERRITORY

Sacramento

Stockton

San Francisco · · Oakland

San Jose

San Joaquin R.

CALIFORNIA

NEW MEXICO TERRITORY

Tulare Lake

San Luis Obispo

Santa Barbara

PACIFIC OCEAN

Los Angeles

Colorado

San Diego

AMERICAN PLACES
Chinatown, San Francisco

Busy, colorful, and thriving, San Francisco's Chinatown is a testament to Chinese immigrants. United through heritage, culture, language, and economics, and living in a new and sometimes unwelcoming country, generations of Chinese immigrants established and still maintain a proud Chinese-American community.

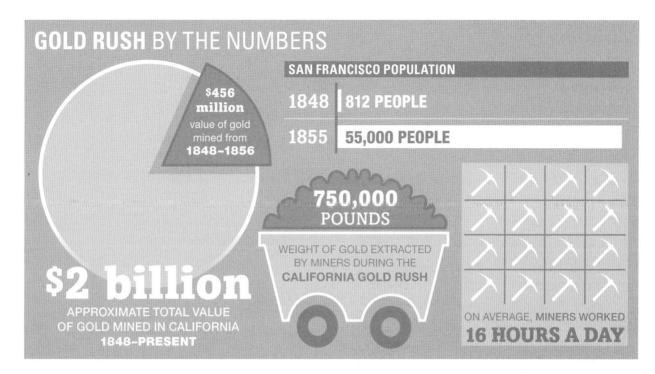

GOLD RUSH BY THE NUMBERS

$456 million
value of gold mined from **1848–1856**

$2 billion
APPROXIMATE TOTAL VALUE OF GOLD MINED IN CALIFORNIA **1848–PRESENT**

SAN FRANCISCO POPULATION

| 1848 | 812 PEOPLE |
| 1855 | 55,000 PEOPLE |

750,000 POUNDS
WEIGHT OF GOLD EXTRACTED BY MINERS DURING THE **CALIFORNIA GOLD RUSH**

ON AVERAGE, MINERS WORKED **16 HOURS A DAY**

NATIVE AMERICAN STRUGGLES

While many immigrants faced prejudice and opposition, the harshest treatment was reserved for the people who had been living in California all along. White miners used Native Americans for cheap labor and made them targets of violence. William Swain was upset by abuse against Native Americans that he witnessed, writing, "Such incidents have fallen under my notice that would make humanity weep and men disown their race." Historians estimate that around 150,000 Native Americans were living in California in 1848, but by 1870, fewer than 30,000 remained. Among the causes for the decline were starvation, violence, and diseases introduced by the miners.

A CITY ARISES

As the Native American population declined, populations of forty-niners and immigrants in northern California cities increased. In March of 1848, the *California Star* newspaper listed the city of San Francisco's population of non–Native Americans as 575 men, 177 women, 60 children— a total of 812 people. Within two years, the city's population had skyrocketed to more than 20,000.

San Francisco's natural wealth lay in its geography, a sheltered port on the Pacific Ocean. Immigrants and forty-niners arriving by ship passed through San Francisco, and many decided to stay. Clever businesspeople established shops, hotels, restaurants, and banks to accommodate the miners' needs, forming the base for what would evolve into a thriving local economy.

The money and people flooding into California also sped up the time it took for it to be granted statehood. In 1848, the federal government purchased the land that included California from Mexico as part of the treaty that ended the Mexican-American War. Just two short years later, California was admitted as the 31st state in the Union.

By the end of the 1850s, the gold rush had ended, but it had lasting effects. Like San Francisco, many cities that got their start during the gold rush still exist. And entrepreneurs who set up shop to sell goods to the miners established brands that are still familiar. In 1852, the bankers Henry Wells and William Fargo opened an office in San Francisco. Wells Fargo Bank remains one of America's top banking institutions. In the same year, Domingo Ghirardelli opened a sweet shop in San Francisco, launching the famous brand of chocolate many people enjoy today.

The California gold rush only lasted a few years, but it helped form a state and change a nation. California would play an increasingly significant role in the national economy.

THINK ABOUT IT

How did the California gold rush affect the economy and population of the United States?

EVERY WOMAN A QUEEN

Luzena Stanley Wilson

Luzena Stanley Wilson was one of the few women to travel to California during the gold rush. She, her husband, and their two young sons left their cabin in Missouri to head west in the spring of 1849. It wasn't long before Wilson got her first inkling that she could make money in California. A man offered to buy a biscuit from her, saying he would pay "$10 for bread made by a woman."

The Wilsons settled in Sacramento and opened a hotel where Luzena did the cooking. Again she found that many miners would pay a premium for a meal made by an experienced female cook. The Wilsons went on to own several successful hotels in different California cities. After Luzena's husband left the family in 1872, she moved to San Francisco and made a living buying and selling real estate. She died in that city in 1902, at the age of 83.

PRIMARY SOURCE

I was a queen. Any woman who had a womanly heart, who spoke a kindly, sympathetic word to the lonely, homesick men, was a queen, and lacked no honor which a subject could bestow. Women were scarce in those days. I lived six months in Sacramento and saw only two.

—from *Luzena Stanley Wilson '49er, Her Memoirs as Taken Down by Her Daughter in 1881,* by Correnah Wilson Wright, 1937

BODIE, CALIFORNIA: GHOST TOWN

Shortly after the initial gold rush, Bodie, California, became a thriving mining town and home to nearly 10,000 people. Now it's a ghost town, an abandoned place that has fallen into ruin after a natural disaster, war, or economic depression. An 1875 mine cave-in led to the discovery of gold in Bodie, which went from a town of a few dozen people to a bustling boomtown. Today it sits in a state of arrested decay, visited by tourists, tumbleweeds, and maybe an occasional ghost.

LONG TOM

Many independent miners used a device called a long tom to separate gold from the California dirt. The largest part of the long tom was a shallow wooden trough about 15 feet long. This had to be placed near a water source, because a steady stream of water needed to flow through it.

A miner would put gold-bearing dirt at the top of the trough. The water washed the dirt through a screen that removed larger rocks. Next, the water flowed into a shallow box with wooden riffles sticking up from the bottom. The gold flakes caught on the riffles while the water and the rest of the dirt flowed out of the box. Shoveling dirt into a long tom all day was back-breaking work.

CRITICAL VIEWING Museum volunteers, or docents, demonstrate the art of using a long tom in the American River in Coloma, California. Based on details you notice in the photo, how did long tom operators use forces of gravity and motion to separate gold from dirt?

HOW THE LONG TOM WORKS

DIRT AND GRAVEL IN
Miners pour pay dirt into the top of the long tom. Water washes over the dirt.

WATER IN

GOLD SEPARATES
Flowing water helps separate gold from rocks and dirt particles.

SCREEN

RIFFLE BOX

RIFFLES CATCH GOLD
Heavy gold flakes get caught in the riffles. Light dirt and sand wash away.

WATER OUT

SETTLING POND

1.1 The Pull of the West

If you had trouble finding work and heard about opportunities in a completely different part of the country, you just might pack up and move. That's exactly what settlers from the eastern half of the United States did in the 19th century. They packed up and moved west.

MAIN IDEA A tough economy and the promise of a rich and exciting future led Americans to look for opportunities in the West.

OPENING THE WEST

The boundaries of the nation shifted dramatically in the early 19th century, and the westward migration of easterners profoundly changed American culture. The West inspired ideals of **individualism**, or a self-reliant independence, and rugged frontier life that dramatically influenced our national self-image and sense of the American past.

In the early 19th century, Americans began to explore, move to, and live in the West. In 1806, Zebulon Pike led an expedition to discover the headwaters of the Arkansas River and was one of the first white men to explore the wilderness of Colorado. Many of these adventurous individuals were fur trappers and explorers, called **mountain men**. They spent most of their time in the wilderness trapping small animals for furs. Every summer from about 1825 to 1840, trappers met with fur traders at temporary markets called **rendezvous** (RAHN-deh-voo) to sell and buy goods and supplies. Trade opportunities like this were one of the economic incentives that drew people to the West.

Several mountain men became legendary. Kit Carson, a successful fur trapper in California, would later use his skills to guide U.S. Army officers in a war with Mexico. Another legend was **Jedediah Smith**. Smith had read of Lewis and Clark's expeditions and decided to explore the West for himself. He would eventually explore more of the unknown territory of the West than any other single person. In 1826, Smith crossed the Mojave (moh-HAH-vee) Desert into southern California. The next year, he hiked through California's high

A Seasoned Mountain Man

Jim Beckwourth's adventures took him from the Everglades of Florida to northern Mexico, southern Canada, and the Pacific coast. While exploring the West, he lived with a Crow tribe for several years. He was also a prospector and a U.S. Army scout, and he learned to overcome many challenges of the frontier.

As they moved west, Americans built new settlements. In this 1868 painting, *Across the Continent* by Frances Palmer, Native Americans on horseback watch from afar as excited settlers greet an incoming train.

mountains, the Sierra Nevada, and became the first white American to travel overland from the East to California and back. Another mountain man who explored the Sierra Nevada was **Jim Beckwourth**. He had been born into slavery but was set free when he was 25. In 1850, he discovered a mountain pass through the Sierra Nevada for settlers to follow as they traveled to northern California. Today, that pass is still called Beckwourth Pass.

The mountain men's explorations opened lands that had previously seemed inaccessible. After the Panic of 1837, many Americans faced economic difficulties. Newly explored lands in the West started to look attractive to unhappy easterners, new immigrants, independent women, and others who were seeking a new start.

MANIFEST DESTINY

In 1845, magazine editor John O'Sullivan wrote an editorial urging the United States to **annex**, or add, Texas as a state. He also wrote that Americans had a "**manifest destiny** to overspread and possess the whole of the continent." The word *manifest* means "obvious," and *destiny* refers to the unavoidable events of the future. The phrase, and the purpose underlying manifest destiny, reflected several cultural assumptions, including the certainty that the United States would—indeed, should—one day stretch from the Atlantic Ocean to the Pacific Ocean. Those who embraced

this concept were driven by more than just the promise of new opportunities. O'Sullivan's editorial described a belief that God intended for white Protestant Americans to take over the continent. Such an idea blatantly ignored the fact that there were already people living on these lands.

For several decades, the federal government pursued the territorial acquisition of western lands. The Oregon Territory promised timber, furs, and rich fisheries. California offered fertile farmland and abundant mineral resources, and both California and Oregon provided ports on the Pacific Ocean for seaboard merchants to ship and receive goods. Texas held deposits of minerals and metals, such as silver. The desire for riches and the belief in manifest destiny inspired settlers and politicians to move westward.

HISTORICAL THINKING

1. **READING CHECK** How did the concept of manifest destiny encourage Americans to move west?

2. **IDENTIFY MAIN IDEAS AND DETAILS** What natural resources served as economic incentives for people moving west?

3. **EVALUATE** Why might lands in the West have seemed inaccessible to many Americans?

1.2 Manifest Destiny

John O'Sullivan might have thought he was onto something when he coined the phrase "manifest destiny." However, he could not have predicted the impact that Americans' movement west would have on the nation's identity.

For the 19th-century Americans already considering moving westward, the idea of manifest destiny—that they had not only the right but also the responsibility to help expand the nation—was quite appealing. Settlers by the hundreds began crossing the Mississippi River and heading west.

John Gast's 1872 painting *American Progress* depicts the "spirit of America" as a goddess-like woman bathed in light and floating westward. She is leading **pioneers**, or people moving to a new and unfamiliar land, as they leave their settled lives and communities behind. The spirit carries a schoolbook, and she strings telegraph wire as she moves across the open land. Notice Gast's use of light and dark in this painting and how Native Americans and wildlife seem to react to the people headed their way.

CRITICAL VIEWING What do you notice about the direction the painting's subjects are facing? How does that reflect the concept of manifest destiny?

🏛 **Autry Museum of the American West, Los Angeles**

Gast painted *American Progress* just a few years after the end of the Civil War. In some ways, the painting's themes of modernization and new frontiers reflect a cultural desire to begin anew.

DOCUMENT ONE

Primary Source: Essay
from "The Great Nation of Futurity,"
by John L. O'Sullivan, 1839

The concept of manifest destiny originated in John L. O'Sullivan's essay about what he perceived as the great future for the United States.

CONSTRUCTED RESPONSE On what authorities does O'Sullivan rest his ideas about the "onward march" of the United States?

The expansive future is our arena. We are entering on its untrodden space, with the truths of God in our minds, beneficent objects in our hearts, and with a clear conscience unsullied by the past. We are the nation of human progress, and who will, what can, set limits to our onward march? Providence is with us, and no earthly power can. We point to the everlasting truth on the first page of our national declaration. In its magnificent domain of space and time, the nation of many nations is destined to manifest to mankind the excellence of divine principles.

DOCUMENT TWO

Primary Source: Artifact
Wheel from a covered wagon, wood and iron, c. 1830

The wheels on the covered wagons that carried the pioneers, like the wagon depicted in *American Progress* at left, were about four feet across. An iron band encircled the outside of the wheel, and iron strengthened the opening for the axle.

CONSTRUCTED RESPONSE What characteristics of the wheel can you see that make it suited to carrying a one-ton load more than 1,000 miles?

DOCUMENT THREE

Primary Source: Diary
from "The Letters and Journals of Narcissa Whitman,"
by Narcissa Whitman, 1836

Some of the first white settlers in the West were missionaries. Narcissa Whitman and her husband Marcus traveled to Oregon Country, hoping to spread Christianity among the Native Americans. Her diaries and letters home capture the experience of traveling the Oregon Trail and living in the Northwest. This excerpt is from July 27, 1836.

CONSTRUCTED RESPONSE How does Whitman describe the hardships of travel to the West?

We are still in a dangerous country; but our company is large enough for safety. Our cattle endure the journey remarkably well. They supply us with sufficient milk for our tea and coffee, which is indeed a luxury. Do not think I regret coming. No, far from it; I would not go back for a world. I am contented and happy, notwithstanding I sometimes get very hungry and weary. Have six week's steady journey before us. Feel sometimes as if it were a long time to be traveling. Long for rest, but must not murmur. Feel to pity the poor Indian women, who are continually traveling in this manner during their lives, and know no other comfort.

SYNTHESIZE & WRITE

1. **REVIEW** Review what you have learned about the cultural, geographic, and political context in which the idea of manifest destiny emerged.

2. **RECALL** On your own paper, write the main ideas about manifest destiny inspired by Gast's painting, the writings of O'Sullivan and Whitman, and the wagon wheel.

3. **CONSTRUCT** Construct a topic sentence that answers this question: In what ways did Americans incorporate the idea of manifest destiny into their decisions about moving west?

4. **WRITE** Using evidence from this chapter and the documents and artifact, write an informative paragraph that supports your topic sentence in Step 3.

1.3 Trails to the West

Think of times when you've had several choices in front of you. In the mid-19th century, westward-bound Americans had to decide which road—or, more accurately, which trail—they would take.

> **MAIN IDEA** Between 1841 and 1866, as many as a half million Americans followed trails to new lives in the West.

TRAVELING BY TRAIL

The story of one of the most important trails to the West begins in 1821, the year that Mexico won its independence from Spain. Under Spanish rule, trade with the United States had been heavily restricted. Mexico was eager to support individual land ownership and trade with the United States. Settlements at Santa Fe and Taos in the New Mexico territory, then part of Mexico, were ideally located for Mexican trade with the westernmost territories.

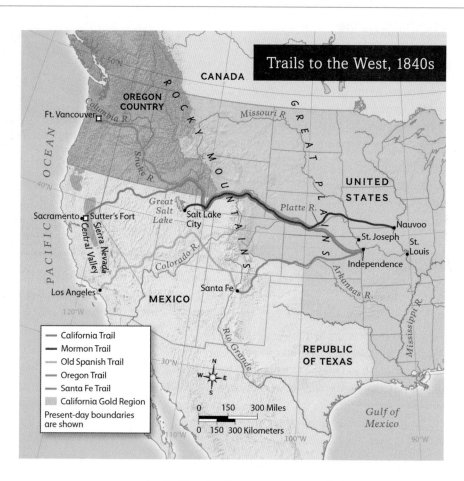

Trails to the West, 1840s

- California Trail
- Mormon Trail
- Old Spanish Trail
- Oregon Trail
- Santa Fe Trail
- California Gold Region

Present-day boundaries are shown

In 1822, a trader named William Becknell opened a new route that covered a distance of more than 900 miles from Independence, Missouri, to Santa Fe. Soon other traders began using this route, which became known as the **Santa Fe Trail**. They hauled their goods in caravans of covered wagons, similar to Conestoga wagons. Near the trail's western end, traders used a branch of the trail called the Cimarron Cutoff so they could avoid crossing the rugged Sangre de Cristo (SAHN-gray day KREE-stoh) Mountains.

From Santa Fe, traders traveled to the Pacific coast along the **Old Spanish Trail**, through territory controlled by Mexico. They brought Mexican woolen goods across the trail to trade for horses in California. Extending across high mountains and the scorching Mojave Desert, it was the most dangerous and difficult of the trails.

In the midst of building a new nation, Mexico struggled to govern its settlements along the American border, where traders and settlers from both countries lived. Cultural clashes over such issues as slavery—which had been outlawed in Mexico—were common.

The Santa Fe Trail represented only one of several important routes to the West. Independence was also the starting point for two other important trails. The **Oregon Trail** led to the Oregon Country in the Northwest. This region included the present-day states of Oregon, Washington, and Idaho as well as parts of Montana and the Canadian province of British Columbia.

In 1846, the United States and Great Britain signed a treaty setting the boundary between their territories In the Oregon Country. The treaty settled disputed land claims between the two nations, and the resulting stability encouraged even more American settlers to move to the **Oregon Territory**, the American portion of what had been Oregon Country. Between 1840 and 1860, from 300,000 to 400,000 Americans traveled the Oregon Trail. By 1860, about 52,000 people had settled in the new state of Oregon. Many settled in the fertile valley of the Willamette River located at the end of the trail.

THE MORMON TRAIL

Some trails were forged by people seeking new economic opportunities. But others were inspired by the religious faiths of the travelers. One of those was the **Mormon Trail**. In 1830, Joseph Smith founded the Mormon religion, the Church of Jesus Christ of Latter-day Saints, in New York. Smith and his followers moved west, establishing a community in Nauvoo, Illinois. There, because of the economic and political power they had achieved, they suffered harassment from their non-Mormon neighbors. When a mob killed Smith, the Mormons' new leader, **Brigham Young**, decided to move even farther west so that he and his fellow Mormons could practice their religion freely.

In 1846, Young led an **exodus**, or mass departure, of Mormons. They traveled westward until they reached the Missouri River near present-day Omaha, Nebraska. After wintering there, they continued west, sometimes following the Oregon Trail. When they neared the **Continental Divide**,

🏛 The National Museum of American History, Washington, D.C.

This sunstone carved from limestone is one of 30 that adorned the grand temple of the Church of Jesus Christ of Latter-day Saints, completed in 1846 in Nauvoo, Illinois, by architect William Weeks. Images of the sun, moon, and stars are important to Mormon symbolism and may pertain to the Old Testament story of Joseph. Joseph Smith said that a sun with a face like this had come to him in a vision.

the high point in the Rocky Mountains that divides the watersheds of the Atlantic and Pacific oceans, they headed southward into territory still owned by Mexico. After an arduous trek over the Rockies, they reached the Great Salt Lake. There, in present-day Utah, Young declared that they had reached their destination, and they established the community of Salt Lake City.

HISTORICAL THINKING

1. **READING CHECK** Where did the Santa Fe, Oregon, and Mormon trails begin and end?

2. **ANALYZE CAUSE AND EFFECT** Why did the Mormons move west from Illinois?

3. **INTERPRET MAPS** What major physical features did all or most of the trails shown on the map share?

1.4 Pioneers and Native Americans

Most people don't enjoy doing chores, even with the help of modern conveniences. Imagine how hard it was for families traveling along the Oregon Trail in the 1840s to prepare meals or wash clothes while also coping with illness and injuries in unfamiliar territory.

MAIN IDEA Pioneers who moved west endured hardships, and their encounters with Native Americans had profound effects on both cultures.

A DIFFICULT JOURNEY

Pioneers heading west usually traveled in groups of covered wagons called **wagon trains**. No matter the destination, the journey was grueling and took several months. Wagon trains crossed rivers and mountains as well as arid lands where water and vegetation were scarce. The long days demanded difficult chores and wearying travel.

Pioneers dealt with severe weather, including sandstorms, snowstorms, and floods. They also fought diseases such as cholera and typhoid. Because of the long distances between outposts, or settlements, running out of food, water, and supplies was a constant worry.

Pioneer women performed tasks such as cooking and cleaning. They also worked alongside men—tending to livestock, gathering supplies, and repairing tools and wagons. Everyone pitched in, no matter who they were or what job needed to be done.

Life on the frontier wagon trains changed conventional gender roles. Excerpts from men's and women's diaries and letters capture both the hope and excitement of seeing new lands, the day-to-day tasks they had to do, and the great losses and hardships endured on the trail. The journal entries below, of a man and a girl, describe very different pioneer experiences.

PRIMARY SOURCES

Today we met a large company, homeward bound. Some of our company purchased two milk cows from them. They say we never can get through, because there is no grass ahead, and the cholera is getting worse. Their wagons are crowded with sick men. Now our hearts began to fail us again and when we reflect that we have hardly made an introduction to our journey, the task becomes harder and we almost get weary of life.

—from "Journal of John Wood," by John Wood, 1852

One pleasant evening some Indian boys wanted to display their skill with bow and arrow. When we gave them a biscuit they would set it up, step off some distance and pierce it with an arrow. Father got a pan of biscuits and he would measure off a distance, set up one and tell them to shoot at it. The one who struck it first got it for his own. They had considerable sport over the biscuits.

—from *One Woman's West*, by Martha Gay Masterson, 1892

Like other mid-19th century painters, Albert Bierstadt depicted the splendor and beauty of the American landscape. He painted this work, *Oregon Trail*, around 1850. What details in this painting convey the challenges and adventures of life on the frontier?

CULTURAL ENCOUNTERS

Westward trails passed through lands inhabited by various Native American tribes. On the Great Plains, pioneers encountered the **Lakota**, and in the Oregon Territory they met the **Nez Perce**. Traders who traveled the Santa Fe Trail to the New Mexico territory interacted with southwestern tribes such as the **Zuni**.

The Lakota, Nez Perce, and Zuni had distinctive customs. Traditionally, the Lakota lived in tepees and hunted bison. The Nez Perce tended to settle along streams that provided a steady supply of food. Up to 30 families could live in one of their roomy lodges. The Zuni lived in adobe houses or dwellings built into cliffs.

Encountering Native Americans was a new experience for pioneers and for the people hearing about such encounters back home. In addition, works of fiction about westward journeys often exaggerated accounts of Native American attacks on pioneers. In reality, attacks were rare. Of the nearly 400,000 people who traveled the Oregon Trail in the mid-19th century, about 400 were killed in attacks by Native Americans. Most encounters were friendly, and Native Americans and settlers engaged in trade and sometimes helped each other.

Even so, as new settlers intruded on Native American land, conflicts did arise. In one instance, a cow wandered away from one of the pioneers traveling on the Oregon Trail and was killed by a Native American. U.S. Army soldiers intervened by talking to the Native American chief. At first everyone behaved reasonably, but misunderstandings and a nervous soldier shooting his gun led to a battle near Fort Laramie, a U.S. military post in present-day Wyoming. By the time it ended, the Native American chief and 29 American soldiers had been killed in what is referred to as the Grattan Massacre of 1854.

HISTORICAL THINKING

1. **READING CHECK** In general, what were interactions between pioneers and Native Americans like?

2. **IDENTIFY MAIN IDEAS AND DETAILS** What kinds of challenges did pioneers heading west in wagon trains face?

3. **EVALUATE** What do we learn about family life on the frontier from the letters and diaries of travelers moving west?

2.1 The Tejanos

When Mexico took control of the territory that later became Texas, the Mexican government was concerned about how few people lived there. The solution? Offer free land and hope people would move there.

MAIN IDEA After achieving independence from Spain, Mexico encouraged American settlement in the territory of Texas.

SPANISH TERRITORY

In the early 1800s, some westward-bound Americans ended up in Spanish territory. What we know today as the state of Texas used to be the Spanish territory called **Tejas** (TAY-hahs). In 1598, Spanish conquistador Juan de Oñate (oh-NYAH-tay) and his soldiers reached the Rio Grande. De Oñate claimed all the land around the river for Spain, leading to 200 years of Spanish rule.

Tejas lay north of the Nueces (noo-AY-suhs) River and extended into present-day Louisiana. Spain established missions throughout the area, starting with San Francisco de los Tejas. Catholic priests and missionaries moved to these missions in order to convert the Coahuiltecan (koh-uh-WEEL-tek-un) and the Caddo (KAH-doh) people. **Presidios**, or military settlements, surrounded most missions. Other Spanish settlers built farms close to the presidios.

Tejas shared a border with the United States. As a result, Spain worried about the influence its northern neighbor might have on the territory. Settlers of Spanish or Mexican descent, called **Tejanos** (tay-HAH-nohs), were forbidden to trade with other countries. Even so, many Americans entered the territory

illegally to do business with Tejanos. Spanish authorities pursued and arrested Americans who did so. Meanwhile, many Native Americans attacked Spanish settlements because they were resentful that Spain limited their chances to trade with the United States and suspicious of the actions of Spanish missionaries. Spain tried to maintain peace with Native Americans in Tejas because it wanted to remain in control of the region. But the Spanish were unable to bring about stability there.

Mexico, c. 1821

A bronze statue of a Tejano sitting astride his horse is part of the striking Tejano Monument, located on the grounds of the Texas state capitol in Austin. The monument honors the contributions of Tejanos and their roles in shaping Tejas—and eventually Texas.

LAND GRANTS AND SETTLERS

After an 11-year war, Mexico won its independence from Spain. As a result, in 1821, the Tejanos found themselves part of Mexico and no longer under Spanish rule. The new nation of Mexico included the lands that make up present-day Texas, New Mexico, Arizona, California, Nevada, and Utah, as well as parts of Colorado and Wyoming.

Few people lived in Tejas, and the Mexican government feared conflicts between Tejano settlements and Native Americans. Hoping that a larger population of settlers would stabilize the territory, Mexico encouraged American immigration and settlement and, unlike Spain, welcomed trade with Americans.

The Mexican government also gave land grants to American farmers and merchants. One American merchant received permission to form a colony even before Mexican independence. In 1820,

Moses Austin persuaded the Spanish governor to allow him to bring a few hundred families to settle in Tejas. He died a year later, before he could carry out his plan, but his son, **Stephen F. Austin**, inherited the land grant. Austin moved 300 American families into southeastern Tejas, establishing the territory's first legal American settlement. A rush of other American immigrants soon followed.

HISTORICAL THINKING

1. **READING CHECK** What influence did Mexican independence have on Americans' presence in Tejas?

2. **IDENTIFY MAIN IDEAS AND DETAILS** What did Mexico hope to accomplish through the land grants?

3. **INTERPRET MAPS** Based on details you notice on the map, describe the borders and territory of Mexico in 1821.

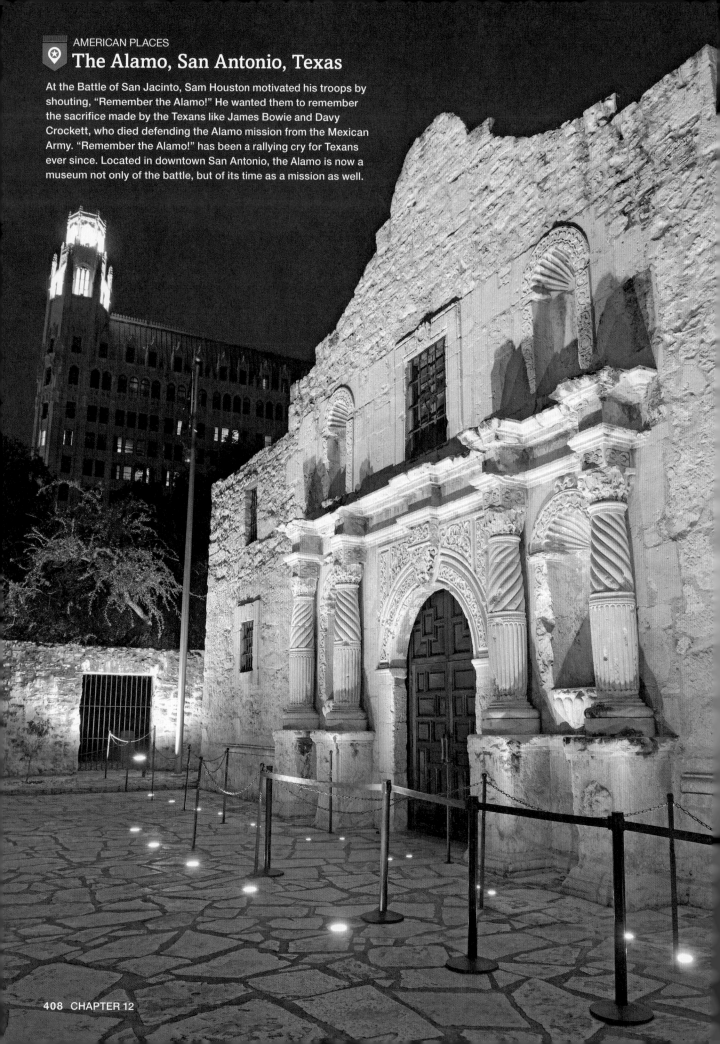

The Alamo, San Antonio, Texas

At the Battle of San Jacinto, Sam Houston motivated his troops by shouting, "Remember the Alamo!" He wanted them to remember the sacrifice made by the Texans like James Bowie and Davy Crockett, who died defending the Alamo mission from the Mexican Army. "Remember the Alamo!" has been a rallying cry for Texans ever since. Located in downtown San Antonio, the Alamo is now a museum not only of the battle, but of its time as a mission as well.

2.2 Settlement and Rebellion

Inviting new friends to your home for a party can sometimes lead to unexpected surprises. Mexico thought that inviting Americans to move to Texas would boost the population. It didn't anticipate what would happen next.

MAIN IDEA Cultural differences and disagreements with the Mexican government led Texans to declare independence from Mexico.

GROWING NUMBER OF SETTLERS

With the opportunity to own a great deal of land in exchange for a small fee, thousands of Americans arrived in Tejas—or Texas, as they called the territory—to take advantage of Mexico's settlement policies. Here, women were able to inherit land grants, and many owned and ran huge, profitable ranches. Women worked alongside men in the day-to-day operations of raising and selling livestock.

Texas quickly became a mix of cultures. Most American settlers were English-speaking Protestants, and the vast majority of Mexicans were Spanish-speaking Catholics. American settlers continued the practice of slavery in Texas, even though Mexico had outlawed slavery in 1829.

Though it had invited American settlement, the Mexican government grew concerned as the population of Texas became more American and less Mexican. By 1830, about 21,000 Americans lived there, including about 1,000 enslaved African Americans. On April 6, 1830, Mexico banned all further American settlement in Texas. Many European countries had already outlawed slavery, and the Mexican government hoped that a stronger European presence would encourage an end to the practice of slavery in the territory.

Texans—Americans and Tejanos alike—who disliked these changes called for more representation within the Mexican government. Revolts in 1832 and 1833 sent the message: Texans wanted Texas statehood within Mexico. General **Antonio López de Santa Anna**, who had recently become the president of Mexico, rejected this demand. Texans rebelled and the Texas War for Independence began.

TEXAS WAR FOR INDEPENDENCE

The war started in October 1835 with the Battle of Gonzales, a victory for Texas. More battles followed, and Santa Anna soon led an army from Mexico City to put down the rebellion. He reached San Antonio by mid-February 1836, where he encountered roughly 180 Texans guarding the **Alamo,** a mission building. For 13 days, 1,800 Mexican soldiers held the Alamo and its defenders under **siege**, which meant no one could leave or enter the building to bring food, supplies, or reinforcements. On March 2, Texans declared themselves a separate nation, the Republic of Texas. On March 6, the Mexican Army breached the Alamo's walls and killed almost everyone inside, including frontiersmen James Bowie, designer of the Bowie knife, and Davy Crockett, a U.S. congressman.

In response, on April 21, **Sam Houston**, the Texan Army's commander, attacked the Mexican Army near the San Jacinto River. He won the **Battle of San Jacinto** (sahn hah-SEEN-toh) and captured Santa Anna. Santa Anna agreed to withdraw and surrender. Texas had achieved independence.

HISTORICAL THINKING

1. **READING CHECK** Why did Texans want independence from Mexico?

2. **ANALYZE CAUSE AND EFFECT** How did the Texans' defeat at the Alamo affect the final outcome of the Texas War for Independence?

3. **DESCRIBE** What opportunities did Tejas offer women who settled and lived there?

2.3 Independence and Annexation

A "political football" is an issue that political opponents fight over. In 1836, the issue of annexing Texas became a political football in the United States, and it would be kicked back and forth for nearly a decade.

> **MAIN IDEA** The annexation of the Republic of Texas as the 28th state caused tension between northern and southern states.

THE LONE STAR REPUBLIC

After the Texas War for Independence, Texas became an independent nation, the Republic of Texas. Texans elected Sam Houston as their first president. The flag of Texas, with a single star, earned the nation the nickname of **Lone Star Republic**. As proud as they were of their victory, Texans knew they were vulnerable to further attacks from Mexico. They also lacked an established economy. Most Texans favored annexation by the United States.

The United States initially rejected this plan, however. In 1836 and 1837, President Andrew Jackson and his successor Martin Van Buren turned down Texas lawmakers' proposals. For one thing, they argued, annexing Texas would hurt American relations with Mexico and perhaps even lead to war. They also knew the American people were divided on the question, primarily because of the issue of slavery.

Before independence, Texas clashed with Mexico over slavery, which was prohibited by Mexican law. The ongoing use of enslaved labor in the Republic of Texas also became a concern for northern states in the United States. Admitting Texas as a state would upset the balance between states that had outlawed slavery and states where slavery was still practiced. Presidents Jackson and Van Buren argued that annexation was not in the best interest of the country.

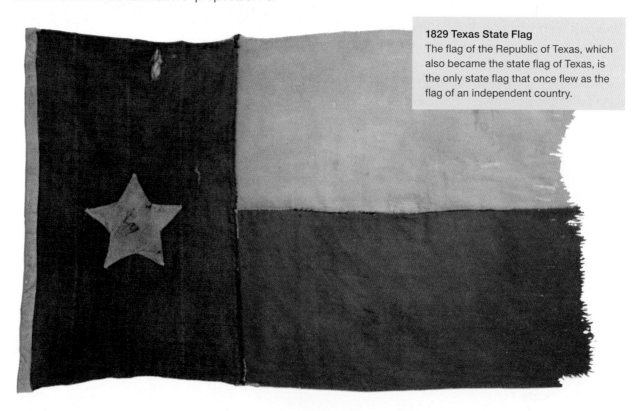

1829 Texas State Flag
The flag of the Republic of Texas, which also became the state flag of Texas, is the only state flag that once flew as the flag of an independent country.

A GLOBAL PERSPECTIVE In recent decades, some Texans have supported a movement for Texas to leave the United States and become an independent republic again. Proponents of this effort believe that the state gives too much power and money to the federal government. Some have compared these views with those advocated by "Brexit," the British movement that voted to leave the European Union (EU) in June 2016. The Texan movement earned a similar nickname, "Texit," a combination of the words *Texas* and *exit*. In this photo, campaigners for and against Brexit pass out flyers in London. What historical precedent might supporters of Texit cite as evidence that Texas should leave the United States?

ANNEXATION OF TEXAS

Texas remained independent for almost 10 years. Then, in 1844, annexation gained a supporter in the White House—**James K. Polk**. Polk had been the Speaker of the House and the governor of Tennessee, but he was not a superstar politician. When the Democrats nominated him for president in 1844, he was an unknown candidate who had little chance of winning. But despite running as an unknown against Henry Clay, the prominent Whig candidate, Polk won the presidency, barely, with 49.5 percent of the popular vote and an electoral college **margin**, or amount by which something is won or lost, of 170–105.

As president, Polk managed to turn his political ambitions into policy. He supported the ideas of manifest destiny and favored the annexation of Texas. He also believed that the United States should take complete control of the Oregon Territory, up to the latitude of 54° 40'. One of Polk's campaign slogans was "Fifty-four forty or fight!" Polk brought an enthusiasm to his presidency for expanding the country. Under his leadership, Texas became the 28th state.

HISTORICAL THINKING

1. **READING CHECK** What were the arguments against the annexation of Texas as a state?

2. **IDENTIFY MAIN IDEAS AND DETAILS** How was Polk's argument for annexation informed by the concept of manifest destiny?

3. **EVALUATE** What made James K. Polk an attractive but unlikely candidate for president?

2.4 Samuel "Sam" Houston
1793–1863

Antonio López de Santa Anna
1794–1876

"Santa Anna, living, can be of incalculable [great] benefit to Texas."—Sam Houston

Houston became known as the "George Washington of Texas." The city of Houston was named after him.

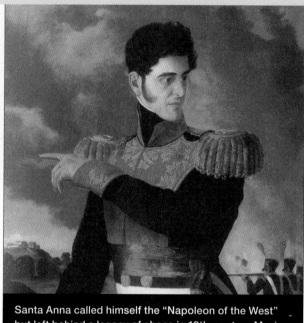

Santa Anna called himself the "Napoleon of the West" but left behind a legacy of chaos in 19th-century Mexico.

Not everyone agreed with Sam Houston about the value of Antonio López de Santa Anna's life. When the Texans won the Battle of San Jacinto, many of Houston's soldiers called for the Mexican leader's execution. After all, Santa Anna hadn't shown any mercy to the Texans at the Alamo. But Houston wanted independence for Texas—not revenge.

CONTRASTING PERSONALITIES

Houston and Santa Anna fought on opposite sides during the Texas War for Independence, but they had a number of things in common. Both pursued careers in the military and in politics. And, in the 1800s, both men were legends and dominant figures in the lands they loved—Houston in Texas and Santa Anna in Mexico.

But that's where the resemblance ended. Houston consistently demonstrated his loyalty and duty to the United States. He fought heroically in the War of 1812 under Andrew Jackson, whom Houston considered his mentor. It was Jackson

who encouraged Houston to enter politics. While living in Tennessee, Houston was first elected to Congress and later became governor of the state.

Santa Anna, on the other hand, often placed self-interest above duty, switching sides based on what was in it for him. He entered the Spanish army at 16 and fought with Spain when the war for Mexican independence broke out. (Mexico was a Spanish colony at that time.) But in 1821, Santa Anna shifted his loyalty and led the Mexican rebels to independence. As a reward, he was appointed governor of the Mexican state of Veracruz.

In 1833, the Mexican people elected Santa Anna president, but he soon lost interest in the office and left the real governing to his vice president. However, when the vice president began reforming the church, state, and army, Santa Anna was furious because the reforms threatened his interests. In response, he used military force to remove his vice president.

CRITICAL VIEWING During the Battle of San Jacinto, Houston was shot in the leg but continued to fight. In this painting by William Huddle, called *Surrender of Santa Anna*, Houston lies on a mat with his leg bandaged, while Santa Anna stands before him. Why do you think Houston's men surround Santa Anna?

CLASHING ARMIES

Resuming authority, Santa Anna introduced a less democratic form of government in Mexico and in Texas. The Texans became dissatisfied with their lack of freedom and, in 1835, began a revolution. They called on Houston, who had relocated to Texas, to lead the rebel force.

From the outset, the Texans were outnumbered. They suffered terrible defeats at the Alamo and in the Texas town of Goliad, where about 350 rebels were taken prisoner and executed. The Texans finally seized their chance in 1836 when Santa Anna and a small number of his soldiers arrived at San Jacinto. Houston organized a surprise attack and quickly overpowered the Mexican Army.

For a time after his embarrassing defeat, Santa Anna fell from favor in Mexico. He returned to power eventually, but as you'll see, American troops would once again bring about his downfall.

As for Houston, he became the first president of the Republic of Texas and served as senator after Texas achieved statehood. He'd just been elected its governor when a number of southern states voted to separate from the United States. When Houston refused to allow Texas to join the southern states, he was removed from office.

HISTORICAL THINKING

1. **READING CHECK** In which two areas did both Houston and Santa Anna pursue careers?

2. **COMPARE AND CONTRAST** How did Houston's treatment of the enemy in the Texas War for Independence differ from the way in which Santa Anna treated his prisoners?

3. **EVALUATE** In what way did Santa Anna's character and judgment affect Texas and Mexico?

2.5 San Jacinto Museum of History La Porte, Texas

III

A museum with a unique location, the San Jacinto is housed in the base of the San Jacinto Monument. It was established as a steward of history to honor those who fought in the Texas War for Independence from Mexico and showcase the history of Texas and the Spanish Southwest. Visitors can view art and artifacts from the Spanish conquest, Spanish colonial life, the Mexican Revolution, the colonization of Mexican Texas, early Texas statehood, and the Civil War. What can you infer about the relationship between Mexico and Texas by examining the artifacts below?

Mexican Badge

This heavy brass badge, likely worn by a soldier in the Mexican Army, features the Mexican military insignia, an eagle perched on a cactus plant. The streamer beneath the eagle's talons reads: "LIBERTAD MEXICANA" (Mexican freedom).

Texas Army Bowie Knife

Alamo hero and knife-fighter Jim Bowie knew what he wanted in a knife. He worked with blacksmiths to create knives like this one that had curved blades and cross-guards to protect hands. It was a handy weapon, useful for hunting, digging, or cutting down trees, as well as in hand-to-hand combat.

Soldiers sharpened the curve on the top of the blade, called a clip point, to inflict a more serious wound as the knife was pulled out.

Santa Anna's Knee Buckle

In the late 1700s, many men wore knee buckles to secure their short pants, or breeches, at the knee. This buckle has 22 square diamonds, a handsome design, and an impressive history. Santa Anna gave this buckle to Sam Houston after Houston defeated him in the Battle of San Jacinto. Historians agree Santa Anna was a strong leader with a dynamic personality, but he also lacked principles and loved military glory, which often led Mexico down the wrong path.

Notice this pistol's unusual octagon-shaped barrel.

Texas Army Percussion Pistol

This wood and brass pistol belonged to Euclid M. Cox, who used it during the 1838 Battle Creek Massacre. A group of 25 Texan surveyors, who were studying the land for its settlement potential, encountered 300 members of the Kickapoo tribe. After failing to heed a warning to leave, the Texans were ambushed. Only seven survived.

Do you think this sword belt would have been a practical accessory? Why or why not?

Texas Army Military Sword Belt

A sword belt like this one, made of gold braid and maroon leather, was an important part of a soldier's uniform. This one belonged to Thomas Jefferson Chambers of the Texas Army. The belt's decorative round buckle is trimmed with leaves and berries and has a silver, five-pointed star set in the center. The two chains attached to the belt end in hooks that Chambers would have fastened to his sword's scabbard, or sheath.

3.1 Tensions with Mexico

When you heat water in a teakettle, pressure builds until the water reaches the boiling point. In the 1840s, tensions between the United States and Mexico reached their boiling point: war.

MAIN IDEA The annexation of Texas upset the balance of slave and free states and led to the Mexican-American War.

POLK'S MISSION

James K. Polk was a firm believer in the concept of manifest destiny. When he became president in 1844, he focused on territorial expansion, including the annexation of Texas and the acquisition of California and Oregon. Southerners favored Polk because of his plans to annex Texas. Since slavery had long been practiced there, Texas would join the Union as a slave state. This infuriated northerners because it meant that slave states would outnumber free states. The threat of an unequal number of slave and free states had already reared its head in 1820, with Missouri's request to become a state. The political firestorm that ensued led to a solution in the Missouri Compromise. That solution proved to be temporary, as Congress voted to annex Texas as a new slave state in 1845.

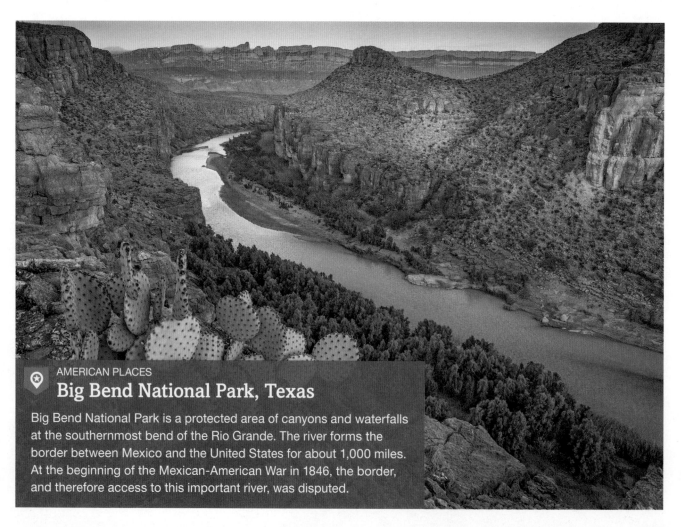

AMERICAN PLACES
Big Bend National Park, Texas

Big Bend National Park is a protected area of canyons and waterfalls at the southernmost bend of the Rio Grande. The river forms the border between Mexico and the United States for about 1,000 miles. At the beginning of the Mexican-American War in 1846, the border, and therefore access to this important river, was disputed.

CROSSING THE NUECES RIVER

Relations between the United States and Mexico had been tense since the creation of the Republic of Texas. Mexican president Antonio López de Santa Anna had signed the Treaties of Velasco, giving Texas its independence, but the Mexican government never formally acknowledged the treaties as legal. Santa Anna had signed the treaties while he was a prisoner of the Texan Army, they argued, and therefore Texas was still a part of Mexico. Given this history, it's not surprising that Texas's annexation further worsened relations between the United States and Mexico.

At the time, Texas extended only as far south as the Nueces River. President Polk insisted that Texas's southern border should be the Rio Grande, much farther south than the Nueces. In July 1845, Polk sent American troops, led by General **Zachary Taylor**, to secure the area between the Rio Grande and the Nueces River. Polk also sent John Slidell, a **diplomat**, or person sent to represent a country, to Mexico City with an offer. Texas would extend to the Rio Grande, and the United States would buy California for $25 million. The Mexican government refused to negotiate.

Hearing about the snub, Polk told Taylor to advance on the Rio Grande. A skirmish between American and Mexican troops near the river gave Polk the excuse he needed to call for war. In an address to Congress, he declared that Mexico "has invaded our territory and shed American blood upon American soil." Even the Whigs, who had wanted to avoid conflict with Mexico, gave in. The **Mexican-American War** started on May 13, 1846.

Although Congress voted overwhelmingly in favor of the war, many Americans opposed Polk's tactics. Notable New Englanders, including John Quincy Adams and James Russell Lowell, claimed the war was a scheme to expand slavery. Henry David Thoreau even landed in jail when he refused to pay taxes to support the war. Abraham Lincoln, then a young congressman from Illinois, agreed with the New Englanders. He demanded an answer from Polk about "the particular spot of soil on which the blood of our citizens was so shed." Despite the protests, the United States remained at war with Mexico for more than a year.

Dallas Historical Society
Dallas, Texas

Zachary Taylor is memorialized as the king of diamonds on this 19th-century playing card. He is wearing a bicorn hat and elaborate epaulettes, or shoulder ornaments—both of which were typical of American and European military officers beginning in the 1790s.

HISTORICAL THINKING

1. **READING CHECK** What did President Polk want from Mexico, and how did the president of Mexico respond?

2. **IDENTIFY MAIN IDEAS AND DETAILS** What were the causes of the Mexican-American War?

3. **EVALUATE** How did President Polk use emotion to persuade Congress to vote for war with Mexico?

3.2 The United States at War

California's state flag features an unusual combination of items: a grizzly bear, a lone red star, and the words "California Republic." The history of this unique flag stems from an event that took place in the 1840s.

MAIN IDEA The United States took control of New Mexico and California after forcing Mexico to surrender at the end of the Mexican-American War.

TERRITORIAL SETTLEMENTS

Despite some Americans' opposition to the Mexican-American War, the United States had the upper hand from the start. On August 18, 1846, General **Stephen Kearny** and his troops marched into Santa Fe, the capital of the New Mexico Territory. They had expected to face strong opposition from Mexican troops and militia, but they found the city unguarded. For unknown reasons, Santa Fe's Mexican governor, Manuel Armijo (ahr-MEE-hoh), had decided not to fight. The United States claimed the New Mexico Territory without a single soldier firing a weapon.

Meanwhile, dramatic events unfolded in California. On June 14, 1846, American settlers took over the town of Sonoma and declared their independence from Mexico. They declared that their land was now the Republic of California. Because of their flag—which featured a grizzly bear— their **insurrection**, or rebellion, would become known as the **Bear Flag Revolt**. American explorer and survey expedition leader **John C. Frémont** headed to Sonoma, where he gave his support to the settlers.

The Republic of California, with Frémont as its elected leader, had a very short life, however. The insurrection had been carried out by a group of settlers who were not connected with, or acting under orders from, the U.S. government. Within days, American forces took control of the area and claimed California for the United States. In August 1846, the U.S. Army also captured the city of Los Angeles, and by November, the conquest was complete.

By 1847, the United States controlled all of California and New Mexico. American military leaders then turned toward Mexico itself. The Mexican Army was busy in the California and New Mexico territories, leaving strategic Mexican cities vulnerable to attack.

State of California Flag
The present-day state flag of California is much like the one used by the California battalion that supported the U.S. Army in taking control of California. It includes the same elements as the Bear Flag of that battalion. The grizzly bear symbolizes strength, the star stands for independence, and the red color represents courage.

CRITICAL VIEWING In this 1847 color print, artist Christian Mayr depicts one of the more dramatic events of the Mexican-American War: General Scott's entrance into Mexico City. Based on what you see in the print, how does the artist represent people's reception of Scott and his troops?

INVADING MEXICO

Zachary Taylor, the leader of the troops that had crossed the Nueces River to spark the war, had enjoyed some success near the Rio Grande. Taylor now entered Mexico, pursuing retreating Mexican troops. He fought Santa Anna at Buena Vista in 1847. Though the battle seemed to be an even fight, Santa Anna withdrew his troops, and Taylor now controlled northern Mexico.

Because Taylor was reluctant to mount a large-scale invasion of Mexico, Polk changed the American strategy. He ordered General **Winfield Scott** to take his troops to Mexico by sea. Scott and his men landed at Veracruz, which they captured after a three-week siege. They then fought their way toward the capital, Mexico City.

After another fierce battle on the outskirts of the city, American troops entered the capital. In September 1847, Scott gained control of Mexico City and raised the flag of the United States.

Mexico had surrendered and the war was over, but politicians were divided about what to do with the conquered territory. Some wanted the United States to claim all of the territory conquered in the war, while others wanted to claim only the disputed territories. Some politicians argued that the United States should claim no territory at all. Any treaty between the United States and Mexico would have to settle this debate.

HISTORICAL THINKING

1. **READING CHECK** What was the Bear Flag Revolt?

2. **EXPLAIN** How did the battles over New Mexico and California territories give the U.S. Army an advantage?

3. **DRAW CONCLUSIONS** Why did some politicians argue that the United States should not claim any territory in Mexico?

3.3 Consequences of the War

Restless Americans dreaming of new opportunities set westward expansion in motion. Then the United States seized vast new western territories in a war with Mexico. Some Americans' dream of manifest destiny seemed to be coming true.

MAIN IDEA After a series of treaties, land purchases, and international agreements, the United States stretched from the Atlantic to the Pacific.

OCEAN TO OCEAN

With the fall of Mexico City, the United States had won the Mexican-American War. The war officially ended in February 1848, when the United States and Mexico signed the **Treaty of Guadalupe Hidalgo**. The treaty set the Rio Grande as the border between Texas and Mexico and, in exchange for $15 million, Mexico gave up its northernmost territories. These territories included present-day California, Nevada, and Utah, as well as parts of Arizona, New Mexico, Colorado, and Wyoming. Upon the signing of the treaty, tens of thousands of people who had previously considered themselves Mexicans became Americans overnight.

The United States now stretched from the Atlantic Ocean to the Pacific Ocean. But the victory over Mexico aggravated an already looming problem.

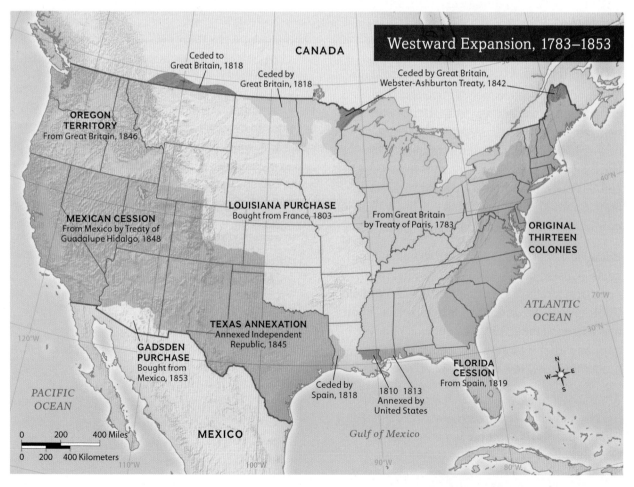

Westward Expansion, 1783–1853

The addition of so much land only worsened conflicts over slavery. The new territories were not part of the Missouri Compromise. What would happen when they gained enough population to become states? Would these states be free states or slave states?

While the Mexican-American War was still in progress, Representative David Wilmot of Pennsylvania introduced a plan called the **Wilmot Proviso**. A **proviso** is a condition attached to a legal document or legislation. The Wilmot Proviso was originally attached to a bill meant to pay for a portion of the Mexican-American War. It called for slavery to be barred from any territory gained from the Mexican-American War. President Polk and other pro-slavery southerners opposed this plan and offered an alternate proposal: to extend the Missouri Compromise line westward. Slavery would be allowed in territories south of the line and prohibited in territories north of it. The Wilmot Proviso passed several times in the House of Representatives but not in the Senate. Without passage of this proviso into law, the subject of slavery in new states remained a major concern.

NEW BORDERS, NORTH AND SOUTH

At the same time the United States was adding land in the West, it began to clash with Great Britain over land in the Northwest: the Oregon Territory. Fortunately, diplomacy, not war, ended this conflict. Lawmakers from the United States and Britain agreed to a compromise, setting the northern border of the United States at the 49th **parallel**, or line of latitude, located 49° N of the equator.

Another puzzle piece of American territory fell into place in 1853, when Mexico sold the United States a sliver of land located along the southern edges of present-day Arizona and New Mexico. This $10 million deal, called the **Gadsden Purchase**, granted the United States land it needed to

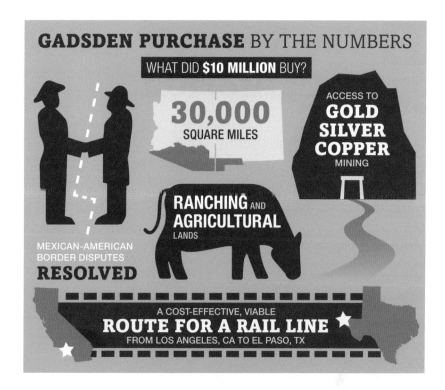

GADSDEN PURCHASE BY THE NUMBERS

WHAT DID **$10 MILLION** BUY?

30,000 SQUARE MILES

ACCESS TO **GOLD SILVER COPPER** MINING

RANCHING AND **AGRICULTURAL** LANDS

MEXICAN-AMERICAN BORDER DISPUTES **RESOLVED**

A COST-EFFECTIVE, VIABLE **ROUTE FOR A RAIL LINE** FROM LOS ANGELES, CA TO EL PASO, TX

complete a southern transcontinental railroad. It also completed the borders of the **contiguous**, or connected, United States.

The Mexican-American War led to a monumental increase in the size of the United States and an important addition to American culture and identity. For generations, Mexican Americans have contributed to and shaped the United States, and their culture has particularly deep roots in the region that once belonged to Spain and Mexico. Place names throughout the Southwest reflect their Hispanic heritage, and Mexican cultural traditions shape life and identity in many southwestern communities. Spanish and Mexican people and their descendants also played a large role in California's story as it moved toward statehood.

HISTORICAL THINKING

1. **READING CHECK** What events finalized the borders of the western United States?

2. **IDENTIFY MAIN IDEAS AND DETAILS** Why did each acquisition of new territory renew conflicts over slavery?

3. **INTERPRET MAPS** Locate present-day state borders on the map. How many states or parts of states were added to U.S. territory between 1803 and 1853?

4.1 The Spanish and Mexicans in California

Maps tell us about geography, but they also tell us about history. Just look at a map of California, and you'll see names such as Los Angeles, Palo Alto, and Sierra Nevada—evidence of a past rooted in Spanish culture.

MAIN IDEA Long before the United States acquired California, Spanish and Mexican settlers were founding missions and settlements there.

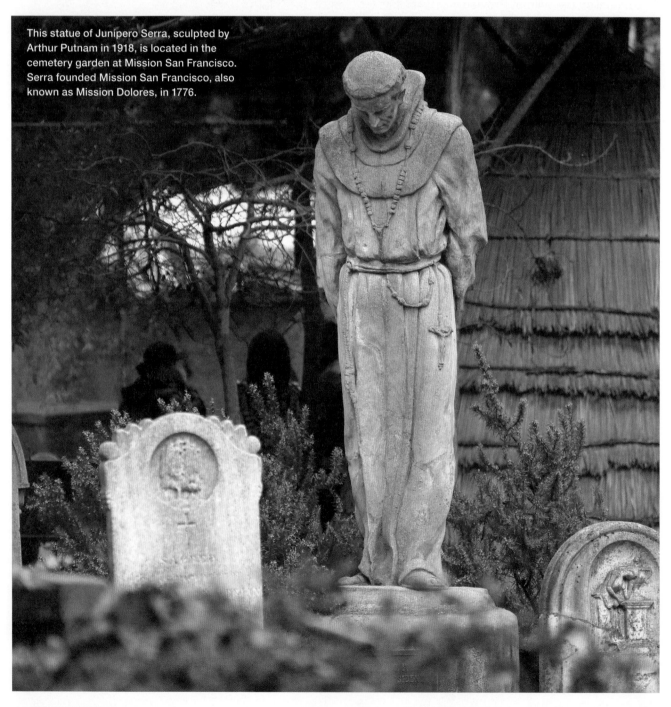

This statue of Junípero Serra, sculpted by Arthur Putnam in 1918, is located in the cemetery garden at Mission San Francisco. Serra founded Mission San Francisco, also known as Mission Dolores, in 1776.

SPANISH MISSIONS IN CALIFORNIA

As you have read, Spanish conquistadors first explored and claimed the area that is now California in the 16th century. The Spanish were slow to settle in California. The colonial government considered California too far north from its base in Mexico for the region to be a priority. In the 1700s, however, British and Russian fur traders expanded westward into the region to take advantage of the land's natural resources. As a defensive measure, Spain sent an expedition to establish communities in southern California in 1769.

One member of the expedition was **Father Junípero Serra** (hoo-NEE-peh-roh SEH-rah), a Catholic priest from Spain. Serra founded the first mission in California at San Diego. His relationship to the Native Americans he sought to convert to Christianity is still the subject of controversy. Some historians see him as a courageous and generous man who worked hard to improve Native American lives. Others point to his participation in the mistreatment and enslavement of Native Americans.

Over time, the Spanish established 21 missions in California. The names of these missions echo the cities that eventually grew up around them, such as San Francisco, Santa Clara, and San Luis Obispo.

The mission system itself was complicated. Mission residents established farms on the nearby lands and tried to convert Native Americans to Christianity. Spanish treatment of Native Americans was often cruel. Many settlers exploited and enslaved Native Americans they encountered near their farms. They pushed thousands of Native Americans off their land and forced hundreds of others to live and work at the missions.

MEXICAN RULE OF CALIFORNIA

When Mexico gained independence from Spain in 1821, California was one of the new nation's northernmost territories. Because of its enormous size and its great distance from Mexico City, California was difficult for Mexico to rule. As in Texas, the local Mexican government was often ineffective and corrupt.

In 1824, Mexico passed an act that granted land to settlers in the form of large estates. These land grants became new estates, called **ranchos**, which consisted of sprawling tracts of land covering thousands of acres. The ranchos formed the basis of the economy of the Mexican settlements in the region. The rancheros, or owners, raised huge herds of cattle and traded hides and the processed fat of the cattle for manufactured goods along the Pacific coast.

The economy expanded as American traders, trappers, farmers, and businesspeople moved into the territory in the decades after Mexican independence. Some received land grants for ranchos or other parcels of land.

One of these new settlers was a Swiss immigrant named **John Sutter**, who received several land grants from the Mexican government to start a colony. In 1843, he built what became known as Sutter's Fort, a huge, high-walled adobe structure at the future site of Sacramento. Sutter kept herds of cattle like other California rancheros, but he also helped diversify the region's economy and agriculture by raising grapes and wheat.

By 1848, Americans who had moved to California accounted for more than half of its non-Native American population. They faced a government they felt did not represent them, and as a result, the Americans entertained the idea of independence from Mexico.

They got their wish with the signing of the Treaty of Guadalupe Hidalgo in 1848. The United States acquired California just in time for an amazing discovery at a sawmill that John Sutter was building in the foothills of the Sierra Nevada.

HISTORICAL THINKING

1. **READING CHECK** Why did the Spanish establish communities in California?

2. **COMPARE AND CONTRAST** How were the histories of Texas and California alike under the rule of Spain and Mexico?

3. **IDENTIFY MAIN IDEAS AND DETAILS** How did the California economy change as American settlers received land grants?

4.2 The Gold Rush

A fever of sorts broke out in the late 1840s. Victims from all around the world quit their jobs, left their families, and set off on long, dangerous journeys. The "illness" they suffered from? Gold fever.

MAIN IDEA The discovery of gold in California in 1848 led to a boom in population and wealth.

EUREKA!

By the late 1840s, Sutter's Fort had become a thriving farm community. Various new projects were underway, including the construction of a sawmill upstream on the American River. You might recall from the American Story in this chapter that this was where workers spotted a few flecks of gold on January 24, 1848. Sutter swore the workers to secrecy, but the word soon got out. The next few years would be chaos for Sutter. His men immediately stopped working, abandoned the colony, and went hunting for gold instead.

At first, **prospectors**, or people in search of valuable resources in the earth, found a wealth of gold deposits that were easy to access. They struck gold by digging into hills or mountainsides, or by panning in rivers or streams. Panning involves using a shallow pan to scoop up gravel from the bed of a stream, dipping the pan in the stream to collect some water, and swishing the water around to wash away dirt, clay, and silt. Heavier materials, including particles of gold, remain in the pan.

When prospectors struck gold, they yelled "Eureka!" *Eureka* is an ancient Greek word that means "I have found it." During the California gold rush, shouts of "Eureka!" expressed the thrill and excitement accompanying the discovery of riches. The word was so closely associated with the gold rush that it would become the California state motto.

News of the gold discovery spread to the East Coast and then around the world. Thousands of people bitten by the "gold bug" began heading west to strike it rich.

CRITICAL VIEWING In 1858, George W. Northrup posed as a prospector for a photo to send home to his family in Minnesota. He is holding a pickaxe, a hoe, a pan, and two pistols. Note that he also has a bag labeled "gold" on his lap. What image do you think Northrup was trying to convey by posing in this way?

PATENT RIVETED CLOTHING

The Best in USE FOR

FARMERS, Mechanics AND MINERS

LEVI STRAUSS & CO, SAN FRANCISCO, CAL.

Levi Strauss's Blue Jeans

One merchant who became rich during the gold rush was **Levi Strauss**. A German immigrant, he arrived in San Francisco in 1850. His goal was to manufacture tents and wagon covers for miners. But after noticing a demand for durable work pants, he began producing trousers made from the tent canvas he had purchased.

People loved the pants. Strauss sold enough to open a factory and started to produce the pants using a denim cloth known as *gênes* in French. Levi Strauss invented blue jeans and founded a company and a unique American brand.

THE FORTY-NINERS

By the following year, around 80,000 new gold-seekers had moved to California. They earned the nickname **forty-niners** because they arrived in 1849. The forty-niners came from all over the United States and the world. Consequently, the mining towns that sprang up to house and feed the forty-niners included diverse mixes of nationalities and cultures. Because slavery was not commonly practiced in California, many free African Americans decided to try their luck in the gold fields. Thousands of immigrants also arrived from China.

Most of the fortune-seekers were single men who hoped to find riches quickly and move on. Others headed to California with plans to settle there permanently. Whether they struck gold or not, many ended up staying. The boom in population created opportunities for all kinds of settlers. With a bit of creativity and business knowledge, people could make a fortune providing goods and services to the miners and other new residents of California.

However, the gold rush did not have a positive impact on everyone. Many people who had long lived in California found their livelihoods destroyed. **Californios**, or residents of Spanish or Mexican descent, had thrived on California's abundant farmland and prosperous ranchos. Newcomers to the area did not respect Californios' customs or legal rights, and in some cases they seized Californios' property. In addition, thousands of Native Americans died at the hands of gold miners or from the diseases that they and other settlers brought into the region.

California's population increased quite rapidly because of the gold rush. Before 1848, about 1,000 non-native people lived there. By the end of 1849, that number reached nearly 100,000. Even though most of the easily found gold deposits had been depleted by then, more fortune-seekers arrived each day. With that fast-growing population came a need for the laws and government that statehood could provide.

HISTORICAL THINKING

1. **READING CHECK** How did the California gold rush start?

2. **ANALYZE CAUSE AND EFFECT** In what ways did the discovery of gold and the migration of the forty-niners affect Californios and others who had long lived in California?

3. **SUMMARIZE** How did the population of California change, and why?

4.3 The Mining Frontier

It's 1849 and you've journeyed to California to hunt for gold. You dreamed of adventure and riches, but the living and working conditions are miserable. Worst of all, you haven't found a speck of gold!

MAIN IDEA A population boom and growing lawlessness caused by the gold rush led to the demand for California statehood.

LIFE IN A MINING CAMP

When 100,000 people crowd into the same region within a short period of time, there are bound to be problems. Few of the single men who rushed west to search for gold were interested in building stable communities. A region that had been mostly rural was suddenly covered with **boomtowns**, or mining camps that grew into crowded towns overnight. These boomtowns had neither strong leadership nor government of any kind. Law enforcement could not keep up with the boomtowns of the gold rush. Thieves and swindlers often got richer than gold miners. Bored miners living far from home spent their free time gambling and fighting with each other.

As you have read, many westward moving pioneers arrived in wagon trains on overland trails. But others decided to travel by ship. Starting on the East Coast, they sailed southward around Cape Horn at the southernmost tip of South America, and then back north to California. Overland trips took from four to six months, and the Cape Horn route took about six months.

Immigrants arrived from many countries, including Chile, Mexico, and China. San Francisco's location made it particularly accessible for people crossing the Pacific Ocean. Immigrants from China were the most numerous. Many settled in California permanently, even though they had not planned on doing so initially.

As a result, these newly established communities included people who spoke different languages, had different customs, and practiced different religions. Sometimes, cultural differences led to misunderstandings or even violence. Among white Americans, prejudices against Native Americans, African Americans, and Chinese immigrants often boiled over into fights. When gold discoveries slowed down, competition for the dwindling gold became more intense. Tensions increased, and so did crime.

Women who moved to boomtowns were far outnumbered by men and faced many challenges. In addition to the hard labor typical of living in a frontier region, they also handled domestic duties for their households. To make extra money, some even took on housekeeping tasks for single men living around them. Many women discovered a liberating independence in California because they could make a good living there. In this frontier region, few laws existed to prohibit women from owning property or businesses. Women opened profitable boarding houses, taverns, and other businesses that catered to the populations of the mining camps. Others tried their luck at mining, and a few even struck gold.

STATEHOOD FOR CALIFORNIA

Many American territories waited years before achieving statehood, but not California. With its population booming and lawlessness plaguing its mining camps, California needed a strong government right away. Since it now easily met the population requirements, many people felt that it was time for California to become a state.

In 1849, territory leaders met at a convention in Monterey to draft a constitution and to make a plan to petition the federal government for statehood. California's first constitution prohibited

San Francisco, 1848

The California gold rush transformed the small mission of San Francisco into a thriving, vibrant city. Between 1848 and 1849, its population rose from 1,000 to 25,000. By 1860, the city had more than 50,000 people. The top illustration shows the city before the gold rush. The bottom lithograph, by the French illustrator Auguste-Victor Deroy, captures the city as he saw it in 1860. How do these two illustrations show how the landscape of San Francisco changed as more people arrived?

San Francisco, 1860

slavery. However, it did not grant civil rights to all of the state's nonwhite or female populations. Like the nation's other states at this time, California's constitution granted only white men the highest level of legal rights and protections.

In September 1850, less than two years after Sutter's workers glimpsed those first specks of gold in a Sierra mountain stream, California became the 31st state. Not surprisingly, its admission as a free state heightened the crisis over slavery that was already threatening to tear the country apart.

HISTORICAL THINKING

1. **READING CHECK** How did the gold rush lead to California's application for statehood?

2. **IDENTIFY MAIN IDEAS AND DETAILS** What opportunities were women able to pursue during the gold rush, and why?

3. **EVALUATE** Did the leaders at the 1849 California constitutional convention support ideas of freedom and equality? Support your response with evidence from the text.

MANIFEST DESTINY

VOCABULARY

Use each of the following vocabulary words in a sentence that shows an understanding of the term's meaning.

1. exodus
    The hurricane warning prompted an exodus of thousands of people from their coastal communities.

2. presidio
3. prospector
4. annex
5. proviso
6. rancho
7. insurrection
8. siege

READING STRATEGY
IDENTIFY MAIN IDEAS AND DETAILS

If you haven't done so already, complete your chart to identify details about Americans' westward movement. Then answer the question.

Main Idea:
Detail:
Detail:
Detail:

9. What factors drove Americans west between 1821 and 1853?

MAIN IDEAS

Answer the following questions. Support your answers with evidence from the chapter.

10. How did the concept of manifest destiny contribute to American expansion? **LESSON 1.1**

11. What groups traveled on the Santa Fe, Oregon, and Mormon Trails? **LESSON 1.3**

12. Why did the Mexican government encourage American settlement in Texas? **LESSON 2.1**

13. Describe the events and outcome of the Battle of the Alamo. **LESSON 2.2**

14. What was James K. Polk's stance on the concept of manifest destiny? **LESSON 2.3**

15. What was the significance of American troops crossing the Nueces River in 1845? **LESSON 3.1**

16. Who participated in the Bear Flag Revolt, and why? **LESSON 3.2**

17. What were the consequences of the Mexican-American War? **LESSON 3.3**

18. Who were the forty-niners? **LESSON 4.2**

19. What did California's first constitution say about slavery? **LESSON 4.3**

HISTORICAL THINKING

Answer the following questions. Support your answers with evidence from the chapter.

20. **IDENTIFY PROBLEMS AND SOLUTIONS** Why did the expansion of the United States create new problems regarding slavery?

21. **MAKE GENERALIZATIONS** How did the ideals of individualism and rugged frontier life shape American identity during the 1800s?

22. **DRAW CONCLUSIONS** Why did the Mexican government regret encouraging American settlement in Texas?

23. **DESCRIBE** In what ways had the borders of the United States changed by the 1850s?

24. **EVALUATE** How did the gold rush provide new opportunities for women, immigrants, and free African Americans?

Look closely at the map of the Mexican-American War. Then answer the questions that follow.

25. What was the final battle of the war, and when did it take place?

26. Based on the map, what type of war were the Mexicans fighting? Explain the reasons for your response.

27. Using the map scale, about what was the greatest distance from the United States that any battle was fought?

28. Which military expedition followed the Gila River? Why might it have done so?

Mexican-American War, 1846–1848

ANALYZE SOURCES

William Gilpin was an explorer, an author, and the first governor of the Colorado Territory. He wrote reports for the government, including "The Untransacted Destiny of the American People" for a U.S. Senate committee in 1846. Read the following excerpt from his report.

29. How were Gilpin's claims similar to President Polk's goals for the United States?

30. What does Gilpin mean when he says that the destiny of Americans is to "subdue the continent?"

Two centuries have rolled over our race upon this continent. From nothing we have become 20,000,000. From nothing we are grown to be . . . the first among nations existing or in history. So much is our destiny—so far, up to this time—transacted, accomplished, certain, and not to be disputed. The untransacted [unfinished] destiny of the American people is to subdue the continent—to rush over this vast field to the Pacific Ocean.

CONNECT TO YOUR LIFE

31. ARGUMENT Think about the way the West represented a new frontier for Americans in the 1800s. Also think about the motivations of pioneers who moved west. Then consider what kinds of frontiers inspire the same kind of exploration today. Identify one present-day frontier that you would like to explore and write a paragraph that presents an argument for exploring the new frontier. In your argument, take into account new technologies and skills that you might need to explore the frontier.

TIPS

- Look back at the chapter and list ways in which expansion affected the United States during the 1800s. Then think about how present-day frontiers inspire exploration today. Make notes and then review them to help you craft your argument.

- Support your argument with examples of similarities and differences. Use evidence from the text and two or three key terms from the chapter to make your claims.

- Conclude your paragraph by restating your argument and summarizing your reasoning.

CHAPTER

13

THE CHANGING AMERICAN
IDENTITY
1830–1860

ESSENTIAL QUESTION
How did immigration and reform influence
American identity?

 AMERICAN STORIES **The Underground Railroad**

SECTION 1 **The Immigrant Experience**
KEY VOCABULARY

assimilate	famine	prejudice
blight	immigrate	push-pull factor
domestic service	Know-Nothing party	steerage
emigrate	nativist	

SECTION 2 **Reforming American Society**
KEY VOCABULARY

asylum	revival meeting
common school movement	Second Great Awakening
craft union	temperance movement
evangelize	transcendentalism
labor union	

SECTION 3 **Abolition and Women's Rights**
KEY VOCABULARY

abolitionist	suffrage
emancipation	Underground Railroad
Seneca Falls Convention	

 AMERICAN **GALLERY**
ONLINE   **Women's Rights**

READING STRATEGY

SYNTHESIZE
When you synthesize, you
combine related ideas into
a single idea, a synthesis.
As you read the chapter,
use a chart like this one
to synthesize ideas about
the ways American identity
changed between 1830
and 1860.

"I went to the woods because I wished to **live deliberately.**"

—Henry David Thoreau

The calm waters of Walden Pond, a lake located in Concord, Massachusetts, reflect the light of sunset. For two years in the 1840s, Henry David Thoreau lived in a cabin at Walden Pond. He wanted to live simply, in nature. His book *Walden*, published in 1854, is based on his years at Walden Pond.

"I think slavery is the next thing to hell."
—Harriet Tubman

CRITICAL VIEWING African-American artist Jacob Lawrence captured the spirit of the Underground Railroad in his moody, nighttime painting called *Forward Together*. Harriet Tubman is believed to be the figure wearing the red cloak on the right. How many other people can you find in the painting?

THE UNDERGROUND
RAILROAD

"When I found I had crossed that line, I looked at my hands to see if I was the same person. There was such a glory over everything; the sun came like gold through trees, and over the fields, and I felt like I was in Heaven."

—Harriet Tubman

CRITICAL VIEWING Based on details in this photograph, what would you infer about photographic practices in the late 1800s?

If you didn't know better,

you might think the Underground Railroad was similar to a city subway. In reality, this amazing railroad never had a single mile of track. In the years before the Civil War, the Underground Railroad was a path to freedom for enslaved African Americans, and its most famous conductor was Harriet Tubman.

Tubman was born into slavery with a different name—Araminta Ross—around 1822 in Dorchester County, Maryland. Minty, as she was called, was first put to work at five years old. By the time she was seven years old, she was cleaning her master's house and taking care of the family's baby. Throughout her childhood and youth, Minty was forced to do difficult jobs, both indoors and out in the fields. She was poorly fed and often beaten by her masters. However, hard work and cruel punishments never crushed Minty's independent nature.

In 1844, Minty married John Tubman, a free black man living in Maryland. Despite her marriage to a free man, she remained enslaved. That meant she could be sold to another owner far from her husband, possibly in the South where conditions for slaves were even worse.

In 1849, Minty learned that she might be sold, so she resolved to flee to Pennsylvania, the free state north of Maryland. As part of her escape, she changed her name to Harriet Tubman. Harriet was her mother's name; Tubman, of course, was her husband's. John Tubman chose to stay in Dorchester County, so Harriet was left to make the risky journey to freedom on her own.

One of the people who helped Tubman escape was a Quaker woman. As you have read, Quakers believed that all people, regardless of skin color, were created equal and that slavery was wrong. This unnamed woman sheltered Tubman for a night and helped her enter the Underground Railroad.

A DIFFERENT KIND OF RAILROAD

The Underground Railroad had no trains, nor was it a single path to freedom. Instead, it was a network of ways that enslaved people could escape to the northern states or Canada. An Underground Railroad "station" was a home or other building in which escaped slaves could take shelter and hide. "Conductors" risked their lives to guide groups of fugitive slaves on the perilous trek from the South and help them navigate the railroad's hidden network.

Because the Underground Railroad operated in deep secrecy, nobody knows exactly how many enslaved people it brought to freedom. One estimate is that around 100,000 people made their way to freedom and safety via the Underground Railroad between 1810 and 1860. Although there were some white supporters of the Underground Railroad, such as the Quakers, free African Americans in the North played the most active role in operating the Underground Railroad. And one of them was Harriet Tubman.

SINGING TO FREEDOM

Escaping slaves needed a secret way to communicate with each other and their conductors. Often they passed messages through songs with a religious theme, called spirituals. Singing while they worked was a tradition among enslaved people, so owners did not suspect an escape was underway when they heard them singing. Harriet Tubman told her biographer that she used the spirituals "Go Down Moses" and "Bound for the Promised Land" to signal to groups of fugitives when they should take cover and when it was safe to come out. "Wade in the Water" was another spiritual used by conductors to communicate with their groups. It was an instruction to jump into a river or stream to shake off possible pursuers.

PRIMARY SOURCE

Wade in the Water. God's gonna trouble the water.
Who are those children all dressed in Red?
God's gonna trouble the water.
Must be the ones that Moses led.
God's gonna trouble the water.

Who are those children all dressed in White?
God's gonna trouble the water.
Must be the ones of the Israelites.
God's gonna trouble the water.

Who are those children all dressed in Blue?
God's gonna trouble the water.
Must be the ones that made it through.
God's gonna trouble the water.

Chorus: *Wade in the Water, wade in the water children.*

THE CODE OF THE RAILROAD

The Underground Railroad used code words to conceal its operations from slave catchers. Several of the code words had their origins in the Bible. Moses—Harriet Tubman's code name—was especially appropriate, because she had a deep faith.

GOSPEL TRAIN the Underground Railroad	**HEAVEN** Canada, freedom
STATION home or other building where slaves could take shelter and hide	**BUNDLES OF WOOD** a group of fugitives that was expected at a station
STATION MASTER person who owned a station and told fugitives how to get to the next station	**STOCKHOLDER** person who donated money, food, or clothing to help the escaping slaves
AGENT person who planned the courses of escapes and contacted the helpers	**LOAD OF POTATOES** fugitives hidden under fruits or vegetables in a farm wagon
MOSES Harriet Tubman (in the Bible, prophet who helped the Israelites escape slavery in Egypt)	**RIVER JORDAN** the Ohio River (a river in Southwest Asia, mentioned in the Bible)

"I was the conductor of the Underground Railroad for eight years, and I can say what most conductors can't say — I never ran my train off the track and I never lost a passenger."

—Harriet Tubman

CRITICAL VIEWING After the Civil War, Harriet Tubman returned to the home she had purchased in Auburn, New York, and began the next phase of her work: caring for elderly African Americans. This photo from c. 1885 shows Tubman (far left) with friends, family members, and some of the aged people she cared for in Auburn. Based on this image and information you have read about Tubman, what conclusions can you draw about the nature of her work and the tasks that motivated and interested her?

CONDUCTOR AND HERO

Once she successfully made her own escape, Tubman decided her family and other slaves should also be free. For her, the best way to do that was to become a conductor herself.

Being a conductor required courage, intelligence, and nerves of steel. Slave catchers were always on the lookout for fugitives. Hired by slave owners to capture escaped slaves, the slave catchers, or bounty hunters as they were sometimes called, were not afraid to use force.

Quick thinking and tough, Tubman was up to the task. According to her own recollections, Tubman made around 19 trips back into Maryland and rescued up to 300 slaves, including her own parents. She gave directions to at least 70 more slaves so they could make their own escapes. Harriet Tubman was one of the most important faces of the Underground Railroad.

When the Civil War broke out, Tubman found other ways to help African Americans and support the Union Army. She worked as a nurse, aiding sick and wounded Union soldiers and escaped slaves. She also acted as spy, passing unnoticed in southern territory disguised as a slave. In 1863, she helped lead Union soldiers and African-American scouts in a raid on the Combahee River in South Carolina. The raid freed over 750 slaves.

After the Civil War, Tubman moved to Auburn, New York, but she did not retire from her mission to help others. She raised money to support schools for freed slaves in the South, participated in antislavery meetings, and campaigned for women's right to vote. She also established a home for elderly and disabled African Americans.

On March 10, 1913, Harriet Tubman died of pneumonia. She was buried in Fort Hill Cemetery in Auburn, New York, with full military honors.

THINK ABOUT IT

Do you think "Underground Railroad" is an appropriate name for the network to aid fugitive slaves? Why or why not? What might such a network be named today?

QUILTED CODES?

Some historians theorize quilts similar to these may have been used to communicate with enslaved people waiting to escape, or with those on the path to freedom. For example, a pattern like the Wagon Wheel could have been hung by seamstresses on plantations. A pattern like the Log Cabin could have been a welcome sight for weary travelers.

The patterns on this quilt may have been used as "maps" for escapees.

The **WAGON WHEEL** design may have told escapees to pack for traveling. It also could have meant escapees would be hiding in a wagon with a secret compartment.

Similar to the Wagon Wheel, the **TUMBLING BLOCKS** pattern might have announced a conductor was in the area, so it was time to pack for the journey.

The **BOW TIE** design could have meant escapees should wear disguises when they journeyed on the Underground Railroad.

The **BEAR PAW** pattern advised passengers to take a hidden path made by bear tracks, which would lead to water and food.

Like the Bow Tie pattern, the **BRITCHES**, or pants, pattern may have told escapees to dress like free people.

The **CROSSROADS** block represented the city of Cleveland, Ohio, one of the main corridors of the Underground Railroad.

The simple design of the **LOG CABIN** may have indicated that a home was a safe house, or a place where escapees could rest.

The floral pattern of the **ROSE WREATH** might have been an announcement that someone had died along the journey to freedom.

HARRIET TUBMAN ON THE $20 BILL?

In 2016, Treasury Secretary Jacob Lew announced his plan to replace President Andrew Jackson with Harriet Tubman on the $20 bill in 2020. However, a new administration entered the White House in 2017. Its leaders suggested they might block the plan or place Tubman on a $2 bill.

1.1 The Lure of America

Imagine sleeping in a small bed in a cramped room on a ship bound for New York City. The sea is rough. You try to ignore how sick you feel. Instead, you think about the new life you will make in America.

> **MAIN IDEA** In the mid-1800s, millions of people from around the world left their homelands and moved to the United States.

PUSH AND PULL

When groups of people decide to move to a new country, they consider two types of reasons for the move. Some reasons push, or encourage people to **emigrate**, or leave their home countries. Other reasons pull, or encourage people to **immigrate**, or move to another country. Together, these reasons are known as **push-pull factors**.

Throughout history, crop failures, overpopulation, religious persecution, and wars have pushed people from their homelands. Immigrants usually chose to move to countries with plenty of land to farm, a better economy, and freedoms that appealed to them. For example, the Pilgrims' disagreements with the Church of England pushed them to leave England. Available land, the chance to earn a living, and the opportunity to practice their religion freely pulled them to North America. In every century that has followed, the promise of a better life has pulled immigrants to the United States from around the world.

Between 1840 and 1870, more than 7.5 million immigrants came to the United States. That's more people than the total U.S. population in 1810. Wars in Europe acted as a push factor on the people there. At the same time, the United States continued to exert pull factors on people experiencing hardship across the oceans.

LOOKING FOR OPPORTUNITIES

As you have read, in 1848, word spread in newspapers around the world that miners had discovered gold in California. Many Chinese men emigrated from China, in hopes of finding work in the American West.

Chinese men weren't the only people to immigrate to the United States or its territories to build new lives. Immigrants from northern Europe—including Britain, Ireland, Germany, and Scandinavia—also traveled across the ocean alone or with their families. Their journeys were often difficult. Many immigrants could only afford to travel in **steerage**, a small, confined space between the main decks of the ship. Steerage class was

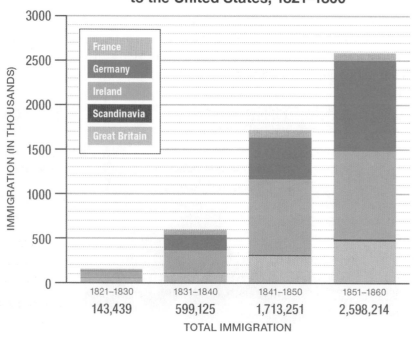

European Immigration to the United States, 1821–1860

IMMIGRATION (IN THOUSANDS)

Legend:
- France
- Germany
- Ireland
- Scandinavia
- Great Britain

1821–1830	1831–1840	1841–1850	1851–1860
143,439	599,125	1,713,251	2,598,214

TOTAL IMMIGRATION

Source: Department of Homeland Security

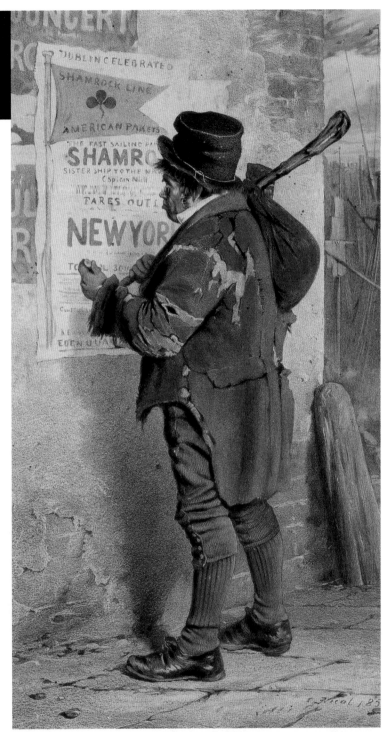

an inexpensive way to travel. However, it was crowded and dark, with almost no comforts. Steerage passengers had to bring mattresses, cooking pots, and even their own food for the voyage. Travelers in steerage class also dealt with rats, lice, and fleas during the journey. Seasickness and other illnesses made the area smelly, unpleasant, and unsanitary. Disease could spread rapidly, which was a problem because any illness put immigrants at risk for rejection when they reached the United States.

As new industries expanded in the northeastern United States, immigrants became an important source of labor. They arrived ready to take whatever work they could find in order to survive. The many job opportunities and the established immigrant population of large American cities encouraged many newcomers to stay in the city of their arrival. In fact, New York City had a large immigration center, called Castle Garden, which accepted new immigrants into the country. Immigrants joined with others from their home countries, and they established neighborhoods where people shared similar customs and traditions and spoke the same language. These neighborhoods grew and became vibrant parts of American culture.

The United States welcomed immigrants throughout the 19th and 20th centuries. Some immigrants decided to uproot their families because they hoped for new opportunities. Others wanted to escape a bleak future, or simply to feed their families.

HISTORICAL THINKING

1. **READING CHECK** Name two push-pull factors that drove mass immigration in the mid-1800s.

2. **ANALYZE GRAPHS** According to the graph, when did the largest number of Irish immigrants move to the United States?

3. **SYNTHESIZE** How do push factors and pull factors work together?

1.2 From Different Countries

You can probably think of a time when you were assigned a tough or boring task you didn't want to do. For some immigrants, only the hardest, lowest-paid work was available when they arrived in their new country.

MAIN IDEA Many immigrants came to the United States to escape food shortages and political conflicts in their home countries.

ESCAPING DISEASE AND POVERTY

Between the 1830s and 1860s, Irish immigrants represented the largest number of newcomers to the United States. Most were poor farmers who had no opportunities to improve their lives in their homeland. For centuries, Britain had claimed sovereignty over Ireland, and many of the Irish were dissatisfied with the oppression of British rule. To make matters worse, the country was experiencing widespread starvation due to the Great Irish Famine. A **famine** is an extreme shortage of food. From 1845 to 1852, a plant disease called **blight** killed the country's entire potato crop. The famine was made worse by the system of farming imposed by the British, because British landlords took what little food the Irish were able to farm. Approximately 1 million people died before the famine was over. For these reasons, or push factors, Irish immigrants came to the United States in record numbers.

Opportunities for jobs and new beginnings were pull factors for many Irish immigrants. American

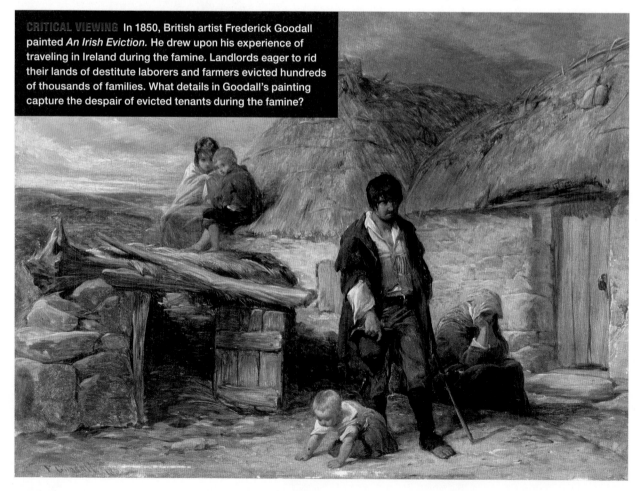

CRITICAL VIEWING In 1850, British artist Frederick Goodall painted *An Irish Eviction.* He drew upon his experience of traveling in Ireland during the famine. Landlords eager to rid their lands of destitute laborers and farmers evicted hundreds of thousands of families. What details in Goodall's painting capture the despair of evicted tenants during the famine?

business owners recruited Irish immigrants because they would work for lower wages than many American workers. While skilled workers such as carpenters or bakers could earn adequate wages, most Irish men were unskilled. They found jobs building railroads, digging canals, and loading cargo onto ships. The work was difficult, dangerous, and paid the lowest wages. For Irish women, unskilled labor meant **domestic service**, or housework in another person's home. Maids and kitchen servants received about a dollar a day in 1870, which was better pay than most factories offered. Plus, domestic service often included food and housing.

Immigrants brought their possessions in large trunks. This handmade wooden trunk with rope handles belonged to a Swedish immigrant.

British immigrants didn't flee from famine, but they did hope to escape from the rigid British class system. Just as in Irish society, few opportunities existed for British farmers to avoid living in poverty. From their perspective, owning inexpensive and fertile American land was a chance at a whole new, and likely better, life.

When they arrived in the United States, most British and Irish immigrants wanted to **assimilate**, or become part of, their new country. But they also held on to their culture and traditions. In the neighborhoods where they lived close to each other, they formed groups and clubs and attended community dances, meals, and church services together. Preserving and maintaining many of their customs and traditions offered a relief from the strain of assimilation.

MOVING TO THE MIDWEST

Poverty and hunger were not the only push factors that affected immigrants. Civil unrest, or open conflict within a society, also encouraged people to leave their home countries. For example, in the middle of the 19th century, areas in Germany experienced a series of revolutions. As a result, many Germans fled to the United States.

German immigrants differed in some ways from other groups of immigrants. One difference was that Germans held diverse religious beliefs. Most German immigrants were Protestants, but some were also Catholics or Jews. Unlike those who came to escape poverty and famine, many German

immigrants were not poor and did not have to travel in steerage. They could afford to continue traveling after they arrived in the country, oftentimes choosing to settle in the farmland between the present-day states of Nebraska and Minnesota. So many of them settled in this region, in fact, that the area became known as the "German Belt."

Especially after the 1860s, immigrants from Sweden, Norway, and Denmark joined the Germans in the upper Midwest. The population of Sweden was growing, farmland was scarce, and the same potato blight that hit Ireland struck Sweden around 1868. Some Swedes and other Scandinavian immigrants sought land in the United States. Others came for the growing number of well-paid factory jobs in midwestern cities such as Chicago and Minneapolis. Immigration increased the population and enriched the culture of the United States, but not all Americans welcomed the newcomers.

HISTORICAL THINKING

1. **READING CHECK** What factors prompted people to emigrate from their home countries?

2. **SYNTHESIZE** What pull factor drew so many different groups to the United States between 1830 and 1860?

3. **MAKE GENERALIZATIONS** What kinds of choices could wealthier immigrants make once they arrived in the United States?

1.3 Central Park New York City

On July 21, 1853, the New York State Legislature set aside more than 750 acres of land in the middle of Manhattan Island to establish America's first major landscaped park. Sensibly called "the Central Park," it was designed by architects and social reformers who believed that great parks would benefit public health and contribute to a "civil society." Central Park sparked the urban park movement, one of the most significant developments in 19th-century America. After several decades of disrepair and neglect, the park was restored during the late 1900s and early 2000s, and it has never been more beautiful, safe, and clean. It proudly represents the American ideals of great public spaces, health and wellness, and the preservation of nature within an urban setting. Which different physical features do you observe in the photo of Central Park?

1.4 Opposition to Immigration

Some people feel afraid when they face something new or unfamiliar. Their fear may make them lash out toward others. In the mid-1800s, some Americans reacted negatively to the arrival of new immigrants.

MAIN IDEA Some native-born Americans tried to restrict immigrants' rights because they feared change and worried about the financial impact of immigration.

FEAR AND JUDGMENT

The numbers of immigrants coming to the United States alarmed some native-born Americans, or Americans who were born in the United States. They feared that the influence of new languages, different religious practices, and new cultural traditions might change the culture of the United States. Their fears inspired many **prejudices**, or broad judgments about groups of people that are not based on reason or fact.

Because many immigrants accepted jobs for very little pay, some native-born Americans believed their own wages would be reduced as a result. Newspaper articles reporting the failed rebellions in Germany gave some Americans the impression that immigrants would try to inspire revolution in the United States. They also worried that local governments would increase taxes and strain public services in order to care for so many poor immigrants. As one American writer put it, "They increase our taxes, eat our bread, and encumber [clog] our streets."

Some elected officials proposed passing **nativist** laws, or laws that favored native-born Americans over immigrants, often focusing on religion. Most native-born Americans were Protestant. Some Protestants formed prejudices against Catholic immigrants entering the country—especially the Irish. Protestants feared that Catholics held an allegiance to a foreign power because the leader of their church, the Pope, reigned over the Catholic Church from Italy. At times, violence erupted between Protestants and Catholics. Anti-Catholic mobs burned a convent, or a dwelling for nuns, near Boston in 1834. Prejudice against Catholics also influenced immigration laws.

EXCLUDING IMMIGRANTS

During the 1840s, nativists organized groups to oppose immigration. One of these groups called itself the American Party. Its leaders told new members to say "I know nothing" if anyone asked what the party did, so people began calling the American Party the **Know-Nothing party**. The party proposed laws that prevented immigrants, especially Irish Catholics, from voting and holding public office. They also wanted to require immigrants to live in the country for 21 years before they could become citizens.

Membership in the party continued to grow. In 1855, 43 members of Congress belonged to the Know-Nothing party. But Congress refused to pass most of the party's proposed legislation, and party members' involvement in violence and corruption in various states made the party increasingly unpopular. By 1860, differing views on slavery broke up the party, but that was not the end of nativist ideas in the United States.

HISTORICAL THINKING

1. **READING CHECK** What issues increased American prejudice toward immigrants in the mid-1800s?

2. **ANALYZE VISUALS** In which different ways do these two political cartoons portray immigrants, native-born Americans, and the political process?

3. **EVALUATE** What role did religion play in nativist prejudices?

These two cartoons from the 1850s reflect nativist attitudes toward immigrants. The first cartoon, published in a Know-Nothing newspaper, portrays an Irish and a German immigrant running away from a voting site with the ballot box, which they have stolen in the midst of a brawl. They are "clothed" in barrels that held whiskey and beer.

The second cartoon, from *Harper's Weekly*, shows a voter being pulled in two directions. On the left, a nativist politician attempts to persuade the voter. On the right, an Irish politician tries to do the same. What different characterizations of immigrant voters are shown in these cartoons?

2.1 The Second Great Awakening

Being part of a large gathering can be exciting and inspiring. In the mid-1800s, some religious events were so popular that they drew huge crowds, much like a music festival or sporting event does today.

MAIN IDEA In the early 19th century, new ideas about religion inspired people to reform problems in society.

A RETURN TO THE CHURCH

As you've read, the Enlightenment was a period in American history when political philosophers applied reason and logic to religion and society. New concepts about equality and government sparked the American Revolution. At the same time, scientific knowledge was expanding. The rush of new ideas caused many people to become skeptical of the power churches seemed to hold. Influenced by the Enlightenment, some people established new religions, such as Unitarianism, that combined the practical ideas of the Enlightenment with the teachings of the Bible.

In the 1790s, some Christians reexamined their religious practices. Many began to believe they should have a direct and emotional relationship with God. This movement is called the **Second Great Awakening**. To revive, or reawaken, religious enthusiasm, many Methodists and Baptists, among other denominations, organized **revival meetings**, or informal religious events held outdoors or in tents. Revivals became very popular because they drew people out of church buildings and into nature. Some preachers drew thousands of spectators. Audience members cried, shook, or rolled on the ground as preachers delivered sermons. Often, preachers **evangelized**, or spread the Christian gospel by delivering dramatic sermons and sharing personal experiences.

Many new believers joined Methodist and Baptist congregations as a result of the revivals. At these events, people felt a sense of freedom in worshiping with their friends and neighbors outside the formal organization of the church.

REFORMING SOCIAL PROBLEMS

One of the most prominent figures of the Second Great Awakening was a former lawyer and religious skeptic, or person who questions something others believe to be true, named **Charles Grandison Finney**. Finney became a fervent, or eager, Christian and preacher after his law studies led him to read and examine the Bible. He used his experience in arguing court cases to persuade others to adopt his beliefs.

Finney was as passionate about social reform as he was about his faith. He believed a just society had the responsibility to improve the lives of all its members. He delivered lively sermons calling for the end of slavery, the improvement of education for all citizens, and women's rights. Many other revivalist preachers shared Finney's views. As a result, religious groups actively promoted social reform causes.

The **temperance movement** was one part of this social reform effort. The word *temperance* means "moderation" or "self-restraint." This movement's proponents crusaded against the overuse of alcohol, which had become an integral part of daily life. On balance, 19th-century Americans consumed a lot of alcohol. In 1830, the average American drank seven gallons of alcohol per year—three times the average amount consumed today. Farmers earned extra money by making whiskey with leftover crops, local economies relied on alcohol sales, and drinking during working hours was commonplace. However, both public drunkenness and alcoholism had become significant social problems.

Temperance reformers approached the issue from different angles. Some wanted to curb the use of alcohol because they feared drunkenness was a threat to social order and economic prosperity. Others, motivated by the fervor of the Second Great Awakening, saw drinking as a sin. Some reformers wanted to protect women and children from neglect and mistreatment resulting from their husbands' and fathers' abuse of alcohol. Finally, medical professionals wanted Americans to limit their alcohol use for health reasons.

The reformers also looked beyond alcohol-related issues. They called attention to poor living conditions in overcrowded cities and advocated for working children's rights in factories and mills. Many, including California pioneer Annie Bidwell, also promoted free public education and voting rights for women.

CRITICAL VIEWING In 1839, J. Maze Burbank captured the fervor of a revival in his painting *Religious Camp Meeting.* Revival meetings were also known as "camp meetings." Most were located on the frontier where churches had yet to be built. How does this painting convey what people who attended this revival meeting might have experienced?

HISTORICAL THINKING

1. **READING CHECK** What was the Second Great Awakening?

2. **DESCRIBE** How did Charles Grandison Finney play a significant role in society?

3. **COMPARE AND CONTRAST** What were the different ways in which reformers approached alcohol consumption in the 19th century?

2.2 Educating and Advocating

When you see a situation that seems unjust, you want to do something about it. Likewise, positive changes in society have often started with one brave person raising his or her voice.

MAIN IDEA Reform movements in the 1830s and 1840s led to improvements in the treatment of mental illness, the prison system, and public education.

EDUCATION FOR ALL

If you were female, African American, or an immigrant, it was hard to get a good education in the United States during the early 19th century. To address the lack of education for girls and women, a number of women established schools for them, including Emma Willard, who founded the Troy Female Seminary in 1821, and Mary Lyon, who founded Mount Holyoke Female Seminary in 1837. Schools and colleges for girls and women were a step forward, but women's literacy rates were still half those of men. Further, most young people

who attended school, whether male or female, came from wealthy families. Many lower-income, working-class, and immigrant children could not afford formal education. They chose work over school to help support their families.

African-American children faced other obstacles in education as well. Laws barred enslaved African Americans from studying at all, and free African Americans could only attend certain

CRITICAL VIEWING Primers were small books used in schools to teach beginning reading and arithmetic. This primer was printed on cloth and sewn together by a Boston printer around 1860. What do you notice about the illustrations used in this primer?

Q is for Quarters, guarded with care.

S is a Sailor, who respected will be.

R is Retreat, may you never be there.

T is a Traitor, that was hung on a tree.

schools. **Prudence Crandall,** an educator from Connecticut, took a bold step to address racism in education. When she opened the Canterbury School for young African-American girls in 1831, her small Connecticut town became the center of controversy. Crandall was arrested several times for unlicensed instruction, the school's water well was poisoned, and townspeople threw eggs and stones at her students. Crandall's school closed in 1834 after a violent mob broke windows and ransacked the classrooms. Clearly, racism against African Americans was not confined to the South.

Individuals and groups worked to correct these injustices and to reform the education system as a whole. The clear solution was to offer every American child a public education. Religious and women's groups campaigned for a public investment in education, or free public schools that would be funded by the collection of property taxes and managed by the local government. This education reform was known as the **common school movement**.

In 1837, **Horace Mann** put the ideas of the common school movement into action. Mann wanted the public education system to be rooted in good citizenship and moral education that would prepare students for society and the workforce. His crusade helped establish a public education system in Massachusetts for students of all social classes, genders, races, ethnicities, and faiths. Soon, other states followed. The Northeast took the lead in establishing free public schools, but the South lagged behind the rest of the nation for several decades.

REFORMING INSTITUTIONS

In the early 1800s, people knew little about what caused mental illnesses or how to treat them. A mental illness is a long-term disorder, such as depression or addiction, that alters one's personality or way of thinking. Those who suffered from such ailments were often feared and misunderstood. Many mentally ill patients ended up living in prisons or poorhouses.

A shocking visit to a prison inspired **Louis Dwight**, a minister from Massachusetts, to help the mentally ill. While visiting inmates, Dwight recognized the need to remove people with mental illnesses from prisons and place them in hospitals called **asylums**. Because of Dwight's efforts, Massachusetts General Hospital opened the state's first asylum at Worcester in 1833.

Dorothea Dix, a teacher from Maine, joined Dwight's cause in 1841 after witnessing mentally ill women shivering in an unheated jail cell. The authorities tried to convince her that, because they were mentally ill, the women could not feel the cold. After that visit, Dix toured hundreds of prisons, jails, and poorhouses. She persuaded state legislators to develop tax-supported systems of care. Her influence helped open more asylums.

At the same time, Dwight, Dix, and others called for improvements in the treatment of prisoners. They believed it was better to rehabilitate inmates, or restore them to health, instead of putting them in solitary confinement, where they were locked up with no human contact. Reformers cited tragedies from the past to make their case.

For instance, in 1821, wardens of Auburn Prison in New York had placed 80 prisoners into solitary confinement for long periods of time. Some prisoners were confined for their entire sentence, which caused many to become mentally ill. In the weeks following their release, many prisoners committed suicide. Soon after, Auburn Prison eliminated solitary confinement for prisoners. The Auburn Prison's change in policies supported the reformers' insistence that solitary confinement damaged prisoners. Reformers went on to fight for prison libraries and literacy classes, programs that can still be found in prisons today.

HISTORICAL THINKING

1. **READING CHECK** How did the common school movement address inequalities in education?

2. **MAKE CONNECTIONS** What connections do you see between the school system Horace Mann helped establish and today's schools?

3. **DRAW CONCLUSIONS** How did American reformers help mentally ill and imprisoned people in the 19th century?

2.3 Fighting for Better Pay

The phrase "strength in numbers" applies to many situations. During the 1830s and 1840s, American workers in many different industries realized that groups were stronger than individuals.

MAIN IDEA During the mid-1800s, American workers banded together and demanded better, safer labor conditions.

LONG DAYS, HARD WORK

By the early 19th century, factory work had become widespread. Working conditions in most factories, however, were far from ideal.

Most factory workers toiled 10 to 14 hours per day, 6 days a week, no matter if they were elderly or 10 years old. They operated large and dangerous machines without safety gear. Many machine operators were maimed or killed on the job. If workers were injured during their shifts, they received no payment or paid time off to recover, and they often lost their jobs.

At the same time, the costs of living, such as rent and groceries, continually rose. Workers wanted better wages. They also wanted their employers to be held responsible for accidents on the job. Individually, workers knew they had little power to change their working conditions. In the 1820s, workers began to organize **labor unions**, or groups that advocate for workers rights and protections. Together, unionized workers had a much more powerful voice in demanding better pay and safer work environments.

A mill worker poses for a photograph around 1850. Many children worked in the textile mills, including this young girl. Her job may have been to straighten strands of cotton as they moved into the loom.

Leather Shoes
These leather baby shoes were produced by a Massachusetts shoe factory during the mid-19th century.

Craftsmen such as carpenters and shoemakers also formed organizations called **craft unions**. Craft unions differed from labor unions because most craftsmen did not work in factories, and they had learned a specialized skill. However, their objectives were the same: better wages and working conditions.

Labor and craft unions made progress in improving workplace conditions. But then in 1836, an economic depression hit the nation. Within a year, many factory workers and craftsmen were unemployed. Those fortunate enough to have jobs saw their wages cut by almost half. Displaced and underpaid workers were willing to take on whatever work they could find, and factory and shop owners knew it. As the economy struggled, the power of labor and craft unions decreased.

A WIN FOR WORKERS

When the economy improved in the early 1840s, unions reorganized. **Sarah Bagley**, a millworker in Lowell, Massachusetts, led the way for women's labor unions. She and her female coworkers worked up to 14 hours a day for lower wages than their male counterparts. In 1844, they joined together and established the **Lowell Female Labor Reform Association (LFLRA)**.

Bagley gave speeches denouncing her employer for not acknowledging the issues the mill workers faced daily. After she stopped working at the mill, she published stories about her experiences. Some politicians disliked her honesty and her critical view of mill owners. But her efforts improved the lives of women in the workforce.

Under the leadership of Bagley, the LFLRA appealed to the Massachusetts legislature to enact laws for shorter workdays. The legislature refused to confront mill owners, who agreed to shorten the workday to 13 hours only after public opinion pressured them into doing so in 1847. The LFLRA continued to advocate for shorter workdays. In 1853, mill owners cut the workday to 11 hours.

The actions of the LFLRA inspired other unions in the Northeast. In 1860, a shoe manufacturer in Massachusetts refused the shoemaker unions' request for wage increases. The shoemakers fought back by organizing a strike, or work stoppage. The workers walked out of the factory in protest. Their bold action encouraged similar strikes across New England. Ultimately, 20,000 shoemakers in 25 towns participated. As a result, most of the employers met the unions' demands. The successful strike emboldened the unions, which grew in strength and numbers and soon began to organize on a national level. Even so, Massachusetts did not pass a 10-hour workday law until 1874.

HISTORICAL THINKING

1. **READING CHECK** Why did factory workers and craftsmen form unions?

2. **SYNTHESIZE** Describe how and why the power of labor unions diminished in the 1830s.

3. **MAKE GENERALIZATIONS** What was work life like for 19th-century laborers?

2.4 Creative Expression

In every civilization, writers and artists ask important questions and help shape and define culture and identity. In the 19th century, American literature and art exploded with creativity.

MAIN IDEA Nineteenth-century American writers and artists helped define what it means to be an American.

AMERICAN AUTHORS ON THE RISE

As reformers advocated for solutions to social problems, writers in the 19th century set out to shape the American identity. Some used the events of American history as their setting. Others reflected social and intellectual movements.

Washington Irving's 1820 story "Rip Van Winkle" was a comment on the dramatic change the American Revolution had brought about. **Henry Wadsworth Longfellow's** poem "Paul Revere's Ride" created an American legend by fictionalizing and bringing to life one of the most exciting events of the Revolution. **James Fenimore Cooper** wrote the first American novel in 1823. *The Pioneers* described life for ordinary Americans on the New York frontier in the late 1700s, before the nation began its westward expansion.

Some 19th-century authors wrote about conflict and individualism. **Nathaniel Hawthorne** wrote during the mid-1800s, but his novel, *The Scarlet Letter,* focused on love and guilt among the Puritans of Massachusetts in the 1640s. **Herman Melville's** *Moby Dick* told the story of Captain Ahab pursuing the great white whale. The novel was Melville's allegory for Americans' reckless westward expansion and obsession with wealth.

One especially rich source of inspiration for some 19th-century writers was **transcendentalism**, an intellectual and social movement of the mid-1800s led by **Ralph Waldo Emerson**. The movement's goal was to transcend, or rise above, the expectations society placed on people. Transcendentalists thought that people should be self-reliant and connected to the natural world. Emerson's book *Nature* reflected these values.

Walt Whitman first published *Leaves of Grass* in 1855. One of the best-known poems in the collection is "Song of Myself," Whitman's celebration of individualism.

PRIMARY SOURCE

I CELEBRATE myself, and sing myself,
And what I assume you shall assume,
For every atom belonging to me as good
belongs to you.
. . .
I too am not a bit tamed, I too am
untranslatable,
I sound my barbaric yawp over the roofs of
the world.

—from "Song of Myself," by Walt Whitman, 1855

One of Emerson's students, **Henry David Thoreau**, lived alone in a simple cabin by Walden Pond for 26 months to write his memoir, *Walden*. **Louisa May Alcott**, the daughter of Bronson Alcott, a transcendentalist, grew up in the company of Emerson and Thoreau. Alcott wrote about family relationships and growing up as a female in the 19th century—the focus of her most successful work, *Little Women*.

Walt Whitman and **Emily Dickinson** forged new paths in poetry by breaking traditional rules. Poetry of the period was flowery and romantic, but Whitman and Dickinson wrote honestly and directly. In his most important work, *Leaves of Grass*, Whitman used free verse, or poetry that doesn't rhyme or depend upon a strict meter. Emily Dickinson also wrote poems that ignored established rules about rhyme and rhythm. She shared them with so few people that even her family members were not aware of all her poems until after her death.

Transcendentalists supported women's rights, abolition, and other social reforms. Organized religion, restrictive laws and social institutions, and industrialization inhibited individuals from fully expressing themselves. Whitman, for example, wrote openly about love as well as same-sex relationships. His work also celebrated laborers, immigrants, and people who were all part of the growing diversity of the nation.

PAINTING AMERICAN BEAUTY

Nineteenth-century visual artists also shaped American identity through landscape paintings that celebrated the diverse beauty of the United States. **Thomas Cole** was one of the early leaders of an art movement known as the **Hudson River School**. In the 1820s, Cole hiked in New York's Catskill Mountains and painted magnificent scenes of the Hudson River Valley. Hudson River School painters became known for their landscapes, which often highlighted people's relationship with nature.

Asher B. Durand and **Frederic Edwin Church**, friends of Cole, were two artists to emerge from the Hudson River School. Cole inspired Durand to switch from painting portraits to painting landscapes. Church painted natural phenomena such as waterfalls, volcanoes, icebergs, and rainbows. A German immigrant and artist named **Albert Bierstadt** painted panoramic scenes of the Rocky Mountains, the Grand Canyon, and the Yosemite Valley using Hudson River School styles.

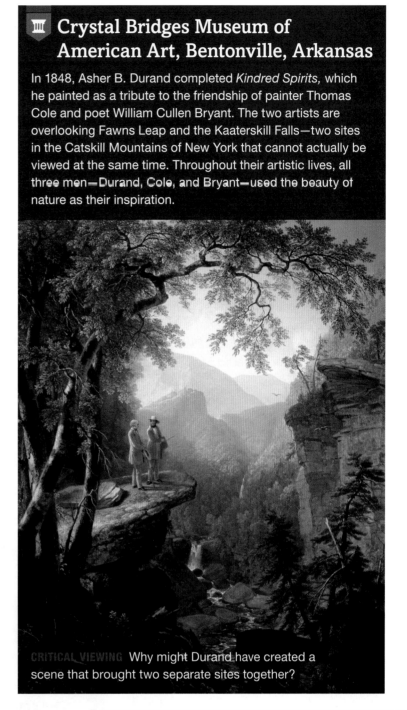

🏛 Crystal Bridges Museum of American Art, Bentonville, Arkansas

In 1848, Asher B. Durand completed *Kindred Spirits*, which he painted as a tribute to the friendship of painter Thomas Cole and poet William Cullen Bryant. The two artists are overlooking Fawns Leap and the Kaaterskill Falls—two sites in the Catskill Mountains of New York that cannot actually be viewed at the same time. Throughout their artistic lives, all three men—Durand, Cole, and Bryant—used the beauty of nature as their inspiration.

CRITICAL VIEWING Why might Durand have created a scene that brought two separate sites together?

HISTORICAL THINKING

1. **READING CHECK** What historical events influenced American literature and art in the 19th century?

2. **DESCRIBE** In what ways did common themes in artistic expression reveal the ideals and aspirations of the new nation?

3. **SYNTHESIZE** How did writers, visual artists, and transcendental thinkers shape American identity in the 19th century?

3.1 The Abolition Movement

Reformers in the 19th century didn't have cell phones or social media to spread the word. Instead, they wrote letters and newspaper articles, gave speeches, and even sent secret messages to communicate their ideas.

| **MAIN IDEA** Brave individuals spoke out about the injustices of slavery in an attempt to end the institution in the United States.

SPEAKING OUT AGAINST SLAVERY

Many reformers who spoke out about social issues were also **abolitionists**, or people who wanted to end slavery. However, some Americans did not agree with abolitionists. Southerners and northerners alike considered abolitionists and their ideas too radical—as well as dangerous, un-Christian, and even unpatriotic.

In 1831, an abolitionist named **William Lloyd Garrison** published the first issue of his newspaper, *The Liberator.* His paper called for the immediate **emancipation**, or freedom, for all enslaved people. **Wendell Phillips**, a wealthy attorney, soon allied with Garrison. He wrote for *The Liberator* and contributed financially to the movement.

In 1839, former President John Quincy Adams argued that the ideals of the Declaration of Independence applied to all people. He called for a constitutional amendment to make every child born in the United States after July 4, 1842, free. He also proposed that no new state could enter the Union if it allowed slavery, but neither idea became law.

Two sisters, **Sarah Grimké** and **Angelina Grimké**, witnessed the cruelty of slavery firsthand while growing up on their parents' plantation in South Carolina. When the sisters took up the abolitionist cause, as some southerners did, their family disowned them. These determined women joined the Quakers and traveled the country giving speeches in support of abolition. In 1863, Angelina

The Iron Collar
One of the most horrifying tools slave owners subjected enslaved people to was the iron collar. They used this device to punish slaves, especially for attempts to escape. The prongs made it impossible to lie down to rest or sleep. They also caught on bushes and underbrush, making it hard to run. Abolitionists pointed to this kind of cruelty in demanding an end to slavery.

William Lloyd Garrison published the weekly newspaper *The Liberator* for 35 years, beginning in 1831. The masthead, or title area, depicts enslaved people before and after liberation.

Grimké married fellow abolitionist **Theodore Weld**, a trainer and recruiter for the American Anti-Slavery Society.

STANDING UP FOR FREEDOM

Both free and enslaved African Americans actively challenged the existence of slavery. **David Walker** was a free African-American man who wrote for *Freedom's Journal*, an abolitionist newspaper. As the owner of a secondhand clothing store in Boston in the 1820s, Walker printed antislavery pamphlets and sewed them into the pockets of clothing he sold to sailors. Walker hoped the pamphlets would reach people in many ports, especially those in the South. One of his pamphlets, entitled *An Appeal to the Coloured Citizens of the World,* became one of the most radical antislavery documents of the movement, and southern states reacted by prohibiting the circulation of abolitionist literature.

Another African-American abolitionist was **Charles Remond**, who was born to a wealthy, free African-American family in Salem, Massachusetts. He worked as an agent of the Massachusetts Anti-Slavery Society, and he traveled and spoke with Garrison, Phillips, and others.

Robert Purvis was the son of a wealthy cotton broker and a free African-American woman. When he was nine years old, his family moved from South Carolina to Philadelphia. As an adult, Purvis became very active in abolition and in the **Underground Railroad**. In fact, he and his wife, **Harriet Forten**, housed escapees in their home, also known as the Purvis "safe house."

At the beginning of the chapter, you read about the courageous work of **Harriet Tubman**. Other African-American women played significant roles in the abolitionist movement as well. **Harriet Jacobs**, born into slavery, escaped to New York in 1842. She published *Incidents in the Life of a Slave Girl* in 1861, considered one of the most extensive slave narratives written by a woman.

Sojourner Truth was also a powerful abolitionist voice. Like Tubman and Jacobs, Truth was born into slavery. When she told a white neighbor that her owner broke his promise to release her, the neighbor paid the owner $20 for her and then set her free. She changed her enslaved name, Isabella, to Sojourner Truth. She captivated people with her simple, clear message: that all people deserved the same rights as white men.

HISTORICAL THINKING

1. **READING CHECK** How did abolitionists work to end slavery?

2. **DRAW CONCLUSIONS** Why did most Americans consider abolitionists' ideas radical?

3. **ANALYZE VISUALS** What details do you notice in the photo, and how might those—and the photo itself—have impacted people who saw it in the mid-1800s?

3.2 Voices Against Slavery

Abolitionists relied on shocking testimonials and appeals to good conscience in their fight to end slavery. They dared to write and publish newspaper articles to condemn the injustices of slavery. Others marshalled their strength to stand on a stage and share the indignities they had witnessed or personally endured.

In the first issue of the *The Liberator*, William Lloyd Garrison called slavery "America's all-conquering sin." He wrote, "I do not wish to think, or to speak, or write, with moderation. . . . I will not equivocate . . . I will not excuse . . . I will not retreat a single inch . . . AND I WILL BE HEARD!" Garrison also helped to found the American Anti-Slavery Society, members of which appear at a convention in New York in this 1850 photo. He would ally with women and men, African American and white, and wealthy and poor in his decades-long fight against slavery.

CRITICAL VIEWING What do you notice about the individuals gathered for a photo at this convention?

DOCUMENT ONE

Primary Source: Speech
from "Address to the Slaves of the United States,"
by William Lloyd Garrison, 1843

When William Lloyd Garrison published this speech in *The Liberator*, slavery had long been the basis for the southern economy. Garrison's passion for the abolitionist cause is evident in the way he addresses enslaved people directly.

CONSTRUCTED RESPONSE How does Garrison describe enslaved people, and what specific actions does he encourage them to take?

We advise you to seize every opportunity to escape from your masters, and, fixing your eyes on the North Star, travel on until you reach a land of liberty. You are not the property of your masters. God never made one human being to be owned by another. Your right to be free, at any moment, is undeniable; and it is your duty, whenever you can, peaceably to escape from the plantations on which you are confined, and assert your manhood.

DOCUMENT TWO

Primary Source: Speech
from "On the Injustice of Slavery," by Sojourner Truth, 1856

Sojourner Truth dictated her life story to Olive Gilbert for her book *Narrative of Sojourner Truth, a Northern Slave,* published in 1850. In the following address to the Friends of Human Progress, Truth shares her grief over the loss of her children. Her story provided clear evidence of the ongoing mistreatment of vast numbers of people who were unable to care for their children or even keep them from being sold.

CONSTRUCTED RESPONSE How does Truth's account reflect the lack of basic freedom enslaved people endured?

I want to know what has become of the love I ought to have for my children? I did have love for them, but what has become of it? I cannot tell you. I have had two husbands, but I never possessed one of my own. I have had five children and never could take one of them up and say, "My child" or "My children," unless it was when no one could see me.

DOCUMENT THREE

Primary Source: Speech
from "What the Black Man Wants,"
by Frederick Douglass, 1865

Frederick Douglass, sitting next to the table in the photo on the left, was an escaped slave who taught himself to read and write. Douglass became one of the most powerful and outspoken opponents of slavery, and proponents, or supporters, of women's rights. He delivered this speech to the Massachusetts Anti-Slavery Society in 1865.

CONSTRUCTED RESPONSE Why does Douglass reject the pity and sympathy of other abolitionists?

I understand the anti-slavery societies of this country to be based on two principles—first, the freedom of the blacks of this country; and, second, the elevation of them. Let me not be misunderstood here. I am not asking for sympathy at the hands of abolitionists, sympathy at the hands of any. What I ask . . . is not benevolence, not pity, not sympathy, but simply justice.

SYNTHESIZE & WRITE

1. **REVIEW** Review what you have learned about 19th-century abolitionists, their ideas and motivations, and their movement.

2. **RECALL** On your own paper, write the main ideas expressed by Garrison, Truth, and Douglass.

3. **CONSTRUCT** Construct a topic sentence that answers this question: In what ways did abolitionists appeal to their fellow citizens' morality in order to gather support to abolish slavery?

4. **WRITE** Using evidence from this chapter and the documents, write an informative paragraph that supports your topic sentence in Step 3.

3.3 Women's Rights and Seneca Falls

Like activists in modern civil rights movements, 19th-century activists in the women's rights movement felt an urgent sense of purpose. And when it came to establishing basic rights for women, failure was impossible.

> **MAIN IDEA** In 1848, supporters of women's rights laid the groundwork for a movement that would change the lives of American women.

LEADERS FOR WOMEN'S RIGHTS

Throughout the early 1800s, women played active roles in social reform and abolition movements. Yet women continued to occupy a secondary place to men in society. When women earned wages outside of the home, their pay was much lower than the wages men received for doing the same job. Married women could not own or purchase property or enter into contracts. Single women had all the property rights a man had but were taxed on that property by a government in which they had no voice. Furthermore, because educational and career opportunities were so limited for women, marriage was often the only possible path to a financially stable life for most women.

The fight for women's rights had its roots in the abolition movement. Female abolitionists gained public speaking and organization experience, and some began to ask why women were not granted the same rights as men. **Elizabeth Cady Stanton** and **Lucretia Mott** were early leaders in the women's rights movement, and both were abolitionists.

Elizabeth Cady came from a wealthy family and received an excellent education at Troy Female Seminary. She married abolitionist Henry Brewster Stanton, became an abolitionist herself, and met many other abolitionists, including Lucretia Mott. Mott was a Quaker from Massachusetts who housed escapees traveling on the Underground Railroad.

In 1848, Mott and Stanton organized the **Seneca Falls Convention** in central New York. There, they issued a "Declaration of Sentiments and Resolutions." The Declaration of Sentiments

Susan B. Anthony shows a document to Elizabeth Cady Stanton, seated, in 1900. In 1902, Anthony wrote to Stanton: "It is fifty-one years since we first met, and we have been busy through every one of them, stirring up the world to recognize the rights of women."

framed the injustices faced by women in familiar language. As you know, the Declaration of Independence introduced the idea that all men are created equal. The Declaration of Sentiments inserted "and women" into that fundamental idea to reinforce the assertion that "all men and women are created equal." In this spirit, Stanton went a

Women's Rights National Historical Park
Seneca Falls, New York

The Women's Rights National Historical Park honors women who produced the Declaration of Sentiments. The statues featured here are the centerpiece of the park's visitors' center lobby. Notice Frederick Douglass standing with the women. Like many women's rights activists, he supported both abolition and women's rights.

a friendship and a political partnership that lasted more than 50 years. They traveled together, delivered speeches to lawmakers, planned campaigns, and published *The Revolution*, a newspaper devoted to women's rights.

During the 1850s and 1860s, issues regarding women's rights became less pressing because of the impending Civil War. However, after the war was over, women's rights activists picked up the cause again. In 1869, Anthony and Stanton founded the **National Woman Suffrage Association**, the first national women's rights organization. Anthony believed that the best way to bring attention to women's suffrage was to violate the law—by voting. When she tried to vote in the 1872 election, she was arrested and fined. Anthony never paid the fine and never went to jail.

step further and included women's **suffrage**, or the right to vote, in the Declaration of Sentiments. She knew opponents of women's suffrage would claim the demand was outrageous, and that it might hinder the acceptance of other ideas about women's rights. But because Stanton believed the right to vote was essential, she and Mott listed it as the first grievance in the Declaration of Sentiments.

CONTINUING THE WORK

In 1851, Sojourner Truth, who had attended Seneca Falls, delivered a powerful speech at the Women's Rights Convention in Ohio. She asked, "Ain't I a woman?" and drew attention to race in the fight for women's rights. Truth was a passionate supporter of equality for men and women of all races. That same year, Elizabeth Cady Stanton met **Susan B. Anthony**. Coming from a Quaker family, Anthony supported both temperance and abolition. The two women began

The campaign for women's rights began in the early 1800s and continued through the rest of the 19th century and into the 20th. Some leaders worked until the day they died. Mott, Stanton, Truth, Anthony, and many other women's rights activists dedicated their lives to securing political and social equality for women.

HISTORICAL THINKING

1. **READING CHECK** What was the Seneca Falls Convention, and why was it significant?

2. **MAKE CONNECTIONS** In what ways were the movements for abolition and women's rights intertwined?

3. **SYNTHESIZE** How did women's rights activists link women's rights to the Founding Fathers' positions on equality and natural rights?

VOCABULARY

Use each of the following vocabulary terms in a sentence that shows an understanding of the term's meaning.

1. nativist
   Members of Congress passed nativist laws to limit the rights of immigrants.

2. blight

3. steerage

4. evangelize

5. labor union

6. revival meeting

7. temperance movement

8. suffrage

9. emancipation

READING STRATEGY
SYNTHESIZE

If you haven't already done so, complete the graphic organizer for this chapter. List at least three ideas and their synthesis. Then answer the question.

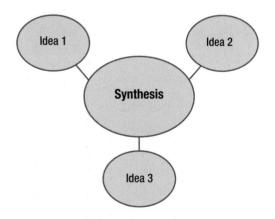

10. In what ways did the American identity change between 1830 and 1860?

MAIN IDEAS

Answer the following questions. Support your answers with evidence from the chapter.

11. Why did many immigrants choose to stay in the city of their arrival? **LESSON 1.1**

12. How did political problems in Europe affect immigration to the United States in the early 1800s? **LESSON 1.2**

13. How did the Know-Nothing party try to limit the freedoms of immigrants to the United States? **LESSON 1.4**

14. What role did religion have in changing the American identity? **LESSON 2.1**

15. What work did Dorothea Dix and Louis Dwight do? **LESSON 2.2**

16. What did the members of the Lowell Female Labor Reform Association seek to change? **LESSON 2.3**

17. From what sources did mid-19th century writers and artists draw their inspiration? **LESSON 2.4**

18. In what ways did abolitionists use print sources to build a case for the abolition of slavery? **LESSON 3.1**

19. Why was Susan B. Anthony arrested in 1872? **LESSON 3.3**

HISTORICAL THINKING

Answer the following questions. Support your answers with evidence from the chapter.

20. **SUMMARIZE** What were the goals of the 19th-century reform movements?

21. **IDENTIFY PROBLEMS AND SOLUTIONS** What problem did Horace Mann seek to solve?

22. **EVALUATE** How did Americans' understanding of the concept of freedom change during the 19th century?

23. **MAKE GENERALIZATIONS** Why did Elizabeth Cady Stanton and Lucretia Mott organize a convention at Seneca Falls?

24. **FORM AND SUPPORT OPINIONS** Which reform effort improved society the most during the 19th century? Support your opinion with evidence from the chapter.

INTERPRET MAPS

The map shows Underground Railroad routes from southern slave states to northern free states. The width of a path on the map corresponds to the number of people following it. Look closely at the map and then answer the questions that follow.

Underground Railroad Routes, 1830–1860

25. What routes indicate that the Underground Railroad was an international network?

26. In what ways did Underground Railroad routes rely on major rivers? Support your answer with details from the map.

ANALYZE SOURCES

Margaret Fuller's *Woman in the Nineteenth Century,* published in 1845, is a transcendentalist argument for women participating fully in society. Fuller points out that women constitute half of humanity. She goes on to argue that women's development contributes to the growth of men, too. Fuller makes the case that men are better off when women are able to lead fulfilling lives.

> Not a few believe, and men themselves have expressed the opinion that . . . the idea of Man, however imperfectly brought out, has been far more so [expressed] than that of Woman . . . that she, the other half of the same thought, the other chamber of the heart of life, needs now take her turn in the full pulsation, and that improvement in the daughters will best aid in the reformation of the sons of this age.

27. Why do you think Fuller describes women as "the other half of the same thought?"

CONNECT TO YOUR LIFE

28. **EXPLANATORY** Think about a 19th-century reform movement and a cause you support today. What common threads can you trace between then and now? Write a paragraph in which you describe how the cause you support can trace its roots to reform movements of the past.

TIPS

• Consider the mix of reforms happening at this time, and list the facts and details that best align with the cause you support.

• Explain your reasons for supporting your cause, and connect them with the reasons of early reformers.

• Use two or three vocabulary terms from the chapter in your paragraph.

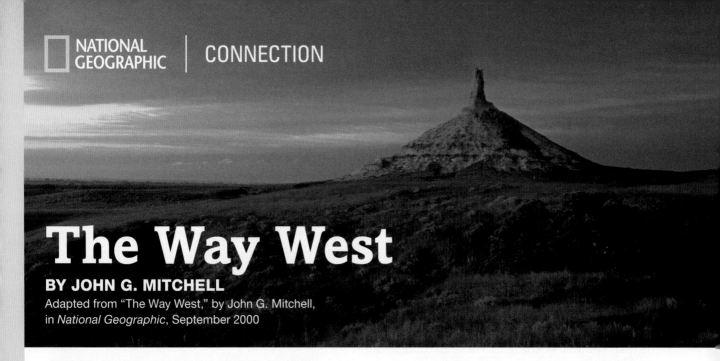

NATIONAL GEOGRAPHIC | CONNECTION

The Way West

BY JOHN G. MITCHELL

Adapted from "The Way West," by John G. Mitchell,
in *National Geographic*, September 2000

The naysayers said it couldn't be done. No one had ever rounded up a party of tenderfoot pioneers, pointed their noses toward sundown, and, without benefit of compass or reliable map, dared them to bet their boots, wagons, and lives against the fearsome 2,000 miles between them and California. But at the far edge of Missouri, where the United States of America had come to a full stop, moving west was on people's minds. They *had* to try it. So in the spring of 1841, a handful of brave souls started out. No matter that they'd have to abandon their wagons on the arid plains and slaughter their livestock to survive in the mountains. All those who stayed the course—34 of them—got to California. It had never been done that way. But they did it.

In 1848, the year Mexico ceded California to the United States and gold was discovered at Sutter's Mill, California could claim a population of 14,000 Anglos and Hispanics. By the end of 1849, emigration by land and sea had pushed the population past 100,000. This number was sufficient for folks to start demanding that the territory be admitted to the Union, which it was on September 9, 1850. In the span of just one generation, even after most of the gold lodes had played out, nearly a quarter million emigrants came into the promised land the old-fashioned way, on foot and by wagon on the California Trail.

By some accounts, the few surviving ruts of that trail reflect one of the greatest human migrations in recorded history. Between the migration's peak years, 1849 to 1852, travelers described the scene as having the appearance of an army on the move. The journey started at the Missouri River, where feeder trails that originated from Independence, Westport Landing, St. Joseph, Council Bluffs, and other frontier towns converged near Fort Kearny on the River Platte. From the Platte's north fork, the trail picked up the Sweetwater River, crossed the Great Divide at South Pass, then dodged one mountain range after another on its way to Fort Hall, a fur post on the Snake River.

A bit beyond Fort Hall, the main trail split and the right fork—the homestretch of the Oregon Trail—continued down the Snake toward Oregon. The left fork turned southwest toward California. In the 1850s, some Oregonians liked to claim that at another place where the trails diverged, a pile of gold-bearing quartz showed the path to California, while a signpost with a written legend guided the traveler toward Oregon. Those who couldn't read, the slur alleged, went to California.

By one estimate, 20,000 people died on the California Trail between 1841 and 1859—an average of 10 graves for every mile. Most died from accidents, disease, contaminated water, inadequate food, or exhaustion from the constant toil. Contrary to what dime novelists would have had the world believe, trouble with Native Americans figured little with the mortality rate on the overland trails. Until 1849, fewer than 50 westward migrant deaths were attributed to Native American attack, and many of those occurred along the pathways to Oregon. However, as the numbers of overlanders increased, so did the fatal encounters. By 1860, pioneer casualties probably totaled close to 400. Even more Native Americans were killed by pioneers.

In the longer view of the great migration, gold was only one of many incentives that lured the wagonfolk west. More lasting was the human hunger for fertile land. But why would a family pack up and set out on a four-month journey when cheap and arable land was still available in the frontier states of the Mississippi Valley?

Perhaps there were as many motives as there were travelers to act on them. A politician might have attributed it all to manifest destiny and the course of empire. But that could not begin to explain the American people's westering tilt, and only the Pacific Ocean would prove big enough to stop it.

For more from *National Geographic*, check out "People of the Horse" online.

UNIT INQUIRY: Organize a Reform Campaign

In this unit, you learned about the ways in which the United States changed in the first part of the 19th century. New national boundaries enlarged the country, and immigrants from around the world enriched the population. Based on your understanding of the text, in what ways did these and other new developments lead to injustices or intensify social problems? What issues did reformers focus on?

ASSIGNMENT

Organize a reform campaign. Identify an injustice or social problem that you learned about in this unit. Then organize a reform campaign. Your plan should include specific actions the campaign could take and communication strategies to broadcast your campaign. Be prepared to present your campaign to the class and explain how it would address the issue you select.

Gather Evidence As you organize your reform campaign, gather evidence from this unit about the different challenges that Americans faced during this time period. Think about the ways in which some developments benefited one group over another. Also consider what principles motivated people to organize reform movements. Use a graphic organizer like this one to help organize your thoughts.

REFORM CAMPAIGN	
ACTIONS	COMMUNICATION

Produce Use your notes to produce descriptions of the specific actions your reform campaign will take and the different audiences it will try to reach. Write a short paragraph on each action and audience using evidence from this unit to support your ideas.

Present Choose a creative way to present your reform campaign to the class. Consider one of these options:

- Create slogans for your campaign that identify the injustice or social problem you are addressing. Carefully consider the campaign message you want to be the most prominent and memorable. Write your slogans on posters, banners, cards, or other forms of visual signage.

- Host a debate that engages different sides of the injustice or social problem your campaign aims to reform. Prepare research memos and talking points for both sides.

- Present your campaign in the character of a reformer from this unit. Research your reformer and consider dressing up as that person.

NATIONAL GEOGRAPHIC | LEARNING FRAMEWORK ACTIVITIES

Research a Mining Boomtown

ATTITUDES Empowerment, Curiosity

KNOWLEDGE Our Human Story

The mining boomtowns of the West were exciting places. In some ways, their remote locations and lack of formal structure allowed different groups a measure of freedom they did not enjoy in 19th-century society. Research the history of a western mining boomtown of your choice. Create a time line that includes major events during the heyday of the town, profiles of important figures and the different groups of people who sought opportunities there, and documents and artwork about the town. Present your research to the class.

Encounter Nature

SKILLS Observation, Collaboration

KNOWLEDGE Our Living Planet

Nineteenth-century artists celebrated the beauty and wonder of the American landscape through visual arts and creative writing. Select a nature site near you to explore. It could be a local park, a beach, a nature trail, or some other site. Explore the nature site you select with a group of classmates. While you are there, take notes on what you observe, including plant life, animals, and birds and the physical features of the site. Gather your notes and present your observations about your site to the class.

UNIT
6 1846–1877

CIVIL WAR AND RECONSTRUCTION

CRITICAL VIEWING Modern-day Civil War reenactors fire a cannon in this photograph of a battle scene. Fighting during the Civil War was fierce and bloody, often resulting in staggering numbers of casualties among both northern and southern soldiers. Improved technologies, including more high-powered cannons, contributed to the high death toll. What details in the photo help convey what fighting in a Civil War battle must have been like?

CIVIL WAR AND
RECONSTRUCTION

THE UNITED STATES

1852
Harriet Beecher Stowe's novel, *Uncle Tom's Cabin*, is published and stirs the debate over slavery. (*cover from 1897 edition of the book*)

1860
Abraham Lincoln is elected president. Soon after, South Carolina secedes from the Union. (*hat worn by Lincoln when he was assassinated in 1865*)

1861
The Civil War begins after the South attacks Fort Sumter, a garrison under federal control.

1850
Congress passes the Compromise of 1850, which seeks to maintain a balance between slave and free states.

1846
Because he lives in a free state, Dred Scott sues for his freedom from slavery after his owner dies.

1840
1850
1860

1848 EUROPE
Nationalism incites unrest and revolution across Europe.

1861 EUROPE
The serfs in Russia are freed.

THE WORLD

1857 ASIA
Indian soldiers, called *sepoys*, revolt against British rule in India. (*illustration of sepoys*)

HISTORICAL THINKING: DETERMINE CHRONOLOGY

How long after Russia freed its serfs did the United States grant African-American men the right to vote?

1870
The 15th Amendment grants voting rights to African-American men. (*1884 glass ballot jar set in a slotted wooden box*)

1865
On April 9, the Civil War ends when southern general Robert E. Lee surrenders to northern general Ulysses S. Grant. On April 15, Lincoln is assassinated. (*Lee signed a letter of surrender at this table.*)

1867
The Reconstruction Acts of 1867 are passed, requiring southern states to satisfy several conditions before they can reenter the Union.

1863
The Union wins the Battle of Gettysburg, but both sides suffer thousands of casualties.

1877
Newly inaugurated president Rutherford B. Hayes puts an end to Reconstruction.

1870

1876 AFRICA
The European scramble for African territory begins.

1880

1864 AMERICAS
Napoleon III crowns Archduke Maximilian emperor of Mexico.

1867 ASIA
The Tokugawa shogunate is overthrown, and Meiji rule brings a period of modernization in Japan. (*Japanese print of a steam engine in a Tokyo station*)

CHAPTER
14

A BROKEN
NATION
1846–1861

ESSENTIAL QUESTION
How did slavery divide the country?

AMERICAN **STORIES** ONLINE **The Pony Express**

AMERICAN **GALLERY** ONLINE **Abraham Lincoln**

READING STRATEGY

IDENTIFY MAIN IDEAS AND DETAILS
When you identify a text's main idea and details, you state the most important idea about a topic and determine which facts support that idea. As you read the chapter, use a graphic organizer like this one to identify main ideas and details relating to the issue of slavery.

Main Idea: Tensions grew between slave states and free states.

Detail	Detail

CRITICAL VIEWING This monumental statue of a seated Abraham Lincoln is situated within the Lincoln Memorial in Washington, D.C. The memorial was completed in 1922, and the statue, designed by sculptor Daniel Chester French, took four years to carve. At 19 feet tall and 19 feet wide, the imposing statue creates a sense of awe and power. What characteristics does Lincoln's face convey?

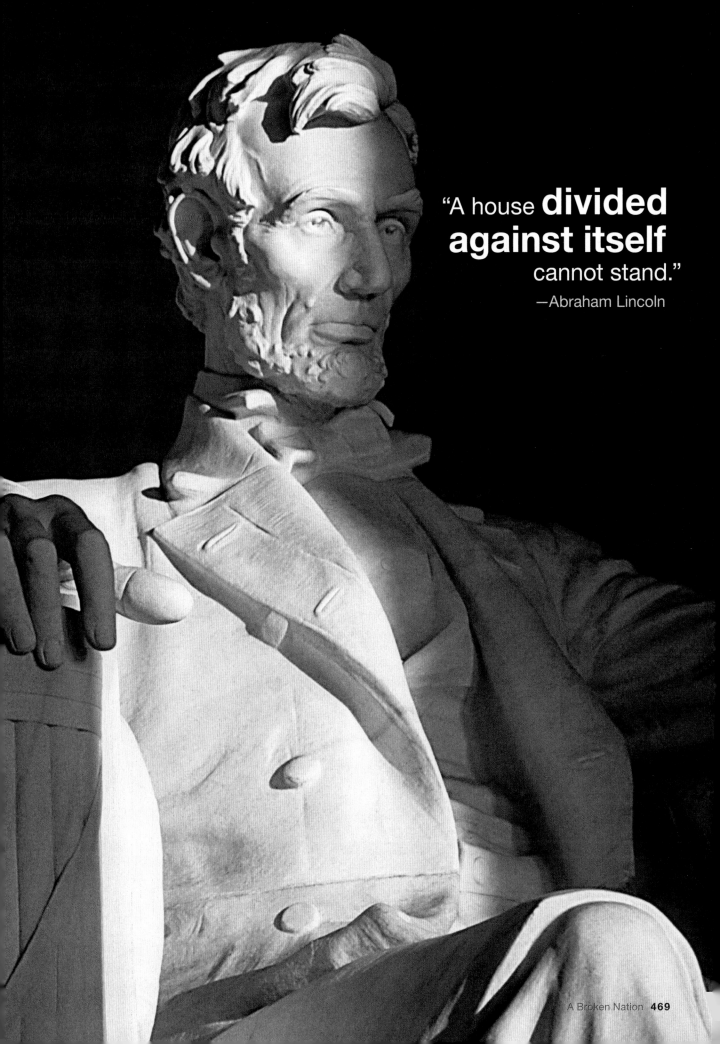

"A house **divided against itself** cannot stand."

—Abraham Lincoln

1.1 Controversy Over Territories

Sometimes friends disagree, and sometimes these disagreements can get out of hand. The United States had gained new territory, but the North and the South couldn't agree on how to use it.

> **MAIN IDEA** Disputes over slavery in new territories and states led to growing tensions between the North and the South.

THE COMPROMISE OF 1850

As the middle of the 19th century approached, slavery had become too divisive, or a cause of conflict, for political leaders to ignore any longer. One of the major issues they debated was whether slaveholding should be allowed in new territories and any new states carved from them.

The Missouri Compromise had temporarily settled the issue in 1820. However, the nation once again split over the debate about the expansion of slavery into newly created western territories and states, especially after the Mexican-American War and the discovery of gold in California. In the run-up to the presidential election of 1848, people hotly argued over the future of the new western territories. Disappointed in the position taken by their parties' presidential candidates, antislavery Whigs and a few antislavery Democrats joined together to create the **Free-Soil Party,** which was dedicated to keeping slavery out of the new territories and states.

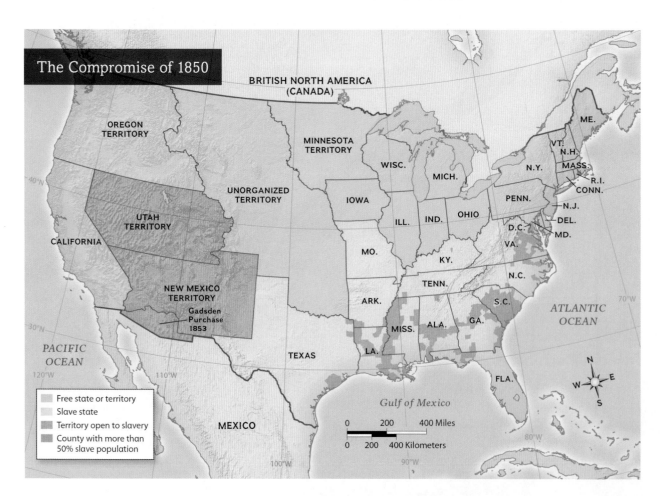

The Compromise of 1850

Legend:
- Free state or territory
- Slave state
- Territory open to slavery
- County with more than 50% slave population

In 1849, a national crisis erupted when California applied for statehood as a free state. For most of the period after the Missouri Compromise, the United States had been evenly split between free states and slave states. Statehood for California would upset this balance and give free states a majority in the U.S. Senate. They already enjoyed a majority in the U.S. House of Representatives. Fearing loss of political power and the possibility that slavery might be outlawed, the slave states threatened to withdraw from the Union.

Remember Henry Clay, the main force behind the Missouri Compromise? In January 1850, he presented a plan for a new compromise. It called for California to be admitted as a free state and for the issue of slavery to be left open in the other territories won from Mexico. Clay and two other famous legislators, John C. Calhoun and Daniel Webster, led a passionate debate over the plan, which lasted for eight months.

Finally, in September, the **Compromise of 1850** became law, preventing the Union from splitting apart. Statehood for California that same year would also give rise to the **Pony Express** in 1860. This mail service, delivered by horseback riders, established communication between the East and the West and so helped keep California connected to the rest with the country.

THE FUGITIVE SLAVE ACT

One of the most controversial parts of the Compromise of 1850 was the **Fugitive Slave Act**. The act strengthened an earlier Fugitive Slave Act passed by Congress in 1793 by enforcing greater penalties on runaways and those who aided them. Under this harsh new act, **federal marshals**, or law enforcers who worked for the U.S. government, could force ordinary citizens to help them capture runaway slaves. In addition, anyone who helped a slave escape faced penalties, as did any marshal who failed to enforce the law. Further, the law denied accused fugitives the right to a trial by jury.

The law provoked bitter anger in the northern states. Many people defied it, and some states passed new laws that protected runaway slaves. Armed groups confronted slave catchers and freed slaves from jails. Nevertheless, slavery continued to expand in the South.

Webster-Calhoun Debate

After Henry Clay proposed his plan, John Calhoun's speech was read in the Senate. Calhoun was too ill to stand and deliver it himself. Three days later, Daniel Webster responded to Calhoun, speaking for more than three hours. In the following excerpts from their speeches, Calhoun speaks for the South, while Webster pleads for saving the Union.

PRIMARY SOURCES

The equilibrium [balance] between [the North and the South] . . . has been destroyed. One section has the exclusive power of controlling the government, which leaves the other without any adequate means of protecting itself against its encroachment and oppression.

—John C. Calhoun, 1850

I wish to speak today, not as a Massachusetts man, nor as a Northern man, but as an American. It is not to be denied that we . . . are surrounded by very considerable dangers to our institutions of government. I speak today for the preservation of the Union. Hear me for my cause.

—Daniel Webster, 1850

HISTORICAL THINKING

1. **READING CHECK** Why did California's application for statehood upset some people?

2. **COMPARE AND CONTRAST** What conflicting views on state and federal authority are revealed in Webster's and Calhoun's speeches?

3. **INTERPRET MAPS** According to the Compromise of 1850, in which territories would settlers be allowed to decide whether slavery would be legal or illegal?

1.2 Slavery and Racism

Enslaved people in the South thought running away from their plantations would change their lives for the better. But would freedom in the North live up to its promise?

| **MAIN IDEA** Racism and slavery were defining forces in the lives of African Americans in both the South and the North.

AFRICAN AMERICANS IN THE SOUTH

While some Americans began to harbor misgivings over slavery, the slave trade continued to thrive in the South. Enslaved people from Africa were no longer imported. But since the children of enslaved people in the United States also became slaves, the slave population grew steadily in the South. By 1860, there were nearly four million enslaved African Americans in the region.

Racism, or the belief that one race is superior to others, was the foundation upon which slavery was built. Many slave owners justified slavery by claiming that African Americans were better off under the care of plantation owners than they would be by caring for themselves. But, as you know, many slaves endured lives of unspeakable cruelty. Laws such as the Fugitive Slave Acts made sure their lives could never improve by sharply curbing their freedom and economic opportunities.

Racist attitudes also affected the lives of the more than 250,000 free African Americans in the South. Local laws prevented them from traveling or assembling in large groups. Free African Americans were also discouraged from

The Impact of Slavery
The damage done to people by slavery is evident in these two photos. The man above, photographed in 1863, is scarred from being whipped, and fear is evident in the faces of the children at the right.

A writer named **Harriet Beecher Stowe** channeled her anger over slavery into a novel called *Uncle Tom's Cabin*. This 1852 painting called *An American Slave Market*, by an artist known only as Taylor, depicts a scene in the novel in which a slave trader purchases a child.

Published in 1852, *Uncle Tom's Cabin* sold 300,000 copies in that year alone and was also turned into popular plays. It dramatically changed the national debate over slavery and racism.

organizing churches, schools, and fraternal orders, or social organizations, like the Masons.

Slavery was central to the economy and culture of the agrarian South. Concerned about the health of the South's economy, southern leaders not only fought for slavery but they also battled against tariffs. They argued that high tariffs favored the industrial North and hurt the South by forcing plantation owners to pay higher prices for manufactured goods.

Some wealthy plantation owners even tried to convince the U.S. government to acquire Cuba from Spain as a slave state. Their proposal was presented in the 1854 Ostend Manifesto and included the provision that the island be taken by force if necessary. The manifesto fell through but became a rallying cry for northern abolitionists, who saw the move as an attempt to extend slavery.

AFRICAN AMERICANS IN THE NORTH

Though some enslaved people dreamed of escaping to the North, those who succeeded found themselves facing many of the challenges they thought they had left behind. Many northerners held the same racist beliefs that were common among southerners. They did not want to live near, work with, or have their children go to school with African Americans. They cared little about ending slavery and looked upon free African Americans with scorn. Even as they worked to try to end the institution of slavery, some abolitionists held racist attitudes toward African Americans.

Discrimination took several forms. Some states passed laws restricting the rights of African Americans to vote, own property, and move about freely. **Segregation**, or the separation of people based on race, was common in northern cities, and African Americans often were forbidden from entering white churches, schools, and many other buildings. They were often blocked from employment for skilled jobs. Free African Americans even feared for their lives. Daily threats included attacks by white mobs and the possibility of being captured and sent back to a life of slavery.

HISTORICAL THINKING

1. **READING CHECK** What was the relationship between racism and slavery?

2. **IDENTIFY MAIN IDEAS AND DETAILS** What forms of discrimination did African Americans face in the North?

3. **COMPARE AND CONTRAST** How were the situations of free African Americans in the North and the South similar?

2.1 A Country in Crisis

In 1820 and again in 1850, compromises had held the United States together. But how many times can you compromise before someone finally cries, "enough already"?

> **MAIN IDEA** The Kansas-Nebraska Act deepened the conflict over slavery and led to the eruption of violence in these territories.

THE KANSAS-NEBRASKA ACT

The discovery of gold in California in 1848 had increased interest in building a railroad to the Pacific coast. **Stephen A. Douglas**, a senator from Illinois, lobbied for the railroad to run through his state. Douglas, who was a great supporter of national expansion, proposed a route stretching from the Illinois city of Chicago west to San Francisco, California.

However, there were problems with this route. Before a railroad could cross the territory west of Minnesota, Iowa, and Missouri, the territory would have to be organized into new states. But the Missouri Compromise had banned slavery in this area. The prospect of new free states infuriated, or enraged, southerners and once again threatened the country's unity.

Douglas introduced a bill that dealt with these issues. It called for the territory to be split into two smaller territories called Kansas and Nebraska, which could then become states. It also called for the repeal of the Missouri Compromise, which would end the long-standing ban on slavery in the North.

The bill, however, did not dictate whether slavery would actually be permitted in the new states. It left that decision to the people. This approach is called **popular sovereignty** (SAHV-run-tee) and allows residents to decide an issue by voting. Douglas had developed this idea, but many northerners, especially in New England, disagreed with it. Despite the strong opposition to popular sovereignty, Douglas managed to push the bill through Congress. It was signed into law in May 1854 as the **Kansas-Nebraska Act**.

Three Compromise Acts, 1820–1854

Free states	Slave states
Territories closed to slavery	Territories open to slavery
Non-U.S. areas	

The Missouri Compromise, 1820–1821

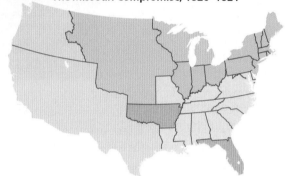

The Compromise of 1850

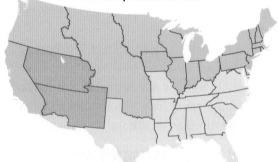

The Kansas-Nebraska Act of 1854

"BLEEDING KANSAS"

Douglas predicted that the Kansas-Nebraska Act would "impart peace to the country [and] stability to the Union." Instead, Kansas became a battleground in the slavery conflict. Antislavery "Free-Soilers," or members of the Free-Soil Party in the North, organized like-minded groups of people to settle in the new territory and vote against slavery there. Free-Soilers hoped that by populating Kansas with people who felt as they did, they could ensure that the territory would become a free state.

But southerners were just as determined to make Kansas a slave state. When elections were held, thousands of slavery supporters from Missouri crossed the border to vote illegally. These "border ruffians," as they were called, were actually not needed because many southerners and slavery supporters already lived in Kansas. Proslavery forces gained control of the legislature in 1855 and passed a series of harsh laws against those who opposed slavery. Antislavery settlers then created their own government within the state and worked through the summer and fall of 1855 to write their own constitution. Over the winter, the Free-Soilers elected a legislature and governor. Groups sympathetic to their cause in the Northeast sent them rifles, while southerners sent a 300-man expedition to support the proslavery settlers.

The situation soon turned violent. In May 1856, a large group of slavery supporters raided the town of Lawrence, Kansas, a free-soil stronghold. They burned down a hotel, destroyed a newspaper office, and threw printing presses into the river. In revenge, a militant, or extremist, abolitionist named **John Brown** led four of his sons and several other men to a proslavery settlement at Pottawatomie (pot-uh-WAH-tuh-mee) Creek. There, they pulled five men out of their houses and brutally murdered them. Federal troops pursued Brown, but he managed to escape. Brown fled north where he was protected by other abolitionists. Because of the violence in Lawrence, Pottawatomie Creek, and other places, Americans

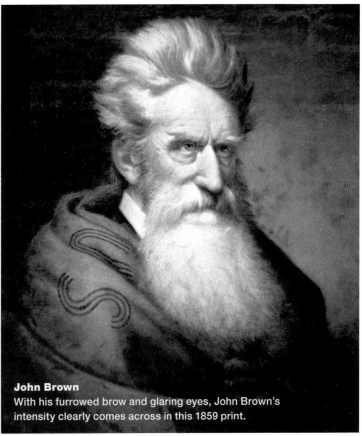

John Brown
With his furrowed brow and glaring eyes, John Brown's intensity clearly comes across in this 1859 print.

began calling the territory "Bleeding Kansas." Eventually, order was restored in Kansas, but the political struggle over slavery continued.

The violence even reached Washington, D.C. Preston Brooks, a representative from South Carolina, had been angered by an antislavery speech given by Massachusetts senator Charles Sumner. When Brooks entered the Senate chamber, he severely beat Sumner with a cane. Soon, the split in the country over slavery would involve the Supreme Court.

HISTORICAL THINKING

1. **READING CHECK** What approach did the Kansas-Nebraska Act take toward the issue of slavery in the Kansas and Nebraska territories?

2. **ANALYZE CAUSE AND EFFECT** What violent incident occurred as a result of a senator's speech opposing slavery?

3. **INTERPRET MAPS** How did U.S. territories represented in the Compromise of 1850 map change after the Kansas-Nebraska Act was passed?

2.2 The Dred Scott Decision

When things are going badly, we like to think that, at least, they can't get any worse. Until, of course, they do.

> **MAIN IDEA** The Dred Scott case and John Brown's attack on Harpers Ferry further divided the North and the South over the issue of slavery.

THE REPUBLICAN PARTY

The Kansas-Nebraska Act caused the political differences in the United States to erupt. The repeal of the Missouri Compromise and the opening of new territories to slavery angered many northerners and deepened North-South divisions in the Whig and Democratic parties. Many northerners began to feel that none of the existing political parties reflected their growing concerns over slavery.

In reaction, antislavery leaders founded a new party in 1854 dedicated to fighting the expansion of slavery. The **Republican Party**, as it was named, found a following among former Whigs, Free-Soilers, Democrats, and Know-Nothings.

Dred Scott was about 60 years old when this photo was taken during his Supreme Court case. His former master's sons purchased and freed Scott after the decision, but he died nine months later.

When the 1856 presidential election approached, the Republicans picked John C. Frémont, who was well-known for his explorations of the West, as their candidate. The Democrats chose **James Buchanan** to represent their party. Buchanan secured the presidency, but Frémont made a strong showing, winning 11 northern states. From the outset, the Republicans proved they were a force to be reckoned with.

DRED SCOTT AND JOHN BROWN

In March of 1857, two days after Buchanan took office, the U.S. Supreme Court issued a decision in *Dred Scott* v. *Sandford*, which had begun in 1846. The case involved a slave named Dred Scott. He had sued for his freedom on the grounds that his master had taken him to live in the free state of Illinois and in the Wisconsin Territory, where slavery was also prohibited.

The Court ruled that Scott should remain a slave, and the **Dred Scott decision** sent shockwaves through the nation. In his explanation of the ruling, Chief Justice **Roger Taney** asserted that "members of the negro African race" were not actually citizens of the United States. Therefore, Scott did not have the right to bring a lawsuit to a federal court. Taney further declared that since slaves were the personal property of slaveholders, Congress had never had the authority to restrict slavery in the territories. This rendered the Missouri Compromise of 1820 unconstitutional. The strongly proslavery decision sparked outrage in the North and raised fears that southerners might try to extend slavery to the whole country. The chasm between North and South grew even wider.

Two years later, yet another dramatic event in the struggle over slavery took center stage. John Brown, the abolitionist responsible for the Pottawatomie Creek massacre in Kansas, led an attack on the town of **Harpers Ferry**, in the part of Virginia that later became West Virginia. He and his armed band of 21 men captured a federal arsenal and a rifle-manufacturing plant and took dozens of hostages. Brown hoped to trigger a

Harpers Ferry National Historical Park, West Virginia

Harpers Ferry is located where the Shenandoah and Potomac rivers meet, as shown in this aerial image taken by National Geographic photographer Ken Garrett. The scene of John Brown's 1859 raid on the armory, the town later became the site of one of the first integrated schools—attended by both former slaves and whites—in the nation.

slave revolt and create an "army of emancipation" that would free slaves across the South. He was wounded and captured, however, and ten of his men were killed. After a short trial, he was hanged just six weeks after the attack. To the dismay of southerners, many northerners refused to condemn Brown. Instead, they viewed him as a hero and a martyr, or a person willing to die for his or her beliefs, to the cause of abolition. The raid at Harpers Ferry increased southerners' fear of slave rebellions and further heightened the tension between the North and the South. As a result, slavery was about to bring the country to the breaking point.

HISTORICAL THINKING

1. **READING CHECK** Why did Dred Scott believe he should be freed from slavery?

2. **IDENTIFY MAIN IDEAS AND DETAILS** What political ideas led to the formation of the Republican Party?

3. **DISTINGUISH FACT FROM OPINION** Is Roger Taney's assertion that "members of the negro African race" were not actually citizens of the United States a fact or opinion? Explain your answer.

2.3 Lincoln and Douglas

Republican Abraham Lincoln and Democrat Stephen Douglas opposed each other in two political races. In 1858, they fought for the U.S. Senate seat in Illinois, which Douglas won. In 1860, they ran against each other for president, with Lincoln the victor. Although both men disliked slavery, they had different views on the issue.

Lincoln and Douglas engaged in a series of debates during their race for the Illinois Senate seat. Their fourth debate was held on September 18, 1858, in Charleston, Illinois. There, Douglas attacked Lincoln by saying that his opponent favored racial equality, an unpopular position at the time, even in the North. The painting below shows Lincoln speaking to the crowd gathered for the outdoor event. Douglas sits to Lincoln's right, waiting his turn to speak.

CRITICAL VIEWING How does the artist portray the debate?

Abraham Lincoln and Stephen A. Douglas Debating at Charleston by Robert Marshall Root, 1918

DOCUMENT ONE

DOCUMENT ONE

Primary Source: Speech
from Abraham Lincoln's speech at the Republican Convention in
Springfield, Illinois, on June 16, 1858

This speech is known as the "House Divided" speech. Lincoln used a
Bible metaphor, comparing the nation to a house, to express his view
of the impact that conflicting laws about slavery were having on the
country as a whole.

CONSTRUCTED RESPONSE What does Lincoln think will happen to
the Union if the division continues?

"A house divided against itself cannot
stand." I believe this government
cannot endure, permanently, half
slave and half free. I do not expect the
Union to be dissolved; I do not expect
the house to fall; but I do expect it will
cease to be divided. It will become all
one thing, or all the other.

DOCUMENT TWO

Primary Source: Speech
from Stephen Douglas's speech at the Lincoln-Douglas
debate in Freeport, Illinois, on August 27, 1858

In a debate held in Freeport, Illinois, Douglas addressed
a question that Lincoln had put to him: Could the people
of a territory keep slavery out? Douglas believed they
could and, in this excerpt, he explains how.

CONSTRUCTED RESPONSE Describe how Douglas
uses cause and effect to explain how people can keep
slavery out of a territory.

The people have the lawful means to introduce
it [slavery] or exclude it as they please, for the
reason that slavery cannot exist a day or an hour
anywhere, unless it is supported by local police
regulations. Those police regulations can only
be established by the local legislature, and if the
people are opposed to slavery they will elect
representatives to that body who will by unfriendly
legislation effectually prevent the introduction of it
into their midst.

DOCUMENT THREE

Primary Source: Political Cartoon
from *Harper's Weekly*, 1860

This political cartoon suggests
that the issue of slavery is tearing
the United States apart. Seen here
are the four candidates in the 1860
presidential election. From left to
right are Abraham Lincoln, Stephen
Douglas, John C. Breckinridge, and
John Bell.

CONSTRUCTED RESPONSE What
details in the cartoon suggest
that slavery is tearing the United
States apart?

SYNTHESIZE & WRITE

1. **REVIEW** Review what you have
   learned about Abraham Lincoln and
   Stephen Douglas and their debates.

2. **RECALL** On your own paper,
   write the main idea expressed in
   each document.

3. **CONSTRUCT** Construct a topic sentence that answers
   this question: What differing positions did Lincoln and
   Douglas take on the issue of slavery?

4. **WRITE** Using evidence from this chapter and the documents,
   write an informative paragraph that supports your topic
   sentence in Step 3.

3.1 The Election of 1860

Say you belong to a club and two groups within it often disagree. Should they try to work things out? Or should one group break away and form a new club? Maybe it depends on whether they're into politics.

MAIN IDEA The growing divide between the North and the South had a strong impact on the 1860 presidential election.

POLITICAL PARTIES BREAK APART

"Bleeding Kansas," the Dred Scott decision, John Brown's raid at Harpers Ferry: each of these developments had left the United States more divided over slavery. The Democratic Party found it harder to hold itself together as tensions grew between its powerful southern faction, or group, and its smaller northern faction. When the two factions could not agree on a candidate for the 1860 presidential election, the party split in two. Northern Democrats nominated Stephen Douglas of Illinois, and southern Democrats nominated **John Breckinridge** of Kentucky.

Around this same time, a group of former Whigs and Know-Nothings founded the conservative **Constitutional Union Party**. It appealed to people who believed that preserving the Union and protecting the

Constitution outweighed concerns about slavery. For the election, **Unionists**, as members of the Constitutional Union Party were called, sought a compromise candidate who could appeal to both northerners and southerners. They chose John Bell, a highly regarded former U.S. senator from Tennessee.

Lincoln Campaign Banner

Lincoln's running mate in the 1860 election was Hannibal Hamlin, a senator from Maine. In this cotton flag, Lincoln's first name is spelled "Abram," possibly to enable his name to appear larger. "Abram" is also the original spelling of the biblical Abraham. The portrait of Lincoln may have been printed sideways so the flag could be hung vertically.

HANNIBAL HAMLIN.

For Vice President

ABRAM LINCOLN.

For President

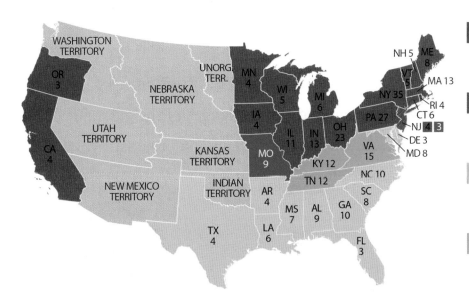

1860 Presidential Election

Lincoln, Republican

Electoral Vote: 180 votes, 59.4%

Popular Vote: 1,866,452 votes, 39.8%

Douglas, Northern Democrat

Electoral Vote: 12 votes, 3.9%

Popular Vote: 1,380,202 votes, 29.5%

Breckinridge, Southern Democrat

Electoral Vote: 72 votes, 23.8%

Popular Vote: 847,953 votes, 18.1%

Bell, Constitutional Unionist

Electoral Vote: 39 votes, 12.9%

Popular Vote: 590,901 votes, 12.6%

THE NOMINATION OF LINCOLN

In May 1860, Republicans gathered in Chicago, Illinois, for their national convention. Party strategists identified four states that would be key to winning the upcoming election: Illinois, Indiana, New Jersey, and Pennsylvania. The first three bordered southern states and were more moderate in their views about slavery than states farther north. The party decided to place its presidential hopes on a moderate from Illinois: Abraham Lincoln.

Born in a one-room log cabin, Lincoln grew up on frontier farms in Kentucky and Indiana. His mother died when he was just nine. Because the family was poor, they moved from place to place, struggling to survive. Young Lincoln developed a love of reading but had to work, so he received very little formal schooling. When Lincoln was 21, he moved with his family to Illinois. There, he taught himself law, built a thriving legal practice, and launched a successful political career. He served four terms in the Illinois state assembly and one term in the U.S. House of Representatives. He failed twice in bids for the U.S. Senate, but that didn't stop him from running for president in 1860.

In the presidential campaign, Lincoln did not try to win over southern voters, and Breckinridge spent little effort on the North. Southerners refused to consider Lincoln because they believed he was too antislavery, while northerners rejected Breckinridge's proslavery views. Bell focused his attention on like-minded Unionists in the states between the North and the South. Douglas, however, campaigned in both the North and the South, defending the Union and warning against voting along sectional lines. Because Bell and Douglas didn't propose enacting laws one way or the other on slavery, they were considered the moderate candidates.

When voters cast their ballots on election day, Lincoln won almost 40 percent of the popular vote, and he captured the electoral votes in every northern state except New Jersey, which he split with Douglas. Not surprisingly, he didn't win any electoral votes in the South. For the most part, voters cast their ballots along regional lines. The election proved they were tired of compromising. And for many southerners, the election also drew a line in the sand that they were not afraid to cross.

HISTORICAL THINKING

1. **READING CHECK** Why were there two Democratic candidates in the 1860 election?

2. **MAKE INFERENCES** Why might Abraham Lincoln's background have appealed to voters?

3. **INTERPRET MAPS** Why did winning just the northern states guarantee that Lincoln would secure the majority of electoral votes?

3.2 Southern States Secede

A crack in a mirror often starts out small, hardly visible. But over time, rough handling causes the crack to deepen and run the length of the glass. Pretty soon, the smallest added pressure will make it snap and break in two.

MAIN IDEA The election of Abraham Lincoln as president in 1860 led southern states to secede from the Union.

1860 campaign buttons feature Lincoln (left) and his running mate, Hamlin (right).

THE SOUTH DEBATES INDEPENDENCE

The South had reached its breaking point. Abraham Lincoln's victory in the 1860 election shocked and angered most southerners. They were suddenly faced with a northern president who had not won a single southern state. In fact, his name had not even appeared on the ballot in most of them. After all, Lincoln represented a party founded by people who wanted to keep slavery out of new territories and states.

Although Lincoln had not called for the abolition of slavery many proslavery southerners felt certain this was his goal. You've already read one excerpt from Lincoln's "House Divided" speech, delivered in 1858. In that speech he also said, "Either the opponents of slavery will arrest the further spread of it, . . . or its advocates [supporters] will push it forward, till it shall become alike lawful in all the States." In the South, many assumed this meant that Lincoln wished to abolish slavery throughout the United States.

On the day after the election, South Carolina's legislature gathered to debate the possibility of **seceding**, or formally withdrawing from the Union and becoming independent. Secession was not a new idea. Slave states had threatened to leave the Union on numerous occasions. In fact, South Carolina had come very close to doing so during the nullification crisis of the 1830s.

Supporters of secession justified it in terms of states' rights. The right that southern leaders most wanted to protect was their perceived right to own slaves. They argued that under the Constitution, the states retained certain rights, including the right to secede. Just as each state had once decided to join the Union, each state could decide to withdraw from it.

VOTES FOR SECESSION

On December 20, 1860, South Carolina became the first state in the nation to secede from the Union. The state's secession came in response to the presidential election of Abraham Lincoln the month before, even though he was not to take office until March 1861. South Carolina decided that Lincoln's presidential win as a Republican—a party that supported the Free-Soil platform, not the end of slavery in territories where it already existed—signaled that it could not continue as part of the United States.

South Carolina was joined by 10 other states in the coming months. In March 1861, the **Confederate States of America**, or the **Confederacy**, united and quickly formed a temporary government in Montgomery, Alabama, and adopted a new constitution. It was much like the U.S. Constitution, but it protected slavery and states' rights.

Jefferson Davis, a Mississippi senator who had spoken out against secession just weeks earlier, was chosen to be the temporary president of the Confederacy. In his inaugural address, Davis placed the blame for the secessions on the Union,

Abraham Lincoln
This 1860 photo by
Alexander Hesler reveals
Lincoln's lined face and
rugged features.

arguing that protecting slavery had been the
"well-known intent" of the Founders. Meanwhile,
the issue of secession was proving to be divisive
in the more northern part of the South. Many
people opposed secession, calling it treason.
They believed secession would be disastrous
for the South. Others thought it would be best to
wait before making a decision. For the time being,
Virginia, Tennessee, North Carolina, and Arkansas
remained in the Union. They still held out hope that
the differences between the North and the South
could be resolved.

HISTORICAL THINKING

1. **READING CHECK** Why did Lincoln's election
   drive southern states to secede from the Union?

2. **MAKE INFERENCES** Why do you think the
   Confederacy adopted a constitution that was
   very similar to the U.S. Constitution?

3. **DRAW CONCLUSIONS** What fundamental
   challenge to the Constitution did secession and
   the doctrine of nullification pose?

3.3 Efforts at Compromise

Who among your friends is the peacemaker? There's usually one who brings those in conflict together and tries to find common ground and iron out differences. Sometimes these efforts pay off. Sometimes they don't.

MAIN IDEA Leaders in the North and the South tried to resolve the secession crisis, but their attempts to reach a compromise failed.

THE CRITTENDEN PLAN

After South Carolina seceded from the Union, John J. Crittenden, a senator from Kentucky, tried to step in as peacemaker. In 1861, he offered a proposal that came to be known as the **Crittenden Plan**. Under the terms of this compromise plan, the federal government would have no power to abolish slavery in the states where it already existed. Further, the Missouri Compromise line would be reestablished and extended all the way to the Pacific Ocean. Slavery would be prohibited in territories north of the line, but in territories south of it, local residents would decide whether to allow slavery.

The proposal found many supporters in both the North and the South, and President James Buchanan pushed for its speedy approval in Congress. President-elect Abraham Lincoln and many Republicans, however, strongly objected to extending slavery in any new territories. After much debate, the Crittenden Plan was defeated in Congress, and the secession crisis continued.

LINCOLN BECOMES PRESIDENT

As his inauguration approached, Lincoln put together his government. For his Cabinet, he purposely chose men who represented competing factions within the Republican Party. Some of them could barely stand one another.

Surprisingly, four of the top positions went to men who had competed with Lincoln for the Republican nomination. He would later defend these appointments by saying, "We needed the strongest men of the party in the Cabinet. These were the very strongest men. Then I had no right to deprive the country of their services." Some have called the men he assembled "a team of rivals."

Lincoln took office on March 4, 1861, as the 16th president of the United States. In his inaugural address, Lincoln spoke sternly and directly about the crisis facing the country. He said his first task was to reunite the nation. Secession was illegal, he declared; no state could simply decide on its own to leave the Union. The Union was therefore

A Perpetual Union

At the beginning of his inaugural address, Lincoln stated that he was going to get directly to the point and talk about the matter of greatest concern to the country at that moment: the threat of southern secession. He assured the South that he did not support freeing its slaves. But he also emphasized that there was no constitutional basis for withdrawing from the Union.

PRIMARY SOURCE

I hold that, in contemplation of universal law and of the Constitution, the Union of these States is perpetual [everlasting]. Perpetuity [This permanence] is implied, if not expressed, in the fundamental law of all national governments. It is safe to assert that no government proper ever had a provision in its organic law [system of laws] for its own termination [end]. . . . The Union will endure forever.

—from Abraham Lincoln's First Inaugural Address, March 4, 1861

Lincoln with His Cabinet and Generals
In this engraving from 1866, Lincoln meets with his Cabinet and military leaders to discuss their response to the South's secession. Lincoln did not want war with the South, but he wanted to be prepared for it if it couldn't be avoided.

still intact, and he vowed to use his powers as president to protect places and property belonging to the federal government. He assured the South, however, that he did not intend to interfere with slavery where it already existed, and there would be no invasion or use of force by the government. "We are not enemies, but friends," Lincoln said. "Though passion may have strained, it must not break our bonds of affection."

Lincoln's words had little effect. The day after his address, a message arrived in Washington from **Fort Sumter**, which lay at the entrance to the harbor in Charleston, South Carolina. The fort was under threat from Confederate forces, and its **garrison**, or defense force, of about 85 federal soldiers would soon run out of food. After South Carolina seceded, the U.S. government

took control of the fort. But in January 1861, local militias prevented a ship from bringing supplies and additional troops to Fort Sumter. President Lincoln wanted to avoid conflict with the South, but a civil war looked more and more likely.

HISTORICAL THINKING

1. **READING CHECK** What compromise did the Crittenden Plan propose?

2. **IDENTIFY MAIN IDEAS AND DETAILS** Who did Lincoln choose to be in his Cabinet, and why did he appoint these individuals?

3. **DRAW CONCLUSIONS** Why did Confederate forces threaten Fort Sumter?

REVIEW

VOCABULARY

Use each of the following terms in a sentence that shows an understanding of the term's meaning.

1. secede
   Southern states <u>seceded</u>, breaking away from the United States.

2. federal marshal

3. racism

4. segregation

5. popular sovereignty

6. Dred Scott decision

7. garrison

8. Confederacy

READING STRATEGY
IDENTIFY MAIN IDEAS AND DETAILS

If you haven't done so already, complete your chart to identify the main ideas and details relating to the issue of slavery. List at least four main ideas and their supporting details. Then answer the question.

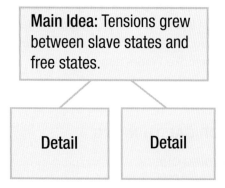

Main Idea: Tensions grew between slave states and free states.

Detail   Detail

9. What impact did Lincoln's "House Divided" speech have on the South and slavery?

MAIN IDEAS

Answer the following questions. Support your answers with evidence from the chapter.

10. How did the Compromise of 1850 help save the Union? **LESSON 1.1**

11. How did segregation affect free African Americans living in northern states? **LESSON 1.2**

12. Why did the Kansas Territory become known as "Bleeding Kansas"? **LESSON 2.1**

13. How did the Supreme Court decision in the Dred Scott case widen the divide between the North and the South? **LESSON 2.2**

14. Why did Jefferson Davis blame the Union for the secession? **LESSON 3.2**

15. Why did the election of Abraham Lincoln cause southern states to secede from the Union? **LESSON 3.2**

16. Under the terms of the Crittenden Plan, how would the issue of slavery be handled south of the Missouri Compromise line? **LESSON 3.3**

HISTORICAL THINKING

17. **SYNTHESIZE** Why didn't the compromises made in the first half of the 19th century last?

18. **DRAW CONCLUSIONS** How did John Brown's raid at Harpers Ferry increase tensions between the North and the South?

19. **MAKE CONNECTIONS** How did slavery as a political, economic, and social institution divide the country and lead to civil war?

20. **IDENTIFY MAIN IDEAS AND DETAILS** Why did the Supreme Court rule that Dred Scott should remain a slave?

21. **FORM AND SUPPORT OPINIONS** Based on the slavery-related developments of the 1850s, was it inevitable that southern states would eventually decide to separate from the Union? Support your opinion with evidence from the chapter.

22. **MAKE INFERENCES** What do you think might have been the strengths and weaknesses of having a "team of rivals" in Lincoln's Cabinet?

INTERPRET MAPS

The map below shows the percentage of enslaved people throughout the United States in 1860. The darkest green shading indicates areas in which more than 50 percent of the residents were enslaved. The lightest green shading indicates areas with no slaves. Look closely at the map and then answer the questions.

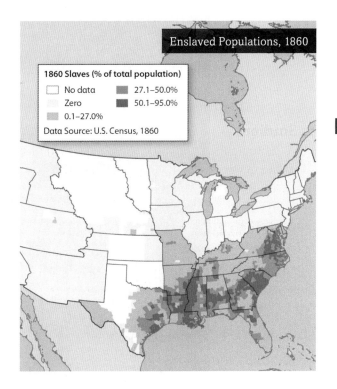

Enslaved Populations, 1860

1860 Slaves (% of total population)
- No data
- Zero
- 0.1–27.0%
- 27.1–50.0%
- 50.1–95.0%

Data Source: U.S. Census, 1860

23. What does this map reveal about the general geographic distribution of slavery across the South?

24. In which sections of the country were there zero populations of enslaved people?

ANALYZE SOURCES

In Harriet Beecher Stowe's novel *Uncle Tom's Cabin,* Eliza is an enslaved woman whose child has been sold to another plantation owner. Rather than see her son turned over to a new slaveholder, Eliza flees with her son in the early spring across the Ohio River to the free state of Ohio. The river is still partly frozen, and she crosses it by jumping from one block of ice to another. Read the following excerpt from the novel and then answer the question.

> Eliza made her desperate retreat across the river just in the dusk of twilight. The gray mist of evening, rising slowly from the river, enveloped her as she disappeared up the bank, and the swollen current and floundering [shifting] masses of ice presented a hopeless barrier between her and her pursuer.

25. What details in the excerpt help build suspense?

CONNECT TO YOUR LIFE

26. **INFORMATIVE** Think about what you have learned about slavery and how deeply it divided the United States. What issues divide the country today? Choose one issue and write a paragraph summarizing it and discussing its impact on the country.

TIPS

- Introduce the topic with a clear main idea statement.

- Develop the topic with relevant facts and concrete details. Be sure to present both sides of the issue.

- Compare the impact of the issue you have chosen to the impact of slavery.

- Provide a concluding statement that follows from and supports the information that you have presented.

CHAPTER
15

BEGINNINGS OF
WAR
1861–1862

ESSENTIAL QUESTION
How did the early years of the Civil War affect people on both sides of the conflict?

AMERICAN STORIES Voices from the Civil War

SECTION 1 War Erupts

KEY VOCABULARY

border state   evacuate   mobilize

cavalry   infantry

SECTION 2 Life in the Army

KEY VOCABULARY

civilian   mortality   trench warfare

ironclad ship   philanthropist

SECTION 3 A War Without End

KEY VOCABULARY

Anaconda Plan   gunboat   pontoon

AMERICAN GALLERY
ONLINE
The Daily Lives of Civil War Soldiers

READING STRATEGY

SUMMARIZE
When you summarize, you restate text in your own words and shorten it, including only the most important main ideas and details. As you read this chapter, use concept clusters like this one to help you summarize important information in the text. In the large oval, list a main idea. In the smaller ovals, note key supporting details. Then use your notes to write your summary.

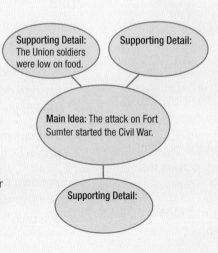

Supporting Detail: The Union soldiers were low on food.

Supporting Detail:

Main Idea: The attack on Fort Sumter started the Civil War.

Supporting Detail:

"War is the remedy our enemies have chosen . . . **let us give them all they want.**"

—General William Tecumseh Sherman

National Geographic photographer Ken Garrett took this photo of the Antietam National Battlefield in Sharpsburg, Maryland. The Battle of Antietam took place on September 17, 1862, and is still considered the bloodiest day in U.S. military history. Garrett shot the photo from the air to capture an area on the battlefield known as Sunken Road, or Bloody Lane, where some of the fiercest fighting took place. The statue standing near the Union lines commemorates a division of Pennsylvania soldiers who fought at Antietam.

VOICES FROM THE
CIVIL WAR

PRIMARY SOURCES

CRITICAL VIEWING Some families camped with their soldiers during the Civil War. What does this photo reveal about the life of this 31st Pennsylvania Infantry soldier and his family?

In the 1860s, an event transformed the lives of all Americans. The Civil War between the northern and southern states would leave no person untouched. In the 1800s, people had limited options for describing their experiences. They used letters and journals, charcoal and paints, and photographs as their voices and means of expression. After the war, they wrote memoirs and recollections to preserve their stories and process their experiences.

You're about to read about the daily lives and hardships of the soldiers, the suffering of civilians in a battle zone, the agony of a family divided, and other struggles of a people divided by war. Through these primary sources, you will gain a firsthand understanding of what it was like to live through the Civil War, one American voice at a time.

JOHN D. BILLINGS

First, [the hardtack biscuits] may have been so hard that they could not be bitten; it then required a very strong blow of the fist to break them.

The second condition was when they were mouldy [moldy] or wet.

The third condition was when from storage they had become infested with maggots and weevils. These weevils were, in my experience, more abundant than the maggots. They were a little slim, brown bug an eighth of an inch in length, having the ability to completely riddle [poke holes in] the hardtack.

But hardtack was not so bad an article of food, even when traversed by insects. Eaten in the dark, no one could tell the difference between it and hardtack that was untenanted. It was no uncommon occurrence for a man to find the surface of his pot of coffee swimming with weevils, after breaking up hardtack in it . . . but they were easily skimmed off and left no distinctive flavour behind.

—from *Hardtack and Coffee,* by John D. Billings, 1888

HARDTACK

In the humorous excerpt from his postwar memoir (left), Union Army soldier John D. Billings describes the challenges of hardtack biscuits, one of the most common camp foods. Hardtack (shown here) is a hard cracker made of flour and water. It was a problematic food, but as you can see, some soldiers actually developed a fondness for it.

Soldiers from both the North and the South learned to live with minimal comfort when they were on the march or in camp. At night, they crowded into small tents, sometimes packed together so tightly, if one soldier wanted to roll over, he had to get his tent mates to roll over, too.

The food tasted awful and was sometimes inedible. When soldiers received "fresh" meat, it had often already gone bad. Preserved meat was so filled with salt that it had to be soaked in water for hours before a soldier even attempted to eat it. In southern camps, these poor rations were likely to run out, especially in the war's later years when many farms in the South had been destroyed.

A SOLDIER'S GEAR

KEPI

BAYONET

RIFLE

CAP BOX

CARTRIDGE BOX

CRITICAL VIEWING Before going off to war, Civil War soldiers often had their photograph taken. For many, it was their last. What do these photographs tell you about the equipment the soldiers carried?

SHELL JACKET

DAGGER

WOOL TROUSERS

CONFEDERATE ARMY SOLDIER

FORAGE CAP

BAYONET

SACK COAT

CAP BOX

RIFLE

WOOL TROUSERS

UNION ARMY SOLDIER

GEORGE ALLEN

A woolen blanket and a piece of shelter tent twisted together, and thrown over our shoulders; haversack [knapsack] loaded with a dozen hard tack and a small piece of "salt horse," little bag of coffee and sugar, . . . all sorts of hats or caps; little to eat, but plenty of ammunition.

—from *Forty-Six Months with the Fourth R.I. Volunteers*, by Corp. George H. Allen, 1887

A SOLDIER'S GEAR

When a Union soldier like George Allen from Rhode Island joined the army, he was, of course, equipped with a rifle. He also received other gear, like a knapsack, a wool blanket, a cartridge box on a shoulder strap, a canteen, a bag for carrying food, and eating utensils. All together, he might find himself carrying 40 to 50 pounds of weapons and gear. But as time went on, most soldiers threw away the items they found to be unnecessary to make marching and moving easier. Corporal Allen's description of the simplicity of his gear after a year of fighting gives a sense of how practicality outweighed comfort.

coffee beans

food sack

cloth for patching

coffee can

tin cup

sewing kit

THE CIVILIANS OF VICKSBURG

As the fighting raged through the border states and the South, civilians often found themselves on the front lines of the war. The people of Vicksburg, Mississippi, experienced life in a battle zone between 1861 and 1863.

Vicksburg sits on a high bluff overlooking the Mississippi River. At the start of the war, the Confederacy controlled Vicksburg, and therefore it controlled the river traffic that passed by the city. The Union Army made multiple attempts to take Vicksburg, and eventually put the city under siege, blocking the paths into town so that no food or ammunition could be brought in. Day and night, Union soldiers rained shells down onto Vicksburg from the opposite side of the Mississippi River. Abandoning their ruined houses, residents dug caves into the hillside beneath the town. As the weeks dragged on, food ran short. People were forced to eat mules, horses, dogs, and rats.

The siege ended on July 4, 1863, when the military commander of the Vicksburg troops surrendered. A chaplain for the southern troops commented, "We surrendered to famine, not to [the northern army]." One woman kept a diary of the civilians' daily life during the siege of Vicksburg. She described the cave she was living in as "suffocating" and like "a living tomb." Read more from her diary in the excerpt below.

April 28, 1863—I never understood before the full force of those questions—what shall we eat? what shall we drink? and wherewithal shall we be clothed?

May 28—The regular siege has continued. We are utterly cut off from the world, surrounded by a circle of fire. The fiery shower of shells goes on day and night. People do nothing but eat what they can get, sleep when they can, and dodge shells. There are three intervals when the shelling stops, either for the guns to cool or for the gunners' meals, I suppose— about eight in the morning, the same in the evening, and at noon. In that time we have to both prepare and eat ours. Clothing cannot be washed or anything else done. I think all the dogs and cats must be killed or starved; we don't see any more pitiful animals prowling around.

—from "A Woman's Diary of the Siege of Vicksburg," published in *The Century Illustrated Monthly Magazine,* 1885

CRITICAL VIEWING The Shirley family, who owned the house shown in this 1863 photograph, were forced to live in a manmade cave, like the ones dug into the ground in the photo, to avoid the cannon fire flying past their home. What does this photo reveal about the impact of the Civil War on the civilian population of cities like Vicksburg?

FAMILIES DIVIDED

They may not look much alike, but David Keener Shriver (left) and Mark Shriver (right) were family members—cousins, in fact—fighting on opposite sides of the Civil War.

David joined up to fight with Company 1 of the Union Army's 190th Regiment of Pennsylvania Volunteers. His cousin Mark was a member of the Confederate Army's 1st Virginia Cavalry. Because the young soldiers' parents were siblings, it's likely loyalty to opposing armies was a source of division and tension in the family.

D.P. CONYNGHAM

I had a Sergeant Driscoll, a brave man, and one of the best shots in the Brigade. When charging at Malvern Hill, a company was posted in a clump of trees, who kept up a fierce fire on us, and actually charged out on our advance. Their officer seemed to be a daring, reckless boy, and I said to Driscoll, "if that officer is not taken down, many of us will fall before we pass that clump."

"Leave that to me," said Driscoll; so he raised his rifle, and the moment the officer exposed himself again bang went Driscoll, over went the officer, his company at once breaking away.

As we passed the place I said, "Driscoll, see if that officer is dead—he was a brave fellow."

I stood looking on. Driscoll turned [the young soldier] over on his back. He opened his eyes for a moment, and faintly murmured "Father," and closed them forever.

I will forever recollect the frantic grief of Driscoll; it was harrowing to witness. [The young soldier] was his son, who had gone South before the war.

—from *The Irish Brigade and Its Campaigns,* by Union Army Capt. D.P. Conyngham, 1867

TRAGIC ENCOUNTERS

Most Americans sided with their home state in the Civil War, but some found it harder to choose a side. Political or personal beliefs, loyalty to the federal government, and pressure from loved ones often made for conflicted soldiers and broken family bonds.

The most heartbreaking tales of the Civil War may be those of families first divided, then reunited as enemies in battle. The personal account of Captain D.P. Conyngham of the Union Army (left) describes a tragic scene he witnessed during the battle at Malvern Hill, Virginia, on July 1, 1862.

CRITICAL VIEWING During the Grand Review in May 1865, the great armies of Grant and Sherman received a hero's welcome in Washington, D.C. What challenges do you think Union soldiers faced after the cheers subsided and they returned to their lives?

LEANDER STILLWELL

I now had only two miles to go, and was soon at the dear old boyhood home. My folks were expecting me, so they were not taken by surprise. There was no "scene" when we met, . . . but we all had a feeling of profound contentment and satisfaction which was too deep to be expressed by mere words.

When I returned home I found that the farm work my father was then engaged in was cutting up and shocking corn. So, the morning after my arrival, September 29th, I doffed my uniform of first lieutenant, put on some of father's old clothes, armed myself with a corn knife, and proceeded to wage war on the standing corn. The feeling I had while engaged in this work was "sort of queer." It almost seemed, sometimes, as if I had been away only a day or two, and had just taken up the farm work where I had left off.

—from *The Story of a Common Soldier of Army Life in the Civil War* by Leander Stillwell, 1920

GOING HOME

For some soldiers, the return home after the Civil War was warm, yet surprisingly undramatic. In his personal account (left), Union soldier Leander Stillwell describes his return home to Illinois.

When the war ended in 1865, thousands of soldiers were mustered out (dismissed from service). But first, for many Union soldiers, there was the Grand Review in Washington, D.C. Over the course of two days in May, thousands of Union troops paraded through the streets of the capital to the applause of large crowds. Then, with the cheers still ringing in their ears, the men returned to their homes.

On the Confederate side, it was harder for soldiers to return home. The war had left southern cities and farms in ruins, and the recovery process would be long and difficult.

Personal accounts shed new light on history.

When you read the words of someone who lived through an event like the Civil War, you draw conclusions that are probably different from those you'd draw from a secondary source like a textbook.

Primary sources like those included in this American Story provide varied perspectives and points of view. They capture the voices of the Civil War and help tell the story of this country-changing event in American history.

THINK ABOUT IT

How useful and credible are primary sources like those included in this American Story in helping you understand soldiers' and civilians' lives during the Civil War?

1.1 Shots at Fort Sumter

Imagine a hot, dry landscape where rain hasn't fallen for months. It would take only a spark to send the whole area up in flames. The spark that ignited the Civil War was the attack on Fort Sumter.

MAIN IDEA Once the northern states declared war and most southern states had seceded, the country waited to see whether the states in between would remain in the Union.

THE SPARK THAT CAUSED THE FIRE

As you have read, President Abraham Lincoln declared that secession was illegal under the Constitution. Southerners, on the other hand, claimed secession as a states' right guaranteed by the document. They decided to secede because they perceived Lincoln's election as a threat to the lawful institution of slavery.

After they split from the Union, the newly formed Confederate states declared that everything owned by the U.S. government within their boundaries now belonged to the Confederacy. Fort Sumter in Charleston, South Carolina, was among the possessions they claimed.

Union major **Robert Anderson**, who was in charge of the fort, had watched the people of Charleston get swept up in secession fever, and he was worried. More than 5,000 Confederate soldiers surrounded Anderson and his men, and the Union soldiers were so low on provisions that they faced starvation. Lincoln sent a message to the southern leaders stating that he was going to send food, but not weapons, to the soldiers at Fort Sumter.

On April 11, 1861, before the Union's provisions arrived, Confederate leaders demanded that the Union troops **evacuate**, or leave, the fort. Otherwise, Confederate forces would take the stronghold by force. Lincoln and Anderson refused to agree to this demand, and the next day, Confederate forces began bombarding the fort from all sides. The shelling lasted for 34 hours. On April 14, with no more food or ammunition, Anderson surrendered.

War was unpopular among northerners, but the attack stirred the Union to action. Lincoln declared South Carolina to be in rebellion and called to form a militia. The Civil War had begun. Its purpose then was not to end slavery but to reunite the nation.

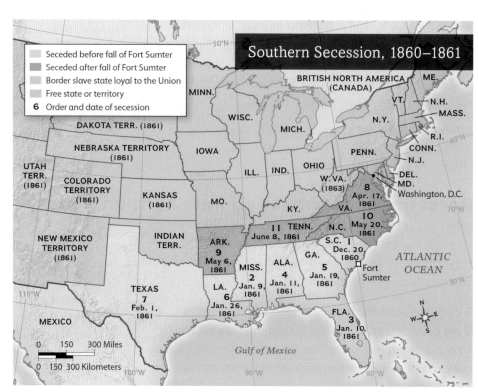

Southern Secession, 1860–1861

- Seceded before fall of Fort Sumter
- Seceded after fall of Fort Sumter
- Border slave state loyal to the Union
- Free state or territory
- 6 Order and date of secession

Fort Sumter

Fort Sumter was built after the War of 1812 with Britain had revealed the need for added defense along the U.S. coast. The five-sided island fort was designed to protect Charleston Harbor. No one was killed during the 1861 bombardment of the fort, but two Union soldiers accidentally died during a 100-gun salute.

THE GEOGRAPHY OF WAR

Within two days of Lincoln's call to arms, Virginia seceded. The Confederacy established its capital at Richmond, Virginia. Soon after, Arkansas, Tennessee, and North Carolina left the Union. However, four states bordering both the Union and the Confederacy—Maryland, Delaware, Missouri, and Kentucky—remained undecided. These states, called the **border states**, lay in the middle ground between the warring North and South and so were very important geographically.

Maryland, for example, bordered Washington, D.C., on three sides. If the state joined the Confederacy, the Union's capital would be completely surrounded by Confederate states. In an effort to keep Maryland in the Union, Lincoln threatened to jail any Confederate soldier who entered the state.

Missouri was also vital to the Union cause. With its large population, Missouri could supply the Union with many soldiers. The state also produced a great deal of food and protected the western side of the Union. In addition, its biggest city, St. Louis, was an important commercial and transportation center.

In Kentucky, both Confederate recruiters and pro-Union leaders tried to sway the state's citizens. But when Confederate forces invaded Kentucky in September 1861, the state asked the federal government for help. Lincoln sent troops to the state, the invaders were driven out, and Kentucky stayed in the Union.

The president gained more ground when 50 counties in northwest Virginia decided to form a new state. The people in those counties no longer wanted to be a part of pro-slavery Virginia and so, in 1863, West Virginia became part of the Union. Overall, Lincoln succeeded in keeping the border states in the Union. He would need all the forces he could gather to prepare for war and fight the long, tough battles ahead.

HISTORICAL THINKING

1. **READING CHECK** What happened after the Confederates attacked Fort Sumter?

2. **SUMMARIZE** Why was it important for the Union to keep the border states out of the Confederacy?

3. **IDENTIFY PROBLEMS AND SOLUTIONS** How did Lincoln deal with Confederate attempts to seize the border states?

1.2 An Early Confederate Victory

Sometimes you jump into something before you're really ready. Without enough time to make a plan or devise a strategy, you could find that you just have to "wing it." In a way, that's what happened to the Union and Confederate armies.

MAIN IDEA Confederate forces gained an early victory by winning the Battle of Bull Run.

Robert E. Lee

Born into a celebrated Virginia family, Robert E. Lee wanted to make a name for himself. He enrolled in the U.S. Military Academy at West Point in New York and was one of only six soldiers in his class who graduated with a clean record of behavior. After graduating, Lee met and married a descendant of Martha Washington, George Washington's wife. During the Mexican-American War, Lee impressed his commanding officer, General Winfield Scott, with his keen military mind. He became an officer in the Confederate Army after turning down Lincoln's offer to command the Union Army. His loyalty to his home state outweighed the president's request.

PREPARING FOR WAR

War had begun, but neither the Union nor the Confederacy was actually prepared for it. In April 1861, the Union forces included only 16,000 professional soldiers, while the Confederacy had fewer than 2,000. Both sides quickly took steps to **mobilize**, or organize and prepare troops for active service.

The North and the South enlisted troops at the local and state levels. A local leader would encourage men to join and serve under his command, or a group of men would get together and elect their commander. Many military units also formed along ethnic lines. Some northern regiments consisted only of European immigrants who communicated in their native language. Germans were the largest European immigrant group fighting for the Union. European immigrants also fought for the South, and a Texas regiment consisting of Mexicans called the Tejas soon joined the Confederate cause as well. Mobilization helped swell the ranks on both sides, but neither army was at full strength.

THE BATTLE OF BULL RUN

The armies were put to the test in July 1861. Hoping to bring a swift end to the war, Lincoln decided to send Union forces to seize Richmond. To carry out his plan, Lincoln first ordered General Irvin McDowell to attack the Confederate forces in Manassas, Virginia, a town less than 100 miles from Richmond. McDowell and his troops were in Washington, D.C., only 40 miles east of Manassas. But McDowell didn't believe his 35,000 volunteers were ready for battle, so he and his troops left

The first official Confederate flag is shown at the left. Often called the "Stars and Bars," it sometimes caused confusion on the battlefield because it looked so much like the U.S. flag. The flag below was first flown by a Virginia regiment. Soon other regiments began using it, but the Confederacy never officially adopted the flag.

Washington, D.C., more than a week later than planned. When the Confederate general stationed in Manassas, P.G.T. Beauregard, learned of the delay, he sent for help. Soon 11,000 more Confederate soldiers arrived to strengthen his forces.

The battle began on July 21, when Union forces crossed a small creek called Bull Run to attack the Confederates. As the Confederate soldiers charged, they unleashed a high-pitched battle cry that could be heard for miles. The earsplitting cry came to be known as the "rebel yell." Many Union soldiers wrote in letters and diaries about the terror the scream inspired.

During the battle, Confederate general Thomas Jackson and his forces filled a gap in the line of Confederate soldiers. He held the line so bravely that another general told his men to take heart from the sight of Jackson, "standing like a stone wall!" Jackson would be known by the nickname **Stonewall Jackson** for the rest of his life. Meanwhile, **J.E.B. Stuart**, the leader of the Virginia Confederate **cavalry**, or soldiers on horseback, watched Union movements on a hill overlooking the battlefield. At a critical point in the battle, Stuart's cavalry charged and scattered the

Union **infantry**, or foot soldiers. The charge forced the Union troops to retreat to Washington, D.C.

The Confederacy won the battle, but both sides suffered heavy casualties: about 3,000 soldiers for the North and more than 1,700 for the South. Another battle at Bull Run would take place more than a year later. Once again, the Confederates, under General **Robert E. Lee**, would win but with staggering casualties: nearly 15,000 for the Union and 9,000 for the Confederacy. These extremely high casualty rates continued to make the war unpopular in the North. Lincoln knew it would be a long and grueling war.

HISTORICAL THINKING

1. **READING CHECK** How did the North and the South prepare for the war?

2. **ANALYZE CAUSE AND EFFECT** How did the first Battle of Bull Run affect the course of the early part of the war?

3. **DRAW CONCLUSIONS** How did this battle reflect the beginnings of a broad pattern of leadership in the North and the South?

1.3 Confederate Memorial Hall New Orleans, Louisiana

Confederate Memorial Hall opened its doors in New Orleans on January 8, 1891. The oldest museum in Louisiana, it celebrates southern heritage and history with a focus on Civil War artifacts from the Confederate Army. In fact, the museum houses one of the largest collections of Confederate memorabilia in the United States, including uniforms and boots, weapons, personal items, and photographs. What challenges and advantages might a museum face in choosing to showcase items from one side of a war rather than from both sides?

Binoculars and Case

These 1863 binoculars and leather case belonged to a Confederate soldier. Cavalry generals—generals who commanded soldiers on horseback—and officers carried binoculars as part of their gear. Confederate soldiers also commonly carried a canteen, blanket roll (similar to a sleeping bag), ammunition and a weapon, and very simple food.

New Yorker William Ketchum designed and patented this Civil War hand grenade.

How might binoculars like these have helped officers on the battlefield?

Ketchum Hand Grenade

Unexploded hand grenades make an interesting addition to any wartime museum exhibit—especially early ones from the Civil War. Confederate and Union soldiers tossed these three- and five-pound hand grenades like darts into enemy territory during battles. The weapons have been recovered from famous battle sites such as Vicksburg and Petersburg.

Tintype Portrait

A photographer captured this 1861 tintype portrait of Sergeant Joseph Corneille, a member of the 22nd Louisiana Infantry, in his full dress uniform. Tintypes were invented in the 1850s and involved the transfer of a photograph to a thin sheet of iron coated with enamel. These portraits were prized possessions. They were also expensive. People bought elaborate frames like the one shown here, so they could put their portraits on display. They also carried them in cases or envelopes so the tintypes would be protected.

Many Civil War soldiers in full uniform had a tintype created before they headed off to battle. Why do you think the soldiers wanted to have these portraits created?

Confederate Battle Flag

Many Confederate regiments designed and adopted their own personalized battle flags during the Civil War. The red and white Van Dorn battle flag shown below was used by the regiments under the command of Confederate general Earl Van Dorn in Louisiana, Missouri, Mississippi, and Arkansas between 1862 and 1863. The 13 white stars represent the 13 Confederate States of America.

2.1 Hardship and Weapons

Siblings fight over all kinds of things: household chores, toys, television programs. During the Civil War, however, some siblings argued over a much larger issue: whether to support the Union or the Confederacy.

> **MAIN IDEA** Soldiers in the Civil War faced difficulties at home and in the field, including dealing with technological advances on the front lines.

A SOLDIER'S LIFE

The Civil War divided not only a nation but also families. Siblings, parents, and even spouses sometimes found themselves on different sides of the debate. It was not uncommon to hear of two brothers serving in opposing armies. No one was spared from these divisions, not even Abraham Lincoln. His brother-in-law, Ben Hardin Helm, was a Confederate general.

Whichever side the soldiers served on, life was difficult and dangerous. For every 30 days in the field, the average soldier engaged in battle one day and drilled, trained, and marched the remaining 29. Army leaders had difficulty keeping track of their units' needs, so supplies didn't always arrive when required. The soldiers were often cold and hungry as a result. Disease killed more men than fighting did.

And now army leaders had more soldiers under their command. After Bull Run, both the Confederate and Union leaders realized they needed larger armies. Farmers under the age of 30 made up about half of the men on both sides. Some older men joined the ranks as well, and boys as young as 12 served as drummers and buglers. About a quarter of the Union volunteers were young immigrants, mainly from Germany, Ireland, Canada, and England. Another group of people, African-American men, could have been drafted into fighting, but it would be several years before either army began to recruit them or even allow them to enlist.

A NEW KIND OF WAR

The Civil War battlefield was far more dangerous than it had been in previous American wars. Advances in technology made fighting more efficient and deadlier than ever. In earlier wars, soldiers carried muskets, which were not very accurate. The inside of a musket's barrel was polished smooth, causing the bullet's flight to be unpredictable. And a man fighting on the battlefield with a musket had to stand within 80 yards of his enemy in order to hit him. All that changed in the 1850s when a new kind of rifle replaced the musket. The grooves carved inside the barrel made the bullet spin as it hurtled toward its target. The spinning made the bullet fly in a straighter line and gave it a greater range—more than 1,000 yards.

Wooden Legs, Iron Arms
Approximately 70,000 soldiers lost limbs during the battles of the Civil War. The government offered veterans money to buy prosthetic, or artificial, arms, feet, and legs, like this one, to replace their missing limbs. Many options made of wood, iron, and leather were soon available. Few, however, were comfortable or functional. Most soldiers chose to use crutches and hooks instead.

CRITICAL VIEWING As this 1862 photograph of the Union Army reveals, Civil War soldiers used heavy guns and fought from trenches. What might have been some of the disadvantages of fighting and living in trenches such as these?

Some Union soldiers had another technological advantage in their hands: the repeating rifle. Instead of having to reload a gun after each shot, a soldier armed with a repeating rifle could fire several times before having to replenish his ammunition. These technological advances would continue to be improved and affect how future wars were fought.

With improvements to both rifles and larger cannons, soldiers increasingly resorted to **trench warfare** during the Civil War. Opposing armies dug lines of trenches, or ditches, roughly parallel to each other. The trenches gave soldiers both a vantage point from which to fire and a place to shelter from incoming rounds of ammunition. Advances in naval technology also brought changes to warfare at sea. Before, ordinary wooden ships were vulnerable to cannon and rifle fire. New **ironclad ships**, or ships plated with thick metal, could withstand this heavy artillery.

Unfortunately, the technology of medical treatment had not transformed as fast as the technology of war. Effective treatments for infections, such as antibiotics, had not yet been invented. **Mortality,**

or the death rate, from wounds and disease was high. And the hundreds of thousands of sick and wounded required medical attention, which in turn created a shortage of people to care for them. Hard-working male doctors and nurses set up hospitals in makeshift buildings and did their best to treat the soldiers, but they struggled to keep up with the flood of patients. The acute need for more caregivers was soon answered, however. Large numbers of women volunteered to provide much-needed care as nurses and administrators.

HISTORICAL THINKING

1. **READING CHECK** What sort of struggles did Civil War soldiers face before they arrived on the battlefield?

2. **DETERMINE WORD MEANING** What context clues help you understand what *replenish* means?

3. **MAKE INFERENCES** What impact do you think technological advances had on the soldiers' mortality rate?

2.2 Women and the War

Think of a time when you stepped up and took on a role you'd never shouldered before. You might have felt uncomfortable about assuming the role, but—like women during the Civil War—you probably felt that you had to do it.

> **MAIN IDEA** Women took an active role in the Civil War, both on the battlefield and at home.

WOMEN ON THE BATTLEFIELD

Just as they had in the American Revolution, women during the Civil War took on roles that brought them closer to the field of battle. Many women, in particular, became nurses. Before the war, society considered it inappropriate for women to care for injured and ill men. The Civil War quickly changed all that. Soon, most nurses were women, and at least one woman, **Mary Edwards Walker**, became a doctor.

In the North, Dorothea Dix and a **philanthropist** named **Clara Barton** led the nursing effort. A philanthropist is someone who actively promotes human welfare. Already known for her work on behalf of the mentally ill, Dix led volunteer nurses in a march on Washington in April 1861, demanding that women be allowed to help the Union forces. As a result, the Secretary of War gave Dix the responsibility of recruiting female nurses. Dix insisted that her volunteers be no younger than 30 years old. More than 2,000 women volunteered. For her part, Barton collected and delivered medical supplies, clothing, and food for Union soldiers throughout the war. She aided wounded Union soldiers and the Confederate prisoners they captured.

In the South, a young woman named **Sally Tompkins** led the effort to provide nursing care through her private hospital in Richmond, which she supported with her own personal fortune. The hospital treated more than 1,300 soldiers during the four years it was open, and it returned more men to the battlefield than any other hospital. In addition, more than 600 nuns from 12 different Catholic religious communities also served as nurses during the war and attended to both Union and Confederate soldiers.

The founder of the American Red Cross, Clara Barton was 29 years old when this photo was taken (1850). A former teacher, Barton was working as a clerk at the U.S. Patent Office in Washington, D.C., when the Civil War began. Determined to support the war effort, she set out to help the soldiers, some of whom were once her students. Soon, Barton was following the Union Army to the battlefields, where she tended to the wounded and dying.

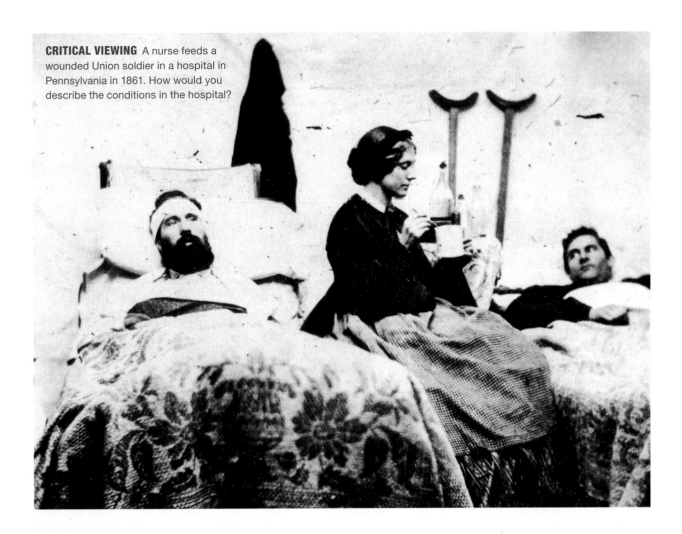

CRITICAL VIEWING A nurse feeds a wounded Union soldier in a hospital in Pennsylvania in 1861. How would you describe the conditions in the hospital?

WOMEN AT HOME

While some women helped on the battlefield, many more did their part at home. When war came, women all over the country took over the roles of their husbands, brothers, and sons in order to keep family farms and businesses running. On small farms, women and children took charge of raising animals and planting, tending, harvesting, and selling crops. On southern plantations, women directed the overseers and enslaved people. In the cities, women took jobs in factories and offices, replacing the men who had left to fight. Many women also volunteered to raise food and money, make clothing, and provide medical supplies for the troops and their communities.

Even for those women who stayed at home, the war sometimes came uncomfortably close. **Civilians**, or people not in the military, who lived near the battlefields had to deal with the sounds and dangers of battle. They could only watch as enemy combatants marched through their towns and raided their homes for supplies. To add to the stress, a family's only means of communicating with husbands and sons at war was through letters. Since troops were constantly on the move, delivering mail to them was difficult. If a soldier was killed or missing in action, the bad news arrived by letter. And since soldiers carried no official identification, many families were not informed at all. If a loved one's letters stopped coming, his family had to assume that he was not coming home.

HISTORICAL THINKING

1. **READING CHECK** How did Dorothea Dix open up the occupation of nursing to women?

2. **SUMMARIZE** What new roles did women play during the Civil War?

3. **ANALYZE CAUSE AND EFFECT** How did the war impact women, combatants, and civilians in different ways?

Photographer Ken Garrett makes a rare appearance in front of the lens at the Burnside Bridge near the Antietam battlefield in Maryland.

"When the photo reaches a wide audience and makes a difference in how we see the world, that is what makes it rewarding."

–Ken Garrett

Through the Lens—
Civil War Photography

For more than 40 years, National Geographic photographer Ken Garrett has documented images of past civilizations for *National Geographic* magazine. He has traveled to every continent, exploring and photographing ancient artifacts and ruins. But his passion for documenting the land and events associated with America's rich history keeps Garrett closer to home. He has found a wealth of subjects to photograph on the Civil War.

Garrett tells the stories of fallen Civil War soldiers through images of famous battlefields and reenactments. He hopes to help people learn from the past and use that knowledge to understand events today. His photographs of Civil War sites are a reminder of the blood shed on both sides of the conflict. The photos convey the emotions, confusion, and determination of the soldiers who fought on what Garrett refers to as "hallowed ground."

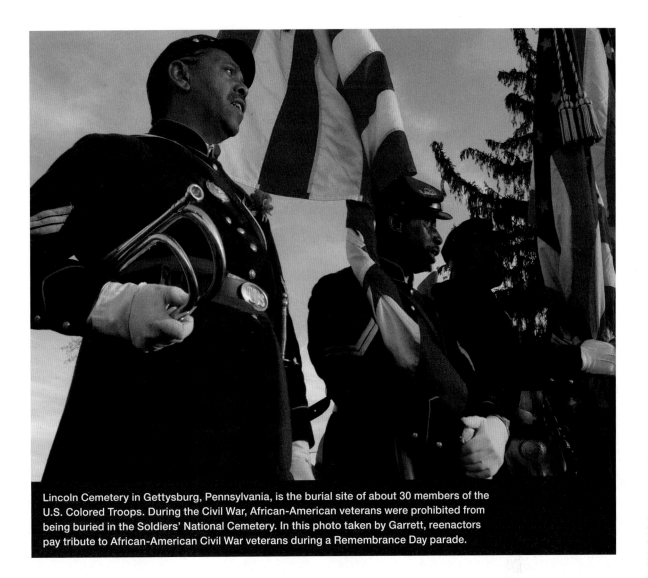

Lincoln Cemetery in Gettysburg, Pennsylvania, is the burial site of about 30 members of the U.S. Colored Troops. During the Civil War, African-American veterans were prohibited from being buried in the Soldiers' National Cemetery. In this photo taken by Garrett, reenactors pay tribute to African-American Civil War veterans during a Remembrance Day parade.

SIZING UP A SITE

When Garrett photographs a Civil War site, he likes to scout the area with a guide who can help him understand the events of the historic battle. The guide's insights help Garrett determine how to use his camera to capture the decisions made during the battle. He uses photography to show why one place was important to defend or what made another a superior place in which to hide, prepare, and attack.

Battery-powered lighting equipment helps Garrett capture the right photograph in the right light or season. "You should try to photograph a site during the season when the action took place," he adds. For example, by photographing Brandy Station, Virginia, during the summer, Garrett was able to provide insight into the heat and humidity both armies endured at this site of the largest cavalry battle in U.S. history.

Gettysburg is Garrett's favorite Civil War battlefield to photograph. "It is a very emotional place, where you really get an understanding of the horror of war. The thought that those boys walked out into that open field to be killed, sometimes by their own brothers, is a shocking realization." Gettysburg is also a popular site for reenactments. These re-creations put contemporary people in the shoes of people from 150 years earlier, bringing history to life and giving us valuable perspective on historic events.

A selection of Garrett's Gettysburg photographs as well as others from his Civil War collection are included in the following photo essay on the Civil War.

HISTORICAL THINKING

MAKE CONNECTIONS Why are Ken Garrett's Civil War photographs relevant today?

Union soldier reenactor, Fauquier County, Virginia

A Civil War Photo Essay

A story doesn't have to be made up of words. A photo essay—a collection of visuals organized to tell a story—can make as powerful a statement as any written words put down on a page.

To tell the story of the Civil War, National Geographic photographer Ken Garrett captures intricate details, sweeping landscapes, and the emotions of reenactors. His photos reveal important details about the uniforms, sites, and battlefields of the Civil War and provide us with insight into the thinking that led up to every battle, determined the fates of thousands of young soldiers, and ultimately transformed a country.

THINK ABOUT IT

How does this photo essay tell a Civil War story with very few words?

Union soldier reenactors, Crooked Run Valley, Virginia

Battle of Bull Run reenactment, Manassas, Virginia

Lincoln Cemetery, burial site for
Gettysburg's African-American soldiers

Pickett's Charge reenactment, Gettysburg, Pennsylvania

Confederate cannon at Pickett's Charge site, Gettysburg, Pennsylvania

Major Ulysses S. Grant statue,
Vicksburg, Mississippi

Graves of unknown soldiers,
Soldiers' National Cemetery,
Gettysburg

Military earthworks, Petersburg
National Battlefield, Virginia

3.1 Different Strategies

Everyone has strengths and weaknesses. You may be good at math and sports but not so great at science and card games. The trick is figuring out how to use what you've got to the best advantage.

MAIN IDEA Both the Union and the Confederacy had advantages and disadvantages, and each came up with strategies for winning the war.

STRENGTHS AND WEAKNESSES

During the Civil War, both the North and the South had strengths and weaknesses. The North had a much larger population than the South. And Union states were home to large cities, which were centers of business and industry. More than 100,000 factories were located in Union states—about five times the industrial capacity of the agrarian South.

The Union also boasted a stronger military infrastructure. It had a navy and many more ships than the South. West Point, the best military academy in the country to train leaders in the midst of war, was in the North. Many northern officers had trained there. However, the South also had talented graduates of West Point leading its soldiers. You may remember that Robert E. Lee graduated from the military academy, and so did Jefferson Davis, the Confederate president.

With its smaller numbers, the South fought the war largely on the defensive. Simply trying to defend itself seemed to be the best way to win the war, at least initially. As a result, most of the fighting took place in Confederate states. But this gave the Confederate forces a geographic advantage. They were fighting in areas they knew well, while the Union Army found itself on unfamiliar ground.

The South also used more offensive tactics to wear down the North. Confederate leaders encouraged private ship owners to intercept and capture northern merchant ships and their cargo in the Atlantic. And some southern generals planned to concentrate their forces and exert pressure on the northern capital of Washington, D.C., which bordered southern states.

MAKING A GAME PLAN

One of the renowned generals who led the Union, Winfield Scott, a hero of the Mexican-American War and the War of 1812, also had a plan. When the Civil War began, Scott was the commander-in-chief of the U.S. Army. In early 1861, he formulated a strategy he hoped would put an end to the war. His plan called for blocking Confederate ports along the Atlantic and Gulf coasts with Union warships. The North hoped to cripple the Confederate war effort and economy by preventing the delivery of weapons and halting cotton exports. Scott also proposed sending troops to gain control of the Mississippi River and capture major cities and river ports, creating divisions in the South.

Scott's massive blockade was risky. No blockade of this size had ever been tried before. There were more than 3,000 miles of coastline to block with fewer than 40 ships! Scott's idea was nicknamed the **Anaconda Plan** after a type of snake that strangles its prey. Within a week after the loss of Fort Sumter, Lincoln ordered the blockade to be carried out, and it was somewhat successful. However, many northern leaders ridiculed the plan. They wanted to take action and fight.

To counter the plan, the South tried to create a cotton shortage on the European market. The Confederacy hoped the shortage would force Great Britain and France, two major cotton consumers, to join the Confederate cause and help break up the Union blockade. The attempt backfired when both countries bought cotton from Egypt and India instead. Meanwhile, the Confederate Army engaged in terrible battles on the ground that would claim many lives and, eventually, give the South greater hope.

SCOTT'S GREAT SNAKE

The Anaconda Plan was meant to strangle the South by cutting off all trade among southern states and allowing the Union to take control of the Mississippi River. Scott believed his plan would put an early end to the war and limit the number of casualties.

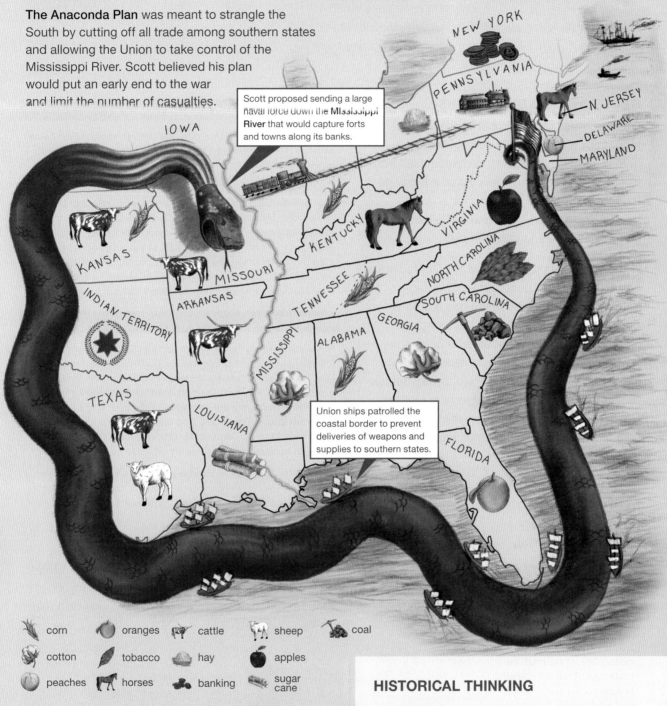

Scott proposed sending a large naval force down the Mississippi River that would capture forts and towns along its banks.

Union ships patrolled the coastal border to prevent deliveries of weapons and supplies to southern states.

corn • oranges • cattle • sheep • coal

cotton • tobacco • hay • apples

peaches • horses • banking • sugar cane

Scott's plan was never fully implemented, but a naval blockade was maintained throughout the war. The blockade succeeded in cutting off the South's resources and probably did shorten the war. But not even Scott knew how the war would develop. He guessed it would go on for two years, not four.

HISTORICAL THINKING

1. **READING CHECK** What was General Scott's strategy for winning the war?

2. **COMPARE AND CONTRAST** What geographic advantages did the South have over the North?

3. **ANALYZE VISUALS** What resources did the Anaconda Plan attempt to prevent from being traded in the South?

3.2 Differences Between North and South

MAIN IDEA At the start of the Civil War, the Union and the Confederacy each had important geographic advantages.

GEOGRAPHIC ADVANTAGES

Geography is critically important in any war. Mountains and rivers can serve as natural defenses, helping an army to defend itself from invaders. Hills can provide a visual advantage for soldiers who are watching for enemy troops. Trees felled in a forest can slow down an army as it tries to pass through.

In the Civil War, the Union and the Confederacy had other types of geographic advantages. You've learned that the Union had a greater population spread across a wide geographic area, which helped boost the size of its army. It also had many industrial centers. As you know, too, the Confederacy had the advantage of fighting the war on familiar terrain. And the South grew abundant cotton, which could be sold to help cover Confederate war expenses.

Read the following text and examine the maps to see how four important geographical factors—population, railroads, industry, and agriculture—critically affected the Civil War.

POPULATION

In 1860, the North had a population of about 18.5 million people, of which about 3.8 million free men were of military age. In contrast, the South had about 5.5 million free persons and 3.5 million enslaved people. Only 1.1 million free men were of military age, and 80 percent of these went to war. This percentage reflects the South's dedication to the cause for independence, since Jefferson Davis and the Confederacy relied on the voluntary cooperation of state governments for troops.

Additionally, 19 of the largest cities in the United States were part of the Union. Because the South was an agricultural society with few industrial cities to attract large populations, the Confederacy had only two, New Orleans and Charleston.

RAIL TRANSPORTATION

As you can see on the large map, the Union had more than twice as many miles of railroad lines as the Confederacy. In the South, most railroads went from Mississippi, Alabama, and Georgia to Charleston, carrying cotton for exporting.

The Civil War was one of the first wars in which railroads played a critical role. The Union and the Confederacy both used railroads to ship equipment, weapons, and troops. Sometimes, officers even sent spies on trains to learn about the opponent's troop movements. However, the Confederacy began the war at a disadvantage. Their railroads were in bad shape, and repairs often had to wait. Many railroad workers had quit to fight the war.

INDUSTRY

Manufacturing, especially of iron and steel, was critically important to both the Union and the Confederacy during the Civil War. The large map shows the location of factories in the North and the South. As you've learned, the majority of the factories were in the North, but the Confederacy did have some in Virginia and other states. The largest Confederate iron works was in Richmond, Virginia. Confederate officers fought to protect their factories because they were so important to the South.

Because the Union did more manufacturing, it was able to produce more of the rifles, cannons, railroad tracks, locomotives, and other materials its army needed for war. That was a definite advantage.

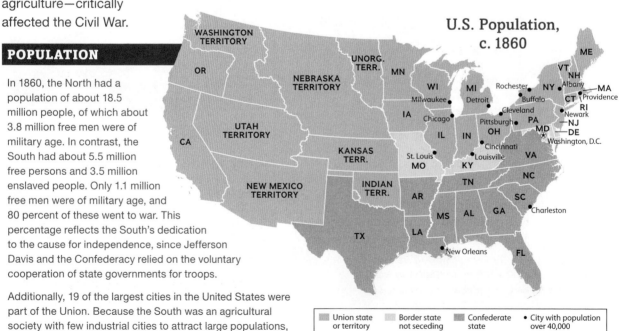

U.S. Population, c. 1860

Union state or territory | Border state not seceding | Confederate state | • City with population over 40,000

Industry and Agriculture in the North and the South, 1850

Legend:
- Textiles
- Other manufacturing
- Cotton
- Railroads

AGRICULTURE

As the map above shows, cotton was king in the South. The region devoted the majority of its economic and technological energy to this cash crop. As a result, the South supplied most of the world's cotton, producing 77 percent of the cotton used by Great Britain, the largest maker of textiles in the world.

Cotton was critical to the Confederacy's ability to raise the huge amounts of money needed to fight a war. In addition to Great Britain, the South exported cotton to France and other European countries and used the profits to buy weapons and equipment and to fund the Confederate government. Even textile mills in the North bought cotton from the South. The Confederacy also borrowed against the promise of future cotton crops to pay for its war efforts.

THINK LIKE A GEOGRAPHER

1. **IDENTIFY MAIN IDEAS AND DETAILS** What geographic advantages did the Confederacy have, and why were they important?

2. **ANALYZE CAUSE AND EFFECT** How did the Union's superiority in rail transportation contribute to its victory in the war?

3. **FORM AND SUPPORT OPINIONS** In your opinion, what was the most important geographic factor in the outcome of the war?

3.3 War in the West and East

You may have heard the phrase "divide and conquer" from a parent or coach. Union military leaders used the same strategy to try to defeat the South.

MAIN IDEA The Union attacked strategic areas in the western and eastern parts of the Confederacy in the early years of the Civil War.

THE BATTLE OF SHILOH

In 1862, Union and Confederate forces clashed in important battles in the western part of the Confederacy. The region had some of the Confederacy's most important assets, including New Orleans, its largest city, and many major ports along the Mississippi River. The North set its sights on capturing the region.

To that end, two Union generals, **Ulysses S. Grant** and **William T. Sherman**, sailed troops on a fleet of 19 riverboats up the Tennessee River. Seven of the vessels were **gunboats**, small, fast ships carrying mounted guns. The fleet successfully captured two key forts in Tennessee, Fort Henry and Fort Donelson, forcing the Confederate Army to retreat. On February 25, the Union Army continued its march across Tennessee with the goal of reaching Corinth, Mississippi—a major rail center—where 20,000 more Union soldiers awaited them. If Grant captured the railroads at Corinth, the Union would control most of the western part of the Confederacy.

However, General Albert Sidney Johnston, the Confederate commander in the region, learned of Grant's plan and ambushed the Union general's forces near a church in Shiloh, Tennessee, on April 6. The larger Confederate forces drove Grant's troops back. By the next day, however, more Union forces had arrived, and Grant led a counterattack. The Confederates conceded defeat and withdrew to Corinth.

The two-day **Battle of Shiloh** was the bloodiest battle in the war to that point. The South lost more than 10,000 men, including General Johnston. Even though it won the battle, the Union Army actually lost more men: about 13,000 soldiers. Because of the high casualty count, some people called for Grant's removal, but Lincoln refused. He is said to have remarked, "I can't spare this man [Grant]; he fights!"

Ulysses S. Grant

After graduating from West Point, Ulysses S. Grant served with General Winfield Scott during the Mexican-American War, as had his Confederate opponent, Robert E. Lee. After the Civil War, Grant became president of the United States in 1868, when he was only 46 years old. His presidency was plagued by scandal, although Grant himself was an honest man.

CRITICAL VIEWING This illustration shows the *Monitor* (in the front) firing its guns at the *Virginia* (in the back) at Hampton Roads Harbor, Virginia. The *Virginia* began its life as a standard steam-powered vessel built in the North, when it was called the *Merrimack*. The Confederates salvaged the *Merrimack* from a navy yard in Norfolk and refitted it as an ironclad. How did the successful use of ironclad ships probably affect future warfare?

THE SEVEN DAYS' BATTLES

Meanwhile, the Union had undertaken another campaign in the eastern part of the Confederacy with the goal of capturing the Confederate capital of Richmond, Virginia. On March 9, 1862, the Confederate ironclad ship, the C.S.S. *Virginia*—also known as the *Merrimack*—faced off against the Union ironclad, the U.S.S. *Monitor*. It marked the first skirmish between ironclad warships. The battle took place in the harbor of Hampton Roads, Virginia, and ended in a standoff.

Lincoln urged General George B. McClellan to continue the advance toward Richmond. McClellan had replaced Winfield Scott as the leader of the Union Army and was a brilliant general. But McClellan's tendency to overestimate the enemy's strength and postpone troop movement often frustrated Lincoln. McClellan eventually set sail with about 120,000 troops to the coast of the Virginia Peninsula. The Union forces battled their way to within a few miles of Richmond. But, fearing that he might be outnumbered, McClellan pulled his men back.

On June 1, rebel forces led by the new commander of the Confederate Army, Robert E. Lee, took advantage of McClellan's caution and moved to protect Richmond. From June 25 to July 1, Lee and his forces went on the attack and fought an offensive war, called the **Seven Days' Battles**. Lee forced McClellan to retreat back down the Virginia Peninsula, but even as they were being pursued, the Union forces still managed to inflict heavy casualties on the Confederates.

Nonetheless, the victory of the Seven Days' Battles boosted southern morale, saved the Confederate capital, and made Lee a hero. But as Lee's star was rising, McClellan's was falling. McClellan's failures made Lincoln's opinion of him sink even lower.

HISTORICAL THINKING

1. **READING CHECK** What did the Union Army hope to accomplish in the western part of the Confederacy in 1862?

2. **SUMMARIZE** Describe the Union advance toward Richmond.

3. **ANALYZE CAUSE AND EFFECT** How did the Seven Days' Battles affect the combatants and the leaders of the war?

Civil War Battles, 1861–1865

Bull Run (Manassas)
July 21, 1861, Aug. 28–30, 1862

Washington, D.C.

MD.

DEL.

Potomac R.

78°W   76°W

Chancellorsville
May 1–4, 1863

Fredericksburg
Dec. 11–15, 1862

Spotsylvania Court House
May 8–21, 1864

38°N

VIRGINIA

James R. Richmond

Seven Days
June 25–July 1, 1862

Appomattox
Court House
(Lee surrenders
to Grant Apr. 9, 1865)

Siege of
Petersburg
June 20, 1864–
Apr. 2, 1865

Hampton Roads
Mar. 8–9, 1862
(Monitor vs.
Merrimack)

Chesapeake Bay

0   25   50 Miles
0   25   50 Kilometers

Main map:

NEW YORK

PENNSYLVANIA

NEW JERSEY

40°N

Antietam
Sept. 17, 1862

Gettysburg
July 1–3, 1863

MD.

DELAWARE

Washington, D.C.

OHIO

INDIANA

ILLINOIS

WEST
VIRGINIA
(1863)

VIRGINIA   Richmond

Appomattox Court House
(Lee surrenders to Grant
Apr. 9, 1865)

Missouri R.

Ohio R.

Louisville

MISSOURI

KENTUCKY

Fort Henry
Feb. 4, 1862

Fort Donelson
Feb. 6, 1862

Tennessee R.

NORTH CAROLINA

Shiloh
Apr. 6–7,
1862

TENNESSEE

Chattanooga
Nov. 23–25, 1863

ARKANSAS

Mississippi R.

Chickamauga
Sept. 19–20, 1863

Wilmington

Kennesaw Mountain
June 27, 1864

Atlanta (occupied
Sept. 2, 1864)

Columbia

SOUTH
CAROLINA

MISSISSIPPI

Jackson

ALABAMA

Montgomery

GEORGIA

Charleston

Fort Sumter
Apr. 12–14, 1861

N
W   E
S

Vicksburg
May 19–July 4, 1863

Natchez

Savannah
(occupied Dec. 21, 1864)

*ATLANTIC
OCEAN*

LOUISIANA

Mobile

Mobile Bay
Aug. 2–23, 1864

Olustee
Feb. 20, 1864

Sanderson

New Orleans
(captured Apr. 25,
1862)

30°N

Gulf of Mexico

FLORIDA

0   100   200 Miles
0   100   200 Kilometers

90°W   80°W

Legend:

Union state
Confederate state
Border state
Union victory
Confederate victory

3.4 Bloody 1862

When a friend lets you down, you likely give him or her one more chance. But at a certain point, you get fed up. As Lincoln realized, you can give someone "just one more chance" only so many times.

> **MAIN IDEA** The bloody battles of Antietam and Fredericksburg exacted a high cost from both Union and Confederate forces.

THE BLOODIEST DAY

You've read about the first Battle of Bull Run in 1861. A second battle took place there in 1862. After driving General George McClellan and his troops back to Washington, D.C., General Robert E. Lee marched his men northward to battle again at Bull Run outside Manassas, Virginia. On the third day of fighting, the Confederates forced the Union soldiers to retreat. Afterward, Lee went on the offensive and marched his troops north into Maryland. He wanted to move the war into the Union states.

President Lincoln called McClellan back into action and ordered him to defend the Union capital. On his way to meet Lee, McClellan got lucky. By chance, a Union soldier found a packet of cigars in a field, dropped by a careless Confederate officer. Wrapped around the cigars were Lee's detailed plans for the assault on Maryland. McClellan learned that Lee's forces were in two groups several miles apart. If McClellan moved quickly, he could destroy Lee's army before the groups joined up. But McClellan acted too late. The Confederate Army met Union soldiers on the battlefield at Antietam (an-TEE-tuhm) Creek near Sharpsburg, Maryland, on September 17.

The casualties for both sides at the **Battle of Antietam** numbered at least 23,000 men. The day of the battle would later be called "America's Bloodiest Day." The Union considered it a victory because Lee's forces left Maryland. But Lincoln was frustrated with McClellan's errors. He said, "If General McClellan does not want to use the army, I would like to borrow it for a time." The president named Ambrose Burnside as the new commander.

THE BATTLE OF FREDERICKSBURG

For his first campaign, General Burnside decided to lead his troops back toward Richmond to try to capture the Confederate capital. To reach Richmond, Burnside marched to Falmouth, near Fredericksburg, Virginia, where he planned to cross the Rappahannock River. The Union troops arrived at Falmouth in December 1862, but Lee's army had got there first and destroyed all the bridges. Burnside ordered army engineers to build floating bridges using **pontoons**, or hollow metal cylinders, but Confederate soldiers shot at the Union engineers while they worked.

Meanwhile, Lee and the rest of his troops dug into the hills above Fredericksburg and readied their artillery. When Burnside finally crossed the Rappahannock River, his forces fought for three days in an unsuccessful effort to take the hills. The Battle of Fredericksburg ended when Burnside retreated across the river.

After so many defeats, northern civilians were becoming restless. They did not like the turn the war had taken, and neither did Lincoln.

HISTORICAL THINKING

1. **READING CHECK** How did McClellan discover Lee's plans at the Battle of Antietam?

2. **SUMMARIZE** How did these two battles reflect broader strategic patterns in the war?

3. **INTERPRET MAPS** Where were most of the Civil War battles fought, in the North or in the South? Explain why.

VOCABULARY

Use each of the following vocabulary words in a sentence that shows an understanding of the term's meaning.

1. cavalry

   The cavalry rode in on their horses to defend their fellow Union soldiers.

2. trench warfare

3. evacuate

4. gunboat

5. ironclad ship

6. mobilize

7. mortality

8. philanthropist

9. civilian

READING STRATEGY
SUMMARIZE

If you haven't done so already, complete your concept cluster of important information discussed in this chapter. Create at least four content clusters and summarize the information in each one. Then answer the question.

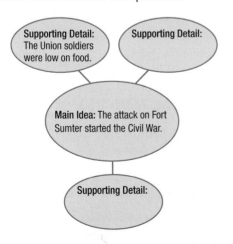

Supporting Detail: The Union soldiers were low on food.

Supporting Detail:

Main Idea: The attack on Fort Sumter started the Civil War.

Supporting Detail:

10. What was life like for a typical soldier in the Union or Confederate army?

MAIN IDEAS

Answer the following questions. Support your answers with evidence from the chapter.

11. How did the call for soldiers affect the states on the border between the North and the South? **LESSON 1.1**

12. Why did the first battle of the Civil War take place near Manassas, Virginia? **LESSON 1.2**

13. What new technological advances in weapons were introduced during the Civil War? **LESSON 2.1**

14. Who made up about half of the men who enlisted in the war on both sides? **LESSON 2.1**

15. What did Sally Tompkins contribute to the war effort? **LESSON 2.2**

16. Why did most of the fighting in the Civil War take place in the Confederate states? **LESSON 3.1**

17. Why did General Grant want to capture the railroads at Corinth, Mississippi? **LESSON 3.3**

18. What did Lee's troops do before Union troops arrived at Falmouth? **LESSON 3.4**

HISTORICAL THINKING

Answer the following questions. Support your answers with evidence from the chapter.

19. **MAKE INFERENCES** Why do you think Lincoln sent a message to southern leaders, stating that he would be sending only food, and not ammunition, to Fort Sumter?

20. **DRAW CONCLUSIONS** How did the attack on Fort Sumter make it clear that war was the necessary step to take toward reunification?

21. **COMPARE AND CONTRAST** What advantages did an ironclad ship have over a wooden ship?

22. **MAKE GENERALIZATIONS** Why was General McClellan unwilling to act quickly when leading the Union Army?

23. **SEQUENCE EVENTS** What were the major early battles of the Civil War? Create a time line of the battles in which you indicate their significance.

INTERPRET VISUALS

Look closely at the photograph of Union soldiers taken during the Civil War, and then answer the questions that follow.

24. What do the men in the photo appear to be doing?

25. What does the photo reveal about the lives of soldiers during the Civil War?

ANALYZE SOURCES

Clara Barton not only gathered supplies and clothing for the Union Army, but she also provided nursing care to wounded Union soldiers on many battlefields, including the Battle of Antietam. In this excerpt from one of her journals, Barton describes the danger she put herself in to help a soldier at Antietam. Read the excerpt and answer the question that follows.

> A man lying upon the ground asked for drink—I stooped to give it, and having raised him with my right hand, was holding the cup to his lips with my left, when I felt a sudden twitch of the loose sleeve of my dress—the poor fellow sprang from my hands and fell back quivering in the agonies of death—a ball [bullet] had passed between my body—and the right arm which supported him—cutting through the sleeve, and passing through his chest from shoulder to shoulder.

26. What happened as Barton was giving the soldier a drink?

CONNECT TO YOUR LIFE

27. **ARGUMENT** The Civil War was a terrible conflict, resulting in great loss of life. But, as you'll learn in the next chapter, the war had positive aspects as well, including helping to put an end to slavery. Think about conflicts in your life. Should they have been avoided, or did some good come out of them? Write a paragraph in which you make an argument for or against conflict.

TIPS

• Make a list of the positive and negative outcomes of conflicts you've experienced.

• Determine whether the positives outweighed the negatives, or vice versa.

• State your position on conflict in a topic sentence and support it with evidence from your own experience.

• Conclude your paragraph with a sentence summarizing your position.

CHAPTER 16

TURNING POINTS OF
THE WAR
1863–1865

ESSENTIAL QUESTION
How did the United States transform during the Civil War?

 AMERICAN STORIES ONLINE The Secret Weapon of the South

SECTION 1 The Emancipation Proclamation

KEY VOCABULARY

Emancipation Proclamation   enlist   stalemate

SECTION 2 Americans at War

KEY VOCABULARY

bond	*habeas corpus*	ration
Conscription Act	Legal Tender Act	scapegoat
draft	quarantine	scurvy
exemption		

SECTION 3 The Tide Turns

KEY VOCABULARY

bluff	Gettysburg Address	total war
flotilla	morphine	veteran

SECTION 4 The War's Aftermath

KEY VOCABULARY

assassinate	Homestead Act	Reconstruction
casualty	jurisdiction	servitude

AMERICAN GALLERY ONLINE Battlefield Medicine

READING STRATEGY

ANALYZE LANGUAGE USE
When you analyze language use, you note how specific word choices shape the meaning or tone of a text. As you read the chapter, use a graphic organizer like this one to help you analyze how word choices help convey the realities of war.

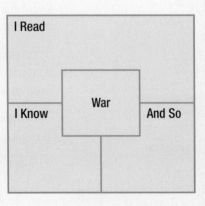

I Read

I Know   War   And So

National Geographic photographer Ken Garrett captures a Union Army reenactor at rest during a Gettysburg Hallowed Ground Remembrance Day parade. The annual event commemorates Lincoln's Gettysburg Address and the cemetery dedication.

"It is well that war is so terrible, **or we would grow too fond of it.**"
— General Robert E. Lee

1.1 Lincoln Issues the Emancipation Proclamation

In a game of tug-of-war, if both sides pull with equal force, neither wins. In the summer of 1862, the Union and Confederate armies were both tugging equally, and President Lincoln had to find a way to end the standoff.

MAIN IDEA In 1863, Abraham Lincoln issued the Emancipation Proclamation, which freed slaves in states under Confederate control.

GIVING PURPOSE TO THE WAR

Before September 17, 1862, the name "Antietam" referred only to a creek near Sharpsburg, Maryland. But by sunset that day, Antietam would become the name of one of the bloodiest battles ever fought on American soil. Despite battle after battle, the war had reached a **stalemate**, with neither side holding a clear path to a final victory. And still, the body count rose.

In both the North and the South, the loss of so many lives led many to question why Americans were fighting against one another. In the midst of all this suffering, President Lincoln sought to define a greater moral purpose for the war. He realized the Union could not defeat the Confederacy without first destroying slavery.

From the beginning of the war, President Lincoln had faced pressure from abolitionists to end slavery. Although personally opposed to the

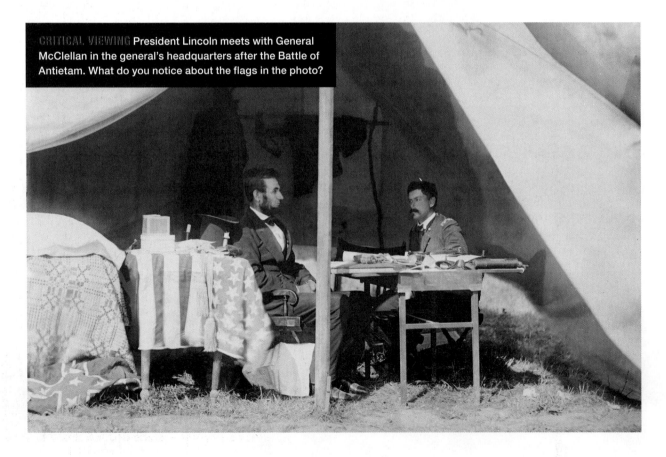

CRITICAL VIEWING President Lincoln meets with General McClellan in the general's headquarters after the Battle of Antietam. What do you notice about the flags in the photo?

institution, Lincoln was initially reluctant to abolish it outright. Instead, he envisioned a gradual end to slavery, with slaveholders being paid for the loss of their property. Northern Democrats, whose support he needed, opposed abolition. Many of them were sympathetic to the South and to the cause of slavery, even as they remained loyal to the Union. They warned Lincoln against the social, economic, and political fallout of bringing an end to slavery, whether slowly or abruptly.

From a military standpoint, however, the institution of slavery gave the Confederacy an advantage over the Union. Slave labor kept the southern agrarian economy running, which meant more white southern men could join the Confederate Army. Although some members of Lincoln's party urged him to allow African-American men to fight on the side of the Union, the president remained hesitant to offend the border states by doing so. By the summer of 1862, Union troops had secured the slave-owning states of Missouri and Kentucky.

FOREVER FREE

The North had been fighting to preserve the Union, but a clearer moral purpose was emerging from the bloodshed. Five days after the Union victory at Antietam, Lincoln shifted the focus of the war. He issued a decree that emancipated, or freed, all Confederate slaves. Lincoln had purposely waited to submit a draft of the **Emancipation Proclamation** to his cabinet because he knew the timing had to be right for such a dramatic move. The five-page document declared that all slaves in rebel states were "thenceforward, and forever free." It committed the government and armed forces of the United States to liberate enslaved people in rebel states. The final draft of the proclamation allowed the Union to accept freed slaves into its fighting forces. On January 1, 1863, Lincoln formally issued the Emancipation Proclamation.

At the time Lincoln wrote the proclamation, approximately 4 million enslaved people lived in the United States. However, the proclamation did not apply to slaves in the Union's slave-holding border states of Maryland, Missouri, Kentucky, Delaware, or West Virginia. Lincoln feared that emancipating slaves in all Union-controlled territories might cause border states to join the Confederacy. The Union couldn't afford that loss.

As you have read, the Declaration of Independence states that "all men are created equal." However, according to the Constitution, enslaved African Americans were not equal citizens with equal rights. By issuing the Emancipation Proclamation, Lincoln began the long process of addressing the vast discrepancies between the words of the Declaration of Independence and the realities experienced by African Americans, both enslaved and free.

Slaveholders in Confederate states did not consider themselves bound by U.S. law, and they refused to acknowledge the proclamation. In order to become free, enslaved people still had to escape to Union-controlled territory. About 500,000 African Americans emancipated themselves by escaping. Some young men who did so fled to Union camps and, after 1863, even joined the Union Army. However, many enslaved people in the South knew nothing about the Emancipation Proclamation until the war was over.

HISTORICAL THINKING

1. **READING CHECK** What were the goals of the Emancipation Proclamation?

2. **MAKE INFERENCES** To what extent did the Emancipation Proclamation extend the principles of the Declaration of Independence?

3. **ANALYZE CAUSE AND EFFECT** What factors affected President Lincoln's decision to issue the Emancipation Proclamation?

1.2 Frederick Douglass 1818–1895

> "The white man's happiness cannot be purchased by the black man's misery." —Frederick Douglass

Frederick Douglass was deeply familiar with the miseries suffered by black men and women living in slavery. Born to an enslaved mother in 1818, he spent the early years of his childhood living on a plantation in Maryland. There, he endured cold and hunger, and he witnessed other slaves being whipped.

BALTIMORE AND BEYOND

When he was around eight years old, Douglass was sent to live in Baltimore with a shipbuilder named Hugh Auld. Auld's wife Sophia taught the young boy the alphabet. Auld quickly put a stop to the lessons because it was illegal to teach a slave to read. However, the child's passion for learning had been ignited, and he taught himself to read and write.

In 1832, Douglass was sent to work on a plantation, where he was regularly beaten and given little to eat. In his own words, he was "broken in body, soul, and spirit" as "the dark night of slavery closed in upon me." Eventually, he returned to Baltimore to work in the shipyards, where he made his escape in 1838 by fleeing to New York City. After his escape, he changed his name to reduce the risk of being found by slave catchers. Before, he had been called Frederick Augustus Washington Bailey. From this point on, he would call himself Frederick Douglass.

🏛 Art Institute of Chicago

This photograph by Samuel J. Miller shows Frederick Douglass in formal dress, staring forcefully at the viewer. Douglass, the most photographed American of the 19th century, insisted on posing this way. He wanted to reteach people how to see African Americans by replacing the stereotype of the oppressed slave with the portrait of a dignified, proud fellow citizen.

FIGHTER FOR FREEDOM

Douglass settled in New Bedford, Massachusetts, where he worked as a laborer and furthered his education by reading widely. In 1841, he made his first speech describing his life in slavery and calling for an end to the brutal practice. It was the beginning of a lifelong career in public speaking.

Douglass's speeches were so eloquent that some people suspected him of simply pretending to be a former slave. They reasoned that a man born in slavery could never have learned to speak with such brilliance. In many ways, Douglass remade how his fellow citizens viewed African Americans.

To tell his full story, Douglass wrote *Narrative of the Life of Frederick Douglass, an American Slave* in 1845. Publishing the autobiography was a special act of courage because it revealed details about his life that might enable slave catchers to find him. He traveled to Great Britain, where he promoted his book and gave lectures. There, he could speak out without fear of being captured. Over the course of his two-year tour, he gained many new friends and supporters, who helped him purchase his freedom.

Back in the United States, Douglass founded an abolitionist newspaper, wrote two more influential books, and continued to speak out. In 1852, he delivered one of his most famous speeches, "The Meaning of July Fourth for the Negro." In it, he asked why enslaved people should celebrate the country's freedom when they did not benefit from it themselves. "We need the storm, the whirlwind, the earthquake," he thundered. "[The] conscience of the nation must be roused."

When the Civil War broke out, Douglass helped recruit African-American soldiers, and he met with President Abraham Lincoln several times. After the war he held various government posts, including U.S. Marshall for the District of Columbia. He continued promoting civil rights for all Americans until his death in 1895.

CRITICAL VIEWING This painting, *Three Great Abolitionists: A. Lincoln, F. Douglass, J. Brown*, was created by William H. Johnson around 1945. Frederick Douglass stands in the middle, clasping hands with Abraham Lincoln on his left and John Brown on his right. Johnson depicted the three using a "primitive" style of painting, characterized by the work's bright colors and two-dimensional figures. Just behind John Brown, African Americans raise their hands in celebration of the abolitionists. What aspects of Civil War–era African-American life are depicted in the background of the painting?

HISTORICAL THINKING

1. **READING CHECK** Why was Douglass in danger of being enslaved again, even after he became well known?

2. **ANALYZE CAUSE AND EFFECT** How did a few lessons from Sophia Auld change the course of Douglass's life?

3. **DRAW CONCLUSIONS** Why do you think Douglass took the Fourth of July as a theme for a speech on slavery?

1.3 African-American Soldiers

Sometimes in war, people put goals ahead of prejudices. During the Civil War, the U.S. military accepted African-American soldiers into its ranks. Defeating the South had become more important than excluding fellow Americans from military service.

MAIN IDEA In 1863, African Americans began to join U.S. military units and proved to be valuable soldiers for the Union.

AFRICAN AMERICANS JOIN THE FIGHT

When the Civil War first began, many free African-American men rushed to **enlist** in, or join, the Union Army, but they were turned away. A 1792 law barred African Americans from joining the U.S. military. At first, members of Lincoln's administration resisted changing this prohibition. But the Emancipation Proclamation reversed the law with its provision that African-American men "will be received into the armed service of the United States," a critical development that affected the war's outcome.

By the end of the Civil War, African-American soldiers in the U.S. Army totaled nearly 180,000, or about 10 percent of total Union enlistments. Additionally, 19,000 African Americans served in the U.S. Navy. African-American troops faced the same danger and fought with as much commitment as white soldiers, but they were not treated equally.

The army assigned African-American soldiers to segregated units commanded by white officers. African-American soldiers received lower wages than most white soldiers until June 1864, when Congress granted equal pay to African-American military units.

Like all 19th-century American women, African-American women were barred from enlisting in the army. Still, some African-American women, including Harriet Tubman, served as nurses, spies, and scouts. As you have read, Tubman led people to freedom on the Underground Railroad. Tubman also worked as a nurse and scouted behind Confederate lines for the Union's 2nd South Carolina Volunteers. In 1863, she helped free 727 slaves at one time during the Combahee River Raid. That raid was the single largest liberation of slaves in American history.

THE 54TH MASSACHUSETTS REGIMENT

In February 1863, the governor of Massachusetts issued the first formal call for African-American soldiers to join the U.S. Army. He selected the **54th Massachusetts** infantry regiment under the command of Colonel **Robert Gould Shaw**, a white officer. In just two weeks, more than 1,000 African Americans enlisted. Charles and Lewis Douglass, two sons of Frederick Douglass, were among them.

On July 18, 1863, the 54th Massachusetts prepared to storm **Fort Wagner**, which guarded the Port of Charleston, South Carolina. At dusk, Shaw gathered 600 of his men on a narrow strip of sand just outside Fort Wagner's walls. He told them, "I want you to prove yourselves. The eyes of thousands will look on what you do tonight."

As night fell, Shaw led his men over the walls of the fort. They were met by 1,700 Confederate soldiers waiting inside the fort. The brutal hand-to-hand combat that followed took its toll: 281 of the 600 charging soldiers were killed, wounded, or captured. Shaw himself was shot in the chest and died instantly. The 54th lost the battle at Fort Wagner, but its valor, or courage, was beyond

▥ Smithsonian National Gallery of Art, Washington, D.C.

In 1897, Augustus Saint-Gaudens unveiled his 14-year project of honoring the members of the 54th Massachusetts in a bronze relief called the Robert Gould Shaw Memorial. The sculpture depicts the regiment marching down Beacon Street in Boston, on its way to fight Confederate troops in South Carolina. The following year in Paris, Saint-Gaudens exhibited a second version of the memorial made of plaster and covered with bronze metallic paint. Today, the bronze-painted sculpture shown above is housed at the Smithsonian National Gallery of Art in Washington, D.C. The original sculpture is located at the Boston African American National Historic Site on Beacon Street, across the street from the Massachusetts State House. An inscription on the Boston memorial reads, "Together they gave to the nation and the world undying proof that Americans of African descent possess the pride, courage, and devotion of the patriot soldier."

question. For his bravery in the fight, **William H. Carney** became the first African American to receive the Congressional Medal of Honor.

For the next two years, the 54th Massachusetts took part in a number of sieges in South Carolina, Georgia, and Florida. The service and bravery of its members helped to win acceptance for other African-American regiments and solidified their importance in the war effort. Despite increased African-American enlistment, the need for more soldiers in both the North and the South grew.

HISTORICAL THINKING

1. **READING CHECK** Why did the Union wait until after the Emancipation Proclamation to enlist African Americans in the army?

2. **DRAW CONCLUSIONS** Why did the 54th Massachusetts gain great respect in the Union Army despite losing its first battle?

3. **ANALYZE LANGUAGE USE** What made the words Colonel Shaw used with his troops before the battle at Fort Wagner particularly effective?

2.1 Conflicts over the Draft

Imagine being told you have to fight in a war you may not even support. Then consider that your wealthy neighbor is told the same thing but can pay someone else to take his place. During the Civil War, many men realized they were getting a bad deal.

MAIN IDEA In reaction to forced military service during the Civil War, people in both the North and the South staged riots.

MILITARY SERVICE IN THE SOUTH

Waging a civil war required a steady supply of men volunteering to fight as soldiers. At first, men from both the North and the South rushed to sign up. However, as battles wore on, numbers of enthusiastic volunteers began to dwindle. The South was first to acknowledge this problem.

When war first broke out, 100,000 southern men volunteered to fight for the Confederacy. But as their yearlong enlistments were ending, many soldiers returned home to their families and farms. In 1862, the Confederate government, worried that its armies would be short of men as the Union was stepping up its attacks, instituted a **draft**, or a mandatory term of military service. The Confederacy required three years of service for all white men between the ages of 18 and 35.

The draft didn't apply to every man equally, however. Wealthy southerners could pay other men to serve in their places. They could also choose to pay a fee of $500—an amount out of reach for most men. Individuals who owned 20 slaves or more were excused from the draft and their voluntary enlistments altogether.

Military **exemptions**, or releases from the obligation to serve, widened the growing divide between rich and poor in the South. A non-slaveholding man named Jasper Collins remarked that exemptions made the Civil War a "rich man's war, and a poor man's fight." Some soldiers deserted, or left, their units. Desertion remained a major problem for the Confederacy throughout the war.

The gap between rich and poor spread beyond military service. Convinced that greedy merchants were hoarding flour and supplies, women rioted in Richmond, the Confederate capital. They smashed storefronts and stole bread and everything else they could grab, from bacon to boots. One young girl explained, "We are starving . . . each of us will take a loaf of bread. That is little enough for the government to give us after it has taken all our men."

DRAFTING SOLDIERS IN THE NORTH

The North also faced the need for new soldiers. Death, disease, and desertion continually reduced the size of the army, so the Union instituted its own draft in the form of a law called the **Conscription Act** in March 1863. Men between 20 and 45 years of age were liable to be drafted into the military, but, as in the South, they could pay to avoid service for $300—a fee only wealthy families could afford. These exemptions ignited draft riots in cities throughout the Northeast.

On July 13, the attempt to enforce the draft in New York City set off the most destructive civil disturbance in the city's history. Rioters torched government buildings. Police struggled for three days to control the riot. Eventually, Union troops had to rush from the battlefields in Pennsylvania to New York City to aid the police. Union soldiers fired into groups of fellow citizens who were rioting. About 300 people, more than half of them police officers and soldiers, were injured, and more than 100 people died, most of them rioters.

Some whites in New York blamed African Americans for the unrest surrounding the draft riots. In fact, African Americans became **scapegoats**, or individuals or groups blamed for the mistakes or faults of others. Some people claimed that African Americans were responsible for the war and that they were taking jobs away from white workers. Angry white rioters killed many African Americans and destroyed their homes. Such violence prompted many African Americans to flee New York City during the draft riots. They feared for their lives.

In an effort to control riots and curb criticism of the war, the Lincoln administration suspended the writ of *habeas corpus*, or the right of an arrested person to be brought before a judge before going to jail. More than 14,000 people were jailed after being accused of disloyalty to the Union. As a result of the riots, some New York men with families who had no other means of financial support received exemptions from the draft.

HISTORICAL THINKING

1. **READING CHECK** Why did both the North and the South enact military drafts?

2. **ANALYZE LANGUAGE USE** How did Jasper Collins describe the Civil War, and why?

3. **COMPARE AND CONTRAST** In what ways were the Confederate and Union drafts similar, and in what ways were they different?

CRITICAL VIEWING In this photo still from the 2016 film *Free State of Jones*, Newton Knight, center, and his fellow soldiers fight off Confederate troops trying to put down their rebellion. What do you notice about the men in the photo?

Open Rebellion in Mississippi

Newton Knight of Mississippi enlisted in the Confederate Army in July 1861. Angered by the law exempting white men who owned 20 or more slaves, Knight deserted his battalion in October 1862. Back home, he witnessed his fellow southerners suffer abuses at the hands of Confederate soldiers, and he decided to form an opposition group. Other deserting soldiers and escaped slaves joined him, and by late 1863, they had organized into the Jones County Scouts.

The Jones County Scouts eventually numbered more than 1,000. To symbolize their open rebellion, Knight and his men raised the American flag over the Jones County courthouse. They evaded capture by disappearing into the swamps, with local civilians supplying them with weapons, food, and information. Though Confederate officers eventually subdued the rebellion, the Jones County Scouts fought against the Confederacy until it fell.

2.2 Paying for War

Raising money to fight a war is difficult. In 1861, the federal government implemented several financial strategies to support the war effort. The Confederate government struggled with hard economic realities as it tried to do the same.

MAIN IDEA During the Civil War, both the North and the South had to devise new methods of funding their war efforts.

FINANCIAL STRATEGIES

War is incredibly expensive. Even though the Union and the Confederacy were both rich by any international standard, neither had ever supported a large army. Thousands of soldiers needed food, shelter, transportation, uniforms, weapons, ammunition, medical care, and a host of other supplies. As the costs increased, leaders on both sides discovered they had only a few choices: loans, new taxes, and the creation of paper money.

In the North, the federal government issued $2 billion worth of treasury **bonds**. Bonds are certificates offered for sale to the public with the promise that the government will pay the money back at a later date, usually with interest. In August 1861, Congress passed the first federal income tax in U.S. history. This law required citizens who earned more than $600 per year to pay a portion of their income to the government to fund the war.

In 1862, Congress passed the **Legal Tender Act**, an act that replaced currencies of individual banks with one national currency. Because the back of the money was colored green, the national notes were soon called "greenbacks." The Union issued $450 million in greenbacks during the war.

The sudden increase in money in the North had unexpected negative consequences. Greedy manufacturers took advantage of federal funds and urgent demand to produce poorly made and even defective goods. Uniforms sometimes fell apart in the first rain or had no buttons. Some shoemakers produced boots with soles made of cardboard. Not surprisingly, these boots didn't last on long

marches. Some suppliers mixed sawdust in with the gunpowder that filled artillery shells. Dishonest businessmen profited from supplying Union troops with spoiled meat. A new word was invented to describe defective war material: *shoddy*.

PRINTING MONEY, SEIZING CROPS

As you have read, the North had a distinct industrial advantage over the agrarian South. It also had the support of the federal government. The South's lack of an industrial base and a strong government made it difficult for the Confederacy to raise funds to pay for war. It tried to borrow money from Britain and France, and it raised taxes to meet expenses. The Confederacy also printed money, but unlike in the North, this strategy resulted in severe inflation: prices for goods increased and the purchasing value of money decreased. The Confederate government also issued war bonds, but most southerners were too poor to buy them. Those wealthy enough to afford bonds soon discovered that inflation was rising faster than the rate of interest on their bonds.

In 1863, the Confederacy passed a law requiring all farmers to give 10 percent of all the crops they raised to the government for use in the war effort. In addition, Confederate citizens were subjected to impressment, a practice that allowed military officers to take anything they thought might be useful to the war effort, including slaves.

Thousands of African Americans were forced to leave their families to perform forced labor for the Confederate military. Many of them rebelled and escaped to the Union lines where they offered their

No matter when or where they are fought, civil wars have devastating consequences for ordinary people. Financial resources of nations are diverted away from supporting citizens in order to pay for war. Young men, and sometimes boys, are forced into military service. Day-to-day lives are disrupted, people are displaced from their homes and countries, and economies are damaged. These characteristics all apply to the civil war that took place after the African country of South Sudan achieved independence in 2011.

During that civil war, government spending on weapons took priority over other responsibilities, thousands of people were killed, and more than 1 million people fled the country. The military limited the movements of those who remained, which meant farmers could not plant crops, trade harvests, or tend livestock. The result was massive starvation and famine by 2016. How might the experience of South Sudanese like the young man shown below be similar to what families in the United States experienced during the Civil War?

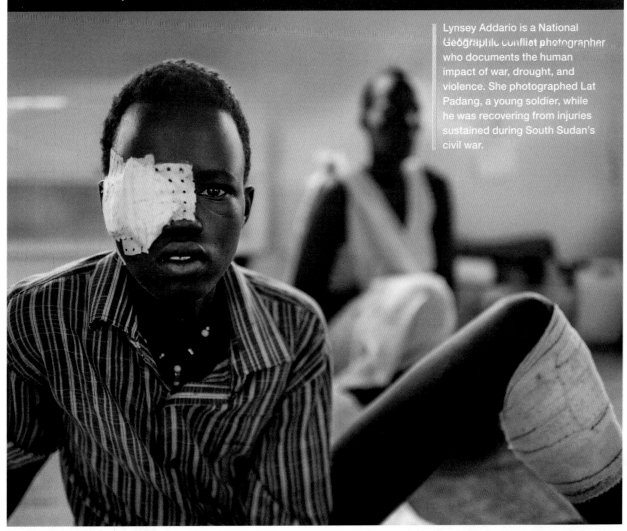

Lynsey Addario is a National Geographic conflict photographer who documents the human impact of war, drought, and violence. She photographed Lat Padang, a young soldier, while he was recovering from injuries sustained during South Sudan's civil war.

labor to the Union. Southern farms and plantations no longer had the labor necessary to grow food and cash crops.

Meanwhile, many southerners watched helplessly as armies stripped their farms of food and livestock. Some farmers grew cotton because it stored well and they thought it would fetch a high price after the war. As a result, the Confederacy devoted land and labor to growing cotton instead of growing food for its hungry citizens.

HISTORICAL THINKING

1. **READING CHECK** What methods did the North and the South use to raise money for the war?

2. **DESCRIBE** In what ways were civilians in the North and the South affected by the war?

3. **COMPARE AND CONTRAST** In terms of its economy and government, what advantages did the North have over the South?

2.3 Wartime Prison Camps

In war, there are always unintended consequences. During the Civil War, neither side was prepared to provide shelter and food for thousands of war prisoners. For those unfortunate enough to be captured, imprisonment could be worse than death.

MAIN IDEA Thousands of soldiers on both sides of the conflict died from exposure and disease in Civil War prison camps.

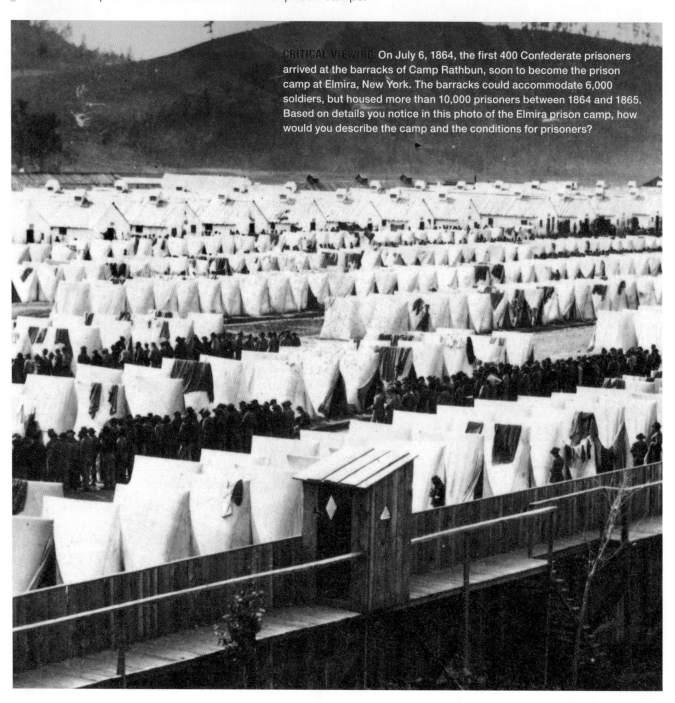

CRITICAL VIEWING On July 6, 1864, the first 400 Confederate prisoners arrived at the barracks of Camp Rathbun, soon to become the prison camp at Elmira, New York. The barracks could accommodate 6,000 soldiers, but housed more than 10,000 prisoners between 1864 and 1865. Based on details you notice in this photo of the Elmira prison camp, how would you describe the camp and the conditions for prisoners?

PRISONERS IN THE NORTH

In the early years of the Civil War, the Union and the Confederacy exchanged prisoners of war rather than maintaining prisons. Cooperation soon broke down between the two sides, however, and captured soldiers were confined in military prison camps on both sides.

Camp Douglas in Illinois received its first prisoners approximately 5,500—in February 1862. It would house more than 26,000 Confederate prisoners by the end of the war. Many prisoners were already sick or wounded when they arrived at the camp, and many died while there due to lack of medical care. Poor sanitation, harsh weather conditions, and reduced **rations**, or supplied food, weakened the remaining prisoners. These circumstances left the prisoners susceptible to infectious diseases such as pneumonia and smallpox. Still others died from **scurvy**, a disease linked to malnutrition and a diet lacking in fruits and vegetables. The total death toll has been estimated to be as many as 6,129 men, the greatest mortality statistic of any Union prison.

Alton was another Illinois prison camp. Originally the first state penitentiary built in Illinois, it closed in 1860, but then reopened in 1862 to relieve overcrowding in other Union prisons. Soon Alton became overcrowded as well. When smallpox swept through the camp in 1862 and 1863, authorities built a hospital on an island in the Mississippi River to **quarantine** infected prisoners, or keep them away from those who had not yet contracted the disease.

Elmira prison camp in New York operated from July 6, 1864, until July 11, 1865. Even though it was set up for 6,000 men, more than 10,000 arrived. Because of overflow, some prisoners camped along the nearby Chemung River.

CAMPS IN THE SOUTH

The largest and most notorious Confederate military prison camp was **Andersonville**, located in Georgia. A creek that flowed through the 16-acre compound provided water for the prisoners, but it quickly became polluted with human waste, making it a perfect breeding ground for contagious diseases. The camp, built for 10,000 men, soon held 33,000 prisoners.

Situated on a 54-acre island in the James River near Richmond, Virginia, Belle Isle prison camp operated from 1862 to 1865, housing more than 30,000 men. In 1864, Surgeon De Witt Peters described the horrific conditions experienced by Union prisoners at Belle Isle.

PRIMARY SOURCE

Laboring under such diseases as chronic diarrhea, . . . scurvy, frost bites, general debility, caused by starvation, neglect, and exposure. Many of [the prisoners] had partially lost their reason. They were filthy in the extreme, covered in vermin. . . . nearly all were extremely emaciated [very thin]; so much so that they had to be cared for even like infants.

—from testimony to the U.S. Sanitary Commission, by De Witt Peters, 1864

Approximately 13,000 of the 45,000 Union prisoners eventually held at Andersonville died because of exposure, starvation, and brutality. Northerners were enraged when they heard about the conditions at the military prison. After the war, Andersonville's commander, Captain **Henry Wirz**, was executed for war crimes.

Overall, between 12 and 16 percent of southern and northern prisoners died in military prison camps during the war. The deplorable prison camp conditions, both in the North and in the South, led to prison reform efforts after the war to build safer, more sanitary, and more humane prisons in the United States.

HISTORICAL THINKING

1. **READING CHECK** What were the general conditions of most Civil War prison camps? Provide evidence to support your answer.

2. **ANALYZE LANGUAGE USE** What words did De Witt Peters use to describe Belle Isle prison camp, and why might he have chosen those words?

3. **ANALYZE CAUSE AND EFFECT** What effect did wartime deaths at prison camps have on the U.S. prison system after the war?

3.1 Battles of Vicksburg and Gettysburg

Sometimes you can recall the exact moment when things suddenly change and get either much better or much worse. For Civil War generals, two battles in particular dramatically shifted the war's direction.

MAIN IDEA The battles of Vicksburg and Gettysburg were the key turning points in the Union's eventual victory in the Civil War.

SPLITTING THE CONFEDERACY

In the first months of 1863, the war was not going well for Union generals. In January, after a disastrous defeat at Fredericksburg, Lincoln replaced General **Ambrose Burnside** with General **Joseph Hooker** as commander of the Army of the Potomac. Then in May, Lee's army defeated Hooker's forces near **Chancellorsville**, Virginia. Hooker resigned after the loss and was replaced by General **George Meade**. Lee lost his own most capable commander when Stonewall Jackson was accidentally shot by one of his own soldiers. However, Lee's victory at Chancellorsville is widely considered his greatest of the entire war.

The battle that ensued further south, in Vicksburg, Mississippi, began to change the course of the war for the Union. By 1863, Vicksburg had been a Confederate stronghold for more than a year. Its position allowed the Confederacy to control a wide part of the region from **bluffs**, or cliffs, 200 feet above the Mississippi River. Capturing the city and silencing Confederate guns became a strategic necessity for the Union.

During the early spring of 1863, Union forces commanded by General Grant tried to find a way to take the city from their vantage point on the western bank of the river. But Confederate troops commanded by General **John C. Pemberton** turned them back. Then in early May, Admiral **David Porter**, under Grant's orders, ran a **flotilla**, or small fleet, of gunboats and barges past Confederate forces at Vicksburg under cover of night. Porter used these vessels to ferry Grant's troops across the river south of the city.

From there, Grant's troops marched northeastward before doubling back toward Vicksburg and cutting the city off from the east. In only three weeks, Grant's men marched 180 miles, won 5 battles, and captured 6,000 prisoners. Vicksburg was now surrounded and under siege. Food ran out and the residents began to starve. Pemberton surrendered on July 4, 1863. The Union victory at the **Battle of Vicksburg** gave the Union control of the Mississippi Valley and split the Confederacy in half. It also convinced President Lincoln of Grant's outstanding military ability.

THE TIDE TURNS AT GETTYSBURG

Despite his victory at Chancellorsville, Lee realized that the North's manpower advantage might be wearing down Confederate troops and that a victory on the attack would boost Confederate morale. He decided that his most effective move was to invade the North again. In late June 1863, Lee's troops advanced into Pennsylvania, where they met Meade's troops at the **Battle of Gettysburg**. At first, Lee succeeded in sending the Union troops into retreat. Then, on July 1, reinforcements arrived for both sides, bringing troop numbers to approximately 90,000 for the Union and about 75,000 for the Confederates. Union forces stopped retreating and stationed themselves on **Cemetery Hill**, where the high vantage point gave them a defensive edge.

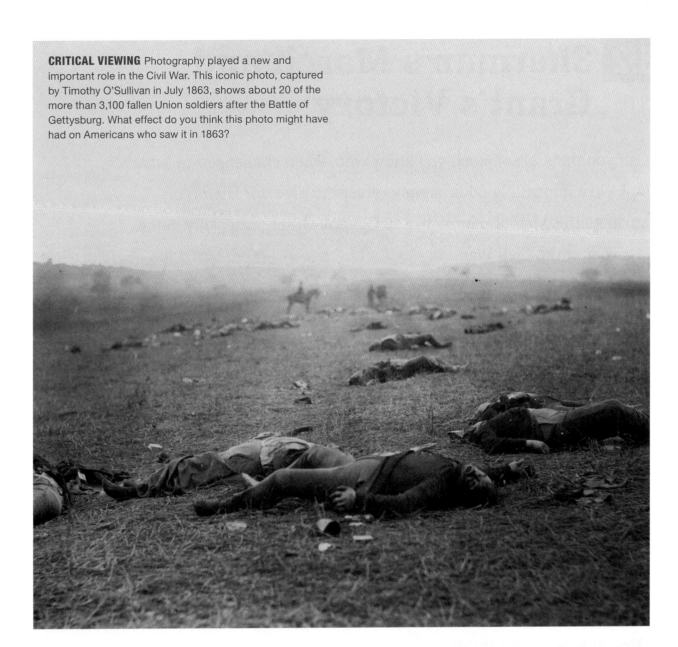

CRITICAL VIEWING Photography played a new and important role in the Civil War. This iconic photo, captured by Timothy O'Sullivan in July 1863, shows about 20 of the more than 3,100 fallen Union soldiers after the Battle of Gettysburg. What effect do you think this photo might have had on Americans who saw it in 1863?

On Friday, July 3, hoping to outflank Union forces on Cemetery Hill, Lee ordered Major General **George Pickett** and about 15,000 of his men to attack the Union troops on a plain just below the hill. Lee's strategy proved disastrous. The Union repelled Pickett's charge, killing or wounding more than half of Pickett's troops. The next day, Lee retreated, eventually crossing the Potomac River to Virginia. This retreat marked a turning point in the war. It put the Confederacy on the defensive and the Union in a favorable position for victory.

On November 19, 1863, President Lincoln delivered the **Gettysburg Address** at the battle site to commemorate the loss of so many men and to dedicate a military cemetery there. Throughout his speech, Lincoln referred to the Declaration of Independence directly and to its ideas. His address reinforced the Declaration's principles of equality and freedom for which the war was fought and for which so many died, and were still dying.

HISTORICAL THINKING

1. **READING CHECK** How did the battles of Vicksburg and Gettysburg affect the Civil War?

2. **IDENTIFY PROBLEMS AND SOLUTIONS** What challenges did Grant and his troops face, and how were they eventually able to capture the city of Vicksburg?

3. **EVALUATE** How did the Union's position on Cemetery Hill contribute to its victory at Gettysburg?

3.2 Sherman's March and Grant's Victory

Can you think of someone you know who, when challenged by what looks like impossible odds, simply refuses to give up? Historians attribute this kind of persistence to General Grant, especially in the last year of the Civil War.

MAIN IDEA Grant and his generals brought the full power of the Union Army down on the South in their campaign to capture the Confederate capital.

MARCHING THROUGH GEORGIA

In March 1864, President Lincoln named Ulysses S. Grant, the victor of Vicksburg, as commanding general of the Union Army. Grant immediately put a plan in place to wear down the Confederacy with a series of widespread and relentless attacks. Following a Union victory at Chattanooga, Tennessee, in 1864, Grant sent General William T. Sherman to deliver destruction to the heart of the Confederacy—Atlanta, Georgia, which Sherman captured in September 1864. This was an important feat because Atlanta was a railroad hub and the industrial center of the Confederacy.

The city was also a symbol of Confederate pride and strength. Its fall made even the most loyal southerners doubt that they could win the war. "Since Atlanta," South Carolinian Mary Chesnut wrote in her diary, "I have felt as if . . . we are going to be wiped off the earth."

From Atlanta, Sherman marched 62,000 Union troops through Georgia to Savannah, located on the Atlantic shore. His goal was to destroy southern property, crops, and other supplies. Early in 1865, Sherman and his men left Savannah, burning their way northward to Columbia, South Carolina. From there, they marched into North Carolina, battling Confederate troops before destroying the Fayetteville arsenal. In Bentonville, the Confederacy challenged Sherman for three days, but his troops gained the upper hand.

A **total war** is one in which all rules and laws of war are ignored and all resources are poured into defeating the enemy no matter what the cost. Sherman waged total war against the Confederacy, and his strategy was brutal and destructive. But it did what it was meant to do. It was a blow to southern morale and fighting

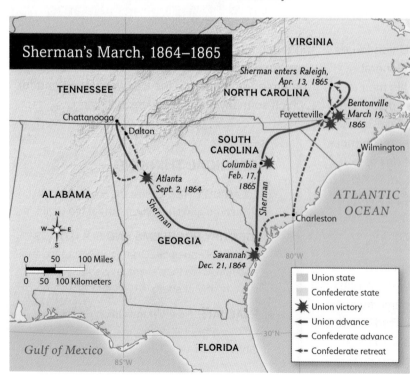

Sherman's March, 1864–1865

TENNESSEE

Chattanooga
Dalton

VIRGINIA

Sherman enters Raleigh, Apr. 13, 1865

NORTH CAROLINA

Fayetteville
Bentonville March 19, 1865
35°N

SOUTH CAROLINA
Columbia Feb. 17, 1865

Wilmington

Atlanta Sept. 2, 1864

ALABAMA

N W E S

GEORGIA

Sherman

Sherman

Charleston

ATLANTIC OCEAN

0   50   100 Miles
0 50 100 Kilometers

Savannah Dec. 21, 1864
80°W

Gulf of Mexico
85°W

FLORIDA

30°N

Union state
Confederate state
Union victory
Union advance
Confederate advance
Confederate retreat

AMERICAN PLACES
Savannah Historic District
Savannah, Georgia

The Savannah Historic District is a National Historic Landmark. James Oglethorpe founded the city in 1733 when Georgia was a British colony. Savannah's distinctive 18th- and 19th-century architecture is reflected in its numerous historic homes, gardens, and monuments. General Sherman used the Greene-Meldrim House, shown here, as a base of operations between 1864 and 1865. The house was built in 1853 in the Gothic Revival architectural style.

capacity. It led to a feeling in the North that the Union was winning the war and so helped with President Lincoln's reelection in November 1864.

Sherman and his troops spared the city of Savannah instead of burning it as they did Atlanta. Why? There are a number of theories, some more plausible than others. One is that Sherman found Savannah too beautiful to burn. Another is that he was lenient because city leaders surrendered before he could enter the city, agreeing they would not put up a fight if he spared life and property. Perhaps the strongest theory is that Savannah had a large port that could prove very useful to the Union.

GRANT FACES LEE

General Grant was pleased with Sherman's success in the South, and he became even more determined to capture Richmond, Virginia, the Confederate capital. The first large battle of Grant's campaign was the **Battle of the Wilderness**, fought in a heavily wooded area west of Fredericksburg and north of Richmond. The armies engaged in battle for two days with heavy casualties, especially on the Union side. Grant refused to retreat. Instead, he moved his army farther south. Lee followed him. On May 8, 1864, Grant attacked Lee's troops near **Spotsylvania**, beginning a battle that raged for 12 days. The Union's Army of the Potomac lost 18,000 men at the Battle of Spotsylvania; the Confederates lost

12,000. In less than three weeks, Grant had lost 33,000 men. On May 31, Lee and Grant collided again at **Cold Harbor**, where Grant's forces were defeated with heavy losses. The Union lost about 13,000 troops; the Confederates lost only 2,500 or fewer.

In 1865, Grant's forces broke through the last line of Richmond's defenses, and the city fell on April 3. Confederate troops and government officials fled Richmond, setting fire to parts of the city as they left to prevent Union troops from using it for shelter and supplies. The Union took control of what was left of the city. The Confederate capital was captured. President Lincoln traveled to Richmond a few days later to see the evidence of this significant Union victory for himself.

HISTORICAL THINKING

1. **READING CHECK** What was Grant's strategy in the South?

2. **ANALYZE LANGUAGE USE** Mary Chesnut used a figurative expression to describe how she felt about the fall of Atlanta. How did she articulate how she felt about the war? Use evidence from the text to support your answer.

3. **MAKE PREDICTIONS** What effect could you predict the Union capture of Richmond would have on the Civil War's outcome?

3.3 Lincoln's Vision

Politicians and public officials use speeches to express their views on public policy. During his political career, Abraham Lincoln delivered a number of speeches, several of which became some of the most formative speeches in U.S. history.

For nearly 100 years, historians believed that no photos existed of Lincoln delivering the Gettysburg Address. But in 1952, National Archives employee Josephine Cobb was examining a crowd shot taken by photographer Mathew Brady at Gettysburg on November 19, 1863. She had the photo enlarged and examined where she thought Lincoln might have been standing in that crowd. And right there, in the middle of the crowd, she identified the out-of-focus—but unmistakable image—of Abraham Lincoln delivering the Gettysburg Address. You can see this rare photo below.

Lincoln was not known as a speaker gifted with a captivating voice or dramatic delivery. Rather, the force of his speeches came from the words themselves. For example, the Gettysburg Address is just 272 words long, and it took only around three minutes for Lincoln to deliver it. But in this succinct address, Lincoln reminded Americans of the foundation on which the United States was built and on which it still rested. Quite intentionally, he framed his words around the principles of liberty and equality as set forth in the Declaration of Independence.

CRITICAL VIEWING Locate Abraham Lincoln in the photograph below. What do you notice about Lincoln's position in the crowd and how it differs from the ways in which the president is protected in public today?

Primary Source: Speech
The Gettysburg Address, by Abraham
Lincoln, November 19, 1863

As president, Lincoln used the
opportunity of a battle site dedication
to appeal to his fellow citizens to take
up "unfinished work" of those who had
died. He begins by situating his words
in time by using the phrase "fourscore
and seven" as a way of expressing the
number 87. The word *score* means 20,
so *fourscore* equals 80. By referring to
87 years ago, Lincoln asks his listeners
to remember the American Revolution
and the nation's founding principles of
liberty and equality.

CONSTRUCTED RESPONSES
What did Lincoln mean by "testing
whether that nation or any nation
so conceived and so dedicated can
long endure"?

What action did Lincoln propose as
the best way to honor those who had
died at Gettysburg?

Fourscore and seven years ago our fathers brought forth on this
continent a new nation, conceived in liberty and dedicated to the
proposition that all men are created equal.

Now we are engaged in a great civil war, testing whether that nation
or any nation so conceived and so dedicated can long endure. We
are met on a great battlefield of that war. We have come to dedicate
a portion of that field as a final resting-place for those who here gave
their lives that that nation might live. It is altogether fitting and proper
that we should do this.

But in a larger sense, we cannot dedicate, we cannot consecrate,
we cannot hallow this ground. The brave men, living and dead who
struggled here have consecrated it far above our poor power to add
or detract. The world will little note nor long remember what we say
here, but it can never forget what they did here.

It is for us the living rather to be dedicated here to the unfinished work
which they who fought here have thus far so nobly advanced. It is
rather for us to be here dedicated to the great task remaining before
us—that from these honored dead we take increased devotion to that
cause for which they gave the last full measure of devotion—that we
here highly resolve that these dead shall not have died in vain, that
this nation under God shall have a new birth of freedom, and that
government of the people, by the people, for the people shall not
perish from the earth.

Primary Source: Speech
from Second Inaugural Address, by Abraham Lincoln,
March 4, 1865

When Lincoln delivered this speech in March 1865, the North was
close to victory. Lincoln did not speak of happiness, nor did he gloat
about the South's impending defeat. Instead, he spoke about his
sadness over the loss of life during the war. Just over a month later, the
president who had saved the Union would be assassinated.

CONSTRUCTED RESPONSE What was Lincoln referring to when
he called on Americans "to bind up the nation's wounds"?

With malice toward none, with charity
for all, with firmness in the right as God
gives us to see the right, let us strive
on to finish the work we are in, to bind
up the nation's wounds, to care for him
who shall have borne the battle and
for his widow and his orphan, to do all
which may achieve and cherish a just
and lasting peace among ourselves
and with all nations.

SYNTHESIZE & WRITE

1. **REVIEW** Review what you have learned
   about the events leading up to Lincoln's
   address at Gettysburg and his Second
   Inaugural Address.

2. **RECALL** On your own paper, write the main
   themes that emerge from the Gettysburg
   Address and this excerpt from Lincoln's
   Second Inaugural Address.

3. **CONSTRUCT** Construct a topic sentence that
   answers this question: What was President
   Lincoln's vision for the United States after
   the Civil War, and how did he try to persuade
   Americans to support that vision?

4. **WRITE** Using evidence from this chapter and
   the documents, write a persuasive paragraph
   that supports your topic sentence in Step 3.

3.4 Appomattox

Forgiving a sibling or a friend after a fight is hard to do. Generals Grant and Lee had a difficult task in front of them when they met to end the war. Grant wondered: Was it better to forgive former enemies, or punish them further?

MAIN IDEA The Civil War ended with the surrender of the Confederacy at a simple ceremony in Virginia.

SURRENDER AT LAST

By the beginning of 1865, war had nearly completely devastated the South. Sherman continued to march through the Carolinas, burning homes, barns, and crops. Knowing the end was near, Confederate president Jefferson Davis sent his vice president, **Alexander Stephens**, to meet with Lincoln on February 3, 1865. His goal was to negotiate peace and bring the war to an end. Not interested in negotiating, Lincoln demanded that the Confederacy surrender completely. Stephens refused, and the war continued.

Meanwhile, General Lee finally had to abandon his defense of Richmond after the Confederate government fled and Union troops marched in to take over the city. But Lee still had hopes of turning the situation around. He tried to move his forces south in order to join other Confederate forces in North Carolina. Lee's army never reached that goal. Union cavalry surrounded Lee and his troops near the Virginia town of **Appomattox Court House**, halting his progress. Following a brief battle, Lee agreed to surrender.

On April 9, 1865, Lee met Grant in the front room of Wilmer McLean's home in Appomattox Court House. Grant arrived in his muddy field uniform, while Lee wore his full dress uniform. Lee accepted Grant's terms of surrender. All Confederate officers and soldiers were pardoned. They could keep their private property, including their horses, which they would need for spring planting. Confederate officers were also allowed to keep their side arms. Grant made sure that Lee's men, many of whom were starving, would receive Union rations. Grant told his officers: "The war is over. The Rebels are our countrymen again."

The Confederacy had fought with courage and endured almost unimaginable hardships. But courage was not enough to defeat the resources and manpower of the far more powerful industrial North. The Union prevailed.

COSTS OF THE WAR

In dollars and cents, the Union spent more than $3 billion on the war; the Confederacy spent about $1 billion. But these amounts of money for military expenditures barely compared to the massive loss of life. Roughly 620,000 men had died: 360,000 Union soldiers and 260,000 Confederate soldiers, the most American lives lost in any conflict to date.

Two out of every three deaths occurred not from battle, but from disease. The most common diseases in army camps were typhoid fever, smallpox, measles, diarrhea, pneumonia, malaria, and tuberculosis. Army surgeons relieved the pain of sick and wounded soldiers by prescribing millions of doses of a highly addictive medication called **morphine**. Morphine worked well to ease wounded soldiers' pain, but many Civil War **veterans**, or people who had served in the military, became addicted to it.

The war had direct economic consequences for American families. The loss of fathers or sons often meant the loss of family breadwinners. Countless wounded veterans were unable to work, and families fell into poverty. Many homes, farms,

To commemorate the centennial anniversary of the end of the Civil War, the National Geographic Society commissioned Tom Lovell to paint *Surrender at Appomattox*. Lee, dressed in gray, signs the surrender terms while Grant and his officers look on. Their meeting was somber, but friendly. Upon signing, Lee is reported to have said, "This will have a very happy effect on my army." Based on details you notice in the painting, how did Grant treat Lee during the signing?

and businesses, particularly in the South, had been destroyed. Lives, careers, and communities had to be rebuilt.

Even after financial costs were recovered, the emotional toll of such intense loss persisted for generations. The war itself became the subject or backdrop for art and literature. In 1862, Louisa May Alcott served as a nurse in Washington, D.C., during the war. She was sent home when she contracted a serious disease called typhoid from the unsanitary conditions in the hospital. In 1863, Alcott published *Hospital Sketches*, a collection of stories crafted from her letters home about her hospital experiences. Thirty-two years later Stephen Crane published *The Red Badge of Courage*, a novel based on the life of Private Henry Fleming. Crane was not yet born when the war broke out, but his novel captured the horrific details of battlefield experiences nonetheless. That Crane's novel still resonated with American readers three decades after the war ended speaks to the profound effect the Civil War had on the country.

HISTORICAL THINKING

1. **READING CHECK** What were the terms of surrender that Grant delivered to Lee?

2. **ANALYZE LANGUAGE USE** What do you think Grant was saying about what it means to be an American when he stated, "The war is over. The Rebels are our countrymen again"?

3. **FORM AND SUPPORT OPINIONS** Explain whether you think the financial losses or personal losses of the war were greater, and support your opinion with information from the text.

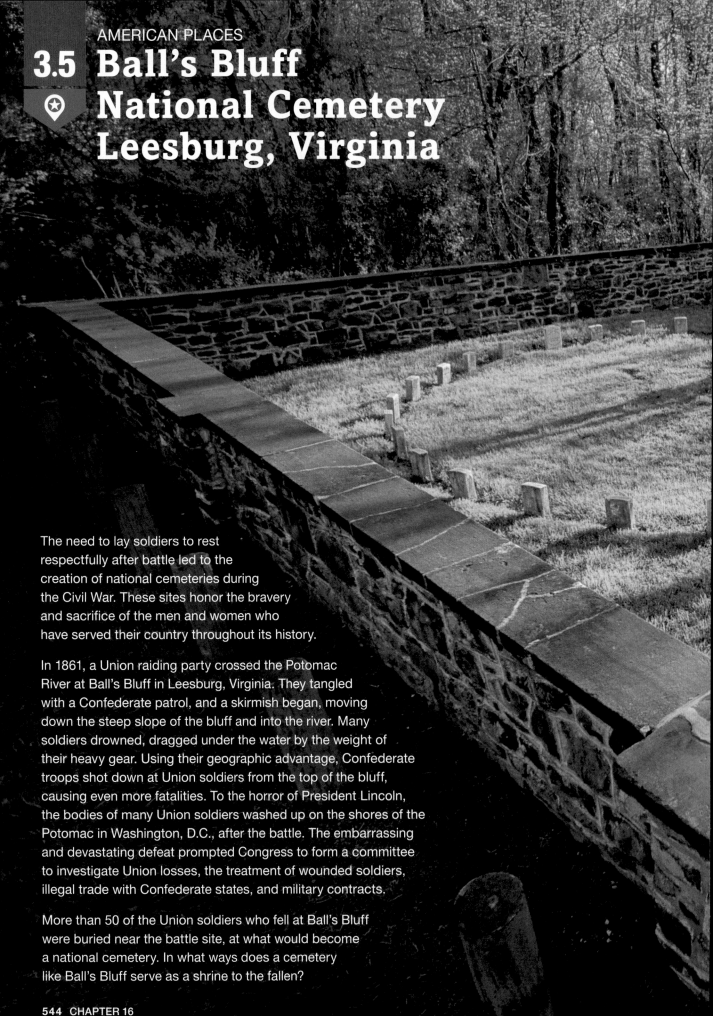

3.5 Ball's Bluff National Cemetery Leesburg, Virginia

The need to lay soldiers to rest respectfully after battle led to the creation of national cemeteries during the Civil War. These sites honor the bravery and sacrifice of the men and women who have served their country throughout its history.

In 1861, a Union raiding party crossed the Potomac River at Ball's Bluff in Leesburg, Virginia. They tangled with a Confederate patrol, and a skirmish began, moving down the steep slope of the bluff and into the river. Many soldiers drowned, dragged under the water by the weight of their heavy gear. Using their geographic advantage, Confederate troops shot down at Union soldiers from the top of the bluff, causing even more fatalities. To the horror of President Lincoln, the bodies of many Union soldiers washed up on the shores of the Potomac in Washington, D.C., after the battle. The embarrassing and devastating defeat prompted Congress to form a committee to investigate Union losses, the treatment of wounded soldiers, illegal trade with Confederate states, and military contracts.

More than 50 of the Union soldiers who fell at Ball's Bluff were buried near the battle site, at what would become a national cemetery. In what ways does a cemetery like Ball's Bluff serve as a shrine to the fallen?

CRITICAL VIEWING The Ball's Bluff National Cemetery is one of the nation's smallest military cemeteries. Established in 1865 as the burial place for Union soldiers killed at Ball's Bluff, only the name of one soldier is known: James Allen, a Union soldier and member of Company H, 15th Massachusetts Infantry. What does the unique perspective of this photo by National Geographic photographer Ken Garrett reveal about the cemetery?

Landmark Amendments and Terrible Loss

The end of slavery was a great moral victory for the nation. But it became a source of rage for some—rage that triggered violence and terrible loss.

MAIN IDEA Abraham Lincoln planned to rebuild the South and restore the Union, but others would have to follow through for him.

SLAVERY IS ABOLISHED

In January 1865, three months before Lee would surrender, Congress passed the **13th Amendment**, which prohibited slavery in the United States. As with all amendments, it was sent to the states for ratification. By December 1865, three-quarters of the states had approved it, and the 13th Amendment was added to the Constitution.

Slavery was over. Georgia, a former Confederate state, provided the final vote needed for ratification. The amendment states, "Neither slavery nor involuntary **servitude** [being enslaved] . . . shall exist within the United States, or any place subject to their **jurisdiction** [the authority to enforce laws within a given area]." The 13th Amendment abolished slavery, but African Americans were not guaranteed full equality under the law until 1868, with the ratification of the **14th Amendment**. African-American men received voting rights when the **15th Amendment** was ratified in 1870.

Outlawing the practice of slavery was a giant step toward equality and justice. However, discrimination and racism did not magically disappear with the passage of the 13th, 14th, and 15th Amendments. African Americans were frequent victims of violence at the hands of whites. With few options for employment, many southern African Americans went back to work on plantations, where they earned poverty-level wages. Further, African Americans could not depend on a legal system that still favored whites.

LINCOLN'S ASSASSINATION

After the Civil War ended, Lincoln's primary goal was, once again, reuniting the nation. He recognized that integrating newly freed African Americans into society and rebuilding the physical and social structures of the South would be a delicate operation. He planned to implement measures to remedy the injustices of slavery, bring the former Confederate states back into the Union, and rebuild the South.

These plans became known as **Reconstruction**. Lincoln knew he would have to act with careful diplomacy in order to carry out these measures without inflaming already volatile racial and sectional tensions. However, he realized some issues would cause an uproar, no matter the diplomacy used in proposing them. For example, on April 11, 1865, he suggested that some African-American men should have the right to vote. As you have read, that right would not be guaranteed for another five years.

Just three days later on April 14, 1865, **John Wilkes Booth**, an actor and Confederate sympathizer, fatally shot Lincoln at Ford's Theatre in Washington, D.C., as the president watched a play. Audience members rushed the president from Ford's Theatre to the Petersen House, a boarding house across the street. Lincoln never regained consciousness, and he died the next morning. For the first time in U.S. history, a sitting president had been **assassinated**, or murdered for political reasons.

On April 21, Lincoln's funeral train began a somber journey to Springfield, Illinois, where he had lived before becoming president. Thousands of Americans lined the train's route to mourn. Lincoln was buried on May 4, 1865.

Vice President **Andrew Johnson** succeeded Lincoln as president. Johnson favored Lincoln's Reconstruction policies, but he lacked Lincoln's leadership skills. Also, Republican congressmen distrusted him because he was a former Democrat and former slaveholder.

Johnson could not stop Congress from enacting harsh penalties on the southern states. In particular, the **Radical Republicans** believed the former Confederacy should be punished for secession and war. Their treatment of the South caused long-standing resentment and discontent among many southerners.

Lincoln's steady leadership had brought an end to the Civil War. Following his death, the nation struggled to regain a true sense of unity as it rebuilt without the leader who had saved it. The far-reaching consequences of his loss were yet to be realized. The morning he died, Lincoln's Secretary of War, Edwin M. Stanton, is reported to have said either, "Now he belongs to the ages" or "Now he belongs to the angels." For Americans in 1865, both statements rang true.

🏛 Chicago History Museum

After Lincoln was shot, he was taken to a small bedroom in the Petersen House and laid in this bed, diagonally, because he was so tall. Today, you can see Lincoln's death bed at the Chicago History Museum. *The Last Hours of Abraham Lincoln,* painted by Alonzo Chappel in 1868, hangs above the bed. It dramatizes Lincoln's last hours, features Mary Todd Lincoln weeping on his chest, and includes many of the people who visited Lincoln before he died.

HISTORICAL THINKING

1. **READING CHECK** How did Lincoln plan to reunite and heal the nation after the Civil War?

2. **ANALYZE LANGUAGE USE** What do you think is meant by the phrase "or any place subject to their jurisdiction" in the 13th Amendment?

3. **EVALUATE** In what ways did Lincoln's assassination affect Reconstruction and attitudes in the South?

4.2 The Legacy of the War

The Civil War was one of the most formative events in American history. Four years of battle and loss resulted in both positive and negative consequences.

MAIN IDEA The Civil War left a legacy of unresolved economic and political issues that would have long-lasting effects on the United States.

REBUILDING THE NATION

Conditions in the North and the South after the Civil War contrasted dramatically. The devastated South struggled to recover from the financial and physical destruction it suffered during the war. Its economy had been based on growing and exporting crops for cash. Invading armies had burned down farms and destroyed crops and fields, and, at least initially, few resources existed to rebuild them. The North's naval blockade of southern exports resulted in plantation owners' financial ruin. The biggest economic blow, however, was the abolition of slavery and the resulting loss of "free" labor. Southern plantation owners would have to find other ways to profit from agriculture as the South rebuilt.

Although the North had suffered some destruction and hundreds of thousands of **casualties**, or dead or injured men, it emerged from the war more prosperous than ever. The war effort had led to a rapid growth of the North's industrial economy. Manufacturing had expanded because of the need to build products necessary to fight the war, from guns to railroad cars to uniforms and shoes. Many northern business owners grew rich on wartime profits and the industrial boom that followed. Even northern agriculture prospered during and after the war, as the Union's farms began using more farm machinery to grow and harvest crops with fewer farmers in the fields. In fewer than 50 years after the Civil War, the expansion of primarily northern manufacturing, mining, and transportation made the United States the world's leading industrial nation.

LAND GRANTS AND HOMESTEADS

The Civil War achieved two significant goals: the preservation of the Union and the abolition of slavery. The United States banned slavery later than some other countries. Great Britain had outlawed slavery throughout its empire, including the British West Indies, with the 1833 **Slavery Abolition Act**. In the Western Hemisphere, many South American countries had already abolished slavery as well, though Brazil didn't outlaw the institution until 1888.

Another result of the war was the greatly expanded power and size of the federal government. The balance of power shifted from individual states and regions to Washington, D.C. The federal government was quick to use its power, and one of its goals was to encourage the settlement and development of the West. The government had already begun to put some of its planned programs in motion even before the end of the Civil War.

The **Morrill Act**, signed into law by President Lincoln on July 2, 1862, provided each state with 30,000 acres of federal land grants for each member of its congressional delegation. The land was then sold to the states, and the proceeds were used to fund public colleges that focused on agriculture and the mechanical arts. These land grants funded 69 colleges, including Cornell University, the Massachusetts Institute of Technology, and the University of Wisconsin at Madison.

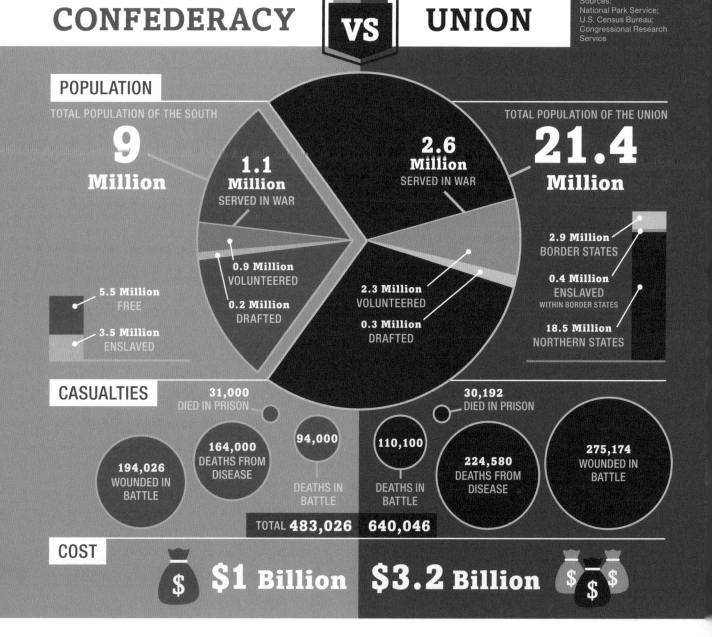

CIVIL WAR BY THE NUMBERS

CONFEDERACY VS UNION

Sources:
National Park Service;
U.S. Census Bureau;
Congressional Research
Service

POPULATION

TOTAL POPULATION OF THE SOUTH

9 Million

1.1 Million
SERVED IN WAR

0.9 Million
VOLUNTEERED

0.2 Million
DRAFTED

5.5 Million
FREE

3.5 Million
ENSLAVED

2.6 Million
SERVED IN WAR

2.3 Million
VOLUNTEERED

0.3 Million
DRAFTED

TOTAL POPULATION OF THE UNION

21.4 Million

2.9 Million
BORDER STATES

0.4 Million
ENSLAVED
WITHIN BORDER STATES

18.5 Million
NORTHERN STATES

CASUALTIES

31,000
DIED IN PRISON

194,026
WOUNDED IN
BATTLE

164,000
DEATHS FROM
DISEASE

94,000
DEATHS IN
BATTLE

30,192
DIED IN PRISON

110,100
DEATHS IN
BATTLE

224,580
DEATHS FROM
DISEASE

275,174
WOUNDED IN
BATTLE

TOTAL **483,026**   **640,046**

COST

$1 Billion   **$3.2 Billion**

The **Homestead Act**, signed into law on May 20, 1862, set in motion a program of public land grants to small farmers. It provided that any adult citizen who headed a family could qualify for a grant of 160 acres of public land by paying a small registration fee and living on the land continuously for five years.

The main task of the country's political leaders, however, was, in Lincoln's words, "to bind up the nation's wounds." Many years would pass before the nation would recover politically, economically, and socially. This struggle would be especially difficult for the South.

HISTORICAL THINKING

1. **READING CHECK** What were the major economic and political impacts of the Civil War on American life?

2. **COMPARE AND CONTRAST** How did the aftermath of the Civil War affect the southern agricultural economy and northern industrial economy differently?

3. **ANALYZE CAUSE AND EFFECT** What effect did the land grants have on education and farming?

REVIEW

VOCABULARY

Use each of the following vocabulary words in a sentence that shows an understanding of the term's meaning.

1. stalemate
   Since they could not agree on a single point, their argument ended in a stalemate.

2. exemption

3. quarantine

4. conscription

5. scapegoat

6. bluff

7. Homestead Act

8. servitude

READING STRATEGY
ANALYZE LANGUAGE USE

If you haven't done so already, complete your graphic organizer to analyze how word choices throughout the text help convey the realities of war. Then answer the question.

I Read
Now we are engaged in a great civil war, testing whether that nation or any nation so conceived and so dedicated can long endure.

I Know	War	And So

9. How do the words used by President Lincoln in the Gettysburg Address help you understand the impact of the Civil War on the United States?

MAIN IDEAS

Answer the following questions. Support your answers with evidence from the chapter.

10. What major change in the war led to Lincoln's decision to issue the Emancipation Proclamation? **LESSON 1.1**

11. What challenges did the members of the 54th Massachusetts face as new members of the U.S. Army? **LESSON 1.3**

12. What provision of the 1863 Conscription Act was most responsible for sparking draft riots throughout the Northeast? **LESSON 2.1**

13. What measures did the North and the South take to pay for the war? **LESSON 2.2**

14. What problems did prison camps in the North and the South share? **LESSON 2.3**

15. Why are the Union victories at Vicksburg and Gettysburg considered turning points in the war? **LESSON 3.1**

16. What was the main military goal of Sherman's march through Georgia? **LESSON 3.2**

17. What were the main provisions of Grant's terms of surrender? **LESSON 3.4**

18. In what ways did Lincoln's assassination affect the treatment of the South during Reconstruction? **LESSON 4.1**

19. How did the federal government support its goal of expansion into western states after the war? **LESSON 4.2**

HISTORICAL THINKING

Answer the following questions. Support your answers with evidence from the chapter.

20. **MAKE CONNECTIONS** In what ways did having a strong central government help Lincoln wage war against the Confederacy?

21. **MAKE INFERENCES** How did the battles fought during Sherman's march through the South reflect broader struggles during the war?

22. **EVALUATE** How and why did the war become a war to end slavery?

23. **DRAW CONCLUSIONS** What is the main reason Lincoln chose Grant to lead the Union armies after the Battle of Vicksburg?

24. **SYNTHESIZE** How did the Civil War change the United States?

25. **FORM AND SUPPORT OPINIONS** What was the most important factor in the Union victory over the Confederacy? Support your opinion with evidence from the text.

26. **SEQUENCE EVENTS** What amendments followed the Civil War, and what meaning did they have? Create an annotated time line to illustrate your answer.

ANALYZE SOURCES

In his 1863 political cartoon, Thomas Nast imagines what impact emancipation would have on African Americans. Look closely at the cartoon and then answer the following questions.

27. How is slavery depicted in this cartoon?

28. How is emancipation depicted in this cartoon?

29. Why does Nast include Lincoln in this cartoon?

30. How might Americans in the North and the South have viewed this cartoon differently? Explain.

CONNECT TO YOUR LIFE

31. **NARRATIVE** Think about the events that became turning points in the Civil War. Connect your knowledge about this time in history to your own life. Have there been any turning points in your life? Do you expect there to be any turning points in your life in the future? Write a paragraph in which you compare turning points on a national scale like those in the Civil War to more personal turning points like those you've experienced or expect to experience in your life.

TIPS

- Make a time line of principal turning points in the Civil War. Then make a time line of possible turning points in your own life.

- Use two or three vocabulary terms from the chapter in your narrative.

- Conclude the narrative with a comment that ties Civil War turning points to your own life.

CHAPTER

17

RECONSTRUCTION
AND THE NEW SOUTH
1865–1877

ESSENTIAL QUESTION
In what ways did Reconstruction both succeed and fail?

 AMERICAN STORIES Freedom Readers

SECTION 1 Rebuilding the Union

KEY VOCABULARY

black codes

Civil Rights Act of 1866

Freedmen's Bureau

impeachment

Presidential Reconstruction

Radical Reconstruction

Reconstruction Acts of 1867

SECTION 2 Reconstruction Changes Daily Life

KEY VOCABULARY

arson

black peonage

Ku Klux Klan

literacy

lynch

sharecropping

social justice

wage economy

SECTION 3 The End of Reconstruction

KEY VOCABULARY

15th Amendment

bribery

Compromise of 1877

Copperhead

corruption

defect

Liberal Republican

literacy test

Panic of 1873

poll tax

AMERICAN GALLERY
ONLINE The Freed Slaves of the Civil War

READING STRATEGY

DRAW CONCLUSIONS
When you draw conclusions, you make a judgment based on what you have read. You analyze the facts, make inferences, and use your own experiences to form your judgment. As you read the chapter, use a diagram like this one to draw conclusions about the impact of Reconstruction on American society.

Facts   Inferences

Reconstruction

Conclusion

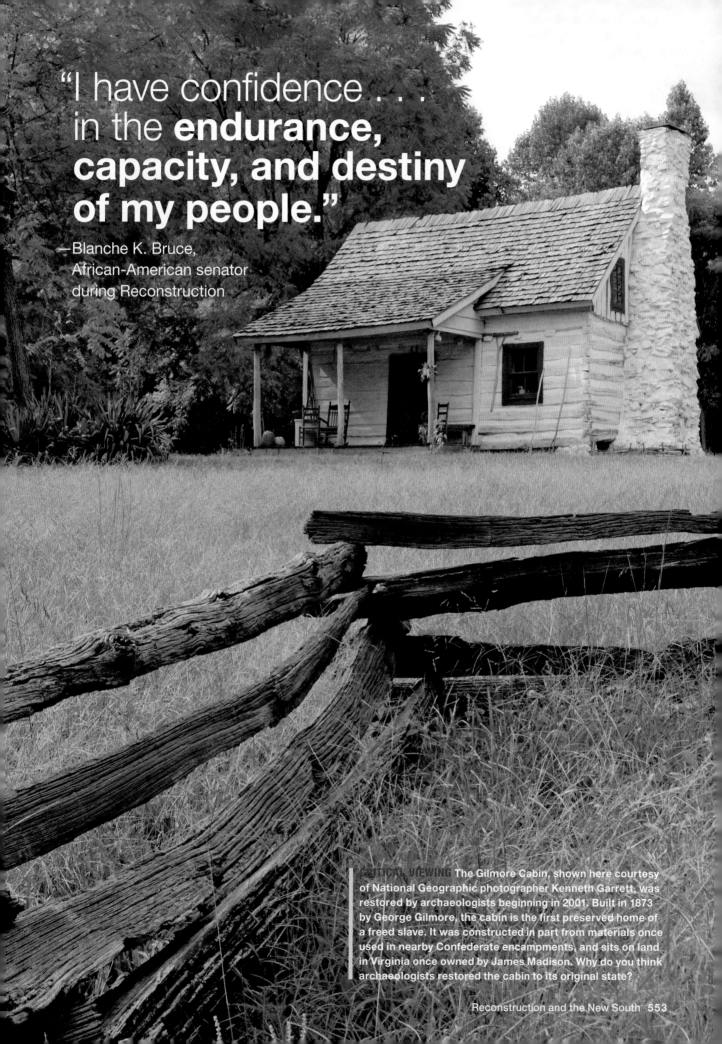

"I have confidence . . . in the **endurance, capacity, and destiny of my people.**"

—Blanche K. Bruce, African-American senator during Reconstruction

CRITICAL VIEWING The Gilmore Cabin, shown here courtesy of National Geographic photographer Kenneth Garrett, was restored by archaeologists beginning in 2001. Built in 1873 by George Gilmore, the cabin is the first preserved home of a freed slave. It was constructed in part from materials once used in nearby Confederate encampments, and sits on land in Virginia once owned by James Madison. Why do you think archaeologists restored the cabin to its original state?

CRITICAL VIEWING This mid-1800s photograph of enslaved women and children outside their southern cabin is unique in a significant way: it shows a young woman reading aloud to the group. How might the ability to read and write have affected the life of a slave before and after the Civil War?

FREEDOM READERS

BY FRAN DOWNEY

Vice President and Publisher,
National Geographic *Explorer* Magazine

African rebellion leaders Nat Turner, Gabriel Prosser,
Touissant L'Ouverture, and Denmark Vesey shared
one important power: literacy. Enslaved people
realized the value of reading, and many risked
everything—including their lives—to learn.
They were America's freedom readers.

When slavery first began in the colonies, slave owners often encouraged their slaves to read. In fact, literacy became a way for slave owners to assert control over them. Slave owners wanted to convert enslaved Africans to Christianity in order to "civilize" them, and believed that all Christians needed to be able to read the Bible. Helping his or her slaves learn to read was a critical part of a slave owner's "civilization" plan. Some slave owners also used scripture to justify the concept of slavery, believing the Bible implied it was acceptable to enslave people.

Many enslaved people had a very different goal in mind as they learned to read and write. They saw it as a way to resist bondage. Like breaking tools, working slowly, and pretending to be ill, learning to read and write was a passive way for the enslaved to revolt against the enslaver. Literate African Americans could learn about the larger world. They could read newspapers, plan escapes and rebellions, and send messages. A few, whose voices you have heard throughout this book, even wrote slave narratives, which exposed the evils of slavery. Instead of a lock that kept them shackled, enslaved people saw literacy as a way to unlock the chains of slavery.

Over time, slave owners began to fear the potential power of literate free and enslaved African Americans. States like North Carolina passed laws that severely punished African-American students and those who helped them. These laws forced African Americans to get inventive. Some slaves tricked their owners into teaching them. Others watched and listened as white children were taught to read, and practiced in secret.

Nat Turner's Rebellion in 1831, as represented by this illustration, panicked the South and prompted legislation that prevented the education, movement, and assembly of enslaved people.

EARLY LAWS AND LITERACY

Southern lawmakers began to outlaw African-American literacy as early as 1740. This date is no coincidence. A year earlier, 20 slaves in South Carolina tried to escape to Florida. This unsuccessful uprising, known as the Stono Rebellion, resulted in the deaths of 60 people. Believing that those who planned the rebellion had used reading and writing to communicate, lawmakers outlawed teaching slaves to write. This law did not impose a penalty on enslaved African Americans, who were considered property. Rather, it punished free people who taught slaves with a fine of 100 pounds.

In the New England Colonies, where slavery was less common, literacy rates among enslaved African Americans were higher. In the 1770s, literate slaves read that many colonists wanted to break from Britain. Believing these revolutionary leaders would be sympathetic to their cause, literate slaves in Massachusetts wrote to the legislature to request their freedom. Enslaved African Americans in Connecticut did the same about five years later. While neither legislature granted the slaves' request, one by one, northern states slowly began to end slavery in the 1780s.

After the American Revolution, African Americans continued to occupy the same social, economic, and political positions in the Northeast. But they began to create institutions to advance their rights and develop communities without racial discrimination. For example, Richard Allen, Absalom Jones, and others founded the African Methodist Episcopal Church in 1816. Additionally, some northern states passed laws to educate their newly emancipated fellow citizens. The state of New York did not abolish slavery until 1827. As a result, the New York African Free School, founded in 1787, became a haven for free African-American students and enslaved people whose owners allowed them to attend.

UNIVERSAL LITERACY?

One of the premises of the new republican government was that the nation's very existence depended on universal literacy—literacy for all. Even Thomas Jefferson, a slave owner himself, argued, "If a nation expects to be ignorant and free, in a state of civilization, it expects what never was and never will be."

Reinforcing the importance of education in the new nation, George Washington declared in his will that the enslaved children he owned who did not have parents should be taught a vocation, or trade, and educated. However, Washington's desire to teach enslaved children to read and write was not shared by most slave owners. In 1800, southern lawmakers passed a new law that restricted all "mental instruction" of both free and enslaved people of African descent, including teaching or simply talking about reading, writing, or mathematics.

The law also prohibited free and enslaved African Americans from gathering between sunset and sunrise. This restriction made it more difficult for African Americans to set up informal schools and gave authorities the right to barge in on anyone who they suspected of holding these "unlawful" meetings. This law punished both free and enslaved lawbreakers with a whipping, stating law officers, or justices of the peace, could "inflict corporal punishment on the offender or offenders . . . not exceeding twenty lashes."

Steel whips like this one from the 1800s were used to terrorize enslaved Africans during the Middle Passage and to punish plantation slaves and free African Americans for violating the rules and laws set forth by state legislatures.

FEARING THE LITERATE

Slave owners' worst fears about literate African Americans were realized in 1829, when David Walker, a free African-American abolitionist, published his *Appeal to the Colored Citizens of the World.* He wanted African Americans, especially slaves, to read his *Appeal,* in which he urged them to resist oppression violently, if necessary. He also argued for racial equality.

Born in North Carolina, Walker was considered free because his mother was free, but he had seen the impact of slavery. Walker became a radical voice against slavery. When authorities in the South discovered the first copies of the *Appeal,* they worried slaves had already been preparing a violent attack. African Americans in Charleston and New Orleans were promptly arrested for distributing Walker's *Appeal,* and a reward was offered for Walker: $10,000 alive, $1,000 dead.

Sunday Morning in Virginia, an oil painting by Winslow Homer, depicts children learning to read in their slave cabin.

LITERACY LAWS CONTINUE

By 1830, southern authorities had taken further steps to curb literacy among African Americans. They prohibited free African Americans, especially those from the North, from meeting with the enslaved, in an attempt to prevent slaves from gaining access to information.

Some northerners also grew concerned about educating free African Americans. You have read about the boarding school Prudence Crandall opened in Connecticut in 1832 for African-American girls. In 1833, the state passed a law requiring all African-American students be residents of the state. Authorities quickly arrested Crandall for violating this law. African Americans from Connecticut were still allowed to attend school, but those from out of state could not. Lawmakers feared migrating students would increase the state's African-American population, resulting in the "injury of the people." This way of thinking contributed to the characterization of free and educated African Americans as a separate and dangerous community.

AFTER THE CIVIL WAR

The Civil War was a watershed event that marked an important shift in American history and the end of slavery. Emancipation brought about many social changes, including the transformation of the

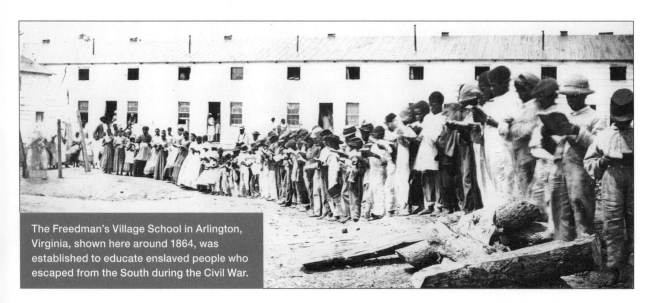

The Freedman's Village School in Arlington, Virginia, shown here around 1864, was established to educate enslaved people who escaped from the South during the Civil War.

RUNAWAY READING

As antiliteracy laws were passed and enforced, enslaved African Americans continued to disregard them. They learned to read and write, and then used these skills to escape slavery. Let's look at some of their remarkable stories.

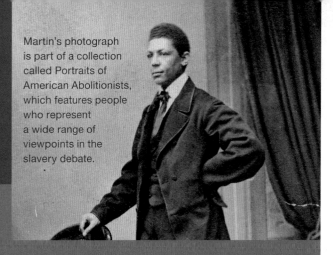

Martin's photograph is part of a collection called Portraits of American Abolitionists, which features people who represent a wide range of viewpoints in the slavery debate.

WILLIS

As valuable as reading was to slaves, writing was equally useful. An enslaved man called Willis used writing to escape slavery. What we know about him comes from a newspaper ad in which he is described as being 30 years old, stooped and downcast, and walking with a limp. On November 25, 1862, Willis ran away from his owner, W.H. Medlin, in South Carolina and headed north. Medlin placed the ad so people would look for Willis, but Willis had a special skill that helped him. To avoid capture, he wrote and signed a note that declared him free. He used his literacy skills to gain his freedom.

MATTIE JACKSON

Slavery crippled bodies and separated families, but it didn't stop people's quest for freedom. When Mattie Jackson was five years old, she and her mother tried to escape from Missouri to Chicago, but they were caught and sold back into slavery. Mattie decided to learn to read and demonstrated her literacy and resistance to slavery openly at times to her owner. When she finally managed to escape to Indiana, Mattie dictated, or spoke the story of her life so someone could record it, and sold the story. She used the money to pay for her education.

JOHN SELLA MARTIN

Runaway slave and abolitionist John Sella Martin (shown above) learned to read by listening. Working in a hotel in Georgia, he secretly listened to white co-workers as they played games and spelled words. By memorizing the sounds and spellings, Martin learned to spell even before he saw the shapes of the letters in the alphabet. He then applied this knowledge by trying to decode signs on the stores he walked by.

Other enslaved people saw Martin spelling words and assumed he could read. One day, three illiterate men gave him a newspaper and dared him to read it to them. Martin thought he might have to pretend he could read it. Instead he found he could read the headline and much of the article, which was about an abolitionist. Amazed and proud, Martin then knew there were abolitionists fighting slavery. And, perhaps even more important, he knew he could read.

Enslaved friends brought Martin newspapers and books they had stolen from their masters so he could practice reading, risking punishment for helping him. For Martin and other slaves, learning to read was one step on the road to freedom.

education system and a significant increase in the literacy rate among African Americans.

During the postwar Reconstruction era, the number of schools for African Americans rose substantially. Newly emancipated African Americans, or freedmen, recognized the value of literacy and education and set out to establish new schools and colleges. In 1865, Congress established an organization called the Freedmen's Bureau to provide support to the newly freed. The bureau aided the spread of African-American

schools in the South, renting buildings for schools, providing books for teachers, and offering protection for students and teachers threatened by the opponents of black literacy. In the face of segregation, violence, and opposition, African Americans would continue to be challenged by the pursuit of equal education for many years.

THINK ABOUT IT

Why might access to public education have been one of the most important outcomes of the Civil War for African Americans?

1.1 Reconstruction Under Andrew Johnson

Imagine you've been fighting with your friend. You both said and did terrible things, but you know it's time to forgive. How do you become friends again? That was the dilemma President Andrew Johnson faced after the Civil War.

MAIN IDEA President Johnson and Congress clashed over different goals for Reconstruction.

LEADING THE WAY

1865 was a rough year. The war had torn the nation in two, and the war's end did not repair this division. Lincoln was dead, and citizens mourned the loss of his thoughtful guidance and strong leadership. The new president, Andrew Johnson, faced the monumental challenge of rebuilding the United States politically, socially, and economically. Many decisions had to be made. How should the Confederate states be readmitted to the Union? Should Confederate leaders be punished? What role should free African Americans play in the country?

Johnson had been an unusual choice as Lincoln's vice president. He was a southerner from Tennessee who had served in Congress as a Democrat. But he was definitely pro-Union, a stance fueled by his dislike for wealthy southern planters. When Tennessee seceded, he remained in the U.S. Senate. Lincoln later appointed Johnson as military governor of Tennessee. During the Civil War, military governors worked to re-establish the governments of southern states conquered by the Union Army.

When the 1864 election rolled around, the Republicans chose Johnson to run as Lincoln's vice president based on his loyalty to the Union. But Johnson didn't support equal rights for African Americans. Like most southern whites, he was deeply prejudiced, which offended many Republicans.

Among the first decisions Johnson made as president was to oversee Reconstruction himself, an approach called **Presidential Reconstruction**. Johnson's plan required Confederate states to ratify the 13th Amendment—which, as you may recall, abolished slavery—and create new governments with new constitutions before they could rejoin the Union.

Although he had repeatedly stated, "Treason is a crime, and crime must be punished," Johnson quickly pardoned, or legally forgave, most Confederates who took an oath of loyalty to the Union. The pardons restored their civil rights and protected their property from being seized. Only wealthy planters and high-ranking Confederate leaders had to apply individually for presidential pardons. Many in Congress felt Johnson's plans were too lenient, or forgiving. Congress wanted Confederates to pay for their actions.

THE FREEDMEN'S BUREAU

Johnson's perceived leniency toward the former rebels was not the only problem Republicans had with his plan. They were equally alarmed that Presidential Reconstruction did not provide a way for African-American men to vote, a right African Americans deeply desired. African Americans also wanted the right to own property. Without the protection of full citizenship and property rights, African Americans worried that white southerners would take away their newly won freedoms and economic opportunities.

Republicans shared their concerns. In 1865, Congress created the Bureau of Refugees, Freedmen, and Abandoned Lands—more popularly known as the **Freedmen's Bureau**—to help the formerly enslaved, as well as impoverished white southerners. Congress appointed General Oliver Otis Howard to run the bureau. Army officers acting as bureau agents provided medicine, food, and clothing to newly freed African Americans and others displaced by the war. The officers also tried to settle former slaves on southern land that had been abandoned or seized during the war. Agents drew up labor contracts between landowners and African-American workers and created courts to settle conflicts between African Americans and whites.

Howard also saw education as a way to improve living conditions and economic opportunities for African Americans. The Freedmen's

Bureau worked with northern aid groups to establish schools for the newly freed. By 1869, approximately 3,000 schools serving more than 150,000 students reported to the bureau. Yet in spite of this progress, neither President Johnson nor most whites were ready to grant full rights to African Americans. As a result, the Republicans in Congress decided to take control of Reconstruction.

HISTORICAL THINKING

1. **READING CHECK** What were the original aims of Reconstruction?

2. **MAKE INFERENCES** Why might Johnson have chosen to be lenient toward many Confederates?

3. **SUMMARIZE** How did the Freedmen's Bureau affect newly freed African Americans?

1.2 Radical Reconstruction

In a debate, you're pitted against a team that wants to make its case as badly as you do. In 1866, the president and Congress both wanted to win control of the South. The struggle deteriorated into name-calling and power grabs.

MAIN IDEA Unhappy with Johnson's Reconstruction plans, the Republican Congress took the responsibility away from him.

JOHNSON VERSUS CONGRESS

Made bold by the lenient terms of Presidential Reconstruction, some southern states refused to ratify the 13th Amendment. They even refused to admit that secession had been illegal. Southern states also passed **black codes**—laws for controlling African Americans and limiting their rights. The codes granted African Americans a few rights, such as the right to marry and pursue a lawsuit in court, but most of the codes dealt with what African Americans could not do. For example, they could not own land, work in certain industries, or serve on a jury.

Congress was furious over the black codes and the leniency of Johnson's Reconstruction plans. As a result, Republicans proposed the **Civil Rights Act of 1866**. The bill granted full equality and citizenship to "every race and color." Johnson vetoed the bill, but Republicans in Congress overrode the veto, and the bill became law. To solidify these rights, Radical Republicans also proposed the 14th Amendment. As you've read, this amendment guarantees citizenship and equal protection under the law to all American-born people. On President Johnson's urging, many southern states refused to ratify the new amendment. It took two years for two-thirds of the states to ratify it.

THE RECONSTRUCTION ACTS OF 1867

Shocked northerners watched as delegates at southern state conventions refused to accept the 14th Amendment. When Republicans won control of Congress in the 1866 elections, they decided it was time to take Reconstruction out of the president's hands. They put themselves in charge of the process by passing the **Reconstruction Acts of 1867**. Their plan of action came to be called **Radical Reconstruction**.

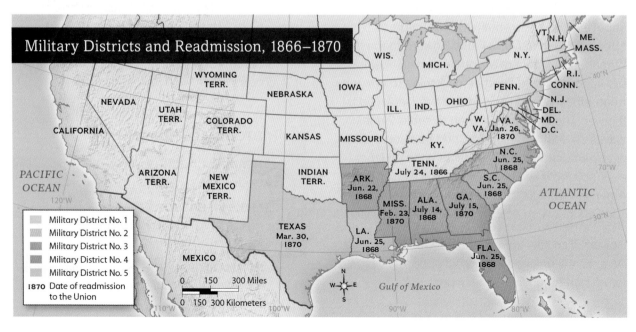

Military Districts and Readmission, 1866–1870

Military District No. 1
Military District No. 2
Military District No. 3
Military District No. 4
Military District No. 5
1870 Date of readmission to the Union

CRITICAL VIEWING Carl Schurz moved from Wisconsin to Missouri, where he was elected U.S. senator in 1868. In this political cartoon from 1872, he is shown as a carpetbagger. What details in the cartoon suggest what southerners thought of Schurz and other carpetbaggers?

Republicans had come to the South to get rich and called them "carpetbaggers," implying they had thrown everything they owned into a cheap suitcase, or carpetbag, and headed south. In reality, most of the Republicans from the North were Union veterans, preachers, teachers, or social workers. Free African Americans made up the rest of the delegates. Most were ministers or teachers.

To prevent Johnson from interfering with Radical Reconstruction, Congress passed the Tenure of Office Act, which prevented the president from removing government officials without Senate approval. The act clearly violated and ignored a Constitutional provision that granted the president the right to hire and fire Cabinet members. Johnson defied the act in August 1867, when he replaced his Secretary of War, Edwin M. Stanton, with Civil War hero Ulysses S. Grant. Stanton had been the only member of Johnson's Cabinet to support Radical Reconstruction. Congress responded by beginning the **impeachment** process, officially charging Johnson with "high crimes and misdemeanors," or extreme misconduct, while in office. They hoped to remove him from the presidency, and this was the first step. But the Senate tried Johnson and acquitted him, or found him not guilty, by one vote.

The Reconstruction Acts placed all of the former Confederate states except Tennessee, which had already officially been readmitted to the Union, into five districts under military rule. Once military leaders decided that order had been established, the states could draw up new constitutions. Each constitution had to accept the 14th Amendment. Then the majority of a state's citizens and the U.S. Congress had to approve the new constitution. Republican delegates were given the task of writing the new state constitutions. Many of the delegates were southern white Republicans who had opposed secession. Those in the South who hated Radical Reconstruction called the southern white Republicans "scalawags," or dishonorable people.

Northern white Republicans also made up a sizeable number of the delegates. Many southerners believed the northern white

HISTORICAL THINKING

1. **READING CHECK** What had to be done before a state could be readmitted to the Union?

2. **DRAW CONCLUSIONS** Why did many in Congress want to remove Johnson from the presidency?

3. **INTERPRET MAPS** Which southern state was the last to be readmitted to the Union?

2.1 Free African Americans Gain a Voice

Think of a time when you've stepped up to be a leader or you've done something hard and unfamiliar. You probably felt both nervous and proud. That may well have been how many African Americans felt as they took part in the political process for the first time.

MAIN IDEA During Radical Reconstruction, African Americans participated in government, established churches of their own, and tried to reestablish kinship structures.

TAKING PUBLIC OFFICE

After Congress passed the Reconstruction Acts, African Americans attained political freedom and wanted to exercise their new political power. As a result, many African-American citizens from the North, newly organized as Republicans, moved to the South hoping to fill appointed or elected government positions. African Americans from the South, some of whom had been free before the war, also sought leadership roles. These men became the backbone of the Republican Party in southern districts with large African-American populations.

African Americans everywhere wanted the ability to make their own choices. Many wanted to be involved in their states' readmission into the Union. Throughout the South, local African-American leaders, ministers, and Republicans encouraged newly freed men to register and vote. Their efforts helped Republican delegates dominate state constitutional conventions in every state except Georgia. African Americans also participated as delegates in all state conventions. Across the South, in fact, African Americans accounted for some 265 delegates out of a total of slightly more than 1,000. Between 1865 and 1877, African Americans influenced the direction of southern politics and elected 22 members of Congress. Republican-dominated legislatures established the first publicly financed education systems in the South, provided debt relief to the poor, and expanded women's rights.

About 600 African Americans also participated directly in the new state legislatures. Although no African Americans were elected governor, several served as lieutenant governors, secretaries of state, judges, or treasurers. **Pinckney Pinchback**, the lieutenant governor of Louisiana, became the acting governor when the state charged his boss with corruption.

African Americans became leaders at the national level when **Hiram Rhodes Revels** and **Blanche K. Bruce** served in the U.S. Senate. Revels, who was born a free man, served in Mississippi's state senate. He went on to fill a U.S. Senate seat left vacant when Mississippi seceded from the Union. He was the first African American to serve in the U.S. Senate. Bruce, who had been born into slavery, also represented Mississippi. He was the second African American to serve in the U.S. Senate and the first to be elected to a full term. In addition, 14 African Americans served in the U.S. House of Representatives during the Reconstruction era.

CHURCH AND FAMILY

Hiram Revels was already familiar in the African-American community in Mississippi through his work as a minister in the African Methodist Episcopal Church. Churches had long been at the center of African-American life. Because ministers were often the most educated members of the community, they became natural leaders—not only in religious matters but also in politics.

Following the Civil War, African Americans quickly established their own churches. The new churches were often Baptist because that denomination allowed each congregation to start a church independently and organize the services the way it wanted. By 1890, about 1.3 million African Americans were members of Baptist churches, mostly in the South. Churches were central to the African-American quest for **social justice**, or fair distribution of opportunities and privileges, including racial equality and rights. In addition to providing a place of worship, African-American churches often served as gathering places for social and political events and housed schools.

Like churches, family life had always been important to African Americans. But as you know, slavery had often split up families when members were sold to different owners. During Reconstruction, many African Americans tried to locate and reunite with their families. They were helped in this effort by the Freedmen's Bureau. In some cases, the bureau succeeded, particularly when the separated members of a family had gone to nearby plantations. Unfortunately, in other cases, family members had been sent far away. Some African Americans traveled hundreds of miles searching for their loved ones—often in vain.

First African Americans in U.S. Congress

The seven men in this print from 1872 are the first African Americans to serve in the U.S. Congress. Together, the seven represented five southern states. From left to right, the men are Senator Hiram Rhodes Revels of Mississippi (who filled the Senate seat that Jefferson Davis had held), Congressman Benjamin S. Turner of Alabama, Congressman Robert C. De Large of South Carolina, Congressman Josiah T. Walls of Florida, Congressman Jefferson F. Long of Georgia, Congressman Joseph Rainey of South Carolina, and Congressman Robert B. Elliot of South Carolina.

HISTORICAL THINKING

1. **READING CHECK** How did African-American political participation help strengthen the Republican Party in the South?

2. **MAKE INFERENCES** Why do you think it was important for African Americans to establish their own churches?

3. **DRAW CONCLUSIONS** Why were African Americans strongly motivated to influence and become leaders in government?

2.2 Education and Land

Like most Americans, you probably consider the education you receive as your right, rather than a privilege. But to African Americans during Reconstruction, school was an important sign of their new freedom.

MAIN IDEA The Freedmen's Bureau made education available to African Americans in the South, but other aspects of their lives changed very little.

AMERICAN PLACES
Howard University
Washington, D.C.

General Oliver Otis Howard's dedication to education is still visible today. Howard University in Washington, D.C., is named after the first commissioner of the Freedmen's Bureau and was the first American university dedicated to the education of African Americans. Howard himself served as the university's president when it occupied just one building. Today, more than 10,000 students are enrolled at the large campus, taking classes in subjects ranging from law to medicine and education.

AN OPPORTUNITY TO LEARN

African Americans appreciated the value of education. Slavery had denied many of them the opportunity to learn, so they saw education as a path to empowerment. **Literacy**, or the ability to read and write, and a solid working knowledge of mathematics gave African Americans the tools they needed to understand labor contracts. Education helped them advance in a **wage economy**, or an economy in which people are paid for their work. With a good education, they could fully participate in the political process and understand their civil rights.

The Freedmen's Bureau helped provide educational opportunities. The bureau and aid groups worked with individual communities to fund, build, and staff hundreds of Freedmen's Schools for African-American children and adults. These schools were often built on land owned by African Americans or housed in their churches. The schools were free, but since most African-American families counted on the labor or income their older children could provide, parents sacrificed a lot to send their children to school.

A shortage of teachers and space meant that schools often had to rotate students in three-hour groups. Typically, teachers worked all day teaching children and then held classes for adults at night. In some schools, however, young people worked and learned alongside adults in the classroom. In return, teachers experienced the satisfaction of teaching enthusiastic and motivated students. By the time the Freedmen's Bureau closed, about 150,000 students had attended classes.

BACK TO WORKING THE LAND

A good education was important to African Americans in the South because it offered their only chance for advancement. For the most part, uneducated African Americans worked the land of white landowners, but they faced discrimination in a southern economy on the edge of collapse. As a result, many former slaves wanted to obtain their own land to farm. Some freed African Americans had this wish fulfilled—at least for a short time.

In January 1865, General William T. Sherman issued Special Field Order No. 15, which set aside the Sea Islands for newly freed African Americans. The Sea Islands were located south of Charleston, South Carolina, and encompassed an area of approximately 400,000 acres. Each family would receive 40 acres to farm and a mule. News of the offer spread quickly, and about 40,000 African Americans rushed to settle on the land. But by the fall of 1865, President Andrew Johnson had overturned Sherman's order. The land was returned to the southern planters who had owned it before the Civil War.

With no land of their own, many African Americans went back to working for white landowners. At first, landowners insisted that the newly freed African Americans work in gangs, as they had under slavery. Over time, however, an agricultural system called **sharecropping** developed. In sharecropping, a farmer raised crops for a landowner in return for part of the money made from selling the crops. Some poor white families, devastated by the war, also took up sharecropping. But they did not face the discrimination that African Americans endured.

Sharecropping often left African-American families in debt to landowners. The sharecroppers needed supplies, such as tools and seeds, to work the land. Landowners would sell or rent the supplies to the sharecroppers on credit and at a high rate of interest. By the time the crops were harvested, sharecroppers had usually run up a large bill and, as a result, would receive very little of the profits from selling the crops. Sharecropping tied African Americans to a landowner's land and resulted in **black peonage**, a sort of economic slavery.

Unable to earn a living as sharecroppers or find other work, many African Americans began moving north or west. Some also fled to escape the terror generated by groups of white southerners.

HISTORICAL THINKING

1. **READING CHECK** How did the Freedmen's Bureau help educate former slaves?

2. **ANALYZE CAUSE AND EFFECT** What factors led to the development of sharecropping in the South?

3. **DRAW CONCLUSIONS** In what way did sharecropping replace slavery?

2.3 Resistance in the South

Terror is a powerful weapon. When combined with racism, its damage can last for generations. A reign of terror in the South set back African-American political gains and broke the Republican Party's hold in the region.

MAIN IDEA Afraid of losing political and economic power, some white southerners used terror tactics against African Americans and Republicans.

THE KU KLUX KLAN

Radical Reconstruction angered many white southerners and created a resistance movement based on racism and discrimination. Few white southerners accepted African Americans as their equals. Sometimes whites turned to violence in an attempt to keep African Americans from voting and exercising other rights. In 1866, white mobs attacked unarmed African-American men, women, and children and rioted in Memphis, Tennessee, and New Orleans, Louisiana. The mobs killed or injured many African Americans. In Memphis, the rioters, who included police officers, committed **arson** by purposefully burning homes, churches, and schools in African-American communities.

That same year, a group of young men in Tennessee founded the **Ku Klux Klan**. Originally intended as a social club, the group's purpose changed dramatically in 1867 when African Americans gained voting rights in the state under the Reconstruction Acts and began holding public office. Thereafter, the Ku Klux Klan, under the leadership of former Confederate officer Nathan Bedford Forrest, dedicated itself to maintaining the social and political power of white people.

To achieve its goals, members of the Klan terrorized and killed African Americans. They also attacked white people who associated with Republicans or supported African-American rights. To conceal their identities and maximize the terror, Klan members rode out at night dressed in hooded costumes. They whipped, tar-and-feathered, and even **lynched**, or hanged, their victims. They also committed arson. The Klan became the face of violent discrimination, carrying out punishments against people whom they felt had overstepped racial boundaries. Boosted by popular sentiment and federal acceptance, the Klan's popularity quickly spread across the South and even beyond.

CRITICAL VIEWING In 1874, this political cartoon by Thomas Nast appeared in *Harper's Weekly*. Why do you think the cartoonist included the words "worse than slavery" over the heads of the African-American family?

A POWER SHIFT

In response, the Republican-dominated Congress passed the Enforcement Acts in 1870 and 1871. The acts made it a crime to use violence or threats to interfere with a citizen's right to vote, hold office, or serve on a jury. The acts authorized the federal government to supervise congressional elections and gave the president the power to enforce the acts. The intent of the acts was to stop Klan activities and protect African-American rights.

Armed with the Enforcement Acts, the federal government took legal action against the Klan in 1871. In state after state, the government charged Klan leaders with crimes. The Klan became less visible, but their scare tactics had already damaged the Republican Party by preventing African Americans from voting. As a result, the Democratic Party began to gain back control in the South, and the number of African-American officeholders fell dramatically.

Meanwhile, many white voters in the North also thought the Radical Republicans had gone too far in promoting African-American rights. Even though the country would elect a Republican president in 1868, Reconstruction was starting to lose steam.

Members of the Ku Klux Klan often wore metal membership badges like these. The 1921 Klan badge on the right is shaped like the hood Klan members wore to scare and intimidate their victims.

HISTORICAL THINKING

1. **READING CHECK** What tactics did the Ku Klux Klan use to terrorize African Americans and white Republicans?

2. **MAKE INFERENCES** Why do you think the Klan's activities were allowed to continue in the South until 1870?

3. **SUMMARIZE** How did Klan activities change the balance of political power in the South?

3.1 Grant's Presidency

Think about how much has been at stake in recent presidential elections. The election of 1868 was similar, especially for Republicans and African Americans. A Democratic victory could deliver the end of Reconstruction.

MAIN IDEA After their party's victory in the 1868 presidential election, Republicans helped pass the 15th Amendment.

THE ELECTION OF GENERAL GRANT

In the 1868 presidential race, the Republicans nominated Ulysses S. Grant, the great Union hero of the Civil War. Although Grant had no experience in government, Republicans believed their candidate would be able to please members of both parties. When Grant accepted the nomination, he said, "Let us have peace." That phrase became a theme for the campaign. Republicans were aware that white voters had become less willing to help African Americans. As a result, the party did not promise to expand Reconstruction or to further promote the rights of African Americans.

The Democrats nominated **Horatio Seymour**, the former governor of New York, as their candidate. Seymour was part of a group of Democrats called the **Copperheads**. As you probably know, a copperhead is a poisonous snake. During the Civil War, this group, who called themselves "Peace Democrats," opposed emancipation and the draft. Republicans called the group "Copperheads" because they believed its members were Confederate sympathizers.

Seymour and the Copperheads relied on fear and racism to attract voters. Seymour criticized the Republicans for their aggressive handling of Reconstruction. He felt the government placed too much importance on African-American rights. His ideals appealed to many midwestern farmers who felt the Republicans did not understand their way of

1868 Campaign Buttons
Grant's running mate was Schuyler (SKY-ler) Colfax, a prominent Radical Republican. The candidates' campaign buttons feature ferrotypes, or photos printed on tin.

life. He also appealed to urban whites who believed free African Americans would move to the North and take their jobs.

Despite Seymour's rhetoric, or use of persuasive language, Grant led the Republicans to victory in the 1868 election. About 500,000 African Americans voted for Grant, helping him receive 53 percent of the ballots. In his inaugural speech, Grant declared, "I shall on all subjects have a policy to recommend, but none to enforce against the will of the people." He promised, unlike Andrew Johnson, to carry out the laws that Congress passed.

THE 15TH AMENDMENT

After the 1868 election, Republicans pushed for the adoption of the **15th Amendment** to the Constitution. Under the amendment's terms, the federal and state governments could not restrict the right to vote because of race, color, or previous condition of servitude—in other words, slavery. The amendment would complete the political reforms sought by Reconstruction. Congress approved the amendment in February 1869 despite Democratic opposition, and it became part of the Constitution in 1870.

The intent of the amendment was to limit the southern states' ability to prevent African Americans from participating in the political process. But the new law did little for African Americans outside the former Confederacy. It also did not restrict or change any of the laws that states had placed on the rights of males to vote, such as charging **poll taxes**. A poll tax is a fee charged when people register to vote. Meanwhile, the Amnesty Act of 1872 removed voting restrictions on most of those who had belonged to the Confederacy.

The adoption of the 13th, 14th, and 15th amendments fundamentally changed the nation by establishing citizenship rights and full equality for anyone born in the United States. However, over the next couple of decades, courts and political interests would undermine the intent of the amendments.

Still, rights and equality were not on the minds of most people in the 1870s. They wanted their elected leaders to pay more attention to problems closer to home, including a severe economic depression. As an Illinois newspaper observed, "the negro is now a voter and a citizen. Let him hereafter take his chances in the battle of life."

HISTORICAL THINKING

1. **READING CHECK** What was the theme of Grant's presidential campaign?

2. **COMPARE AND CONTRAST** What differing views characterized the Republican and Democratic presidential candidates in the election of 1868?

3. **DRAW CONCLUSIONS** Why would a poll tax prevent African Americans from voting?

3.2 The Election of 1876

With our 24/7 online news feed, it can be hard to focus on one important problem when other issues arise. But this also happened in the 1870s, when scandals and economic woes distracted Americans from Reconstruction.

MAIN IDEA As scandals and a depression arose, a compromise reached over a contested election brought Reconstruction to an end.

SCANDAL AND PANIC

Ulysses S. Grant had been an effective general, but he proved to be a poor administrator. He often relied on Congress to make the types of decisions he should have made as the country's leader. He also was unable to keep his party from splintering into different factions, or groups, each promoting a different political viewpoint. The **Liberal Republicans** were among these factions. They believed the government had become too large and too powerful. They favored free trade and an end to Reconstruction. In American politics of the 1870s, the word *liberal* referred to someone who embraced these ideas.

Leading up to the election of 1872, the Liberal Republicans **defected**, or broke away, from the Republican Party and formed an alliance with Democrats. They nominated Horace Greeley, a newspaper editor from New York City, as the Democratic presidential candidate. Greeley's main goal was to end Reconstruction, but that was not enough to appeal to voters. Grant easily won re-election.

But accounts of dishonest behavior plagued Grant's second term. These scandals involved **bribery**, or offers of money or privileges in exchange for political favors. Financial

wrongdoing among legislators and Cabinet members surfaced. For instance, Congress investigated Secretary of War William Belknap for **corruption**, another word for dishonesty. Congress accused Belknap of accepting cash gifts from army suppliers, which led to his resignation.

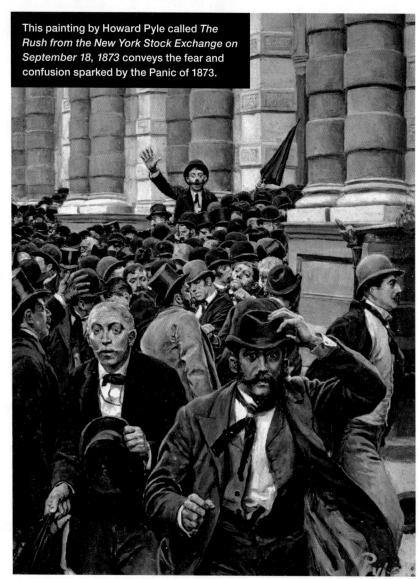

This painting by Howard Pyle called *The Rush from the New York Stock Exchange on September 18, 1873* conveys the fear and confusion sparked by the Panic of 1873.

The Election of 1876

Hayes (Republican)

Uncontested Electoral: 165 votes

Electoral Vote: 185 votes, 50.1%

Popular Vote: 4,034,311 votes, 48.5%

Tilden (Democrat)

Uncontested Electoral: 184 votes

Electoral Vote: 184 votes, 49.9%

Popular Vote: 4,288,546 votes, 51.5%

Territories, No Returns

Contested Electoral Votes

Twenty electoral votes from Florida, Louisiana, Oregon, and South Carolina were contested, or disputed, following charges of voter fraud. The controversial election was finally settled by the Compromise of 1877. All 20 votes went to Hayes, giving him the win by one electoral vote.

WASH. TERR.

MONTANA TERR.

DAKOTA TERR.

MN 5

NH 5

VT 5

ME 7

OR 2 1

IDAHO TERR.

WYOMING TERR.

WI 10

MI 11

NY 35

MA 13

NV 3

UTAH TERR.

NE 3

IA 11

IL 21

IN 15

OH 22

PA 29

RI 4

CT 6

NJ 9

LA 6

CO 3

KS 5

MO 15

WV 5

VA 11

DE 3

MD 8

KY 17

ARIZONA TERR.

NEW MEXICO TERR.

INDIAN TERR.

AR 6

TN 12

NC 10

SC 7

TX 8

LA 8

MS 8

AL 10

GA 11

FL 4

To make matters worse, economic disaster struck in 1873 when bank and railroad failures triggered an economic crisis called the **Panic of 1873**. Many people lost their money when banks closed and lost their jobs when businesses collapsed. As unemployment rose, the country slid into a depression that lasted six years.

END OF RECONSTRUCTION

As the depression wore on, economic concerns overshadowed the nation's interest in Reconstruction. In 1876, two court cases dealt a further blow to the cause of African Americans' civil rights. The U.S. Supreme Court ruled in *U.S.* v. *Cruikshank* that the civil rights amendments only allowed the federal government to prevent states from abusing African Americans' civil rights. The job of punishing individuals fell to the states. In *U.S.* v. *Reese,* the Court ruled that the 15th Amendment only made it illegal to deny a person the right to vote based on race. States could use other criteria, such as **literacy tests**, or tests of one's ability to read and write, to exclude voters.

By the 1876 presidential election, Democrats had regained control of several southern states and the U.S. House of Representatives. Democrats nominated Samuel J. Tilden as their candidate. The Republican nominee was **Rutherford B. Hayes**. The race was extremely close, with election results in several states disputed. Congress created an electoral commission to decide the election, but while it

met, Democrats and Republicans got together to negotiate a deal. In what came to be called the **Compromise of 1877**, Democrats agreed to award the victory to Hayes if Republicans agreed to end Reconstruction and pull federal troops out of the South. The deal was struck.

In the end, Reconstruction fell short of its goals. It had raised and then dashed hopes that African Americans would achieve equality. To some degree, African Americans made advances. But to help African Americans overcome the effects of hundreds of years of slavery and racism entirely would have required a great expansion of federal power. Still, although the promise of the 13th, 14th, and 15th amendments remained unfulfilled during Reconstruction, these amendments became the legal basis for the civil rights movement of the 1960s.

HISTORICAL THINKING

1. **READING CHECK** What views did Liberal Republicans promote?

2. **ANALYZE CAUSE AND EFFECT** What impact did the 1872 Amnesty Act, the 1876 election, and the withdrawal of federal troops from the South have on civil rights for African Americans?

3. **INTERPRET MAPS** How many contested electoral votes did Tilden need to win the election?

VOCABULARY

Use each of the following vocabulary words in a sentence that shows an understanding of the term's meaning.

1. black codes
   Southern states used black codes to restrict the rights of African Americans.

2. corruption

3. Freedmen's Bureau

4. impeachment

5. Radical Reconstruction

6. sharecropping

7. 15th Amendment

8. Panic of 1873

READING STRATEGY
DRAW CONCLUSIONS

If you haven't done so already, complete your diagram to draw conclusions about the impact of Reconstruction on American society. Then answer the question.

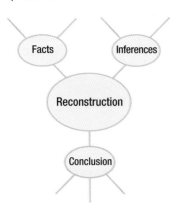

9. How did Reconstruction redefine what it meant to be an American?

MAIN IDEAS

Answer the following questions. Support your answers with evidence from the chapter.

10. Why was President Johnson at odds with many Republicans? **LESSON 1.1**

11. What did Presidential Reconstruction fail to do for African Americans? **LESSON 1.1**

12. What legislation did Congress propose to counteract Johnson's Reconstruction plans? **LESSON 1.2**

13. Why did African Americans often establish Baptist churches? **LESSON 2.1**

14. Why was education a symbol of their new freedom to African Americans in the South? **LESSON 2.2**

15. What was the goal of the Ku Klux Klan? **LESSON 2.3**

16. How did the 15th Amendment fail African Americans? **LESSON 3.1**

17. What was the Compromise of 1877? **LESSON 3.2**

HISTORICAL THINKING

Answer the following questions. Support your answers with evidence from the chapter.

18. **DRAW CONCLUSIONS** What did the outcome of Johnson's impeachment trial indicate about the power of Radical Republicans in the Senate?

19. **EVALUATE** What did the election of Blanche K. Bruce to the U.S. Senate probably mean to African Americans?

20. **ANALYZE CAUSE AND EFFECT** What impact did Reconstruction have on the political and social structures of the North and the South?

21. **MAKE INFERENCES** Why do you think some states charged poll taxes and made voters take literacy tests?

22. **MAKE CONNECTIONS** How were the 13th, 14th, and 15th amendments connected to Reconstruction?

INTERPRET PHOTOGRAPHS

The lives and work of sharecroppers remained largely unchanged for decades after the end of the Civil War. Look closely at the photograph of a sharecropper in Mississippi taken in the 1930s. Then answer the questions that follow.

23. How would you describe the work the woman is doing?

24. In what way is this work similar to that performed by enslaved persons?

ANALYZE SOURCES

In his second inaugural address delivered on March 4, 1873, Ulysses S. Grant discussed the problems African Americans still faced in the South. Read the following excerpt from the speech and answer the question.

> The effects of the late civil strife have been to free the slave and make him a citizen. Yet he is not possessed of the civil rights which citizenship should carry with it. This is wrong, and should be corrected. To this correction I stand committed, so far as Executive influence can avail [be of service or help].
>
> Social equality is not a subject to be legislated upon, nor shall I ask that anything be done to advance the social status of [an African American], except to give him a fair chance to develop what there is good in him, give him access to the schools, and when he travels let him feel assured that his conduct will regulate the treatment and fare [prices charged, food, material] he will receive.

25. Based on the excerpt, what is Grant's position on African-American civil rights?

CONNECT TO YOUR LIFE

26. **EXPOSITORY** Review the reasons many African Americans saw the opportunity for education as a way to improve their lives. Think about an activity you enjoy doing, for instance, reading comic books or playing basketball. Write a paragraph explaining how your education helps you better enjoy that activity.

TIPS

• Pick an activity you enjoy doing. Use an idea web to brainstorm what school subjects are involved in doing that activity.

• Conclude your paragraph with a comment about how your education has enabled you to enjoy the activity.

• Have you addressed the topic? Revise or rewrite your paragraph, as needed.

NATIONAL GEOGRAPHIC | CONNECTION

Lincoln's Funeral Train

by Adam Goodheart

Adapted from "How Abraham Lincoln's Funeral Train Made History," by Adam Goodheart, news.nationalgeographic.com, April 18, 2015

On the drizzly morning of April 19, 1865, when the train carrying the murdered president's coffin pulled out of Washington's central depot, it embarked on a journey that resonated deeply with many chapters of his life. As a 27-year-old novice state legislator in the 1830s, he was already advocating the construction of new train lines. He later served as an attorney for the Illinois Central and other companies.

In 1861, when Lincoln journeyed to Washington for his first inauguration, he traveled farther to reach the White House than any previous president-elect. As he made his way through midwestern and northern states, he reassured Americans that the nation would be saved. The trip itself was a powerful statement. It was a reminder of the 30,000 miles of steel that already bound the nation together, of the industrial economy that was vaulting the North ahead of the South, and of plans to build a transcontinental line joining Atlantic to Pacific.

Four years later, the funeral trip that carried Lincoln home for burial in Springfield, Illinois, was designed to recall the earlier journey. On the second day of travel, as it crossed the border between Maryland and Pennsylvania, the train rode over tracks that just a few years earlier had been used by slaves escaping to freedom. During the Civil War, trains laden with wounded soldiers often passed here as well, trundling their human burden from Virginia battlefields to the Union military hospitals in Pennsylvania.

On the 1865 trip, just two cars made the entire journey. One carried high-ranking military personnel and members of the Lincoln family. The other was the funeral car itself, named the United States. It had been completed in February 1865 as a lavish presidential office on wheels, a 19th-century version of Air Force One. It boasted gilded wood, etched glass, and wheels designed to accommodate tracks of varying gauges. For the funeral trip, it was draped inside and out in heavy black cloth fringed with silver.

The train's passage through towns and villages, usually in darkness, was an unparalleled event. "As we sped over the rails at night, the scene was the most pathetic ever witnessed," wrote one member of the entourage. "At every crossroads, the glare of innumerable torches illuminated the whole population from [old] age to infancy kneeling on the ground, and their clergymen leading in prayers and hymns."

Especially in the rural Midwest, ordinary Americans felt a connection with Lincoln that went beyond the tragedy of his assassination. Like him, they had suffered the agonies and triumphs of four years of war, and this emotional journey was bound up with memories of the railroad, too. It was at the local depots—the same ones where the funeral train now passed—that, long before, many had caught their last glimpses of sons and brothers who would never return. It was here that civilians brought the bandages, clothing, food, and flags that they contributed to the war effort. It was here that the first news of defeats and losses on distant battlefields arrived, carried by the telegraph lines that ran along the tracks.

For the 150th anniversary of the funeral journey, some people resurrected memories of when Lincoln's funeral car carried history through the midwestern heartland. It stopped in Springfield for a reenactment of the Lincoln funeral, two days shy of the actual anniversary.

A coffin—empty, of course—was unloaded onto a horse-drawn hearse and driven to the old Illinois State House for an all-night vigil. The next day, it was taken to Oak Ridge Cemetery. As in 1865, the last few miles of the homeward journey were powered by horses, not steam engines. But the ghostly presence of the railroad, like that of the murdered president himself, hovered somewhere close at hand.

For more from National Geographic, check out "Civil War Battlefields" online.

UNIT INQUIRY: Develop a Conflict Resolution Strategy

In this unit, you learned about the issues that fueled the Civil War and about the challenges that the United States faced after the war ended. Based on your understanding of the text, what unresolved conflicts eventually drove Americans to war? How did these conflicts get resolved? How did the Civil War and Reconstruction shape the American identity?

ASSIGNMENT

Develop a strategy that you think would have been successful in resolving one of the conflicts that Americans wrestled with before, during, and after the Civil War. Since you have knowledge about how events unfolded, your strategy should take into consideration the factors that led to conflict. Be prepared to present your strategy to the class and explain your reasoning.

Gather Evidence As you plan your strategy, gather evidence from this unit about the different ways in which conflicts and the way Americans did or didn't resolve them shaped the American identity. Also think about what Americans hoped to achieve through war and how the war affected ordinary citizens. Make a list of the causes and consequences of the war and address the most significant ones in your strategy. Use a graphic organizer like this one to help organize your thoughts.

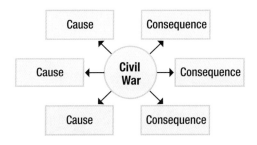

Produce Use your notes to produce descriptions of the causes and consequences of the Civil War. Write a short paragraph on each, using evidence from this unit to support your ideas.

Review Your Paragraphs Is the writing appropriate for your audience? Do you meet the purpose of the assignment? Revise or edit as needed.

Present Choose a creative and engaging way to present your conflict negotiation strategy to the class. Consider one of these options:

- Play the role of a diplomat and explain why a peaceful solution or compromise is preferable to a full-scale civil war.

- Write a dialogue between two people, one from the North and one from the South, that describes their perspectives on the causes and consequences of the Civil War.

- Create a multimedia presentation using paintings, photographs, and excerpts of documents to illustrate what caused the war, the realities of the war, and the consequences of the war.

 LEARNING FRAMEWORK ACTIVITIES

Create an Illustrated Time Line

SKILL Observation

KNOWLEDGE Our Human Story

Keeping track of events and their details can be a challenge, but understanding how events flow and relate to each other is how we make sense of them. Create an illustrated time line of the events surrounding the Civil War. You can organize events and details horizontally or vertically and illustrate the events you find most compelling. Include important dates and people. When you have completed your time line, share your work with the class.

Compose a Letter Home

ATTITUDE Empowerment

SKILLS Collaboration, Communication

In any war, letters from the front reveal the hard realities facing people on the front lines. Imagine that you are a soldier, medic, or reporter during the Civil War. Write a letter home that describes your experiences. Include specific details about time and place and observations about the people around you. Consider working with a partner who, as the recipient of your letter home, writes a letter back. When you have completed your letter or letters, present them to the class.

To look at American life and culture at the turn of the 20th century

Your U.S. History course concludes just as the country has survived a divisive Civil War and Reconstruction. Now Americans were ready to define a new, optimistic national identity.

Fred Hiebert
▶ Watch the Why Study U.S. History? video

THE WORLD'S FAIR OF 1893

The Civil War and Reconstruction had brought about deep social changes, and it was clear that divisions among the American people couldn't just be legislated away. Facing rapid industrial growth and increasing immigration, many Americans were uneasy about the country's direction.

In the late 1880s, America's thought leaders looked for a way to unify people and pointed to the successful 1851 Crystal Palace Exhibition, a world's fair in London. The idea for a World's Columbian Exposition in the United States to celebrate the 400th anniversary of Columbus's landing in the New World took hold. New York, St. Louis,

Postcards and posters for the World's Columbian Exposition often featured aerial color illustrations similar to the one shown here. The Exposition covered more than 600 acres along Chicago's lakefront.

Washington, D.C., and Chicago all lobbied to host the fair, and Chicago outbid its competition.

The city had emerged from the Great Chicago Fire of 1871 eager to express its optimistic energy, and prominent leaders approached the world's fair with enthusiasm. Architect Daniel Burnham and landscape architect Frederick Law Olmsted took on the challenge of turning a boggy stretch of real estate along Chicago's lakefront into a venue for millions of visitors. Burnham's directive to his team was "Make no little plans."

And the fair was unforgettable. Many of its buildings were intended to be only temporary, so the facades were covered in a mixture of plaster, cement, and jute fiber. The fair became known as the "White City," both because the buildings gleamed with white stucco and because of its extensive use of new electric street lights.

Among many amazing displays, the fair included life-size reproductions of Columbus's three ships. The most popular attraction was the 250-foot high Ferris wheel designed by engineer George Washington Gale Ferris. Each of its 36 cars could accommodate up to 60 people. The *John Bull* locomotive, built in 1831, chugged its way from Washington, D.C., to Chicago to participate in the fair. Historian Frederick Jackson Turner famously lectured on the end of the American frontier, even as Buffalo Bill Cody set up his "Wild West" show just outside the gates. But the fair's exhibitions on culture—and some noticeable omissions—provoked controversy.

PERCEPTIONS OF AMERICAN CULTURE

Following the example of the 1889 Paris fair, in which anthropologists created displays of "living villages" of people from Africa and Asia, in Chicago, a Midway had been set aside as a sort of living outdoor museum of humans from less-developed areas of the world. The Midway displayed an African village and a "Streets of Cairo" exhibit, among others. The contrast between the lofty grandeur of the White City and the displays on the Midway reflected the differences among Americans about their society and future.

Both women and African Americans protested their lack of representation in the fair. If the World's

This view of the administration and electrical buildings reveals the fair's dramatic architecture.

Columbian Exposition was seen by some as defining American culture, important sectors of the population had pretty much been overlooked.

In the end, the World's Columbian Exposition captured the positive momentum of a country ready to become a world leader. More than 45 nations participated in the fair, and 26 million guests strolled through its grounds. Of the fair's nearly 200 buildings, only two still stand. The Palace of Fine Arts eventually became the Museum of Science and Industry, and the Art Institute of Chicago moved into the World's Congress Building after the fair closed. Today's visitors to Chicago can still experience firsthand a couple of the grand buildings that provided a snapshot of American life at a critical moment in time.

Your American Story

As you've been studying American history, you've been collecting thoughts and recollections about your life in the United States. Time to put it all together.

 Use your History Notebook to help you write about—and share—your own American story.

STUDENT REFERENCES

This famous Civil War battlefield in Gettysburg, Pennsylvania is a peaceful place today.

CITIZENSHIP
HANDBOOK

This Citizenship Handbook will help you take a detailed look at our two most important documents: the Declaration of Independence and the U.S. Constitution, which contains the Bill of Rights. The handbook includes notes to help you understand the formal language and difficult concepts contained in the more than 225-year-old documents. At the end of the handbook, you will learn about citizenship and the rights and responsibilities that come along with it. You will also find out how you can build and practice citizenship skills.

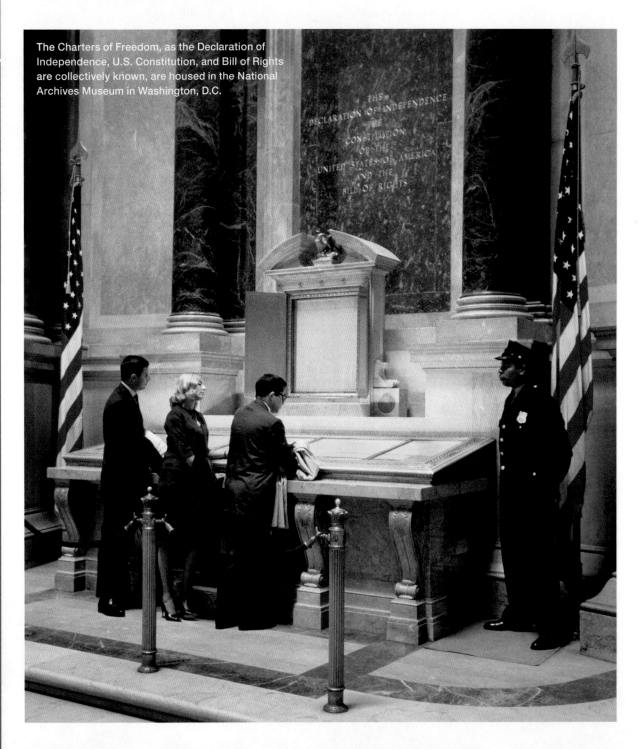

The Charters of Freedom, as the Declaration of Independence, U.S. Constitution, and Bill of Rights are collectively known, are housed in the National Archives Museum in Washington, D.C.

DECLARATION OF INDEPENDENCE

Introduction

The American colonists wrote the Declaration of Independence in 1776 to call for their separation and independence from Britain. During the first half of the 1700s, the colonists had lived in relative isolation from British authority and largely governed themselves. They modeled their colonial governments on Parliament, Britain's legislative body, by forming elected assemblies similar to the House of Commons. Unlike the British legislature, however, elected officials in the assemblies lived in the areas they represented. The colonists believed that representatives who lived among the people who elected them would better understand local interests and needs. They had no representatives in Parliament and sometimes resented what they felt to be unfair treatment by Britain.

GROWING RESENTMENT

The colonists' resentment grew after they fought alongside the British in the French and Indian War. The Americans had joined the fight so that they could expand their settlements westward into Native American territory. After Britain won the war against the French in 1763, however, the British government issued a proclamation stating that colonists could not settle west of the Appalachian Mountains. To make matters worse, British king George III charged a series of taxes against the colonists to help pay for the war. The king believed that the role of a colony was to support the mother country—in this case, Britain.

Crying "No taxation without representation," the colonists protested against the British legislation. As tensions rose, violence erupted in 1770 with the Boston Massacre, resulting in the deaths of five colonists at the hands of British soldiers. Three years later, colonists demonstrated their anger over a law on the sale of tea by staging the Boston Tea Party in Boston Harbor. A group of colonists boarded British ships and threw more than 300 crates of tea overboard.

Finally, in 1775, feelings on both sides reached the boiling point. After British troops learned that the colonists had stored weapons in Concord, Massachusetts, the troops marched to the town. Colonial militiamen rushed to face down the British soldiers in nearby Lexington. Shots rang out at what would later be called the first battle of the American Revolution.

DECLARING INDEPENDENCE

Colonial delegates to the two Continental Congresses met in Philadelphia in 1774 and 1775. Some delegates called for the colonies to separate completely from Britain. While the 1775 Congress debated the issue, a committee was formed to write an official document to declare independence from Britain. The committee included Thomas Jefferson, John Adams, and Benjamin Franklin, three of America's Founding Fathers.

Jefferson became the principal author of the Declaration of Independence. Like many American colonists, Jefferson had been deeply influenced by the Enlightenment, a movement that spread from Britain to the colonies in the 1700s. Enlightenment thinkers, such as John Locke, claimed that humans were born free and equal and that a leader could rule only with the consent of the people.

Inspired by the Enlightenment philosophy of unalienable, or natural, rights, Jefferson called for "Life, Liberty, and the Pursuit of Happiness" in the Declaration. These unalienable rights, he insisted, could not be taken away. Jefferson also drew on the principles of freedom contained in the Magna Carta as he wrote the document. On July 4, 1776, the delegates to the Continental Congress adopted the Declaration of Independence. In 1782, more than six years after the first shots were fired, the American Revolution officially ended. The American colonists had fought for and won their freedom and independence from Britain.

THE DECLARATION OF INDEPENDENCE

IN CONGRESS, JULY 4, 1776

The Declaration begins by explaining why the colonists want to break away from Britain and become independent. The Founding Fathers believed it was important to explain why they wanted to take this step.

The unanimous Declaration of the thirteen united States of America, When in the Course of human events, it becomes necessary for one people to dissolve the political bands which have connected them with another, and to assume among the powers of the earth, the separate and equal station to which the Laws of Nature and of Nature's God entitle them, a decent respect to the opinions of mankind requires that they should declare the causes which impel them to the separation.

The American colonists believed people are born equal and have rights that should be kept safe by the government. The Declaration explains that government is necessary to make sure people keep their natural rights; for example, the right to life, liberty, and the pursuit of happiness.

Once a government takes such rights away, the people must work to change or overthrow the government.

Such action is taken very seriously but is necessary because of King George's treatment of the colonies.

We hold these truths to be self-evident, that all men are created equal, that they are endowed by their Creator with certain unalienable Rights, that among these are Life, Liberty and the pursuit of Happiness.—That to secure these rights, Governments are instituted among Men, deriving their just powers from the consent of the governed, —That whenever any Form of Government becomes destructive of these ends, it is the Right of the People to alter or to abolish it, and to institute new Government, laying its foundation on such principles and organizing its powers in such form, as to them shall seem most likely to effect their Safety and Happiness. Prudence, indeed, will dictate that Governments long established should not be changed for light and transient causes; and accordingly all experience hath shown, that mankind are more disposed to suffer, while evils are sufferable, than to right themselves by abolishing the forms to which they are accustomed. But when a long train of abuses and usurpations, pursuing invariably the same Object evinces a design to reduce them under absolute Despotism, it is their right, it is their duty, to throw off such Government, and to provide new Guards for their future security.—Such has been the patient sufferance of these Colonies; and such is now the necessity which constrains them to alter their former Systems of Government. The history of the present King of Great Britain is a history of repeated injuries and usurpations, all having in direct object the establishment of an absolute Tyranny over these States. To prove this, let Facts be submitted to a candid world.

The Declaration goes on to explain exactly what King George has done. This section is commonly referred to as the list of grievances.

The king has refused to approve laws that people need.

He has refused his Assent to Laws, the most wholesome and necessary for the public good.

He has forbidden his Governors to pass Laws of immediate and pressing importance, unless suspended in their operation till his Assent should be obtained; and when so suspended, he has utterly neglected to attend to them. He has refused to pass other Laws for the accommodation of large districts of people, unless those people would relinquish the right of Representation in the Legislature, a right inestimable to them and formidable to tyrants only.

He has called together legislative bodies at places unusual, uncomfortable, and distant from the depository of their public Records, for the sole purpose of fatiguing them into compliance with his measures.

He has dissolved Representative Houses repeatedly, for opposing with manly firmness his invasions on the rights of the people.

He has refused for a long time, after such dissolutions, to cause others to be elected; whereby the Legislative powers, incapable of Annihilation, have returned to the People at large for their exercise; the State remaining in the mean time exposed to all the dangers of invasion from without, and convulsions within.

He has endeavored to prevent the population of these States; for that purpose obstructing the Laws for Naturalization of Foreigners; refusing to pass others to encourage their migrations hither, and raising the conditions of new Appropriations of Lands.

He has obstructed the Administration of Justice, by refusing his Assent to Laws for establishing Judiciary powers.

He has made Judges dependent on his Will alone, for the tenure of their offices, and the amount and payment of their salaries.

He has erected a multitude of New Offices, and sent hither swarms of Officers to harass our people, and eat out their substance.

He has kept among us, in times of peace, Standing Armies without the Consent of our legislatures.

He has affected to render the Military independent of and superior to the Civil power.

Laws are needed, but the king has failed to approve or disapprove them, so no new laws can be put into effect. He has claimed that unless people in the colonies give up the right to have representatives in their own government in America, he will not pass laws those people need.

The king has put an end to lawmaking bodies that opposed laws representatives believed were harmful to people's rights.

After the legislatures were dismissed, some colonies had no laws to protect them.

Judges have been appointed who favor the king's interests.

The king has sent soldiers to America, without the agreement of its lawmakers. He has made his soldiers more powerful than the colonists.

DECLARATION OF INDEPENDENCE

The king has allowed others to pass and enforce new laws in the colonies.

He has combined with others to subject us to a jurisdiction foreign to our constitution, and unacknowledged by our laws; giving his Assent to their Acts of pretended Legislation:

For example:
- making sure that soldiers who kill colonists are given a fake trial and not held accountable for murder;
- stopping American trade with other countries;
- taxing without permission;
- often refusing the right of trial by jury;
- sending colonists far away to be tried in courts for things they have not done;
- abolishing laws made by the colonies;
- stopping lawmaking groups in America and declaring that only the British government can make laws for people in America.

For Quartering large bodies of armed troops among us:

For protecting them, by a mock Trial, from punishment for any Murders which they should commit on the Inhabitants of these States:

For cutting off our Trade with all parts of the world:

For imposing Taxes on us without our Consent:

For depriving us in many cases, of the benefits of Trial by Jury:

For transporting us beyond Seas to be tried for pretended offences

For abolishing the free System of English Laws in a neighboring Province, establishing therein an Arbitrary government, and enlarging its Boundaries so as to render it at once an example and fit instrument for introducing the same absolute rule into these Colonies:

For taking away our Charters, abolishing our most valuable Laws, and altering fundamentally the Forms of our Governments:

For suspending our own Legislatures, and declaring themselves invested with power to legislate for us in all cases whatsoever.

The colonists claim that the king has essentially given up ("abdicated") his power to govern in America—because he refuses to protect America and has started a war against the colonies.

He has abdicated Government here, by declaring us out of his Protection and waging War against us.

He has plundered our seas, ravaged our Coasts, burnt our towns, and destroyed the lives of our people.

In a way that has almost never been seen before, the king is now sending soldiers from other countries to harm and kill Americans.

He is at this time transporting large Armies of foreign Mercenaries to complete the works of death, desolation and tyranny, already begun with circumstances of Cruelty & perfidy scarcely paralleled in the most barbarous ages, and totally unworthy the Head of a civilized nation.

DECLARATION OF INDEPENDENCE

He has constrained our fellow Citizens taken Captive on the high Seas to bear Arms against their Country, to become the executioners of their friends and Brethren, or to fall themselves by their Hands.

He has excited domestic insurrections amongst us, and has endeavored to bring on the inhabitants of our frontiers, the merciless Indian Savages, whose known rule of warfare, is an undistinguished destruction of all ages, sexes and conditions.

> He has encouraged conflict among Americans and incited Native Americans to attack the colonists.

In every stage of these Oppressions We have Petitioned for Redress in the most humble terms: Our repeated Petitions have been answered only by repeated injury. A Prince whose character is thus marked by every act which may define a Tyrant, is unfit to be the ruler of a free people.

> We have repeatedly and unsuccessfully made formal requests for this behavior to stop. The king has become cruel and oppressive.

Nor have We been wanting in attentions to our British brethren. We have warned them from time to time of attempts by their legislature to extend an unwarrantable jurisdiction over us. We have reminded them of the circumstances of our emigration and settlement here. We have appealed to their native justice and magnanimity, and we have conjured them by the ties of our common kindred to disavow these usurpations, which, would inevitably interrupt our connections and correspondence. They too have been deaf to the voice of justice and of consanguinity. We must, therefore, acquiesce in the necessity, which denounces our Separation, and hold them, as we hold the rest of mankind, Enemies in War, in Peace Friends.

> We have appealed to the British people, pointing out the injustice of our treatment and our close ties to them ("consanguinity"), but they have ignored us. So we have no choice but to consider them our enemies.

We, therefore, the Representatives of the united States of America, in General Congress, Assembled, appealing to the Supreme Judge of the world for the rectitude of our intentions, do, in the Name, and by Authority of the good People of these Colonies, solemnly publish and declare, That these United Colonies are, and of Right ought to be Free and Independent States; that they are Absolved from all Allegiance to the British Crown, and that all political connection between them and the State of Great Britain, is and ought to be totally dissolved; and that as Free and Independent States, they have full Power to levy War, conclude Peace, contract Alliances, establish Commerce, and to do all other Acts and Things which Independent States may of right do. And for the support of this Declaration, with a firm reliance on the protection of divine Providence, we mutually pledge to each other our Lives, our Fortunes and our sacred Honor.

> For all of these reasons, we declare that the United Colonies are free and independent states with no further allegiance to Britain. Because we are free, we can declare war, declare peace, make agreements to work with other countries, establish commerce, and participate in all other activities allowed by independent states.

CONSTITUTION OF THE UNITED STATES

Introduction

In 1787, after much debate, delegates at the Constitutional Convention in Philadelphia, known as the Framers, signed the U.S. Constitution, which became the supreme law of the land in the United States. Considering the size and complexity of the United States today and its position as a world power, the U.S. Constitution is relatively simple. It consists of a Preamble, 7 articles, and currently 27 amendments, based on the 7 key principles discussed below. About the simplicity of the Constitution, John Adams wrote, "Our Constitution was made only for a moral and religious People. It is wholly inadequate to the government of any other."

1. Popular Sovereignty This principle addresses the idea that people together create a social contract in which they agree to be governed.

2. Republicanism In a republic, citizens have the power and authority to make decisions as to how they are governed. The citizens elect representatives, and the representatives then have the power to make and enforce laws.

3. Federalism A government operating under federalism features a strong central government, but states do not lose all rights and power. The federal government holds some powers, which are enumerated, or listed, powers. The states have other powers, which are reserved, or unwritten, powers. And some powers are concurrent powers, which means that they may be practiced by both the federal government and the state governments.

4. Separation of Powers To reduce the potential for abuse of power, the government was divided into three branches: the legislative branch (made up of the Senate and the House of Representatives), which makes the laws; the executive branch (led by the president), which enforces the laws; and the judicial branch (made up of the U.S. Supreme Court and additional federal courts), which interprets the laws.

5. Checks and Balances Each branch of the government provides a check for the others, which means that it can limit the power of those branches. Such checks provide a balance among the three branches. For example, while the legislative branch can make laws, the judicial branch interprets them and decides if those laws are constitutional. And while the president can veto a law made by Congress, Congress can override a presidential veto.

6. Limited Government A strong central power was important to those who developed the Constitution. Still, the Framers believed the strong central government should not be allowed to abuse its power by providing particular rights to some groups or taking away rights from others. This principle of government seeks to protect rights by limiting the power of the central government.

7. Individual Rights Amendments, or articles added to the Constitution, have become part of the U.S. Constitution over the years. The first 10 amendments, known as the Bill of Rights, were added in 1791. These amendments address many individual rights, such as freedom of religion, freedom of speech, and the right to trial by jury. The Bill of Rights was added to the Constitution to ensure that all states would accept and ratify this new plan for government.

THE CONSTITUTION

Preamble **We the People** of the United States, in Order to
form a more perfect Union, establish Justice, insure domestic Tranquility,
provide for the common defense, promote the general Welfare, and
secure the Blessings of Liberty to ourselves and our Posterity, do ordain
and establish this Constitution for the United States of America.

Article I Legislative Branch

SECTION 1: CONGRESS

All legislative Powers herein granted shall be vested in a Congress
of the United States, which shall consist of a Senate and House
of Representatives.

SECTION 2: THE HOUSE OF REPRESENTATIVES

1 The House of Representatives shall be composed of Members
chosen every second Year by the People of the several States, and
the Electors in each State shall have the Qualifications requisite for
Electors of the most numerous Branch of the State Legislature.

2 No Person shall be a Representative who shall not have attained to
the Age of twenty five Years, and been seven Years a Citizen of the
United States, and who shall not, when elected, be an Inhabitant of
that State in which he shall be chosen.

3 *Representatives and direct Taxes shall be apportioned among the
several States which may be included within this Union, according
to their respective Numbers, which shall be determined by adding to
the whole Number of free Persons, including those bound to Service
for a Term of Years, and excluding Indians not taxed, three fifths of
all other Persons.* The actual Enumeration shall be made within three
Years after the first Meeting of the Congress of the United States, and
within every subsequent Term of ten Years, in such Manner as they
shall by Law direct. The Number of Representatives shall not exceed
one for every thirty Thousand, but each State shall have at Least one
Representative; and until such enumeration shall be made, the State
of New Hampshire shall be entitled to choose three, Massachusetts
eight, Rhode-Island and Providence Plantations one, Connecticut five,
New-York six, New Jersey four, Pennsylvania eight, Delaware one,
Maryland six, Virginia ten, North Carolina five, South Carolina five, and
Georgia three.

4 When vacancies happen in the Representation from any State, the
Executive Authority thereof shall issue Writs of Election to fill such
Vacancies.

5 The House of Representatives shall choose their Speaker and other
Officers; and shall have the sole Power of Impeachment.

NOTE Boldfaced headings,
section numbers, margin notes, and
questions have been inserted to
help you understand and interpret
this complex document. Passages
that are no longer part of the
Constitution have been printed in
italic type.

PREAMBLE
**UNDERSTANDING THE
CONSTITUTION** The phrase
"We the People" begins the Preamble
to the Constitution. The Preamble
states the "why" and the "how" of
Americans' agreement to be governed.
The Preamble also states that the
Constitution will define the government
and that the document will be a
social contract.

ARTICLE I
**UNDERSTANDING THE
CONSTITUTION Section 2**
The House of Representatives
provides one of the most direct ways
in which citizens can participate in
the political process. People can
communicate with representatives by
mail, email, and phone, and by visiting
the lawmakers' offices.

**UNDERSTANDING THE
CONSTITUTION 2.3** Each state
can have one representative for every
30,000 people in the state. The phrase
"their respective Numbers" refers to
the states' populations. Today every
state has a population greater than
30,000, but the Constitution made
sure that states with fewer people had
a representative. The Constitution
indicates the initial numbers of
representatives for each of the original
13 states.

HISTORICAL THINKING In 2.3, the
italicized phrase "three fifths of all
other persons" refers to enslaved
people. Why do you think slaves were
not counted in the same way as free
persons?

**UNDERSTANDING THE
CONSTITUTION 2.5** The Speaker
presides over sessions of Congress,
but the Constitution says nothing
about what the Speaker or other
officers will do.

UNDERSTANDING THE CONSTITUTION 3.1 The Constitution originally provided for the election of senators by the state legislatures, but the 17th Amendment changed that in 1913 with the election of senators by voters.

UNDERSTANDING THE CONSTITUTION 3.2 The terms of senators are staggered. One class of senators begins their term in an even-numbered year, the next class begins two years later, and the third class begins two years after that.

HISTORICAL THINKING In the previous section, the Constitution states the House has the power of impeachment, and in 3.6, it says the Senate tries impeachments. Why do you think the Constitution separates these powers?

HISTORICAL THINKING Only two U.S. presidents have been impeached: Andrew Johnson in 1868 and William Clinton in 1998, but neither was convicted by the Senate. Why do you think impeachment is part of the Constitution?

Visitors with tickets could observe President Andrew Johnson's impeachment trial from the gallery of the Senate. Each ticket was valid for one day in March through May 1868, indicated by the ticket's color.

UNDERSTANDING THE CONSTITUTION 4.2 In 1933, the 20th Amendment changed the starting date for meetings of Congress to January 3.

SECTION 3: THE SENATE

1 The Senate of the United States shall be composed of two Senators from each State, chosen by the Legislature thereof, for six Years; and each Senator shall have one Vote.

2 Immediately after they shall be assembled in Consequence of the first Election, they shall be divided as equally as may be into three Classes. The Seats of the Senators of the first Class shall be vacated at the Expiration of the second Year, of the second Class at the Expiration of the fourth Year, and of the third Class at the Expiration of the sixth Year, so that one third may be chosen every second Year; and if Vacancies happen by Resignation, or otherwise, during the Recess of the Legislature of any State, the Executive thereof may make temporary Appointments until the next Meeting of the Legislature, which shall then fill such Vacancies.

3 No Person shall be a Senator who shall not have attained to the Age of thirty Years, and been nine Years a Citizen of the United States, and who shall not, when elected, be an Inhabitant of that State for which he shall be chosen.

4 The Vice President of the United States shall be President of the Senate, but shall have no Vote, unless they be equally divided.

5 The Senate shall choose their other Officers, and also a President pro tempore, in the Absence of the Vice President, or when he shall exercise the Office of President of the United States.

6 The Senate shall have the sole Power to try all Impeachments. When sitting for that Purpose, they shall be on Oath or Affirmation. When the President of the United States is tried, the Chief Justice shall preside: And no Person shall be convicted without the Concurrence of two thirds of the Members present.

7 Judgment in Cases of Impeachment shall not extend further than to removal from Office, and disqualification to hold and enjoy any Office of honor, Trust or Profit under the United States: but the Party convicted shall nevertheless be liable and subject to Indictment, Trial, Judgment and Punishment, according to Law.

SECTION 4: CONGRESSIONAL ELECTIONS

1 The Times, Places and Manner of holding Elections for Senators and Representatives, shall be prescribed in each State by the Legislature thereof; but the Congress may at any time by Law make or alter such Regulations, except as to the Places of choosing Senators.

2 *The Congress shall assemble at least once in every Year, and such Meeting shall be on the first Monday in December, unless they shall by Law appoint a different Day.*

SECTION 5: RULES

1 Each House shall be the Judge of the Elections, Returns and Qualifications of its own Members, and a Majority of each shall constitute a Quorum to do Business; but a smaller Number may adjourn from day to day, and may be authorized to compel the Attendance of absent Members, in such Manner, and under such Penalties as each House may provide.

2 Each House may determine the Rules of its Proceedings, punish its Members for disorderly Behavior, and, with the Concurrence of two thirds, expel a Member.

3 Each House shall keep a Journal of its Proceedings, and from time to time publish the same, excepting such Parts as may in their Judgment require Secrecy; and the Yeas and Nays of the Members of either House on any question shall, at the Desire of one fifth of those Present, be entered on the Journal.

4 Neither House, during the Session of Congress, shall, without the Consent of the other, adjourn for more than three days, nor to any other Place than that in which the two Houses shall be sitting.

SECTION 6: PAY AND EXPENSES

1 The Senators and Representatives shall receive a Compensation for their Services, to be ascertained by Law, and paid out of the Treasury of the United States. They shall in all Cases, except Treason, Felony and Breach of the Peace, be privileged from Arrest during their Attendance at the Session of their respective Houses, and in going to and returning from the same; and for any Speech or Debate in either House, they shall not be questioned in any other Place.

2 No Senator or Representative shall, during the Time for which he was elected, be appointed to any civil Office under the Authority of the United States, which shall have been created, or the Emoluments whereof shall have been increased during such time; and no Person holding any Office under the United States, shall be a Member of either House during his Continuance in Office.

SECTION 7: PASSING LAWS

1 All Bills for raising Revenue shall originate in the House of Representatives; but the Senate may propose or concur with Amendments as on other Bills.

2 Every Bill which shall have passed the House of Representatives and the Senate, shall, before it become a Law, be presented to the President of the United States; If he approve he shall sign it, but if not he shall return it, with his Objections to that House in which it shall have originated, who shall enter the Objections at large on their Journal, and proceed to reconsider it. If after such Reconsideration two thirds of that House shall agree to pass the Bill, it shall be sent, together with the Objections, to the other House, by which it shall likewise be reconsidered, and if approved by two thirds of that House, it shall become a Law. But in all such Cases the Votes of both Houses shall be determined by yeas and Nays, and the Names of the Persons voting for and against the Bill shall be entered on the Journal of each House respectively. If any Bill shall not be returned by the President within ten Days (Sundays excepted) after it shall have been presented to him, the Same shall be a Law, in like Manner as if he had signed it, unless the Congress by their Adjournment prevent its Return, in which Case it shall not be a Law.

3 Every Order, Resolution, or Vote to which the Concurrence of the Senate and House of Representatives may be necessary (except on a question of Adjournment) shall be presented to the President of the United States; and before the Same shall take Effect, shall be approved by him, or being disapproved by him, shall be re-passed by two thirds of the Senate and House of Representatives, according to the Rules and Limitations prescribed in the Case of a Bill.

SECTION 8: POWERS OF CONGRESS

1 The Congress shall have Power To lay and collect Taxes, Duties, Imposts and Excises, to pay the Debts and provide for the common Defense and general Welfare of the United States; but all Duties, Imposts and Excises shall be uniform throughout the United States;

2 To borrow Money on the credit of the United States;

3 To regulate Commerce with foreign Nations, and among the several States, and with the Indian Tribes;

4 To establish an uniform Rule of Naturalization, and uniform Laws on the subject of Bankruptcies throughout the United States;

5 To coin Money, regulate the Value thereof, and of foreign Coin, and fix the Standard of Weights and Measures;

6 To provide for the Punishment of counterfeiting the Securities and current Coin of the United States;

7 To establish Post Offices and post Roads;

8 To promote the Progress of Science and useful Arts, by securing for limited Times to Authors and Inventors the exclusive Right to their respective Writings and Discoveries;

9 To constitute Tribunals inferior to the supreme Court;

10 To define and punish Piracies and Felonies committed on the high Seas, and Offences against the Law of Nations;

11 To declare War, grant Letters of Marque and Reprisal, and make Rules concerning Captures on Land and Water;

UNDERSTANDING THE CONSTITUTION Section 8 Section 8 provides a list of 17 specific powers given to Congress and empowers it "to make all laws" necessary to support those functions. Additionally, the first paragraph of the section empowers Congress to provide for the "general welfare" of the nation. However, the Constitution includes little detail on how some of these powers should be carried out.

HISTORICAL THINKING How does the Constitution balance the power of Congress to raise and support armies?

UNDERSTANDING THE CONSTITUTION 8.3 Regulating commerce with foreign nations means controlling imports and exports to provide maximum benefit for U.S. businesses and consumers. Regulating commerce between states means maintaining a common market among the states, with no restrictions. Remember that at the time the Constitution was written, Native Americans traded fur and other items with U.S. citizens.

HISTORICAL THINKING What problems might arise if the United States did not have a common coinage?

12 To raise and support Armies, but no Appropriation of Money to that Use shall be for a longer Term than two Years;

13 To provide and maintain a Navy; To make Rules for the Government and Regulation of the land and naval Forces;

14 To provide for calling forth the Militia to execute the Laws of the Union, suppress Insurrections and repel Invasions;

15 To provide for organizing, arming, and disciplining, the Militia, and for governing such Part of them as may be employed in the Service of the United States, reserving to the States respectively, the Appointment of the Officers, and the Authority of training the Militia according to the discipline prescribed by Congress;

16 To exercise exclusive Legislation in all Cases whatsoever, over such District (not exceeding ten Miles square) as may, by Cession of particular States, and the Acceptance of Congress, become the Seat of the Government of the United States, and to exercise like Authority over all Places purchased by the Consent of the Legislature of the State in which the Same shall be, for the Erection of Forts, Magazines, Arsenals, dock-Yards, and other needful Buildings;—And

17 To make all Laws which shall be necessary and proper for carrying into Execution the foregoing Powers, and all other Powers vested by this Constitution in the Government of the United States, or in any Department or Officer thereof.

SECTION 9: RESTRICTIONS ON CONGRESS

1 *The Migration or Importation of such Persons as any of the States now existing shall think proper to admit, shall not be prohibited by the Congress prior to the Year one thousand eight hundred and eight, but a Tax or duty may be imposed on such Importation, not exceeding ten dollars for each Person.*

2 The Privilege of the Writ of Habeas Corpus shall not be suspended, unless when in Cases of Rebellion or Invasion the public Safety may require it.

3 No Bill of Attainder or ex post facto Law shall be passed.

4 *No Capitation, or other direct, Tax shall be laid, unless in Proportion to the Census or Enumeration herein before directed to be taken.*

5 No Tax or Duty shall be laid on Articles exported from any State.

6 No Preference shall be given by any Regulation of Commerce or Revenue to the Ports of one State over those of another: nor shall Vessels bound to, or from, one State, be obliged to enter, clear, or pay Duties in another.

UNDERSTANDING THE CONSTITUTION Section 9
Section 9 lists specific areas in which Congress may not legislate. These include laws governing the importation of slaves—a provision made obsolete with the abolition of slavery (9.1); holding a person without charging him or her with a crime (9.2); passing an act that declares a specific person guilty of a crime ("bill of attainder") (9.3); and making an action illegal after it has been committed ("ex post facto") (9.3).

UNDERSTANDING THE CONSTITUTION 9.4 A "capitation tax" is a tax charged on an individual.

UNDERSTANDING THE CONSTITUTION 9.6 Congress cannot pass laws that favor commerce in one state over that of another. For example, Congress cannot pass a law requiring shipping to go through a particular state's port.

7 No Money shall be drawn from the Treasury, but in Consequence of Appropriations made by Law; and a regular Statement and Account of the Receipts and Expenditures of all public Money shall be published from time to time.

8 No Title of Nobility shall be granted by the United States: And no Person holding any Office of Profit or Trust under them, shall, without the Consent of the Congress, accept of any present, Emolument, Office, or Title, of any kind whatever, from any King, Prince, or foreign State.

SECTION 10: LIMITING THE AUTHORITY OF STATES

1 No State shall enter into any Treaty, Alliance, or Confederation; grant Letters of Marque and Reprisal; coin Money; emit Bills of Credit; make any Thing but gold and silver Coin a Tender in Payment of Debts; pass any Bill of Attainder, ex post facto Law, or Law impairing the Obligation of Contracts, or grant any Title of Nobility.

2 No State shall, without the Consent of the Congress, lay any Imposts or Duties on Imports or Exports, except what may be absolutely necessary for executing its inspection Laws: and the net Produce of all Duties and Imposts, laid by any State on Imports or Exports, shall be for the Use of the Treasury of the United States; and all such Laws shall be subject to the Revision and Control of the Congress.

3 No State shall, without the Consent of Congress, lay any Duty of Tonnage, keep Troops, or Ships of War in time of Peace, enter into any Agreement or Compact with another State, or with a foreign Power, or engage in War, unless actually invaded, or in such imminent Danger as will not admit of delay.

Article II The Executive Branch
SECTION 1: ELECTING THE PRESIDENT

1 The executive Power shall be vested in a President of the United States of America. He shall hold his Office during the Term of four Years, and, together with the Vice President, chosen for the same Term, be elected, as follows

2 Each State shall appoint, in such Manner as the Legislature thereof may direct, a Number of Electors, equal to the whole Number of Senators and Representatives to which the State may be entitled in the Congress: but no Senator or Representative, or Person holding an Office of Trust or Profit under the United States, shall be appointed an Elector.

UNDERSTANDING THE CONSTITUTION Section 10 Section 10 sets out actions that the states are not permitted to take on their own: for example, entering into a treaty, coining money, or passing laws that interfere with contracts.

HISTORICAL THINKING How can Section 10 be used to prove that the secession of the southern states was unconstitutional?

ARTICLE II
UNDERSTANDING THE CONSTITUTION Section 1 Section 1 describes a detailed process for choosing the president. This process was replaced in 1804 by another detailed in the 12th Amendment.

UNDERSTANDING THE CONSTITUTION 1.2 Each state determines how its electors are chosen, but all follow the same principle. Voters cast their ballots for a ticket consisting of a president and a vice president. In most states, whoever wins the most votes in the state wins all that state's electoral votes.

HISTORICAL THINKING Some Americans believe voters should directly elect the president. Do you agree or disagree? Explain.

3 *The Electors shall meet in their respective States, and vote by Ballot for two Persons, of whom one at least shall not be an Inhabitant of the same State with themselves. And they shall make a List of all the Persons voted for, and of the Number of Votes for each; which List they shall sign and certify, and transmit sealed to the Seat of the Government of the United States, directed to the President of the Senate. The President of the Senate shall, in the Presence of the Senate and House of Representatives, open all the Certificates, and the Votes shall then be counted. The Person having the greatest Number of Votes shall be the President, if such Number be a Majority of the whole Number of Electors appointed; and if there be more than one who have such Majority, and have an equal Number of Votes, then the House of Representatives shall immediately choose by Ballot one of them for President; and if no Person have a Majority, then from the five highest on the List the said House shall in like Manner choose the President. But in choosing the President, the Votes shall be taken by States, the Representation from each State having one Vote; A quorum for this Purpose shall consist of a Member or Members from two thirds of the States, and a Majority of all the States shall be necessary to a Choice. In every Case, after the Choice of the President, the Person having the greatest Number of Votes of the Electors shall be the Vice President. But if there should remain two or more who have equal Votes, the Senate shall choose from them by Ballot the Vice President.*

4 The Congress may determine the Time of choosing the Electors, and the Day on which they shall give their Votes; which Day shall be the same throughout the United States.

5 No Person except a natural born Citizen, or a Citizen of the United States, at the time of the Adoption of this Constitution, shall be eligible to the Office of President; neither shall any Person be eligible to that Office who shall not have attained to the Age of thirty five Years, and been fourteen Years a Resident within the United States.

6 *In Case of the Removal of the President from Office, or of his Death, Resignation, or Inability to discharge the Powers and Duties of the said Office, the Same shall devolve on the Vice President, and the Congress may by Law provide for the Case of Removal, Death, Resignation or Inability, both of the President and Vice President, declaring what Officer shall then act as President, and such Officer shall act accordingly, until the Disability be removed, or a President shall be elected.*

7 The President shall, at stated Times, receive for his Services, a Compensation, which shall neither be increased nor diminished during the Period for which he shall have been elected, and he shall not receive within that Period any other Emolument from the United States, or any of them.

UNDERSTANDING THE CONSTITUTION 1.3 The italicized text refers to how vice presidents were originally elected. Voters cast ballots for presidential candidates, and the one who came in second became vice president. Today, a presidential candidate selects a running mate, and voters cast a single vote for the entire ticket.

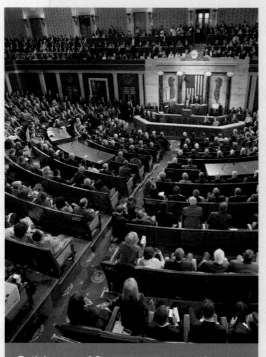

Both houses of Congress convene each year in the House chamber to hear the president's State of the Union address. In this photo, Congress listens as President Barack Obama delivers his 2016 address.

UNDERSTANDING THE CONSTITUTION 1.8 Every president has taken the same oath of office, saying these exact words at the inauguration.

UNDERSTANDING THE CONSTITUTION Section 2 Section 2 outlines the president's authority. Among other duties, the president is commander in chief of the armed forces, has the power to make treaties, and can appoint ambassadors and Supreme Court justices. However, the treaties and appointments are subject to approval by the Senate.

HISTORICAL THINKING On what "extraordinary occasions" might a president wish to address both houses of Congress?

UNDERSTANDING THE CONSTITUTION Section 4 In the phrase "high crimes and misdemeanors," the word *high* does not mean "more serious" but rather refers to highly placed public officials.

8 Before he enter on the Execution of his Office, he shall take the following Oath or Affirmation:—"I do solemnly swear (or affirm) that I will faithfully execute the Office of President of the United States, and will to the best of my Ability, preserve, protect and defend the Constitution of the United States."

SECTION 2: EXECUTIVE POWERS

1 The President shall be Commander in Chief of the Army and Navy of the United States, and of the Militia of the several States, when called into the actual Service of the United States; he may require the Opinion, in writing, of the principal Officer in each of the executive Departments, upon any Subject relating to the Duties of their respective Offices, and he shall have Power to grant Reprieves and Pardons for Offences against the United States, except in Cases of Impeachment.

2 He shall have Power, by and with the Advice and Consent of the Senate, to make Treaties, provided two thirds of the Senators present concur; and he shall nominate, and by and with the Advice and Consent of the Senate, shall appoint Ambassadors, other public Ministers and Consuls, Judges of the supreme Court, and all other Officers of the United States, whose Appointments are not herein otherwise provided for, and which shall be established by Law: but the Congress may by Law vest the Appointment of such inferior Officers, as they think proper, in the President alone, in the Courts of Law, or in the Heads of Departments.

3 The President shall have Power to fill up all Vacancies that may happen during the Recess of the Senate, by granting Commissions which shall expire at the End of their next Session.

SECTION 3: THE PRESIDENT AND CONGRESS

He shall from time to time give to the Congress Information of the State of the Union, and recommend to their Consideration such Measures as he shall judge necessary and expedient; he may, on extraordinary Occasions, convene both Houses, or either of them, and in Case of Disagreement between them, with Respect to the Time of Adjournment, he may adjourn them to such Time as he shall think proper; he shall receive Ambassadors and other public Ministers; he shall take Care that the Laws be faithfully executed, and shall Commission all the Officers of the United States.

SECTION 4: IMPEACHMENT

The President, Vice President and all civil Officers of the United States, shall be removed from Office on Impeachment for, and Conviction of, Treason, Bribery, or other high Crimes and Misdemeanors.

Article III The Judiciary Branch

SECTION 1: SUPREME COURT AND LOWER COURTS

The judicial Power of the United States, shall be vested in one supreme Court, and in such inferior Courts as the Congress may from time to time ordain and establish. The Judges, both of the supreme and inferior Courts, shall hold their Offices during good Behavior, and shall, at stated Times, receive for their Services, a Compensation, which shall not be diminished during their Continuance in Office.

The Supreme Court justices posed for this photo in 2017. In the top row, from left to right, are Elena Kagan, Samuel Alito, Jr., Sonia Sotomayor, and Neil Gorsuch. In the bottom row, from left to right, are Ruth Bader Ginsburg, Anthony Kennedy, John Roberts, Jr. (chief justice), Clarence Thomas, and Stephen Breyer.

SECTION 2: AUTHORITY OF THE SUPREME COURT

1 The judicial Power shall extend to all Cases, in Law and Equity, arising under this Constitution, the Laws of the United States, and Treaties made, or which shall be made, under their Authority;—to all Cases affecting Ambassadors, other public Ministers and Consuls;—to all Cases of admiralty and maritime Jurisdiction;—to Controversies to which the United States shall be a Party;—*to Controversies between two or more States;—between a State and Citizens of another State;—between Citizens of different States;—between Citizens of the same State claiming Lands under Grants of different States, and between a State, or the Citizens thereof, and foreign States, Citizens or Subjects.*

2 In all Cases affecting Ambassadors, other public Ministers and Consuls, and those in which a State shall be Party, the supreme Court shall have original Jurisdiction. In all the other Cases before mentioned, the supreme Court shall have appellate Jurisdiction, both as to Law and Fact, with such Exceptions, and under such Regulations as the Congress shall make.

3 The Trial of all Crimes, except in Cases of Impeachment, shall be by Jury; and such Trial shall be held in the State where the said Crimes shall have been committed; but when not committed within any State, the Trial shall be at such Place or Places as the Congress may by Law have directed.

SECTION 3: TREASON

1 Treason against the United States, shall consist only in levying War against them, or in adhering to their Enemies, giving them Aid and Comfort. No Person shall be convicted of Treason unless on the Testimony of two Witnesses to the same overt Act, or on Confession in open Court.

2 The Congress shall have Power to declare the Punishment of Treason, but no Attainder of Treason shall work Corruption of Blood, or Forfeiture except during the Life of the Person attainted.

ARTICLE III
UNDERSTANDING THE CONSTITUTION 2.1 The italicized portion of this section was changed in 1795 by the 11th Amendment, which states that the Judicial Department does not have jurisdiction in matters between states or between a foreign country and a U.S. state.

UNDERSTANDING THE CONSTITUTION 2.2 When the Supreme Court serves as an appeals court, it reviews decisions made by lower courts.

UNDERSTANDING THE CONSTITUTION Section 3 Treason is the only crime specifically defined in the Constitution. Between 1954 and 2016, one person was charged with treason for collaborating in the production of propaganda videos for the terrorist group al-Qaeda.

Article IV States and Citizens

SECTION 1: MUTUAL RESPECT AMONG STATES

Full Faith and Credit shall be given in each State to the public Acts, Records, and judicial Proceedings of every other State. And the Congress may by general Laws prescribe the Manner in which such Acts, Records and Proceedings shall be proved, and the Effect thereof.

SECTION 2: CITIZENS OF STATES AND OF THE UNITED STATES

1 The Citizens of each State shall be entitled to all Privileges and Immunities of Citizens in the several States.

2 A Person charged in any State with Treason, Felony, or other Crime, who shall flee from Justice, and be found in another State, shall on Demand of the executive Authority of the State from which he fled, be delivered up, to be removed to the State having Jurisdiction of the Crime.

3 *No Person held to Service or Labor in one State, under the Laws thereof, escaping into another, shall, in Consequence of any Law or Regulation therein, be discharged from such Service or Labor, but shall be delivered up on Claim of the Party to whom such Service or Labor may be due.*

SECTION 3: NEW STATES

1 New States may be admitted by the Congress into this Union; but no new State shall be formed or erected within the Jurisdiction of any other State; nor any State be formed by the Junction of two or more States, or Parts of States, without the Consent of the Legislatures of the States concerned as well as of the Congress.

2 The Congress shall have Power to dispose of and make all needful Rules and Regulations respecting the Territory or other Property belonging to the United States; and nothing in this Constitution shall be so construed as to Prejudice any Claims of the United States, or of any particular State.

SECTION 4: PROTECTION OF STATES BY THE UNITED STATES

The United States shall guarantee to every State in this Union a Republican Form of Government, and shall protect each of them against Invasion; and on Application of the Legislature, or of the Executive (when the Legislature cannot be convened), against domestic Violence.

Article V Amending the Constitution

1 The Congress, whenever two thirds of both Houses shall deem it necessary, shall propose Amendments to this Constitution, or, on the Application of the Legislatures of two thirds of the several States, shall call a Convention for proposing Amendments, which, in either Case, shall be valid to all Intents and Purposes, as Part of this Constitution, when ratified by the Legislatures of three fourths of the several States, or by Conventions in three fourths thereof, as the one or the other Mode of Ratification may be proposed by the Congress; **2** Provided that no Amendment which may be made prior to the Year One thousand eight hundred and eight shall in any Manner affect the first and fourth Clauses in the Ninth Section of the first Article; and that no State, without its Consent, shall be deprived of its equal Suffrage in the Senate.

Article VI The Supreme Law of the Land

1 All Debts contracted and Engagements entered into, before the Adoption of this Constitution, shall be as valid against the United States under this Constitution, as under the Confederation.

2 This Constitution, and the Laws of the United States which shall be made in Pursuance thereof; and all Treaties made, or which shall be made, under the Authority of the United States, shall be the supreme Law of the Land; and the Judges in every State shall be bound thereby, any Thing in the Constitution or Laws of any State to the Contrary notwithstanding.

3 The Senators and Representatives before mentioned, and the Members of the several State Legislatures, and all executive and judicial Officers, both of the United States and of the several States, shall be bound by Oath or Affirmation, to support this Constitution; but no religious Test shall ever be required as a Qualification to any Office or public Trust under the United States.

ARTICLE V
UNDERSTANDING THE CONSTITUTION Article 5
This article describes the process for amending the Constitution but states that the first and fourth clauses in Article 1's ninth section cannot be amended before 1808. Remember that these clauses refer to the importation of slaves and to a tax charged on an individual.

ARTICLE VI
UNDERSTANDING THE CONSTITUTION Article 6
This article states that all judges and legislators must uphold and be bound by the Constitution, the supreme law of the land. When any state law or part of a law conflicts with the Constitution or federal laws and treaties, the federal law is the one that must be followed. This concept was important to keep the states of the new nation united in their dealings with each other, with foreign powers, and with the federal government.

HISTORICAL THINKING What might happen if a state established laws that contradicted those in the Constitution?

Today, "the people" referred to in the Constitution includes all adult U.S. citizens.

Article VII
UNDERSTANDING THE CONSTITUTION Article 7

On June 21, 1788, New Hampshire became the 9th state to ratify the Constitution and make it the law of the United States. The Framers clearly stated in Article 7 that the Constitution required the approval of only 9 states, not the 13 then in existence. However, the Framers wanted each state to ratify the Constitution through a state convention. They knew the new nation's survival depended on the populous and wealthy states of Virginia and New York, which were slow to ratify. After lengthy debates, first Virginia and then New York gave approval, becoming the 11th and 12th states to ratify the Constitution. But Rhode Island was the main roadblock to unanimous approval. It officially joined the United States only after being told the state would be treated like a foreign government if it did not.

HISTORICAL THINKING Do you think your state would ratify the Constitution today? Why or why not?

Article VII Ratification

The Ratification of the Conventions of nine States, shall be sufficient for the Establishment of this Constitution between the States so ratifying the Same.

[Here appears some text noting corrections that were made on the original copy of the document.]

Done in Convention by the Unanimous Consent of the States present the Seventeenth Day of September in the Year of our Lord one thousand seven hundred and Eighty seven and of the Independence of the United States of America the Twelfth In witness whereof We have hereunto subscribed our Names,

G°. Washington
President and deputy from Virginia

Massachusetts
Nathaniel Gorham
Rufus King

New York
Alexander Hamilton

Delaware
George Read
Gunning Bedford, Jr.
John Dickinson
Richard Bassett
Jacob Broom

Virginia
John Blair
James Madison, Jr.

Pennsylvania
Benjamin Franklin
Thomas Mifflin
Robert Morris
George Clymer
Thomas Fitzsimons
Jared Ingersoll
James Wilson
Gouverneur Morris

New Hampshire
John Langdon
Nicholas Gilman

New Jersey
William Livingston
David Brearley
William Paterson
Jonathan Dayton

Connecticut
William Samuel Johnson
Roger Sherman

North Carolina
William Blount
Richard Dobbs Spaight
Hugh Williamson

South Carolina
John Rutledge
Charles Cotesworth Pinckney
Charles Pinckney
Pierce Butler

Maryland
James McHenry
Daniel of St. Thomas Jenifer
Daniel Carroll

Georgia
William Few
Abraham Baldwin

Introduction

Individual rights are fundamental to liberty. As you've read, the Magna Carta influenced the Declaration of Independence, but it also helped inspire the Bill of Rights. The people who came to America from Britain had enjoyed the freedoms granted to them under both the Magna Carta and the English Bill of Rights. They believed they were entitled to these rights when they settled their colonies. After the American Revolution, the new country's leaders wanted citizens' individual freedoms to become law. In 1787, Thomas Jefferson wrote to James Madison, "[A] bill of rights is what the people are entitled to against every government on earth, general or particular, and what no just government should refuse."

As a result, a list of basic citizenship rights became a permanent part of the Constitution. The following is a transcription of the first 10 amendments to the Constitution in their original form: the Bill of Rights. As you'll see, over time, more amendments were added to the Constitution to address issues that arose as the nation grew and changed.

The Preamble to the Bill of Rights

Congress of the United States begun and held at the City of New York, on Wednesday the fourth of March, one thousand seven hundred and eighty nine.

THE Conventions of a number of the States, having at the time of their adopting the Constitution, expressed a desire, in order to prevent misconstruction or abuse of its powers, that further declaratory and restrictive clauses should be added: And as extending the ground of public confidence in the Government, will best ensure the beneficient ends of its institution.

RESOLVED by the Senate and House of Representatives of the United States of America, in Congress assembled, two thirds of both Houses concurring, that the following Articles be proposed to the Legislatures of the several States, as amendments to the Constitution of the United States, all, or any of which Articles, when ratified by three fourths of the said Legislatures, to be valid to all intents and purposes, as part of the said Constitution; viz.

UNDERSTANDING THE PREAMBLE *Viz* is Latin for "that is to say" or "namely."

UNDERSTANDING AMENDMENT 1 The determination to protect religious freedom arose in part from Thomas Jefferson's 1786 Statute for Religious Freedom, which he composed for Virginia's legislature. In his statute, Jefferson called for religious liberty and the separation of church and state.

HISTORICAL THINKING Why do you think the Framers insisted there should be "no law respecting an establishment of religion"?

UNDERSTANDING AMENDMENT 2 This amendment has been hotly debated for decades. Many Americans believe the amendment grants them the right to possess guns. Others think gun ownership should be controlled.

HISTORICAL THINKING Do you think the Framers intended to grant all Americans the right to own guns or just those in militias? Explain your ideas.

UNDERSTANDING AMENDMENT 3 This amendment stemmed from the colonists' experience during the American Revolution. Back then, British soldiers could come into colonists' homes and demand food and shelter. This isn't an issue anymore.

ARTICLES in addition to, and Amendment of the Constitution of the United States of America, proposed by Congress, and ratified by the Legislatures of the several States, pursuant to the fifth Article of the original Constitution.

Amendment 1 (1791)

Congress shall make no law respecting an establishment of religion, or prohibiting the free exercise thereof; or abridging the freedom of speech, or of the press; or the right of the people peaceably to assemble, and to petition the Government for a redress of grievances.

Amendment 2 (1791)

A well regulated Militia, being necessary to the security of a free State, the right of the people to keep and bear Arms, shall not be infringed.

Amendment 3 (1791)

No Soldier shall, in time of peace be quartered in any house, without the consent of the Owner, nor in time of war, but in a manner to be prescribed by law.

Amendment 4 (1791)

The right of the people to be secure in their persons, houses, papers, and effects, against unreasonable searches and seizures, shall not be violated, and no Warrants shall issue, but upon probable cause, supported by Oath or affirmation, and particularly describing the place to be searched, and the persons or things to be seized.

Amendment 5 (1791)

No person shall be held to answer for a capital, or otherwise infamous crime, unless on a presentment or indictment of a Grand Jury, except in cases arising in the land or naval forces, or in the Militia, when in actual service in time of War or public danger; nor shall any person be subject for the same offence to be twice put in jeopardy of life or limb; nor shall be compelled in any criminal case to be a witness against himself, nor be deprived of life, liberty, or property, without due process of law; nor shall private property be taken for public use, without just compensation.

Amendment 6 (1791)

In all criminal prosecutions, the accused shall enjoy the right to a speedy and public trial, by an impartial jury of the State and district wherein the crime shall have been committed, which district shall have been previously ascertained by law, and to be informed of the nature and cause of the accusation; to be confronted with the witnesses against him; to have compulsory process for obtaining witnesses in his favor, and to have the Assistance of Counsel for his defence.

Amendment 7 (1791)

In Suits at common law, where the value in controversy shall exceed twenty dollars, the right of trial by jury shall be preserved, and no fact tried by a jury, shall be otherwise re-examined in any Court of the United States, than according to the rules of the common law.

Amendment 8 (1791)

Excessive bail shall not be required, nor excessive fines imposed, nor cruel and unusual punishments inflicted.

Amendment 9 (1791)

The enumeration in the Constitution, of certain rights, shall not be construed to deny or disparage others retained by the people.

Amendment 10 (1791)

The powers not delegated to the United States by the Constitution, nor prohibited by it to the States, are reserved to the States respectively, or to the people.

UNDERSTANDING AMENDMENTS 4–6 These three amendments protect people who are suspected of a crime or being tried for one.

- Amendment 4 says that police must have a good reason ("probable cause") before they can seize, or take someone's possessions.
- Amendment 5 means that a person has the right to remain silent when charged with a crime. The amendment is the basis for the Miranda rights warning, which requires police to tell those they arrest their rights.
- Amendment 6 guarantees those accused of a crime to a speedy and public trial.

UNDERSTANDING AMENDMENT 7 This amendment provides the right to a trial by jury. Common law is unwritten law created by judges that apply to all people.

UNDERSTANDING AMENDMENT 8 This amendment proclaims that no punishment should be "excessive" or "cruel and unusual." In other words, the harshness of the punishment should match the seriousness of the crime.

HISTORICAL THINKING How might this amendment be used to either justify or oppose the death penalty as punishment for a crime?

UNDERSTANDING AMENDMENTS 9 and 10 Amendment 9 promises that other rights not stated in the Bill of Rights, such as the right to travel freely, are still covered. Amendment 10 says each state has the power to make laws that are not covered by the Constitution, including laws about starting a business.

UNDERSTANDING AMENDMENT 11

According to this amendment, the United States has no power in lawsuits against individual states.

UNDERSTANDING AMENDMENT 12

This amendment established the electoral college, which decides who the president and vice president will be. The electoral college was challenged in 2000 and 2016, when the candidates who won the popular vote (Al Gore in 2000 and Hillary Clinton in 2016) lost the elections to George W. Bush and Donald Trump, respectively.

HISTORICAL THINKING Do you think presidential elections should be decided by the electoral college? Explain why or why not.

Amendment 11 (1798)

[**Note:** Article 3, Section 2, of the Constitution was modified by the 11th Amendment.]

The Judicial power of the United States shall not be construed to extend to any suit in law or equity, commenced or prosecuted against one of the United States by Citizens of another State, or by Citizens or Subjects of any Foreign State.

Amendment 12 (1804)

[**Note:** Part of Article 2, Section 1, of the Constitution was replaced by the 12th Amendment.]

The Electors shall meet in their respective states and vote by ballot for President and Vice-President, one of whom, at least, shall not be an inhabitant of the same state with themselves; they shall name in their ballots the person voted for as President, and in distinct ballots the person voted for as Vice-President, and they shall make distinct lists of all persons voted for as President, and of all persons voted for as Vice-President, and of the number of votes for each, which lists they shall sign and certify, and transmit sealed to the seat of the government of the United States, directed to the President of the Senate; —the President of the Senate shall, in the presence of the Senate and House of Representatives, open all the certificates and the votes shall then be counted; —The person having the greatest number of votes for President, shall be the President, if such number be a majority of the whole number of Electors appointed; and if no person have such majority, then from the persons having the highest numbers not exceeding three on the list of those voted for as President, the House of Representatives shall choose immediately, by ballot, the President. But in choosing the President, the votes shall be taken by states, the representation from each state having one vote; a quorum for this purpose shall consist of a member or members from two-thirds of the states, and a majority of all the states shall be necessary to a choice. *And if the House of Representatives shall not choose a President whenever the right of choice shall devolve upon them, before the fourth day of March next following, then the Vice-President shall act as President, as in case of the death or other constitutional disability of the President.* The person having the greatest number of votes as Vice-President, shall be the Vice-President, if such number be a majority of the whole number of Electors appointed, and if no person have a majority, then from the two highest numbers on the list, the Senate shall choose the Vice-President; a quorum for the purpose shall consist of two-thirds of the whole number of Senators, and a majority of the whole number shall be necessary to a choice. But no person constitutionally ineligible to the office of President shall be eligible to that of Vice-President of the United States.

Amendment 13 (1865)

[**Note:** A portion of Article 4, Section 2, of the Constitution was superseded by the 13th Amendment.]

SECTION 1: Neither slavery nor involuntary servitude, except as a punishment for crime whereof the party shall have been duly convicted, shall exist within the United States, or any place subject to their jurisdiction.

SECTION 2: Congress shall have power to enforce this article by appropriate legislation.

Amendment 14 (1868)

[**Note:** Article 1, Section 2, of the Constitution was modified by Section 2 of the 14th Amendment.]

SECTION 1: All persons born or naturalized in the United States, and subject to the jurisdiction thereof, are citizens of the United States and of the State wherein they reside. No State shall make or enforce any law which shall abridge the privileges or immunities of citizens of the United States; nor shall any State deprive any person of life, liberty, or property, without due process of law; nor deny to any person within its jurisdiction the equal protection of the laws.

UNDERSTANDING AMENDMENT 14 Section 1 This section defines citizenship and ensures that all citizens enjoy the same rights and the same protections by the law.

SECTION 2: Representatives shall be apportioned among the several States according to their respective numbers, counting the whole number of persons in each State, excluding Indians not taxed. But when the right to vote at any election for the choice of electors for President and Vice-President of the United States, Representatives in Congress, the Executive and Judicial officers of a State, or the members of the *Legislature thereof, is denied to any of the male inhabitants of such State, being twenty-one years of age, and citizens of the United States,* or in any way abridged, except for participation in rebellion, or other crime, the basis of representation therein shall be reduced in the proportion which the number of such male citizens shall bear to the whole number of male citizens twenty-one years of age in such State.

UNDERSTANDING AMENDMENT 14 Section 2 This section overrides the Three-Fifths Compromise in Article I. As a result of this amendment, each citizen is counted as a whole person—except Native Americans.

SECTION 3: No person shall be a Senator or Representative in Congress, or elector of President and Vice-President, or hold any office, civil or military, under the United States, or under any State, who, having previously taken an oath, as a member of Congress, or as an officer of the United States, or as a member of any State legislature, or as an executive or judicial officer of any State, to support the Constitution of the United States, shall have engaged in insurrection or rebellion against the same, or given aid or comfort to the enemies thereof. But Congress may by a vote of two-thirds of each House, remove such disability.

UNDERSTANDING AMENDMENT 14 Sections 3 and 4 These sections of the amendment refer to those who supported or fought for the Confederacy.

SECTION 4: The validity of the public debt of the United States, authorized by law, including debts incurred for payment of pensions and bounties for services in suppressing insurrection or rebellion, shall not be questioned. But neither the United States nor any State shall assume or pay any debt or obligation incurred in aid of insurrection or rebellion against the United States, or any claim for the loss or emancipation of any slave; but all such debts, obligations and claims shall be held illegal and void.

SECTION 5: The Congress shall have the power to enforce, by appropriate legislation, the provisions of this article.

Amendment 15 (1870)

SECTION 1: The right of citizens of the United States to vote shall not be denied or abridged by the United States or by any State on account of race, color, or previous condition of servitude—

SECTION 2: The Congress shall have the power to enforce this article by appropriate legislation.

Amendment 16 (1913)

[**Note:** Article 1, Section 9, of the Constitution was modified by the 16th Amendment.]

The Congress shall have power to lay and collect taxes on incomes, from whatever source derived, without apportionment among the several States, and without regard to any census or enumeration.

UNDERSTANDING AMENDMENT 15 As a result of this amendment, African-American men were granted voting rights. No woman of any race or color could vote. Unfortunately, even after this amendment was passed, some states passed laws that required taxes, tests, and other unfair requirements for people to be permitted to vote.

HISTORICAL THINKING Why do you think the 13th, 14th, and 15th amendments are sometimes referred to as the "Reconstruction amendments"?

In this illustration, a group of men who helped bring about the 15th Amendment, including Abraham Lincoln, Hiram Revels, and Frederick Douglass, watch as President Ulysses S. Grant signs the amendment.

Amendment 17 (1913)

[**Note:** Article 1, Section 3, of the Constitution was modified by the 17th Amendment.]

The Senate of the United States shall be composed of two Senators from each State, elected by the people thereof, for six years; and each Senator shall have one vote. The electors in each State shall have the qualifications requisite for electors of the most numerous branch of the State legislatures.

When vacancies happen in the representation of any State in the Senate, the executive authority of such State shall issue writs of election to fill such vacancies: Provided, That the legislature of any State may empower the executive thereof to make temporary appointments until the people fill the vacancies by election as the legislature may direct.

This amendment shall not be so construed as to affect the election or term of any Senator chosen before it becomes valid as part of the Constitution.

Amendment 18 (1919)

Repealed by the 21st Amendment.

SECTION 1: *After one year from the ratification of this article the manufacture, sale, or transportation of intoxicating liquors within, the importation thereof into, or the exportation thereof from the United States and all territory subject to the jurisdiction thereof for beverage purposes is hereby prohibited.*

SECTION 2: *The Congress and the several States shall have concurrent power to enforce this article by appropriate legislation.*

SECTION 3: *This article shall be inoperative unless it shall have been ratified as an amendment to the Constitution by the legislatures of the several States, as provided in the Constitution, within seven years from the date of the submission hereof to the States by the Congress.*

Amendment 19 (1920)

The right of citizens of the United States to vote shall not be denied or abridged by the United States or by any State on account of sex.

Congress shall have power to enforce this article by appropriate legislation.

UNDERSTANDING AMENDMENT 18 Known as the Prohibition Amendment, the 18th Amendment was repealed only 14 years later, in 1933, by the 21st Amendment. Alcohol was associated with social problems including abuse of women and children.

HISTORICAL THINKING Why do you think the 18th Amendment was repealed?

Federal agents pour a barrel filled with beer down a sewer during Prohibition.

UNDERSTANDING AMENDMENT 19 With the passage of the 19th Amendment, all women received the right to vote in all states. Prior to ratification of this amendment, a number of states already permitted women to vote.

HISTORICAL THINKING Why was it important to add an amendment to the Constitution granting women voting rights and not just leave the matter to individual states?

UNDERSTANDING AMENDMENT 20 This amendment is often called the "Lame Duck Amendment." In government, a lame duck is an elected official whose term in office is about to end. So, for instance, a president who has already served two terms is a lame duck. Officials who have not won re-election are also considered lame ducks.

HISTORICAL THINKING Why do you think it is more difficult for so-called lame-duck officials to enact legislation?

Amendment 20 (1933)

[**Note:** Article 1, Section 4, of the Constitution was modified by Section 2 of the 20th Amendment. In addition, a portion of the 12th Amendment was superseded by Section 3.]

SECTION 1: The terms of the President and the Vice President shall end at noon on the 20th day of January, and the terms of Senators and Representatives at noon on the 3d day of January, of the years in which such terms would have ended if this article had not been ratified; and the terms of their successors shall then begin.

SECTION 2: The Congress shall assemble at least once in every year, and such meeting shall begin at noon on the 3d day of January, unless they shall by law appoint a different day.

SECTION 3: If, at the time fixed for the beginning of the term of the President, the President elect shall have died, the Vice President elect shall become President. If a President shall not have been chosen before the time fixed for the beginning of his term, or if the President elect shall have failed to qualify, then the Vice President elect shall act as President until a President shall have qualified; and the Congress may by law provide for the case wherein neither a President elect nor a Vice President elect shall have qualified, declaring who shall then act as President, or the manner in which one who is to act shall be selected, and such person shall act accordingly until a President or Vice President shall have qualified.

SECTION 4: The Congress may by law provide for the case of the death of any of the persons from whom the House of Representatives may choose a President whenever the right of choice shall have devolved upon them, and for the case of the death of any of the persons from whom the Senate may choose a Vice President whenever the right of choice shall have devolved upon them.

SECTION 5: Sections 1 and 2 shall take effect on the 15th day of October following the ratification of this article.

SECTION 6: This article shall be inoperative unless it shall have been ratified as an amendment to the Constitution by the legislatures of three-fourths of the several States within seven years from the date of its submission.

Amendment 21 (1933)

SECTION 1: The eighteenth article of amendment to the Constitution of the United States is hereby repealed.

SECTION 2: The transportation or importation into any State, Territory, or possession of the United States for delivery or use therein of intoxicating liquors, in violation of the laws thereof, is hereby prohibited.

SECTION 3: This article shall be inoperative unless it shall have been ratified as an amendment to the Constitution by conventions in the several States, as provided in the Constitution, within seven years from the date of the submission hereof to the States by the Congress.

Amendment 22 (1951)

SECTION 1: No person shall be elected to the office of the President more than twice, and no person who has held the office of President, or acted as President, for more than two years of a term to which some other person was elected President shall be elected to the office of the President more than once. But this Article shall not apply to any person holding the office of President when this Article was proposed by the Congress, and shall not prevent any person who may be holding the office of President, or acting as President, during the term within which this Article becomes operative from holding the office of President or acting as President during the remainder of such term.

SECTION 2: This article shall be inoperative unless it shall have been ratified as an amendment to the Constitution by the legislatures of three-fourths of the several States within seven years from the date of its submission to the States by the Congress.

UNDERSTANDING AMENDMENT 21 This amendment repealed the 18th Amendment and ended Prohibition.

UNDERSTANDING AMENDMENT 22 Franklin D. Roosevelt served three terms as president of the United States and was elected to a fourth term shortly before he died in 1945. All presidents before Roosevelt served two terms. Within months of Roosevelt's death, Republicans in Congress presented the 22nd Amendment for consideration.

HISTORICAL THINKING Do you think the U.S. president should be limited to serving two terms? Why or why not?

UNDERSTANDING AMENDMENT 23 Although the District of Columbia is the official seat of the U.S. government, it is a federal territory, not a state, and has only a nonvoting representative in Congress. Washington, D.C., began as a very small community. However, by 1960, more than 760,000 people who paid federal taxes and could be drafted to serve in the military lived in the District. The states ratified Amendment 23 in 1961 to give the residents of the District the right to have their votes counted in the presidential elections.

UNDERSTANDING AMENDMENT 24 This amendment abolished poll taxes, election fees charged by states to keep low-income and mostly African-American citizens from voting. The amendment was passed in response to the demands of the civil rights movement of the 1960s, which condemned the poll tax.

HISTORICAL THINKING What impact did the poll tax probably have on election results?

Amendment 23 (1961)

SECTION 1: The District constituting the seat of Government of the United States shall appoint in such manner as the Congress may direct:

A number of electors of President and Vice President equal to the whole number of Senators and Representatives in Congress to which the District would be entitled if it were a State, but in no event more than the least populous State; they shall be in addition to those appointed by the States, but they shall be considered, for the purposes of the election of President and Vice President, to be electors appointed by a State; and they shall meet in the District and perform such duties as provided by the twelfth article of amendment.

SECTION 2: The Congress shall have power to enforce this article by appropriate legislation.

Amendment 24 (1964)

SECTION 1: The right of citizens of the United States to vote in any primary or other election for President or Vice President, for electors for President or Vice President, or for Senator or Representative in Congress, shall not be denied or abridged by the United States or any State by reason of failure to pay any poll tax or other tax.

SECTION 2: The Congress shall have power to enforce this article by appropriate legislation.

Amendment 25 (1967)

[Note: Article 2, Section 1, of the Constitution was affected by the 25th Amendment.]

SECTION 1: In case of the removal of the President from office or of his death or resignation, the Vice President shall become President.

SECTION 2: Whenever there is a vacancy in the office of the Vice President, the President shall nominate a Vice President who shall take office upon confirmation by a majority vote of both Houses of Congress.

SECTION 3: Whenever the President transmits to the President pro tempore of the Senate and the Speaker of the House of Representatives his written declaration that he is unable to discharge the powers and duties of his office, and until he transmits to them a written declaration to the contrary, such powers and duties shall be discharged by the Vice President as Acting President.

SECTION 4: Whenever the Vice President and a majority of either the principal officers of the executive departments or of such other body as Congress may by law provide, transmit to the President pro tempore of the Senate and the Speaker of the House of Representatives their written declaration that the President is unable to discharge the powers and duties of his office, the Vice President shall immediately assume the powers and duties of the office as Acting President.

Thereafter, when the President transmits to the President pro tempore of the Senate and the Speaker of the House of Representatives his written declaration that no inability exists, he shall resume the powers and duties of his office unless the Vice President and a majority of either the principal officers of the executive department or of such other body as Congress may by law provide, transmit within four days to the President pro tempore of the Senate and the Speaker of the House of Representatives their written declaration that the President is unable to discharge the powers and duties of his office. Thereupon Congress shall decide the issue, assembling within forty-eight hours for that purpose if not in session. If the Congress, within twenty-one days after receipt of the latter written declaration, or, if Congress is not in session, within twenty-one days after Congress is required to assemble, determines by two-thirds vote of both Houses that the President is unable to discharge the powers and duties of his office, the Vice President shall continue to discharge the same as Acting President; otherwise, the President shall resume the powers and duties of his office.

UNDERSTANDING AMENDMENT 25 The 25th Amendment was ratified in 1967 to set up procedures to follow if a president becomes disabled while in office. It was proposed after the assassination of President John F. Kennedy in 1963. Following his death, some people began to wonder what would have happened if he'd survived the shooting but been unable to govern. This amendment provides for an orderly transfer of power.

HISTORICAL THINKING Why is there a plan of succession for the presidency?

President Richard Nixon signs the 26th Amendment in 1971. Looking on are members of the youth choir Young Americans.

UNDERSTANDING AMENDMENT 26 The voting age had been 21 since 1868. However, while the United States fought the Vietnam War in the 1960s and 1970s, people began to question why 18-year-old men could be drafted to serve in the military but could not vote. As a result, the 26th Amendment was passed by Congress and ratified by the states on July 1, 1971.

Through the progressive expansion of voting rights, the Constitution has provided ever-increasing opportunities for citizens to participate in the political process.

HISTORICAL THINKING Why do you think many Americans questioned the fairness of denying voting rights to 18-year-olds, especially to those who could be drafted to go to war?

Amendment 26 (1971)

[**Note:** Amendment 14, Section 2, of the Constitution was modified by Section 1 of the 26th Amendment.]

SECTION 1: The right of citizens of the United States, who are eighteen years of age or older, to vote shall not be denied or abridged by the United States or by any State on account of age.

SECTION 2: The Congress shall have power to enforce this article by appropriate legislation.

Amendment 27 (1992)

No law, varying the compensation for the services of the Senators and Representatives, shall take effect, until an election of Representatives shall have intervened.

Citizenship and You

Imagine your parents have given you the right to play a computer game during your free time. To keep enjoying this right, you have some responsibilities. You're responsible for having your homework and chores done before you play the game. You're responsible for using the computer according to your family's or school's rules. Similarly, our responsibilities as citizens balance the rights we receive as citizens. Let's take a closer look at the whats, whys, and hows of **citizenship**—being a full member of a country in exchange for certain responsibilities.

AS DEFINED BY THE FRAMERS

As you have observed by studying the U.S. Constitution and Bill of Rights, privileges and rights like citizenship and voting have been contested, reshaped, and amended over time. We started with the freedoms outlined by the Framers, but many contributions have been made throughout history by Americans who have worked to expand our rights. These include the civil rights of individuals and minorities, the right to participate in government, the right to speak freely, the right to a fair trial, and many others. The efforts of those activists have helped us move forward in our continuing struggle to become a more perfect union—a struggle that continues today.

A COUNTRY WITHOUT RULES?

Picture this: You arrive at school on the first day of classes, but no schedules are available for the students. Nobody knows the school rules. Teachers and office workers can't answer any questions, and no one has been assigned a locker. Everything is completely disorganized and confusing.

This is similar to what would happen in a government without clear rules—or laws—that define the rights and responsibilities of its citizens. Order, organization, equality, and safety would all suffer without these laws. Is it fair that a government makes the laws that define the rights and responsibilities of a nation? In essence, a democratic government IS the people of its nation. The people who serve in the government and make its laws are elected by people across the country. So, these lawmakers represent the people of that country.

In the United States, we work to be *good citizens* by obeying laws, *participatory citizens* by voting and serving on juries, and *socially-just citizens* by standing up for the rights of others. Read on to learn more about the rights and responsibilities of citizenship.

While you might not be old enough to vote in the United States, you have many other rights, and as you'll see, those rights come with responsibilities.

THINK ABOUT IT

SUMMARIZE How have the rights and responsibilities of U.S. citizens been defined and changed over time?

The Rights and Responsibilities of Citizens

In the United States, citizens have many rights, regardless of whether they were born here or came here from another country. Knowing their rights helps citizens understand the responsibilities they have to balance and support their rights. Rights are simple: they are established in the U.S. Constitution and Bill of Rights. Responsibilities are pretty simple, too. Mostly they consist of simply doing what is right and showing good character. As you read, think about specific actions you might take to be a good, participatory, and socially-just citizen.

BECOMING A CITIZEN

Some residents of the United States are citizens because they were born in the country. Others came from foreign countries to legally enter and live in the United States. They worked to become citizens through an immigration process called **naturalization**. People becoming naturalized citizens work hard to learn the laws, rights, and responsibilities of American citizenship. They take a citizenship test and are sworn in as citizens during a naturalization ceremony. Immigrants enhance the diversity of the United States and have contributed greatly throughout history. It is a proud day when they become U.S. citizens who can enjoy the rights of citizens listed below.

Rights of Citizens
Right to freedom of religion
Right to freedom of speech
Right to freedom of the press
Right to assemble
Right to trial by jury (in specific types of cases)
Right to vote
Right to buy and sell property
Right to freely travel across the country and to leave and return to the country

LIMITS ON RIGHTS

By now, you're probably pretty familiar with the basic rights of citizens as guaranteed in the Constitution. It's worth noting there are limitations that apply to some of these rights. Some of these restrictions were built into the laws that established the rights. Others have come into being because of cases that have come before the Supreme Court and tested various rights. For example, it's true that as stated in the First Amendment to the U.S. Constitution, people have the right to free speech—to say what they are thinking without fear of the government punishing them for expressing their thoughts or ideas. But this freedom of speech is not absolute. For example, suppose someone shouted "Fire!" in a movie theater or crowded shopping mall when there actually was no fire. That person would not be protected by the right to free speech, as his or her clearly intentional "speech" could cause harm to others.

CIVIC RESPONSIBILITIES

U.S. citizens have two different types of responsibilities: civic and personal. **Civic responsibilities** include voting, paying taxes, and serving on juries. **Personal responsibilities** include respecting others, helping in the community, standing up for others, and staying informed about issues.

If people didn't exercise their civic responsibilities, rights would not exist. In the United States, for example, many people take for granted their right to vote and don't bother to vote at all. Perhaps they don't consider the fact that the right to vote is a privilege that doesn't exist in all countries. People in many countries do not have the opportunity to elect officials who will represent them and make decisions that determine how everyone will be governed.

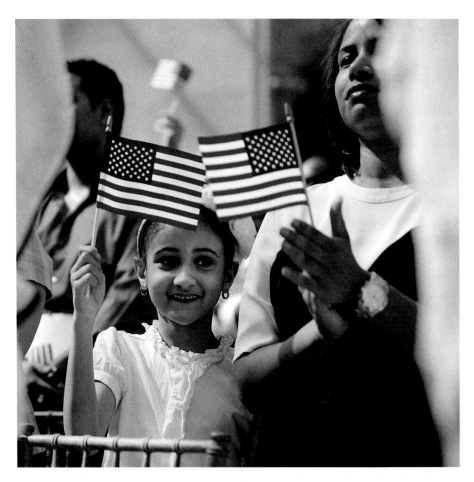

A six-year old stands in proud support as her mother receives her citizenship. This naturalization ceremony took place in 2014 in the Metropolitan Museum of Art in New York City.

Because people in the United States have the right to vote, they have a corresponding responsibility to exercise that right. They are also responsible for being informed voters. Voters have an obligation to use reliable sources to learn about candidates who are running for office. Voters must determine the similarities and differences between the candidates' positions on issues and use evidence to analyze the credibility of their claims. Similarly, voters have the same obligation to inform themselves about new laws before casting votes in favor of or against them.

How can a young person exercise civic responsibilities related to voting if he or she is not old enough to vote? You can participate in mock elections or student government elections in your school. You can create posters and pamphlets to encourage adults to vote, or volunteer to help with a candidate's campaign. Remember, the decisions of voters impact people of every age.

PERSONAL RESPONSIBILITIES

When you think of your personal responsibilities as a citizen, consider the choices you make in terms of your actions. Being a responsible citizen means behaving in ways that are right, moral, and just, and acting in a way that benefits you and those around you. Considering the rights of all people, not just the rights of a select few, will help you be a personally responsible citizen.

Citizens have many personal responsibilities, such as being open-minded, respecting the opinions of others, and showing respect for the beliefs and individuality of people with different backgrounds. People of any age can take on personal responsibilities by doing community service projects, standing up for the rights of others, and respecting all people regardless of ethnicity, nationality, gender identity, sexual orientation, or beliefs. Living up to these personal responsibilities helps citizens contribute to an environment of respect and caring.

THINK ABOUT IT

EXPLAIN How does a democracy depend on people fulfilling their civic and personal responsibilities?

Building and Practicing Citizenship Skills

Building citizenship skills is like building muscle. It takes hard work and repetition, but the rewards pay off for everyone. Some citizenship skills, such as helping raise voter participation, will require you to seek out specific opportunities. Others, such as refusing to tolerate bullying, can be exercised whenever appropriate situations arise. Citizenship affords many rights and requires many responsibilities. Enjoying these rights and responsibilities is the reward of being a good citizen.

The following chart includes ways you can build and apply citizenship skills and become an active participant in our democracy. Study the chart and check out the Active Citizenship for the Environment Activities in this program's online resources. Then brainstorm more ways you can be a good, participatory, socially-just citizen.

THINK ABOUT IT

DESCRIBE What citizenship project would you be interested in undertaking, and how would you carry it out?

Citizenship in Action

Responsibilities	Citizenship Projects: Ways to Take Action
Become informed.	• Read books and articles from reliable sources. • Attend, watch, or read transcripts of debates and speeches. • Watch broadcast journalists on reliable cable and digital sources. • Ask questions of others who are well informed.
Make decisions based on facts.	• Think about whether you are acting on emotion or fact. • Use reliable sources to evaluate statements you hear and read. • Check reliable sources to see if others' statements are accurate.
Listen to the opinions of others. Discuss differences of opinion in a kind and civil manner.	• When friends or acquaintances express opinions that differ from yours, explain why you disagree, if you do. • Use appropriate language and remain calm as you discuss opinions. If the other person refuses to be calm or civil, end the conversation and walk away.
Respect the value of individuals. Respect differences among people.	• Enjoy the differences among people. • Make friends with people who are different from you. • Volunteer in your community to interact with and help others.
Stand up for rights of others. Work to stop bullying.	• Do not stand by silently when someone is being bullied. Speak up. If you do not feel safe, immediately seek the help of an adult. • Write articles and blog posts about the importance of stopping the act of bullying. Develop or participate in an antibullying program.
Volunteer in your community.	• Determine how your skills and interests could help someone else. • Talk with your parents, teachers, and friends to learn what types of volunteer services your community needs. • Make volunteering a regular part of your life. You could consider serving food to the homeless, collecting clothing or canned goods to help a local shelter, cleaning or restoring a local park or playground, or tutoring students who are struggling with their school work.

Responsibilities	Citizenship Projects: Ways to Take Action
Express political opinions.	• Write a letter or an email to a newspaper editor about an issue that concerns you. • Use clear and concise language. Edit your letter carefully.
Obey the law.	• Become familiar with the laws in your state, city, and town that apply to people your age.
Pay taxes.	• Read more about your local and state taxes, and what the revenue is used for. • Recognize that you are already paying sales taxes when you purchase many items.
Lobby for change.	• Form a lobbying committee with other students to influence legislation or public policy. • Establish a goal for your lobbying campaign. • Identify whom to lobby. (Who are the people who can help you accomplish your goal?) • Find information and statistics to support your goal. • Get public support for your cause. You might consider gathering signatures on a petition or creating flyers to publicize your campaign. • Present your case to the appropriate individuals.
Accept responsibility for your actions.	• If someone asks about a mistake you have made, tell the truth. • Ask what you might do to make up for the mistake.
Participate in the democratic process.	• Ask a teacher to organize a trip to a local courtroom to see the law in action. • Contact a local political candidate whose ideas you support to see how you might help with his or her campaign. • Plan and/or participate in mock elections, student government elections, and student government meetings. • With the help of a parent or teacher, seek opportunities to participate in a naturalization ceremony. • Research how you and your classmates can participate in National History Day at a state or national level.

One way of practicing citizenship is by volunteering.

GLOSSARY

A

abolition *n.* (a-buh-LIH-shuhn) the act of putting an end to something, such as slavery (page 357)

abolitionist *n.* (a-buh-LIH-shuhn-ihst) a person who wants to end slavery (page 454)

African diaspora *n.* (A-frih-kuhn DY-as-poh-rah) the removal of Africans from their homelands to the Americas (page 74)

agrarian *adj.* (ah-GRAR-ee-ehn) related to agriculture or farming (page 374)

Agricultural Revolution *n.* (AHG-rihkuhl-chuhr-uhl REV-oh-luh-shuhn) the transition in human history from hunting and gathering food to planting crops and raising animals (page 9)

Alien and Sedition Acts *n.* (AY-lee-uhn AND sih-DIH-shun AKTS) a series of four laws passed to keep certain groups from immigrating to the United States; the laws gave the government power to expel aliens living in the United States and targeted U.S. citizens who criticized the U.S. government (page 301)

alliance *n.* (ah-LY-ans) an agreement between nations to fight each other's enemies or otherwise collaborate; a partnership (page 111)

amendment *n.* (uh-MEND-muhnt) a formal change to a law, usually referring to a formal change to the U.S. Constitution (page 263)

American System *n.* (uh-MAIR-uh-kuhn SIHS-tuhm) a policy of promoting the U.S. industrial system through the use of tariffs, federal subsidies to build roads and other public works, and a national bank to control currency (page 350)

Anaconda Plan *n.* (a-nuh-KAHN-duh PLAN) a military strategy during the Civil War in which the North planned to set up a blockade around the southern coast to ruin the South's economy and secure ports on the Mississippi River; much as a huge snake, like an anaconda, crushes its prey (page 512)

annex *v.* (a-NEX) to add (page 399)

antebellum *adj.* (an-tih-BEH-luhm) before the American Civil War (page 348)

antifederalist *n.* (an-tee-FEH-duh ruh-list) a person who opposed the U.S. Constitution of 1787 because of its emphasis on a strong national government (page 262)

apprentice *n.* (ah-PREHN-tis) a person who learns a craft or trade by working with a skilled member of that craft or trade (page 129)

arable *adj.* (AIR-ah-bl) able to grow crops; fertile (page 140)

arson *n.* (AR-son) the purposeful burning of buildings illegally (page 568)

Articles of Confederation *n.* (AHR-TIH-kuhls UHV kuhn-feh-duh-RAY-shuhn) a set of laws adopted by the United States in 1777 that established each state in the union as a republic, replaced by the Constitution in 1789 (page 222)

artillery *n.* (ahr-TIH-luh-ree) large guns that can fire over a long distance (page 203)

artisan *n.* (AR-tih-san) a person skilled at making things by hand (page 136)

B

assassinate *v.* (uh-SA-suh-nayt) to murder for political reasons (page 546)

assimilate *v.* (ah-SIM-ih-late) to adopt the culture or way of life of the nation in which one currently lives; to become absorbed in a culture or country (page 376, 441)

asylum *n.* (uh-SY-luhm) a hospital dedicated to treating the mentally ill (page 449)

attorney general *n.* (uh-TUR-NEE JEN-ruhl) a member of the president's Cabinet, whose primary role is to represent the United States before the Supreme Court (page 289)

backcountry *n.* (BAK-kuhn-tree) the western part of the Southern Colonies just east of the Appalachian Mountains (page 134)

banish *v.* (BA-nish) to send away as punishment, usually without hope of return (page 101)

bayonet *n.* (BAY-uh-nuht) a sharp blade attached to the end of a rifle (page 228)

Bering Land Bridge *n.* (BARE-ingh LAND BRIJ) a piece of land between Alaska and Siberia that was above sea level 13,000 years ago and allowed early humans to cross into North America (page 6)

Bill of Rights *n.* (BIHL UHV RITES) the first 10 amendments to the U.S. Constitution; a list of guarantees to which every person in a country is entitled (page 263)

black codes *n.* (BLAK KOHDZ) laws passed by southern states immediately after the Civil War for controlling African Americans and limiting their rights; repealed by Reconstruction in 1866 (page 562)

black peonage *n.* (BLAK PE-eh-nij) economic slavery that tied African Americans to sharecropping landlords' lands (page 567)

blight *n.* (BLYT) a fungus or an insect that causes plants to dry up and die (page 440)

blockade *v.* (blah-KAYD) to block ships from entering or leaving a harbor (page 228)

bluff *n.* (BLUHF) a cliff (page 536)

bond *n.* (BAHND) a certificate offered for sale to the public with the promise that the government will pay the money back at a later date (page 532)

boomtown *n.* (BOOM-town) a town that experiences a great population increase in only a short time period (page 426)

border state *n.* (BOR-dur STAYT) at the time of the Civil War, a state that bordered both Union and Confederate states, namely Maryland, Kentucky, Delaware, Missouri, and West Virginia (page 497)

Boston Massacre *n.* (BAWS-tuhn MA-sih-kur) the 1779 incident in which British soldiers fired on locals who had been taunting them (page 188)

Boston Tea Party *n.* (BAWS-tuhn TEE PAR-tee) the 1773 incident in which the Sons of Liberty boarded British ships and dumped their cargo in protest of British taxes on the colonists (page 191)

boycott *n.* (BOY-kaht) a form of protest that involves refusing to purchase goods or services (page 183)

bribery *n.* (BRY-buh-ree) offers of money or privileges to those in power in exchange for political favors (page 572)

burgeon *v.* (BUR-jehn) to grow quickly (page 146)

C

Cabinet *n.* (KAB-niht) the heads of the departments that assist the U.S. president (page 287)

Californio *n.* (kal-uh-fowr-nee-oh) a resident of California who was of Spanish or Mexican descent and lived there before the gold rush (page 425)

caravan *n.* (KARE-uh-van) a group of people and animals traveling together, usually for trade (page 42)

caravel *n.* (KER-uh-vehl) a small, fast ship used by Spanish and Portuguese explorers (page 40)

cash crop *n.* (KASH KRAHP) a crop grown for sale rather than for use by farmers (page 132)

casualty *n.* (KAH-zhuhl-tee) a dead or injured person (page 548)

cavalry *n.* (KA-vuhl-ree) army troops who fight on horseback (page 499)

cede *v.* (SEED) to give up (page 296)

charter *n.* (CHAHR-tuhr) a written grant establishing an institution and detailing members' rights and privileges (page 92)

chattel slavery *n.* (CHA-tuhl SLAY-veh-ree) a system in which enslaved people have no human rights and are classified as goods (page 72)

checks and balances *n.* (CHEKS AND BAH-luhn-suhz) the system established by the U.S. Constitution that gives each of the branches of government the power to limit the power of the other two (page 258)

Chief Justice *n.* (CHEEF JUH-stuhs) the head of the judicial branch of the government; presides over the Supreme Court (page 289)

chiefdom *n.* (CHEEF-duhm) a large community of people ruled by a chief (page 9)

circumnavigate *v.* (sur-cuhm-NAV-ih-gayt) to travel completely around Earth (page 62)

citizenship *n.* (SIH-tuh-zuhn-ship) the condition of having the opportunities and duties of citizens (page R33)

civic responsibility *n.* (SIH-vihk rih-spawn-suh-BIHL-uh-tee) responsibility that is either required or essential that people perform, such as voting, paying taxes, and serving on juries (page R34)

Civil Rights Act of 1866 *n.* (SIH-vuhl RITES AKT UHV 1866) a bill granting full equality and citizenship to "every race and color" (page 562)

civilian *n.* (suh-VIHL-yuhn) a person who is not in the military (page 505)

civilization *n.* (sih-vuhl-ih-ZAY-shun) a society with a highly developed culture and technology (page 24)

Columbian Exchange *n.* (kuh-LUM-bee-uhn ehks-CHAYNJ) the exchange of plants, animals, microbes, people, and ideas between Europe and the Americas following Columbus's first voyage to the Western Hemisphere (page 70)

commerce clause *n.* (KAH-murs KLAWZ) a provision in Article 1 of the U.S. Constitution granting Congress the power to make laws concerning foreign trade as well as trade among the states and with Native American nations (page 260)

committee of correspondence *n.* (kuh-MIH-tee UHV KAWR-uh-spahn-dunts) in the Revolutionary era, a group of colonists whose duty it was to spread news about protests against the British (page 191)

commodity *n.* (kuh-MAH-duh-tee) a trade good (page 142)

common market *n.* (KAH-muhn MAHR-kuht) a group of countries or states that allows the members to trade freely among themselves (page 261)

common school *n.* (KAH-muhn SKOOL) a colonial elementary school (page 129)

common school movement *n.* (KAH-muhn SKOOL MOOV-muhnt) an educational reform movement in the 1830s that promoted free public schools funded by property taxes and managed by local governments (page 449)

Compromise of 1877 *n.* (KAHM-pruh-myz UHV 1877) a deal in which Democrats agreed to make Rutherford B. Hayes president if Republicans ended Reconstruction and pulled federal troops out of the South (page 573)

Conestoga wagon *n.* (kah-nuh-STOH-guh WA-guhn) a kind of wagon, made by German settlers in North America, that could carry heavy loads (page 143)

confederacy *n.* (kon-FED-ur-uh-see) an agreement among several groups, states, or governments to protect and support one another in battle or other endeavors (page 111)

Confederacy *n.* (kon-FED-ur-uh-see) the 11 southern states that seceded from the Union to form their own nation, the Confederate States of America (page 482)

conformity *n.* (kuhn-FAWR-mih-tee) an obedience to a set of beliefs (page 144)

conquistador *n.* (kon-KEE-stuh-dohr) a Spanish conqueror who sought gold and other riches in the Americas (page 56)

Conscription Act *n.* (kuhn-SKRIHP-shuhn AKT) a law instituted by the Union in 1863 stating that men between the ages of 20 and 45 years of age were liable to be drafted into the military but they could pay $300 to avoid service (page 530)

constitution *n.* (kahn-stuh-TOO-shuhn) a document that organizes a government and states its powers (page 250)

constitutionalism *n.* (kahn-stuh-TOO-shuh-nuh-lih-zuhm) the concept of governing based on a constitution (page 251)

contiguous *adj.* (kuhn-TIH-gyuh-wuhs) connected (page 421)

Continental Army *n.* (kahn-tuh-NEHN-tuhl AHR-mee) the American army formed in 1775 by the Second Continental Congress and led by General George Washington (page 203)

Continental Divide *n.* (kahn-tuh-NEHN-tuhl duh-VYD) the high point in the Rocky Mountains that divides the watersheds of the Atlantic and Pacific oceans (page 403)

convert *v.* (kuhn-VERT) to persuade to change one's religious beliefs (page 43)

Copperhead *n.* (KAH-pur-hed) a negative nickname for Democrats who opposed emancipation of enslaved people and the draft (page 570)

corruption *n.* (kuh-RUHP-shuhn) dishonesty, unlawfulness (page 572)

GLOSSARY

cotton gin *n.* (KAH-tuhn JIHN) a machine that separates the cotton seeds and hulls from the cotton boll (tuft of cotton) (page 346)

counterattack *n.* (KOWN-tur uh-TAK) an attack made in response to a previous attack (page 227)

craft union *n.* (KRAFT YOON-yuhn) a labor union that advocates for workers' rights and protections, whose members are specialized skilled workers or craftsmen (page 451)

credit *n.* (KREH-diht) the privilege of purchasing something or borrowing money and paying the money back over time (page 254)

Crittenden Plan *n.* (KRIHT-uhn-duhn PLAN) a proposal that stated the federal government would have no power to abolish slavery in the states where it already existed; it reestablished and extended the Missouri Compromise line to the Pacific Ocean (page 484)

Currency Act *n.* (KUR-uhn-see AKT) the British law that regulated paper money in the American colonies (page 181)

customs *n.* (KUH-stuhmz) the taxes placed on imported and exported goods (page 327)

D

Declaration of Independence *n.* (deh-kluh-RAY-shun UHV ihn-duh-PEHN-duhns) the document declaring U.S. independence from Great Britain, adopted July 4, 1776 (page 208)

defect *v.* (dih-FEKT) to break away (page 572)

defensive war *n.* (dih-FEHN-sihv WOR) a war to protect one's own land, on familiar ground, from outside attackers (page 222)

delegate *n.* (DEH-lih-guht) a person chosen or elected to represent a group of people (page 256)

depression *n.* (dee-PREH-shuhn) a period of slow economic activity when many people are without work (page 383)

desert *v.* (dih-ZURT) to run away from the army or another branch of the military to avoid military service (page 231)

diplomat *n.* (DIH-pluh-mat) a person sent to another nation to represent his or her country's interests (page 417)

dissenter *n.* (dih-SEHN-tur) a person who strongly disagrees with official policy (page 100)

diversity *n.* (duh-VUR-suh-tee) a wide variety (page 143)

doctrine *n.* (DAHK-truhn) a principle or set of beliefs accepted by a group (page 109)

doctrine of nullification *n.* (DAHK-truhn UHV nuh-luh-fuh-KAY-shuhn) a doctrine that said a state could nullify, or reject, a federal law they felt was unconstitutional, held by some southern politicians before the Civil War (page 374)

domestic service *n.* (duh-MEHS-tihk SUR-vuhs) housework in another person's home, performed as a job (page 441)

domesticate *v.* (duh-MEHS-tih-kayt) to raise plants and animals for human benefit and consumption (page 27)

domestication *n.* (duh-mehs-TIH-kay-shuhn) the practice of raising animals and growing plants for human benefit (page 9)

draft *n.* (DRAFT) a mandatory term of military service (page 530)

Dred Scott decision *n.* (DRED SKAHWT dih-SIH-zhuhn) a Supreme Court decision that African Americans held no rights as citizens and that the Missouri Compromise of 1820 was unconstitutional; Dred Scott, the escaped slave at the center of the case, was returned to slavery (page 476)

drumlin *n.* (DRUHM-luhn) a smooth-sloped hill made of glacial sediments (page 204)

dual sovereignty *n.* (DOO-uhl SAH-vuh-ruhn-tee) the concept that state governments have certain powers the federal government cannot overrule (page 257)

duty *n.* (DOO-tee) a tax on imports (page 181)

E

earthworks *n.* (URTH-wurks) human-made land modifications (page 204)

economic activity *n.* (eh-kuh-NAH-mihk ak-TIH-vuh-tee) actions that involve the production, distribution, and consumption of goods and services (page 114)

Electoral College *n.* (ee-lehk-TAWR-uhl KAH-lihj) the group that elects the U.S. president; each state receives as many electors as it has congressional representatives and senators combined (page 258)

emancipation *n.* (ih-man-suh-PAY-shuhn) the ending of slavery (page 454)

Emancipation Proclamation *n.* (ih-man-suh-PAY-shuhn prah-kluh-MAY-shuhn) an 1863 document issued by Abraham Lincoln that freed all slaves living in Confederate-held territory during the American Civil War (page 525)

embargo *n.* (ihm-BAHR-goh) a law that restricts commerce with one or more nations (page 327)

Embargo Act of 1807 *n.* (ihm-BAHR-goh AKT UHV 1807) a federal legislation that stopped all foreign imports from entering American harbors (page 327)

emigrate *v.* (EH-muh-grayt) to move away from a country in order to live in another (page 438)

encomienda *n.* (en-coe-mee-AYN-dah) a system in Spain's American colonies in which wealthy settlers were given plots of land and allowed to enslave the people who lived there (page 66)

Enlightenment *n.* (ihn-LY-tuhn-muhnt) an intellectual movement that emphasized the use of reason to examine previously accepted beliefs (page 149)

enlist *v.* (ehn-LIST) to join (page 528)

envoy *n.* (AHN-voy) an ambassador (page 300)

espionage *n.* (EH-spee-uh-nahj) the practice of spying to obtain information (page 232)

evacuate *v.* (ih-VA-kyoo-wayt) to leave a location, usually for one's own protection (page 496)

evangelize *v.* (ih-VAN-juh-lyz) to spread one's religious beliefs through public speaking and personal witness (page 446)

executive branch *n.* (ihg-ZEH-kyuh-tihv BRANCH) the section of the U.S. government headed by the president; responsible for enforcing the law (page 258)

exemption *n.* (ihg-ZEHMP-shuhn) a release from obligations (page 530)

exodus *n.* (EHK-suh-duhs) a mass departure (page 403)

expertise *n.* (ehk-spur-TEEZ) an expert knowledge or skill (page 241)

F

factory system *n.* (FAK-tuh-ree SIHS-tuhm) a method of production in which large crews of people perform work in one location (page 336)

famine *n.* (FA-muhn) an extreme lack of crops or food causing widespread hunger (page 440)

federal *adj.* (FEH-duh-ruhl) relating to a government where power is shared between the central, national government and that of states or provinces (page 250)

federal marshal *n.* (FEH-duh-ruhl MAHR-shuhl) a law enforcement officer who works for the United States government (page 471)

federalism *n.* (FEH-duh-ruh-lih-zuhm) the support of a government where power is shared between the central, national government and that of states or provinces (page 257)

federalist *n.* (FEH-duh-ruh-lihst) a person who supported the U.S. Constitution of 1787 as it was written during the process of ratification (page 262)

feudalism *n.* (FEW-dahl-izm) a political and social system in which a vassal receives protection from a lord in exchange for obedience and service (page 36)

15th Amendment *n.* (15th uh-MENDmuhnt) an amendment to the Constitution that says that federal and state governments cannot restrict the right to vote because of race, color, or previous condition of servitude (page 570)

financier *n.* (fih-nuhn-SIHR) a person who lends or manages money for a business or undertaking (page 229)

First Continental Congress *n.* (FURST kahn-tuh-NEHN-tuhl KAHN-gruhs) the 1774 meeting of representatives from all American colonies to decide on a response to the Intolerable Acts (page 195)

flotilla *n.* (flo-TIHL-ah) a small fleet (page 536)

fortification *n.* (fawr-tuh-fuh-KAY-shuhn) a structure built to protect a place from attack (page 227)

forty-niner *n.* (for-tee-NY-nur) one of the thousands of prospective miners who traveled to California seeking gold in 1849 (page 425)

framers *n.* (FRAYM-urz) delegates to the 1787 Constitutional Convention who helped shape the content and structure of the U.S. Constitution (page 256)

Freedmen's Bureau *n.* (FREED-muhns BYOOR-oh) the Bureau of Refugees, Freedmen, and Abandoned Lands, created by Congress in 1865 to help former slaves, as well as poor white southerners (page 561)

French Revolution *n.* (FRENCH re-vuh-LOO-shuhn) the 1789 rebellion against the French monarchy that sought to put an end to upper-class privilege and demanded equality for the lower classes (page 297)

fugitive slave clause *n.* (FYOO-juh-tihv SLAYV KLAWZ) a provision in Article 4 of the U.S. Constitution that prevented free states from emancipating enslaved workers who had escaped from their masters in other states (page 260)

Fundamental Orders of Connecticut *n.* (fuhn-duh-MEHN-tahl AWR-duhr UHV kuh-NEH-tih-kuht) a founding document of the Connecticut colony that listed 11 laws and stood as the framework for governing the colony (page 101)

G

Gadsden Purchase *n.* (GADZ-duhn PUHR-chuhs) a sale of land in 1853 from Mexico to the United States that established the current U.S. southwestern border (page 421)

galleon *n.* (GAL-eeahn) a large sailing ship used especially by the Spanish in the 16th and 17th centuries (page 62)

garrison *n.* (GAIR-uh-suhn) a defense force of soldiers (page 485)

geographic perspective *n.* (jee-uh-GRA-fihk pur-SPEHK-tihv) the examination of how geography affects people and culture (page 34)

geology *n.* (jee-AH-luh-jee) the study of the processes that shape Earth's rocks and landforms (page 204)

Gettysburg Address *n* (GEH-teez-burg uh-DREHS) an 1863 speech delivered by President Lincoln to commemorate the loss of life at the Battle of Gettysburg and to dedicate a military cemetery (page 537)

glacial period *n.* (GLAY-shuhl PEER-ee-uhd) a period of time in history during which huge sheets of ice covered much of Earth (page 5)

Great Awakening *n.* (GRAYT uh-WAY-kuhn-ing) a series of Protestant religious revivals that swept across the American colonies (page 148)

grievance *n.* (GREE-vuhnts) an objection or reason to complain (page 181)

gristmill *n.* (GRIHST-mihl) a building that houses machinery for grinding grain (page 140)

guerrilla *adj.* (guh-RIH-luh) relating to an independent military group that uses methods such as sneak attacks and sabotage (page 237)

gunboat *n.* (GUHN-boht) a small, fast ship carrying mounted guns (page 516)

H

habeus corpus *n.* (HA-be-as COR-pus) the right of an arrested person to be brought before a judge before going to jail (page 531)

hacienda *n.* (hah-see-EHN-dah) a large plantation in a Spanish-speaking colony (page 66)

heretic *n.* (HAYR-eh-tik) a person who holds beliefs different from the teachings of the Catholic Church (page 61)

Hessians *n.* (HEH-shuhnz) German soldiers hired by the British to fight during the American Revolution (page 206)

hierarchy *n.* (HY-uh-rahr-kee) the classification of a group of people according to ability or to economic, social, or professional standing (page 36)

Homestead Act *n.* (HOHM-stehd AKT) an act that started a program of public land grants to small farmers (page 549)

GLOSSARY

human geography *n.* (HYOO-muhn jee-AH-gruh-fee) the study of how people and their cultures are affected by physical geography and how human activities affect the environment (page 34)

humanism *n.* (HYOO-muh-nih-zhum) a movement that focuses on the importance of the individual (page 39)

hunter-gatherer *n.* (HUHN-tuhr GAHTH-ur-ur) a human who hunts animals and gathers wild plants to eat (page 7)

I

ice age *n.* (AISS AJ) a period of time in history during which huge sheets of ice covered much of Earth (page 5)

immigrate *v.* (IH-muh-grayt) to permanently move to another country (page 438)

immunity *n.* (ih-MYOO-nih-tee) a protection against disease, either natural or induced by vaccination (page 70)

impeachment *n.* (ihm-PEECH-muhnt) the official charge of a president with misconduct while in office (page 563)

implied power *n.* (ihm-PLYD POW-ur) a power not explicitly stated in the Constitution (page 351)

impressment *n.* (ihm-PRESS-muhnt) the act of forcing men into military or naval service (page 327)

inauguration *n.* (uh-NAW-gyuh-ray-shun) the ceremony that marks the beginning of a presidency (page 287)

incumbent *n.* (ihn-KUHM-buhnt) the person currently in office; the incumbent president is the current president (page 314)

indentured servant *n.* (ihn-DEHN-churd SUR-vuhnt) a person under contract to work, usually without pay, in exchange for free passage to the colonies (page 93)

Indian Removal Act *n.* (IHN-dee-uhn rih-MOO-vuhl AKT) a law that ended the U.S. government's earlier policy of respecting the rights of Native Americans to remain on their land (page 376)

Indian Territory *n.* (IHN-dee-uhn TAIR-uh-tawr-ee) the area of land in present-day Oklahoma and parts of Kansas and Nebraska to which Native Americans were forced to migrate (page 376)

indigo *n.* (IHN-dih-goh) a plant that produces a blue dye for cloth (page 132)

individualism *n.* (ihn-duh-VIHJ-wuh-lih-zuhm) self-reliant independence (page 398)

Industrial Revolution *n.* (ihn-DUH-stree-uhl rev-oh-LUH-shuhn) an era in which widespread production by machinery replaced goods made by hand (page 336)

infantry *n.* (IHN-fuhn-tree) foot soldiers (page 499)

inflation *n.* (ihn-FLAY-shuhn) a decrease in the value of money that causes an increase in the price of goods and services (page 382)

institution *n.* (ihn-stuh-TOO-shuhn) an established and accepted practice in a society or culture (page 74)

insurrection *n.* (ihn-suh-REK-shun) a rebellion (page 418)

interchangeable part *n.* (ihn-tur-CHAYN-juh-buhl PAHRT) parts of a mechanism that can be substituted one for another (page 338)

interstate slave trade *n.* (IHN-tur-stayt SLAYV TRAYD) the buying and selling of slaves within the United States (page 347)

Intolerable Acts *n.* (ihn-TAHL-ruh-buhl AKTS) the British laws passed to punish the people of Boston after the Boston Tea Party; also called the Coercive Acts (page 194)

ironclad ship *n.* (I-urn-klahd SHIP) a ship armored with iron plates to protect it from cannon fire (page 503)

Iroquois League *n.* (IHR-uh-kwoy) the confederation of five Iroquois-speaking nations: the Mohawk, Oneida, Onondaga, Cayuga, and Seneca; later joined by the Tuscarora (page 29)

irrigation *n.* (eer-uh-GAY-shun) the supply of water to fields using human-made systems (page 24)

J

Jacksonian democracy *n.* (jak-SOH-nee-uhn dih-MAH-kruh-see) a political movement that celebrated the common man and defended the will of the people, named for President Andrew Jackson (page 370)

joint-stock company *n.* (JOYNT STAHK KUHM-puh-nee) a company whose shareholders own stock in the company (page 92)

judicial branch *n.* (joo-DIH-shehl BRANCH) the section of the U.S. government that includes the courts and legal system, led by the Supreme Court; responsible for interpreting the law (page 258)

judicial review *n.* (joo-DIH-shuhl rih-VYOO) the power to invalidate any law the Supreme Court deems unconstitutional, even if it has been passed by Congress and signed into law by the president (page 318)

Judiciary Act of 1801 *n.* (joo-DIH-shee-air-ee AKT UHV 1801) the federal legislation that reduced the number of justices on the Supreme Court from 6 to 5 (page 318)

jurisdiction *n.* (jur-uhs-DIHK-shuhn) the authority to enforce laws within a given area (page 546)

K

kayak *n.* (KAI-yak) a canoe with a light frame and a small opening on top in which to sit (page 26)

King Philip's War *n.* (KING FIH-luhps WOR) a violent conflict between Native Americans and English colonists from New England, who were aided by Native American allies (page 106)

Know-Nothing Party *n.* (NOH-NUH-thing PAHR-tee) a political party formed in the 1850s to oppose immigration, also called the American Party (page 444)

Ku Klux Klan *n.* (KOO KLUHKS KLAN) the group whose purpose was to maintain the social and political power of white people (page 568)

L

labor union *n.* (LAY-bur YOON-yuhn) a voluntary association of workers that uses its power to negotiate better working conditions (page 450)

Legal Tender Act *n.* (LEE-guhl TEHN-dur AKT) an act that replaced the notes of individual banks with a unified national currency (page 532)

legislative branch *n.* (LEH-jeh-slay-tihv BRANCH) the section of the U.S. government led by Congress; responsible for making the law (page 258)

GLOSSARY

levy *v.* (LEH-vee) to require the payment of a tax (page 105)

libel *n.* (LY-buhl) the publishing of lies (page 152)

Liberal Republicans *n.* (LIH-buh-ruhl rih-PUH-blih-kuhnz) a group during the 1870s who believed the government had become too large and too powerful (page 572)

literacy *n.* (LIH-tur-uh-see) the ability to read and write (page 567)

literacy test *n.* (LIH-tur-uh-see TEST) test of one's ability to read and write (page 573)

loose interpretation *n.* (LOOS ihn-tur-pruh-TAY-shuhn) an understanding of the Constitution as one that gives Congress and the president broad powers (page 294)

Louisiana Purchase *n.* (lu-ee-zee-A-nuh PUR-chuhs) a treaty between France and the United States in which a large area of land between the Mississippi River and the Rocky Mountains was purchased (page 321)

Loyalist *n.* (LOY-uh-lihst) an American colonist who supported Britain during the American Revolution (page 198)

lynch *v.* (LINCH) to hang someone illegally by mob action (page 568)

M

manifest destiny *n.* (MAN-uh-fehst DEHS-tuh-nee) the idea that the United States had the right and the obligation to expand its territory across North America to the Pacific Ocean (page 399)

manor system *n.* (MA-nur SIHS-tuhm) an economic system in which peasants are bound to a lord and work his land, or manor, in exchange for food and shelter (page 37)

margin *n.* (MAHR-juhn) the amount by which something is won or lost (page 411)

market revolution *n.* (MAHR-kuht revuh-LOO-shuhn) the transition from a pre-industrial economy to a market-oriented, capitalist economy (page 336)

matrilineal *adj.* (ma-truh-LIN-ee-uhl) relating to descendants traced through the mother (page 29)

Mayflower Compact *n.* (MAY-flow-uhr KAHM-pakt) a shipboard contract signed by the Pilgrims on the Mayflower before they landed in North America, binding them to abide by their own laws and establish a civil society (page 100)

megafauna *n.* (MEH-guh-faw-nuh) the large animals of a particular area in the world or a particular time in history (page 6)

mercantilism *n.* (MUHR-kuhn-teel-ih-zuhm) an economic policy that gives a country sole ownership of the trade occurring in its colonies (page 52)

mercenary *n.* (MUR-suh-nair-ee) a soldier who is paid to fight for a country other than his or her own (page 222)

mestizo *n.* (mes-TEE-zoh) a person who has mixed Spanish and Native American ancestry (page 66)

Middle Passage *n.* (MIH-duhl PA-sihj) the long trip across the Atlantic Ocean by which enslaved Africans were brought to the Americas; the second leg of the triangular trade route (page 73)

midwife *n.* (MIHD-wyf) a person who is trained to help deliver babies (page 146)

migrate *v.* (MY-grayt) to move from one place to another (page 27)

militia *n.* (muh-LIH-shuh) military force made up of local citizens to help protect their town, land, or nation (page 178)

minuteman *n.* (MIH-nuht-man) an American colonial militia member who was ready to join in combat at a moment's notice (page 196)

mission *n.* (MIH-shuhn) a Christian church settlement established to convert native peoples (page 66)

missionary *n.* (MIH-shuh-nair-ee) a person who tries to spread Christianity to others (page 53)

Missouri Compromise *n.* (mih-ZUR-ee KAHM-pruh-myz) an agreement that stated the people of Missouri could own slaves and be admitted to the Union along with Maine, a free state (page 352)

mobilize *v.* (MOH-buh-lyz) to organize and prepare troops for war (page 498)

monopoly *n.* (muh-NAH-puh-lee) the complete and exclusive control of an industry by one company (page 351)

Monroe Doctrine *n.* (muhn-ROH DAHK-truhn) an approach to foreign policy that stated the American continents were no longer under European influence (page 353)

morphine *n.* (MOR-feen) a powerful painkiller (page 542)

mortality *n.* (mor-TAH-luh-tee) the death rate (page 503)

mountain men *n.* (MOWN-tuhn MEHN) the American fur trappers and explorers who began to explore and move west (page 398)

N

national debt *n.* (NA-shuh-nuhl DEHT) the amount of money a government owes to all its creditors, including to other nations and to companies from which it purchases goods and services (page 290)

nationalism *n.* (NA-shuh-nuh-lih-zuhm) the concept of loyalty and devotion to one's nation (page 350)

nativist *n.* (NAY-tih-vihst) a person who believes native-born people should be favored more than immigrants (page 444)

natural resource *n.* (NACH-uh-ruhl REE-sawrs) a material or substance found in nature that can be used to sustain a society or exploited for economic gain, such as minerals, water, or living things (page 114)

natural rights *n.* (NACH-uh-ruhl RYTS) rights such as life or liberty that a person is born with (page 149)

naturalization *n.* (NACH-uh-ruh-lih-ZAY-shuhn) the process of becoming a U.S. citizen for people who are not native-born citizens (page R34)

navigation *n.* (nav-ih-GAY-shuhn) the science of finding position and planning routes, often used in relation to seafaring (page 40)

Navigation Acts *n.* (nav-ih-GAY-shuhn AKTS) a series of laws passed by the English Parliament to protect English shipping by restricting the transport of goods to and from the English colonies (page 125)

neutrality *n.* (noo-TRA-luh-tee) the refusal to take sides or become involved (page 111)

GLOSSARY

Northwest Ordinance of 1787 *n.* (nawrth-WEHST AWR-duh-nuhns UHV 1787) a legislation adopted by Congress to establish stricter control over the government of the Northwest Territory (page 252)

Northwest Passage *n.* (nawrth-WEHST PA-sihj) a passage by water between the Atlantic and Pacific oceans along the northern coast of North America (page 60)

O

oasis *n.* (oh-AY-sihs) a fertile place with water in a desert (page 42)

ordinance *n.* (AWR-duh-nuhns) an official law, decree, or directive (page 252)

Ordinance of 1785 *n.* (AWR-duh-nuhns UHV 1785) a federal law that set up a system to allow settlers to purchase land in the undeveloped West (page 252)

overseer *n.* (OH-vur-see-ur) a supervisor (page 134)

P

pacifist *n.* (PA-suh-fihst) a person who stands against war and violence (page 239)

Panic of 1837 *n.* (PA-nihk UHV 1837) the widespread fear of a failing economy that caused the beginning of a U.S. economic recession that lasted until 1840 (page 383)

Panic of 1873 *n.* (PA-nihk UHV 1873) an economic crisis triggered by bank and railroad failures (page 573)

parallel *n.* (PAIR-uh-lehl) a line of latitude (page 421)

Parliament *n.* (PAHR-luh-muhnt) the legislative body of England, and, later, Great Britain (page 150)

passive resistance *n.* (PA-sihv rih-ZIHS-tuhns) a nonviolent refusal to obey authority and laws (page 349)

Patriot *n.* (PAY-tree-uht) an American colonist who supported the right of the American colonies to govern themselves (page 198)

persecute *v.* (PUR-seh-kyoot) to punish, particularly because of beliefs or background (page 61)

personal responsibility *n.* (PURS-uh-nuhl rih-SPAWN-suh-BIHL-uh-tee) responsibility that is not required but that contributes to a more civil society, such as respecting and standing up for others' rights, helping in the community, and staying informed (page R34)

philanthropist *n.* (fuh-LAN-thruh-pihst) someone who actively promotes human welfare (page 504)

physical geography *n.* (FIH-zih-kuhl jee-AH-gruh-fee) the study of Earth's exterior physical features (page 34)

Piedmont *n.* (PEED-mont) a relatively flat area between the Appalachian Mountains and the coastal plain (page 134)

pilgrimage *n.* (PILL-gruhm-ij) a religious journey (page 45)

pioneer *n.* (py-uh-NIHR) a settler moving to a new and unfamiliar land (page 400)

plantation *n.* (plan-TAY-shuhn) a large farm; on southern plantations slaves worked to grow and harvest crops (page 66)

Pleistocene epoch *n.* (PLEIS-toh-seen EH-puhk) a period in the history of Earth in which large animals and plants existed and glaciers covered Earth (page 5)

poll tax *n.* (POHL TAKS) a fee charged when people register to vote (page 571)

pontoon *n.* (pahn-TOON) a portable, cylindrical float used to build a temporary bridge (page 519)

popular sovereignty *n.* (PAH-pyuh-lur SAHV-run-tee) the idea that the residents of a region or nation decide an issue by voting (page 474)

potlatch *n.* (PAHT-lach) a gift-giving ceremony practiced by the Kwakiutl and Haida Native American tribes (page 26)

power base *n.* (POW-ur BAYS) an area or group of people providing the biggest influence over a political candidate (page 294)

precedent *n.* (PREH-suh-duhnt) a prior event or decision that serves as an example for events or decisions that follow (page 286)

prejudice *n.* (PREH-juh-duhs) a broad judgment about a group of people not based on reason or fact (page 444)

Presidential Reconstruction *n.* (preh-zuh-DEN-shuhl ree-kuhn-STRUHK-shuhn) a policy that stated Confederate states must ratify the 13th Amendment and create new governments with new constitutions before they could rejoin the Union (page 560)

presidio *n.* (prih-SIH-dee-oh) a military post or settlement (page 406)

printing press *n.* (PRIHN-ting PREHS) an invention that used movable metal type to print pages (page 39)

privateer *n.* (PRY-vah-teer) an armed but privately owned ship that acts under the authority of a government to participate in warfare; or a sailor on such a ship (page 62)

Proclamation of 1763 *n.* (prah-kluh-MAY-shuhn UHV 1763) a law requiring colonists to stay east of a line drawn on a map along the crest of the Appalachian Mountains (page 178)

profit *n.* (PRAH-fuht) the amount of money left for a business after expenses are deducted (page 40)

prophet *n.* (PRAH-fuht) someone who is believed to deliver messages from God or some other divine source (page 329)

proprietor *n.* (pruh-PRY-uh-tuhr) a person with ownership of a colony, including the right to manage and distribute land and to establish government (page 112)

prospector *n.* (PRAH-spek-tur) a person who searches in the earth for valuable resources, such as gems or precious metals (page 424)

Protestant *n.* (PRAH-teh-stant) a follower of the Reformation in Christianity (page 39)

provision *n.* (pruh-VIH-zhuhn) a legal condition that anticipates future needs (page 244)

provisions *n.* (pruh-VIH-zhuhnz) the supplies of food, water, and other items needed for a journey (page 124)

proviso *n.* (pruh-VY-zoh) a condition attached to a legal document or legislation (page 421)

push-pull factor *n.* (PUSH PUL FAK-tur) a reason why people immigrate, such as lack of economic opportunity or freedom in one country and the promise of a better life in another (page 438)

GLOSSARY

Q

quarantine *v.* (KWAWR-uhn-teen) to keep infected people away from those who have not yet contracted a disease (page 535)

Quartering Act *n.* (KWAWR-tuh-ring AKT) one of several British laws that required American colonists to provide housing and food for British soldiers stationed in North America (page 178)

quinine *n.* (KWHY-nyn) a substance made from the bark of a tree that is an effective remedy for malaria (page 71)

R

racism *n.* (RAY-sih-zuhm) the belief that one race is better than others (page 472)

radical *n.* (RA-dih-kuhl) a person who supports complete social or political change (page 297)

Radical Reconstruction *n.* (RA-dih-kuhl ree-kuhn-STRUHK-shuhn) the name given to the Republicans' plan in passing the Reconstruction Acts of 1867 (page 562)

rancho *n.* (RAN-choh) land granted by Mexico to settlers in the form of large estates in what is now California (page 423)

ratify *v.* (RA-tuh-fy) to approve formally, by vote (page 250)

rations *n.* (RA-shuhnz) supplied food (page 535)

raw material *n.* (RAW muh-TIHR-ee-uhl) the basic substances and elements used to make products (page 114)

reaper *n.* (REE-pur) a machine that cuts stalks of wheat or oats (page 339)

Reconstruction *n.* (ree-kuhn-STRUHK-shuhn) the effort to rebuild and reunite the United States following the Civil War (page 546)

Reconstruction Acts of 1867 *n.* (ree-kuhn-STRUHK-shuhn AKTS UHV 1867) acts that put the Republican Congress in charge of Reconstruction instead of the president (page 562)

reinforcements *n.* (ree-uhn-FAWRS-muhnts) more soldiers and supplies sent to help military troops engage in warfare (page 224)

religious freedom *n.* (rih-LIH-juhs FREE-duhm) the right to practice the religion of one's choosing without government interference (page 126)

rendezvous *n.* (RAHN-deh-voo) a temporary market where trappers met to trade and socialize (page 398)

repeal *v.* (rih-PEEL) to cancel or nullify, especially a law (page 183)

republic *n.* (RE-puhb-lik) a form of government in which the people elect representatives to speak for them and enact laws based on their needs (page 222)

republican motherhood *n.* (rih-PUH-blih-kuhn MUH-thur-hud) the idea that women should raise their children to be good citizens who participated in the government (page 356)

Republican Party *n.* (rih-PUH-blih-kuhn PAHR-tee) a political party founded in 1854 by antislavery leaders (page 476)

republicanism *n.* (rih-PUH-blih-kuh-nih-zuhm) a government in which people choose representatives to make their laws (page 244)

revenue *n.* (REH-vuh-noo) income; money that is received (page 180)

revival meeting *n.* (rih-VY-vuhl MEE-ting) an informal religious gathering meant to inspire people to join the faith, often held outdoors or in tents (page 446)

royal colony *n.* (ROY-uhl KAH-luh-nee) a colony ruled by a monarch through an appointed governor (page 112)

S

salutary neglect *n.* (SAL-yuh-tair-ee nih-GLEKT) the policy of the British government to not strictly enforce its colonial policies (page 151)

salvation *n.* (sal-VAY-shuhn) the act of being forgiven for wrongdoings or sins (page 148)

scapegoat *n.* (SKAYP-goht) an individual or group blamed for the mistakes or faults of others (page 531)

scurvy *n.* (SCUR-vee) a disease linked to malnutrition and a diet lacking in fruits and vegetables (page 535)

secede *v.* (seh-SEED) to formally withdraw from a nation or organization in order to become independent (page 482)

secession *n.* (seh-SEHSH-ehn) the act of formally withdrawing from an organization, a nation, or any other group in order to be independent (page 375)

Second Continental Congress *n.* (SEHK-und kahn-tuh-NEHN-tuhl KAHN-gruhs) a group of leaders of the American colonies who met to address the problem of British tyranny, declared independence in 1776, and led the United States through the American Revolution (page 203)

Second Great Awakening *n.* (SEHK-und GRAYT uh-WAYK-ning) an American Protestant movement based on revival meetings and a direct and emotional relationship with God (page 446)

sectionalism *n.* (SEHK-shnuh-lih-zuhm) a loyalty to whichever section or region of the country one was from, rather than to the nation as a whole (page 352)

sedition *n.* (sih-DIH-shuhn) the act of provoking rebellion (page 301)

segregation *n.* (seh-grih-GAY-shuhn) the separation of people based on race (page 473)

self-governance *n.* (SELF GUH-vur-nuhnts) the control of one's own affairs; the control of community affairs and laws by those who live there rather than by an outside ruler or monarch (page 105)

Seneca Falls Convention *n.* (SEH-nih-kuh FAWLS kuhn-VEHN-shuhn) an 1848 women's rights convention organized by Elizabeth Cady Stanton and Lucretia Mott in Seneca Falls, New York (page 458)

separation of powers *n.* (seh-puh-RAY-shuhn UHV POW-urs) the division of governmental power among the three branches of U.S. government: the executive branch, the judicial branch, and the legislative branch (page 258)

separatist *n.* (SEH-prah-tihst) a person in the 16th and 17th centuries who wished to leave the Church of England (page 100)

GLOSSARY

serf *n.* (SURF) a person who lived and worked on the private land of a landowner such as a noble or medieval lord (page 37)

servitude *n.* (SUR-vuh-tood) the state of being enslaved (page 546)

sharecropping *n.* (SHAIR-krahp-ing) an agricultural system in which a farmer raises crops for a landowner in return for part of the money made from selling the crops (page 567)

Shays's Rebellion *n.* (SHAYZ rih-BEL-yuhn) the 1786–1787 uprising of Massachusetts farmers in protest of high taxes (page 255)

siege *n.* (SEEJ) a tactic in which a military force surrounds a city in an attempt to take control of it (page 409)

skirmish *n.* (SKUR-mish) a small, short-lasting battle (page 231)

slash-and-burn agriculture *n.* (SLASH AND BURN A-grih-kuhl-chur) a method of clearing fields for planting that involves cutting and setting fire to existing trees and plants (page 29)

slave importation clause *n.* (SLAYVE ihm-pohr-TAY-shuhn KLAWZ) a provision in Article 1 of the U.S. Constitution that established that the United States would not consider prohibiting the international slave trade in the United States until 1808 (page 260)

slavery *n.* (SLAY-veh-ree) a social system in which human beings take complete control of others (page 72)

slogan *n.* (SLOH-guhn) a catchy phrase meant to attract and keep attention (page 370)

smallpox *n.* (SMAWL-poks) a deadly virus that causes a high fever and small blisters on the skin (page 56)

smuggle *v.* (SMUH-guhl) to import or export goods illegally (page 125)

social justice *n.* (SOH-shuhl JUH-stuhs) the fair distribution of opportunities and privileges, including racial equality (page 565)

Sons of Liberty *n.* (SUHNS UHV LIH-bur-tee) the groups of merchants, shopkeepers, and craftsmen who successfully opposed the Stamp Act by establishing networks to boycott British goods (page 183)

sovereign *adj.* (SAH-vuh-ruhn) having the right to self-rule or independent government (page 250)

spiritual *n.* (SPIHR-ih-chuh-wuhl) a religious song based on scripture and biblical figures in the Bible, first sung by enslaved people in the South (page 349)

spoils system *n.* (SPOY-uhlz SIHS-tuhm) the practice of rewarding political backers with government jobs (page 373)

stalemate *n.* (STAYL-mayt) a situation in which neither side in a conflict is able to win (page 524)

Stamp Act *n.* (STAMP AKT) the British law requiring colonists to purchase a stamp for official documents and published papers (page 182)

states' rights *n.* (STAYTS RITES) the concept that individual states have rights that the federal government cannot violate (page 301)

statute *n.* (STA-choot) a formal, written law (page 267)

steamboat *n.* (STEEM-boht) a boat outfitted with steam boiler engines to power the paddle wheels that propel it forward (page 339)

steerage *n.* (STEER-ehg) the inferior section of a ship housing passengers who pay the lowest fare for the journey (page 438)

steppe *n.* (STEP) a vast, grassy plain (page 42)

Stono Rebellion *n.* (STOH-noh rih-BEL-yuhn) a 1739 revolt by enslaved Africans against their owners (page 137)

strict interpretation *n.* (STRIHKT ihn-tur-pruh-TAY-shuhn) an understanding of the Constitution as one in which the Constitution is strictly followed as it was written (page 294)

strike *n.* (STRYK) a work stoppage in order to force an employer to comply with demands (page 336)

subsidy *n.* (SUHB-suh-dee) government funds for improvements or support of commerce (page 350)

subsistence farming *n.* (suhb-SIHS-tuhnts FAHR-ming) the practice of producing enough food for a farmer and his family but not enough to sell for profit (page 123)

suffrage *n.* (SUH-frihj) the right to vote (page 459)

Sugar Act *n.* (SHU-gur AKT) the British law that lowered the duty on molasses to cut out smuggling, so that the British would get the revenue (page 181)

Supreme Court *n.* (soo-PREEM KORT) the highest court in the United States (page 258)

T

tariff *n.* (TAIR-uhf) a tax on imports and exports (page 290)

Tariff of Abominations *n.* (TAIR-uhf UHV uh-bah-muh-NAY-shuhns) the term used by southerners to refer to the Tariff of 1828 because it stirred feelings of disgust and hatred (page 374)

Tea Act *n.* (TEE AKT) the British law stating that only the East India Company was allowed to sell tea to the American colonists (page 191)

telegraph *n.* (TEHL-uh-graf) a machine that sends messages long distances by sending electrical pulses in code over electrical wires (page 339)

temperance movement *n.* (TEHM-pur-uhns MOOV-mehnt) 19th-century reform movement that encouraged the reduction or elimination of alcoholic beverage consumption (page 446)

tepee *n.* (TEE-pee) a cone-shaped tent made of bison hides (page 27)

terrain *n.* (tuh-RAYN) the physical features of the land (page 204)

textile *n.* (TEHKS-ty-uhl) the cloth and clothing made from cotton and other raw materials (page 336)

Three-Fifths Compromise *n.* (THREE FIFTHS KAHM-pruh-myz) the agreement that determined that only three-fifths of the total population of enslaved persons in a state would be counted for purposes of taxation and representation (page 260)

tolerance *n.* (TAH-luh-runts) the acceptance of others (page 144)

total war *n.* (TOH-tuhl WOR) a war in which all rules and laws of war are ignored and all resources are used for defeating the enemy (page 538)

GLOSSARY

Townshend Acts *n.* (TOWN-sehnd AKTS) a set of British laws that placed duties on tea, glass, paper, lead, and paint; required colonists to purchase from Britain (page 186)

trading post *n.* (TRAYD-ing POHST) a small settlement established for the purpose of exchanging goods (page 155)

Trail of Tears *n.* (TRAYL UHV TEHRS) the route the Cherokees and other Native Americans took during their forced migration from the southeast United States to Oklahoma (page 381)

traitor *n.* (TRAY-tohr) a person who betrays his or her own people, nation, or cause (page 99)

trans-Saharan *adj.* (tran-suh-HAHR-uhn) across the Sahara (page 42)

transcendentalism *n.* (tran-sehn-DEHN-tuh-li-zuhm) an intellectual and social movement of the 1830s and 1840s that called for rising above society's expectations (page 452)

treason *n.* (TREE-zuhn) the crime of aiding the enemy of one's nation or plotting to overthrow one's nation; the act of being disloyal to one's nation (page 375)

treaty *n.* (TREE-tee) a peace agreement (page 158)

Treaty of Greenville *n.* (TREE-tee UHV GREEN-vihl) a treaty between the United States and a number of Native American nations in which the Native American nations gave up their lands in present-day Ohio and Indiana to the United Sates (page 296)

Treaty of Paris of 1783 *n.* (TREE-tee UHV PAIR-uhs UHV 1783) the binding agreement between Britain and the United States in which Britain acknowledged American independence, and the initial borders of the United States were determined (page 244)

trench warfare *n.* (TREHNCH WOR-fair) a battle strategy that uses a system of ditches to give soldiers a protected place from which to fire during battle (page 503)

triangular trade *n.* (try-ANG-gyuh-lur TRAYD) a transatlantic trade network formed by Europe, West Africa, and the Americas (page 73)

tributary *n.* (TRIH-byoo-tair-ee) a creek, stream, or river that flows into a larger river or other body of water (page 112)

truce *n.* (TROOS) an agreement to stop fighting (page 379)

tundra *n.* (TUHN-druh) the flat treeless land found in arctic and subarctic regions (page 26)

tyranny *n.* (TEER-uh-nee) unjust rule by an absolute ruler (page 181)

U

unalienable right *n.* (uhn-AY-lee-uhn-ah-buh RITE) a right that cannot be taken away (page 208)

unconstitutional *adj.* (uhn-KAHNT-stuh-too-shnuhl) an idea or law that goes against the principles of the U.S. Constitution (page 318)

Underground Railroad *n.* (uhn-dur-GROWND RAYL-rohd) a network of people who worked together to help African Americans escape from slavery from the southern United States to the northern states or to Canada before the Civil War (page 455)

Unionist *n.* (YOON-yuh-nihst) a member of the Constitutional Union Party (page 480)

unorganized territory *n.* (uhn-AWR-guh-nyzd TAIR-uh-tawr-ee) lands governed by the federal government but not belonging to any state (page 353)

V

vassal *n.* (VA-suhl) in the medieval European feudal system, a person, usually a lesser nobleman, who received land and protection from a feudal lord in exchange for obedience and service (page 36)

veteran *n.* (VEH-tuh-ruhn) a person who has served in the military (page 542)

veto *v.* (VEE-toh) to formally reject a decision or proposal made by a legislature (page 383)

viceroy *n.* (VYSE-roy) a governor of Spain's colonies in the Americas who represented the Spanish king and queen (page 58)

viceroyalty *n.* (vyse-ROHY-uhl-tee) a territory governed by a viceroy (page 58)

voting rights *n.* (VOHT-ing RITES) the laws that tell who can vote and when; the civil right to vote (page 370)

W

wage economy *n.* (WAYJ ih-KAH-nuh-mee) an economy in which people are paid for their work (page 567)

wagon train *n.* (WA-guhn TRAYN) a large group of covered wagons that traveled together across the North American continent as American pioneers moved westward (page 404)

War Hawk *n.* (WOR HAWK) a person who approved of and encouraged war; an American who favored war with Great Britain in 1812 (page 329)

War of 1812 *n.* (WOR UHV 1812) the war against Great Britain that James Madison declared (page 330)

watershed *n.* (WAH-tuhr-shed) an area of land that includes a particular river or lake and all the bodies of water that flow into it (page 64)

Whig Party *n.* (WIHG PAHR-tee) a political party formed to oppose the policies of Andrew Jackson, who the party believed had exceeded his power as president (page 384)

Whiskey Rebellion *n.* (HWIH-skee rih-BEL-yuhn) a series of violent protests among farmers in western Pennsylvania against a tax on whiskey (page 297)

writ *n.* (RIHT) a legal document (page 318)

writs of assistance *n.* (RIHTS UHV uh-SIHS-tuhns) a legal document giving authorities the right to enter and search a home or business (page 186)

X

XYZ Affair *n.* (X Y Z uh-FAIR) the meeting with French agents after France began seizing American ships in the late 18th century in an effort to prevent U.S. trade with Britain (page 301)

Y

yellow fever *n.* (YEH-loh FEE-vur) an often fatal disease carried by mosquitoes in tropical climates (page 320)

abomination *n.* (uh-bah-muh-NAY-shuhn) a thing worthy of hatred or disgust (page 374)

acclaim *n.* (uh-KLAYM) enthusiastic praise (page 293)

acquisition *n.* (a-kwuh-ZIH-shuhn) the act of obtaining something as one's own; an item obtained (page 37)

allegory *n.* (A-luh-gor-ee) a story told through symbols, in which the characters and other story elements represent human actions and emotions (page 452)

ardent *adj.* (AHR-duhnt) very eager; passionate (page 290)

arduous *adj.* (AHR-juh-wuhs) difficult; requiring great effort to achieve (page 403)

arid *adj.* (AIR-uhd) extremely dry (as a desert) (page 24)

covenant *n.* (KUH-vuh-nuhnt) an agreement or promise between two parties (page 179)

divisive *adj.* (duh-VY-sihv) causing angry dissent and disunity (page 470)

dumbfounded *adj.* (DUHM-fownd-uhd) at a loss for words (page 58)

encompass *v.* (ihn-KUHM-puhs) to form a circle around; to surround; to include (page 567)

fertile *adj.* (FUR-tuhl) capable of growing plants (page 24)

fervor *n.* (FUR-vur) an intense feeling (page 447)

formidable *adj.* (FOR-mih-duh-buhl) awe inspiring, usually in a menacing way (page 223)

iconography *n.* (ai-kuh-NAH-gruh-fee) the representative objects or symbols of a culture or religion (page 131)

indispensable *adj.* (ihn-dih-SPENT-suh-buhl) necessary; cannot be done without (page 103)

intervene *v.* (ihn-tur-VEEN) to interfere, usually to force or prevent an action (page 405)

intimidate *v.* (ihn-TIH-muh-dayt) to use threats, usually to make someone do one's bidding (page 379)

legacy *n.* (LEH-guh-see) a body of knowledge or accomplishment from the past (page 250)

lenient *adj.* (LEE-nee-uhnt) tolerant; easygoing (page 560)

manor *n.* (MA-nur) an estate, or the central house on an estate (page 64)

martyr *n.* (MAHR-tur) a person who sacrifices his or her life or something of great value for the good of a cause (page 477)

mechanized *adj.* (MEH-kuh-nyzd) carried out entirely or in part with machines (page 336)

militant *adj.* (MIHL-uh-tuhnt) combative and aggressive; acting as one fighting a war (page 475)

monetary *adj.* (MAH-nuh-tair-ee) taking the form of money (page 311)

nullify *v.* (NUH-luh-fy) to negate, especially in legal terms (page 374)

offensive *n.* (uh-FENT-sihv) the fighting initiated by one side in a war (page 231)

orthodox *adj.* (OR-thuh-dahks) following a strict religious doctrine (page 101)

pardon *v.* (PAHR-duhn) to forgive or excuse (page 560)

philosophy *n.* (fuh-LAH-suh-fee) the basic beliefs of a person or group (page 39)

prestigious *adj.* (preh-STIH-juhs) having a reputation of quality, esteem, and respect (page 370)

prosthetic *n.* (prahs-THEH-tihk) an artificial limb or body part (page 502)

rehabilitate *v.* (ree-uh-BIH-luh-tayt) to restore to previous health or reputation (page 449)

replenish *v.* (rih-PLEH-nish) to fill up again (page 503)

rhetoric *n.* (REH-tuh-rihk) the way words are used to express an idea, usually to persuade (page 570)

shrapnel *n.* (SHRAP-nuhl) the sharp pieces of an exploded shell or cannonball (page 172)

specimen *n.* (SPE-suh-muhn) one example of something from nature, such as a certain plant, animal, or mineral (page 308)

sphere *n.* (SFEER) an area defining one's function or authority (page 336)

survey *n.* (sur-VAY) a measurement to establish land boundaries (page 252)

susceptible *adj.* (suh-SEHP-tuh-buhl) open to being affected or influenced by something (page 535)

tenure *n.* (TEHN-yur) the act of holding something of value, such as land or an important position, or the term during which such a thing is held (page 563)

valor *n.* (VA-lur) the quality of great courage or bravery (page 528)

GLOSARIO

A

abolición *s.* acto de poner fin a algo, como la esclavitud (página 357)

abolicionista *s.* persona que quería que la esclavitud terminara (página 454)

acatamiento *s.* obediencia a un conjunto de creencias (página 144)

actividad económica *s.* operaciones de producción, distribución y consumo de bienes y servicios (página 114)

afluente *s.* arroyo, riachuelo o río que desemboca en un río más grande o en otra masa de agua (página 112)

agente federal *(marshal) s.* agente del orden público que trabaja para el gobierno de los Estados Unidos (página 471)

agrario(a) *adj.* relativo al campo o la agricultura (página 374)

agricultura de subsistencia *s.* modo de producir suficientes alimentos para el granjero y su familia, pero no para la venta (página 123)

agricultura de tala y quema *s.* método de despejar los campos para sembrar cultivos que consiste en cortar y quemar los árboles y las plantas existentes (página 29)

alfabetizar *s.* enseñar a leer y escribir (página 567)

alianza *s.* acuerdo entre naciones para luchar en contra de los enemigos de cada una o para colaborar entre ellas; pacto (página 111)

alistarse *v.* unirse a la milicia (página 528)

anexar *v.* agregar (página 399)

antifederalista *s.* persona que se oponía a la Constitución de EE. UU. de 1787 porque el énfasis de esta era un gobierno nacional poderoso (página 262)

aparcería *s.* sistema agrícola en donde los jornaleros levantan la cosecha de un terrateniente a cambio de recibir una parte de la venta de dichas cosechas (página 567)

aprendiz *s.* persona que aprende un arte u oficio manual trabajando junto a un experto en ese arte u oficio (página 129)

arancel *s.* impuesto a las importaciones y exportaciones (página 290)

arancel de aduana *s.* impuesto a las importaciones (página 181)

arancel de las abominaciones *s.* término usado por los sureños para referirse al arancel de 1828 porque lo consideraban odioso y opresivo (página 374)

artesano *s.* persona que realiza a mano objetos con gran destreza (página 136)

Artículos de la Confederación *s.* conjunto de leyes adoptado por los Estados Unidos en 1777, que establecía cada estado de la Unión como una república, reemplazado por la Constitución en 1789 (página 222)

artillería *s.* cañones y armas largas que disparan a gran distancia (página 203)

asimilar *v.* adoptar la cultura o forma de vida de la nación donde se vive (página 376, 441)

Asunto XYZ *s.* reunión con agentes franceses luego de que Francia comenzara a capturar barcos estadounidenses para prevenir el comercio entre EE. UU. y Gran Bretaña (página 301)

autonomía *s.* control de sus propios asuntos por parte de uno mismo; control de los asuntos y leyes de una comunidad por parte de aquellos que viven en ella y no por parte de un monarca o gobernante ajeno (página 105)

B

baja *s.* persona muerta o herida en combate (página 548)

barco de vapor *s.* barco equipado con calderas de vapor que impulsaban ruedas giratorias para hacerlo navegar (página 339)

base de poder *s.* zona o grupo de personas que provee la mayor influencia sobre un candidato político (página 294)

bayoneta *s.* cuchillo afilado que se une a la boca de un fusil (página 228)

bloquear *v.* cortar la entrada o salida de barcos de una bahía (página 228)

boicot *s.* forma de protesta que rechaza la compra de bienes o servicios (página 183)

bono *s.* bono *s.* certificado puesto a la venta al público por el gobierno con la promesa de pagar esa cantidad en una fecha posterior (página 532)

C

caballería *s.* tropas de un ejército que luchan montadas a caballo (página 499)

Cabeza de Cobre *s.* apodo peyorativo para designar a los miembros del Partido Demócrata que en los estados de la Unión se oponían a la emancipación de los esclavos y al reclutamiento (página 570)

cacicazgo *s.* comunidad de personas regida por un cacique o jefe (página 9)

californio *s.* residente de California de descendencia española o mexicana y que vivía allí antes de la fiebre del oro (página 425)

Camino de Lágrimas *s.* ruta que los cheroquis y otras tribus norteamericanas tomaron durante su migración forzada desde el sureste de los Estados Unidos hacia Oklahoma (página 381)

cañonero *s.* embarcación rápida y pequeña que llevaba cañones (página 516)

capataz *s.* supervisor (página 134)

carabela *s.* barco pequeño y rápido usado por los exploradores españoles y portugueses (página 40)

caravana *s.* grupo de personas y animales que viajan juntos, usualmente para comerciar (página 42)

caravana *s.* grupo grande de carretas cubiertas, una detrás de otra, donde viajaban los pioneros a través de Norteamérica hacia el Oeste (página 404)

carreta Conestoga *s.* tipo de carreta diseñada por colonos alemanes en Norteamérica para llevar cargas pesadas (página 143)

GLOSARIO

caso Dred Scott *s.* decisión de la Corte Suprema que dictaminó que los afroamericanos no tenían derechos como ciudadanos y que invalidó el Compromiso de Missouri de 1820; Dred Scott, el esclavo en cuestión, fue devuelto a la esclavitud (página 476)

cateador *s.* persona que busca en la tierra recursos minerales valiosos, especialmente piedras y metales preciosos (página 424)

cazador-recolector *s.* ser humano que cazaba animales y recolectaba plantas silvestres para su alimentación (página 7)

ceder *v.* renunciar (página 296)

cédula real *s.* título por escrito que concede el establecimiento de una institución y que detalla derechos y privilegios de los miembros (página 92)

chivo expiatorio *s.* individuo o grupo culpado por los errores o las faltas de otros (página 531)

circunnavegar *v.* viajar por completo alrededor de la Tierra (página 62)

ciudad en auge *s.* ciudad cuya población aumenta repetinamente y en grandes cantidades (página 426)

ciudadanía *s.* la condición de tener los derechos y deberes de los ciudadanos (página R33)

civil *s.* persona que no es militar (página 505)

civilización *s.* sociedad con una cultura y una tecnología muy desarrolladas (página 24)

cláusula *s.* condición adjunta a un documento legal o ley (página 421)

cláusula de comercio *s.* disposición del Artículo 1 de la Constitución de EE. UU., que otorga al Congreso el poder de hacer leyes con respecto al comercio internacional, entre estados y con las naciones indígenas (página 260)

cláusula de esclavo fugitivo *s.* disposición del Artículo 4 de la Constitución de EE. UU., que prohíbe a los estados libres la liberación de trabajadores esclavos que se hayan escapado de sus amos en otros estados (página 260)

cláusula de importación de esclavos *s.* disposición del Artículo 1 de la Constitución de EE. UU., que establece que los Estados Unidos no considerará prohibir el comercio internacional de esclavos en el país hasta 1808 (página 260)

clientelismo *s.* práctica que recompensa a los partidarios políticos con puestos en el gobierno (página 373)

códigos negros *s.* leyes aprobadas por los estados sureños inmediatamente después de la Guerra Civil para controlar y limitar los derechos de los afroamericanos; fueron revocadas durante la Reconstrucción en 1866 (página 562)

Colegio electoral *s.* grupo que elige al presidente de los EE. UU.; cada estado tiene un número de electores igual al número de sus representates y senadores en el Congreso (página 258)

colonia real *s.* colonia gobernada por un monarca a través de un gobernador designado (página 112)

comercio de esclavos interestatal *s.* la compra y venta de esclavos dentro de los Estados Unidos (página 347)

comercio triangular *s.* red transatlántica de comercio formada por Europa, África Occidental y las Américas (página 73)

comité de correspondencia *s.* en la época de la independencia, grupo de colonos cuyo deber era hacer correr la voz para la organización de protestas contra los británicos (página 191)

Compra de Gadsden *s.* venta de tierras de México a los Estados Unidos en 1853, que estableció la frontera suroeste actual de los EE. UU. (página 421)

Compra de Louisiana *s.* tratado entre Francia y los Estados Unidos, por el cual fue comprada una gran extensión de tierras entre el río Mississippi y las montañas Rocosas (página 321)

Compromiso de 1877 *s.* acuerdo mediante el cual el Partido Demócrata se comprometió a reconocer a Hayes como presidente a cambio de que los Republicanos concluyeran la Reconstrucción y retiraran a las tropas federales del Sur (página 573)

Compromiso de las tres quintas partes *s.* acuerdo en el cual se determinó que solo tres quintas partes de la población total de esclavos en un estado se tomarían en cuenta para objetivos de impuestos y representación (3/5) (página 260)

Compromiso de Missouri *s.* acuerdo que estableció que Missouri podía tener esclavos y a su vez ser admitido a la Unión junto con Maine, un estado libre (página 352)

confederación *s.* acuerdo entre varios grupos, estados o gobiernos para protegerse y apoyarse unos a otros en batallas u otros emprendimientos (página 111)

Confederación *s.* los 11 estados que se separaron de la Unión para formar su propia nación: los Estados Confederados de América (página 482)

conquistador *s.* explorador español que buscaba oro y otras riquezas en las Américas (página 56)

constitución *s.* documento que organiza los poderes de un gobierno y los estados (página 250)

constitucionalismo *s.* sistema de gobernar basándose en una constitución (página 251)

contiguo *adj.* junto a algo (página 421)

contraataque *s.* ataque en respuesta a un ataque previo (página 227)

contrabandear *v.* importar y exportar productos de manera ilegal (página 125)

Convención de Seneca Falls *s.* convención por los derechos de la mujer, organizada por Elizabeth Cady Stanton y Lucretia Mott en Seneca Falls, Nueva York, en 1848 (página 458)

convertir *v.* persuadir a alguien para que cambie sus creencias religiosas (página 43)

corrupción *s.* deshonestidad, ilegalidad (página 572)

corsario *s.* buque mercante privado autorizado por un gobierno para perseguir a las embarcaciones enemigas siguiendo las leyes de guerra, o un marinero a bordo ese tipo de barco (página 62)

Corte Suprema *s.* la corte o tribunal más alto de justicia en EE. UU. (página 258)

crédito *s.* privilegio para comprar algo o pedir prestado dinero, devolviendo el dinero con el tiempo (página 254)

cuarentena *v.* acción de mantener aislados a quienes han contraído alguna enfermedad de aquellas personas que aún no han sido infectadas (página 535)

cuenca *s.* área de tierra que incluye un río o lago en particular y todos los cuerpos de agua que afluyen al mismo (página 64)

cultivable *adj.* apto para cultivos; fértil (página 140)

cultivo comercial *s.* cultivo plantado para la venta y no para el consumo del granjero (página 132)

D

Decimoquinta Enmienda *s.* enmienda efectuada a la Constitución de los Estados Unidos de América, que establece que los gobiernos federal y estatal no pueden limitar el derecho al voto en virtud de la raza, el color de la piel o por una condición previa de esclavitud (página 570)

Declaración de Derechos *s.* las diez primeras enmiendas a la Constitución de EE. UU.; lista de garantías a las que tienen derecho todas las personas del país (página 263)

Declaración de Independencia *s.* documento que declara la independencia de los Estados Unidos de Gran Bretaña, emitido el 4 de julio de 1776 (página 208)

delegado *s.* persona elegida para representar a un grupo de personas (página 256)

democracia jacksoniana *s.* movimiento político que honraba al hombre común y defendía la voluntad del pueblo; su nombre deriva de Andrew Jackson (página 370)

depresión *s.* período de baja actividad económica, cuando muchas personas se quedan sin trabajo (página 383)

derecho al voto *s.* ley que establece quién puede votar y cuándo; derecho civil a votar (página 370)

derecho estatal *s.* concepto de que los estados individuales tienen derechos que el gobierno federal no puede violar (página 301)

derecho inalienable *s.* derecho que no se puede quitar (página 208)

derechos naturales *s.* derechos de una persona desde su nacimiento, como a la vida o a la libertad (página 149)

derogar *v.* cancelar o revocar, especialmente una ley (página 183)

desertar *v.* huir del ejército o de otra fuerza armada para evitar el servicio militar (página 231)

desertar *v.* abandonar una obligación o causa (página 572)

desmotadora de algodón *s.* máquina que separa las fibras de algodón de sus semillas y vainas (página 346)

desterrar *v.* expulsar a alguien de un territorio como castigo, generalmente sin la esperanza de regresar (página 101)

destino manifiesto *s.* idea de que los Estados Unidos tenían el derecho y la obligación de expandir su territorio a través de Norteamérica hacia el océano Pacífico (página 399)

deuda nacional *s.* cantidad de dinero que un país debe a todos sus acreedores, que incluyen otros países y compañías a las que compra bienes y servicios (página 290)

diáspora africana *s.* el traslado de africanos de su lugar natal a las Américas (página 74)

difamación *s.* publicación con la intención de desacreditar (página 152)

diplomático *s.* persona enviada a otro país para representar los intereses del suyo propio (página 417)

Discurso de Gettysburg *s.* discurso pronunciado en 1863 por el presidente Lincoln para conmemorar a los caídos en la Batalla de Gettysburg, y para instaurar un cementerio militar en ese sitio (página 537)

disidente *s.* persona que se separa de la creencia u opinión de la mayoría (página 100)

disposición *s.* condición legal que anticipa necesidades futuras, o para evitar un mal (página 244)

diversidad *s.* amplia variedad (página 143)

divisoria continental *s.* punto alto en las montañas Rocosas que marca la divisoria de aguas, o vertientes hidrográficas, que van a los océanos Atlántico y Pacífico (página 403)

doble soberanía *s.* sistema en el cual los gobiernos de los estados tienen ciertos poderes que el gobierno federal no puede desautorizar (página 257)

doctrina *s.* conjunto de ideas o creencias aceptadas por un grupo (página 109)

doctrina de anulación *s.* doctrina que decía que un estado podía anular o rechazar una ley federal si creía que era inconstitucional, apoyada por un político sureño antes de la Guerra Civil (página 374)

Doctrina Monroe *s.* enfoque de política exterior que expresaba que las Américas ya no estaban bajo el influjo europeo (página 353)

domesticación *s.* práctica de criar animales y cultivar plantas para el beneficio humano (página 9)

domesticar *v.* cultivar plantas y criar animales para que sean útiles a los seres humanos (página 27)

drumlin *s.* montículo pequeño de laderas lisas formado por sedimentos glaciares; también llamado "cresta de una colina" (página 204)

E

economía asalariada *s.* economía donde se remunera a los trabajadores (página 567)

Ejército Continental *s.* ejército norteamericano formado en 1775 en el Segundo Congreso Continental y liderado por el general George Washington (página 203)

emancipación *s.* fin de la esclavitud (página 454)

embargo *s.* ley que limita o prohíbe el comercio con una o más naciones (página 327)

emigrar *v.* irse de un país para vivir en otro (página 438)

en ejercicio *adj.* persona que ocupa el cargo en el presente; el presidente en ejercicio es el presidente actual (página 314)

GLOSARIO

encomienda *s.* sistema de España en sus colonias en América, en el cual colonos ricos recibían terrenos y se les permitía esclavizar a las personas que allí vivían (página 66)

enmienda *s.* cambio oficial a una ley, generalmente con respecto a un cambio oficial a la Constitución de EE. UU. (página 263)

enviado *n.* embajador (página 300)

escaramuza *s.* lucha de corta duración (página 231)

esclavitud *s.* sistema social en el cual unas personas toman control total sobre otras (página 72)

esclavitud como propiedad personal *s.* sistema según el cual las personas esclavizadas no tienen ningún derecho humano y se clasifican como bienes (página 72)

escorbuto *s.* enfermedad vinculada a la malnutrición y a una dieta carente de frutas y verduras (página 535)

escuela común *(common school)* *s.* nombre que se le daba a la escuela primaria en las colonias (página 129)

eslogan *s.* frase breve y fácil de recordar hecha para atraer y llamar la atención (página 370)

espionaje *s.* práctica de espiar para obtener información (página 232)

espiritual *s.* canto religioso basado en figuras bíblicas y de las escrituras de la Biblia cristiana, cantado por primera vez por los esclavos del Sur (página 349)

estado fronterizo *s.* estado que limitaba tanto con los estados de la Unión como con los estados Confederados, específicamente Maryland, Kentucky, Delaware, Missouri y Virginia Occidental (página 497)

estancamiento *s.* situación en la que ninguna de las partes de un conflicto tiene posibilidad de ganar (página 524)

estatuto *s.* ley oficial escrita (página 267)

estepa *s.* planicie amplia y cubierta de hierbas (página 42)

evacuar *v.* dejar un lugar, generalmente para evitar el peligro (página 496)

evangelizar *v.* predicar las creencias de una religión mediante charlas públicas y testimonios personales (página 446)

examen de lectoescritura *s.* prueba aplicada para evaluar la capacidad de alguien para leer y escribir (página 573)

exención *s.* librar de obligaciones a alguien (página 530)

éxodo *s.* salida masiva de personas (página 403)

expandirse *v.* extenderse; aumentar de manera rápida (página 146)

F

factor de expulsión o atracción *s.* razón por la cual las personas migran, por ejemplo, por falta de oportunidades económicas o de libertad en un país y la promesa de una vida mejor en otro país (página 438)

federal *adj.* gobierno en el cual el poder es compartido entre el gobierno nacional central y el de los estados o provincias (página 250)

federalismo *s.* apoyo al gobierno en el cual el poder es compartido entre el gobierno nacional central y los estados o provincias (página 257)

federalista *s.* persona que apoyaba la Constitución de EE. UU. de 1787 según se redactó durante el proceso de ratificación (página 262)

feudalismo *s.* sistema político y social en el que un vasallo recibe protección de un señor feudal a cambio de prestarle obediencia y servicio (página 36)

fiebre amarilla *s.* enfermedad, con frecuencia mortal, transmitida por mosquitos en climas tropicales (página 320)

filántropo(a) *s.* persona que promueve activamente el bienestar de los demás (página 504)

financista *s.* persona que presta o maneja dinero para un negocio u emprendimiento (página 229)

fiscal general *s.* miembro del Gabinete del presidente, cuyo papel principal es representar a los EE. UU. ante la Corte Suprema (página 289)

flotilla *s.* flota pequeña o compuesta de buques de menor calado (página 536)

fortificación *s.* estructura construida para proteger un lugar de un ataque (página 227)

forty-niner *(buscador de oro)* *s.* uno de los miles de futuros mineros que viajaron a California a buscar oro en 1849 (página 425)

Framers **(autores de la Constitución)** *s.* término histórico para los delegados en la Convención Constitucional de 1787, quienes ayudaron a crear y redactar la Constitución de los Estados Unidos (página 256)

G

Gabinete *s.* los jefes de los departamentos que asisten al presidente de los EE. UU. (página 287)

galeón *s.* buque de vela grande usado especialmente por los españoles en los siglos XVI y XVII (página 62)

ganancia *s.* cantidad de dinero que sobra después de descontar los gastos (página 40)

geografía física *s.* estudio de las características físicas externas de la Tierra (página 34)

geografía humana *s.* estudio de la influencia que tiene la geografía física sobre las personas y su cultura, así como de los efectos que producen las actividades humanas sobre el medio ambiente (página 34)

geología *s.* estudio de los cambios que formaron las rocas y los accidentes geográficos de la Tierra (página 204)

Glaciación *s.* período en la historia durante el cual inmensas capas de hielo cubrían gran parte de la superficie terrestre (página 5)

Gran Despertar *s.* serie de avivamientos religiosos protestantes que se extendieron por las colonias en Norteamérica (página 148)

guarnición *s.* tropa de defensa (página 485)

Guerra de 1812 *s.* guerra contra Gran Bretaña declarada por James Madison (página 330)

guerra de trincheras *s.* estrategia de guerra que usa un sistema de zanjas de protección desde donde los soldados disparan durante la batalla (página 503)

guerra defensiva *s.* guerra para proteger su propio país de ataques extranjeros, luchada en tierras conocidas (página 222)

Guerra del rey Philip *s.* conflicto violento entre indígenas americanos y colonos ingleses de Nueva Inglaterra, ayudados estos últimos por indígenas aliados (página 106)

guerra sin cuartel *s.* guerra en la cual se ignoran todos los convenios bélicos y se usan todos los recursos para vencer al enemigo (página 538)

guerrillero(a) *adj.* que usa tácticas de ataque encubiertas y sabotajes (página 237)

H

hábeas corpus *s.* derecho de una persona arrestada para comparecer ante un juez antes de ser encarcelada (página 531)

hacienda *s.* plantación grande en una colonia española (página 66)

Halcón de Guerra *s.* persona partidaria de la guerra; estadounidense que estaba a favor de la guerra contra Gran Bretaña en 1812 (página 329)

hambruna *s.* escasez extrema de cultivos o alimentos, que causa hambre generalizada (página 440)

hereje *s.* persona que tiene creencias diferentes a las enseñanzas de la Iglesia Católica (página 61)

***Hessians* (hesianos)** *s.* soldados alemanes contratados por los británicos para luchar durante la Guerra de Independencia (página 206)

Hijos de la Libertad *s.* grupos de mercaderes, comerciantes y artesanos que se organizaron con éxito para rechazar la Ley del Timbre mediante el boicot a los productos británicos (página 183)

hombres de montaña *s.* cazadores y comerciantes de pielesconocidos como tramperos que contribuyeron con la exploración del Oeste (página 398)

huelga *s.* huelga s. interrupción del trabajo para forzar a un empleador a cumplir con ciertas demandas (página 336)

humanismo *s.* movimiento basado en la importancia del individuo (página 39)

I

Ilustración *s.* movimiento intelectual caracterizado por el uso de la razón para revisar creencias aceptadas anteriormente (página 149)

imponer *v.* requerir el pago de un impuesto (página 105)

imprenta *s.* invención que usaba letras móviles de metal para imprimir páginas (página 39)

impuesto electoral *s.* cuota impuesta a los ciudadanos al registrarse en el padrón electoral (página 571)

incendio intencional *s.* incendio ilegal provocado de manera deliberada en contra de propiedades y edificios (página 568)

inconstitucional *adj.* idea o ley que va en contra de los principios de la Constitución de los EE. UU. (página 318)

independizarse *v.* separarse oficialmente de una nación u organización para hacerse independiente (página 482)

indiferencia saludable *s.* política del gobierno británico que evitaba que sus leyes en las colonias se cumplieran estrictamente (página 151)

índigo *s.* planta que produce un tinte azul para teñir telas (página 132)

individualismo *s.* independencia autosuficiente (página 398)

infantería *s.* tropas de soldados a pie (página 499)

inflación *s.* disminución en el valor de una moneda que causa el aumento en el precio de bienes y servicios (página 382)

ingreso *s.* recaudación de dinero; dinero que se recibe (página 180)

inmigrar *v.* llegar a vivir a un país de manera permanente (página 438)

inmunidad *s.* protección contra una enfermedad, ya sea natural o provocada por vacunación (página 70)

institución *s.* práctica establecida y aceptada en una sociedad o una cultura (página 74)

insurrección *s.* rebelión (página 418)

intercambio colombino *s.* intercambio de plantas, animales, microbios, personas e ideas entre Europa y las Américas después del primer viaje de Colón al Hemisferio Occidental (página 70)

interpretación estricta *s.* un entendimiento de la Constitución en el cual la Constitución debe ser seguida estrictamente como fue redactada (página 294)

interpretación flexible *s.* un entendimiento de la Constitución que le da al Congreso y al presidente amplios poderes (página 294)

***ironclad* (barco blindado)** *s.* barco revestido con planchas de hierro para protegerlo del fuego de los cañones (página 503)

irrigación *s.* suministro de agua a los campos mediante el uso de sistemas hechos por el hombre (página 24)

J

jerarquía *s.* clasificación de un grupo de personas de acuerdo con su capacidad o con su posición económica, social o profesional (página 36)

Juicio Político *s.* acusación formal para destituir a un presidente en funciones a causa de malos manejos en su administración (página 563)

jurisdicción *s.* poder o autoridad concedida a alguien para aplicar la ley en determinado territorio (página 546)

justicia social *s.* régimen caracterizado por una justa distribución de las oportunidades y los privilegios, incluyendo la igualdad racial (página 565)

K

kayak *s.* canoa con un armazón liviano y con una pequeña abertura superior para sentarse (página 26)

GLOSARIO

Ku Klux Klan *s.* grupo clandestino cuyo propósito era mantener el poder social y político de la comunidad blanca en los Estados Unidos (página 568)

L

leal a Gran Bretaña *s.* colono que apoyaba a Gran Bretaña en la Guerra de Independencia (página 198)

Ley de Alojamiento *s.* una de varias leyes británicas que exigía a los colonos proporcionar vivienda y comida a los soldados británicos en Norteamérica (página 178)

Ley de Asentamientos Rurales (Ley de Homestead) *s.* ley que impulsó un programa para otorgar tierras públicas a pequeños agricultores (página 549)

Ley de Conscripción *s.* ley promulgada en 1863 por la Unión mediante la cual se estipulaba que todos los hombres de entre 20 y 45 años de edad podrían ser reclutados en el ejército, pero también podían pagar $300 dólares para evitar el servicio militar (página 530)

Ley de Derechos Civiles de 1866 *s.* proyecto de ley que les otorgaba plena igualdad y ciudadanía a los estadounidenses de "cualquier color y raza" (página 562)

Ley de Desalojo de los Indígenas *s.* ley que terminó con una ley anterior de los EE. UU. que respetaba los derechos de los indígenas norteamericanos a permanecer en sus tierras (página 376)

Ley de Embargo de 1807 *s.* legislación federal que prohibió la entrada de todas las importaciones extranjeras a los puertos estadounidenses (página 327)

Ley de Judicatura de 1801 *s.* legislación federal que redujo de 6 a 5 la cantidad de jueces de la Corte Suprema (página 318)

Ley de la Moneda *s.* ley británica que regulaba el papel moneda en las colonias de Norteamérica (página 181)

Ley del Azúcar *s.* ley británica que rebajaba el arancel de aduana a la melaza importada para disminuir su contrabando, y así los británicos recibían las ganancias (página 181)

Ley del Té *s.* ley británica que otorgaba a la Compañía Británica de las Indias Orientales el monopolio de la venta del té en las colonias (página 191)

Ley del Timbre *s.* ley británica que exigía a los colonos la compra de un timbre para documentos oficiales y materiales impresos (página 182)

Ley sobre Moneda de Curso Legal *s.* ley que reemplazó los billetes emitidos por los bancos privados con una moneda unificada a nivel nacional (página 532)

Leyes de Extranjería y Sedición *s.* serie de cuatro leyes aprobadas para prevenir que ciertos grupos inmigraran a los Estados Unidos; las leyes dieron al gobierno el poder para expulsar extranjeros que vivían en el país y perseguir a ciudadanos estadounidenses críticos del gobierno (página 301)

Leyes de Navegación *s.* leyes aprobadas por el Parlamento inglés para proteger las compañías navieras inglesas al restringir el transporte de bienes desde y hacia las colonias inglesas (página 125)

Leyes de Townshend *s.* grupo de leyes británicas que imponían aranceles de aduana a las importaciones de té, vidrio, papel, plomo y pintura; los colonos tenían que comprar estos productos a Gran Bretaña (página 186)

Leyes Intolerables *s.* leyes británicas aprobadas para castigar a la gente de Boston después del Motín del Té; llamadas también Leyes Coercitivas (página 194)

Leyes para la Reconstrucción de 1867 *s.* leyes que le otorgaban al Congreso Republicano el poder necesario para llevar a cabo la Reconstrucción, por encima del Presidente (página 562)

libertad de religión *s.* derecho a practicar la religión que uno desee sin intervención del gobierno (página 126)

Liga Iroquesa *s.* confederación compuesta por cinco naciones de habla iroquesa: los mohawk, los oneida, los onondaga, los cayuga y los seneca; más tarde se sumaron los tuscarora (página 29)

linchar *v.* ejecución ilegal por parte de una turba (página 568)

M

madres republicanas *(Republican Motherhood)* *s.* término histórico que describía la idea de que las mujeres debían educar a sus hijos como buenos ciudadanos participantes del gobierno (página 356)

magnicidio *v.* el asesinato de una persona muy importante por su cargo o poder (página 546)

margen *s.* la cantidad de diferencia por la que se gana o se pierde algo (página 411)

Masacre de Boston *s.* incidente en 1779, en el cual soldados británicos dispararon contra personas locales que los estaban insultando (página 188)

materia prima *s.* materia o sustancia básica necesaria para la fabricación de un producto (página 114)

matrilineal *adj.* relacionado con los descendientes que provienen de la madre (página 29)

megafauna *s.* animales gigantescos, o muy grandes, que habitan un área particular o que vivieron en un período histórico determinado (página 6)

mercado común *s.* grupo de países o estados que permite que sus miembros comercien libremente entre ellos (página 261)

mercancía *s.* bien comerciable (página 142)

mercantilismo *s.* política económica que le da a un país la propiedad exclusiva del comercio en sus colonias (página 52)

mercenario *s.* soldado al que se le paga para luchar por un país que no es el suyo (página 222)

mestizo *s.* persona que tiene ascendencia mixta española e indígena americana (página 66)

migrar *v.* mudarse de un lugar a otro (página 27)

milicia *s.* fuerza militar compuesta por ciudadanos civiles locales con el fin de proteger su pueblo, tierra o nación (página 178)

miliciano *s.* miembro de la milicia colonial que estaba dispuesto a luchar en cualquier momento (página 196)

misión *s.* asentamiento de una iglesia cristiana establecida para convertir a las personas indígenas (página 66)

misionero *s.* persona que se esfuerza por divulgar el cristianismo a los demás (página 53)

molino harinero *s.* pieza donde estaba la maquinaria que molía los granos (página 140)

monopolio *s.* el control total y exclusivo de una industria por parte de una sola compañía (página 351)

morfina *s.* potente analgésico (página 542)

mortalidad *s.* tasa de muertes (página 503)

Motín del Té *s.* incidente en 1773, en el cual los Hijos de la Libertad subieron a bordo de barcos británicos y botaron al mar los cargamentos de té en protesta por los impuestos británicos a los colonos (página 191)

movilizar *v.* organizar y preparar tropas para la guerra (página 498)

movimiento de escuelas comunes *(common schools)* *s.* movimiento de reforma a la educación en la década de 1830 para promover escuelas públicas gratuitas financiadas por la recolección de impuestos a la propiedad y manejadas por los gobiernos locales (página 449)

movimiento por la moderación *s.* movimiento de reforma del siglo XIX que buscaba reducir o eliminar el consumo de bebidas alcohólicas (página 446)

N

nacionalismo *s.* concepto de lealtad y devoción al país de uno (página 350)

nativist (antiinmigrante) *s.* término histórico para aquella persona que creía que los nacidos en un lugar debían tener más privilegios que los inmigrantes (página 444)

naturalización *s.* el proceso de convertirse en ciudadano estadounidense para quienes no son ciudadanos nativos (página R34)

navegación *s.* ciencia que consiste en determinar la ubicación de un barco y en planificar rutas, a menudo usado para referirse a los viajes por mar (página 40)

neutralidad *s.* negativa a tomar parte en un conflicto entre otros (página 111)

O

oasis *s.* lugar fértil con agua en un desierto (página 42)

Oficina de Libertos *s.* Oficina para Refugiados, Hombres Libres y Tierras Abandonadas, creada por el Congreso en 1865 para brindar ayuda a los afroamericanos que habían sido esclavos, así como a los sureños blancos más pobres (página 561)

orden de asistencia *s.* documento legal que daba a las autoridades el derecho de entrar y registrar una casa o negocio (página 186)

orden judicial *s.* documento legal (página 318)

ordenanza *s.* mandato, decreto o ley oficial (página 252)

Ordenanza de 1785 *s.* Ordenanza de 1785 s. ley federal que creó un sistema que permitía a los colonos comprar tierras en el oeste (página 252)

Ordenanza del Noroeste de 1787 *s.* legislación adoptada por el Congreso para establecer un control más estricto sobre el gobierno del Territorio del Noroeste (página 252)

Órdenes Fundamentales de Connecticut *s.* acta de fundación de la colonia de Connecticut que establecía 11 leyes y fue el marco de gobierno de la colonia (página 101)

P

pacifista *s.* persona que se resiste a la guerra y a la violencia (página 239)

Pacto del *Mayflower* *s.* documento que firmaron los peregrinos a bordo del Mayflower antes de llegar a Norteamérica, que los vinculaba a obedecer sus propias leyes y establecer una sociedad civil (página 100)

Pánico de 1837 *s.* episodio de temor por una caída de la economía, que causó el comienzo de una recesión económica en los EE. UU. hasta 1840 (página 383)

Pánico de 1873 *s.* crisis económica desencadenada por la quiebra de algunos bancos y empresas ferroviarias (página 573)

paralelo *s.* línea de latitud (página 421)

Parlamento *s.* cámara legislativa de Inglaterra, y después de Gran Bretaña (página 150)

partera *s.* persona entrenada para atender partos (página 146)

partes intercambiables *s.* partes de un mecanismo que pueden ser sustituidas unas por otras (página 338)

Partido de los *Know-Nothing* *s.* partido político que se formó alrededor de 1850 para oponerse a la inmigración, y cuyos miembros secretos contestaban "no sé nada" (know nothing) a cualquier pregunta; también se llamó American Party (página 444)

Partido de los *Whigs* *s.* partido político que se opuso a las políticas de Andrew Jackson, de quien consideraban que tenía demasiado poder (página 384)

Partido Republicano *s.* partido político fundado en 1845 por líderes antiesclavistas (página 476)

pasaje medio *s.* el largo viaje a través del océano Atlántico durante el cual los africanos esclavizados eran llevados a las Américas; segunda etapa de la ruta del comercio triangular (página 73)

paso del noroeste *s.* canal entre los océanos Atlántico y Pacífico a lo largo de la costa norte de América del Norte (página 60)

patriota *s.* colono que apoyaba el derecho de las colonias en Norteamérica a gobernarse a sí mismas (página 198)

peregrinación *s.* viaje religioso (página 45)

pericia *s.* conocimiento de una ciencia o habilidad (página 241)

perseguir *v.* castigar, en particular debido a creencias o antecedentes (página 61)

GLOSARIO

perspectiva geográfica *s.* examen de la influencia que tiene la geografía sobre las personas y su cultura (página 34)

pesos y contrapesos *n.* sistema establecido en la Constitución de EE. UU. que da a cada una de las ramas del gobierno el poder para controlar a las otras dos (página 258)

Piedmont *s.* región relativamente plana entre los montes Apalaches y la llanura costera (página 134)

pionero *s.* colono que va a una tierra nueva y desconocida (página 400)

plaga *s.* hongos o insectos que causan que las plantas se sequen y mueran (página 440)

Plan Anaconda *s.* estrategia militar durante la Guerra Civil, en la cual el Norte planeó un bloqueo alrededor de las costas sureñas para arruinar la economía del Sur y tomar los puertos en el Mississippi; al igual que una enorme serpiente, como la anaconda, estrangula a su presa (página 512)

Plan de Crittenden *s.* propuesta que establecía que el gobierno federal no tuviera poderes para abolir la esclavitud en los estados donde ya existía; reestablecía y extendía el límite del Compromiso de Missouri hasta el océano Pacífico (página 484)

plantación *s.* granja grande; en las plantaciones del Sur, los esclavos trabajaban plantando y cosechando cultivos (página 66)

Pleistoceno *s.* período en la historia de la Tierra durante el cual existieron animales y plantas gigantescos, y grandes extensiones de tierra se cubrieron de hielo (página 5)

poder ejecutivo *s.* rama del gobierno de EE. UU. presidida por el presidente; responsable de que se cumpla la ley (página 258)

poder implícito *s.* poder que no está explícito en la Constitución (página 351)

poder judicial *s.* rama del gobierno de EE. UU., que incluye las cortes o tribunales y el sistema legal, presidida por la Corte Suprema; responsable de interpretar las leyes (página 258)

poder legislativo *s.* rama del gobierno de EE. UU. presidida por el Congreso; responsable de hacer las leyes (página 258)

pontón *s.* flotador cilíndrico portable, que se usaba para construir un puente temporal (página 519)

potlatch *s.* ceremonia de entrega de obsequios practicada por las tribus indígenas norteamericanas kwakiutl y haida (página 26)

prebélico *adj.* anterior a la Guerra Civil de los Estados Unidos (página 348)

precedente *s.* suceso anterior o resolución que sirve de ejemplo para sucesos o resoluciones futuras (página 286)

prejuicio *s.* juicio generalizado acerca de un grupo de personas que no está basado en razones o hechos (página 444)

presidente de la Corte Suprema *s.* jefe máximo del poder judicial del gobierno; preside la Corte Suprema (página 289)

presidio *s.* puesto o asentamiento militar (página 406)

Primer Congreso Continental *s.* reunión en 1774 de los representantes de todas las colonias norteamericanas para dar una respuesta a las Leyes Intolerables (página 195)

Proclamación de 1763 *s.* ley que establecía que los colonos debían mantenerse al este de una línea dibujada en un mapa, a lo largo de la cima de los montes Apalaches (página 178)

Proclamación de Emancipación *s.* documento de 1863, emitido por Abraham Lincoln, que abolió la esclavitud en los estados gobernados por la Confederación durante la Guerra Civil de los Estados Unidos (página 525)

profeta *s.* alguien de quien se cree que trae mensajes de Dios o de cualquier otra fuente divina (página 329)

propietario *s.* dueño de una colonia, que tenía el derecho a manejar y distribuir tierras y a establecer un gobierno (página 112)

protestante *s.* seguidor de la Reforma en el cristianismo (página 39)

provisiones *s.* conjunto de alimentos, agua y otras cosas reservadas para un viaje (página 124)

psiquiátrico *s.* hospital o clínica donde se trata a los enfermos mentales (página 449)

puente de Beringia *s.* territorio entre Alaska y Siberia que se encontraba por encima del nivel del mar hace unos 13,000 años, lo que permitió el paso a grupos humanos que migraban hacia Norteamérica (página 6)

puesto comercial *s.* pequeño asentamiento establecido con el propósito de intercambiar bienes (página 155)

Q

quinina *s.* sustancia hecha de la corteza de un árbol que es un remedio eficaz contra la malaria (página 71)

R

ración *s.* porción de comida suministrada (página 535)

racismo *s.* creencia de que una raza es mejor que otras (página 472)

radical *n.* persona partidaria de cambios sociales o políticos extremos (página 297)

rancho *s.* terreno cedido por México a los colonos, en forma de grandes fincas, en lo que hoy es California (página 423)

ratificar *v.* aprobar formalmente mediante el voto (página 250)

Rebelión de *Shays* *s.* revuelta de los granjeros de Massachusetts en protesta por los altos impuestos, ocurrida entre 1786 y 1787 (página 255)

rebelión del Stono *s.* revuelta de esclavos africanos en contra de sus dueños ocurrida en 1793 (página 137)

Rebelión del Whiskey *s.* serie de protestas violentas de los granjeros del oeste de Pennsylvania contra un impuesto al whiskey (página 297)

GLOSARIO

reclamación *s.* objeción o motivo para quejarse (página 181)

reclutamiento forzoso *s.* acto que obliga a los hombres a prestar el servicio militar o naval (página 327, 530)

Reconstrucción *s.* etapa posterior a la Guerra de Secesión caracterizada por el anhelo de reunificar a los Estados Unidos de América (página 546)

Reconstrucción Presidencial *s.* política impulsada para obligar a los estados confederados a ratificar la Decimotercera Enmienda y a formar nuevos gobiernos, regidos por nuevas constituciones, como condición para poder reintegrarse a la Unión (página 560)

Reconstrucción Radical *s.* nombre dado al plan del Partido Republicano que buscaba aprobar las Leyes de Reconstrucción de 1867 (página 562)

recurso natural *s.* material o sustancia que se encuentra en la naturaleza que se usa para mantener una sociedad o para ser explotado con fines económicos, como minerales, agua, seres vivos (página 114)

refuerzos *s.* más soldados y suministros que se envían para ayudar a las tropas en batalla (página 224)

regionalismo *s.* lealtad a cualquier sección o región del país de donde una persona es, en vez de a la nación como tal (página 352)

rendezvous *s.* mercado temporal donde los tramperos y cazadores se encontraban para comerciar y socializar (página 398)

república *s.* forma de gobierno en la cual la gente elige a sus representantes para hablar por ellos y aprobar leyes según sus necesidades (página 222)

republicanismo *s.* gobierno en el que la gente elige a sus representantes para crear las leyes (página 244)

Republicanos liberales *s.* grupo durante la década de 1870 que pretendía contrarrestar el creciente tamaño y poderío del gobierno (página 572)

resistencia pasiva *s.* negativa no violenta a obedecer a la autoridad y las leyes (página 349)

responsabilidad cívica *s.* responsabilidad que es obligatoria o esencial para las personas, como votar, pagar impuestos y servir en jurados (página R34)

responsabilidad personal *s.* responsabilidad que no es obligatoria pero que contribuye a una sociedad más civilizada, como respetar y defender los derechos de los demás, ayudar a la comunidad y mantenerse informado (página R34)

reunión de reavivamiento *s.* reunión religiosa informal que buscaba avivar la fe en la religión del grupo, y que generalmente se hacía en carpas o al aire libre (página 446)

revisión judicial *s.* poder de la Corte Suprema para invalidar cualquier ley que considere inconstitucional, incluso si fue aprobada por el Congreso o firmada por el presidente (página 318)

revolución agrícola *s.* transición de la dependencia de recolectar plantas salvajes y cazar animales, a cultivar cosechas y criar animales (página 9)

revolución del mercado *s.* transición de una economía preindustrial a una economía capitalista, o sea orientada hacia el mercado (página 336)

Revolución francesa *s.* rebelión de 1789 contra la monarquía francesa que buscó poner fin al privilegio de las clases altas y demandó igualdad para las clases más bajas (página 297)

Revolución industrial *n.* época en que la producción de bienes hechos con máquinas reemplazó de manera generalizada a los productos hechos a mano (página 336)

Revolución neolítica *s.* transición, en la historia de la humanidad, de una forma de vida basada en la caza y recolección a una forma productora agrícola y ganadera (página 9)

risco *s.* peñasco (página 536)

S

salvación *s.* acto de ser perdonado por su deidad (dios) y así quedar libre de pecado (página 148)

secesión *s.* acto de separación formal de una nación o de un territorio para ser independiente (página 375)

sedición *s.* alzamiento contra la autoridad (página 301)

segadora *s.* máquina que corta las plantas de trigo y avena (página 339)

segregación *s.* separación de las personas de acuerdo a su raza (página 473)

Segundo Congreso Continental *s.* grupo de líderes de las colonias norteamericanas que se reunieron para tratar el tema de la tiranía británica, declarar la independencia en 1776 y conducir la Guerra de Independencia hasta formar los Estados Unidos (página 203)

Segundo Gran Despertar *s.* movimiento protestante estadounidense basado en las reuniones de reavivamiento y en una relación directa y emocional con Dios (página 446)

separación de poderes *s.* división de poderes gubernamentales entre las tres ramas del gobierno de los EE. UU.: el poder ejecutivo, el poder judicial y el poder legislativo (página 258)

separatista *s.* persona que quería dejar la Iglesia de Inglaterra (página 100)

servicio doméstico *s.* trabajo o tareas del hogar que hace una o varias personas en la casa de otro (página 441)

servidumbre *s.* sistema social en el cual unas personas toman control total sobre otras (página 546)

servidumbre negra *s.* esclavitud de tipo económico que condenaba a los trabajadores afroamericanos a permanecer como aparceros de los terratenientes (página 567)

siervo *s.* persona que vivía y trabajaba en la tierra perteneciente a un noble o a un señor feudal (página 37)

sindicato de oficio *s.* sindicato que defiende los derechos y protecciones de los trabajadores, cuyos miembros se especializan en el mismo oficio de quienes defienden (página 451)

GLOSARIO

sindicato de trabajadores *s.* asociación voluntaria de trabajadores que usa su poder para negociar condiciones mejores de trabajo (página 450)

sirviente ligado por contrato *s.* persona obligada por contrato a trabajar, generalmente sin paga, a cambio de un boleto gratis a las colonias (página 93)

Sistema americano (American System) *s.* política para promover el sistema industrial de los EE. UU. mediante aranceles, subsidios federales para construir carreteras y otras obras públicas y un banco nacional para controlar la moneda (página 350)

sistema de fábrica *n.* método de producción en el que grandes grupos de operarios trabajaban en un solo lugar (página 336)

sistema de señorío *s.* sistema económico en el cual los campesinos están vinculados a un señor feudal y trabajan su tierra, o señorío, a cambio de comida y vivienda (página 37)

sitio *s.* táctica militar durante la cual las tropas de soldados rodean una ciudad para intentar apoderarse de ella (página 409)

soberanía popular *s.* idea de que los residentes de una región o país deciden sobre un tema mediante el voto (página 474)

soberano *adj.* que posee la autoridad para gobernarse o que es un gobierno independiente (página 250)

soborno *s.* dádiva en dinero o en privilegios que se da subrepticiamente a funcionarios a cambio de favores políticos (página 572)

sociedad por acciones *s.* compañía cuyos accionistas poseen acciones en la propia compañía (página 92)

subsidio *s.* fondo del gobierno para mejoras y apoyo al comercio (página 350)

sufragio *s.* derecho al voto (página 459)

T

tasa de aduana *s.* impuesto sobre bienes importados y exportados (página 327)

telégrafo *s.* máquina que envía mensajes a grandes distancias mediante señales eléctricas en código a través de cables eléctricos (página 339)

tercera clase *s.* término histórico para la sección inferior de un barco en la que viajaban los que pagaban el boleto más barato (página 438)

terraplén *s.* movimiento de tierra hecho por el hombre, que se levanta como defensa (página 204)

terreno *s.* características físicas de la tierra (página 204)

Territorio Indígena *s.* área de tierra, en lo que hoy es Oklahoma y parte de Kansas y Nebraska, a la cual fueron obligados a migrar los indígenas norteamericanos (página 376)

territorio no organizado *s.* tierras bajo el gobierno federal pero que no le pertenecían a ningún estado (página 353)

textil *s.* tela o tejido hecho de algodón u otras materias primas (página 336)

tierras fronterizas (backcountry) *s.* la zona oeste de las Colonias del Sur justo al este de los montes Apalaches (página 134)

tipi *s.* tienda de campaña que tiene forma de cono y que está hecha con pieles de búfalo (página 27)

tiranía *s.* abuso de poder injusto por parte de un gobernante absoluto (página 181)

tolerancia *s.* aceptación de otros (página 144)

toma de posesión *s.* ceremonia que marca el comienzo de una presidencia (página 287)

traición *s.* delito cometido por ayudar al enemigo o planear un derrocamiento; falta de lealtad a su propia nación (página 375)

traidor *s.* persona que traiciona a su propia gente, nación o causa (página 99)

transahariano *adj.* que cruza el Sahara (página 42)

trascendentalismo *s.* movimiento intelectual y social en las décadas de 1830 y 1840 que pedía ir más allá de lo que la sociedad esperaba de cada uno (página 452)

tratado *s.* acuerdo de paz (página 158)

Tratado de Greenville *s.* tratado entre los Estados Unidos y varias naciones indígenas en el cual las naciones indígenas cedieron sus tierras a los Estados Unidos, en lo que hoy es Ohio e Indiana (página 296)

Tratado de París de 1783 *s.* Tratado de París de 1783 acuerdo entre Gran Bretaña y los Estados Unidos, en el cual Gran Bretaña reconoce la independencia de sus colonias en Norteamérica y se determinan los límites iniciales de los Estados Unidos (página 244)

tregua *s.* acuerdo para dejar de luchar (página 379)

Tren Clandestino *s.* red de personas que trabajaron juntas para ayudar a los afroamericanos a escapar de la esclavitud en los estados sureños de los EE. UU. hacia los estados del Norte y Canadá antes de la Guerra Civil (página 455)

tundra *s.* terreno plano y sin árboles de las regiones ártica y subártica (página 26)

U

unionista *s.* miembro del Partido de la Unión Constitucional (página 480)

V

vasallo *s.* en el sistema feudal medieval europeo, era una persona, usualmente un noble de menor rango, que recibía tierras y protección de un señor feudal a cambio de prestarle obediencia y servicio (página 36)

vetar *v.* rechazar oficialmente una decisión o propuesta dictada por el poder legislativo (página 383)

veterano *s.* persona que sirvió al ejército (página 542)

virreinato *s.* territorio gobernado por un virrey (página 58)

virrey *s.* gobernador de las colonias españolas en las Américas que representaba al Rey y la Reina de España (página 58)

viruela *s.* virus mortal que causa fiebre alta y pequeñas ampollas en la piel (página 56)

abarcar *v.* formar un círculo en torno a algo; redondear; incluir (página 567)

abominable *a.* digno de odio o malestar (página 374)

aclamación *s.* elogio entusiasta (página 293)

activista *a.* combativo y determinado; que actúa como si combatiera en una guerra (página 475)

adquisición *s.* acción de obtener algo en calidad de propiedad; artículo obtenido por alguien (página 37)

alegoría *s.* historia contada a través de símbolos, donde los personajes y otros elementos narrativos representan acciones y emociones humanas (página 452)

ardiente *a.* quien se muestra muy ansioso o apasionado en el objetivo de realizar su deseo (página 290)

arduo *a.* difícil; que requiere de un gran esfuerzo para poder lograrse (página 403)

árido *a.* extremadamente seco (como un desierto) (página 24)

delimitación *s.* acción mediante la cual se miden y establecen los límites entre dos o más áreas territoriales (página 252)

divisivo *a.* que causa disenso y desunión con ánimo de discordia (página 470)

espécimen *s.* muestra de alguna criatura o parte de la naturaleza, tal como una planta, un animal o un mineral (página 308)

fértil *a.* capaz de dar vida, como parir crías o hacer crecer plantas (página 24)

fervor *s.* sentimiento o celo muy intenso hacia algo, generalmente espiritual (página 447)

filosofía *s.* conjunto de creencias argumentadas por una persona o por un grupo (página 39)

formidable *a.* asombroso, generalmente de manera temible (página 223)

iconografía *s.* objetos o símbolos representativos de una cultura o religión (página 131)

indispensable *a.* necesario; algo de lo que no se puede prescindir (página 103)

indulgente *a.* tolerante; comprensible (página 560)

intervenir *v.* interferir, generalmente para provocar o prevenir una acción (página 405)

intimidar *v.* servirse de amenazas, por lo general para obligar a alguien a hacer lo que se le exige (página 379)

legado *s.* conjunto de conocimientos o realizaciones transmitido de una generación a otra (página 250)

mártir *s.* persona que sacrifica su vida o algo de gran valor en beneficio de una causa superior (página 477)

mecanizado *a.* que ha sido realizado íntegra o parcialmente por máquinas (página 336)

metralla *s.* conjunto de pedazos filosos lanzados por un proyectil, una granada o, incluso, por una bala de cañón (página 172)

monetario *a.* que tiene, representa o asume la forma del dinero (página 311)

nulificar *v.* eliminar o negar, especialmente en términos legales anular algo (página 374)

ofensiva *s.* lucha iniciada por uno de los bandos que participan en una guerra o disputa (bélica, política, personal e, incluso, deportiva) (página 231)

ortodoxo *a.* que sigue una doctrina religiosa de manera estricta (página 101)

pacto *s.* acuerdo o promesa que negocian dos o más partes en conflicto (página 179)

perdonar *v.* eximir, excusar a otra persona de alguna culpa por voluntad propia (página 560)

perplejo *a.* quien se queda de pronto sin palabras para expresar sus ideas o emociones (página 58)

prestigioso *a.* que cuenta con una reputación de calidad, estima y respeto (página 370)

prótesis *s.* miembro, extremidad o parte artificial del cuerpo humano (página 502)

quinta *s.* finca o casa principal de una hacienda (página 64)

rehabilitar *v.* restaurar la salud o la reputación original (página 449)

rellenar *v.* volver a poner todo el contenido que originalmente tenía algo (página 503)

retórica *s.* manera de usar las palabras para expresar una idea, comúnmente para persuadir (página 570)

soberanía *s.* área donde se puede ejercer a plenitud la función o la autoridad de una entidad (página 336)

susceptible *a.* capaz de percibir la acción o intención de otra persona (página 535)

tenencia *s.* acción de ostentar algo valioso, como un terreno o una posición relevante, o el período durante el cual dicho cargo u objeto es ostentado (página 563)

valentía *s.* tener gran valor, coraje o voluntad para enfrentar cualquier obstáculo (página 528)

INDEX

INDEX, CONTINUED

SKILLS INDEX

ACKNOWLEDGMENTS

 CENGAGE

National Geographic Learning gratefully acknowledges the contributions of the following National Geographic Explorers and affiliates to our program:

Ken Garrett, National Geographic Photographer
Fredrik Hiebert, National Geographic Archaeologist-in-Residence
Kathryn Keane, Vice President, National Geographic Exhibitions
John Kelly, National Geographic Explorer
William Kelso, National Geographic Explorer
William Parkinson, National Geographic Explorer
Robert Reid, National Geographic Digital Nomad
Andrés Ruzo, National Geographic Explorer
Pardis Sabeti, National Geographic Explorer
Donald Slater, National Geographic Explorer

Photographic Credits

IFC, IBC Mark Summers/National Geographic Learning. **ii** (t) Meriwether Lewis & William Clark © 2004 United States Postal Service. All rights reserved. Used with Permission. (b) Lyn Alweis/The Denver Post/Getty Images. **iii** (l) Mark Thiessen/National Geographic Creative. (c) Mary Lynne Ashley Photography/National Geographic Learning. (r) National Geographic Creative. **iv** (tl) Marcie Goodale/National Geographic Learning. (tr) Brian Nelson/National Geographic Learning. (cl) ©Kenneth Garrett Photography. (cr) Robert Reid/National Geographic Creative. (bl) KMK/ National Geographic Creative. (br) Andrés Ruzo/National Geographic Creative. **v** (tl) ©Kenneth Garrett Photography. (tcl) ©David Kilper/WUSTL. (tcr) IRA BLOCK/National Geographic Creative. (tr) Robert Reid/National Geographic Creative. (bl) Chiun-Kai Shih/National Geographic Creative. (br) ©Khiem DoBa. **vi** RALPH LEE HOPKINS/National Geographic Creative. **vii** The Departure of the Mayflower for England in 1621, 1941 (oil on canvas)/Wyeth, Newell Convers (1882–1945)/Private Collection/Bridgeman Images. **viii–ix** (spread) Washington Crossing the Delaware River, 25th December 1776, 1851 (oil on canvas) (copy of an original painted in 1848)/Leutze, Emanuel Gottlieb (1816–68)/Metropolitan Museum of Art, New York, USA/Bridgeman Images. **x–xi** (spread) ©Ken Garrett Photography. **xii–xiii** (spread) Barney Burstein/Getty Images. **xiv–xv** (spread) Jennifer Counter/Moment/Getty Images. **xvi** Mapping Specialists/National Geographic Learning. **xvii** (l) Damon Winter/The New York Times/Redux. (r) ©National Museum of the American Indian, Smithsonian Institution 14/9624. **xviii** aimintang/Getty Images. **xix** (t) Portrait of Thomas Jefferson, 1805 (oil on canvas)/Peale, Rembrandt (1778–1860)/NEW YORK HISTORICAL SOCIETY/© Collection of the New-York Historical Society, USA/Bridgeman Images. (b) Erik Sampers/Getty Images. **0–1** (spread) RozanneHakala/ Getty Images. **1** (tl) Mark Thiessen/National Geographic Creative. (br) ©Bruce Davidson/Magnum Photos. **2** © Fried Hiebert (Helen Hiebert). **3** (t) ©National Postal Museum/Smithsonian. (br) Mark Summers/National Geographic Learning. **4** (bg) Daniel Gomes Lacerda/EyeEm/Getty Images. **6** ©Levi Stroud/Michigan News. (inset) Mapping Specialists/National Geographic Learning. **7** ©National Museum of the American Indian, Smithsonian Institution (6/8904). Photo by NMAI Photo Services. **8** (t) Nicolle Rager Fuller, National Science Foundation. (c) Philippe Psaila/Science Source. **9** IRA BLOCK/National Geographic Creative. **10** (l) Marilyn Angel Wynn/Getty Images. (tr) Werner Forman/Getty Images. (cr1) Marilyn Angel Wynn/Getty Images. (cr2) IRA BLOCK/National Geographic Creative. (br) Werner Forman/Getty Images. **11** (bl) IRA BLOCK/National Geographic Creative. (tr) National Museum of the American Indian, Smithsonian Institution 5/4385. (cr) Heritage Image Partnership Ltd / Alamy Stock Photo. (cl) Aldo Tutino/Art Resource, NY. (br) Mask with antlers, 1400-1600 (wood & bone)/Mississippian culture (c.800-1500)/DIRK BAKKER PHOTOGRAPHY/Private Collection/Bridgeman Images. **12–13** (spread) RALPH LEE HOPKINS/National Geographic Creative. **14** (tr) Victor R. Boswell,

Jr./National Geographic Creative. (tl) Simon Dannhauer/Shutterstock. com. (br) WernerForman/Getty Images. **15** (t) Inca mask (gold with red & green paint), Peruvian School/MuseoArqueologia, Lima, Peru/ Photo Boltin Picture Library/The Bridgeman Art Library. (cr) akg-images/ The Image Works. (bl) Fine Art Images/Fine Art Images/Superstock. **16–17** (spread) Danita Delimont/Alamy Stock Photo. **18–19** (spread) Josh Miller Photography/Aurora Photos. **20** ©Ken Stanback/500px. **21** kenneth-cheung/Getty Images. **22** (tr) ©Mark Malijan Photography. (b) ©Mark Malijan Photography. **23** Werner Forman/ Getty Images. **24** Werner Forman Archive/Bridgeman Images. **26** George H. H. Huey/age fotostock. **28** Tony Linck/Superstock. **30** IRA BLOCK/National Geographic Creative. **31** ©David Kilper/WUSTL. **32–33** (spread) ©National Museum of the American Indian, Smithsonian Institution 9/7850 & 9/7851. **32** (bl) ©National Museum of the American Indian, Smithsonian Institution 20/2175. **33** (tr) ©National Museum of the American Indian, Smithsonian Institution 14/9624. **34** (t) Werner Forman/Getty Images. (bl) Smithsonian American Art Museum, Washington, DC/Art Resource, NY. (br) Werner Forman/Universal Image Group/Getty Images. **37** Bettmann/ Getty Images. **38** J. Paul Getty Museum, Los Angeles, USA/Bridgeman Images. **41** Chris Lawrence/Alamy Stock Photo. **43** ©Trevor Cole/500px. **44** ©JaumeCusidó/500px. **46** BibliothequeNationale de France/National Geographic Creative. **47** Abraham Cresques/Getty Images. **50–51** (spread) The Columbus Foundation. **52** James L. Stanfield/National Geographic Creative. **53** AP Images/Elaine Thompson. **54** Alfredo DagliOrti/The Art Archive at Art Resource, NY. **55** ©The New York Public Library Digital Collections. **56** Museum of Fine Arts, Houston, Texas, USA/Gift of Alfred C. Glassell, Jr./Bridgeman Images. **57** Private Collection/Bridgeman Images. **58** George H. H. Huey/AlamyStockPhoto. **61** Cleveland Museum of Art, OH, USA/Bridgeman Images. **62** National Portrait Gallery. **63** Interfoto. **65** (t) MARKLEY BOYER/National Geographic. (b) Robert Clark/National Geographic Creative. **67** Spring Images/Alamy Stock Photo. **68** Damon Winter/The New York Times/Redux. **69** George Musil/Getty Images. **72** Library of Congress Prints and Photographs Division [LC-USZ62-44000]. **75** (t) Elsa Hahne for Whitney Plantation. (b) ©British Library, London, UK/British Library Board. All Rights Reserved/Bridgeman Images. **78** JON FOSTER/National Geographic Creative. **80–81** (spread) The Departure of the Mayflower for England in 1621, 1941 (oil on canvas) , Wyeth, Newell Convers (1882-1945) / Private Collection / Bridgeman Images. **82** (tr) Robert Clark/National Geographic Creative. (cl) bpk, Berlin/Art Resource, NY. (b) ClaudineVM/Getty Images. **83** (b) ViewStock/AGE Fotostock. (c) The Trustees of the British Museum/Art Resource, NY. (b) Science & Society Picture Library/Getty Images. **84–85** (spread) Joe Raedle/Getty Images News/Getty Images. **86** Photo Researchers, Inc/Alamy Stock Photo. **87** The Trustees of the British Museum/Art Resource, NY. **88** Anna Pomaville/Getty Images. (inset) ©David Stahle, University of Arkansas. **89** Peter Newark American Pictures/Bridgeman Images. **90** (t) The Trustees of the British Museum/Art Resource, NY. (b)Mark Thiessen/National Geographic Creative. **91** The Trustees of the British Museum/Art Resource, NY. **92** Cameron Davidson/Getty Images. **93** (b) Pocahontas, c. 1852 (oil on canvas)/Sully, Thomas (1783–1872)/VIRGINIA HISTORICAL SOCIETY/Virginia Historical Society, Richmond, Virginia, USA/Bridgeman Images. (tl) Pocahontas (c. 1595–1617) 1616 (oil on canvas)/English School, (17th century)/PETER NEWARK'S PICTURES/Private Collection/Bridgeman Images. (tr) W. LANGDON KIHN/National Geographic Creative. **94** (tr) ©Historic Jamestowne. (bl) Robert Clark/National Geographic Creative. **95** (tr) Robert Clark/National Geographic Creative. (tl) ©Historic Jamestowne. (b) ©Historic Jamestowne. **96** IRA BLOCK/National Geographic Creative. **97** Art Resource, NY. **99** The Burning of Jamestown, 1676, illustration from 'Colonies and Nation' by Woodrow Wilson, pub. in Harper's Magazine, 1901 (litho)/Pyle, Howard (1853–1911) (after)/Private Collection/Bridgeman Images. **100** ©Pilgrim Hall Museum. **101** ROBERT SISSON/National Geographic Creative. **102** Head of Squanto (wood)/American School, (17th century)/Private Collection/Bridgeman Images. **103** Kean Collection/Getty Images. **104** T. J. Kirkpatrick/Getty Images News/Getty Images. **107** (tl) North Wind Picture Archives/Alamy Stock Photo. (tr) H. S. Photos/Alamy Stock Photo. (b) H. S. Photos/Alamy Stock photo. **109** US Capitol. **111** CPC Collection/Alamy Stock photo. **113** (t) Kevin Fleming/Corbis/VCG/

Getty Images. (b) Richard Ellis/Alamy Stock Photo. **116** AP Images/ BRUCE PARKER. **117** The Washington Post/Getty Images. **120–121** (spread) Jon Bilous/Shutterstock.com. **122** ReinhardDirscherl/Alamy Stock Photo. **123** Science & Society Picture Library/Getty Images. **125** Blackbeard the pirate (coloured engraving)/English School, (19th century)/PETER NEWARK'S PICTURES/Private Collection/ Bridgeman Images. **127** Ralph Earl Gentleman with Attendant, 1785– 88 Oil on canvas 30 . x 25 . in. Courtesy of the New Britain Museum of American Art Harriet Russell Stanley Fund 1948. 6. **128** Joseph Sohm/Getty Images. **129** Bettmann/Getty Images. **130** ©Nathan Hamilton. (inset) ©Donald Slater. **131** ©Donald Slater. **133** (bl) ©Courtesy, Georgia Archives, Vanishing Georgia Collection, sap094. (br) ©Courtesy, Georgia Archives, Vanishing Georgia Collection, sap093. **135** zrfphoto/Getty Images. **136** Bill Grant/Alamy Stock Photo. **137** ©Division of Culture & the Arts, National Museum of American History, Behring Center, Smithsonian Institution. **138** OlaudahEquiano alias GustavusVassa, a slave, 1789 (mezzotint)/ BRITISH LIBRARY/British Library, London, UK/ Bridgeman Images. **142** ©The Metropolitan Museum of Art. Image source: Art Resource, NY. **143** ©JC Shamrock/500px. **145** Quaker Meeting (oil on canvas), English School, (18th–19th century)/Museum of Fine Arts, Boston, Massachusetts, USA/Bequest of Maxim Karolik/The Bridgeman Art Library. **147** (bl) czarny_bez/Getty Images. (br) Warming pan, probably from Boston, 1780–90 (brass & maple or birch)/American School, (18th century)/ HISTORIC NEW ENGLAND/Historic New England, Boston, Massachusetts, USA/Bridgeman Images. **149** George Whitefield preaching, Collet, John (c. 1725–80)/Private Collection/The Bridgeman Art Library. **150** Heritage Image Partnership Ltd/Alamy Stock Photo. **151** Portrait of King James II, c. 1690 (oil on canvas)/English School, (17th century)/National Portrait Gallery, London, UK/Bridgeman Images. **152** Bettmann/Getty Images. **153** (tl) Bettmann/Getty Images. (b) ©The New York Times. **156** Ball-Headed Tomahawk Club (wood and brass), American School/Ashmolean Museum, University of Oxford, UK/Bridgeman Images. **157** AKG Images. **159** Pontiac (1720–69) 1763 (oil on canvas), Stanley, John Mix (1814–72)/Private Collection/Peter Newark American Pictures/The Bridgeman Art Library. **162** (l) Philip Straub/National Geographic Creative. (r) Robert Clark/ National Geographic Creative. **164–165** (spread) Washington Crossing the Delaware River, 25th December 1776, 1851 (oil on canvas) (copy of an original painted in 1848), Leutze, Emanuel Gottlieb (1816–68)/ Metropolitan Museum of Art, New York, USA/The Bridgeman Art Library. **166** (t) Joseph Sohm; Visions of America/Corbis. (c) Don Troiani/Corbis. (br) Mike Randolph/Masterfile/Corbis. **167** (t) Fraser Hall/robertharding/Corbis. (b) Gianni DagliOrti/Corbis. **168–169** (spread) Kenneth Garrett. **170** Richard Freeda/Aurora Photos. **171** Richard Freeda/Aurora Photos. **172–173** (spread) AP Images/Ric Tapia. **173** National Postal Museum, Smithsonian. **174** KevorkDjansezian/Getty Images News/Getty Images. **175** (tl) Ken Cedeno/ Corbis. (bl) HALSTEAD; DIRCK/Corbis. (tr) Tim Sloan/AFP/ Getty Images. (br) Apollo 11 Commander Neil Armstrong/NASA Kennedy Space Center (NASA-KSC)/National Aeronautics and Space Administration (NASA). **176–177** (spread) ©National Musuem of American History. **177** ©National Musuem of American History. **178** North Wind Picture Archives/The Image Works. **179** Library of Congress Geography and Map Division Washington, D. C. 20540- 4650 USA dcu. **180** Alfredo DagliOrti/Art Resource, NY. **181** (tl) North Wind Picture Archives/The Image Works. (r) The Colonial Williamsburg Foundation. Gift of the Lasser family. **182** The New York Public Library/Art Resource, NY. **183** (t) Sons of Liberty Bowl, from Boston, 1768 (silver)/Revere, Paul (1735–1818)/MUSEUM OF FINE ARTS, BOSTON/ Museum of Fine Arts, Boston, Massachusetts, USA. (b) ACME Imagery/ SuperStock. **184** National Portrait Gallery, Smithsonian Institution/Art Resource, NY. **185** John Paul Bonanno. **186** Art Resource. **187** Private Collection/Art Resource, NY. **189** (t) Art Resource, NY. (b) Death of Crispus Attucks at the Boston Massacre, 5th March, 1770, 1856 (chromolitho)/ Champney, James Wells (1843–1903)/AMERICAN ANTIQUARIAN SOCIETY/American Antiquarian Society, Worcester, Massachusetts, USA/ Bridgeman Images. **190** Eric Gaillard/Reuters. **192** ©Museum of the American Revolution. **192–193** ©Museum of the American Revolution. **193** ©Museum of the American Revolution. **194** 3LH/SuperStock. **195** James McWilliams/Alamy Stock Photo. **196** Concord Musuem. **197** John Burke/Getty Images. **199** Marcelo Baez/ National Geographic Learning. **200–201** (spread) Brian Jannsen/Alamy Stock Photo. **202** Richard Timberlake/TimberlakePhotos LLC. **203** Niday Picture Library/Alamy Stock Photo. **206** Division of Military History and Diplomacy, National Museum of American History. **208** 4X5 Collection/SuperStock. **209** Hisham Ibrahim/Exactostock-1598/

SuperStock. **210** 3LH/ SuperStock. **214–215** (spread) ©Crossroads of the American Revolution NHA. **216–217** (spread) aimintang/Getty Images. **218** Valley Forge National Historical Park/US National Park Service. **220** Courtesy National Park Service, Museum Management Program and The George C. Neumann Collection, Valley Forge National Historical Park. **221** (l) Courtesy National Park Service, Museum Management Program and The George C. Neumann Collection, Valley Forge National Historical Park. (r) Courtesy National Park Service, Museum Management Program and Valley Forge National Historical Park. **223** (t) ©Glenn Cantor. (b) Library of Congress, Rare Book and Special Collections Division. **225** (l) George Romney/Getty Images. (r) ©Joseph Brant Museum/Museums of Burlington. **226** shyflygirl/Getty Images. **227** ©Early American. **229** Franklin at the court of France, 1778, receiving the homage of his genius and the recognition of his country's advent among the nations, 1853 (hand-coloured mezzotint)/Jolly, Baron (18th-19th century) (after)/BOSTON ATHENAEUM/© Boston Athenaeum, USA/ Bridgeman Images. **230–231** (spread) SuperStock/Getty Images. **233** (t) Abigail Smith Adams, c. 1766 (pastel on paper)/Blyth, Benjamin (c. 1746–c. 1786)/MASSACHUSETTS HISTORICAL SOCIETY/ Massachusetts Historical Society, Boston, MA, USA/Bridgeman Images. (b) Culver Pictures/The Art Archive at Art Resource, NY. **234** ©Beverly Historical Society & Museum. **235** ©Saturday Evening Post Archive. **236–237** (spread) ©Swamp Fox Murals Trail Society, Manning, Clarendon County, SC, www. swampfoxtrail.com. **240** Architect of the Capitol. **241** raclro/Getty Images. **242** Paul Grossmann/Tetra Images/ Getty Images. **245** National Archives, Washington, D. C. **248–249** (spread) Rick Wilking/REUTERS. **250** Everett Collection Inc/Alamy Stock Photo. **251** RGB Ventures/ SuperStock/Alamy Stock Photo. **253** Prisma/ Superstock. **254** Photograph courtesy of the Pocumtuck Valley Memorial Association, Memorial Hall Museum, Deerfield, Massachusetts. **255** IllustratedHistory/Alamy Stock Photo. **256** National Archives. **257** Joseph Sohm/Getty Images. **259** (tl) Library of Congress, Prints & Photographs Division, Reproduction number LC-DIGdet- 4a26389. (tr) Everett Collection Historical/Alamy Stock Photo. (b) Classic Image/Alamy Stock Photo. **261** Life of George Washington—The Farmer, pub. 1853 (colourlitho)/Stearns, Junius Brutus (1810–85)/ STAPLETON COLLECTION/Private Collection/Bridgeman Images. **263** The Signing of the Constitution of the United States in 1787, 1940 (oil on canvas)/Christy, Howard Chandler (1873–1952)/Hall of Representatives, Washington D. C. , USA/Bridgeman Images. **264** Mrs James Warren (Mercy Otis) c. 1763 (oil on canvas)/Copley, John Singleton (1738–1815)/MUSEUM OF FINE ARTS, BOSTON/Museum of Fine Arts, Boston, Massachusetts, USA/Bridgeman Images. **267** JAMES P. BLAIR/National Geographic Creative. **269** Mark Summerfield/Alamy Stock Photo. **270** LOUIS S. GLANZMAN/ National Geographic Creative. **272** Dan Westergren / National Geographic Creative. **274-275** (spread) Richard T. Nowitz/Corbis Documentary/Getty Images. **276** Christian Heeb/Prisma/SuperStock. **277** (t) BROKEN ARROW, US poster art, from left: Jeff Chandler, Debra Paget, James Stewart, 1950, TM and Copyright ©20th Century Fox Film Corp. All rights reserved./courtesy Everett Collection. (b) Chad Coppess/South Dakota Department of Tourism. **278** (t) Philip Scalia / Alamy Stock Photo. (b) Stillman Rogers/Alamy Stock Photo. **279** WILLIAM ALBERT ALLARD/National Geographic Creative. **280–281** (spread) KENNETH GARRETT/National Geographic Creative. **282** (t) Lyn Alweis/The Denver Post/Getty Images. (b) STEPHANE GAUTIER/AGE Fotostock. **283** (tl) United States, Eagle Motif Painted Wooden Infantry Drum Circa 1810–20/Private Collection/Photo. Don Troiani/Bridgeman Images. (tr) Larasoul/ Getty Images. (b) HaraldSund/Getty Images. **284–285** (spread) Pat & Chuck Blackley/Alamy Stock Photo. **286** George Washington, 1796–1803 (oil on canvas)/Stuart, Gilbert (1755–1828)/CLARK ART INSTITUTE/Sterling and Francine Clark Art Institute, Williamstown, Massachusetts, USA/ Bridgeman Images. **287** ©Mark Finkenstaedt/Mount Vernon Museum. **288** Photographs in the Carol M. Highsmith Archive, Library of Congress, Prints and Photographs Division. **290** akova/Getty Images. **291** Getty Images. **292–293** (spread) Theo Wargo/Getty Images. **295** Richard Levine/ Alamy Stock Photo. (inset) Michael McDonald/Alamy Stock Photo. **296** Washington Reviewing the Western Army at Fort Cumberland, Maryland, after 1795 (oil on canvas)/Kemmelmeyer, Frederick (d.1821) (attr. to)/Metropolitan Museum of Art, New York, USA/ Bridgeman Images. **297** AKG Images. **298** ©Mount Vernon Ladies Association. **300–301** (spread) AFP/Getty Images. **304–305** (spread) ©Chris Gibson/500px. **306–307** (spread) Sam Abell/National Geographic Creative. **307** Everett Collection Inc/Alamy Stock photo. **308** ©Missouri History Museum, St. Louis. **309** Sam Abell/National

Geographic Creative. **308–311** (spread) Marc Moritsch/Getty Images. **311** (t) Greg Vaughn/Alamy Stock photo. (b) Division of Political History, National Museum of American History, Smithsonian Institution. **312** IRA BLOCK/National Geographic Creative. **313** (tl) ©American Philosophical Society. (cl) (bl) (br)©Missouri History Museum, St. Louis. **314** ©Gift of Mr. and Mrs. Gherardi Davis and Ellen King/The New-York Historical Society. All Rights Reserved. **316** Collection of the New-York Historical Society/Bridgeman Images. **317** Edwin Remsberg/Newscom/Dreams of the Blue Communications (Visual&Written)/Charlottesville/Virginia/USA. **319** L. Toshio Kishiyama/ Getty Images. **321** Johnny Stockshooter/ age fotostock/Superstock. **324** Sam Abell/National Geographic Creative. **325** Sam Abell/National Geographic Creative. **326** Don Mason/AGE Fotostock. **328** ©National Museum of the American Indian. **329** Bettmann/Getty Images. **330** Richard T. Nowitz/ Science Source. **331** © 2004 White House Historical Association. **334–335** (spread) iStock/Getty Images Plus/Getty Images. **338** (l-Images/ Alamy Stock Photo. **339** Blaine Harrington III/Getty Images. **342–343** (spread) Erik Sampers/Getty Images. **344** (tl) StudioSmart/ Shutterstock.com (br) ©From the Collections of The Henry Ford. **345** (©From the Collections of The Henry Ford. **346** The Athenaeum. **347** ©Slave Dwelling Project. **348** (t) Chicago History Museum, ICHi-052442. (b) ©Chicago Historical Society. **349** ©A slave family in a Georgia cotton field, c. 1860 (b/w photo), American Photographer, (19th century)/Private Collection/Peter Newark American Pictures/ Bridgeman Images. **351** (l) Fotosearch/Getty Images. (r) Peter Steiner/ Alamy Stock Photo. **353** ©Bruce White for the White House Historical Association/Collection of the James Monroe Museum and Memorial Library. **354** Bettmann/Getty Images. **356** Knowledge is Power, (oil on canvas), Guy, Seymour Joseph (1824-1910)/Private Collection/Photo © Christie's Images/Bridgeman Images. **357** The Beecher Family, c. 1860 (b/w photo), American Photographer, (19th century)/Schlesinger Library, Radcliffe Institute, Harvard University/The Bridgeman Art Library. **360** Russell, Charles Marion (1865–1926)/Private Collection/Peter Newark American Pictures/ The Bridgeman Art Library. **362** (t) Mark Thiessen/National Geographic Creative. (b) ©2007 Delaware County (PA) History. **363** ©Wilbur Hall/Haverford Township Historical Society. **364–365** (spread) Barney Burstein/Getty Images. **366** (tl) Everett Collection/ age fotostock. (tr) The Last Stand at the Alamo, 6th March 1836 (colourlitho), Wyeth, Newell Convers (1882–1945)/Private Collection/The Bridgeman Art Library. (b) chrisbrignell/Getty Images. **367** (tl) World History Archive/Alamy Stock Photo. (tr) Library of Congress, Prints and Photographs Division, LC-DIG-ppmsca-07531. (b) Steve Allen Travel Photography/Alamy Stock Photo. **368–369** (spread) WimWiskerke/Alamy Stock Photo. **371** (t) Peter Turnley/Getty Images. (bl) Azad Lashkari/REUTERS. (bc) Omar Sobhani/©REUTERS. (br) RIZWAN TABASSUM/Getty Images. **372** ©Armed Forces History Division, National Museum of American History, Smithsonian Institution. **373** (t) National Portrait Gallery, Smithsonian Institution; transfer from the National Gallery of Art; gift of the A. W. Mellon Educational and Charitable Trust, 1942; Frame conserved with funds from the Smithsonian Women's Committee. (b) National Archives and Records Administration. **375** ClassicStock/Alamy Stock Photo. **377** ©National Museum of the American Indian. **378** Gary Cameron/REUTERS. **379** Portrait of Black Hawk (1767–1838) by Homer Henderson c. 1870 (oil on canvas)/ King, Charles Bird (1785–1862) (after)/ CHICAGO HISTORY MUSEUM/Chicago History Museum, USA/Bridgeman Images. **381** ©David Fitzgerald/Cherokee Heritage Center. **382** (t) ©Courtesy of the Federal Reserve Bank of San Francisco. (b) Library of Congress Prints and Photographs Division[LC-USZ62-89594]. **384** ©Jeff R. Bridgman Antiques, Inc. **385** (t) Album/Prisma/Album/Superstock. (c) Bettmann/Getty Images. (b) Fine Art/Getty Images. **387–388** (spread) JAMES L. AMOS/National Geographic Creative. **390–391** (spread) PiriyaPhotography/Getty Images. **392** ©Division of Work & Industry, National Museum of American History, Smithsonian Institution. **393** Courtesy of the California History Room, California State Library, Sacramento, California. **394** Garden Photo World/ David C Phillips/Getty Images. **396** (t) Superstock. (b)Photo Tan Yilmaz/Getty Images. **397** Citizen of the Planet/Alamy Stock Photo. **398** Universal History Archive/Getty Images. **399** Across the Continent: 'Westward the Course of Empire Takes it's Way', pub. by Currier and Ives, New York, 1868 (colourlitho), Palmer, Frances Flora Bond (Fanny) (c. 1812–76) (after)/Museum of the City of New York, USA/Bridgeman Images. **400** American Progress, 1872 (oil on canvas)/ Gast, John (1842–1896)/CHRISTIES IMAGES/Private Collection/Bridgeman Images. **401** RuslanSemichev/Shutterstock. com. **403** ©Smithsonian Institution, National Museum of American

History, Division of Home and Community Life. **405** Oregon Trail (oil on canvas tacked over board), Bierstadt, Albert (1830–1902)/ Private Collection/Photo Christie's Images/ Bridgeman Images. **407** ©HerronStock.com. **408** Robin Jerstad/Alamy Stock Photo. **410** ©Star of the Republic Museum. **411** Kevin Coombs/REUTERS. **412** (l) Sam Houston, c. 1851 (oil on canvas)/Flintoff, Thomas (1809–92)/ MUSEUM OF FINE ARTS, HOUSTON/Museum of Fine Arts, Houston, Texas, USA/Bridgeman Images. (r) UniversalImagesGroup/ Getty Images. **413** ©State Preservation Board, Austin, Texas. **414** (©San Jacinto Museum of History. **415** ©San Jacinto Museum of History. **416** IngeJohnsson/Alamy Stock Photo. **417** Playing card: King of Diamonds (colourlitho), American School, (19th century)/ Dallas Historical Society, Texas, USA/Bridgeman Image. **418** (b) ©The Art Archive/The Picture Desk, Inc. **419** The New York Public Library/Art Resource, NY. **422** Jim Wilson/The New York Times/ Redux. **424** Gold Rush prospector, 1849 (b/w photo)/American Photographer, (19th century)/PETER NEWARK'S PICTURES/Private Collection/Bridgeman Images. **425** Pictorial Press Ltd/Alamy Stock Photo. **427** (t) Print Collector/Getty Images. (b) Archive Images/ Alamy Stock Photo. **430–431** (spread) Tetra Images/Getty Images. **432–433** (spread) ARS, NY, Photo: The Jacob and Gwendolyn Lawrence Foundation/Art Resource, NY. **434** Library of Congress Prints and Photographs Division [LC-USZ62-7816]. **436** George Eastman House/Getty Images. **437** (t) © Rebecca Ray/National Geographic Learning. (b) © United States Department of the Treasury. **439** Outward Bound, The Quay of Dublin, engraved by T. H. Maguire, 1854 (colourlitho) (see 189921), Nicol, J (19th century) (after)/Collection of the New York Historical Society, USA/ Bridgeman Images. **440** An Irish Eviction (oil on panel)/Goodall, Frederick (1822–1904)/LEICESTER ARTS AND MUSEUMS SERVICE/New Walk Museum & Art Gallery, Leicester, UK/ Bridgeman Images. **441** ©National Museum of American History. **442–443** (spread) ©Robert Pettus/500px. **445** (t) American 'Know-Nothing' Party Cartoon, 1854 (engraving), American School, (19th century)/Private Collection/Peter Newark American Pictures/ Bridgeman Images. (b) Everett Collection Historical/Alamy Stock Photo. **447** ©Old Dartmouth Historical Society-New Bedford Whaling Museum. **448** Primer (printed textile), American School, (19th century)/Private Collection/Photo Civil War Archive/ Bridgeman Images. **450** © Library of Congress. **451** image copyright © The Metropolitan Museum of Art. Image source: Art Resource, NY. **453** Tomas Abad/Alamy Stock Photo. **454** Esclave/Photo Gerald Bloncourt/Bridgeman Images. **455** MPI/Getty Images. **456** Fotosearch/Getty Images. **458** Library of Congress/Getty Images. **459** Jim West/Alamy Stock Photo. **462** JIM RICHARDSON/National Geographic. **464–465** (spread) Jennifer Counter/ Moment/Getty Images. **466** (tl) Schomburg Center, NYPL/Art Resource, NY. (tr) ©National Museum of American History, Political History. (b) Pictorial Press Ltd/Alamy Stock Photo. **467** (tr) ©National Museum of American History Smithsonian. (tl) ©Chicago History Museum. (b) John Stevenson/ Getty Images. **468–469** (spread) DamirFrkovic/ Masterfile. **472** (l) National Portrait Gallery, Smithsonian Institution/Art Resource, NY. (r) Schomburg Center, NYPL/Art Resource, NY. **473** Iberfoto/Superstock. **475** John Brown, 1859 (colourlitho), Balling, Ole Peter Hansen (1823–1906)/Private Collection/Peter Newark American Pictures/Bridgeman Images. **476** Pictorial Press Ltd/Alamy Stock Photo. **477** ©Kenneth Garret Photography. **478** Abraham Lincoln and Stephen A. Douglas debating at Charleston, Illinois on 18th September 1858, 1918 (oil on canvas), Root, Robert Marshall (1863–1937)/Private Collection/ Bridgeman Images. **479** Niday Picture Library/Alamy Stock Photo. **480** Niday Picture Library/Alamy Stock Photo. **482** Everett Collection Inc/Alamy Stock Photo. **483** Abraham Lincoln (1809–65) 1860 (b/w photo), Hesler, Alexander (1823–95)/Private Collection/ Peter Newark American Pictures/Bridgeman Images. **485** Charles Phelps Cushing/ClassicStock/Getty Images. **488–489** (spread) ©Kenneth Garrett Photography. **490** The Library of Congress. **491** ©Armed Forces History Division, National Museum of American History, Smithsonian Institution. **492** (t) The Library of Congress. (b) ©Armed Forces History Division, National Museum of American History, Smithsonian Institution. **493** Smithsonian American Art Museum, Washington, DC/Art Resource, NY. **494** ©Historical Society of Carroll County. **495** ©The Library of Congress. **497** ©Jason Demek/500px. **498** Library of Congress, Prints & Photographs Division, Reproduction number LC-DIG-cwpb-04402 (digital file from original neg.)LC-B8172-0001 (b&w film neg.). **499** (l) ©Chicago Historical Society. (r) ©Confederate Memorial Hall Museum, New Orleans. **500** ©Confederate Memorial Hall Museum. **501** ©Confederate Memeorial Hall Museum. **502** Wellcome Images/

Science Source. **503** Science & Society Picture Library/Getty Images. **504** ©Clara Barton National Historic Site/National Parks Service. **505** Fotosearch/Getty Images. **506** ©George Ohrstrom II. **507** ©Kenneth Garrett Photography. **508** ©Kenneth Garrett Photography. **509** ©Kenneth Garrett Photography. **510** ©Kenneth Garrett Photography. **511** ©Kenneth Garrett Photography. **513** National Geographic Learning. **516** Library of Congress, Prints & Photographs Division, LC-DIG-cwpb-07310. **517** Library of Congress, Prints & Photographs Division, LC-DIG-ppmsca-31277. **521** Library of Congress, Prints & Photographs Division, LC-DIG-stereo-1s02987. **522–523** (spread) ©Kenneth Garrett Photography. **524** Library of Congress, Prints & Photographs Division, LC-DIG-cwpb-04351. **526** The Art Institute of Chicago, IL, USA/Major Acquisitions Centennial Endowment/Bridgeman Images. **527** Smithsonian American Art Museum, Washington, DC/Art Resource, NY. **529** B Christopher/ Alamy Stock Photo. **531** The Everett Collection. **533** LynseyAddario/ Getty Reportage. **534** Library of Congress, Prints & Photographs Division, LC-DIG-ppmsca-33993. **537** Library of Congress, Prints & Photographs Division, LC-B8184-7964-A. **539** Ian Dagnall/Alamy Stock Photo. **540** Library of Congress, Prints & Photographs Division, LC-DIG-ds-03106. **543** TOM LOVELL/National Geographic Creative. **544–545** (spread) ©Kenneth Garrett Photography. **547** Chicago History Museum, USA/Bridgeman Images. **551** Library of Congress, Prints & Photographs Division, LC-DIG-pga-03898. **552–553** (spread) Kenneth Garrett Photography. **554** Hulton Archive/Staff/Getty Images. **556** Library of Congress. **557** (t) SSPL/Science Museum/Art Resource, NY. (b) Library of Congress. **558** (t) Sunday morning in Virginia, 1877 (oil on canvas)/Homer, Winslow (1836–1910)/ CINCINNATI ART MUSEUM/Cincinnati Art Museum, Ohio, USA/ Bridgeman Images. (b) National Archives Washington DC/The Art Archive at Art Resource, NY. **559** ©Collection of the Massachusettes Historical Society. **561** Victor Cardoner/Moment Open/ Getty Images. **563** Bettmann/Getty Images. **565** Library of Congress Prints and Photographs Division Washington, D. C. **566** Angus Osborn/ Getty Images. **568** MPI/Getty Images. **569** (l) Everett Collection Historical/Alamy Stock photo. (r) Universal Images Group/Art Resource, NY. **570** ©National Parks Service. **571** Library of Congress Prints and Photographs Division Washington, D. C. **572** The Rush from the New York Stock Exchange on September 18, 1873, from 'A History of the Last Quarter Century' by E. Benjamin Andrews, published in Scribner's Magazine, July 1895 (oil on canvas), Pyle, Howard (1853–1911)/Delaware Art Museum, Wilmington, USA/The Bridgeman Art Library. **575** MPI/Getty Images. **576** Library of Congress, Prints and Photographs Division, LC-DIG-ppmsca-23855. **578** (t) Mark Thiessen/National Geographic Creative. (b) Niday Picture Library/Alamy Stock Photo. **579** Library of Congress/Getty Images. **R0–R1** (spread) GREG DALE/ National Geographic Creative. **R2** Bettmann/Getty Images. **R10** Bygone Collection/Alamy Stock Photo. **R15** SAUL LOEB/Getty Images. **R17** ©REUTERS/Jonathan Ernst. **R19** National Archives. **R26** Library of Congress, Prints & Photographs Division, LC-DIG-pga-03453. **R27** Library of Congress, Prints & Photographs Division, LC-USZ62-123257. **R32** Bettmann/ Getty Images. **R33** Tetra Images/Shutterstock.com. **R35** Spencer Platt/Getty Images. **R37** Hill Street Studios/Eric Raptosh/Getty Images.

Illustration Credits

Unless otherwise indicated, all illustrations are created by Lachina and all maps are created by Mapping Specialists.